# Microsoft® Office
# 2016 IN PRACTICE
# powerpoint
## COMPLETE

# Microsoft® Office 2016 IN PRACTICE

# powerpoint

## COMPLETE

Pat Graves
**EASTERN ILLINOIS UNIVERSITY**

Randy Nordell
**AMERICAN RIVER COLLEGE**

Mc
Graw
Hill
Education

MICROSOFT OFFICE 2016: IN PRACTICE POWERPOINT COMPLETE
Published by McGraw-Hill/Irwin, a business unit of The McGraw-Hill Companies, Inc., 1221 Avenue of
the Americas, New York, NY, 10020. Copyright © 2017 by The McGraw-Hill Companies, Inc. All rights

Some ancillaries, including electronic and print components, may not be available to customers outside the
United States.

This book is printed on acid-free paper.

1 2 3 4 5 6 7 8 9 RMN 19 18 17 16

ISBN 978-1-259-76269-7
MHID 1-259-76269-6

Chief Product Officer, SVP Products & Markets: *G. Scott Virkler*
Managing Director: *Scott Davidson*
Executive Brand Manager: *Wyatt Morris*
Executive Director of Development: *Ann Torbert*
Senior Product Developer: *Alan Palmer*
Executive Marketing Managers: *Tiffany Russell & Debbie Clare*
Director, Content Design & Delivery: *Terri Schiesl*
Program Manager: *Mary Conzachi*
Content Project Manager: *Rick Hecker*
Buyer: *Jennifer Pickel*
Designer: *Matt Backhaus*
Cover Image: © *Chris Ryan/Getty Images*
Senior Digital Product Analyst: *Thuan Vinh*
Compositor: *SPi Global*
Printer: *RR Donnelley*

**Library of Congress Cataloging-in-Publication Data**

Names: Graves, Pat R., author. | Nordell, Randy, author.
Title: Microsoft Office 2016 : in practice Powerpoint complete / Pat Graves,
    Randy Nordell.
Description: New York, NY : McGraw-Hill Education, [2017]
Identifiers: LCCN 2016021657 | ISBN 9781259762697 (alk. paper)
Subjects: LCSH: Microsoft PowerPoint (Computer file) | Presentation graphics software.
Classification: LCC P93.53.M534 G728 2017 | DDC 005.5/8—dc23
LC record available at https://lccn.loc.gov/2016021657

# dedication

Brent, thank you for the many ways you have helped me while I worked on this book. Your love and support mean so much to me. I also appreciate my friends who shared their expertise and provided content for projects.

—Pat Graves

Bob and Lanita, thank you for generously allowing me to use the cabin where I completed much of the work on this book. Don and Jennie, thank you for teaching me the value of hard work and encouraging me throughout the years. Kelsey and Taylor, thank you for keeping me young at heart. Kelly, thank you for your daily love, support, and encouragement. I could not have done this without you. I'm looking forward to spending more time together on our tandem!

—Randy Nordell

# brief contents

# contents

## CHAPTER 3: PREPARING FOR DELIVERY AND USING A SLIDE PRESENTATION   P3-146

## CHAPTER 4: CUSTOMIZING IMAGES, ILLUSTRATIONS, AND THEMES   P4-209

# about the authors

## PAT GRAVES, Ed.D.

Pat Graves is a professor emeritus at Eastern Illinois University in Charleston, Illinois. She taught at the high school level before receiving her doctorate in education from the University of Memphis. At Eastern Illinois University, she taught in the School of Business for 20 years. Pat has been an author of PowerPoint textbooks for McGraw-Hill Education since 2002. When not writing, she travels, spends time with family and friends, enjoys the music city of Nashville, and appreciates the peacefulness of the Tennessee mountains.

## RANDY NORDELL, Ed.D.

Randy Nordell is a professor of business technology at American River College in Sacramento, California. He has been an educator for over 25 years and has taught at the high school, community college, and university levels. He holds a bachelor's degree in business administration from California State University, Stanislaus, a single-subject teaching credential from Fresno State University, a master's degree in education from Fresno Pacific University, and a doctorate in education from Argosy University. Randy is the lead author of the *Microsoft Office 2013: In Practice* and *Microsoft Office 2016: In Practice* series of texts. He is also the author of *101 Tips for Online Course Success* and *Microsoft Outlook 2010*. Randy speaks regularly at conferences on the integration of technology into the curriculum. When not teaching and writing, he enjoys spending time with his family, cycling, skiing, swimming, backpacking, and enjoying the California weather and terrain.

# What We're About

We wrote *Microsoft Office 2016: In Practice* to meet the diverse needs of both students and instructors. Our approach focuses on presenting Office topics in a logical and structured manner, teaching concepts in a way that reinforces learning with practice projects that are transferrable, relevant, and engaging. Our pedagogy and content are based on the following beliefs.

## Students Need to Learn and Practice Transferable Skills

Students must be able to transfer the concepts and skills learned in the text to a variety of projects, not simply follow steps in a textbook. Our material goes beyond the instruction of many texts. In our content, students practice the concepts in a variety of current and relevant projects *and* are able to transfer skills and concepts learned to different projects in the real world. To further increase the transferability of skills learned, this text is integrated with SIMnet so students also practice skills and complete projects in an online environment.

## Your Curriculum Drives the Content

The curriculum in the classroom should drive the content of the text, not the other way around. This book is designed to allow instructors and students to cover all the material they need to in order to meet the curriculum requirements of their courses no matter how the courses are structured. *Microsoft Office 2016: In Practice* teaches the marketable skills that are key to student success. McGraw-Hill's Custom Publishing site, **Create,** can further tailor the content material to meet the unique educational needs of any school.

## Integrated with Technology

Our text provides a fresh and new approach to an Office applications course. Topics integrate seamlessly with SIMnet with 1:1 content to help students practice and master concepts and skills using SIMnet's interactive learning philosophy. Projects in SIMnet allow students to practice their skills and receive immediate feedback. This integration with SIMnet meets the diverse needs of students and accommodates individual learning styles. Additional textbook resources found in SIMnet (Resources and Library sections) integrate with the learning management systems that are widely used in many online and onsite courses.

## Reference Text

In addition to providing students with an abundance of real-life examples and practice projects, we designed this text to be used as a Microsoft Office 2016 reference source. The core material, uncluttered with exercises, focuses on real-world use and application. Our text provides clear step-by-step instructions on how readers can apply the various features available in Microsoft Office in a variety of contexts. At the same time, users have access to a variety of both online (SIMnet) and textbook practice projects to reinforce skills and concepts.

# instructor walkthrough

## Textbook Learning Approach

*Microsoft Office 2016: In Practice* uses the *T.I.P.* approach:
- **T**opic
- **I**nstruction
- **P**ractice

### Topic
- Each Office application section begins with foundational skills and builds to more complex topics as the text progresses.
- Topics are logically sequenced and grouped by topics.
- Student Learning Outcomes (SLOs) are thoroughly integrated with and mapped to chapter content, projects, end-of-chapter review, and test banks.
- Reports are available within SIMnet for displaying how students have met these Student Learning Outcomes.

### Instruction (How To)
- *How To* guided instructions about chapter topics provide transferable and adaptable instructions.
- Because *How To* instructions are not locked into single projects, this textbook functions as a reference text, not just a point-and-click textbook.
- Chapter content is aligned 1:1 with SIMnet.

### Practice (Pause & Practice and End-of-Chapter Projects)
- Within each chapter, integrated Pause & Practice projects (three to five per chapter) reinforce learning and provide hands-on guided practice.
- In addition to Pause & Practice projects, each chapter has 10 comprehensive and practical practice projects: Guided Projects (three per chapter), Independent Projects (three per chapter), Improve It Project (one per chapter), and Challenge Projects (three per chapter). Additional projects can also be found in the Library or Resources section of SIMnet.
- Pause & Practice and end-of-chapter projects are complete content-rich projects, not small examples lacking context.
- Select auto-graded projects are available in SIMnet.

# Chapter Features

All chapters follow a consistent theme and instructional methodology. Below is an example of chapter structure.

Main headings are organized according to the ***Student Learning Outcomes (SLOs)***.

---

**SLO 1.1**

### Creating, Opening, and Saving Presentations

PowerPoint provides several ways to start, view, and save a presentation. Save a presentation if you will need to access it again. If you close the presentation your content is lost.

---

video, PowerPoint has all the tools you need. You can use PowerP computer projection equipment in meeting rooms, for self-running individuals, or for presentations shown on the web. This chapter cov and editing a PowerPoint presentation.

### STUDENT LEARNING OUTCOMES (SLOs)

After completing this chapter, you will be able to:

**SLO 1.1** Create, open, and save a presentation (p. P1-3).

**SLO 1.2** Work with slides, layouts, placeholders, and text (p. P1-1

**SLO 1.3** Navigate between slides and organize content by repro rearranging slides (p. P1-23).

**SLO 1.4** Change theme colors and fonts (p. P1-29).

**SLO 1.5** Insert headers and footers to add identifying informatio

**SLO 1.6** Insert, resize, and align a picture from a file (p. P1-37).

**SLO 1.7** Apply and modify transition effects to add visual intere

**SLO 1.8** Preview a presentation and print slides, handouts, and

**SLO 1.9** Apply presentation properties (p. P1-45).

---

**A list of Student Learning Outcomes begins each chapter. All chapter content, examples, and practice projects are organized according to the chapter SLOs.**

---

### CASE STUDY

*Throughout this book you have the opportunity to put into practice the application features that you are learning. Each chapter begins with a case study that introduces you to the Pause & Practice projects in the chapter. These Pause & Practice projects give you a chance to apply and practice key skills. Each chapter contains three to five Pause & Practice projects.*

***Hamilton Civic Center*** *(HCC) is a nonprofit community fitness center that partners with*

the local hospital for educational events. Doctors and nurses provide classes on a variety of health and wellness issues for adults. HCC also works with local schools to support their academic programs and sponsors events for children.

In this chapter, you develop a presentation about training for an upcoming marathon that is being promoted to HCC members.

---

**The *Case Study* for each chapter is a scenario that establishes the theme for the entire chapter. Chapter content, examples, figures, Pause & Practice projects, SIMnet skills, and projects throughout the chapter are closely related to this case study content. The three to five Pause & Practice projects in each chapter build upon each other and address key case study themes.**

***How To*** instructions enhance transferability of skills with concise steps and screen shots.

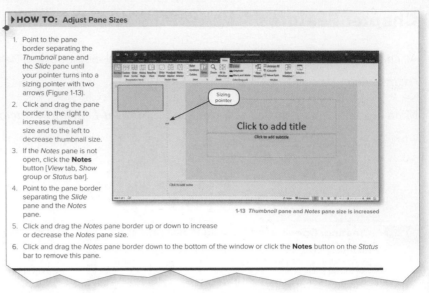

**HOW TO: Adjust Pane Sizes**

1. Point to the pane border separating the *Thumbnail* pane and the *Slide* pane until your pointer turns into a sizing pointer with two arrows (Figure 1-13).
2. Click and drag the pane border to the right to increase thumbnail size and to the left to decrease thumbnail size.
3. If the *Notes* pane is not open, click the **Notes** button [*View* tab, *Show* group or *Status* bar].
4. Point to the pane border separating the *Slide* pane and the *Notes* pane.
5. Click and drag the *Notes* pane border up or down to increase or decrease the *Notes* pane size.
6. Click and drag the *Notes* pane border down to the bottom of the window or click the **Notes** button on the *Status* bar to remove this pane.

1-13 *Thumbnail pane and Notes pane size is increased*

**How To instructions are easy-to-follow concise steps. Screen shots and other figures fully illustrate How To topics.**

Students can complete hands-on exercises in either the Office application or in SIMnet.

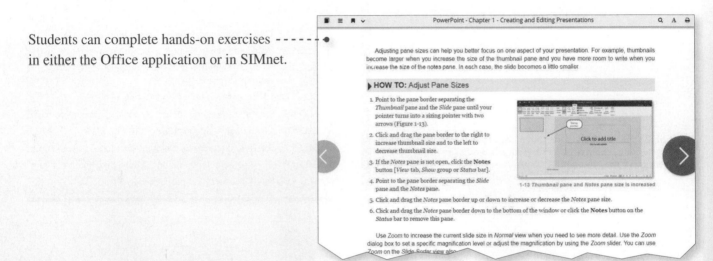

**Pause & Practice projects, which each covers two to three of the student learning outcomes in the chapter, provide students with the opportunity to review and practice skills and concepts. Every chapter contains three to five Pause & Practice projects.**

***Pause & Practice 1-1:*** Create a presentation and develop text content.

***Pause & Practice 1-2:*** Apply a presentation theme, change theme colors and fonts, and edit content.

***Pause & Practice 1-3:*** Add interest with pictures and apply transitions, and print supplements.

**MORE INFO**

For instructions to set up a *OneDrive* account, refer to *SLO Intro.1: Using Windows 10* in *Intro Chapter 1: Windows 10, Office 2016, and File Management.*

***More Info*** provides readers with additional information about chapter content.

*Another Way* notations teach alternative methods of accomplishing the same task or feature such as keyboard shortcuts.

Marginal notations present additional information and alternative methods.

## End-of-Chapter Projects

Ten learning projects at the end of each chapter provide additional reinforcement and practice for students. Many of these projects are available in SIMnet for completion and automatic grading.

- *Guided Projects (three per chapter):* Guided Projects provide guided step-by-step instructions to apply Office features, skills, and concepts from the chapter. Screen shots guide students through the more challenging tasks. End-of-project screen shots provide a visual of the completed project.
- *Independent Projects (three per chapter):* Independent Projects provide students further opportunities to practice and apply skills, instructing students what to do, but not how to do it. These projects allow students to apply previously learned content in a different context.
- *Improve It Project (one per chapter):* In these projects, students apply their knowledge and skills to enhance and improve an existing document. These are independent-type projects that instruct students what to do, but not how to do it.
- *Challenge Projects (three per chapter):* Challenge Projects are open-ended projects that encourage creativity and critical thinking by integrating Office concepts and features into relevant and engaging projects.

# Appendix

- *Office 2016 Shortcuts:* Appendix A covers the shortcuts available in Microsoft Office and within each of the specific Office applications. Information is in table format for easy access and reference.

# Additional Resources in SIMnet

Students and instructors can find the following resources in the Library section in SIMnet.

## Student Resources

- **Data Files:** Files contain start files for all Pause & Practice, Capstone, and end-of-chapter projects.
- **SIMnet Resources:** Resources provide getting started and informational handouts for instructors and students.
- **Check for Understanding:** A combination of multiple choice, fill-in, matching, and short answer questions are available at the end of each SIMbook chapter in SIMnet to assist students in their review of the skills and concepts covered in the chapter.

## Capstone Projects

- **Integrating Applications:** Projects provide students with the opportunity to learn, practice, and transfer skills using multiple Office applications.
- **Integrating Skills:** Projects provide students with a comprehensive and integrated review of all of the topics covered in each application (Word, Excel, Access, and PowerPoint). Available in individual application texts.

## Appendices

- **Business Document Formats:** Appendix B is a guide to regularly used business document formatting and includes numerous examples and detailed instructions.

## Instructor Resources

- **Instructor's Manual:** An Instructor's Manual provides teaching tips and lecture notes aligned with the PowerPoint presentations for each chapter. The manual also includes the solutions for online **Check for Understanding** questions.
- **Test Bank:** The extensive test bank integrates with learning management systems (LMSs) such as Blackboard, WebCT, Desire2Learn, and Moodle.
- **PowerPoint Presentations:** PowerPoint presentations for each chapter can be used in onsite course formats for lectures or can be uploaded to LMSs.
- **SIMnet Resources:** These resources provide getting started and informational handouts for instructors.
- **Solution Files:** Files contain solutions for all Pause & Practice, Capstone, Check for Understanding, and end-of-chapter projects.

# acknowledgments

## REVIEWERS

We would like to thank the following instructors, whose invaluable insights shaped the development of this series.

Scott Straub
College of Western Idaho

Jeremy Eason
West Georgia Technical College

Linda Johnsonius
Murray State University

Barbara West
Central Georgia Technical College

Yvonne Galusha
University of Iowa

Jean Finley
Asheville Buncombe Technical Community College

Candace S. Garrod
Red Rocks Community College

Marianne Dougherty
Middlesex County College

Adam Rosen
LIM College

Robert Doyle
Dona Ana Community College

Pamela Silvers
Asheville-Buncombe Technical Community College

Lisa Cady
University of Arkansas - Fort Smith

Richard Johnsen
County College of Morris

Joan Butler
Manchester Community College

Robert Nichols
College of DuPage

Anna Tsipenyuk
LIM College

Brian Fox
Santa Fe College

Leilani Benoit
Dona Ana Community College

Uma Sridharan
Presbyterian College

Marianne Daugharthy
College of Western Idaho

Tom Moore
Kapiolani Community College

Diane Morris
Tyler Junior College

Brenda McFarland
Asheville-Buncombe Technical Community College

Mitch Pendleton
LDS Business College

Tony Hunnicutt
College of the Ouachitas

Jeanine Taylor
Bryan University

Darin Bell
Treasure Valley Community College

Martha Guzman
Taller San Jose

Mary Jean Blink
Mount St. Joseph University

Ralph Dickerson
The Atlanta Workforce Development Agency

Robert LaRocca
Keiser University

Jenna Dulak
Hilbert College

Carole Eustice
Clark College

Brad West
Sinclair Community College

Gwyn Ebie
Colorado Mountain College

Susan Paulsen
Community College of Vermont

Karen A. Myers
Fisher College

Gary Judd
Trinity Baptist College

Letty Barnes
Lake Washington Institute of Technology

Tiffinee Morgan
West Kentucky Community and Technical College

Carol Lee
Central Georgia Technical College

Ronald Creel
Troy University

John Sehloff
Bethany Lutheran College

Samuel Gabay
Chicago ORT Technical Institute

Bonnie Armendariz
Bakersfield College, Bakersfield California

Sherry E. Jacob
Jefferson Community and Technical College

Tuncay Bayrak
Western New England University

Mandy Burrell
Holmes community college

Denver Riffe
American National University

Dan Lowrance
LDS Business College

Velma Latson
Bowie State University

Marilyn Mendoza
Franklin Career Institute

Lisa McCool
Alfred State College

Pamela Sorensen
Santa Rosa Junior College

Peggy Batchelor
Furman University

Larry Fudella
Erie Community College

Chet Cunningham
Madisonville Community College

Lauri Smedley
Sacramento City College

Gary Ewen
Colorado Christian University

Amanda Hardin
Mississippi Delta Community College

Rob Durrance
Keiser University

Alli Vainshtein
Riverland Community College

George C. Holder
Cloud County Community College

Colin Onita
University of Akron

Melissa Nemeth
Indiana University Kelley School of Business

Keith Conn
Cleveland Institute of Electronics

Phil Young
Baylor University

Laura Earner
Saint Xavier University

Josanne Ford
Metropolitan Career Center Computer Technology Institute

Darla Hunt
Maysville Community and Technical College

Christopher VanOosterhout
Muskegon Community College

Mark Webb
Illinois Central College

David Raney
Cuyamaca College

Christine Wolfe
Ohio University Lancaster

Dan Guerra
Community Business College

Samuel Abraham
Siena Heights University

Sandra Carriker
North Shore Community College

Shelly Smith
Valley College- Beckley

Tahir Aziz
Long Beach City College

Kin Lam
Medgar Evers College/CUNY

Sherry Grosso
University of South Carolina

Regena Aye
Allen Community College

Paul Weaver
Bossier Parish Community College

Brian McDaniel
Palo Alto College

Stephen Arney
Washburn Institute of Technology

Lynn Wermers
North Shore Community College

Lois McWhorter
Somerset Community College

J. Kirk Atkinson
Western Kentucky University

Salina Chahal
UEI College

Dana Fellows
Whiteside Area Career Center

John Golofski
Everest Institute

Eileen Dewey
Rose State College

Nasser Tadayon
Southern Utah University

Tina Denmark
Montgomery College

Delores Vance
Hazard Community and Technical College

Brad Thomas
Olivet Nazareth University

Steven Mark Sachs
Los Angeles Valley College

Andrew Smith
Marian University

Nelly Delessy
Miami Dade COllege

Richard Patterson
Peirce College

Michael Goeken
Northwest Vista College

Janice Flegle
Thomas Edison State College

Sara Rutledge
Mount Aloysius College

Seyed Roosta
Albany State University

Jim Flannery
Central Carolina Community College

Lynn Krausse
Bakersfield College

Kay Hammond
Lindenwood University

Penny Pereira
Indiana University-Purdue University Fort Wayne

Kevin Lambert
Southeast Kentucky Community and Technical College

Adam Rosen
LIM College

Cheri Whalen
Odessa College

Karr Dyal
LIM College

Shirley Birenz
New York University College of Dentistry

Jose Valdes
IBMC College

Gary DeLorenzo
California University of Pennsylvania

Kristin Roberts
Grand Rapids Community College

Michael Gray
Lane Community College

Ed Jaramillo
Peninsula College

Debasish Banerjee
Western Carolina University

Jenny Elshtain
Indiana University East

Sarah Rencher
Coconino Community College

Debbi Dybevik
Washtenaw Community College

Ann Kiefer
Chippewa Valley Technical College

Keff Lagoditz
American International College

Barbara Lave
Clark College

Morris Pondfield
Towson University

Peter Meggison
Massasoit Community College

Anne Acker
Jacksonville University

Gary Mosley
Southern Wesleyan University

Patrick J. Nedry
Monroe County Community College

Wasim A. Alhamdani
Kentucky State University

Bruce Baginski
Craven Community College

Diane Kosharek
Madison Area Technical College (Madison College)

Christina Shaner
Evergreen Valley College

Thomas Magliolo
Alvin Community College

Dmitriy Kupis
St. Joseph's College

Craig Brigman
Liberty University

Janak Shah
Berkeley college

Gary McFall
Purdue University

Phil Feinberg
Palomar College

Sheila Sicilia
Onondaga Community College

Randy Hollifield
McDowell Technical Community College

Bala R. Subramanian
Kean University

Marie Schmitz
Erie Community College

David Bell
Pacific Union College

Jack Tan
University of Wisconsin - Eau Claire

Richard Brown
Loyola University Maryland

Narcissus Shambare
College of Saint Mary

S. E. Rouse
University of Southern Mississippi

Robert Doyle
Dona Ana Community College

David Welch
Nashville State Community College

Chen Ye
Purdue University Calumet

Bahadir Akcam
Western New England University

Frank Lucente
Westmoreland County Community College

Ted Janicki
University of Mount Olive

Kenneth R. Mayer, Jr.
Lipscomb University

Tamar Mosley
Meridian Community College

Pat McMahon
South Suburban College

Maureen Greenbaum
Union County College

Paulinus Ozor-Ilo
Gadsden State Community College

Michael Haugrud
Minnesota State University Moorhead

John Finley
Columbus State University

Philip Reaves
University of West Georgia
Cerro Coso Community College

Michael Leih
Trevecca Nazarene University

Shahla Durany
Tarrant County College - South Campus

Gary Sibbitts
St. Louis Community College at Meramec

Sandro Marchegiani
University of Pittsburgh at Johnstown

Sambit Bhattacharya
Fayetteville State University

Christine Peterson
Saint Paul College

C. Steven Hunt
Morehead State University

Shirley Nagg
Everest College

Ruth Parker
Rowan-Cabarrus Community College

Cecil Lawson
Evergreen Valley College

Adnan Turkey
DeVry College of New York

Janet Nicolaus
Mitchell Technical Institute

Mohammad Morovati
College of Dupage

Anthony Kapolka
Wilkes University

Steven Singer
Kapi'olani Community College

Bill Mills
East Texas Baptist University

Michele Schutte
Delaware Technical Community College - Terry Campus

Mark Evans
American National University

Syed Raza
Talladega College

Pam Gilmore
Reedley College

Philip Kim
Walsh University

Jeanann Boyce
Montgomery College

MaryJo Slater
Community College of Beaver County

JoAnn Brannen
Abraham Baldwin Agricultural College

Robert Patrick Sheridan
Northeast Iowa Community College

Sherry Muse
American Institute

Marcus Lacher
Minnesota State Community and Technical College

John Hupp
Columbus State University

Bernard Ku
Austin Community College

Theresa Meza
James Sprunt Community College

Jeremy A. Pittman
Coahoma Community College

LeAnne Lovering
Augusta Technical College

Lois Ann ONeal
Rogers State University

Lucy DeCaro
College of the Sequoias

Fredrick Bsharah
Cape Cod Community College

Timothy Holston
Mississippi Valley State University

Robert Balicki
Wayne County Community College District

Anita Beecroft
Kwantlen Polytechnic University

Margaret Cooksey
Tallahassee Community College

Susan Jackson
University of New Mexico-Valencia Campus

Beverly Forney
Clackamas Community College

Yves Durand
Keiser University

Cindi Nadelman
New England College

Susan Mahon
Collin College

Anthony Cameron
Fayetteville Tech Comm College

W. Randy Somsen
Brigham Young University-Idaho

Leanne Ruff
Blue Ridge Community College

Jan Wilms
Union University

Diane Bigger
LDS Business College

Michael Kurhan
Burlington County College

Vincent Yip
Umpqua Community College

Cheryl Jordan
San Juan College

Md Manzoor Murshed
Upper Iowa University

Pengtao Li
California State University, Stanislaus

George Sweiss
Governors State University Ill

Sharon M. Hope
Maria College

Ann Konarski
Baker College - Port Huron

Saiid Ganjalizadeh
Metropolitan School of Professional Studies

Brittany Bright
University of Arkansas

Iftikhar Sikder
Cleveland State University

Robin Fuller
Mississippi Gulf Coast Community College

Trude Pang
Kapiolani Community College

Tanya Patrick
Clackamas Community College

Tom Sill
Northwest University

Diane Franklin
Uintah Basin Applied Technology College

Cameron Spears
Hillsborough Community College

Kristi Smith
Allegany College of Maryland

Philip H. Nielson
Salt Lake Community College

Angela Nino
Richland College

Rajkumar Kempaiah
College of Mount Saint Vincent

Jeff Hansen
Treasure Valley Community College

J. F. Pauer
Bowling Green State University Firelands Campus

Ryan Carter
Mayland Community College

Kungwen (Dave) Chu
Purdue University Calumet

Bruce Haft
Glendale College

Tahir Aziz
J. Sargeant Reynolds Community College

Mercedes N. Alafriz
University of Phoenix/WIU

Dusty Anderson
Bluefield College

Keith Grubb
Rowan-Cabarrus Community College

Denise Reimer
Iowa Lakes Community College

Michael Sisk
Cleveland Community College

Anna Beavers
Laney College

Ted Tedmon
North Idaho College

Paulette Bell
Santa Rosa Junior College

Kevin Wyzkiewicz
Delta College

Uma Sridharan
Presbyterian College

Frank Tatum
Patrick Henry Community College

Jean Welsh
Lansing Community College

Karen Poland
Bryant and Stratton College

Aaron Tenenbaum
Brooklyn College

Susan Burden
Moberly Area Community College

Jim Patterson
Paradise Valley Community College

Richard Johnsen
County College of Morris

Ann Henry
Opportunity Center, Inc.,
ServiceSource - Delaware

Cathy Urbanski
Chandler-Gilbert College

Panda Jones
Gwinnett Technical College

Roni Ettleman
Atchison High School

Georgia Vanderark
Stark State College

Kevin Bradford
Somerset Community College - KCTCS

Shan Bhagoji
Monroe College

Anita Laird
Schoolcraft College

Carmen M. Aponte
Ana G. Mendez University System

Roberto Ordonez
Southern Adventist University

Marni Ferner
University of North Carolina Wilmington

Alisa Kadenic-Newman
NHTI

Andrea Langford
Ohio Valley Goodwill Industries

Barbara Schwartz
Pine Manor College

Carolyn Hill
Tallahassee Community College

Tracy Richardson
Eastern Maine Community College

Steve Nichols
Metropolitan Community College

Adell Brooks
Hinds Community College

Don Gaber
University of Wisconsin - Eau Claire

Laurie Zouharis
Suffolk University

Jill Fisher
Indian Capital Technology Center—Bill Willis Campus

Daniel Lowrance
Salt Lake Community College

Dee Hobson
Richland College

Matthew Macarty
University of New Hampshire

Jackie Porter
El Centro College

Alton Tripp
Northern Virginia Community College

Jan Repnow
Minot State University

Muhammad Obeidat
Southern Poly State University

Kirk McLean
LIM College

Saiid Ganjalizadeh
Northern Virginia Community College

Masoud Naghedolfeizi
Fort Valley State University

Kevin Fishbeck
University of Mary

Judy Smith
University District of Columbia

Mary Williams
University of Akron

Lisa Cady
University of Arkansas - Fort Smith (UAFS)

Phyllis Hutson
Southern Arkansas University Tech

Madison Ngafeeson
Northern Michigan University

Mandy Reininger
Chemeketa Community College

Lennie Alice Cooper
Miami Dade College - North Campus

Robert Pavkovich
Fortis College

Augustine Brennan
Erie Community College South

Judy Paternite
Kent State University Geauga

Brian Bradley
College of DuPage

Wilma Andrews
Virginia Commonwealth University
Anna Fitzpatrick
Rowan College at Gloucester County
Abdul Sattar
Bridgewater State University
Annette Kerwin
College of DuPage
Carolyn Barren
Macomb Community College
Matthew Marie
Aquinas College
Michael C. Theiss
University of Wisconsin Colleges
Kimberly Campbell
Eastern Maine Community College
Kamiyar Maleky
American River College
Chris Cheske
Lakeshore Technical College
Teresa Ferguson
Seattle Vocational Institute
Candace S. Garrod
Red Rocks Community College
Amiya K. Samantray
Marygrove College
Alex Morgan
DeAnza College
Howard Divins
DuBois Business College
Reshma R. Tolani
Charter College
Melinda White
Seminole State College
Michelle Thompson
Hillsborough Community College
Roy Stewart
Harris-Stowe State University
Joan Butler
Manchester Community College
Gary Moore
Caldwell Community College and Technical
Institute
Brian Downs
Century College
Mitch Pendleton
LDS Business College
Meg Stoner
Santa Rosa Junior College
Orletta E. Caldwell
Grand Rapids Community College
Julia Basham
Southern State Community College
Mary Ann Culbertson
Tarrant County College Northwest Campus
Michael Carrington
Northern Virginia Community College
Freddy Barton
Tampa Vocational Institute
Sandy Keeter
Seminole State College
Harold Gress, Jr.
Wilson College
Sujing Wang
Lamar University
Brent Nabors
Clovis Community College Center
Dennis Walpole
University of South Florida
LaToya Smith
Piedmont Community College
Kyu Lee
Saint Martin's University
Lacey Lormand
University of Louisiana at Lafayette
Rebecca Bullough
College of the Sequoias
Mark Vancleve
Terronez
Raj Parikh
Westwood College

Carolyn Carvalho
Kent State University
Gerry Young
Vance Granville Community College
Marie Hartlein
Montgomery County Community College
Doug Read
Ball State University
Marie Guest
North Florida Community College
Gloria Sabatelli
Butler County Community College
Rose Steimel
Kansas Wesleyan University
Ronald Johnson
Central Alabama Community College
Eddie Bannister
Keiser University-Pembroke Pines, FL
Gustavo Diaz
Broward College
Pamela Lewis
Wilson Community College
James Schaap
Grand Rapids Community College
Gregory Latterell
Alexandria Technical and Community College
David Lewis
Bryant and Stratton College
Pamela Van Nutt
American National University - Martinsville,
VA
Cheryl Miller
Bay College
James Anderson
Bay College
Darryl Habeck
Milwaukee Area Technical College
Dorvin Froseth
United Tribes Technical College
Wade Graves
Grayson College
Brenda McFarland
Asheville-Buncombe Technical Community
College
Cherie M. Stevens
South Florida State College
Sandra Tavegia
The Community College of Baltimore County
Robyn Barrett
St Louis Community College - Meramec
Sharon Breeding
Bluegrass Community and Technical College
Theodore Tielens
Mt. San Jacinto
Lynda Hodge
Guilford Technical Community College
James Graves
College of Southern Maryland
Mike Michaelson
Palomar College
Kristi Parker
Baptist Bible College
Cheri Broadway
Jacksonville University
Anna Tsipenyuk
LIM College
Pamela Silvers
Asheville-Buncombe Technical Community
College
Clarence Stokes
American River College
Cheryl D. Green
Delgado Community College
Kenneth N. Bryant
Kentucky State University
James Cammack
Lamar State College Port Arthur
Bryan Moss
San Jacinto College
Becky McAfee
Hillsborough Community College

David Gomillion
Northern Michigan University
Steven Bale
Truckee Meadows Community College
Julie Craig
Scottsdale Community College
Ashley Harrier
Hillsborough Community College
Brian Fox
Santa Fe College
Alicen Flosi
Lamar University
Karl Smart
Central Michigan University
David Little
High Point University
Paula Gregory
Yavapai College
Gary Sorenson
Northwest Technical College, Bemidji
Linda Lau
Longwood University
Frank Clements
State College of Florida
Keith Hood
Indiana Purdue Fort Wayne
Timothy Ely
Harcum College
Deborah Sahrbeck
North Shore Community College,
Danvers, MA
Barbara West
Central Georgia Technical College
Shondra Greene
Albany State University
Amy Giddens
Central Alabama Community College
Dishi Shrivastava
University of North Florida
Patricia Frederick
Del Mar College
Bill Hammerschlag
Brookhaven College
Vinzanna Leysath
Allen University
Robert Nichols
College of DuPage
Corrine Sweet
Darton State College
Michael Magro
Shenandoah University
Vijay K Agrawal
University of Nebraska at Kearney
Timothy Ely
Harcum College
Rosie L. Inwang
Olive-Harvey College
Milledge Mosby
Prince George's Community College
Michael Torguson
Rogue Community College
Linda Phelps
Northwest Arkansas Community College
Corey DeLaplain
Keiser University Online
Lisa Lopez
Southern Wesleyan University
John Marek
Houston Community College
Lori Krei
Iowa Lakes Community College
Sharon Sneed
Eastfield Community College
Michael C. Johnson
ACD Computer College
Ben Martz
Northern Kentucky University
Russ Dulaney
Rasmussen College
Linda Johnsonius
Murray State University

Ionie Pierce
LIM College
Jo Ann Koenig
Indiana University-Purdue University
Indianapolis
James Reneau
Shawnee State University
Wanda Gibson
Consolidated School of Business
David Milazzo
Niagara County Community College
John S. Galliano
University of Maryland University College
Lee Janczak
Lackawanna College
Philip Raphan
Broward College North Campus
Larry Schulze
San Antonio College
David Easton
Waubonsee Community College
Doug Baker
Kent State University
Alanna Duley
College of Western Idaho
Helen Slack
Mahoning County Career and Technical Center
Carolyn Golden
Huston-Tillotson University
Terri Tiedeman
Southeast Community College
Edwin Harris
University of North Florida
Jeff Lehman
Huntington University
Aimee Durham
Rowan-Cabarrus Community College
Denise Askew
Rowan-Cabarrus Community College
Curby Simerson
Randolph Community College
Cindi Albrightson
Southwestern Oklahoma State University
Amanda Kaari
Central Georgia Tech
Ruben Ruiz
Morton College
Riza Marjadi
Murray State University
Annette Yauney
Herkimer Couny Community College
Donna Maxson
Lake Michigan College
Benjamin White
Bainbridge State College
Joy Flanders
Central Methodist University
Jill McCollum
Southern Arkansas University Tech
Sonya Sample
Greenville Technical College
Michelle Chappell
Henderson Community College
Shawn Brown
Ashland Community and Technical College
Sherry Cox
Broward College
Bonnie J. Tuggle-Ziglar
Brookstone College of Business
Fernando Wilches
Ana G. Mendez University System
Doreen Palucci
Wilmington University
Thomas Seeley
Urbana University
Victor Wotzkow
New Professions Technical Institute
Ahmed Kamel
Concordia College, Moorhead
Marie Campbell
Idaho State University-College of Technology

Sue McCrory
Missouri State University

Somone Washington
Broward College Online

Johnnie Nixon
King's College

Gloria Hensel
Matanuska-Susitna College University of Alaska Anchorage

Gary Cotton
American River College,

Kingsley Meyer
University of Rio Grande / Rio Grande Community College

Martha Merrill
Pellissippi State Community College

Olusade Ajayi
Germanna Community College

Pat Pettit
Millikin University

Mary Evens
Clark College

Michelle Masingill
North Idaho College

Mark Douglas
Our Lady of the Lake University

Rhonda Lucas
Spring Hill College

Anita Sutton
Germanna Community College

S. E. Beladi
Broward College

Ronda Thompson
Keene State College

Lyn Snyder
Owens Community College

Mark Connell
SUNY at Cortland

Guarionex Salivia
Minnesota State University

David Arevigian
Monroe County Community College

Verlan Erickson
Western Dakota Technical Institute

John Robinson
Cumberland County College

Allan Greenberg
New York University

Debra Adams
Mott Community College

Bobbie Hawkins
Southwest TN Community College

Nancy Stephens
Chemeketa Community College

Jeremy Harris
Evangel University

Kim Mangan
Manor College

Judith Scheeren
Westmoreland County Community College

Darrelyn Relyea
Grays Harbor College

Jay F. Miller
Union College, Barbourville

Deborah Franklin
Bryant and Stratton College

Nina Fontenot
South Louisiana Community College

Jim Speers
Southeastern Oklahoma State University

Jennifer Klenke
East Central College

Young Baek
Los Angeles City College

Carl Rebman
University of San Diego

Shelly Knittle
Alaska Career College

Natunya Johnson
Holmes Community College

Linda Lemley
Pensacola State College

Ranida Harris
Indiana University Southeast

Kelly Young
Lander University

Karin Stulz
Northern Michigan University

Cathie Phillips
Lamar State College-Orange

James Brown
Central Washington University

H. Roger Fulk
Rhodes State College

Dan Britton
Chemeketa Community College

Olivia Kerr
El Centro College

Michelle Dawson
Missouri Southern State University

Dianne Hargrove
College of Health Care Professions

Shannon Shoemaker
SUNY Delhi

Bruce Caraway
Lone Star College - University Park

Richard DiRose
Hillsborough Community College - South Shore

TECHNICAL EDITORS

Karen May
Blinn College

Andrea Nevill
College of Western Idaho

Richard Finn
Moraine Valley Community College

Chris Anderson
North Central Michigan College

Gena Casas
Florida State College

Leon Blue
Pensacola State College

Mary Carole Hollingsworth
Georgia Perimeter College

Amie Mayhall
Olney Central College

Julie Haar
Alexandria Technical and Community College

Diane Santurri
Johnson & Wales University

Ramona Santa Maria
Buffalo State College

Thank you to the wonderful team at McGraw-Hill for your confidence in us and support throughout this project. Alan, Wyatt, Tiffany, Debbie, Rick, and Julianna, we thoroughly enjoy working with you all! A special thanks to Debbie Hinkle for her thorough and insightful review of the series. Thank you also to Laurie Zouharis, Amie Mayhall, Sarah Clifford, Rebecca Leveille, Jane Holcombe, and all of the reviewers and technical editors for your expertise and invaluable insight, which helped shape this book.

—Pat and Randy

**Intro Chapter**

# Windows 10, Office 2016, and File Management

## CHAPTER OVERVIEW

Microsoft Office 2016 and Windows 10 introduce many new features, including cloud storage for your files, Office file sharing, and enhanced online content. The integration of Office 2016 and Windows 10 means that files are more portable and accessible than ever when you use *OneDrive*, Microsoft's free online cloud storage. The new user interface for Office 2016 and Windows 10 allows you to work on tablet computers and smartphones in a consistent working environment that resembles that of your desktop or laptop computer.

### STUDENT LEARNING OUTCOMES (SLOs)

After completing this chapter, you will be able to:

SLO Intro.1    Explore the features of Windows 10 (p. OI-2).

SLO Intro.2    Use the basic features of Office 2016 and navigate the Office 2016 working environment (p. OI-10).

SLO Intro.3    Create, save, close, and open Office files (p. OI-17).

SLO Intro.4    Customize the view and display size in Office applications and work with multiple Office files (p. OI-25).

SLO Intro.5    Print, share, and customize Office files (p. OI-28).

SLO Intro.6    Use the *Ribbon*, tabs, groups, dialog boxes, task panes, galleries, and the *Quick Access* toolbar (p. OI-33).

SLO Intro.7    Use context menus, mini toolbars, keyboard shortcuts, and function keys in Office applications (p. OI-37).

SLO Intro.8    Organize and customize Windows folders and Office files (p. OI-42).

## CASE STUDY

*Throughout this book you have the opportunity to put into practice the application features that you are learning. Each chapter begins with a case study that introduces you to the Pause & Practice projects in the chapter. These Pause & Practice projects give you a chance to apply and practice key skills in a realistic and practical context. Each chapter contains three to five Pause & Practice projects.*

American River Cycling Club (ARCC) is a community cycling club that promotes fitness. ARCC members include recreational cyclists who enjoy the exercise and camaraderie as well as competitive cyclists who compete in road, mountain, and cyclocross races throughout the cycling season. In the Pause & Practice projects, you incorporate many of the topics covered in the chapter to create, save, customize, manage, and share Office 2016 files.

*Pause & Practice Intro-1:* Customize the Windows *Start* menu and *Taskbar*, create and save a PowerPoint presentation, create a folder, open and rename an Excel workbook, and use Windows 10 features.

*Pause & Practice Intro-2:* Modify the existing document, add document properties,

customize the Quick Access toolbar, export the document as a PDF file, and share the document.

*Pause & Practice Intro-3:* Copy and rename files, create a folder, move files, create a zipped folder, and rename a zipped folder.

---

SLO INTRO. 1

# Using Windows 10

Windows 10 is the ***operating system*** that controls computer functions and the working environment. Windows 10 uses the familiar ***Windows desktop***, ***Taskbar***, and ***Start menu***, and you can customize the working environment. You can install traditional applications (***apps***), such as Microsoft Office, to your computer. Also, you can add modern apps from the Microsoft Store similar to how you add an app to your smartphone. Your ***Microsoft account*** is used to store your Microsoft settings, download apps from the Microsoft Store, and connect you to Microsoft Office, *OneDrive*, and *Office Online*.

## Windows 10

The Windows 10 operating system controls interaction with computer hardware and software applications. ***Windows 10*** has a revised user interface that utilizes an updated ***Start menu***, where you can select and open a program. Alternatively, you can use the *Taskbar* on the Windows desktop, which has the familiar look of previous versions of Windows. When you log in to Windows 10 using your Microsoft account, it synchronizes your Windows, Office, and ***OneDrive*** cloud storage among computers.

## Microsoft Account

In Windows 10 and Office 2016, your files and account settings are portable. In other words, your Office settings and files can travel with you and be accessed from different computers. You are not restricted to a single computer. When you sign in to Windows 10 using your Microsoft account (user name and password), Microsoft uses this information to transfer your Windows and Office 2016 settings to the computer you are

Intro-1 Create a Microsoft account

using. Your Microsoft account not only signs you in to Windows and Office but also to other free Microsoft online services, such as *OneDrive* and ***Office Online***. If you don't have a Microsoft account, you can create a free account at https://signup.live.com (Figure Intro-1).

## Windows Desktop and Taskbar

The Windows desktop is the working area of Windows. When you log in to Windows, the desktop displays (Figure Intro-2). The *Taskbar* displays at the bottom of the desktop. You can open programs and folders from the *Taskbar* by clicking on an icon on the *Taskbar* (see Figure Intro-2). You can pin apps and other Windows items, such as the *Control Panel* or *File Explorer*, to the *Taskbar* (see "Customize the Taskbar" later in this section).

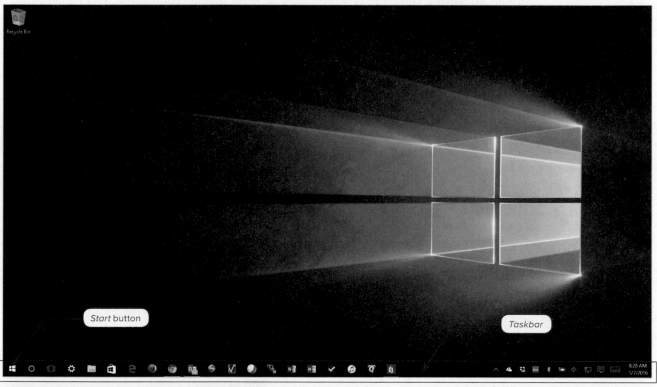

Intro-2  Windows desktop and *Taskbar*

Intro-3  Windows *Start* menu

## Start Menu

Windows 10 utilizes a redesigned *Start* menu (Figure Intro-3), that you open by clicking the **Start button** located in the bottom left of the *Taskbar*. From the *Start* menu, you can open programs, files, folders, or other Windows resources. The *Start* menu is divided into two main sections. The left side of the *Start* menu displays **Most Used** items, buttons to open the **File Explorer** and **Settings** windows, the **Power** button, and **All apps**, which displays an alphabetical listing of all applications installed on your computer. The right side of the *Start* menu displays apps as tiles (large and small buttons) you can click to open an application or window.

You can customize which apps and items appear on either side of the *Start* menu, arrange and group apps on the *Start* menu, resize the *Start* menu, and display the *Start* menu as a **Start page** when you log in to Windows (similar to the *Start* page in Windows 8 and 8.1). See "Customize the Start Menu" later in this section for information about customizing the *Start* menu.

## Add Apps

Windows 10 uses the term *apps* generically to refer to applications and programs. Apps include the Windows 10 Weather app, Microsoft Excel program, Control Panel, Google Chrome, or *File Explorer*. Many apps are preinstalled on a Windows 10 computer, and you can add apps to your computer. You can install an app such as Office 2016 or Quicken by downloading it from a web site or from a program DVD. These are referred to as ***traditional apps***.

The ***Microsoft Store*** app is preinstalled on Windows 10 computers. You can also install apps such as Netflix, Trip Advisor, and The Weather Channel from the Microsoft Store. These apps are referred to as ***modern apps*** and look and function similar to apps you install on your smartphone. Many apps in the Microsoft Store are free and others are available for purchase.

### ▶HOW TO: Add an App from the Microsoft Store

1. Click the **Start** button to open the *Start* menu.
2. Click the **Store** button (tile) to open the Microsoft Store app (Figure Intro-4).
   - If the *Store* tile is not available on the *Start* menu, click **All apps** on the *Start* menu, scroll down, and click **Store** in the alphabetic listing of all apps.
3. Select an app in the Microsoft Store (Figure Intro-5).
   - The Microsoft Store has different categories of apps.
   - You can search for apps by typing key words in the *Search* box in the upper right.
   - When you select an app, a description and screen shots of the app displays.
4. Click the **Free**, **Free trial**, or price button to install the app.
   - You must have a payment method stored in your Microsoft account to purchase apps from the Microsoft Store.
5. Click **Open** to open the installed app.
   - When you install an app, the app is listed in the *Recently added* area on the *Start* menu and *All apps* list of applications.

Intro-4 **Store** button on the **Start** menu

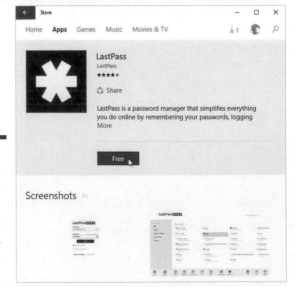

## Customize the Start Menu

When you start using Windows 10 or after you have installed either traditional or modern apps, you can customize what appears on your *Start* menu and resize the *Start*

Intro-5 Install an app from the Microsoft Store

menu. When you **pin** an app to the *Start* menu, the app tile remains on the right side of the *Start* menu. Pin the apps you most regularly use, unpin the apps you don't want to display on the *Start* menu, and rearrange and resize apps tiles to your preference.

▶ **HOW TO:** Customize the Start Menu

1. Move an app tile by clicking and dragging the app tile to a new location on the *Start* menu. The other app tiles shuffle to accommodate the placement of the app tile.

2. Remove an app tile from the *Start* menu by right-clicking the app tile you want to remove and selecting **Unpin from Start** from the context menu (Figure Intro-6).
   - The app tile is removed from the *Start* menu, but the program or task is not removed from your computer.

Intro-6  Unpin an app from the *Start* menu

3. Pin an app tile to the *Start* menu by clicking **All apps** at the bottom of the *Start* menu, right-clicking the app to pin, and selecting **Pin to Start** (Figure Intro-7).
   - Drag the newly added app tile to the desired location on the Start menu.

Intro-7  Pin an app to the *Start* menu

4. Resize an app tile by right-clicking the app tile, selecting **Resize**, and selecting **Small**, **Medium**, **Wide**, or **Large**.
   - Some apps only have *Small*, *Medium*, and *Wide* size options.

5. Turn on or off the live tile option by right-clicking the app tile and selecting **Turn live tile on** or **Turn live tile off**.
   - Live tile displays rotating graphics and options on the app tile. When this option is turned off, the name of the app displays on the tile.

6. Uninstall an app by right-clicking the app you want to uninstall and selecting **Uninstall**.
   - Unlike the unpin option, this option uninstalls the program from your computer, not just your *Start* menu.

7. Resize the *Start* menu by clicking and dragging the top or right edge of the *Start* menu.

8. Use a full screen *Start* menu by clicking the **Start** button to open the *Start* menu, selecting **Settings** to open the *Settings* window, clicking the **Personalization** button, clicking the **Start** option at the left, selecting **Use Start full screen**, and clicking the **X** in the upper right to close the *Settings* window (Figure Intro-8).
   - The *Start* menu expands to the full screen when opened.

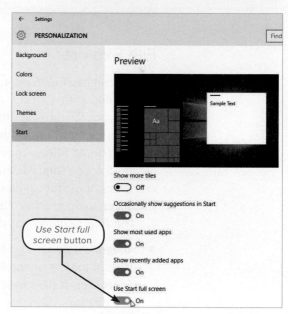

Intro-8  Use full screen *Start* menu

## Customize the Taskbar

The *Taskbar* is located at the bottom of the Windows desktop, and you can quickly open an app by clicking a button on the *Taskbar* rather than opening it from the *Start* menu. You can customize the *Taskbar* by pinning, unpinning, and rearranging apps on the *Taskbar*.

## ▶ HOW TO: Customize the Taskbar

1. Pin an app to the *Taskbar* by clicking the *Start* menu, right-clicking an app, clicking **More**, and selecting **Pin to taskbar** (Figure Intro-9).
   - You can also pin an app to the *Taskbar* from the *All apps* list in the *Start* menu.
2. Unpin an app from the *Taskbar* by right-clicking an app on the *Taskbar*, and selecting **Unpin from taskbar** (Figure Intro-10).
   - You can also unpin apps from the *Taskbar* by right-clicking the app in the *Start* menu, clicking **More**, and selecting **Unpin from taskbar**.
3. Rearrange apps on the *Taskbar* by clicking and dragging the app to the desired location on the *Taskbar* and release.

Intro-9 Pin an app to the *Taskbar*

Intro-10 Unpin an app from the *Taskbar*

> ### MORE INFO
> If using a touch screen, you can press and hold an app on the *Start* menu or *Taskbar* to display the app options.

## File Explorer

The redesigned *File Explorer* in Windows 10 is a window that opens on your desktop where you can browse for files stored on your computer (Figure Intro-11). You can open a file or folder, move or copy items, create folders, and delete files or folders. Click the **Start** button and select **File Explorer** to open a *File Explorer* window.

The *File Explorer* has different areas:

- ***Navigation pane***: The *Navigation* pane displays folders on the left. The ***Quick access*** area at the top of the *Navigation* pane displays shortcuts to favorite folders. You can pin or unpin folders in the *Quick access* area of the *Navigation* pane.
- ***Navigation buttons***: The navigation buttons (*Back*, *Forward*, *Recent location*, and *Up*) are located directly above the *Navigation* pane and below the *Ribbon*. Use these buttons to navigate a File Explorer window.
- ***Folder pane***: When you select a folder in the *Navigation* pane, the contents of the folder displays in the *Folder* pane to the right of the *Navigation* pane. Double-click a folder or file in the *Folder* pane to open it.
- ***Ribbon***: The *Ribbon* at the top of the *File Explorer* is collapsed by default. When you click a tab on the *Ribbon*, it expands to display the options on the tab. The main tabs of

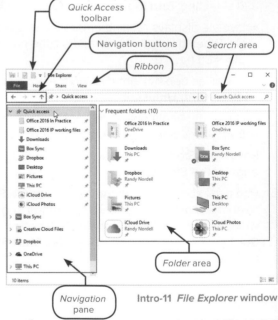

Intro-11 *File Explorer* window

the *Ribbon* are *File*, *Home*, *Share*, and *View*. Other context-sensitive tabs open when you select certain types of files. For example, the *Picture Tool Manage* tab opens when you select a picture file.

- **Quick Access toolbar**: The *Quick Access* toolbar is above the *Ribbon*. From the *Quick Access* toolbar, you can click the **New Folder** button to create a new folder or **Properties** to display the properties of a selected file or folder. You can add buttons, such as *Rename*, to the *Quick Access* toolbar.
- **Search**: The *Search* text box is located on the right of the *File Explorer* window below the *Ribbon*. Type key words in the *Search* text box to find files or folders.

## OneDrive

*OneDrive* is a cloud storage area where you can store files in a private and secure online location that you can access from any computer. When you store your files in *OneDrive*, the files are actually saved on both your computer and on the cloud. *OneDrive* synchronizes your files so when you change a file it is automatically updated on the *OneDrive* cloud.

With Windows 10, the **OneDrive folder** is one of your storage location folder options, similar to your *Documents* or *Pictures* folders (Figure Intro-12). You can save, open, and edit your *OneDrive* files from a *File Explorer* folder. Your *OneDrive* folder looks and functions similar to other Windows folders.

In addition to the *OneDrive* folder on your computer, you can also access your *OneDrive* files online using an Internet browser such as Microsoft Edge, Google Chrome, or Mozilla Firefox. When you access *OneDrive* online using a web browser, you can upload files, create folders, move and copy files and folders, and create Office files using *Office Online* (*Office Online* is discussed in *SLO Intro.2: Using Office 2016*).

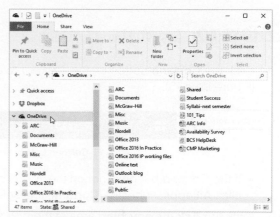

Intro-12 *OneDrive* folder in a *File Explorer* window

### ▶HOW TO: Use OneDrive Online

1. Open an Internet browser window and navigate to the *OneDrive* web site (www.onedrive.live.com), which takes you to the *OneDrive* sign in page.
   - You can use any Internet browser to access *OneDrive* (Microsoft Edge, Google Chrome, Mozilla Firefox).
2. Click the **Sign in** button, type your Microsoft account email address, and click **Next**.
3. Type your Microsoft account password and click **Sign in** (Figure Intro-13). You are taken to your *OneDrive* page.
   - If you are on your own computer, check the **Keep me signed in** box to stay signed in to *OneDrive* when you return to the page.

Intro-13 Log in to *OneDrive* online

- The different areas of *OneDrive* are listed under the *OneDrive* heading on the left (Figure Intro-14).
- Click **Files** to display your folders and files in the folder area.
- At the top of the page, buttons and drop-down menus list the different actions you can perform on selected files and folders.

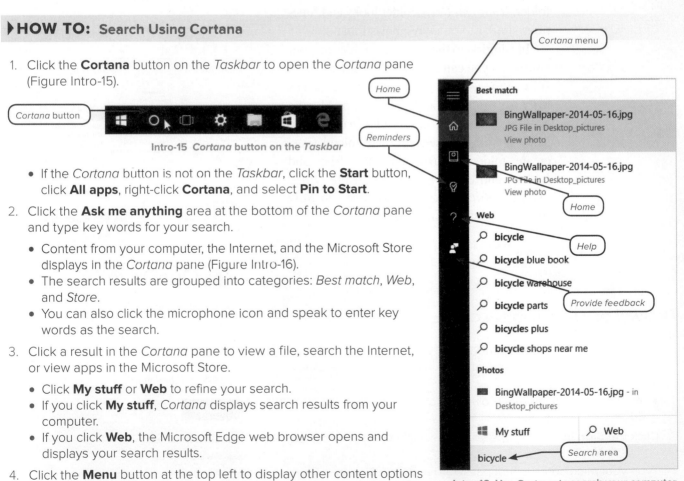

Intro-14 *OneDrive* online environment

## Cortana

In addition to using the search tools in the *File Explorer*, you can also use **Cortana**, which is new in Windows 10. While the search feature in the *File Explorer* searches only for content on your computer, *Cortana* searches for content on your computer, on the Internet, and in the Microsoft Store. You can either type key words for a search or use voice commands to search for content.

When you open *Cortana*, other content, such as weather, upcoming appointments, and popular news stories, displays in the *Cortana* pane.

▶ **HOW TO: Search Using Cortana**

1. Click the **Cortana** button on the *Taskbar* to open the *Cortana* pane (Figure Intro-15).

   Intro-15 *Cortana* button on the *Taskbar*

   - If the *Cortana* button is not on the *Taskbar*, click the **Start** button, click **All apps**, right-click **Cortana**, and select **Pin to Start**.

2. Click the **Ask me anything** area at the bottom of the *Cortana* pane and type key words for your search.

   - Content from your computer, the Internet, and the Microsoft Store displays in the *Cortana* pane (Figure Intro-16).
   - The search results are grouped into categories: *Best match*, *Web*, and *Store*.
   - You can also click the microphone icon and speak to enter key words as the search.

3. Click a result in the *Cortana* pane to view a file, search the Internet, or view apps in the Microsoft Store.

   - Click **My stuff** or **Web** to refine your search.
   - If you click **My stuff**, *Cortana* displays search results from your computer.
   - If you click **Web**, the Microsoft Edge web browser opens and displays your search results.

4. Click the **Menu** button at the top left to display other content options in the *Cortana* pane (see Figure Intro-16).

   - The other content options are *Home*, *Notebook*, *Reminders*, *Help*, and *Feedback*.

Intro-16 Use *Cortana* to search your computer, the Internet, and the Microsoft Store

## Task View

A new feature to Windows 10 is **Task View**. *Task View* displays all open apps and windows as tiles on your desktop, and you can choose which item to display or close. This feature is very helpful when you have multiple items open and want to select or close one.

**▶HOW TO:** Use Task View

1. Click the **Task View** button on the *Taskbar* (Figure Intro-17).
   - All open apps and windows display on the desktop (Figure Intro-18).

Intro-17  *Task View* button on the *Taskbar*

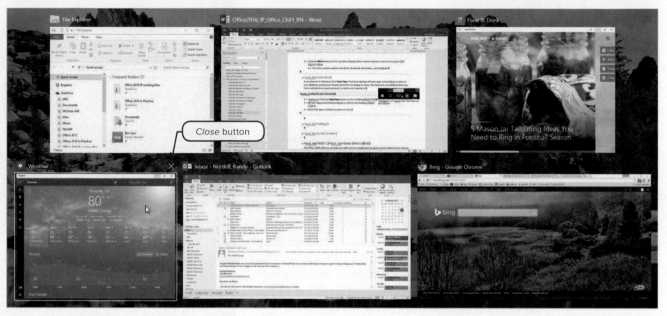

Intro-18  *Task View* with open apps and windows displayed on the desktop

2. Select the app or window to open or close.
   - Click a tile to open an app. The app opens and *Task View* closes.
   - Click the **X** in the upper right corner of an app to close an app. *Task View* remains open when you close an app.

## Settings

In Windows 10, the **Settings** window is the redesigned *Control Panel* (although the *Control Panel* is still available). The *Settings* window is where you change global Windows settings, customize the Windows environment, add devices, and manage your Microsoft account. Click the **Settings** button on the *Taskbar* or *Start* menu to open the *Settings* window (Figure Intro-19). The following categories are available in the *Settings* window:

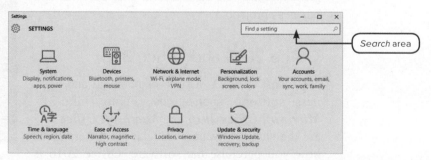

Intro-19  *Settings* window

- **System**: Display, notifications, apps, and power
- **Devices**: Bluetooth, printers, and mouse
- **Network & Internet**: Wi-Fi, airplane mode, and VPN
- **Personalization**: Background, lock screen, and colors
- **Accounts**: Your account, sync settings, work, and family
- **Time & Language**: Speech, region, and date
- **Ease of Access**: Narrator, magnifier, and high contrast
- **Privacy**: Location and camera
- **Update & Security**: Windows Update, recovery, and backup

> **MORE INFO**
>
> If you can't find an item in *Settings*, use the *Search* dialog box (*Find a setting*) in the upper right corner and type key words. If *Settings* is not available on the *Taskbar*, you can find it in the *All apps* list on the *Start* menu.

## Action Center

The **Action Center** in Windows 10 provides a quick glance of notifications and buttons to open other commonly used settings and features in Windows. The *Action Center* displays notifications such as emails and Windows update notifications. Or you can click an action button to turn on or off features or open other windows or apps such as the *Settings* menu (*All Settings* button) or OneNote (*Note* button). Click the **Action Center** button on the right side of the *Taskbar* to open the *Action Center* pane on the right side of your screen (Figure Intro-20).

Intro-20 *Action Center*

## Using Office 2016

Office 2016 includes common software applications such as Word, Excel, Access, and PowerPoint. These applications give you the ability to work with word processing documents, spreadsheets, presentations, and databases in your personal and business projects.

### Office 2016 and Office 365

Microsoft Office is a suite of personal and business software applications (Figure Intro-21). **Microsoft Office 2016** and **Microsoft Office 365** are the same software products; the difference is how you purchase the software. Office 2016 is

Intro-21 Microsoft Office application tiles on the *Start* menu

the traditional model of purchasing the software, and you own that software for as long as you want to use it. Office 365 is a subscription that you pay monthly or yearly, similar to how you purchase Netflix or Spotify. If you subscribe to Office 365, you automatically receive new versions of the software when they are released.

The common applications typically included in Microsoft Office 2016 and 365 are described in the following list:

- **Microsoft Word**: Word processing software used to create, format, and edit documents such as reports, letters, brochures, and resumes.
- **Microsoft Excel**: Spreadsheet software used to perform calculations on numerical data such as financial statements, budgets, and expense reports.
- **Microsoft Access**: Database software used to store, organize, compile, and report information such as product information, sales data, client information, and employee records.
- **Microsoft PowerPoint**: Presentation software used to graphically present information in slides such as a presentation on a new product or sales trends.
- **Microsoft Outlook**: Email and personal management software used to create and send email and create and store calendar items, contacts, and tasks.
- **Microsoft OneNote**: Note-taking software used to take and organize notes, which can be shared with other Office applications.
- **Microsoft Publisher**: Desktop publishing software used to create professional-looking documents containing text, pictures, and graphics such as catalogs, brochures, and flyers.

## Office Desktop Apps, Office Universal Apps, and Office Online

**Office desktop apps** are the full-function Office 2016 or 365 programs installed on your computer (PC or Mac). Both Office 2016 and Office 365 are considered Office desktop apps. Because of the increased popularity and capabilities of tablets and mobile devices, Office software is also available for both tablets and smartphones. **Office universal apps** are the Office 365 programs that can be installed on tablets or other mobile devices. Office universal apps do not have the full range of advanced features available in Office desktop applications, but Office universal apps provide users the ability to create, edit, save, and share Office files using many of the most common features in the Office suite of programs.

> **MORE INFO**
>
> Office universal apps are also referred to as **Office mobile apps**.

Intro-22 *Office Online*

**Office Online** is free online software from Microsoft that works in conjunction with your Microsoft account and *OneDrive* (Figure Intro-22). With *Office Online*, you can work with Office files online through a web browser, even on computers that do not have Office 2016 or 365 installed. This is a useful option when you use a computer at a computer lab or use a friend's computer that does not have Office installed.

You can access *Office Online* from your *OneDrive* web page to create and edit Word documents, Excel workbooks, PowerPoint presentations, and OneNote notebooks. *Office Online* is a scaled-down version of Office 2016/365 and not as robust in terms of features, but you can use it to create, edit, print, share, and collaborate on files. If you need more advanced features, you can open *Office Online* files in Office 2016.

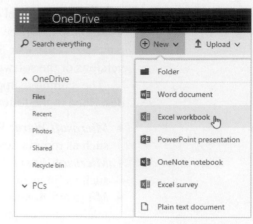

> **MORE INFO**
>
> Microsoft Access is not available in *Office Online* or as an Office universal app.

## ▶HOW TO: Create an Office Online File

1. Open an Internet browser Window, navigate to the *OneDrive* web site (www.onedrive.live.com), and log in to *OneDrive*. If you are not already logged in to *OneDrive*, use the following steps.

   - Click the **Sign in** button, type your Microsoft account email address, and click **Next**.
   - Type your Microsoft account password and click **Sign in** to open your *OneDrive* page.

Intro-23 Create an Office Online file from your online *OneDrive* page

2. Click the **New** button and select the type of *Office Online* file to create (Figure Intro-23).

   - A new file is created and opens in the *Office Online* program.
   - The new file is saved in your *OneDrive* folder (both online and on your computer).

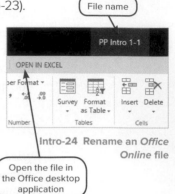

File name

3. Rename the file by clicking on the file name at the top of the file, typing a new file name, and pressing **Enter** (Figure Intro-24).

   - You can also click the **File** tab to open the *Backstage* view, select *Save As*, and choose **Save As** or **Rename**.
   - Click the **OPEN IN [OFFICE APPLICATION]** button (for example **OPEN IN EXCEL**) to open the file in the Office desktop application (see Figure Intro-24).

Intro-24 Rename an *Office Online* file

Open the file in the Office desktop application

4. Close the browser tab or window to close the file.

   - *Office Online* automatically saves the file as you make changes.

## Open an Office Desktop Application

When using Windows 10, you open an Office desktop application by clicking the application tile on the *Start* menu or the application icon on the *Taskbar*. If your *Start* menu and *Taskbar* do not have the Office applications displayed, click the **Start** button, select **All apps**, and select **Word 2016**, **Excel 2016**, **Access 2016**, or **PowerPoint 2016** to launch the application (Figure Intro-25).

You can also use *Cortana* to quickly locate an Office desktop app (Figure Intro-26).

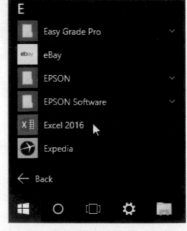

Intro-25 Open an Office desktop app from the *All apps* area on the *Start* menu

Intro-26 Use *Cortana* to find and open an app

## Office Start Page

Most of the Office applications (except Outlook and OneNote) display a ***Start page*** when you launch the application (Figure Intro-27). From this *Start* page, you can create a new blank file (for example a Word document, an Excel workbook, an Access database, or a PowerPoint presentation), create a file from an online template, search for an online template, open a recently used file, or open another file. These options vary depending on the Office application.

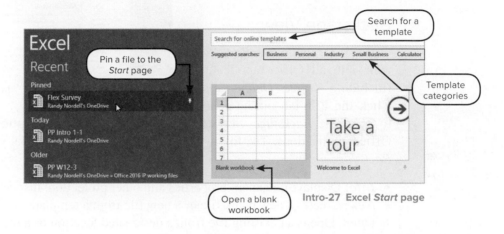

Intro-27 Excel *Start* page

▶ **HOW TO: Use the Office Start Page**

1. Open a file listed in the *Recent* area on the left side of the *Start* menu by clicking the file to open. The file opens in the working area of the Office application.

   - The *Recent* area on the left side of the *Start* page lists files you have recently used and files that are pinned to the *Start* page.

2. Open a new blank file by clicking the **Blank *[file type]*** tile (*Blank workbook*, *Blank document*, etc.) to the right of the *Recent* area.

   - You can also press the **Esc** key to exit the *Start* page and open a new blank file.

3. Open an existing file that is not listed in the *Recent* area by clicking the **Open Other Workbooks** link (Figure Intro-28). The *Open* area on the *Backstage* view displays.

   - Click the **Browse** button to open the *Open* dialog box where you can locate and open a file.
   - You can also select a different location, *OneDrive* or *This PC*, and select a file to open.

4. Open a template by clicking a template file on the right or searching for templates.

   - Search for a template by typing key words in the *Search* area on the *Start* page.
   - Click a link to one of the categories below the *Search* area to display templates in that category.

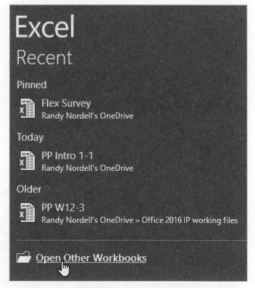

Intro-28 *Open Other Workbooks* link on the *Start* page

5. Pin a frequently used file to the *Start* page by clicking the **Pin** button.
   - The *Pin* button is on the right side of items listed in the *Recent* area and at the bottom right of templates displayed in the *Templates* area (to the right of the *Recent* area).
   - Pinned files display at the top of the *Recent* area.

> **MORE INFO**
>
> In Access, you have to open an existing database or create a new one to enter the program.

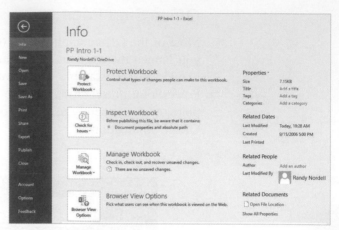

Intro-29 *Backstage* view in Excel

## Backstage View

Office incorporates the ***Backstage view*** into all Office applications (including *Office Online* apps). Click the **File** tab on the *Ribbon* to open the *Backstage* view (Figure Intro-29). *Backstage* options vary on the different Office applications. The following list describes common tasks you can perform from the *Backstage* view:

- ***Info***: Displays document properties and other protection, inspection, and version options.
- ***New***: Creates a new blank file or a new file from a template or theme.
- ***Open***: Opens an existing file from a designated location or a recently opened file.
- ***Save***: Saves a file. If the file has not been named, the *Save As* dialog box opens when you select this option.
- ***Save As***: Opens the *Save As* dialog box.
- ***Print***: Prints a file, displays a preview of the file, or displays print options.
- ***Share***: Invites people to share a file or email a file.
- ***Export***: Creates a PDF file from a file or saves as a different file type.
- ***Close***: Closes an open file.
- ***Account***: Displays your Microsoft account information.
- ***Options***: Opens the *[Application] Options* dialog box (for example *Excel Options*).

## Office Help—Tell Me

In all the Office 2016/365 applications, ***Tell Me*** is the new help feature (Figure Intro-30). This new help feature displays the commands in the Office application related to your search. The *Help* feature in older versions of Office displayed articles describing the feature and how

to use it. The new *Tell Me* feature provides command options that take you directly to a command or dialog box. For example if you type *PivotTable* in the *Tell Me* search box in Excel, the results include the option to open the *Create PivotTable* dialog box, as well as other options such as *Recommended PivotTables* and *Summarize with PivotTable*.

Intro-30 *Tell Me* search box

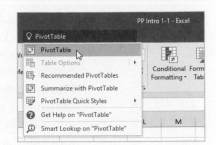

# ▶HOW TO: Use Tell Me

1. Place your insertion point in the **Tell Me** search box at the top of the *Ribbon* (see Figure Intro-30).

2. Type key words for the command or feature for which you are searching.

3. Select an option from the list of displayed search results (Figure Intro-31).

- When you select a search result, it may apply a command, open a dialog box, or display a gallery of command choices.

Intro-31 *Tell Me* search results

> ▶ ANOTHER WAY
>
> **Alt+Q** places the insertion point in the *Tell Me* dialog box.
> The previous *Help* feature is still available in Office 2016/365. Press **F1** to open the *Help* dialog box.

## Mouse and Pointers

If you are using Office on a desktop or laptop computer, use your mouse (or touch pad) to navigate around files, click tabs and buttons, select text and objects, move text and objects, and resize objects. The following table lists mouse and pointer terminology used in Office:

### Mouse and Pointer Terminology

| Term | Description |
| --- | --- |
| *Pointer* | When you move your mouse, the pointer moves on your screen. A variety of pointers are used in different contexts in Office applications. The following pointers are available in most of the Office applications (the appearance of these pointers varies depending on the application and the context used): <br> • *Selection pointer:* Select text or an object. <br> • *Move pointer:* Move text or an object. <br> • *Copy pointer:* Copy text or an object. <br> • *Resize pointer:* Resize objects or table columns or rows. <br> • *Crosshair:* Draw a shape. |
| *Insertion point* | The vertical flashing line indicating where you type text in a file or text box. Click the left mouse button to position the insertion point. |
| *Click* | Click the left mouse button. Used to select an object or button or to place the insertion point in the selected location. |
| *Double-click* | Click the left mouse button twice. Used to select text. |
| *Right-click* | Click the right mouse button. Used to display the context menu and the mini toolbar. |
| *Scroll* | Use the scroll wheel on the mouse to scroll up and down through your file. You can also use the horizontal or vertical scroll bars at the bottom and right of an Office file window to move around in a file. |

## Touch Mode and Touch Screen Gestures

The new user interface in Windows 10 and Office 2016 has improved touch features to facilitate the use of Windows and the Office applications on a tablet computer or smartphone. On tablets and smartphones, you use a touch screen rather than using a mouse, so the process of selecting text and objects and navigating around a file is different from a computer without a touch screen.

In Office 2016/365, *Touch mode* optimizes the Office working environment when using a computer with a touch screen to provide more space between buttons and commands. Click the **Touch/Mouse Mode** button on the *Quick Access* toolbar (upper left of the Office app window) and select **Touch** from the drop-down list to enable *Touch* mode (Figure Intro-32). To turn off *Touch* mode, select **Mouse** from the *Touch/Mouse Mode* drop-down list.

Intro-32 Turn on *Touch* mode

> **MORE INFO**
>
> The *Touch/Mouse Mode* button displays on the *Quick Access* toolbar when using a touch-screen computer.

The following table lists common gestures used when working on a tablet or smartphone (these gestures vary depending on the application used and the context):

## Touch Screen Gestures

| Gesture | Used To | How To |
|---------|---------|--------|
| **Tap** | Select text or an object or position the insertion point. Double tap to edit text in an object or cell. | |
| **Pinch** | Zoom in or resize an object. | |
| **Stretch** | Zoom out or resize an object. | |
| **Slide** | Move an object or selected text. | |
| **Swipe** | Select text or multiple objects. | |

> **MORE INFO**
>
> Window 10 has a *Tablet mode* that optimizes all of Windows and apps for touch screens. When you turn on the *Tablet mode* feature in Windows, the *Touch mode* in Office apps turns on automatically. Click the **Action Center** button on the Windows *Taskbar* and click the **Tablet mode** button to turn on this feature in Windows.

# Creating, Saving, Closing, and Opening Files

Creating, saving, opening, and closing files is primarily done from the *Start* page or *Backstage* view of the Office application you are using. These areas provide you with many options and a central location to perform these tasks. You can also use shortcut commands to create, save, and open files.

## Create a New File

When you create a new file in an Office application, you can create a new blank file or a new file based on a template (in PowerPoint, you can also create a presentation based on a theme). On the *Start* page, click **Blank [file type]** to create a new blank file in the application you are using (in Word, you begin with a blank document; in Excel, a blank workbook; in Access, a blank desktop database; and in PowerPoint, a blank presentation).

> ## ▶ HOW TO: Create a New File from the Start Page

1. Open the Office application you want to use. The *Start* page displays when the application opens (Figure Intro-33).

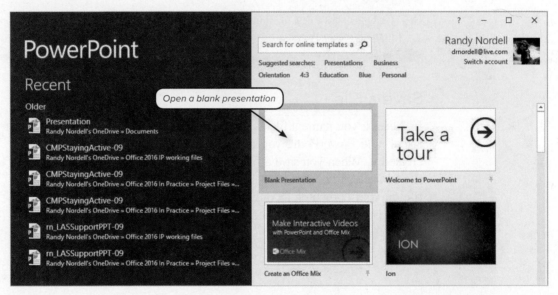

Intro-33 *Start* page in PowerPoint

2. Click **Blank [file type]** or select a template or theme to use for your new blank file. A new file opens in the application you are using.

   - The new file is given a generic file name (for example *Document1, Book1,* or *Presentation1*). You can name and save this file later.
   - When creating a new Access database, you are prompted to name the new file when you create it.
   - A variety of templates (and themes in PowerPoint only) display on the *Start* page, but you can search for additional online templates and themes using the *Search* text box at the top of the *Start* page.

---

> ## ▶ MORE INFO
> **Esc** closes the *Start* page and takes you into the Office application (except in Access).

If you have been using an application already and want to create a new file, you create it from the *Backstage* view. From the *Backstage* view, the new file options are available in the *New* area.

> **HOW TO:** Create a New File from the Backstage View

1. Click the **File** tab to display the *Backstage* view.
2. Select **New** on the left to display the *New* area (Figure Intro-34).
3. Click **Blank [file type]** or select a template or theme to use in your new blank file. A new file opens in the application.
   - The new file is given a generic file name (*Document1*, *Book1*, or *Presentation1*). You can name and save this file later.
   - When you are creating a new Access database, you are prompted to name the new file when you create it.

Intro-34    *New* area on the *Backstage* view in PowerPoint

> **ANOTHER WAY**
>
> **Ctrl+N** opens a new file from within an Office application. In Access, **Ctrl+N** opens the *New* area in the *Backstage* view.

## Save a File

In Access, you name a file as you create it, but in Word, Excel, and PowerPoint, you name a file after you have created it. When you save a file, you type a name for the file and select the location to save the file. You can save a file on your computer, an online storage location such as *OneDrive*, or portable device, such as a USB drive.

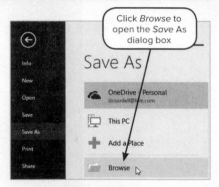

Click *Browse* to open the *Save As* dialog box

Intro-35 *Save As* area on the *Backstage* view in PowerPoint

> **HOW TO:** Save a File

1. Click the **File** tab to display the *Backstage* view.
2. Select **Save** or **Save As** on the left to display the *Save As* area (Figure Intro-35).
   - If the file has not already been saved, clicking *Save* or *Save As* takes you to the *Save As* area on the *Backstage* view.
3. Click the **Browse** button to open the *Save As* dialog box (Figure Intro-36).
   - You can also select a different location (*OneDrive* or *This PC*) and select a folder from the list of folders at the right to open the *Save As* dialog box.
4. Select a location to save the file in the *Folder* list on the left.

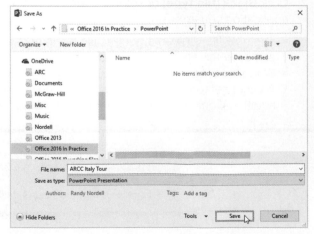

Intro-36 *Save As* dialog box

5. Type a name for the file in the *File name* area.
   - By default, Office selects the file type, but you can change the file type from the *Save as type* drop-down list.
6. Click **Save** to close the dialog box and save the file.

> **ANOTHER WAY**
>
> **Ctrl+S** opens the *Save As* area on the *Backstage* view when a file has not been named. If a file has already been named, **Ctrl+S** saves the file without opening the *Backstage* view.

> **MORE INFO**
>
> If you save a file in *OneDrive*, you have access to that file from any computer with Internet access. Also, you can share and collaborate on files stored in *OneDrive*. *OneDrive* is one of the folders in the *Save As* dialog box.

## Create a New Folder When Saving a File

When saving files, it is a good idea to create folders to organize your files. Organizing your files in folders makes it easier to find your files and saves you time when you are searching for a specific file (see *SLO Intro.8: Organizing and Customizing Folders and Files* for more information on this topic). When you save an Office file, you can also create a folder in which to store that file.

> **HOW TO: Create a New Folder When Saving a File**

1. Click the **File** tab to display the *Backstage* view.
2. Select **Save As** on the left to display the *Save As* area.
3. Click **Browse** to open the *Save As* dialog box.
4. Select a location to save the file in the *Folder* list on the left.
5. Click the **New Folder** button to create a new folder (Figure Intro-37).
6. Type a name for the new folder and press **Enter**.

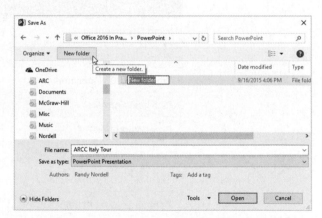

Intro-37 Create a new folder

> **ANOTHER WAY**
>
> **F12** opens the *Save As* dialog box (except in Access). On a laptop, you might have to press **Fn+F12**. See more about the *Fn* (Function) key in *SLO Intro.7: Using Context Menus, the Mini Toolbars, and Keyboard Shortcuts*.

## Save As a Different File Name

After you have saved a file, you can save it again with a different file name. If you do this, you have preserved the original file, and you can continue to revise the second file for a different purpose.

> **HOW TO:** Save as a Different File Name

1. Click the **File** tab to display the *Backstage* view.
2. Select **Save As** on the left to display the *Save As* area.
3. Click the **Browse** button to open the *Save As* dialog box.
4. Select a location to save the file in the *Folder* list on the left.
5. Type a new name for the file in the *File name* area.
6. Click **Save** to close the dialog box and save the file.

## Office 2016 File Types

When you save an Office file, by default Office saves the file in the most recent file format for that application. You also have the option of saving files in older versions of the Office application you are using. For example, you can save a Word document as an older version to share with or send to someone who uses an older version of Word. Each file has an extension at the end of the file name that determines the file type. The ***file name extension*** is automatically added to a file when you save it. The following table lists common file types used in the different Office applications:

### Office File Types

| File Type | Extension | File Type | Extension |
|-----------|-----------|-----------|-----------|
| Word Document | *.docx* | Access Database | *.accdb* |
| Word Template | *.dotx* | Access Template | *.accdt* |
| Word 97-2003 Document | *.doc* | Access Database (2000-2003 format) | *.mdb* |
| Rich Text Format | *.rtf* | PowerPoint Presentation | *.pptx* |
| Excel Workbook | *.xlsx* | PowerPoint Template | *.potx* |
| Excel Template | *.xltx* | PowerPoint 97-2003 Presentation | *.ppt* |
| Excel 97-2003 Workbook | *.xls* | Portable Document Format (PDF) | *.pdf* |
| Comma Separated Values (CSV) | *.csv* | | |

## Close a File

You can close a file using the following different methods:

- Click the **File** tab and select **Close** on the left.
- Press **Ctrl+W**.
- Click the **X** in the upper right corner of the file window. This method closes the file and the program if only one file is open in the application.

When you close a file, you are prompted to save the file if it has not been named or if changes were made after the file was last saved (Figure Intro-38). Click **Save** to save and close the file or click **Don't Save** to close the file without saving. Click **Cancel** to return to the file.

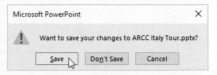

## Open an Existing File

You can open an existing file from the *Start* page when you open an Office application or while you are working on another Office file.

▶**HOW TO: Open a File from the Start Page**

1. Open an Office application to display the *Start* page.
2. Select a file to open in the *Recent* area on the left (Figure Intro-39). The file opens in the Office application.
    - If you select a file in the *Recent* area that has been renamed, moved, or on a storage device not connected to the computer, you receive an error message.
3. Alternatively, click the **Open Other [file type]** (for example *Open Other Presentations*) (see Figure Intro-39) link to open the *Open* area of the *Backstage* view (Figure Intro-40).

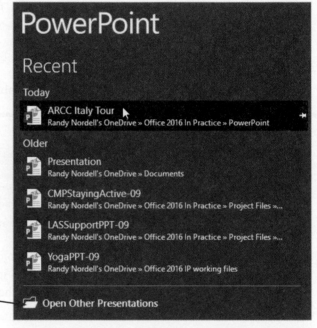

Intro-39 Open a file from the *Start* page

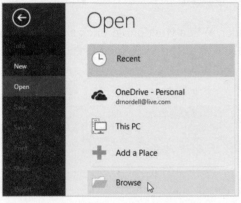

Intro-40 *Open* area on the *Backstage* view

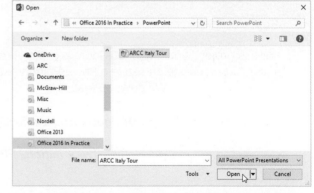

4. Click the **Browse** button to open the *Open* dialog box (Figure Intro-41).
5. Select a location from the *Folder* list on the left.
6. Select the file to open and click the **Open** button.
    - If the file opens in *Protected View,* click the **Enable Editing** button to allow you to edit the file.

Intro-41 *Open* dialog box

When working on a file in an Office application, you might want to open another file. You can open an existing file from within an Office application from the *Open* area on the *Backstage* view.

## ▶HOW TO: Open a File from the Backstage View

1. Click the **File** tab from within an open Office application to open the *Backstage* view.
2. Click **Open** on the left to display the *Open* area on the *Backstage* view (see Figure Intro-40).
3. Click the **Browse** button to open the *Open* dialog box (see Figure Intro-41).
   - You can also select a file to open from the list of *Recent* files on the right of the *Open* area on the *Backstage* view.
4. Select a location from the *Folder* list on the left.
5. Select the file to open and click the **Open** button.
   - If the file opens in *Protected View*, click the **Enable Editing** button to allow you to edit the file.

> **ANOTHER WAY**
>
> Press **Ctrl+F12** to open the *Open* dialog box when you are in the working area of an Office application (except in Access). On some laptops, you might have to press **Fn+Ctrl+F12**.

You can also open a file from a *File Explorer* folder. When you double-click a file in a *File Explorer* folder, the file opens in the appropriate Office application. Windows recognizes the file name extension and launches the correct Office application.

## PAUSE & PRACTICE: INTRO-1

For this project, you log in to Windows using your Microsoft account, customize the Windows *Start* menu and *Taskbar*, create and save a PowerPoint presentation, create a folder, open and rename an Excel workbook, and use Windows 10 features.

File Needed: ***ARCC2018Budget-Intro.xlsx*** *(Student data files are available in the* Library *of your SIMnet account)*
Completed Project File Names: ***[your initials] PP Intro-1a.pptx*** and ***[your initials] PP Intro-1b.xlsx***

1. Log in to Windows using your Microsoft account if you are not already logged in.
   a. If you don't have a Microsoft account, you can create a free account at https://signup.live.com.
   b. If you are using a computer on your college campus, you may be required to log in to the computer using your college user name and password.

2. Customize the *Start* menu to include Office 2016 apps. If these apps tiles are already on the *Start* menu, skip steps 2a–e. You can pin other apps of your choice to the *Start* menu.
   a. Click the **Start** button at the bottom left of your screen to open the *Start* menu.

b. Click **All apps** at the bottom left of the *Start* menu (Figure Intro-42). The list of apps installed on the computer displays on the left side of the *Start* menu.

c. Locate and right-click **Access 2016** and select **Pin to Start** (Figure Intro-43). The app displays as a tile on the right side of the *Start* menu.

d. Repeat step 2c to pin **Excel 2016**, **PowerPoint 2016**, and **Word 2016** apps to the *Start* menu.

e. Display the *Start* menu and drag these Office app tiles so they are close to each other.

f. Click the **Start** button (or press the **Esc** key) to close the *Start* menu.

Intro-42 *All apps* button on the *Start* menu

3. Use *Cortana* and the *Start* menu to pin Office 2016 apps to the *Taskbar*.

a. Click the **Cortana** button (to the right of the *Start* button) on the *Taskbar* and type Access. *Cortana* displays content matching your search.

b. Right-click the **Access 2016** option near the top of the *Cortana* pane and select **Pin to taskbar** (Figure Intro-44). The app pins to the *Taskbar*.

c. Click the **Start** button to open the *Start* menu.

d. Right-click the **Excel 2016** tile on the right side of the *Start* menu, click **More**, and select **Pin to taskbar**. The app pins to the *Taskbar*.

e. Use either of the methods described above to pin the **PowerPoint 2016** and **Word 2016** apps to the *Taskbar*.

f. Drag the Office apps on the *Taskbar* to rearrange them to your preference.

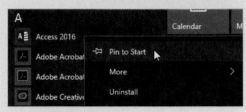

Intro-43 Pin Access 2016 app to *Start* menu

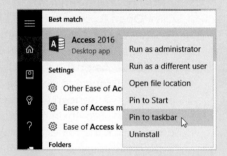

Intro-44 Use *Cortana* to find an Office app and pin it to the *Taskbar*

4. Create a PowerPoint presentation and save the presentation in a new folder.

a. Click the **PowerPoint 2016** app tile on your *Start* menu to open the application.

b. Click **Blank Presentation** on the PowerPoint *Start* page to create a new blank presentation.

c. Click the **Click to add title** placeholder and type American River Cycling Club to replace the placeholder text.

d. Click the **File** tab to open the *Backstage* view and click **Save As** on the left to display the *Save As* area.

e. Click **Browse** to open the *Save As* dialog box (Figure Intro-45).

f. Select a location to save the file from the *Folder* list on the left. If the *OneDrive* folder is an option, select **OneDrive**. If it is not, select the **Documents** folder in the *This PC* folder. You can also save to a portable storage device if you have one.

g. Click the **New Folder** button to create a new folder.

h. Type American River Cycling Club as the name of the new folder and press **Enter** (Figure Intro-46).

i. Double-click the **American River Cycling Club** folder to open it.

Intro-45 *Save As* area on the *Backstage* view in PowerPoint

j. Type [your initials] PP Intro-1a in the *File name* area.

k. Click **Save** to close the dialog box and save the presentation. Leave the file and PowerPoint open.

5. Open an Excel file and save as a different file name.

a. Return to the Windows *Start* menu.

b. Click the **Excel 2016** app button on the *Taskbar* to open it.

c. Click the **Open Other Workbooks** link on the bottom left of the Excel *Start* page to display the *Open* area of the *Backstage* view.

d. Click **Browse** to open the *Open* dialog box (Figure Intro-47).

e. Browse to your student data files and select the *ARCC2018Budget-Intro* file.

f. Click **Open** to open the workbook. If the file opens in *Protected View*, click the **Enable Editing** button.

g. Click the **File** tab to open the *Backstage* view.

h. Click **Save As** on the left to display the *Save As* area and click **Browse** to open the *Save As* dialog box.

i. Locate the **American River Cycling Club** folder (created in step 4h) in the *Folder* list on the left and double-click the folder to open it.

j. Type [your initials] PP Intro-1b in the *File name* area.

k. Click **Save** to close the dialog box and save the workbook. Leave the file and Excel open.

6. Use the *Tell Me* feature in Excel to find a command.

a. Click the **Tell Me** search box on the *Ribbon* of the Excel window and type PivotTable (Figure Intro-48).

b. Click **PivotTable** to open the *Create PivotTable* dialog box.

c. Click the **X** in the upper right corner of the *Create PivotTable* dialog box to close it.

7. Open the *Microsoft Store* app, the *Action Center*, and the *Settings* window.

a. Click the **Cortana** button and type Microsoft Store.

b. Click **Store** at the top of the *Cortana* pane to open the *Store* app.

c. Click **Apps** in the top left and browse the available apps in the Microsoft Store.

d. Click the **Minimize** button in the upper right corner of the *Store* window to minimize this app (Figure Intro-49). The app is still open, but it is minimized on the *Taskbar*.

e. Click the **Action Center** button on the right side of the *Taskbar* to display the *Action Center* pane at the right (Figure Intro-50).

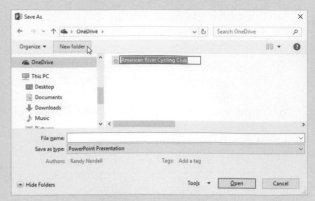

Intro-46 Create a new folder from the *Save As* dialog box

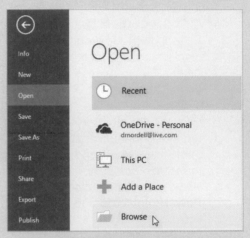

Intro-47 *Open* area on the *Backstage* view

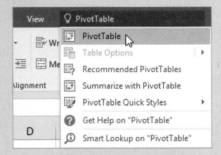

Intro-48 Use the *Tell Me* feature to find a command

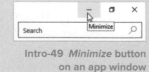

Intro-49 *Minimize* button on an app window

Intro-50 Windows 10 *Action Center*

f.  Click **All settings** to open the *Settings* window.

g.  Click the **Find a setting** search box, type Printer, and view the search results.

h.  Click the **Minimize** button to minimize the *Settings* windows to the *Taskbar*.

8. Use the *Task View* feature to open and close apps and windows.

a.  Click the **Task View** button on the left side of the *Taskbar* (Figure Intro-51). All of the open apps and windows are tiled on the Windows desktop.

b.  Click the **Store** app to open it. *Task View* closes and the *Store* app displays on your Windows desktop.

c.  Click the **Task View** button again.

d.  Click the **X** in the upper right corner to close each open app and window. You may be prompted to save changes to a file.

e.  Click the **Task View** button again or press **Esc** to return to the desktop.

Intro-51 *Task View* button on the *Taskbar*

 **Working with Files**

When you work with Office files, a variety of display views are available. You can change how a file displays, adjust the display size, work with multiple files, and arrange the windows to view multiple files. Because most people work with multiple files at the same time, Office makes it easy and intuitive to move from one file to another or to display multiple document windows at the same time.

### File Views

Each of the different Office applications provides you with a variety of ways to view your document. In Word, Excel, and PowerPoint, the different views are available on the *View tab* (Figure Intro-52). You can also change views using the buttons on the right side of the *Status bar* at the bottom of the file window (Figure Intro-53). In Access, the differ-

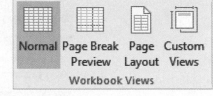

Intro-52 *Workbook Views* group on the *View* tab in Excel

Intro-53 PowerPoint views on the *Status* bar

ent views for each object are available in the *Views* group on the *Home* tab.

The following table lists the views that are available in each of the different Office applications:

### File Views

| Office Application | Views | Office Application | Views |
|---|---|---|---|
| **Word** | *Read Mode*<br>*Print Layout*<br>*Web Layout*<br>*Outline*<br>*Draft* | **Access**<br>*(Access views vary depending on active object)* | *Layout View*<br>*Design View*<br>*Datasheet View*<br>*Form View*<br>*SQL View*<br>*Report View*<br>*Print Preview* |
| **Excel** | *Normal*<br>*Page Break Preview*<br>*Page Layout*<br>*Custom Views* | **PowerPoint** | *Normal*<br>*Outline View*<br>*Slide Sorter*<br>*Notes Page*<br>*Reading View*<br>*Presenter View* |

## Change Display Size

You can use the **Zoom** feature to increase or decrease the display size of your file. Using *Zoom* to change the display size does not change the actual size of text or objects in your file; it only changes the size of your display. For example, if you change the *Zoom* level to 120%, you increase the display of your file to 120% of its normal size (100%), but changing the display size does not affect the actual size of text and objects in your file. You could also decrease the *Zoom* level to 80% to display more of your file on the screen.

You can increase or decrease the *Zoom* level several different ways. Your *Zoom* options vary depending on the Office application you are using.

- **Zoom level** *on the Status* bar (Figure Intro-54): Click the + or − button to increase or decrease *Zoom* level in 10% increments.
- **Zoom group** *on the View tab* (Figure Intro-55): The *Zoom* group includes a variety of *Zoom* options. The options vary depending on the Office application.
- **Zoom dialog box** (Figure Intro-56): Click the **Zoom** button in the *Zoom* group on the *View* tab or click the **Zoom level** on the *Status* bar to open the *Zoom* dialog box.

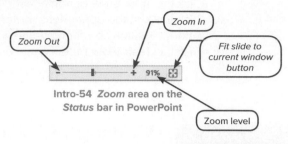

Intro-54 *Zoom* area on the *Status* bar in PowerPoint

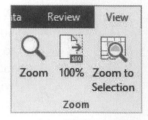

Intro-55 *Zoom* group in Excel

> **MORE INFO**
>
> The *Zoom* feature is only available in Access in *Print Preview* view when you are working with reports.

## Manage Multiple Open Files and Windows

When you are working on multiple files in an Office application, each file is opened in a new window. You can **minimize** an open window to place the file on the Windows *Taskbar* (the bar at the bottom of the Windows desktop), **restore down** an open window so it does not fill the entire computer screen, or **maximize** a window so it fills the entire computer screen. The *Minimize, Restore Down/Maximize*, and *Close* buttons are in the upper right of a file window (Figure Intro-57).

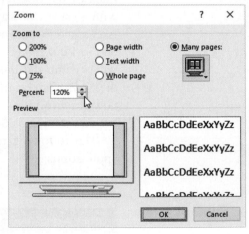

Intro-56 *Zoom* dialog box in Word

> **MORE INFO**
>
> You can open only one Access file at a time. If you open another Access file, the first one closes.

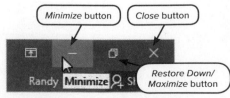

Intro-57 Window options buttons

- *Minimize*: Click the **Minimize** button (see Figure Intro-57) to hide the active window. When a document is minimized, it is not closed. It is minimized to the *Taskbar* so the window is not displayed on your screen. Place your pointer on the application icon on the Windows *Taskbar* to display thumbnails of open files. You can click an open file thumbnail to display the file (Figure Intro-58).

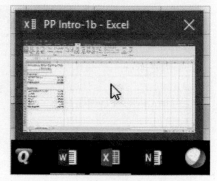

Intro-58 Display minimized file on the *Taskbar*

- *Restore Down/Maximize*: Click the **Restore Down/ Maximize** (see Figure Intro-57) button to decrease the size of an open window or maximize the window to fill the entire screen. This button toggles between *Restore Down* and *Maximize*. When a window is restored down, you can change the size of a window by clicking and dragging a border of the window. You can also move the window by clicking and dragging the title bar at the top of the window.
- *Close*: Click the **Close** button (see Figure Intro-57) to close the window. If there is only one open file, the Office application also closes when you click the *Close* button on the file.

You can switch between open files or arrange the open files to display more than one window at the same time. The following are several methods to do this:

- *Switch Windows button*: Click the **Switch Windows** button [*View* tab, *Window* group] (not available in Access) to display a drop-down list of open files. Click a file from the drop-down list to display the file.

> **ANOTHER WAY**
>
> Click the Windows **Task View** button on the *Taskbar* to tile all open windows and apps on the desktop.

- *Windows Taskbar*: Place your pointer on an Office application icon on the Windows *Taskbar* to display the open files in that application. Click a file thumbnail to display it (see Figure Intro-58).
- *Arrange All button*: Click the **Arrange All** button [*View* tab, *Window* group] to display all windows in an application. You can resize or move the open file windows.

## Snap Assist

The *Snap Assist* feature in Windows provides the ability to position an open window to the left or right side of your computer screen and fill half the screen. When you snap an open window to the left or right side of the screen, the other open windows tile on the opposite side where you can select another window to fill the opposite side of the computer screen (Figure Intro-59).

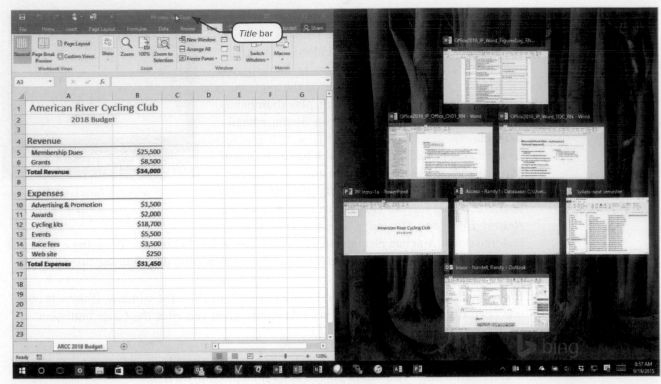

Intro-59 Windows *Snap Assist* feature

## ▶HOW TO: Use Snap Assist

1. Click the **title bar** of an open window.
2. Drag it to the left or right edge of the computer screen and release the pointer.
   - The window snaps to the side of the screen and fills half of the computer screen (see Figure Intro-59).
   - The other open windows and apps display as tiles on the opposite side.
   - If you're using a touch screen computer, you can use *Snap Assist* by pressing and holding the title bar of an open window and dragging to either side of the computer screen.
3. Select a tile of an open window or app to fill the other half of the screen.

> **MORE INFO**
>
> *Snap Assist* also allows you to snap a window to a quadrant (quarter rather than half) of your screen. Drag the **title bar** of an open window to one of the four corners of your computer screen.

### SLO INTRO. 5

## Printing, Sharing, and Customizing Files

On the *Backstage* view of any of the Office applications, you can print a file and customize how a file is printed. You can also export an Office file as a PDF file in most of the Office applications. In addition, you can add and customize document properties for an Office file and share a file in a variety of formats.

## Print a File

You can print an Office file if you need a hard copy. The *Print* area on the *Backstage* view displays a preview of the open file and many print options. For example, you can choose which page or pages to print and change the margins of the file in the *Print* area. Print settings vary depending on the Office application you are using and what you are printing.

**▶HOW TO:** Print a File

1. Open the file you want to print from a Windows folder or within an Office program.
2. Click the **File** tab to open the *Backstage* view.
3. Click **Print** on the left to display the *Print* area (Figure Intro-60).
   - A preview of the file displays on the right. Click the **Show Margins** button to adjust margins or **Zoom to Page** button to change the view in the *Preview* area. The *Show Margins* button is only available in Excel.
4. Change the number of copies to print in the *Copies* area.
5. Click the **Printer** drop-down list to choose from available printers.
6. Customize what is printed and how it is printed in the *Settings* area.
   - The *Settings* options vary depending on the Office application you are using and what you are printing.
   - In the *Pages* area (*Slides* area in PowerPoint), you can select a page or range of pages (slides) to print.
   - By default all pages (slides) are printed when you print a file.
7. Click the **Print** button to print your file.

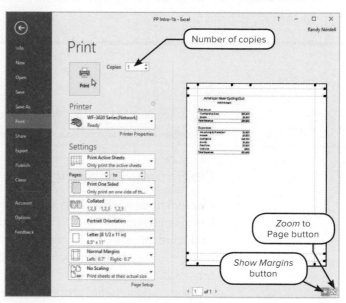

Intro-60 *Print* area on the *Backstage* view

---

▶ **ANOTHER WAY**

Press **Ctrl+P** to open the *Print* area on the *Backstage* view.

---

## Export as a PDF File

***Portable document format***, or ***PDF***, is a specific file format that is often used to share files that are not to be changed or to post files on a web site. When you create a PDF file from an Office application file, you are actually exporting a static image of the original file, similar to taking a picture of the file.

The advantage of working with a PDF file is that the format of the file is retained no matter who opens the file. PDF files open in the Windows Reader app or Adobe Reader, which is free software that is installed on most computers. Because a PDF file is a static image of a file, it is not easy for other people to edit your files. When you want people to be able to view a file but not change it, PDF files are a good choice.

## ▶HOW TO: Export a File as a PDF File

1. Open the file you want to export as a PDF file.
2. Click the **File** tab and click **Export** to display the *Export* area on the Backstage view (Figure Intro-61).
3. Select **Create PDF/XPS Document** and click the **Create PDF/XPS**. The *Publish as PDF or XPS* dialog box opens.
   - XPS (XML Paper Specification) format is an alternative to a PDF file. XPS is a Microsoft format and is not widely used.
4. Select a location to save the file.
5. Type a name for the file in the *File name* area.
6. Click **Publish** to close the dialog box and save the PDF file.
   - A PDF version of your file may open. You can view the file and then close it.

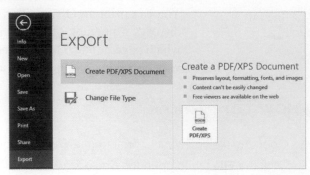

Intro-61 *Export* a file as a PDF file

---

▶

### MORE INFO

Microsoft Word can open PDF files, and you can edit and save the file as a Word document.

---

## Document Properties

***Document properties*** are hidden codes in a file that store identifying information about that file. Each piece of document property information is called a ***field***. You can view and modify document properties in the *Info* area of the *Backstage* view.

Some document properties fields are automatically generated when you work on a file, such as *Size*, *Total Editing Time*, *Created*, and *Last Modified*. Other document properties fields, such as *Title*, *Comments*, *Subject*, *Company*, and *Author*, can be modified. You can use document property fields in different ways such as inserting the *Company* field in a document footer.

Intro-62 Document properties

## ▶HOW TO: View and Modify Document Properties

1. Click the **File** tab and click **Info**. The document properties display on the right (Figure Intro-62).
2. Click the text box area of a field that can be edited and type your custom document property information.
3. Click the **Show All Properties** link at the bottom to display additional document properties.
   - Click **Show Fewer Properties** to collapse the list and display fewer properties.
   - This link toggles between *Show All Properties* and *Show Fewer Properties*.
4. Click the **Back** arrow to return to the file.

## Share a File

Windows 10 and Office 2016 have been enhanced to help you share files and collaborate with others. The *Share* area on the *Backstage* view lists different options for sharing files from within an Office application. When you save a file to your *OneDrive*, Office provides a variety of options to share your file (Figure Intro-63). The two main sharing options are ***Share with People*** and ***Email***. Within these two categories, you have a variety of ways to share a file with others. Your sharing options vary depending on the Office application you are using. The following list describes the sharing options available in the Office applications:

Intro-63 *Share* options on the *Backstage* view

- **Word**: *Share with People, Email, Present Online*, and *Post to Blog*
- **Excel**: *Share with People* and *Email*
- **Access**: No *Sharing* option on the *Backstage* view
- **PowerPoint**: *Share with People, Email, Present Online*, and *Publish Slides*

---

### ▶HOW TO: Share a File

1. Click the **File** tab to open the *Backstage* view and select **Share** on the left.
   - If your file is not saved in *OneDrive*, you are directed to first save the file to the cloud (*OneDrive*). Click the **Save to Cloud** button and save your file in *OneDrive*.
   - If your file is not saved to *OneDrive*, you will not have all available sharing options.
2. Share a *OneDrive* file with others by clicking **Share with People** on the left and then clicking the **Share with People** button on the right (see Figure Intro-63).
   - The *Backstage* view closes and the *Share* pane opens on the right side of the file (Figure Intro-64).
   - Alternatively, click the **Share** button in the upper right corner of the Office application window to open the *Share* pane (Figure Intro-65).
   - Type an email address in the *Invite people* text box. If you want to share the file with more than one person, separate email addresses with a semicolon.
   - Select **Can edit** or **Can view** from the permission drop-down list, which controls what others can do with your file.
   - You can include a message the recipients will receive.
   - Click the **Share** button below the message to send a sharing email to recipients.
   - Alternatively, click the **Get a sharing link** option at the bottom of the *Share* pane to create an *edit link* or *view-only link* (Figure Intro-66). You can then copy the sharing link and email it to others or post it in an online location.

Intro-64 *Share* pane

Intro-65 *The Share button* opens the *Share* pane

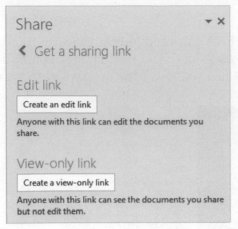

Intro-66 *Get a sharing link* options in the *Share* pane

3. Share a file through email by clicking the **Email** button on the left side of the *Share* area on the *Backstage* view and selecting an option (Figure Intro-67).

Intro-67 *Email* share options in the *Share* area on the *Backstage* view

- These *Email* share options use Microsoft Outlook (email and personal management Office application) to share the selected file through email.
- The *Email* share options include *Send as Attachment*, *Send a Link*, *Send as PDF*, *Send as XPS*, and *Send as Internet Fax*.
- A description of each of these *Email* share options are provided to the right of each option.

> **MORE INFO**
>
> Sharing options are also available if you save files to other online storage locations such as Dropbox and Box.

## Program Options

Using the program options, you can apply global changes to the Office program. For example, you can change the default save location to your *OneDrive* folder or you can turn off the *Start* page that opens when you open an Office application.

Click the **File** tab and select **Options** on the left to open the **[Program] Options** dialog box (Word Options, Excel Options, etc.) (Figure Intro-68). Click one of the categories on the left to display the category options on the right. The categories and options vary depending on the Office application you are using.

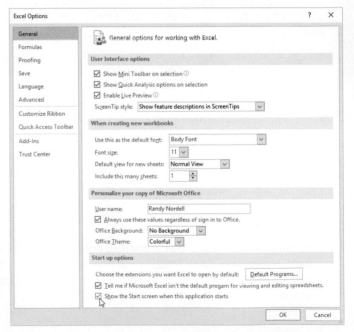

Intro-68 *Excel Options* dialog box

# Using the Ribbon, Tabs, and Quick Access Toolbar

You can use the *Ribbon*, tabs, groups, buttons, drop-down lists, dialog boxes, task panes, galleries, and the *Quick Access* toolbar to modify your Office files. This section describes different tools you can use to customize your files.

## The Ribbon, Tabs, and Groups

The ***Ribbon***, which appears at the top of an Office file window, displays the many features available to use on your files. The *Ribbon* is a collection of ***tabs***. On each tab are ***groups*** of features. The tabs and groups that are available on each Office application vary. Click a tab to display the groups and features available on that tab.

Some tabs always display on the *Ribbon* (for example the *File* tab and *Home* tabs). Other tabs are ***context-sensitive***, which means that they only appear on the *Ribbon* when you select a specific object. Figure Intro-69 displays the context-sensitive *Table Tools Field* tab that displays in Access when you open a table.

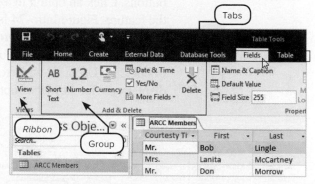

Intro-69 Context-sensitive *Table Tools Fields* tab displayed

## Ribbon Display Options

The *Ribbon* displays by default in Office applications, but you can customize how the *Ribbon* displays. The ***Ribbon Display Options*** button is in the upper right corner of an Office application window (Figure Intro-70). Click the **Ribbon Display Options** button to select one of the three options:

- ***Auto-Hide Ribbon***: Hides the *Ribbon*. Click at the top of the application to display the *Ribbon*.
- ***Show Tabs***: *Ribbon* tabs display. Click a tab to open the *Ribbon* and display the tab.
- ***Show Tabs and Commands***: Displays the *Ribbon* and tabs, which is the default setting in Office applications.

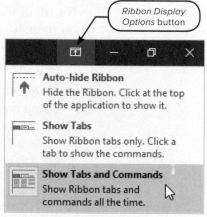

Intro-70 *Ribbon Display Options*

> **MORE INFO**
>
> **Ctrl+F1** collapses or expands the *Ribbon*.

## Buttons, Drop-Down Lists, and Galleries

Groups on each of the tabs contain a variety of ***buttons***, ***drop-down lists***, and ***galleries***. The following list describes each of these features and how they are used:

- ***Button***: Applies a feature to selected text or object. Click a button to apply the feature (Figure Intro-71).

- *Drop-down list*: Displays the various options available for a feature. Some buttons are drop-down lists only, so when you click one of these buttons the drop-down list of options appears (Figure Intro-72). Other buttons are *split buttons*, which have both a button you click to apply a feature and an arrow you click to display a drop-down list of options (Figure Intro-73).
- *Gallery*: Displays a collection of option buttons. Click an option in a gallery to apply the feature. Figure Intro-74 is the *Styles* gallery. You can click the **More** button to display the entire gallery of options or click the **Up** or **Down** arrow to display a different row of options.

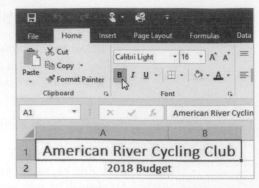

Intro-71 *Bold* button in the *Font* group on the *Home* tab

Up and Down buttons

More button

Intro-74 *Styles* gallery in Word

Intro-72 *Orientation* drop-down list

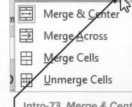

Intro-73 *Merge & Center* split button—button and drop-down list

Click the arrow on a split button to display the drop-down list

## Dialog Boxes, Task Panes, and Launchers

Not all of the features that are available in an Office application are displayed in the groups on the tabs. Additional options for some groups display in a *dialog box* or *task pane*. A *launcher*, which is a small square in the bottom right of some groups, opens a dialog box or displays a task pane when you click it (see Figure Intro-76).

- *Dialog box*: A new window that opens to display additional features. You can move a dialog box by clicking and dragging the title bar, which is the top of the dialog box where the title is displayed. Figure Intro-75 shows the *Format Cells* dialog box that opens when you click the *Alignment* launcher in Excel.

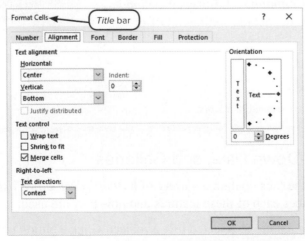

Title bar

Intro-75 *Format Cells* dialog box

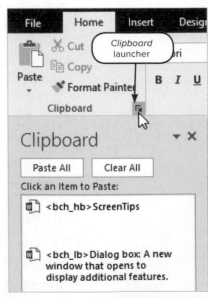

Clipboard launcher

Intro-76 *Clipboard* pane

- **Task pane**: Opens on the left or right of the Office application window. Figure Intro-76 shows the *Clipboard* pane, which is available in all Office applications. Task panes are named according to their feature (for example *Clipboard* pane or *Navigation* pane). You can resize a task pane by clicking and dragging its left or right border. Click the **X** in the upper right corner to close a task pane.

## ScreenTips

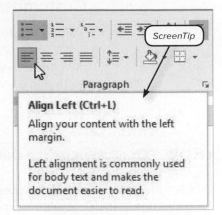

Intro-77 *Align Left ScreenTip*

**ScreenTips** display descriptive information about a button, drop-down list, launcher, or gallery selection. When you place your pointer on an item on the *Ribbon*, a *ScreenTip* displays information about the selection (Figure Intro-77). The *ScreenTip* appears temporarily and displays the command name, keyboard shortcut (if available), and a description of the command.

## Radio Buttons, Check Boxes, and Text Boxes

Dialog boxes and task panes contain a variety of features you can apply using *radio buttons*, *check boxes*, *text boxes*, *drop-down lists*, and other buttons (Figure Intro-78).

- **Radio button**: A round button you click to select one option from a list of options. A selected radio button has a solid dot inside the round button.
- **Check box**: A square button you click to select one or more options. A check appears in a check box you have selected.
- **Text box**: An area where you can type text.

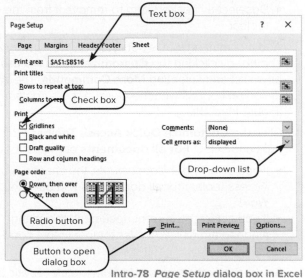

Intro-78 *Page Setup* dialog box in Excel

A task pane or dialog box may also include drop-down lists or other buttons that open additional dialog boxes. Figure Intro-78 shows the *Page Setup* dialog box in Excel, which includes a variety of radio buttons, check boxes, text boxes, drop-down lists, and other buttons that open additional dialog boxes (for example the *Print* and *Options* buttons).

## Quick Access Toolbar

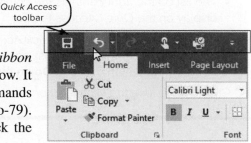

Intro-79 *Quick Access* toolbar

The **Quick Access toolbar** is located above the *Ribbon* on the upper left of each Office application window. It contains buttons to apply commonly used commands such as *Save*, *Undo*, *Redo*, and *Open* (Figure Intro-79). The *Undo* button is a split button. You can click the button to undo the last action performed or you can click the drop-down arrow to display and undo multiple previous actions.

## Customize the Quick Access Toolbar

You can customize the *Quick Access* toolbar to include features you regularly use, such as *Quick Print*, *New*, and *Spelling & Grammar*. The following steps show how to customize the *Quick Access* toolbar in Word. The customization process is similar for the *Quick Access* toolbar in the other Office applications.

> **HOW TO:** Customize the Quick Access Toolbar

1. Click the **Customize Quick Access Toolbar** drop-down list on the right edge of the *Quick Access* toolbar (Figure Intro-80).

2. Select a command to add to the *Quick Access* toolbar. The command displays on the *Quick Access* toolbar.
   - Items on the *Customize Quick Access Toolbar* drop-down list with a check mark are commands that are displayed on the *Quick Access* toolbar.
   - Deselect a checked item to remove it from the *Quick Access* toolbar.

3. Add a command that is not listed on the *Customize Quick Access Toolbar* by clicking the **Customize Quick Access Toolbar** drop-down list and selecting **More Commands**. The *Word Options* dialog box opens with the *Quick Access Toolbar* area displayed (Figure Intro-81).

4. Click the **Customize Quick Access Toolbar** drop-down list on the right and select **For all documents** or the current document.
   - If you select *For all documents*, the change is made to the *Quick Access* toolbar for all documents you open in Word.
   - If you select the current document, the change is made to the *Quick Access* toolbar in that document only.

5. Select the command to add from the alphabetic list of commands on the left and click the **Add** button.
   - If you can't find the command you're looking for, click the **Choose commands from** drop-down list and select **All Commands**.
   - The list on the right contains the commands that display on the *Quick Access* toolbar.

6. Rearrange commands on the *Quick Access* toolbar by selecting a command in the list on the right and clicking the **Move Up** or **Move Down** button.

7. Click **OK** to close the *Word Options* dialog box.

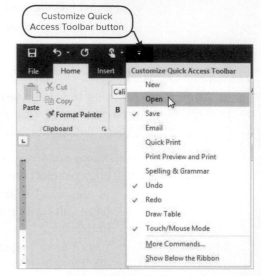

Intro-80 Add a command to the *Quick Access* toolbar

Intro-81 Customize the *Quick Access* toolbar in the *Word Options* dialog box

**SLO INTRO. 7**

# Using Context Menus, the Mini Toolbars, and Keyboard Shortcuts

Most of the commands you use for formatting and editing your files display in groups on the tabs. But many of these features are also available using content menus, mini toolbars, and keyboard shortcuts. You can use these tools to quickly apply formatting or other options to text or objects.

## Context Menu

A *context menu* displays when you right-click text, a cell, or an object such as a picture, drawing object, chart, or *SmartArt* (Figure Intro-82). The context menu is a vertical list of options, and the options are context-sensitive, which means they vary depending on what you right-click.

Context menus include options that perform an action (*Cut* or *Copy*), open a dialog box or task pane (*Format Cells* or *Hyperlink*), or display a drop-down list of selections (*Filter* or *Sort*).

## Mini Toolbar

The *mini toolbar* is another context menu that displays when you right-click or select text, a cell, or an object in your file (see Figure Intro-82). The mini toolbar is a horizontal rectangular menu that lists a variety of formatting options. These options vary depending on what you select or right-click. The mini toolbar contains a variety of buttons and drop-down lists. The mini toolbar typically displays above the context menu. The mini toolbar automatically displays when you select text or an object, such as when you select a row of a table in Word or PowerPoint.

Intro-82 Context menu and mini toolbar

## Keyboard Shortcuts

You can also use a *keyboard shortcut* to quickly apply formatting or perform commands. A keyboard shortcut is a combination of keyboard keys that you press at the same time. These can include the **Ctrl**, **Shift**, **Alt**, letter, number, and function keys (for example **F1** or **F7**). The following table lists common Office keyboard shortcuts.

## Common Office Keyboard Shortcuts

| Keyboard Shortcut | Action or Displays | Keyboard Shortcut | Action or Displays |
|---|---|---|---|
| Ctrl+S | Save | Ctrl+Z | Undo |
| F12 | *Save As* dialog *box* | Ctrl+Y | Redo or Repeat |
| Ctrl+O | *Open* area on the *Backstage* view | Ctrl+1 | Single space |
| Shift+F12 | *Open* dialog box | Ctrl+2 | Double space |
| Ctrl+N | New blank file | Ctrl+L | Align left |
| Ctrl+P | *Print* area on the *Backstage* view | Ctrl+E | Align center |
| Ctrl+C | Copy | Ctrl+R | Align right |
| Ctrl+X | Cut | F1 | *Help* dialog box |
| Ctrl+V | Paste | F7 | *Spelling* pane |
| Ctrl+B | Bold | Ctrl+A | Select All |
| Ctrl+I | Italic | Ctrl+Home | Move to the beginning |
| Ctrl+U | Underline | Ctrl+End | Move to the end |

> **MORE INFO**
> See Appendix A for additional Office 2016 keyboard shortcuts.

## Function Keys on a Laptop

Intro-83 Function key

When using a laptop computer, function keys perform specific Windows actions on your laptop, such as increase or decrease speaker volume, open Windows *Settings*, or adjust the screen brightness. So when using a numbered function key, such as **F12** as a shortcut to open the *Save As* dialog box in an Office application, you may need to press the ***function key*** (**Fn** or **fn**) on your keyboard in conjunction with a numbered function key to activate the command (Figure Intro-83). The *function key* is typically located near the bottom left of your laptop keyboard next to the *Ctrl* key.

## PAUSE & PRACTICE: INTRO-2

For this project, you work with a document for the American River Cycling Club. You modify the existing document, add document properties, customize the *Quick Access* toolbar, export the document as a PDF file, and share the document.

File Needed: ***ARCCTraining-Intro.docx*** *(Student data files are available in the Library of your SIMnet account)*
Completed Project File Names: ***[your initials] PP Intro-2a.docx*** and ***[your initials] PP Intro-2b.pdf***

1. Open Word 2016 and open the ***ARCCTraining-Intro*** file from your student data files. If the file opens in *Protected View*, click the **Enable Editing** button.

2. Save this document as [your initials] PP Intro-2a in the *American River Cycling Club* folder in your *OneDrive* folder.

   a. In *Pause & Practice Intro-1*, you created the *American River Cycling Club* folder in *OneDrive* or other storage area. Save this file in the same location.

   b. If you don't save this file in *OneDrive*, you will not be able to complete steps 7 and 9 in this project.

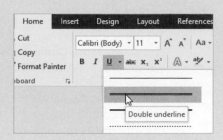

Intro-84 Apply *Double underline* to selected text.

3. Use a button, drop-down list, and dialog box to modify the document.

   a. Select the first heading, "**What is Maximum Heart Rate?**"

   b. Click the **Bold** button [*Home* tab, *Font* group].

   c. Click the **Underline** drop-down arrow and select **Double underline** (Figure Intro-84).

   d. Click the **launcher** in the *Font* group [*Home* tab] to open the *Font* dialog box (Figure Intro-85).

   e. In the *Size* area, select **12** from the list or type12 in the text box.

   f. In the *Effects* area, click the **Small caps** check box to select it.

   g. Click **OK** to close the dialog box and apply the formatting changes.

   h. Select the next heading, "**What is Target Heart Rate?**"

   i. Repeat steps 3b–g to apply formatting to selected text.

Intro-85 *Font* dialog box

4. Add document properties.

   a. Click the **File** tab to display the *Backstage* view.

   b. Select **Info** on the left. The document properties display on the right.

   c. Click the **Add a title** text box and type ARCC Training.

   d. Click the **Show All Properties** link near the bottom to display additional document properties.

   e. Click the **Specify the subject** text box and type Heart rate training.

   f. Click the **Specify the company** text box and type American River Cycling Club.

   g. Click the **Back** arrow on the upper left to close the *Backstage* view and return to the document.

5. Customize the *Quick Access* toolbar.

   a. Click the **Customize Quick Access Toolbar** drop-down arrow and select **Open** (Figure Intro-86).

   b. Click the **Customize Quick Access Toolbar** drop-down arrow again and select **Spelling & Grammar**.

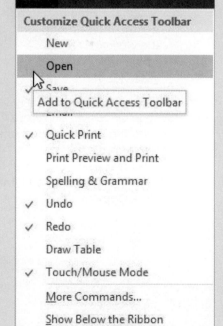

Intro-86 *Customize Quick Access Toolbar* drop-down list

c. Click the **Customize Quick Access Toolbar** drop-down arrow again and select **More Commands**. The *Word Options* dialog box opens (Figure Intro-87).

d. Select **Insert Comment** in the list of commands on the left.

e. Click the **Add** button to add it to your *Quick Access* toolbar list on the right.

f. Click **OK** to close the *Word Options* dialog box.

g. Click the **Save** button on the *Quick Access* toolbar to save the document.

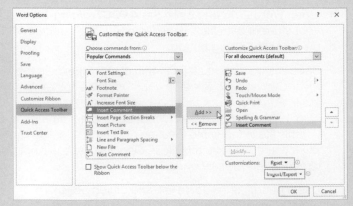

Intro-87 Customize the *Quick Access* toolbar in the *Word Options* dialog box

6. Export the file as a PDF file.

a. Click the **File** tab to go to the *Backstage* view.

b. Select **Export** on the left.

c. Select **Create PDF/XPS Document** and click the **Create PDF/XPS** button. The *Publish as PDF or XPS* dialog box opens (Figure Intro-88).

d. Select the **American River Cycling Club** folder in your *OneDrive* folder as the location to save the file.

e. Type [your initials] PP Intro-2b in the *File name* area.

f. Deselect the **Open file after publishing** check box if it is checked.

g. Select the **Standard (publishing online and printing)** radio button in the *Optimize for* area.

h. Click **Publish** to close the dialog box and create a PDF version of your file.

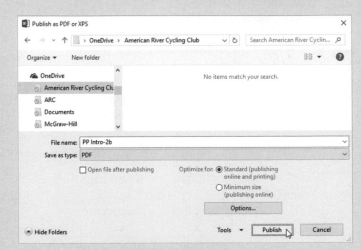

Intro-88 *Publish as PDF or XPS* dialog box

7. Get a link to share a document with your instructor. If your file is not saved in *OneDrive*, skip steps 7 and 9.

a. Click the **Share** button in the upper right of the Word window. The *Share* pane opens on the right side of your document.

b. Click **Get a sharing link** at the bottom of the *Share* pane.

c. Click the **Create an edit link** button.

d. Click **Copy** to copy the edit link (Figure Intro-89).

Intro-89 Copy a sharing link

8. Save and close the document (Figure Intro-90).

# American River Cycling Club
www.arcc.org          Cycling...a way of life          info@arcc.org

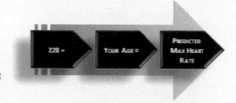

## WHAT IS MAXIMUM HEART RATE?

The maximum heart rate is the highest your pulse rate can get. To calculate your **predicted maximum heart rate**, use this formula:

*(Example: a 40-year-old's predicted maximum heart rate is 180.)*

Your actual maximum heart rate can be determined by a graded exercise test. Please note that some medicines and medical conditions might affect your maximum heart rate. If you are taking medicines or have a medical condition (such as heart disease, high blood pressure, or diabetes), always ask your doctor if your maximum heart rate/target heart rate will be affected.

220 –     YOUR AGE =     PREDICTED MAX HEART RATE

## WHAT IS TARGET HEART RATE?

You gain the most benefits and decrease the risk of injury when you exercise in your target heart rate zone. Usually this is when your exercise heart rate (pulse) is 60 percent to 85 percent of your maximum heart rate. Do not exercise above 85 percent of your maximum heart rate. This increases both cardiovascular and orthopedic risk and does not add any extra benefit.

When beginning an exercise program, you might need to gradually build up to a level that is within your target heart rate zone, especially if you have not exercised regularly before. If the exercise feels too hard, slow down. You will reduce your risk of injury and enjoy the exercise more if you don't try to over-do it.

To find out if you are exercising in your target zone (between 60 percent and 85 percent of your maximum heart rate), use your heart rate monitor to track your heart rate. If your pulse is below your target zone (see the chart below), increase your rate of exercise. If your pulse is above your target zone, decrease your rate of exercise.

## MAX AND TARGET HEART RATES

| AGE | PREDICTED MAX HEART RATE | TARGET HEART RATE (60-85% OF MAX) |
|---|---|---|
| 20 | ✔ 200 | 120-170 |
| 25 | ✔ 195 | 117-166 |
| 30 | ✔ 190 | 114-162 |
| 35 | ✔ 185 | 111-157 |
| 40 | ✔ 180 | 108-153 |
| 45 | ✔ 175 | 105-149 |
| 50 | ✔ 170 | 102-145 |
| 55 | ✔ 165 | 99-140 |
| 60 | ✔ 160 | 96-136 |
| 65 | ✔ 155 | 93-132 |
| 70 | ✔ 150 | 90-128 |

Intro-90  PP Intro-2a completed

9. Email the sharing link to your instructor.
   a. Using your email account, create a new email to send to your instructor.
   b. Include an appropriate subject line and a brief message in the body.
   c. Press **Ctrl+V** to paste the link to your document in the body of the email.
   d. Send the email message.

# Organizing and Customizing Folders and Files

The more you use your computer to create and use files, the more important it is to stay organized. You can use *folders* to store related files, which makes it easier for you to find, edit, and share your files. For example, you can create a folder for the college you attend. Inside the college folder, you can create a folder for each of your courses. Inside each of the course folders you might create a folder for student data files, solution files, and group projects. Folders can store any type of files; you are not limited to Office files.

## Create a Folder

In *SLO Intro.3: Creating, Saving, Closing, and Opening Files*, you learned how to create a new folder when saving an Office file in the *Save As* dialog box. You can also create a Windows folder using *File Explorer*. You can create folders inside other folders.

---

### ▶ HOW TO: Create a Windows Folder

1. Click the **Start** button and select **File Explorer** to open a *File Explorer* window.
   - Your folders and computer locations are listed on the left.
2. Select the location in the *Navigation* pane on the left where you want to create a new folder.
3. Click **Home** tab, and click the **New folder** button [*New* group]. A new folder is created (Figure Intro-91).
   - The *New Folder* button is also on the *Quick Access* toolbar in the *File Explorer* window.
4. Type the name of the new folder and press **Enter**.

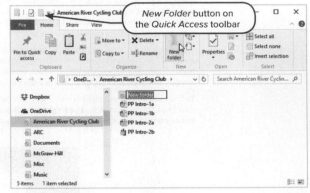

Intro-91 Create a new Windows folder

---

> **ANOTHER WAY**
>
> **Ctrl+Shift+N** creates a new folder in a Windows folder.

## Move and Copy Files and Folders

Moving a file or folder is cutting it from one location and pasting it in another location. Copying a file or folder creates a copy of it, and you can paste in another location so the file or folder is in two or more locations. If you move or copy a folder, the files in the folder are moved or copied with the folder. Move or copy files and folders using the *Move to* or *Copy to* buttons on the *Home* tab of *File Explorer*, keyboard shortcuts (**Ctrl+X, Ctrl+C, Ctrl+V**), or the drag-and-drop method.

To move or copy multiple folders or files at the same time, press the **Ctrl** key and select multiple items to move or copy. Use the **Ctrl** key to select or deselect multiple non-adjacent files or folders. Use the **Shift** key to select a range of files or folders. Click the first file or folder in a range, press the **Shift** key, and select the last file or folder in the range to select all of the items in the range.

## ▶ HOW TO: Move or Copy a File or Folder

1. Click the **Start** button and select **File Explorer** to open a *File Explorer* window.
2. Select a file or folder to move or copy.
   - Press the **Ctrl** key to select multiple files or folders.
3. Click the **Home** tab in the *File Explorer* window.
4. Click the **Move to** or **Copy to** button [*Organize* group] and select the location where you want to move or copy the file or folder (Figure Intro-92).

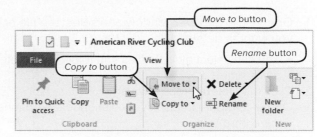

Intro-92 Move or copy a selected file or folder

- If the folder you want is not available, select **Choose location** to open the *Move Items* or *Copy Items* dialog box.
- To use the keyboard shortcuts, press **Ctrl+X** to cut the file or folder or **Ctrl+C** to copy the file or folder from its original location, go to the desired new location, and press **Ctrl+V** to paste it.
- To use the drag-and-drop method to move a file or folder, select the file or folder and drag and drop to the new location.
- To use the drag-and-drop method to copy a file or folder, press the **Ctrl** key, select the file or folder, and drag and drop to the new location.

> ▶ **ANOTHER WAY**
>
> Right-click a file or folder to display the context menu where you can select **Cut**, **Copy**, or **Paste**.

## Rename Files and Folders

You can rename a file or folder in a *File Explorer* window. When you rename a file or folder, only the file or folder name changes, and the contents of the file or folder do not change.

## ▶ HOW TO: Rename a File or Folder

1. Click the **Start** button and select **File Explorer** to open a *File Explorer* window.
2. Select the file or folder you want to rename.
3. Click the **Rename** button [*Home* tab, *Organize* group] (see Figure Intro-92).
4. Type the new name of the file or folder and press **Enter**.

> ▶ **ANOTHER WAY**
>
> Select a file or folder to rename, press **F2**, type the new name, and press **Enter**. You can also right-click a file or folder and select **Rename** from the context menu.

## Delete Files and Folders

You can also easily delete files and folders. When you delete a file or folder, it is moved from its current location to the ***Recycle Bin*** on your computer where deleted items are stored. If a file or folder is in the *Recycle Bin*, you can restore this item to its original location or move it to a different location. You also have the option to permanently delete a file or folder; the item is deleted and not moved to the *Recycle Bin*. If an item is permanently deleted, you do not have the restore option.

> **HOW TO:** Delete Files and Folders

1. Open a *File Explorer* window and select the file or folder you want to delete.
   - You can select multiple files and folders to delete at the same time.
2. Click the **Delete** drop-down arrow [*Home* tab, *Organize* group] to display the list of delete options (Figure Intro-93).
   - The default action when you click the *Delete* button (not the drop-down arrow) is *Recycle*.
3. Delete a file by selecting **Recycle**, which moves it to the *Recycle Bin*.
   - *Recycle* deletes the item(s) and moves it to the *Recycle Bin*.
   - When you *Recycle* an item, you are not by default prompted to confirm the deletion. Select **Show recycle confirmation** from the *Delete* drop-down list to receive a confirmation dialog box each time you delete or recycle an item.
4. Permanently delete a file by selecting **Permanently delete**. A confirmation dialog box opens. Click **Yes** to confirm the deletion.
   - *Permanently delete* deletes the item(s) from your computer.

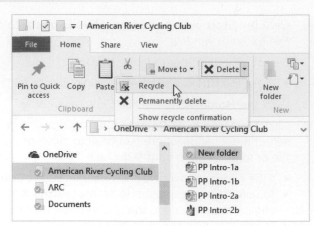

Intro-93 Delete selected folder

> **ANOTHER WAY**
> Press **Ctrl+D** or the **Delete** key on your keyboard to recycle selected item(s).
> Press **Shift+Delete** to permanently delete selected item(s).

## Create a Zipped (Compressed) Folder

If you want to share multiple files or a folder of files with classmates, coworkers, friends, or family, you can *zip* the files into a *zipped folder* (also called a *compressed folder*). For example, you can't attach an entire folder to an email message, but you can attach a zipped folder to an email message. Compressing files and folders decreases their size. You can zip a group of selected files, a folder, or a combination of files and folders, and then share the zipped folder with others through email or in a cloud storage location such as *OneDrive*.

> **HOW TO:** Create a Zipped (Compressed) Folder

1. Open a *File Explorer* window.
2. Select the file(s) and/or folder(s) you want to zip (compress).
3. Click the **Zip** button [*Share* tab, *Send* group] (Figure Intro-94). A zipped folder is created.
   - The name of the zipped folder is the name of the first item you selected to zip. You can rename this folder.
   - The icon for a zipped folder looks similar to the icon for a folder except it has a vertical zipper down the middle of the folder.

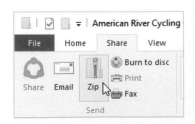

Intro-94 Create a zipped folder

## Extract a Zipped (Compressed) Folder

If you receive a zipped folder via email or download a zipped folder, save the zipped folder to your computer and then you can *extract* its contents. Extracting a zipped folder creates a regular Windows folder from the zipped folder.

### ▶ HOW TO: Extract a Zipped (Compressed) Folder

1. Select the zipped folder to extract.
2. Click the **Compressed Folder Tools** tab.
3. Click the **Extract all** button (Figure Intro-95). The *Extract Compressed (Zipped) Folders* dialog box opens (Figure Intro-96).
4. Click **Extract** to extract the folder.
   - Both the extracted folder and the zipped folder display in the folder where they are located.
   - If you check the **Show extracted files when complete** check box, the extracted folder will open after extracting.

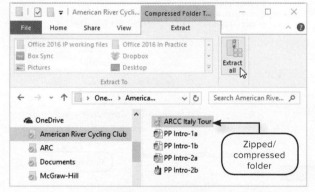

Intro-95 Extract files from a zipped folder

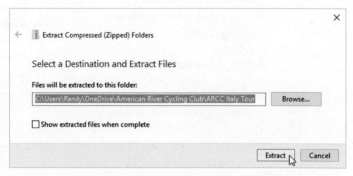

Intro-96 *Extract Compressed (Zipped) Folders* dialog box

For this project, you copy and rename files in your *OneDrive* folder on your computer, create a folder, move files, create a zipped folder, and rename a zipped folder.

Files Needed: *[your initials] PP Intro-1a.pptx, [your initials] PP Intro-1b.xlsx, [your initials] PP Intro-2a.docx, [your initials] PP Intro-2b.docx,* and **ARCC_Membership-Intro.accdb** *(Student data files are available in the* Library *of your SIMnet account)*
Completed Project File Names: *[your initials] PP Intro-1a.pptx, [your initials] PP Intro-1b.xlsx, [your initials] PP Intro-2a.docx, [your initials] PP Intro-2b.docx, [your initials]PP Intro-3.accdb,* and **ARCC Italy Tour-2018** (zipped folder)

1. Copy and rename a file.
   a. Click the Windows **Start** button and click **File Explorer** to open a *File Explorer* window. If *File Explorer* is not available on the *Start* menu, use *Cortana* to find and open a *File Explorer* window.
   b. Browse the *File Explorer* window to locate your student data files.
   c. Select the **ARCC_Membership-Intro** file.
   d. Click the **Copy to** button [*Home* tab, *Organize* group] and select **Choose location** from the drop-down list to open the *Copy Items* dialog box.
   e. Browse to locate the *American River Cycling Club* folder you created in *Pause & Practice: Intro-1.*
   f. Select the **American River Cycling Club** folder and click the **Copy** button to copy the **ARCC_Membership-Intro** file to the *American River Cycling Club* folder (Figure Intro-97). The *Copy Items* dialog box closes and the file is copied.
   g. In the open *File Explorer* window, browse to locate the *American River Cycling Club* folder and double-click the folder to open it.
   h. Click the **ARCC_Membership-Intro** file in the *American River Cycling Club* folder to select it.
   i. Click the **Rename** button [*Home* tab, *Organize* group], type [your initials] PP Intro-3 as the new file name, and press **Enter** (Figure Intro-98).

2. Create a new folder and move files.
   a. With the *American River Cycling Club* folder still open, click the **New folder** button [*Home* tab, *New* group] (see Figure Intro-98).
   b. Type ARCC Italy Tour as the name of the new folder and press **Enter**.

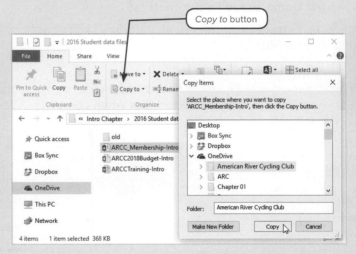

Intro-97 *Copy Items* dialog box

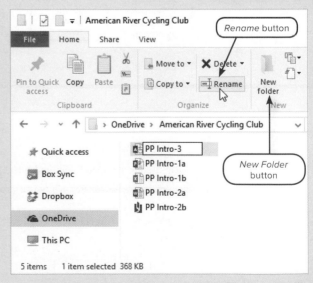

Intro-98 Rename a file

c.  Select the *[your initials] PP Intro-1a* file.
d.  Press the **Ctrl** key, select the *[your initials] PP Intro-1b*, *[your initials] PP Intro-2a*, *[your initials] PP Intro-2b*, and *[your initials] PP Intro-3* files, and release the **Ctrl** key. All five files should be selected.
e.  Click the **Move to** button [*Home* tab, *Organize* group] and select **Choose location** to open the *Move Items* dialog box (Figure Intro-99).
f.  Browse to locate the *ARCC Italy Tour* folder in the *Move Items* dialog box.
g.  Select the **ARCC Italy Tour** folder and click the **Move** button to move the selected files to the *ARCC Italy Tour* folder.
h.  Double-click the **ARCC Italy Tour** folder to open it and confirm the five files are moved.
i.  Click the **Up** or **Back** arrow above the *Navigation* pane to return to the *American River Cycling Club* folder (see Figure Intro-99).

3.  Create a zipped folder.
    a.  Select the **ARCC Italy Tour** folder.
    b.  Click the **Zip** button [*Share* tab, *Send* group]. A zipped (compressed) folder is created.
    c.  Place the insertion point at the end of the zipped folder name, type –2018, and press **Enter** (Figure Intro-100).

4.  Email the zipped folder to your instructor.
    a.  Use your email account to create a new email to send to your instructor.
    b.  Include an appropriate subject line and a brief message in the body.
    c.  Attach the **ARCC Italy Tour-2018** zipped folder to the email message and send the email message.

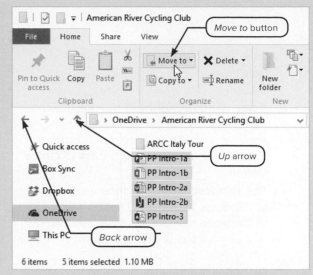

Intro-99  Move selected files to a different folder

Intro-100  Create a zipped folder

# Chapter Summary

**Intro.1** Explore the features of Windows 10 (p. OI-2).

- **Windows 10** is a computer operating system.
- A **Microsoft account** is a free account you create. When you create a Microsoft account, you are given an email address, a **OneDrive** account, and access to **Office Online**.
- The **Windows desktop** is the working area of Windows 10 and the **Taskbar** displays at the bottom of the desktop. You can rearrange icons on and pin applications to the *Taskbar*.
- Use **Start menu** in Windows 10 to select a task. You can pin applications to the *Start* menu and customize the arrangement of apps.
- **Most Used** items, **File Explorer**, **Settings**, the **Power** button, and **All apps** options display to the left of the *Start* menu.
- **Apps** are the applications or programs installed on your computer. App buttons are arranged in tiles on the Windows 10 *Start* menu.
- The **Microsoft Store** is a Windows 10 app you use to search for and install apps on your computer.
- You can install both **traditional apps** and **modern apps** in Windows 10.
- You can customize the *Start* menu and *Taskbar* to add, remove, or arrange apps.
- The *File Explorer* is a window that displays files and folders on your computer.
- *OneDrive* is the cloud storage area where you can store files in a private and secure online location.
- In Windows 10, the **OneDrive folder** is one of your file storage location options.
- You can access your *OneDrive* folders and files using an Internet browser window.
- **Cortana** is a search tool in Windows 10 used to locate information on your computer and the Internet.
- **Task View** displays all open apps and windows as tiles on your desktop where you can select an app or window to display or close.
- **Settings** is the redesigned *Control Panel* where you change many Windows settings.

- The **Action Center** displays notifications and buttons to open many common Windows settings and features.

**Intro.2** Use the basic features of Office 2016 and navigate the Office 2016 working environment (p. OI-10).

- **Office 2016** is application software that includes **Word**, **Excel**, **Access**, **PowerPoint**, **Outlook**, **OneNote**, and **Publisher**.
- *Office 2016* and **Office 365** include the same application products, but they differ in how you purchase them.
- **Office desktop apps** are the full-function Office 2016 or 365 products you install on your laptop or desktop computer.
- **Office universal apps** are a scaled-down version of Office applications you install on a tablet or mobile device.
- **Office Online** is free online software that works in conjunction with your online *Microsoft* account.
- When you open each of the Office applications, a **Start page** displays where you can open an existing file or create a new file.
- In the **Backstage view** in each of the Office applications, you can perform many common tasks such as saving, opening an existing file, creating a new file, printing, and sharing.
- **Tell Me** is the Office help feature that displays Office commands related to specific topics.
- Use the mouse (or touch pad) on your computer to navigate the pointer on your computer screen. Use the pointer or click buttons to select text or objects.
- When using Office 2016 on a touch-screen computer, use the touch screen to perform actions. You can choose between **Touch Mode** and **Mouse Mode** in Office applications.

**Intro.3** Create, save, close, and open Office files (p. OI-17).

- You can create a new Office file from the *Start* page or *Backstage* view of the Office application you are using.
- When you save a file for the first time, assign the file a file name.

- You can create folders to organize saved files, and you can save a file as a different file name.
- A variety of different file types are used in each of the Office applications.
- You can close an Office file when you are finished working on it. If the file has not been saved or changes have been made to the file, you are prompted to save the file before closing.
- In each of the Office applications, you can open an existing file from the *Start* page or from the *Open* area on *Backstage* view.

**Intro.4** Customize the view and display size in Office applications and work with multiple Office files (p. OI-25).

- Each Office application has a variety of display views.
- You can select an application view from the options on the **View tab** or the view buttons on the **Status bar**.
- The **Zoom** feature changes the display size of your file.
- You can **minimize**, **restore down**, or **maximize** an open Office application window.
- You can work with multiple Office files at the same time and switch between open files.
- **Snap Assist** enables you to arrange an open window on one side of your computer screen and select another window to fill the other side of the screen.

**Intro.5** Print, share, and customize Office files (p. OI-28).

- You can print a file in a variety of formats. The *Print* area on the *Backstage* view lists your print options and displays a preview of your file.
- You can export a file as a **PDF (portable document format)** file and save the PDF file to post to a web site or share with others.
- **Document properties** store information about a file.
- You can share Office files in a variety of ways and allow others to view or edit shared files. To share a file with others, save the file in *OneDrive*.

- Program options are available on the *Backstage* view. You can use the program options to apply global changes to an Office application.

**Intro.6** Use the *Ribbon,* tabs, groups, dialog boxes, task panes, galleries, and the *Quick Access* toolbar (p. OI-33).

- The **Ribbon** appears at the top of an Office window. It contains **tabs** and **groups** with commands to format and edit files.
- The **Ribbon Display Options** provides different ways the *Ribbon* displays in Office applications.
- Within groups on each tab are a variety of **buttons**, **drop-down lists**, and **galleries**.
- **Dialog boxes** contain additional features not always displayed on the *Ribbon*.
- Click the **launcher** in the bottom right corner of some groups to open a dialog box for that group.
- A **ScreenTip** displays information about commands on the *Ribbon*.
- Dialog boxes contain **radio buttons**, **check boxes**, **drop-down lists**, and **text boxes** you can use to apply features.
- The **Quick Access toolbar**, which contains buttons that allow you to perform commands, displays in all Office applications in the upper left.
- You can add or remove commands on the *Quick Access* toolbar.

**Intro.7** Use context menus, mini toolbars, keyboard shortcuts, and function keys in Office applications (p. OI-37).

- A **context menu** displays when you right-click text or an object. The context menu contains different features depending on what you right-click.
- The **mini toolbar** is another context menu that displays formatting options.
- You can use **keyboard shortcuts** to apply features or commands.
- Some of the numbered **function keys** perform commands in Office applications. On laptops, you may have to press the function key (**Fn** or **fn**) to activate the numbered function keys.

**Intro.8** Organize and customize Windows folders and Office files (p. OI-42).

- *Folders* store and organize your files.
- You can create, move, or copy files and folders. Files stored in a folder are moved or copied with that folder.
- You can rename a file to change the file name.
- When you delete a file or folder, it is moved to the *Recycle Bin* on your computer by

default. Alternatively, you can permanently delete files and folders.

- You can *zip* files and/or folders into a *zipped (compressed) folder* to email or share multiple files as a single file.
- When you receive a zipped folder, you can *extract* the zipped folder to create a regular Windows folder and access its contents.

## Check for Understanding

The SIMbook for this text (within your SIMnet account) provides the following resources for concept review:

- Multiple choice questions
- Short answer questions
- Matching exercises

For these projects, you use your *OneDrive* to store files. If you don't already have a Microsoft account, see *SLO Intro.1: Using Windows 10* for information about creating a free personal Microsoft account.

## Guided Project Intro-1

For this project, you organize and edit files for Emma Cavalli at Placer Hills Real Estate. You extract a zipped folder, rename files, manage multiple documents, apply formatting, and export as a PDF file.
[Student Learning Outcomes Intro.1, Intro.2, Intro.3, Intro.4, Intro.5, Intro.6, Intro.7, Intro.8]

---

Files Needed: ***CavalliFiles-Intro*** (zipped folder) *(Student data files are available in the* Library *of your SIMnet account)*
Completed Project File Names: ***PHRE*** folder containing the following files: ***BuyerEscrowChecklist-Intro***, ***CavalliProspectingLetter-Intro***, *[your initials]* ***Intro-1a.accdb***, *[your initials]* ***Intro-1b.xlsx***, *[your initials]* ***Intro-1c.docx***, and *[your initials]* ***Intro-1d.docx***

---

### Skills Covered in This Project

- Copy and paste a zipped folder.
- Create a new folder in your *OneDrive* folder.
- Extract a zipped folder.
- Move a file.
- Rename a file.
- Open a Word document.

- Use *Task View* to switch between two open Word documents.
- Save a Word document with a different file name.
- Change display size.
- Use a mini toolbar, keyboard shortcut, context menu, and dialog box to apply formatting to selected text.
- Export a document as a PDF file.

---

1. Copy a zipped folder and create a new *OneDrive* folder.
   a. Click the Windows **Start** button and click **File Explorer** to open the *File Explorer* window. If *File Explorer* is not available on the *Start* menu, use *Cortana* to find and open the *File Explorer* window.
   b. Browse in the *File Explorer* window to locate your student data files.
   c. Select the ***CavalliFiles-Intro*** zipped folder from your student data files and press **Ctrl+C** or click the **Copy** button [*Home* tab, *Clipboard* group] to copy the folder.
   d. Select your ***OneDrive*** folder on the left of the *File Explorer* window, and click the **New folder** button [*Home* tab, *New* group] to create a new folder. If you don't have *OneDrive* available, create the new folder in a location where you store your files.
   e. Type PHRE and press **Enter**.
   f. Press **Enter** again to open the *PHRE* folder or double-click the folder to open it.
   g. Press **Ctrl+V** or click the **Paste** button [*Home* tab, *Clipboard* group] to paste the copied ***CavalliFiles-Intro*** zipped folder in the *PHRE* folder.

2. Extract a zipped folder.
   a. Select the ***CavalliFiles-Intro*** zipped folder.
   b. Click the **Compressed Folder Tools Extract** tab and click the **Extract all** button. The *Extract Compressed (Zipped) Folders* dialog box opens.
   c. Uncheck the **Show extracted files when complete** box if it is checked.
   d. Click the **Extract** button (Figure Intro-101). The zipped folder is extracted, and the *PHRE* folder now contains two *CavalliFiles-Intro* folders. One folder is zipped and the other is a regular folder.

e.  Select the zipped **CavalliFiles-Intro** folder and click the **Delete** button [*Home* tab, *Organize* group] to delete the zipped folder.

3.  Move and rename files.
    a.  With the *PHRE* folder still open, double-click the **CavalliFiles-Intro** folder to open it.
    b.  Click the first file, press and hold the **Shift** key, and click the last file to select all four files.
    c.  Press **Ctrl+X** or click the **Cut** button [*Home* tab, *Clipboard* group] to cut the files from the current location (Figure Intro-102).
    d.  Click the **Up** arrow to move up to the *PHRE* folder.
    e.  Press **Ctrl+V** or click the **Paste** button [*Home* tab, *Clipboard* group] to paste and move the files.
    f.  Select the **Cavalli files-Intro** folder and press **Delete** to delete the folder.
    g.  Select the **CavalliPHRE-Intro** file and click the **Rename** button [*Home* tab, *Organize* group].
    h.  Type [your initials] Intro-1a and press **Enter**.
    i.  Right-click the **FixedMortgageRates-Intro** file and select **Rename** from the context menu.
    j.  Type [your initials] Intro-1b and press **Enter**.

4.  Open two Word documents and rename a Word document.
    a.  Press the **Ctrl** key and click the **BuyerEscrowChecklist-Intro** and **CavalliProspectingLetter-Intro** files to select both files.
    b.  Press the **Enter** key to open both files in Word. If the files open in *Protected View*, click the **Enable Editing** button.
    c.  Press the **Task View** button on your *Taskbar* (Figure Intro-103). All open windows display as tiles on your desktop.
    d.  Select the **BuyerEscrowChecklist-Intro** document.
    e.  Click the **File** tab to open the *Backstage* view and select **Save As** on the left.
    f.  Click the **Browse** button to open the *Save As* dialog box.
    g.  Type [your initials] Intro-1c in the *File name* text box and click **Save**. The file is saved in the *PHRE* folder.
    h.  Click the **X** in the upper right corner of the Word window to close the document. The *CavalliProspectingLetter-Intro* document remains open.

5.  Change display size and edit and rename a Word document.
    a.  Press the **Task View** button on your *Taskbar* and select the **CavalliProspectingLetter-Intro** document.

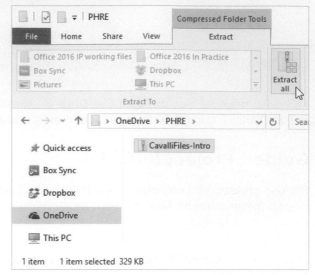

Intro-101 Extract a zipped folder

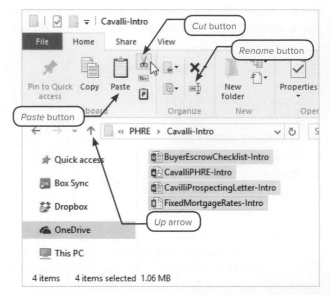

Intro-102 *Cut* files to move from a folder

Intro-103 *Task View* button on the *Taskbar*

b. Click the **Zoom In** or **Zoom Out** button in the bottom right of the document window to change the display size to **120%** (Figure Intro-104).

c. Select "**Placer Hills Real Estate**" in the first body paragraph of the letter and the mini toolbar displays (Figure Intro-105).

d. Click the **Bold** button on the mini toolbar to apply bold formatting to the selected text.

e. Select "**Whitney Hills resident**" in the first sentence in the second body paragraph and press **Ctrl+I** to apply italic formatting to the selected text.

Intro-105 Use the mini toolbar to apply formatting

f. Select the text that reads "**Emma Cavalli**," below "Best regards,".

g. Right-click the selected text and select **Font** from the context menu to open the *Font* dialog box.

h. Check the **Small Caps** box in the *Effects* area and click **OK** to close the *Font* dialog box.

i. With "**Emma Cavalli**" still selected, click the **Bold** button [*Home* tab, *Font* group].

j. Click the **File** tab, select **Save As** on the left, and click the **Browse** button to open the *Save As* dialog box.

k. Type [your initials] Intro-1d in the *File name* text box and click **Save**.

6. Export a Word document as a PDF file.

a. With the *[your initials] Intro-1d* still open, click the **File** tab to open the *Backstage* view.

b. Select **Export** on the left, select **Create PDF/XPS Document** in the *Export* area, and click the **Create PDF/XPS** button (Figure Intro-106). The *Publish as PDF or XPS* dialog box opens.

c. Deselect the **Open file after publishing** check box if it is checked.

d. Select the **Standard (publishing online and printing)** radio button in the *Optimize for* area.

e. Type [your initials] Intro-1e in the *File name* text box and click **Publish**.

f. Click the **File** tab to open the *Backstage* view and select **Save** on the left.

g. Click the **X** in the upper right corner of the Word window to close the document and Word.

Intro-106 Export as a PDF file

7. Your *PHRE* folder should contain the files shown in Figure Intro-107.

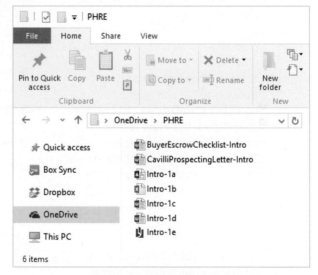

Intro-107 Intro-1 completed

OI-53

# Guided Project Intro-2

For this project, you modify an Excel file for Hamilton Civic Center. You create a folder, rename a file, add document properties, use *Tell Me* to search for a topic, share the file, and export a file as a PDF file.
[Student Learning Outcomes Intro.1, Intro.2, Intro.3, Intro.5, Intro.6, Intro.7, Intro.8]

File Needed: ***HCCYoga-Intro.xlsx*** *(Student data files are available in the* Library *of your SIMnet account)*
Completed Project File Names: ***[your initials] Intro-2a.xlsx*** and ***[your initials] Intro-2b.pdf***

## Skills Covered in This Project

- Open Excel and an Excel workbook.
- Create a new folder.
- Save an Excel workbook with a different file name.
- Add document properties to a file.
- Use *Tell Me* to search for a topic.
- Open a Word document.
- Share a file.
- Export a file as a PDF file.

1. Open Excel 2016 and open an Excel workbook.
   a. Click the Windows **Start** button and click **Excel 2016** to open this application. If Excel 2016 is not available on the *Start* menu, click the **Cortana** button on the *Taskbar*, type Excel, and then click **Excel 2016** in the search results to open it.
   b. From the Excel *Start* page, click **Open Other Workbooks** to display the *Open* area of the *Backstage* view.
   c. Click the **Browse** button to open the *Open* dialog box.
   d. Browse to the location where your student data files are stored, select the ***HCCYoga-Intro*** file, and click **Open** to open the Excel workbook. If the file opens in *Protected View*, click the **Enable Editing** button.

2. Save a file as a different file name in your *OneDrive* folder.
   a. Click the **File** tab to open the *Backstage* view and select **Save As** on the left.
   b. Click the **Browse** button to open the *Save As* dialog box.
   c. Select the **OneDrive** folder on the left and click the **New folder** button to create a new folder (Figure Intro-108). If *OneDrive* is not a storage option, select another location to create the new folder.
   d. Type HCC and press **Enter**.
   e. Double-click the **HCC** folder to open it.
   f. Type [your initials] Intro-2a in the *File name* area and click **Save** to close the dialog box and save the file.

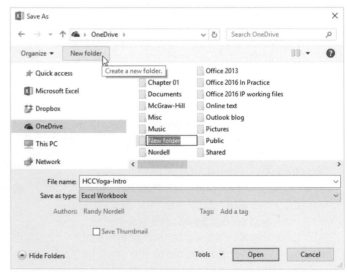

Intro-108 Create a new folder from the *Save As* dialog box

3. Add document properties to the Excel workbook.
   a. Click the **File** button to open the *Backstage* view and select **Info** on the left if it is not already selected. The document properties displays on the right.
   b. Place your insertion point in the *Title* text box ("Add a title") and type Yoga Classes as the worksheet title.

c. Click the **Show All Properties** link at the bottom of the list of properties (Figure Intro-109).

d. Place your insertion point in the *Company* text box and type Hamilton Civic Center as the company name.

e. Click the **Back** arrow in the upper left of the *Backstage* window to return to the Excel workbook.

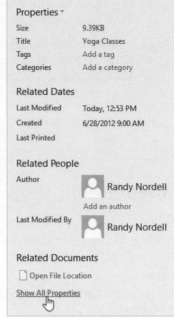

Intro-109 Add document properties

4. Use *Tell Me* to search for a topic.

a. Click the **Tell Me** search box at the top of the *Ribbon* and type Cell formatting (Figure Intro-110).

b. Select **Get Help on "Cell formatting"** to open the *Excel 2016 Help* dialog box.

c. Click the first result link to display information about the topic.

d. Click the **Back** arrow to return to the search list.

e. Click the **X** in the upper right corner to close the *Excel 2016 Help* dialog box.

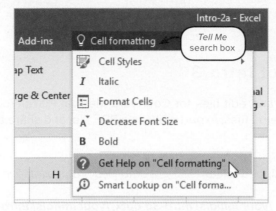

Intro-110 Use *Tell Me* to search for a topic

5. Share an Excel workbook with your instructor. If your file is not saved in *OneDrive*, skip step 5.

a. Click the **Share** button in the upper right of the Excel worksheet. The *Share* pane opens on the right side of the worksheet (Figure Intro-111).

b. Type your instructor's email address in the *Invite people* area.

c. Select **Can edit** from the drop-down list below the email address if it is not already selected.

d. Type a brief message in the body text box.

e. Click the **Share** button.

f. Click the **X** in the upper right corner of the *Share* pane to close the pane.

g. Press **Ctrl+S** to save the worksheet.

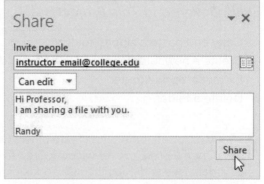

Intro-111 *Share* pane

6. Export an Excel file as a PDF file.

a. Click the **File** tab to open the *Backstage* view.

b. Select **Export** on the left, select **Create PDF/XPS Document** in the *Export* area, and click the **Create PDF/XPS** button (Figure Intro-112). The *Publish as PDF or XPS* dialog box opens.

c. Deselect the **Open file after publishing** check box if it is checked.

Intro-112 Export as a PDF file

d.  Select the **Standard (publishing online and printing)** radio button in the *Optimize for* area.

e.  Type [your initials] Intro-2b in the *File name* text box and click **Publish**.

7. Save and close the Excel file.

a.  Click the **File** tab to open the *Backstage* view and select **Save** on the left.

b.  Click the **X** in the upper right corner of the Excel window to close the file and Excel.

## Independent Project Intro-3

For this project, you organize and edit files for Courtyard Medical Plaza. You extract a zipped folder, delete a folder, move files, rename files, export a file as a PDF file, and share a file.
[Student Learning Outcomes Intro.1, Intro.2, Intro.3, Intro.5, Intro.8]

File Needed: ***CMPFiles-Intro*** (zipped folder) *(Student data files are available in the* Library *of your SIMnet account)*

Completed Project File Names: ***[your initials] Intro-3a.pptx***, ***[your initials] Intro-3a-pdf.pdf***, ***[your initials] Intro-3b.accdb***, ***[your initials] Intro-3c.xlsx***, and ***[your initials] Intro-3d.docx***

### Skills Covered in This Project

- Copy and paste a zipped folder.
- Create a new folder in your *OneDrive* folder.
- Extract a zipped folder.
- Delete a folder.

- Move a file.
- Rename a file.
- Open a PowerPoint presentation.
- Export a file as a PDF file.
- Open a Word document.
- Share a file.

1. Copy a zipped folder and create a new *OneDrive* folder.

a.  Open a *File Explorer* window, browse to locate the ***CMPFiles-Intro*** zipped folder in your student data files and copy the zipped folder.

b.  Go to your *OneDrive* folder and create a new folder named **Courtyard Medical Plaza** within the *OneDrive* folder. If *OneDrive* is not a storage option, select another location to create the new folder.

2. Paste a copied folder, extract the zipped folder, and move files.

a.  Paste the zipped folder in the *Courtyard Medical Plaza* folder.

b.  Extract the zipped folder and then delete the zipped folder.

c.  Open the ***CMPFiles-Intro*** folder and move all of the files to the *Courtyard Medical Plaza* folder.

d.  Return to the *Courtyard Medical Plaza* folder to confirm the four files were moved.

e.  Delete the ***CMPFiles-Intro*** folder.

3. Rename files in the *Courtyard Medical Plaza* folder.

a.  Rename the ***CMPStayingActive-Intro*** PowerPoint file to [your initials] Intro-3a.

b.  Rename the ***CourtyardMedicalPlaza-Intro*** Access file to [your initials] Intro-3b.

c.  Rename the ***EstimatedCalories-Intro*** Excel file to [your initials] Intro-3c.

d.  Rename the ***StayingActive-Intro*** Word file to [your initials] Intro-3d.

4. Export a PowerPoint file as a PDF file.

a.  From the *Courtyard Medical Plaza* folder, open the ***[your initials] Intro-3a*** file. The file opens in PowerPoint. If the file opens in *Protected View*, click the **Enable Editing** button.

b.  Export this file as a PDF file. Don't have the PDF file open after publishing and optimize for **Standard** format.

c.  Save the file as **[your initials] Intro-3a-pdf** and save in the *Courtyard Medical Plaza* folder.

d.  Close the PowerPoint file and exit PowerPoint.

5.  Share a file with your instructor. If your files are not saved in *OneDrive*, skip step 5.

a.  Return to your *Courtyard Medical Plaza* folder and open the **Intro-3d** file. The file opens in Word. If the file opens in *Protected View*, click the **Enable Editing** button.

b.  Open the *Share* pane.

c.  Type your instructor's email address and select **Can edit** from the permission drop-down list.

d.  Type a brief message and **Share** the file.

e.  Close the *Share* pane.

f.  Save and close the document and exit Word.

6.  Close the *File Explorer* window containing the files for this project (Figure Intro-113).

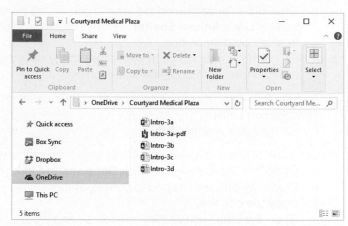

Intro-113  Intro-3 completed

# Independent Project Intro-4

For this project, you modify a Word file for Life's Animal Shelter. You create a folder, rename a document, add document properties, modify a document, create a sharing link, export a document as a PDF file, and create a zipped folder.

[Student Learning Outcomes Intro.1, Intro.2, Intro.3, Intro.5, Intro.6, Intro.7, Intro.8]

---

File Needed: ***LASSupportLetter-Intro.docx*** *(Student data files are available in the* Library *of your SIMnet account)*

Completed Project File Names: ***[your initials] Intro-4a.docx***, ***[your initials] Intro-4b.pdf***, and ***LAS files*** (zipped folder)

---

### Skills Covered in This Project

- Open a Word document.
- Create a new folder.
- Save a file with a different file name.

- Apply formatting to selected text.
- Add document properties to the file.
- Create a sharing link.
- Export a file as a PDF file.
- Create a zipped folder.

---

1.  Open a Word document, create a new folder, and save the document with a different file name.

a.  Open Word 2016.

b.  From the Word *Start* page, open the ***LASSupportLetter-Intro*** document from your student data files. If the file opens in *Protected View*, click the **Enable Editing** button.

c. Open the **Save As** dialog box and create a new folder named **LAS** in your *OneDrive* folder. If *OneDrive* is not a storage option, select another location to create the new folder.

d. Save this document in the *LAS* folder and use [your initials] Intro-4a as the file name.

2. Apply formatting changes to the document using a dialog box, keyboard shortcut, and mini toolbar.
   a. Select "**To**:" in the memo heading and use the launcher to open the *Font* dialog box.
   b. Apply **Bold** and **All caps** to the selected text.
   c. Repeat the formatting on the other three memo guide words "**From**:," "**Date**:," and "**Subject**:".
   d. Select "**Life's Animal Shelter**" in the first sentence of the first body paragraph and press **Ctrl+B** to apply bold formatting.
   e. Select the first sentence in the second body paragraph ("**Would you again consider** . . .") and use the mini toolbar to apply *italic* formatting.

3. Add the following document properties to the document:
   *Title*: Support Letter
   *Company*: Life's Animal Shelter

4. Get a link to share this document with your instructor and email your instructor the sharing link.
   a. Open the *Share* pane and click **Get a sharing link** at the bottom of the *Share* pane.
   b. Create an edit link to send to your instructor.
   c. Copy the edit link.
   d. Open the email you use for this course and create a new email message to send to your instructor.
   e. Type your instructor's email address, include an appropriate subject line, and type a brief message in the body of the email message.
   f. Paste (**Ctrl+V**) the sharing link in the body of the email message and send the message.
   g. Click the **Task View** button on the Windows *Taskbar* and select the *Intro-4a* document to display this document.
   h. Close the *Share* pane.
   i. Use the **Save** command on the *Quick Access* toolbar to save the file before continuing.

7. Export this document as a PDF file.
   a. Export this file as a PDF file. Don't have the PDF file open after publishing and optimize for **Standard** format.
   b. Save the file as [your initials] Intro-4b and save in the *LAS* folder.
   c. Save and close the document and exit Word.

8. Create a zipped folder.
   a. Using *File Explorer*, open the **LAS** folder in your *OneDrive* folder.
   b. Select the two files and create a zipped folder.
   c. Rename the zipped folder **LAS files**.

9. Close the open *File Explorer* window (Figure Intro-114).

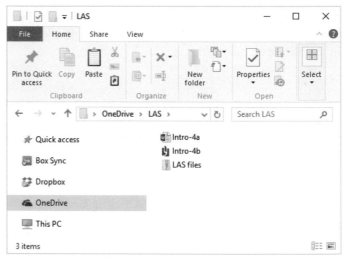

Intro-114 Intro-4 completed

# Challenge Project Intro-5

For this project, you create folders to organize your files for this class and share a file with your instructor.
[Student Learning Outcomes Intro.1, Intro.5, Intro.8]

Files Needed: Student data files for this course
Completed Project File Name: Share a file with your instructor

Using *File Explorer*, create *OneDrive* folders to contain all of the student data files for this class. Organize your files and folders according to the following guidelines:

- Create a *OneDrive* folder for this class.
- Create a *Student data files* folder inside the class folder.
- Copy and paste the student data files in the *Student data files* folder.
- Extract student data files and delete the zipped folder.
- Create a *Solution files* folder inside the class folder.
- Inside the *Solution files* folder, create a folder for each chapter.
- Create a folder to store miscellaneous class files such as the syllabus and other course handouts.
- Open one of the student data files and share the file with your instructor.

# Challenge Project Intro-6

For this project, you save a file as a different file name, customize the *Quick Access* toolbar, share a file with your instructor, export a file as a PDF file, and create a zipped folder.
[Student Learning Outcomes Intro.1, Intro.2, Intro.3, Intro.5, Intro.6, Intro.8]

File Needed: Use an existing Office file
Completed Project File Names: *[your initials] Intro-6a* and *[your initials] Intro-6b*

Open an existing Word, Excel, or PowerPoint file. Save this file in a *OneDrive* folder and name it [your initials] Intro-6a. If you don't have any of these files, use one from your Pause & Practice projects or select a file from your student data files.

With your file open, perform the following actions:

- Create a new folder on OneDrive and save the file to this folder using a different file name.
- Customize the *Quick Access* toolbar to add command buttons. Add commands such as *New*, *Open*, *Quick Print*, and *Spelling* that you use regularly in the Office application.
- Share your file with your instructor. Allow your instructor to edit the file.
- Export the document as a PDF file. Save the file as [your initials] Intro-6b and save it in the same *OneDrive* folder as your open file.
- Zip the files in the folder.

# Microsoft® Office

## IN PRACTICE

# powerpoint

# Creating and Editing Presentations

## CHAPTER OVERVIEW

Microsoft PowerPoint is the leading presentation software. Whether you need to create a quick display or a very polished presentation with dazzling graphics, creative animation effects, and video, PowerPoint has all the tools you need. You can use PowerPoint for slide shows with computer projection equipment in meeting rooms, for self-running presentations viewed by individuals, or for presentations shown on the web. This chapter covers the basics of starting and editing a PowerPoint presentation.

**POWERPOINT**

### STUDENT LEARNING OUTCOMES (SLOs)

After completing this chapter, you will be able to:

**SLO 1.1**   Create, open, and save a presentation (p. P1-3).

**SLO 1.2**   Work with slides, layouts, placeholders, and text (p. P1-14).

**SLO 1.3**   Navigate between slides and organize content by reproducing and rearranging slides (p. P1-23).

**SLO 1.4**   Change theme colors and fonts (p. P1-29).

**SLO 1.5**   Insert headers and footers to add identifying information (p. P1-33).

**SLO 1.6**   Insert, resize, and align a picture from a file (p. P1-37).

**SLO 1.7**   Apply and modify transition effects to add visual interest (p. P1-40).

**SLO 1.8**   Preview a presentation and print slides, handouts, and outlines (p. P1-42).

**SLO 1.9**   Apply presentation properties (p. P1-45).

## CASE STUDY

*Throughout this book you have the opportunity to put into practice the application features that you are learning. Each chapter begins with a case study that introduces you to the Pause & Practice projects in the chapter. These Pause & Practice projects give you a chance to apply and practice key skills. Each chapter contains three to five Pause & Practice projects.*

***Hamilton Civic Center*** *(HCC) is a nonprofit community fitness center that partners with* the local hospital for educational events. Doctors and nurses provide classes on a variety of health and wellness issues for adults. HCC also works with local schools to support their academic programs and sponsors events for children.

In this chapter, you develop a presentation about training for an upcoming marathon that is being promoted to HCC members.

**Pause & Practice 1-1:** Create a presentation and develop text content.

**Pause & Practice 1-2:** Apply a presentation theme, change theme colors and fonts, and edit content.

**Pause & Practice 1-3:** Add interest with pictures and apply transitions, and print supplements.

# Creating, Opening, and Saving Presentations

PowerPoint provides several ways to start, view, and save a presentation. Always save your presentation if you will need to access it again. If you close the presentation before saving it, your content is lost.

## Create a Presentation

When PowerPoint first opens, you can start a new presentation or open an existing presentation that is listed on the left. Clickable images called *thumbnails* have a name below each one. If you prefer to work on text content only, click the **Blank Presentation** thumbnail to go directly to your first slide so you can begin developing content.

Other thumbnails represent built-in *Themes* that provide a unified look for all the slides in a presentation. Most themes have color or graphic treatments that create a background design. When you click a theme, a dialog box opens where you can choose from four or more *Variants* showing different color combinations. Variants may have different graphics, too. Once these choices are made, you can start developing content.

The following three How-to Boxes explain several different ways to start a presentation.

---

▶ **HOW TO:** Create a Presentation When First Opening PowerPoint

1. Open PowerPoint and you will see the *Backstage* view (Figure 1-1).
2. Click **Blank Presentation** to go directly to your first slide.

*Or*

3. Click a **Theme** to open a dialog box (Figure 1-2).
4. Click the arrow buttons below the slide example to see how colors are applied to different layouts.

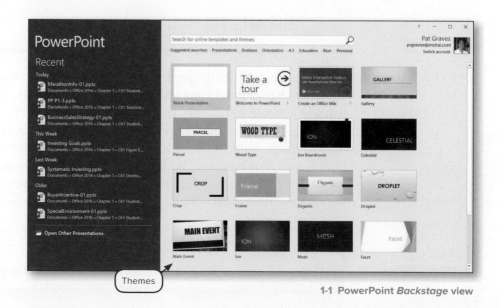

1-1 PowerPoint *Backstage* view

5. Select one of four *Variants* on the right that provide different color combinations.

6. Click **Create**.

1-2 Theme *Variants*

When you create a new presentation, PowerPoint assigns a generic name, such as *Presentation1*, that appears in the title bar. Additional new presentations are named in the same way. When you save the presentation with a new name, that name appears in the title bar.

> **MORE INFO**
>
> When your content is complete, save your presentation (discussed on pages P1-10 – P1-12) and then close it by clicking the **File** tab and then clicking **Close**. To close PowerPoint, click the **Close** button (an **X**) in the upper right corner of the title bar. If you click the **Close** button before saving, your presentation will automatically close or you will be asked if you want to save your presentation if changes have been made.

## ▶ HOW TO: Create a New Presentation When PowerPoint Is Open

1. Click the **File** tab to open the *Backstage* view.
2. Click **New** and use one of these methods to start a presentation:
   - Select a *Theme*, select a *Variant*, and click **Create** to open the presentation with the selected theme and colors.
   - Double-click a *Theme* to open the presentation with that theme and the default *Variant* colors.
   - Double-click **Blank Presentation** to go directly to your first slide.

*Or*

3. Press **Ctrl+N** to open a new blank presentation.

A theme simplifies the process of creating professional looking presentations by providing consistent background graphics, colors, and font settings. A ***template*** contains the characteristics of a theme and usually provides sample content you can edit or delete if you want only the background a template provides. Many themes and templates are available in PowerPoint by searching online when you start a new presentation, or they can be downloaded at Office.com. You can save downloaded themes and templates so they are available for future use. *SLO 1.4: Changing Theme Colors and Fonts* provides information about searching within PowerPoint and customizing theme settings.

> **MORE INFO**
>
> Your computer must be connected to the Internet to download themes and templates.

## ▶ HOW TO: Create a New Presentation from Online Templates and Themes

1. Click the **File** tab to open the *Backstage* view.

2. Click **New**. In the search box, type a word, such as small business, and click the **Start searching** button (Figure 1-3). Available templates and themes appear.

   - Filter your results by typing the word **and** and then typing a second search word such as travel.
   - Click the **Start searching** button to search again.

*Or*

3. Click one of the *Suggested searches* for general topics and available templates and themes will appear.

   - Filter your results by clicking one of the terms in the *Category* list on the right (Figure 1-4).
   - Filter your results by typing the word **or** before another search word and searching again.

4. Click a thumbnail to open a dialog box to review other slides in addition to the title slide. Some templates include a description (Figure 1-5).

5. Click **Create** and the presentation opens.

   - The presentation may contain sample content that you need to delete before adding your content.

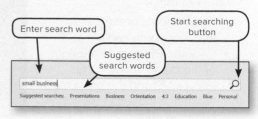

1-3 Search for online themes and templates

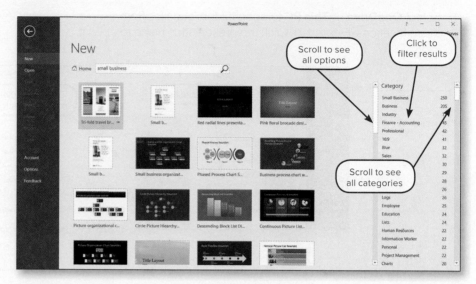

1-4 Search results for online themes and templates

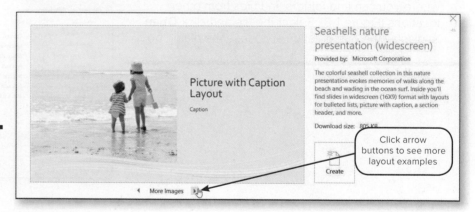

1-5 Template with description and sample content

You can use an existing presentation to start a new presentation. To do this, open a presentation file from a source such as your computer, USB drive, local network, cloud space such as *OneDrive*, or an email attachment.

## ▶ HOW TO: Open a Recent Presentation

1. Start PowerPoint and click the **File** tab to open the *Backstage* view.

2. Click **Open** to display the *Open* area on the *Backstage* view.

3. Select **Recent** and click a presentation name on the right to open it.

   - If you open a presentation frequently, you can pin it.
   - Click the **Pin** icon to the right of the presentation name (Figure 1-6) and the presentation name moves to the top in a *Pinned* area.

*Or*

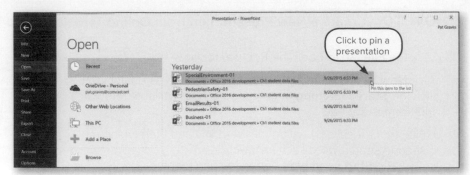

1-6  Pin a presentation in the *Open* area on the *Backstage* view

4. Select **OneDrive** or **This PC** to open folders and files from these locations (Figure 1-7). Click the presentation name to open it.

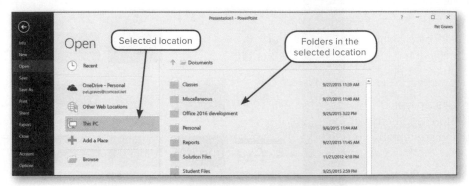

1-7  Folders in *This PC*

*Or*

5. Click **Browse** and the *Open* dialog box appears where you can find folders and files from other locations (Figure 1-8). Select the file and click **Open** to display the presentation and close the dialog box.

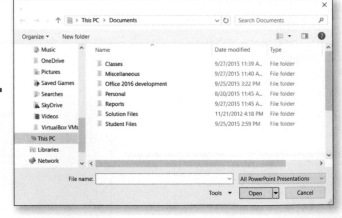

1-8  *Open* dialog box

> **MORE INFO**
>
> For instructions to set up a *OneDrive* account, refer to *SLO Intro.1: Using Windows 10* in *Intro Chapter 1: Windows 10, Office 2016, and File Management*.

> **ANOTHER WAY**
>
> **Ctrl+O** opens the *Backstage* view where you can open a presentation. **Ctrl+F12** opens the *Open* dialog box. Some laptops require **Fn+Ctrl+F12**.

**PowerPoint 2016** Chapter 1  Creating and Editing Presentations

## Views

PowerPoint provides different views to help you create slides, organize them, and display them in a slide show. When you start a new presentation, it opens in **Normal** view. The *Ribbon* displays across the top of the window and has nine tabs with commands organized in groups (Figure 1-9). Additional tabs, such as the *Drawing Tools Format* tab, open depending on what you are doing. Several tabs contain commands similar to those in Word, whereas other tabs display features that are unique to PowerPoint.

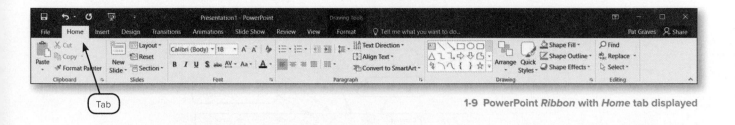

1-9 PowerPoint *Ribbon* with *Home* tab displayed

The area below the *Ribbon* is divided into panes where you create and work on slides: A *Thumbnail* pane is on the left and a *Slide* pane is on the right. A *Notes* pane may display below the slide. You can change views using commands on the *View* tab [*Presentation Views* group] (Figure 1-10) or the *View* buttons on the *Status* bar at the bottom of the window.

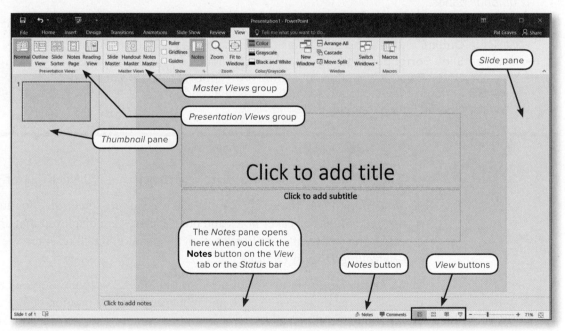

1-10 *Normal* view with *View* tab and *Notes* pane displayed

The *View* tab has five *Presentation Views* that include the following:

- **Normal View**: The default view where you enter content and move between slides as you develop them. Click the *Normal* button or the *Notes* button to open a *Notes* pane below the slide to add speaker notes for individual slides.
- **Outline View**: The left pane displays slide titles and bulleted text instead of slide thumbnails.

- *Slide Sorter View*: Slides appear as thumbnails so it is easy to reorganize slides and apply transition effects to control how the slides advance.
- *Notes Page View*: Each slide appears at the top of a page with space below the slide where you can type speaker notes.
- *Reading View*: The slide show displays at full-screen or another window size controlled by the viewer. Navigation controls are in the *Status* bar at the bottom of the window.

The *Master Views* group includes the following: **Slide Master**, **Handout Master**, and **Notes Master**. These views are used to change formatting that affects the whole presentation.

The *View* buttons located on the *Status* bar provide easy access to different PowerPoint views regardless of which *Ribbon* tab is currently open (Figure 1-11).

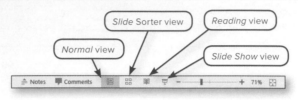

1-11 *View* buttons

▶**HOW TO:** Change Views

1. Click the **View** tab. Note that *Normal* is selected in the *Presentation Views* group and you can see the *Slide* and *Thumbnail* panes.
2. Observe the changes as you access each different view using buttons on the *View* tab or *Status* bar:
   - Click the **Outline** button and text appears on the left instead of slide thumbnails.
   - Click the **Slide Sorter** button to display all slide thumbnails in your presentation.
   - Click the **Notes Page** button and your current slide appears at the top of a page.
   - Click the **Reading View** button to see your slides in a window.
   - Click the **Normal** button to return to *Normal* view.

The following two more views are very important for the delivery of your presentation:

- *Slide Show View*: Slides appear one at a time at full-screen size for audience viewing.
- *Presenter View*: Speaker notes and other features are displayed that are helpful for delivering a presentation. For more on this feature, see "Presenter View" in *SLO 3.5: Controlling Display Options*.

While developing your presentation, test it in *Slide Show* view so you can see the content in the way your audience will see it, and rehearse your presentation before using it.

Start a presentation slide show from the beginning by pressing **F5**; start with the current slide by clicking the **Slide Show** button on the *Status* bar. You may also use buttons on the *Slide Show* tab (Figure 1-12).

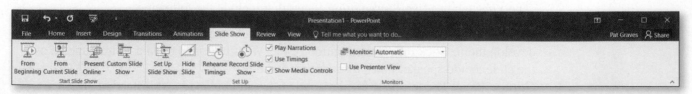

1-12 *Slide Show* tab

## ▶ HOW TO: Start a Presentation from the Slide Show Tab

1. Click the **Slide Show** tab.
2. Click the **From Beginning** button [*Start Slide Show* group] to display slides from the beginning, regardless of which slide is the current slide.
3. Click the **From Current Slide** button to display slides starting with the current slide.
4. Move through the slides by clicking the screen or pressing one of several keys on the keyboard: **spacebar**, **Enter**, **Page Down**, **Down** arrow, or **N**.

Adjusting pane sizes can help you better focus on one aspect of your presentation. For example, thumbnails become larger when you increase the size of the thumbnail pane and you have more room to write when you increase the size of the notes pane. In each case, the slide becomes a little smaller.

## ▶ HOW TO: Adjust Pane Sizes

1. Point to the pane border separating the *Thumbnail* pane and the *Slide* pane until your pointer turns into a sizing pointer with two arrows (Figure 1-13).

2. Click and drag the pane border to the right to increase thumbnail size and to the left to decrease thumbnail size.

3. If the *Notes* pane is not open, click the **Notes** button [*View* tab, *Show* group or *Status* bar].

4. Point to the pane border separating the *Slide* pane and the *Notes* pane.

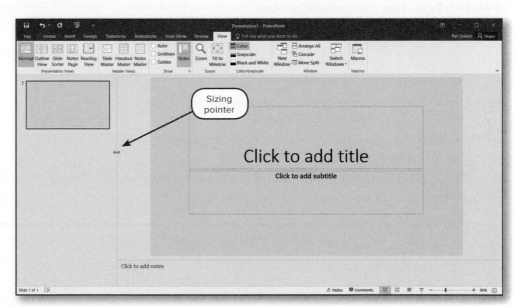

1-13 *Thumbnail* pane and *Notes* pane size is increased

5. Click and drag the *Notes* pane border up or down to increase or decrease the *Notes* pane size.

6. Click and drag the *Notes* pane border down to the bottom of the window or click the **Notes** button on the *Status* bar to remove this pane.

Use **Zoom** to increase the current slide size in *Normal* view when you need to see more detail. Use the *Zoom* dialog box to set a specific magnification level or adjust the magnification by using the *Zoom* slider. You can use *Zoom* on the *Slide Sorter* view also.

### ▶HOW TO: Use the Zoom Dialog Box

1. Click the **Zoom** button [*View* tab, *Zoom* group] and the *Zoom* dialog box opens.
2. Select a preset zoom percentage such as 200% (Figure 1-14) or enter a percentage number, such as 150%.
3. Click **OK**. The slide size is increased and you can see only a portion of the slide.
4. Click the **Zoom** button again, select **Fit**, and click **OK** to return to the default setting so the entire slide displays.

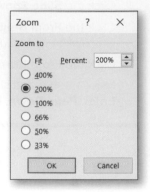

1-14 *Zoom* dialog box

The *Zoom* controls are located on the right side of the *Status* bar and the current slide size percentage is shown. At 100%, the slider is in the center. Drag the slider or click the **Zoom** buttons to adjust the slide size.

### ▶HOW TO: Use the Zoom Controls

1. Click the **Zoom Out** button several times to decrease the view to 50% (Figure 1-15).
2. Drag the **Zoom** slider to the center.
3. Click the **Zoom In** button several times to increase the view to 150%.
4. Click the line on the left or right of the **Zoom** slider to increase or decrease the percentage.
5. Click the **Fit slide to current window** button to return to the default setting.
6. Click the percentage to open the *Zoom* dialog box. Select a percentage and click **OK** to close the dialog box.

1-15 *Zoom* controls

## Save and Close a Presentation

PowerPoint assigns each new presentation a generic name such as *Presentation1*. When you save the presentation for the first time, change the generic name to a more meaningful name.

### ▶HOW TO: Save a Presentation

1. Click the **File** tab to open the *Backstage* view.
2. Click **Save** or **Save As** to display the *Save As* area (Figure 1-16).
3. Select the location where you want to save your presentation: *OneDrive, Other Web Locations,* or *This PC.*
   - Select an appropriate folder. If you select the wrong folder, click the blue **Up** arrow and select again.
   - Type a file name in the box that appears at the top and click the **Save** button

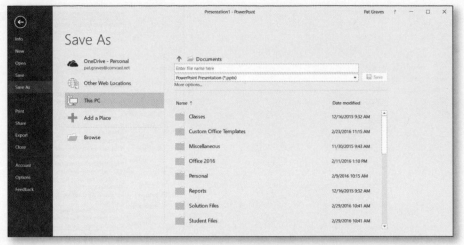

1-16 *Save As* area on the *Backstage* view

4. Click the **Browse** button to open the *Save As* dialog box (Figure 1-17).

   - Browse to the appropriate folder to save the file.
   - Type the presentation name in the *File name* area and click the **Save** button.

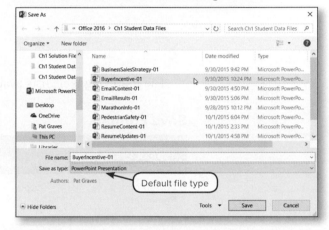

Default file type

1-17 *Save As* dialog box

When saving for the first time, you can also click the **Save** button on the *Quick Access* toolbar, or press **Ctrl+S**, to open the *Save As* area on the *Backstage* view. As you revise your presentation, simply clicking the **Save** button on the *Quick Access* toolbar will resave it with the same name in the same location.

If you want to create a second version of that file, then click the **File** tab and then click **Save As** to resave it with a different name in the same or different location. The original presentation is not affected by any changes you make to the second presentation.

**ANOTHER WAY**

Press **F12** to open the *Save As* dialog box.

You can save PowerPoint presentations in a variety of formats. By default, PowerPoint 2016 presentations are saved with the .pptx file extension. To change the type of presentation format, select the format of your choice from the *Save as type* area in the *Save As* dialog box (Figure 1-18).

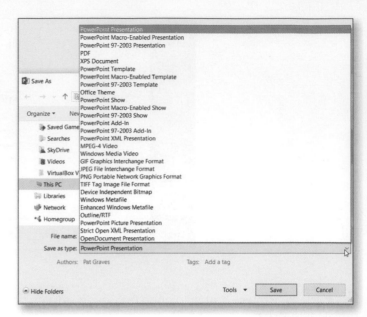

1-18 *Save As* file types

The following table lists available formats that are most commonly used for PowerPoint:

## Save Formats

| Type of Presentation | File Extension | Uses of This Format |
|---|---|---|
| PowerPoint Presentation | .pptx | PowerPoint presentation compatible with 2007–2016 software versions that use an XML-enabled file format. This is the default file format. |
| PowerPoint 97-2003 Presentation | .ppt | PowerPoint presentation compatible with 1997–2003 software versions. Newer software features are not supported. |
| PDF (Portable Document Format) | .pdf | Similar to pictures of slides, with each slide shown as a separate page. The file size may be smaller than the original presentation, so this format often works well for presentations distributed electronically. |
| PowerPoint Template | .potx | PowerPoint template that can be used to format presentations. |
| Windows Media Video or Mpeg-P4 Video | .wmv or .mp4 | PowerPoint presentation saved as a video that will play on many media players. Three resolution sizes are available, and all create large file sizes. |
| Outline/RTF | .rtf | A presentation text-only outline with a small file size for easy sharing. |
| PowerPoint Picture Presentation | .pptx | PowerPoint presentation that converts each slide into an image. It helps to reduce file size or create images for inclusion in other documents. |
| Open Document Presentation | .odp | PowerPoint presentation that can be opened in applications that use the Open Document Presentation format, such as Google.Docs or OpenOffice.org. |

> ### MORE INFO
> Other file formats are used to save individual slides or images on slides. These graphic file formats include .jpg, .png, .tif, .bmp, .wmf, or .emf. These formats are explained on page P1-38.

When you are finished with a presentation, save your final version and then close the presentation by clicking the **File** tab, and then clicking **Close** or clicking the **Close** button [**X**] in the upper right corner of the title bar.

## Share and Export Options

From the *Backstage* view you have options for *sharing* (Figure 1-19) or *exporting* (Figure 1-20) your presentation using different file formats. Not all classroom computer lab configurations permit access to shared online sites or network locations.

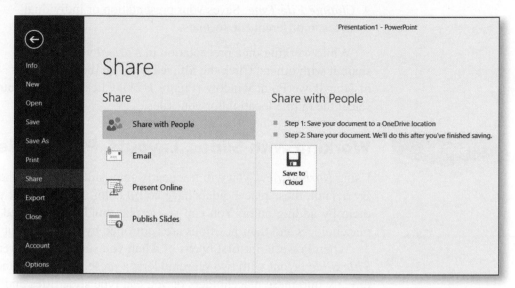

1-19 *Share* options

### Share

- *Share with People*: Saves your presentation to a *OneDrive* location so you can share it with others.
- *Email*: Sends your presentation as an attachment in the file type you choose.
- *Present Online*: Requires a Microsoft Account so people can link to your slide show through a web browser.
- *Publish Slides*: Sends presentation files to a shared library or SharePoint site.

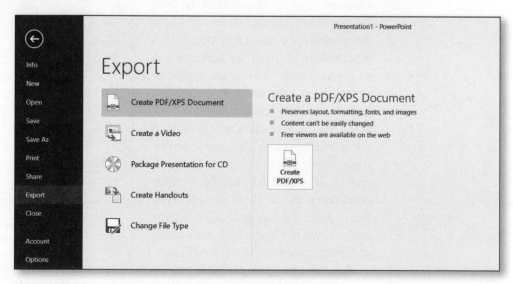

1-20 *Export* options

## Export

- *Create PDF/XPS Document*: Preserves formatting and reduces file size for easier distribution.
- *Create a Video*: Saves your presentation as a video.
- *Package Presentation for CD*: Saves your presentation and all linked or embedded files.
- *Create Handouts*: Transfers slides and notes to a Word document that you can re-format.
- *Change File Type*: Saves your presentation or individual slides in different file formats.

1-21 *Share* button

While working on a presentation in *Normal* view, you can share it with others. Click the **Share** button on the upper right of your PowerPoint window (Figure 1-21). Click **Save to Cloud** and then select the online location for your files.

## SLO 1.2

# Working with Slides, Layouts, Placeholders, and Text

Using *Normal* view, you will frequently enter slide text and other objects using **placeholders**. By default, these placeholders have no fill color or border, but you may choose to emphasize them by adding color. You can resize placeholders as needed to fit content. The available placeholders and their positions are controlled by the particular **layout** that you choose.

When PowerPoint first opens or when you start a blank presentation, the first slide has a *Title Slide* layout with two placeholders: a presentation title and a subtitle. You can add text directly into these placeholders or you can type slide titles and bulleted text in *Outline* view. The font, font size, and alignment are preset, but you can change them as you develop your presentation. Keep in mind that text should be brief, straight to the point, and easy to read.

## Add Slides and Choose Layouts

To insert additional slides, you click the **New Slide** button on the *Home* tab. After a title slide, PowerPoint automatically inserts a *Title and Content* layout. This layout is used for developing most slides; it has a placeholder for the slide title and a placeholder for inserting bulleted text or content such as pictures, tables, or charts. From that point forward, each time you click the top of the **New Slide** button, you add a new slide with the same layout as the previous one (unless you use the *Title Slide* layout again). If you click the **New Slide** drop-down arrow (bottom half), you see a gallery of layouts, such as the ones shown in Figure 1-22, for a blank presentation using the *Office Theme*.

Layouts provide a starting point for your slide designs. You can change

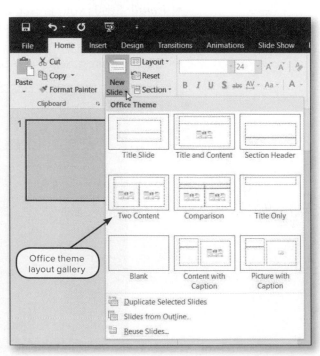

1-22 Slide layouts

layouts or customize each slide for the content you are developing. The available layouts vary based on the current theme. The most common layouts are described in the following table:

## Slide Layouts

| Layout Name | Layout Description |
| --- | --- |
| *Title Slide* | A layout used for a presentation's opening slide. It contains a title and a subtitle placeholder. |
| *Title and Content* | A layout used for the body of a presentation. It contains a placeholder for the slide title and a larger placeholder for many different kinds of content. |
| *Section Header* | This layout is similar to a Title Slide layout and usually has a slightly different appearance. It can divide a lengthy presentation or introduce different topics or speakers. |
| *Two Content* | This layout has a slide title placeholder and two smaller content placeholders to display either two brief lists or a list and a graphic object, such as a picture or chart. |
| *Comparison* | A layout that is similar to the Two Content layout, but it works better for comparing two lists because it provides a heading area above each content placeholder. |
| *Title Only* | A layout with only one placeholder for the title (usually at the top) of the slide. |
| *Blank* | This layout has no placeholders. |
| *Content with Caption* | A layout that is similar to the Two Content layout, but one area is designated for content, such as a table or chart, while the other area is meant for descriptive text. |
| *Picture with Caption* | This layout has a large area for a picture and another area for descriptive text. |

---

▶ **HOW TO:** **Choose and Change Slide Layouts**

1. Choose a layout for a new slide using one of these methods:
   - Click the **New Slide** button [*Home* tab, *Slides* group] to insert a slide with the default layout.
   - Click the **New Slide** drop-down arrow [*Home* tab, *Slides* group] and select a layout from the layout gallery. The current theme name will appear at the top.
2. Change the layout of a selected slide by following these steps:
   - Click the **Layout** button [*Home* tab, *Slides* group].
   - From the layout gallery, select a different layout.
   - Repeat this process to try another layout.
3. Click the **Undo** button [*Quick Access* toolbar] to remove the layout change.

## Enter Text in Placeholders

When you first see placeholders on slides, they appear as boxes with a thin, dotted border. When you click inside the placeholder, it becomes active with a blinking insertion point where you can type or edit text (Figure 1-23). Click the border to select the placeholder and the line becomes solid (Figure 1-24). In both cases, ***sizing handles*** that are small white circles appear on the corners and sides. A ***rotation handle*** that is a circular arrow appears at the top.

Dotted line border as it first appears

**Click to add title**

Click to make the placeholder active with an insertion point

**1-23 Placeholders for text**

By default, PowerPoint automatically fits text in a placeholder. Therefore, keep the wording of titles concise so the text does not become too small. Depending on the font that is used, title text for individual slides is usually 36–44 points. When using the *Title Slide* layout, the title text is usually 54–72 points.

1-24 Selected placeholder to move or resize

### MORE INFO

A point is a unit of measurement in typography used to represent the height of text characters and the space between lines. The number of points in one inch is 72. The widescreen slide size is 13.33" × 7.5" (*Width* × *Height*).

In body placeholders, a bullet (a small symbol such as a circle or square) automatically appears when you type text and press **Enter**. Bullets help mark the beginning of a line, so people recognize items as separate. You can also add subpoints that are indented below a bulleted item. Be sure your list is very concise, usually no more than six items, and the text size is 20–28 points. Larger font sizes are very important if you are presenting in a large room so your audience can read slide text from a distance. However, if you are preparing a presentation to be viewed on a computer or online, you can use smaller font sizes.

Bulleted lists are appropriate when items require no particular order. If you need to show items in order, use a numbered list instead.

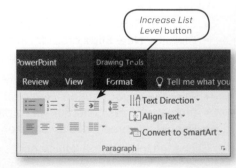

1-25 Paragraph group on the *Home* tab

### ▶HOW TO: Work with Lists

1. Click after the first bullet in the body placeholder and type text.
2. Press **Enter** to type another bulleted item using the same list level.
3. Press **Tab** or click the **Increase List Level** button [*Home* tab, *Paragraph* group] (Figure 1-25) to indent a bulleted item to the right (Figure 1-26).
4. Use *Outline View* to enter several text slides. *Outline View* displays all slide titles and bulleted text in the left pane.
   - Click the **Outline View** button [*View* tab, *Presentation Views* group].
   - Position your insertion point at the beginning of a bulleted item and press **Shift+Tab** or click the **Decrease List Level** button [*Home* tab, *Paragraph* group] (Figure 1-27) to move a bulleted item to the left to create a slide title.
   - Change text capitalization as needed for a title (Figure 1-28).

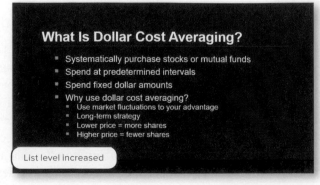

1-26 Bulleted list slide

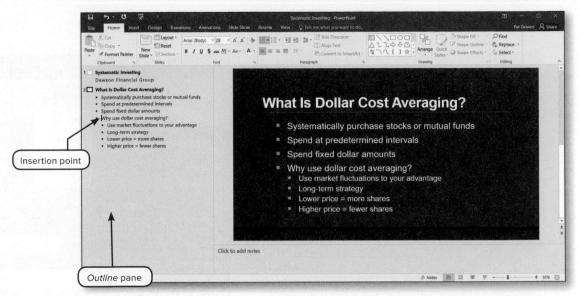

1-27 Slide with bulleted text before list level changes

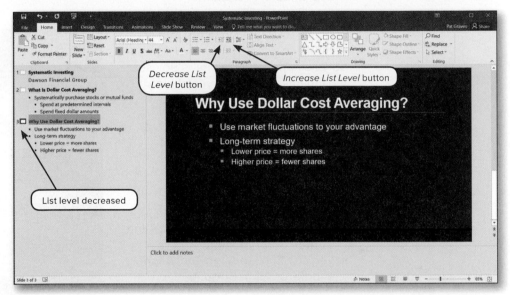

1-28 New slide created by decreasing the list level

5. Convert a bulleted list to a numbered list by selecting the text to be changed and then clicking the **Numbering** button [*Home* tab, *Paragraph* group].

> **MORE INFO**
>
> To move from the title to the body placeholder, press **Ctrl+Enter**. If you are in the last placeholder, press **Ctrl+Enter** to create a new slide.

## Align, Move, and Resize Placeholders

How text is positioned within placeholders is controlled by *horizontal alignment* and *vertical alignment*. A small margin automatically appears in placeholders so the text within them does not touch the border.

## ▶HOW TO: Align Text and Placeholders

1. Align selected text within placeholders horizontally or vertically using these options:

   - *Horizontal*: Choose **Align Left**, **Center**, **Align Right**, or **Justify** (aligns text on both the left and right) [*Home* tab, *Paragraph* group]. *Justify* is rarely used on slides because it can cause irregular spacing between words.
   - *Vertical*: Click **Align Text** [*Home* tab, *Paragraph* group] and then choose **Top**, **Middle**, or **Bottom** (See Figure 1-29).

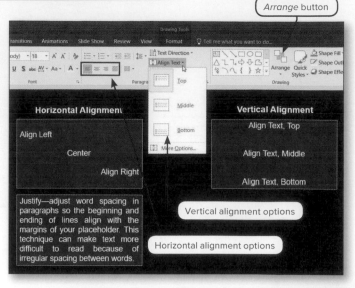

1-29 *Align Text* within placeholders

2. Align selected placeholders with one another. The same drop-down list of options appears on two tabs, so use the tab that is most convenient to you.

   - Click the **Arrange** button [*Home* tab, *Drawing* group] and then choose **Align**.
   - Click the **Align** button [*Drawing Tools Format* tab, *Arrange* group].

3. Choose an alignment option from the drop-down list (Figure 1-30):

   - *Horizontal*: Choose **Align Left**, **Align Center**, or **Align Right**.
   - *Vertical*: Choose **Align Top**, **Align Middle**, or **Align Bottom**.

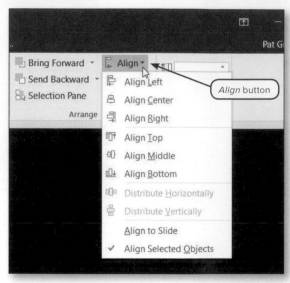

1-30 *Align* options

Move a placeholder by pointing to its border so your pointer changes to a move arrow (with four points) (Figure 1-31). Click to select the placeholder and drag it to a new position. Use the same technique for moving other objects such as shapes and pictures.

To increase or decrease placeholder size, point to a corner or side *sizing handle* until your pointer changes to a *resize pointer* (with two points) (see Figure 1-31). As you drag to resize, your pointer changes to a crosshair and the area you will keep is grayed out (Figure 1-32). When you release the pointer, the circle handles appear again. Drag a corner sizing handle (with a diagonal resize pointer) to change both the horizontal and vertical dimensions at the same time.

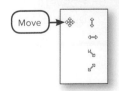

1-31 Move and resize pointers

1-32 Resize a placeholder

You can control the way placeholders and other objects are resized by pressing one of three keys as you drag:

- *Ctrl*: The placeholder size changes from a fixed center point.
- *Shift*: The height and width proportions are maintained as the size changes.
- *Ctrl+Shift*: The placeholder resizes from the center and remains in proportion.

Another way to precisely resize a placeholder is to enter the exact dimensions in the *Size* group on the *Drawing Tools Format* tab (Figure 1-33).

All of these techniques for moving, aligning, and resizing also apply to pictures and other objects. If you don't like a change that you made, click the **Reset** button in the *Slides* group on the *Home* tab.

1-33 *Size* group

## Edit Text

Notice that your pointer changes when you are working with text. When you see a blinking insertion point, PowerPoint is waiting for you to type text. When you point to text, your pointer changes to a text selection tool so you can click and drag to select text.

Much like Word, commands for editing text are on the *Home* tab in the following groups (from left to right) (Figure 1-34):

- *Clipboard group*: **Cut**, **Copy**, **Paste**, and **Format Painter**.
- *Font group*: Character formatting commands such as **Bold**, **Italic**, **Underline**, **Case**, **Font**, and **Font Size**.
- *Paragraph group*: Paragraph formatting commands such as **Align**, **Bullets**, **Numbering**, and **Increase List Level**.

1-34 *Clipboard*, *Font*, and *Paragraph* groups on the *Home* tab

Also, many text formatting options are available on the mini toolbar (Figure 1-35), which appears when text is selected. You can undo or redo actions using commands on the *Quick Access* toolbar.

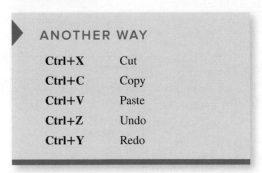

| ANOTHER WAY | |
|---|---|
| **Ctrl+X** | Cut |
| **Ctrl+C** | Copy |
| **Ctrl+V** | Paste |
| **Ctrl+Z** | Undo |
| **Ctrl+Y** | Redo |

1-35 Mini toolbar

---

▶**HOW TO:** Delete Text

1. Press **Delete** to remove text to the right of the insertion point.
2. Press **Backspace** to remove text to the left of the insertion point.
3. Select text and press **Delete** to remove several words at one time.

---

Click outside a text placeholder to deselect it. Handles no longer appear.

## Change Text Case

Text *case* refers to how text is capitalized. In several themes, text appears in a placeholder in uppercase (all capital) letters. Be careful when using uppercase letters, because they may not be as easy to read as text with initial caps (the first letter only is capitalized). People can generally read lowercase text faster than uppercase text. Also, uppercase words in email are thought to represent shouting, and this negative connotation might carry over to your presentation if you overuse capital letters. Use uppercase letters when you really want to emphasize selected words or brief phrases.

▶**HOW TO:** Change Case

1. Select the text to be changed.
2. Click the **Change Case** button [*Home* tab, *Font* group].
3. Choose from the options **Sentence case.**, **lowercase**, **UPPERCASE**, **Capitalize Each Word**, or **tOGGLE cASE** (Figure 1-36).

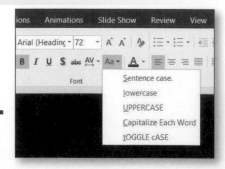

1-36 *Change Case* options

## Change List Bullet Symbols

You can change the bullet symbol in a placeholder if it seems inappropriate or if its color blends too much with the slide background.

▶**HOW TO:** Change Bullet Symbols

1. Select the text or placeholder where you want to change the bullet.
   - Select text in the placeholder to change the bullet for one or more bulleted items.
   - Select the bulleted placeholder to change all bullets in the placeholder.
2. Click the **Bullets** drop-down arrow [*Home* tab, *Paragraph* group] and then select **Bullets and Numbering** to open the *Bullets and Numbering* dialog box (Figure 1-37).
3. Select one of the pre-defined bullets.
4. Enter a different number in the *Size* box to increase or decrease the bullet size.
5. Click the **Color** button to select a different bullet color.
6. Click the **Customize** button to open the *Symbol* dialog box (Figure 1-38), where you can select from many symbols displayed in several fonts.

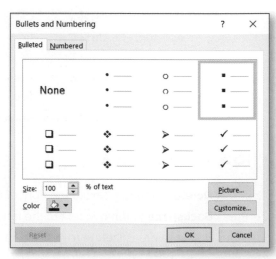

1-37 *Bullets and Numbering* dialog box

7. Select a symbol and a *Character code* appears. This is a unique number that your computer uses to identify the symbol you have chosen.

8. Click **OK** to add that symbol to the *Bullets and Numbering* dialog box.

9. Select the bullet and click **OK** to change the bullets on selected text.

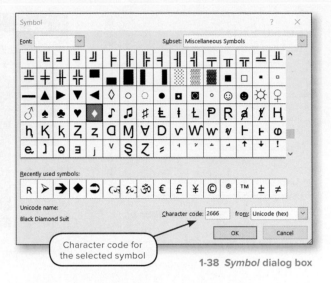

Character code for the selected symbol

1-38 *Symbol* dialog box

The three ***Wingdings*** fonts have most of the available character bullets from the *Symbols* dialog box. You can also select picture bullets that are more decorative from the *Bullets and Numbering* dialog box.

## The Format Painter

To copy formatting from text, shapes, or pictures and apply these settings to another selection, use the ***Format Painter***. You can apply the changes on the same slide or on different slides.

▶ **HOW TO:** Use the Format Painter

1. Select the text or other object with the format that you want to copy.
2. Click **Format Painter** [*Home* tab, *Clipboard* group] (see Figure 1-34). Your pointer changes to a paintbrush.
3. Move the paintbrush over the text or other object that you want to change and click to apply the formatting.
4. Apply the change to multiple selections by double-clicking the **Format Painter** button.
5. Press **Esc** to stop formatting.

## Reuse Slides from Another Presentation

You can add slides from another presentation without opening it as long as you can access the location where it is stored.

▶ **HOW TO:** Reuse Slides

1. Click between two slides in the thumbnail area where you want one or more new slides inserted. A red line between the slides indicates your insertion point.
2. Click the **New Slide** drop-down arrow [*Home* tab, *Slides* group] and select **Reuse Slides** from the bottom of the layout gallery. The *Reuse Slides* pane automatically opens.
3. Click the **Browse** button in the *Reuse Slides* pane and then click **Browse File** (Figure 1-39).

1-39 *Reuse Slides* pane

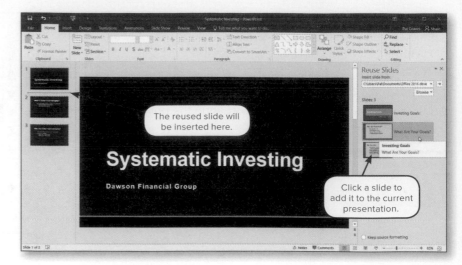

1-40 Reuse slides

4. Find the location where your presentation with the slides you need is saved and select the file name.

5. Click **Open**. The slides in this second presentation appear in the *Reuse Slides* pane with text showing their titles (Figure 1-40).

6. Click the slides you want to insert in your current presentation.

   - By default, the reused slides will appear with the formatting of your current presentation.
   - If you want the inserted slides to retain their design from the original presentation, select the **Keep source formatting** checkbox at the bottom of the *Reuse Slides* pane before inserting them.

7. Click the **Close** button at the top of the *Reuse Slides* pane.

> **MORE INFO**
>
> When task panes open, they are docked on the right side of the PowerPoint window. If you have a wide computer screen and you are using PowerPoint in a window size that does not fill the screen, you can drag a pane away from the window so your slide size becomes larger. Double-click the pane to dock it on the right of the window again.

## Check Spelling and Word Usage

PowerPoint's **AutoCorrect** feature repairs many simple errors such as changing "teh" to "the" or "recieve" to "receive" as you enter text on your slides. You can customize *AutoCorrect* options to include words that you frequently misspell or abbreviate when the word should be spelled.

PowerPoint will automatically add a red, wavy line below words it does not recognize. Use the **Spelling** feature to correct errors at any time during a presentation but always when you are making your final adjustments. You still need to carefully read the content to find any words that may have been missed, such as names or words that might not be in the spelling dictionary. If your audience sees mistakes when viewing your slide show, your credibility is undermined.

## ▶ HOW TO: Check Spelling

1-41 *Spelling* button on the *Review* tab

1. Click the **Spelling** button [*Review* tab, *Proofing* group] (Figure 1-41). The *Spelling* pane opens on the right (Figure 1-42).
2. Consider each word that is identified and whether or not the suggested spelling is correct.
3. Click the **Audio** button on the *Spelling* pane to hear the word pronounced.
4. Click the **Change** button to insert a suggested spelling; click the **Ignore** button if you want to skip the suggestion.
5. Click **OK** when the spell check is complete. The *Spelling* pane automatically closes.

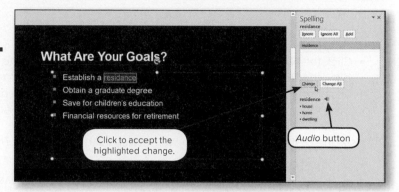

1-42 *Spelling* pane

If you want to replace an awkward word or one that is used too frequently, use PowerPoint's ***Thesaurus*** to find a more appropriate word.

## ▶ HOW TO: Use the Thesaurus

1. Click the word you want to change.
2. Click the **Thesaurus** button [*Review* tab, *Proofing* group]. The *Thesaurus* pane opens and the selected word appears in the search box (Figure 1-43). Words with similar meanings appear below it.
3. Click a word in this list to see more options; click the **Back** arrow to return to the original list.
4. Click the **Down** arrow on the right of a word in this list and choose **Insert**. The selected word on your slide is replaced with the new word.
5. Click the **Close** button at the top of the *Thesaurus* pane.

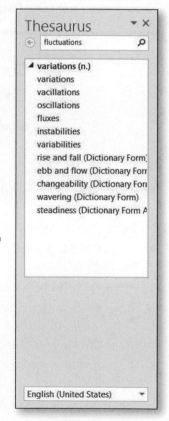

1-43 *Thesaurus* word choices

 **SLO 1.3**

# Navigating between Slides and Organizing Content

When developing a presentation, you might need to move between slides as ideas occur to you or when you have new information to add. You can rearrange slides at any time. Always examine your sequence carefully when all slides are complete. The final order must be logical to you and to your audience.

## Navigate between Slides

In *Normal* view, you can move between slides by clicking the **Next Slide** and **Previous Slide** buttons, clicking scroll arrows, or dragging the scroll box to the right of the window. You can also click thumbnails or use keyboard shortcuts.

### ▶ HOW TO: Navigate between Slides

1. Use one of these methods to move between slides using the scroll bar and buttons on the right.
   - Click the **Next Slide** button or the **Scroll Down** arrow to go to the next slide.
   - Click the **Previous Slide** button or **Scroll Up** arrow to go to the previous slide.
   - Click above or below the scroll box to move between slides one at a time.
   - Drag the *Scroll* box up or down to move to a specific slide, using the slide indicator (Figure 1-44).
2. Use one of these methods to move between slides using the *Thumbnail* pane.
   - Click a slide thumbnail to make that slide active.
   - Click between slide thumbnails to select a position for a new slide. A red line indicates your insertion point.
3. Press the following shortcut keys:

   | | |
   |---|---|
   | First slide | **Home** |
   | Last slide | **End** |
   | Next slide | **Page Down** or **Down** arrow |
   | Previous slide | **Page Up** or **Up** arrow |

1-44 Navigate between slides

## Copy, Paste, and Duplicate Slides

To reuse a slide's content or format, copy the thumbnail. It is stored in your computer's temporary storage area called the ***Clipboard***. The original slide remains in its position. Paste the copied slide where you need it and edit the text.

### ▶ HOW TO: Copy and Paste Slides

1. Select the thumbnail of the slide to be copied (Figure 1-45).
2. Press **Ctrl+C** or click the **Copy** button [*Home* tab, *Clipboard* group] to copy the slide.
   - You can also right-click a slide thumbnail and select **Copy** from the context menu.
3. Move the insertion point to the place between slides where you want the copied slide to appear. A red line indicates your insertion point.
4. Press **Ctrl+V** or click the **Paste** button [*Home* tab, *Clipboard* group].
   - You can also right-click a slide thumbnail and select **Paste** from the context menu.
5. Edit the text on the new slide as needed.

1-45 Copy and paste a selected slide

Duplicating also creates a second copy of a slide. You can drag the second slide to a different position.

▶ **HOW TO:** Duplicate Slides

1. Select the thumbnail of the slide to be duplicated.
2. Press **Ctrl+D** to duplicate the slide. The second slide appears immediately after the original slide and the new slide is selected.
   - You can also right-click a slide thumbnail and select **Duplicate Slide** from the context menu.

## Select Multiple Slides

If you need to make the same changes to more than one slide, you can select more than one slide thumbnail.

▶ **HOW TO:** Select Multiple Slides

1. Select multiple adjacent slides (in order) by selecting the first slide and then pressing **Shift** while you click the last slide (Figure 1-46).
2. Select multiple nonadjacent slides (not in order) by selecting the first slide and then pressing **Ctrl** while you click each of the slides you need to select (Figure 1-47).

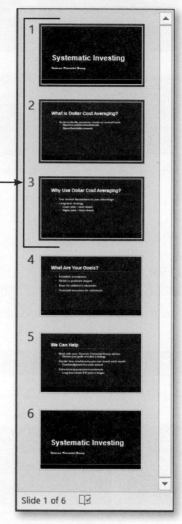

1-46 Adjacent slides selected

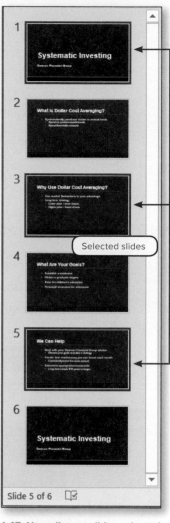

1-47 Nonadjacent slides selected

## Rearrange Slide Order

You can rearrange slides at any time while developing a presentation. In the *Thumbnail* pane you can drag slide thumbnails up or down. On the *Outline* view, you can drag the slide icons. You can also cut slides and paste them into different positions. However, when your presentation has more slides than can be seen in the *Thumbnail* pane, it is best to rearrange slides using *Slide Sorter* view (Figure 1-48).

The *Slide Sorter* view enables you to see your presentation as a whole. The thumbnails are arranged from left to right in rows. By default, they are shown at a 100% size. Click buttons on the *Status* bar to change this percentage. The **Zoom In** button will increase the slide thumbnail size if you need to see the slide content better; the **Zoom Out** button will decrease the slide thumbnail size and you see more slides at one time.

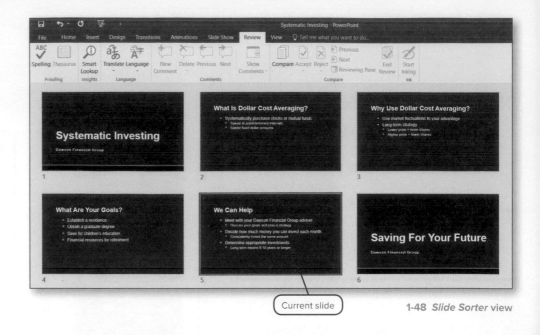

Current slide

1-48 *Slide Sorter* view

1. Click the **Slide Sorter** button on the *Status* bar.
2. Click the **Zoom In** or **Zoom Out** buttons to adjust the size of the thumbnails.
3. Click and drag the slide thumbnails into their new positions (Figure 1-49).

1-49 Slides rearranged

## Delete Slides

Remove slides by deleting slide thumbnails in *Normal* view and *Slide Sorter* view or by deleting the slide icon in *Outline* view. You can also use the **Cut** button on the *Home* tab in the *Clipboard* group. This method is helpful because if you change your mind about the deletion later, you can paste the deleted slides back into the presentation from the *Clipboard*.

## ▶ HOW TO: Delete Slides

1. Right-click the slide thumbnail (or the *Slide* icon in *Outline* view). Click **Delete Slide** from the context menu.

*Or*

2. Select the slide thumbnail (or the *Slide* icon in *Outline* view). Press **Delete** or click **Cut** [*Home* tab, *Clipboard* group].

---

# PAUSE & PRACTICE: POWERPOINT 1-1

For this project, you develop the text for a presentation about upcoming marathon events at the Hamilton Civic Center. This presentation promotes event preparation for participants. You start with a blank presentation, add slides, reuse slides from another presentation, and change formatting.

---

File Needed: ***Marathon Info-01.pptx*** *(Student data files are available in the* Library *of your SIMnet account.)*
Completed Project File Name: ***[your initials] PP P1-1.pptx***

---

1. Open PowerPoint and click **Blank Presentation** to start a new presentation.
   a. If PowerPoint is already open, press **Ctrl+N** or click the **File** tab, click **New**, and then click **Blank Presentation**.

2. Name and save the presentation.
   a. Press **F12** to open the *Save As* dialog box.
   b. Browse to the location where you want to save your files and double-click to open the appropriate folder (Figure 1-50). If necessary, click the **New Folder** button, type a name for the new folder, and then double-click to open it.
   c. Type [your initials] PP P1-1 in the *File name* area.
   d. Verify that the *Save as type* area says "PowerPoint Presentation."
   e. Click **Save**. The *Save As* dialog box closes.

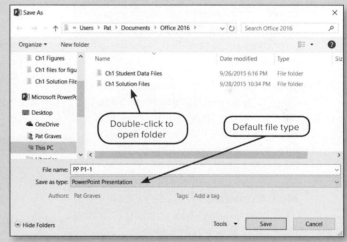

1-50 *Save As* dialog box

3. Display slide 1. Type the following text in the placeholders:

   Title:      Take the Right Steps

   Subtitle:   Train for a Marathon

4. Click the **New Slide** button [*Home* tab, *Slides* group] twice to add two new slides. The slide thumbnails will appear blank, but the slides have the *Title and Content* layout with two placeholders. Type the following text on slides 2 and 3:

Slide 2 Title:          What Is Your Goal?
Bulleted items:
- Run the second half faster
- Beat a time you've run before
- Or
- Finish the marathon

Slide 3 Title:          Start Early to Be Ready
Bulleted items:
- Begin 5-16 weeks in advance
- Get a physical check up
- Prepare gear for running
- Join a training group
- Enjoy camaraderie
- Be accountable
- Run 3-4 times a week

5. Change a slide layout and adjust the text.
   a. Display slide 3 and click the **Layout** button [*Home* tab, *Slides* group]. Next, select the **Two Content** layout.
   b. Select the last four bulleted items on the left placeholder and press **Ctrl+X** to cut them.
   c. Click the right placeholder and press **Ctrl+V** to paste them.
   d. Delete any extra bullets by placing your insertion point on that line and pressing **Backspace**.
   e. Select the middle two bulleted items on the right placeholder and press **Tab** or click the **Increase List Level** button [*Home* tab, *Paragraph* group] to format them as indented subpoints under the first-level item (Figure 1-51).

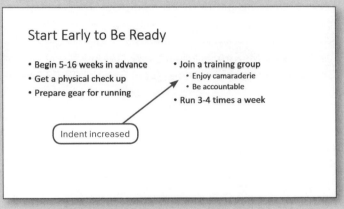

1-51 *Two Content* layout

6. Insert three slides from another presentation.
   a. Display slide 3. Click the **New Slide** drop-down arrow and select **Reuse Slides**.
   b. On the *Reuse Slides* pane, click the **Browse** button; then select **Browse File** and locate your student data files.
   c. Select the presentation *MarathonInfo-01* and click **Open**. (This presentation has spelling errors that you will fix later.)
   d. Click three slides (Figure 1-52) to insert them: "Practice Runs," "Eat Energy Foods," and "Get Running Apparel."
   e. Close the *Reuse Slides* pane.

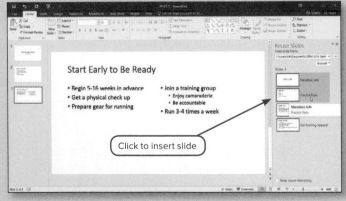

1-52 Reuse slides

7. Rearrange slides.
   a. Click the thumbnails and drag them up or down so the six slides are in this order: "Take the Right Steps," "What is Your Goal?," "Start Early to Be Ready," "Get Running Apparel," "Eat Energy Foods," and "Practice Runs."

8. Insert and duplicate a new slide.
   a. Display slide 6. Click the **New Slide** drop-down arrow and select the **Title Only** layout.
   b. Type Look It UP! in the title placeholder on slide 7. (Figure 1-53).
   c. Select the title text and change the font size to **72 pt**.
   d. Select this slide thumbnail and press **Ctrl+D** to duplicate it to create slide 8.

9. Edit and duplicate a slide.
   a. Display slide 8. Replace the title with the text Mark It DOWN!.
   b. Select this slide thumbnail and press **Ctrl+D** to duplicate it to create slide 9.

10. Display slide 9. Change the title text to See You THERE!

11. Click the **Spelling** button [*Review* tab, *Proofing* group] and correct each of the spelling errors ("performance," "soreness," "banana," and "yogurt").

12. Save and close the presentation (Figure 1-54). You will continue to work on this presentation for *Pause & Practice 1-2* and *Pause & Practice 1-3*.

**1-53 Placeholder text resized**

**1-54 PP P1-1 completed**

SLO 1.4

## Changing Theme Colors and Fonts

In PowerPoint, you can quickly change theme colors and fonts using the *Design* tab. If you want to make additional theme changes, use the *Slide Master* tab. The **Slide Master** stores information about slide backgrounds, layouts, colors, and fonts for each theme. In this section, you change theme colors and fonts using both of these tabs so you can learn to choose the method that is most efficient for what you need to change.

When you start a new presentation and search online for templates and themes, you may find backgrounds with artwork or pictures that match your topic perfectly. The file names you see below each thumbnail do not distinguish between themes and templates. Many of the presentations that appear in a search will have the PowerPoint default file extension (*.pptx*). Those saved as template files will have a different file extension (*.potx*). Depending on how your software is set up, you may not see these file extensions when you open files.

You can search through general categories or enter a specific search word to get more targeted results. Themes and templates are provided by Microsoft and other companies.

Your searches will provide results that include the following:

- *Theme*: A slide show with only background graphics and text treatments but no content. Different layouts control where slide objects are positioned. You can control design elements with the *Slide Master* to create custom designs.
- *Template*: A slide show with the characteristics of a theme but also with sample content on several slides. You can edit the content or remove individual slides that you do not need for your presentation. You can control design elements with the *Slide Master* to create custom designs.
- *Template, title slide only*: While the thumbnail may show a title slide, that slide might be the only content in the presentation. Other slides may be blank or have no related graphic background. The *Slide Master* has not been used.
- *Template, individual slide only*: Thumbnails may show only a diagram or chart that can be revised for a new presentation. Usually, the *Slide Master* has not been used.
- *Different slide sizes*: Two slide sizes will appear. The thumbnails that have an almost square appearance are shown in a 4:3 **aspect ratio**, the ratio of width to height, which was the standard for many years. The thumbnails in a wide-screen size are shown in PowerPoint's default 16:9 aspect ratio, which reflects the shape of current computer screens.

People who frequently see presentations become very familiar with the slide show designs that appear in common software. So seeing a slide show with a contemporary looking design that truly matches the topic is refreshing. Caring enough to match your theme to your topic speaks volumes to people about your preparedness and competence. Consider carefully what you select so the design is suitable for your topic and for how your slide show is used.

▶ **HOW TO: Apply a Theme to an Existing Presentation**

1. Click the **Design** tab.
2. Click the **More** button in the *Themes* gallery to see additional themes.
3. Point to a thumbnail to see a live preview of that theme on the current slide (Figure 1-55).
4. Click the thumbnail to apply the theme.

1-55 *Design* tab and *Themes* gallery

## Change Theme Colors

When changing theme colors, select colors that are appropriate for your topic. Also consider where you will present. Because of room lighting, colors for a slide show projected on a large screen are not as clear or vibrant as what you see on a computer screen directly in front of you. These differences can influence your color choices. Be sure your text is easy to read with a high contrast between the text and background colors (dark on light or light on dark).

Every presentation, even a blank one, begins with a set of colors that have been chosen to work well together. With each built-in theme, PowerPoint provides *Variants* on the *Design* tab that show different theme colors and some variants have different graphics. Many more theme colors are available.

► **HOW TO: Change Theme Colors Using the Design Tab**

1. Click the **Design** tab.
2. Click the **More** button [*Variants* group].
3. Select **Colors** and a drop-down list appears showing theme colors (Figure 1-56).
4. Point to a set of theme colors and you see a live preview of those colors on your current slide. The blank, Office theme will show a live preview only if the background colors have changed.
5. Click the colors or a theme name to apply it to all slides.

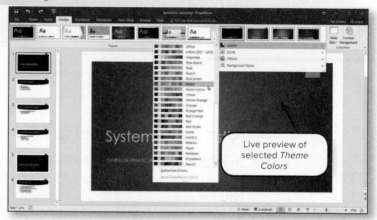

1-56 *Design* tab and *Theme Colors*

The first two colors in each color theme represent the background and text colors; the remaining six show accent colors. Once you select theme colors, you can apply a *Background Style* to change to a light or dark variation of background and text colors. Click the **More** button [*Design* tab, *Variants* group] and select **Background Styles**. Point to a color in the gallery to see a live preview; click a color to apply it.

Not all of the themes you find online permit color changes in the same way. It depends on how the background design was created. For more on customizing theme colors, see *SLO 3.1: Creating Custom Theme and Background Colors*.

## Change Theme Fonts

Select your fonts carefully. Some fonts seem very traditional and serious; others appear more playful and flamboyant. Use fonts that are appropriate for your presentation topic.

Consider how legible the font is with the background color you are using. Letters can appear very thin and are not easy to read unless you apply bold. Also consider issues related to where you present. The lighting and room size affect how readable the text is on a large screen and you must use large font sizes. If you are designing a presentation to be displayed for a single person on your notebook or tablet computer, you can use smaller font sizes.

Every presentation, even a blank one, begins with a pair of *Theme Fonts*. The heading font is used for slide titles and the body font is used for all other text. Sometimes the same font is used for both. You can view or change *Theme Fonts* from the *Design* tab or from the *Slide Master* tab.

### ▶ HOW TO: Change Theme Fonts Using the Design Tab

1. Click the **Design** tab.
2. Click the **More** button [*Variants* group].
3. Select **Fonts** and a drop-down list appears showing theme fonts (Figure 1-57).
4. Point to a pair of theme fonts and you see a live preview of those fonts applied to the current slide.
5. Click a theme font pair to apply it to all slides.

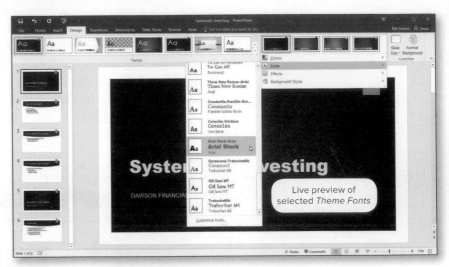

1-57 *Design* tab and *Theme Fonts*

## Use the Slide Master to Change Theme Colors and Fonts

It is best to use the *Slide Master* tab to change theme colors or theme fonts when you are also changing other design elements. For example, you could customize slide layouts or background graphics by adding a company logo to all slides in a presentation. Each *Slide Master* has a variety of layouts, shown in the pane at the left, that control positioning of different types of content. If you are adding graphics or changing only specific layout colors, then select only the layout you want to change. Changes made on the first layout at the top of this pane generally apply to all other layouts.

### ▶ HOW TO: Change Theme Colors and Fonts Using the Slide Master

1. Click the **View** tab.
2. Click the Slide Master button [*Master Views* group] (Figure 1-58) to open the *Slide Master* tab.
3. Scroll up to select the first layout, the *Slide Master* layout, at the top of the *Thumbnails* pane so your changes will affect all layouts.
4. Click the **Colors** button [*Background* group] and a drop-down list appears showing theme colors (Figure 1-59).
5. Point to a set of theme colors and you see a live preview of those colors on your current *Slide Master* layout.
6. Click the colors or a theme color name to apply it to all *Slide Master* layouts.

1-58 *Slide Master* button on the *View* tab

7. Click the **Background Styles** button [*Slide Master* tab, *Background* group] to change the background to light or dark variations (Figure 1-60).

   - You can apply different *Background Styles* to various *Slide Master* layouts.
   - This feature is available on the *Design* tab, also.

8. Click the **Fonts** button [*Slide Master* tab, *Background* group] and a drop-down list appears showing theme fonts.

9. Point to a pair of theme fonts and you see a live preview of those fonts applied to the current layout.

10. Click a theme font pair to apply it to all layouts.

11. Click the **Close Master View** button [*Slide Master* tab, *Close* group].

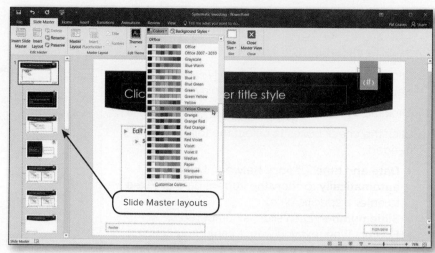

1-59 *Slide Master* tab and *Theme Colors*

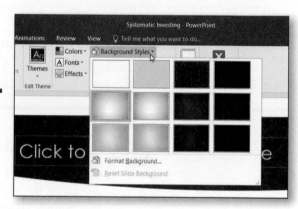

1-60 *Background Styles*

---

# Inserting Headers and Footers

If you want to include identifying information on all slides of a presentation, use the *Header & Footer* command on the *Insert* tab (Figure 1-61). **Footers** are displayed on every slide with placeholders for the date and time, slide number, and footer text. These placeholders often appear across the bottom of the slide, but they may appear in different places depending on the theme. You can choose to show footers on all slides or only on selected slides.

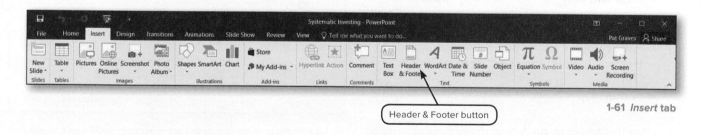

1-61 *Insert* tab

## Create a Slide Footer

When you enter information using the *Header and Footer* dialog box, placeholders appear on the slides. You can move these placeholders if you wish.

## ▶ HOW TO: Create a Slide Footer

1. Click the **Insert** tab.

2. Click the **Header & Footer** button [*Text* group]. The *Header and Footer* dialog box displays.

3. Click the **Slide** tab (Figure 1-62).

4. Click the check boxes to select the following as needed:

   - **Date and time**: Choose between **Update automatically** to show the current date or **Fixed** to enter a specific date.
   - **Slide number**: Each slide is numbered.
   - **Footer**: Type text you want to appear on each slide.

5. Check the box for **Don't show on title slide** if you do not want footer information to appear on any slide created with the *Title Slide* layout.

6. Apply your choices by clicking one of these buttons:

   - **Apply:** the settings are applied to the current slide only.
   - **Apply to All:** the settings are applied to all slides.

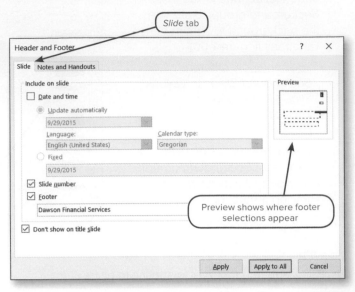

1-62 *Slide* tab in the *Header and Footer* dialog box

## Create a Notes and Handouts Header

Because notes and handouts are usually printed documents, they can include *header* information that appears at the top of each page. Control all settings for notes and handouts in the same way you control slide footers.

## ▶ HOW TO: Create a Notes and Handouts Header

1. Click the **Insert** tab.

2. Click the **Header & Footer** button [*Text* group]. The *Header and Footer* dialog box displays.

3. Click the **Notes and Handouts** tab (Figure 1-63).

4. Click the check boxes to select the following as needed:

   - **Date and time**: Choose between **Update automatically** to show the current date or **Fixed** to enter a specific date.
   - **Page number**: Each page is numbered.
   - **Header**: Type text you want to appear on each page.
   - **Footer**: Type text you want to appear on each page.

5. Click the **Apply to All** button to apply your settings to all pages.

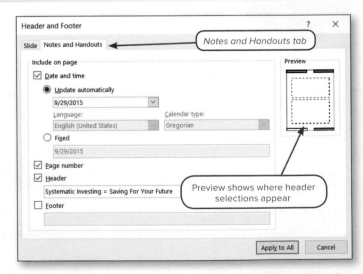

1-63 *Notes and Handouts* tab in the *Header and Footer* dialog box

If you leave items blank in the *Header and Footer* dialog box, empty placeholders show on your slide, but no information appears in *Slide Show* view.

For this project, you continue working on the presentation about training for a marathon. You add a theme then change theme colors and fonts to revise two individual slides. Finally, you add a footer to your slides and add page numbering to the notes and handout pages.

File Needed: *[your initials] PP P1-1.pptx*
Completed Project File Name: *[your initials] PP P1-2.pptx*

1. Open the presentation you completed in *Pause & Practice 1-1*.
   a. Click the **File** tab to open the *Backstage* view and click **Open** on the left.
   b. Click **Browse** to open the *Open* dialog box.
   c. Locate the folder where you want to save this file.
   d. Select the **[your initials] PP P1-1** presentation and click **Open**.

2. Rename and save the presentation.
   a. Click the **File** tab to open the *Backstage* view and select **Save As** on the left.
   b. Click **Browse** to open the *Save As* dialog box.
   c. Locate the folder where your files are saved.
   d. Change the file name to [your initials] PP P1-2.
   e. Click **Save** to save the presentation and close the *Save As* dialog box.

3. Apply a theme.
   a. Click the **Design** tab.
   b. Click the **More** button [*Themes* group] to open the *Themes* gallery (Figure 1-64).
   c. Click the **Facet** theme so it is applied to all slides.

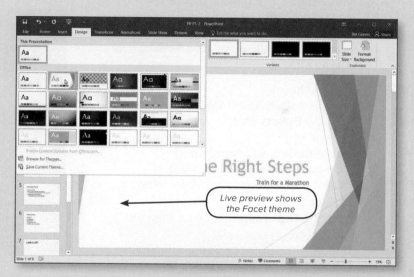

*Live preview shows the Facet theme*

1-64 *Themes gallery*

4. Change theme colors and the background style.
   a. Click the **More** button [*Design* tab, *Variants* group] and select **Colors**.
   b. Scroll down the list and select the **Aspect** theme.
   c. Click the **More** button again and select **Background Styles**.
   d. Select **Style 4**, which applies a solid black background (Figure 1-65).

5. Change theme fonts.
   a. Click the **More** button [*Design* tab, *Variants* group] and select **Fonts**.
   b. Scroll down the list and click the **TrebuchetMS** font pair (Figure 1-66).

1-65 *Background Styles*

6. Modify and move the title.
   a. Display slide 1. Select the title placeholder and apply these font changes: **60 pt.**, **Bold** [*Home* tab, *Font* group], and **Align Left** [*Home* tab, *Paragraph* group].
   b. Click the **Arrange** button [*Home* tab, *Drawing* group], select **Align**, and select **Align Top**.
   c. Select the word **Right**. Click the **Change Case** button [*Home* tab, *Font* group] and select **UPPERCASE**.
   d. Resize the placeholder by dragging the right horizontal sizing handle so the text fits on one line.

7. Modify and move the subtitle.
   a. Select the subtitle placeholder on slide 1 and apply these font changes: **36 pt.**, **Bold** [*Home* tab, *Font* group], and **Align Left** [*Home* tab, *Paragraph* group].
   b. Move the subtitle placeholder below the title and select both placeholders.
   c. Click the **Arrange** button [*Home* tab, *Drawing* group], select **Align**, and then select **Align Left**.

8. Change the bullet.
   a. Display slide 2. Select the bulleted text and click the **Bullets** drop-down arrow [*Home* tab, *Font* group].
   b. Select **Bullets and Numbering**.
   c. Change the *Size* to **100%** of text.
   d. Click the **Color** button and select **Red, Accent 2** (Figure 1-67).
   e. Click the **Customize** button to open the *Symbol* dialog box.
   f. Change the *Subset* to **Geometric Shapes** (Figure 1-68). Select the **Black Square** (Character code 25A0).
      • If the **Wingdings** font is available, select a similar symbol (Character code 110).
   g. Click **OK** to insert the symbol and close the *Symbol* dialog box. Click **OK** again to close the *Bullets and Numbering* dialog box.
   h. Click to position your insertion point before the word "**Or**" on the third bulleted item.
   i. Press **Backspace** to remove the bullet from this item only. Apply **bold**.

9. Add a slide footer.
   a. Display slide 2 and click the **Header & Footer** button [*Insert* tab, *Text* group].
   b. On the *Slide* tab, select **Slide number** and **Footer** (Figure 1-69).

1-66 Change *Theme* font

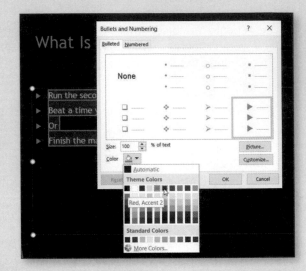

1-67 Change bullet size and color

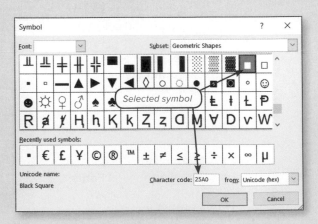

1-68 *Symbol* dialog box

c. In the *Footer* text box, type Take the Right Steps, Train for a Marathon.

d. Select **Don't show on title slide**.

e. Click the **Apply** button. The dialog box closes and the footer appears only on this slide.

f. Press **Shift** and click the footer and the page number placeholders to select them both. Increase the font size to **18 pt**. [*Home* tab, *Font* group].

10. Save and close the presentation (Figure 1-70).

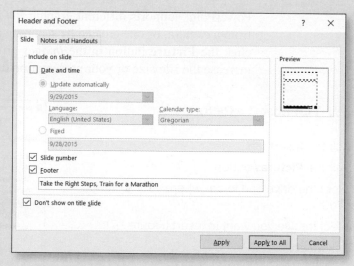

1-69 *Header and Footer* dialog box with changes

1-70 PP P1-2 completed

## Working with a Picture from a File

An old adage says "A picture is worth a thousand words." That saying is still true today, because pictures bring a sense of realism to a presentation. Select pictures appropriate for your topic. Include pictures obtained from web sites only if you have the permission of the image owner to avoid copyright infringement. For academic purposes, you may include images if you reference their sources as you would any other research citation.

## Insert a Picture

PowerPoint supports different graphic file types, so you can insert almost any digital image from a camera, or one created by scanning a document, into a slide show. To insert a picture, click the **Picture** button in the *Images* group on the *Insert* tab. Be aware that pictures can increase the file size of your presentation dramatically.

### ▶ HOW TO: Insert a Picture

1. Click the **Insert** tab.
2. Click the **Pictures** button.
3. Select the drive and folder where your picture is saved.
4. Select the file you want to insert (Figure 1-71).
5. Click **Insert**.

1-71 *Insert Picture* dialog box

### ▶ ANOTHER WAY

Once you have located your picture file, insert the picture by double-clicking the file name.

The following table lists the more commonly used graphic file formats for pictures and illustrations.

## Graphic File Formats

| Picture File Type | Extension | Uses of This Format |
|---|---|---|
| JPEG (Joint Photographic Experts Group) | .jpg | Used for photographs and complex graphics. Handles gradual color blending well. Produces a smaller file size than most other formats. Transparency is not supported. |
| PNG (Portable Network Graphics) | .png | Used for photographs and complex graphics. Supports transparency so areas removed from the image appear blank on the slide. |
| GIF (Graphics Interchange Format) | .gif | Suited for line art and simple drawings because it is limited to 256 colors. Used for simple animated graphics. Does not handle gradual color blending well. Supports transparency. |
| Windows Metafile and Enhanced Windows Metafile | .wmf and .emf | Used for simple 16-bit or 32-bit graphics. |
| Device Independent Bitmap | .bmp | Images usually display well in their original size, but if you increase size, the image will be distorted. |
| TIFF (Tagged Image File Format) | .tiff | Designed for print publications. Produces high-quality images with large file sizes. Supports transparency. |

## Resize a Picture

To resize a picture, point to a sizing handle (white circle on the border) and drag it. Dragging the corner sizing handles will maintain correct proportions because they move diagonally to change both horizontal and vertical dimensions at the same time. Dragging the side handles can cause distortion because the height or width is changed independently.

You can precisely resize a picture by entering dimensions in the *Size* group on the *Picture Tools Format* tab (Figure 1-72) that appears when a picture is selected. When you change the *Height* or *Width* measurement [*Size* group], the other measurement will automatically adjust.

Reset Picture button    Enter sizes    **1-72** *Picture Tools Format* tab

Maintain the correct ratio between height and width to avoid distorting the image. You can make a picture smaller and still retain its clarity, but some pictures cannot be made larger without becoming blurred or distorted. If you change the size incorrectly, restore the picture's original dimensions by clicking the **Reset Picture** button [*Picture Tools Format* tab, *Adjust* group] and selecting **Reset Picture & Size**. Depending on the picture's resolution, you may need to resize it again to fit your slide.

## Align a Picture

As you place pictures and other graphic objects on slides, consider how they are aligned. Everything on the slide should align in some way. You can align selected pictures and other objects with each other or on the slide in the same way you align placeholders (see *Align, Move, and Resize Placeholders* in *SLO 1:2 Working with Slides, Layouts, Placeholders, and Text*.) Click the **Align** button [*Picture Tools Format* tab, *Arrange* group] and select the alignment from the drop-down list (Figure 1-73):

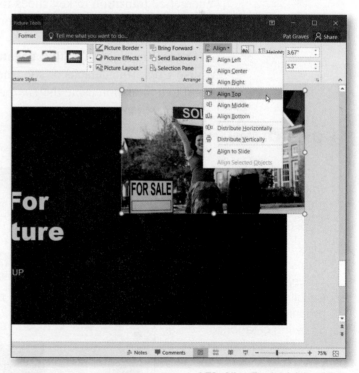

**1-73** *Align Top* and *Align Right*

- *Horizontal alignment*: **Align Left**, **Align Center**, or **Align Right**
- *Vertical alignment*: **Align Top**, **Align Middle**, or **Align Bottom**

The picture shown in Figure 1-73 displays the following alignment: **Align Right**, **Align Top**, and **Align to Slide**.

**SLO 1.7** | **Applying and Modifying Transitions**

A *transition* is the visual effect of movement that occurs when one slide changes to the next slide. Each transition effect in PowerPoint provides a different type of movement. You can find these in the *Transition to This Slide* gallery on the *Transitions* tab (Figure 1-74).

1-74 *Transitions* tab

Each slide can have only one transition. You can set transitions for one slide at a time in *Normal* view or apply the same transition to all slides. If you want to use different transitions, select thumbnails in *Normal* view or *Slide Sorter* view and click a transition to apply it to those slides. Once a transition has been applied, an icon symbolizing movement appears with the slide thumbnail.

Although it is possible to apply different transitions on every slide in a presentation, it is neither practical nor advisable. People are very accustomed to PowerPoint use today and know that slides are going to change. Random movements using many different transitions do not entertain an audience and may be distracting or even annoying. Control movement skillfully to reinforce your message. For example, you could apply a "quiet" transition for most of your presentation (sort of like turning pages in a book or an e-reader) and then apply a more "energetic" transition to key slides to grab attention or signal the beginning of a new topic. Use the *Slide Sorter* view to see more slides at once and decide which slides might benefit from a different movement.

In the *Timing* group, the **Advance Slide** options control whether slides advance **On Mouse Click** (the default) or after the number of seconds that you specify. You can also add sound to a transition using the *Timing* group.

▶ **HOW TO: Apply Transitions**

1.  Select the slide thumbnail where you want a transition to appear.

2.  Click the **Transitions** tab.

3.  Click the **More** button [*Transition to This Slide* group] to see additional transitions (Figure 1-75) organized by the following categories:

    - *Subtle*
    - *Exciting*
    - *Dynamic Content*

4.  Apply one transition to all slides in the presentation.

    - Select a transition effect.

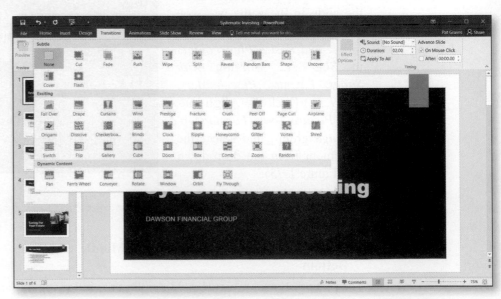

1-75 *Transitions* gallery

- Select **On Mouse Click** [*Timing* group] if it is not already selected.
- Click the **Apply to All** button [*Timing* group].

5. Apply a different transition to selected slides.

- Click the **Slide Sorter** button on the *Status* bar.
- Press **Ctrl** as you click to select one or more slides that should have a different transition.
- Click to apply a different transition effect and the movement is displayed on the selected slides.
- Select **On Mouse Click** [*Timing* group] if it is not already selected. (Figure 1-76).

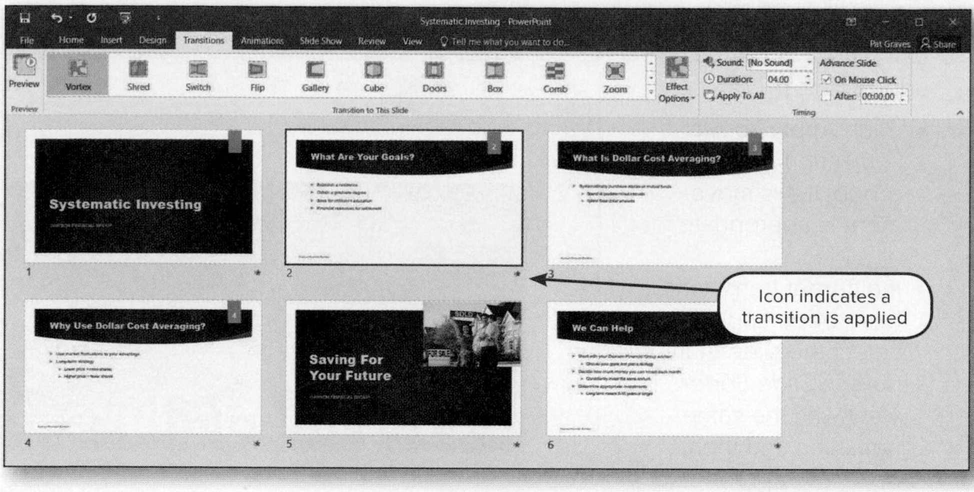

**1-76** Change transitions on selected slides in *Slide Sorter* view

6. Preview slides in different views to test the movement.

- *Slide Sorter* view: Click the **Slide Sorter** button on the *Status* bar. Select a slide thumbnail and click **Preview** [*Transitions* tab, *Preview* group]. Repeat for other slides.
- *Normal* view: Click the **Normal View** button on the *Status* bar. Select a slide and click **Preview**. Click the **Next Slide** button to advance from slide to slide.
- *Slide Show* view: Click the **Slide Show** tab and press **N** to advance from slide to slide.
- Click the **From Beginning** button [*Start Slide Show* group] to view the slide show from the first slide. Click to advance from slide to slide.

---

*Duration*, shown in seconds, controls how fast the slides change. Duration seconds vary based on the selected transition effect. Movement might be barely visible if the duration is fast; a slower duration of five or more seconds will cause the movement to be much more noticeable. Enter a different number to change the duration and experiment to see what works best for your content.

## Select Effect Options

*Effect Options* control the direction of transition movement. Each transition can have only one effect option, but most transitions provide two or more options from which you can choose. You can apply these options as you are setting up your transitions or later when you are editing your presentation.

▶ **HOW TO:** Select Effect Options

1. Select a slide with a transition.
2. Click the **Effect Options** button [*Transition* tab, *Transition to This Slide* group] to see a drop-down list showing directional movements (Figure 1-77).
3. Select an effect option to apply it.

4. Apply the effect option to multiple transitions if appropriate:

- Click **Apply To All** [*Transition* tab, *Timing* group] if this movement is appropriate for all slides.
- If different transitions have been applied, select the slide thumbnails in *Slide Sorter* view with the same transition and then apply the appropriate effect option.

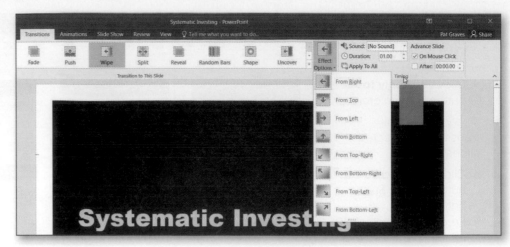

1-77 Transition *Effect Options*

5. Preview the slides in *Slide Show* view to test all transitions and effect options.

---

## Exploring Print Options

You may want to proofread your presentation content on paper or review the slides with a colleague. Or you may want to prepare audience handouts or your own printed materials to use while you are giving the presentation. PowerPoint 2016 provides convenient ways to preview and print presentation slides, handouts, notes pages, or outlines.

### Preview a Presentation

Before printing, check your slides to ensure everything looks as you intended. The *Backstage* view [*File* tab, *Print* button] displays each slide or handout page in your presentation as it will look when printed. Use the navigation controls at the bottom of the window to go through the slides or pages one at a time. You can also use the scroll bar on the right. Adjust slide or page size using the *Zoom* controls on the lower right.

The look of your slides in *Backstage* view is influenced by the selected printer. The preview image shows in color if you are printing with a color printer or in **grayscale** (shades of black) if you are printing with a printer that prints only black. In a work setting, you may have a small desktop printer for printing rough draft copies with black print and a network printer for printing more expensive, high-quality color pages.

If you design slides in color and plan to print slides or handouts in grayscale, preview your slides in grayscale to confirm that all text is readable. You may need to adjust a few colors to get good results.

In *Backstage* view, select a printer from the available list of local and network printers. **Print Settings** are shown as buttons with the current setting displayed. Click the list arrow for a list of the following options:

- *Which Slides to Print*: Choose *Print All Slides*, *Print Selection*, *Print Current Slide*, or *Custom Range* using slide numbers entered in the *Slides* box (slides 1–3 or slides 1–3, 5, 8)
- *What to Print*: Choose *Full Page Slides*, *Notes Pages*, *Outline*, or *Handouts*. You can print handouts with 1, 2, 3, 4, 6, or 9 slides on a page with the sequence of slides arranged horizontally or vertically. You can also specify *Frame Slides*, *Scale to Fit Paper* (increases slide size), or *High Quality*.

- *Print Side*: Choose between *Print One Sided* or *Print on Both Sides*. You can choose to *Flip pages on long edge* or *Flip pages on short edge* to control how pages will turn if they are bound together at the top or side like a book. However, not all printers can print on both sides, so you may not see these options.
- *Print Order*: Choose between *Collated* and *Uncollated*. Usually slides print in order (collated), but you may want to print multiple copies page by page (uncollated).
- *Orientation*: Choose between *Landscape* and *Portrait*. By default, slides print in landscape orientation; notes and handouts print in portrait orientation. This option is not available if you are printing full-size slides.
- *Color Range*: Choose among *Color*, *Grayscale*, or *Pure Black and White*.

Below the print *Settings* in *Backstage* view, you can click the **Edit Header & Footer** link to open the *Header and Footer* dialog box and then enter or revise information on the *Notes and Handouts* tab.

## Print a Slide

The default print settings print each slide on letter-size paper. Adjust print settings as needed to print the current or selected slides.

**▶ HOW TO: Print a Slide in Grayscale**

1. Click the **File** tab.
2. Click **Print** on the left.
3. Select an appropriate printer.
4. Locate the *Settings* area. Click the list arrow for each box and choose options from the drop-down list, such as the following:
   - *Which Slides to Print*: **Print Current Slide**
   - *What to Print*: **Full Page Slides**
   - *Print Order*: **Collated**
   - *Color Range*: **Grayscale** (Figure 1-78)
5. Enter the number of copies, if you need more than one.
6. Click the **Print** button at the top.

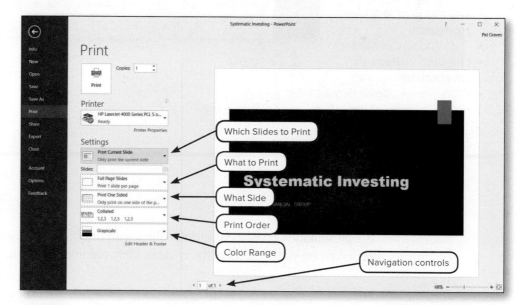

1-78 Print settings for a full-size slide

## Print a Handout

*Handouts* print one to nine slides on a page. You can use these pages as audience handouts or for your own reference during a presentation. Selecting *Scale to Fit Paper* increases the slide size. *Framing* shows the shape of slides, which is helpful when printing slides with a white background on white paper. Depending on the number of slides, changing the page orientation to landscape may increase slide size.

When preparing handouts for an audience, consider which slides will be important for the audience to have. You can specify which slides to include and perhaps reduce the number of pages required for printing.

---

### ▶ HOW TO: Print a Handout for Selected Slides in Color

1. Click the **File** tab.
2. Click **Print** on the left.
3. Select a color printer.
4. Locate the *Settings* area. Click the list arrow for each box and choose options from the drop-down list, such as the following:
   - *Which Slides to Print*: Type the specific slides needed (1, 3–4, 6) in the *Slides* box to print a *Custom Range*.
   - *What to Print*: **6 Slides Horizontal**
   - *Print Order*: **Collated**
   - *Orientation*: **Portrait Orientation**
   - *Color Range*: **Color** (Figure 1-79)
5. Type the number of copies, if you need more than one.
6. Click the **Print** button at the top.

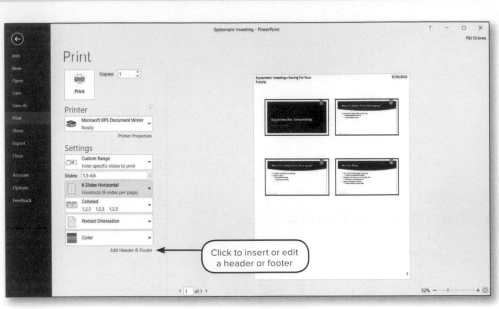

1-79 Print settings for a handout

---

## Print an Outline

If a presentation consists of mostly slides with titles and bulleted lists, printing an outline is a very concise way to display the content. Only the text is shown.

---

### ▶ HOW TO: Print an Outline in Pure Black and White

1. Click the **File** tab.
2. Click the **Print** button on the left.
3. Select an appropriate printer.
4. Locate the *Settings* area. Click the list arrow and choose options from the drop-down list, such as the following:
   - *Which Slides to Print*: **Print All Slides**
   - *What to Print*: **Outline**
   - *What Side*: **Print One Sided**
   - *Print Order*: **Collated**

- *Orientation*: **Portrait Orientation**
- *Color Range*: **Pure Black and White**
(Figure 1-80)

5. Enter the number of copies, if you need more than one.

6. Click the **Print** button at the top.

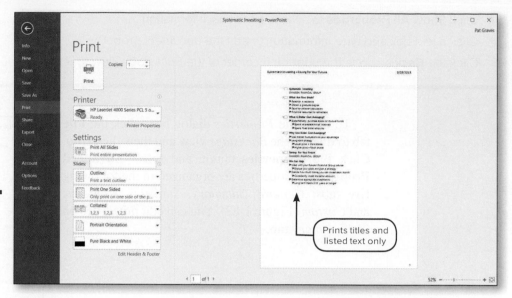

1-80 Print settings for an outline

# Applying Properties

PowerPoint automatically records information called ***properties***, or ***metadata***, that identify details of your presentation to help you manage and track files. Some information is generated automatically such as the file size, creation date, and number of slides. These details are not visible in the presentation; they appear on the *Backstage* view or the *Properties* dialog box. Items shown with fields can be edited by inserting your own content such as title and author. Properties can be viewed by others who use the presentation.

---

▶ **HOW TO:** Add Properties Using Backstage View

1. Click the **File** tab to display the *Backstage* view.

2. Click **Info** if it is not already selected.

3. Point to the properties listed on the right. The property field names are followed by the information for the current presentation.

- Some properties cannot be changed because they are automatically generated.
- A text box with a red border indicates a property field where the information can be edited (Figure 1-81). Click the box to add your content.

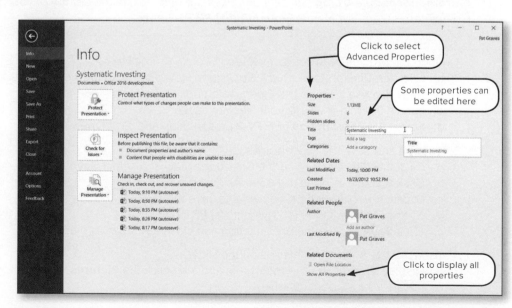

1-81 Document properties on the *Backstage* view

4. Click **Show All Properties** to access additional information.
5. Click a text box and type information to edit the document property.
6. Click the **Back** arrow in the upper left corner of the *Backstage* view to return to your presentation.

To open the *Properties* dialog box, click the **File** tab to display the *Backstage* view and then click **Info**. Click the **Properties** button and select **Advanced Properties**. Properties are organized in the following five tabs: *General*, *Summary*, *Statistics*, *Contents*, and *Custom* (Figure 1-82). You can edit properties on the *Summary* tab.

1-82 *Properties* dialog box

## PAUSE & PRACTICE: POWERPOINT 1-3

For this final Pause & Practice project, you finish the presentation about training for a marathon. You insert, resize, and align several pictures, apply transitions, change the presentation properties, and print a handout.

**Files Needed: *[your initials] PP P1-2.pptx, RunnersGroup-01.jpg, RunnerWoman-01.jpg*,** and ***MarathonSchedule-01.jpg*** *(Student data files are available in the* Library *of your SIMnet account.)*
Completed Project File Name: ***[your initials] PP P1-3.pptx***

1. Open the presentation you completed in *Pause & Practice 1-2*.
   a. Click the **File** tab to open the *Backstage* view and click **Open** on the left.
   b. Click **Browse** to open the *Open* dialog box.
   c. Locate the folder where your files are saved.
   d. Select the ***[your initials] PP P1-2*** presentation and click **Open**.

2. Rename and save the presentation.
   a. Click the **File** tab to open the *Backstage* view and select **Save As** on the left.
   b. Click **Browse** to open the **Save As** dialog box.
   c. Locate the folder where you want to save this file.
   d. Change the file name to [your initials] PP P1-3.
   e. Click **Save** to save the presentation and close the *Save As* dialog box.

3. Insert, resize, and align a picture on the slide.
   a. Display slide 1. Click the **Insert** tab, and then click the **Pictures** button [*Images* group].
   b. Locate your student data files.

c. Select **RunnersGroup-01** and click **Insert** (or double-click the file name) to insert the picture (Figure 1-83).

d. With the picture selected, click the **Align** button [*Picture Tools Format* tab, *Arrange* group].
   - Select **Align Bottom**.
   - Repeat to select **Align Right**.

e. Drag the picture's left horizontal sizing arrow to resize the picture so the *Width* is **8.5"** (Figure 1-84).
   - Because the picture is already blurred to reflect the speed of running, it looks fine when you stretch the picture.
   - If necessary, move the subtitle so it is between the title and picture.

1-83 Picture of runners inserted

4. Insert and align a picture.
   a. Display slide 6. Click the **Insert** tab and click the **Pictures** button.
   b. Locate your student data files.
   c. Select **RunnerWoman-01** and click **Insert** (or double-click the file name) to insert the picture.
      - No resizing is required for this picture.
   d. Select the picture and click the **Align** button [*Picture Tools Format* tab, *Arrange* group] and select **Align Right**.

1-84 Picture resized and aligned

5. Add a new slide and insert a picture of a table.
   a. With slide 6 displayed. Click the **New Slide** drop-down arrow [*Home* tab, *Slides* group].
   b. Select the **Title Only** layout.
   c. Type the title **Upcoming Marathons**.
   d. Click the **Insert** tab, and then click the **Pictures** button [*Images* group].
   e. Locate your student data files.
   f. Select **MarathonSchedule-01** and click **Insert** (or double-click the file name) to insert the picture.
   g. Increase the picture *Width* to **8.5"** (*Picture Tools Format* tab, *Size* group).
   h. Move the table so it is approximately centered in the black area (Figure 1-85).

1-85 Picture of a table inserted and positioned

6. Adjust placeholder size and alignment.
   a. Display slide 8. Select the title placeholder and resize it horizontally on the right side so the text fits in the placeholder without extra horizontal space or word wrapping.
   b. Click the **Align** button [*Drawing Tools Format* tab, *Arrange* group] and select **Align Left**. Repeat to select **Align Top** (Figure 1-86).
   c. Display slide 9. Repeat steps 6a and 6b using **Align Center** and **Align Bottom**.

1-86 Title placeholder aligned top and left

d.  Display slide 10. Repeat steps 6a and 6b using **Align Right** and **Align Middle**.
e.  Change the font color for the word "THERE!" on slide 10 to **Tan, Text 2** [*Home* tab, *Font* group].

7.  Apply one transition to all slides.
    a.  Click the **Slide Sorter** button [*Status* bar].
    b.  Click the **Transitions** tab.
    c.  Click the **Wipe** transition from the gallery.
    d.  Click **Effect Options** [*Transition* tab, *Transition to This Slide* group].
    e.  Select **From Left** (Figure 1-87).

1-87 Transition *Effect Options*

    f.  Click **Apply To All** [*Transition* tab, *Timing* group].

8.  Select each of the following slides and apply different transitions (listed first) and effect options to emphasize the content.
    Slide 2: **Zoom**, **In**
    Slide 7: **Doors**, **Vertical**
    Slide 8: **Pan**, **From Bottom**
    Slide 9: **Pan**, **From Top**
    Slide 10: **Pan**, **From Left**

9.  Test transition movements.
    a.  In *Slide Sorter* view, press **Ctrl+A** to select all slides.
    b.  Click **Preview** [*Transitions* tab] to see the movements.
    c.  Select the first slide and click the **Slide Show** button [*Status* bar].
    d.  Click to advance each slide so you can see the movements in *Slide Show* view. At the end, click or press **Esc** to exit *Slide Show* view.

10. Change presentation properties.
    a.  Click the **File** tab to open the *Backstage* view.
    b.  Click **Info** on the left if it is not already selected. The properties display on the right.
    c.  Click the *Title* field and type Train for a Marathon.
    d.  Click the **Properties** button, then select **Advanced Properties** to open the *Properties* dialog box (Figure 1-88).

1-88 *Properties* dialog box

e. Click the **Summary** tab and type the following information in the respective fields:

*Title*: Train for a Marathon (already entered)
*Subject*: Athletic Event Promotion
*Author*: Your Name *(unless it already appears)*
*Comments*: This presentation will be shown at the Civic Center to explain how to get ready for upcoming marathon events.

f. Click **OK** to close the *Properties* dialog box and return to *Backstage* view.

11. Print slides as a handout. If your computer is not connected to a printer, skip step e.
    a. Click the **Print** button on the left.
    b. Select the appropriate printer.
    c. Change the following *Settings* by clicking the list arrow for each option (repeat as necessary for more than one change) (Figure 1-89):
    *Which Slides to Print*: **Print All Slides**
    *What to Print*: **Handouts, 6 Slides Horizontal, Frame Slides, Scale to Fit Paper**
    *Print Order*: **Collated**
    *Orientation*: **Portrait**
    *Color Range*: **Grayscale** (or **Color** if you prefer)

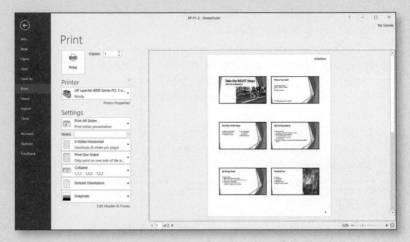

1-89 *Print* settings

    d. Preview the handout by clicking the navigation buttons to see both pages.
    e. Click the **Print** button at the top of the *Backstage* view.
    f. If necessary, click the **Back** button to close *Backstage* view.

12. Press **Ctrl+S** to save the presentation (or click **Save** on the *File* tab or the *Quick Access* toolbar). Close the presentation (Figure 1-90).

1-90 PP P1-3 completed

# Chapter Summary

**1.1** Create, open, and save a presentation (p. P1-3).

- You can start developing presentation content with a blank presentation, a *Theme*, an existing presentation, or a *Template*.
- PowerPoint views enable you to look at your content in different ways.
- The *Zoom* feature allows you to adjust the size of the current slide.
- The standard file format for presentation files has an extension of *.pptx*.
- In *Backstage* view, PowerPoint provides a variety of save and send options. For example, you can save a presentation as a PDF file or email a presentation file as an attachment.
- Additional themes and templates are available by searching online through PowerPoint or downloading them at Office.com.

**1.2** Work with slides, layouts, placeholders, and text (p. P1-14).

- Use *placeholders* for presentation text and objects such as pictures, tables, and charts. You can resize, reposition, and align text placeholders on slides.
- The *New Slide* button displays a gallery of slide layouts with placeholders arranged for different content.
- You can change fonts using commands on the *Home* tab or the mini toolbar.
- *Change Case* changes the way words are capitalized.
- In bulleted lists, you can change the bullet symbol, size, and color.
- Use the *Format Painter* to copy formatting from one object and apply it to another object.
- The *Reuse Slides* feature enables you to insert slides from another presentation.
- Although potential spelling errors are automatically marked, you also can use the *Spelling* dialog box to check for errors.
- Use the *Thesaurus* to find synonyms for words in your presentation.

**1.3** Navigate between slides and organize content by reproducing and rearranging slides (p. P1-23).

- You can move selected slides using a variety of methods to rearrange their sequence.

- Copy, paste, duplicate, and delete slides using the *Slides* pane or *Slide Sorter* view.

**1.4** Change theme colors and fonts (p. P1-29).

- Presentation themes provide a cohesive look through the consistent use of background designs, colors, and font treatments.
- Consider the topic and tone of your presentation when choosing theme colors and fonts.

**1.5** Insert headers and footers to add identifying information (p. P1-33)

- Both headers and footers are used for notes pages and handouts. They are applied to all pages or to individual pages.
- Footers usually appear at the bottom of slides but can appear in other locations. They are applied to all slides, all slides except the title slide, or to individual slides.

**1.6** Insert, resize, and align a picture from a file (p. P1-37).

- PowerPoint supports different graphic file types; you can insert almost any digital image into slide shows.
- Use *sizing handles* or enter exact dimensions to increase or decrease a picture's size.
- Avoid distortion when resizing pictures by maintaining accurate height and width ratios.
- You can align pictures with one another or with the slide.

**1.7** Apply and modify transition effects to add visual interest (p. P1-40).

- A *transition* is the visual effect that appears when one slide changes into another slide.
- The *Effect Options* command enables you to control the direction of transition movement.
- You can apply transitions to one slide, multiple slides, or to all slides in a presentation.

**1.8** Preview a presentation and print slides, handouts, and outlines (p. P1-42).

- *Backstage* view allows you to examine each slide in your presentation before printing.
- The printer you select influences how slides appear in *Backstage* view.
- *Grayscale* shows shades of black.

- **Print Settings** control which slides to print, what to print, and the print order, orientation, and color range.

**1.9** Apply presentation properties (p. P1-45).

- **Properties** are automatically recorded in your presentation file.
- You can add properties such as subject, keywords, or category to help manage and track files.
- Edit properties in *Backstage* view under *Info* or by opening the *Properties* dialog box.

## Check for Understanding

The SIMbook for this text (within your SIMnet account) provides the following resources for concept review:

- Multiple choice questions
- Matching exercises
- Short answer questions

## Guided Project 1-1

Jason Andrews is a sales associate for Classic Gardens and Landscaping (CGL) and frequently talks to customers when they visit the CGL showroom. For this project, you prepare a presentation he can use when introducing customers to CGL services.
[**Student Learning Outcomes 1.1, 1.2, 1.3, 1.4, 1.5, 1.6**]

Files Needed: ***GardenView-01.jpg*** and ***CGLLogo-01.png*** *(Student data files are available in the* Library *of your SIMnet account.)*
Completed Project File Name: ***[your initials] PowerPoint 1-1.pptx***

### Skills Covered in This Project

- Create a new presentation using a theme.
- Change theme colors and background style.
- Change theme fonts.
- Add slides.
- Change font size.
- Rearrange slides.
- Use the *Format Painter.*
- Insert a footer.
- Check spelling.
- Adjust placeholder position.
- Insert, align, and resize a picture.
- Save a presentation.

1. Create a new presentation using a theme.
   a. Click the **File** tab, and then click **New**.
   b. Double-click the **Ion** theme (Figure 1-91).

2. Save the presentation as [your initials] PowerPoint 1-1.

1-91 *Ion* theme selected

3. Change the theme colors.
   a. Click the **Design** tab.
   b. Click the **More** button [*Variants* group] to select each of the following options:
      *Colors*: Scroll down the list and select the **Paper** theme.
      *Background Styles*: Select **Style 3** from the gallery (Figure 1-92).
      *Fonts*: Select the **Candara** font group.

4. Type the following text in the placeholders on slide 1. Press **Ctrl+Enter** to move between placeholders.
   *Title*: Creating Beautiful Outdoor Spaces
   *Subtitle*: Jason Andrews, Sales Associate

5. Format the title and subtitle.
   a. Apply **bold** and **shadow** [*Home* tab, *Font* group] format to both the title and subtitle.
   b. Change the title font size to **66 pt**. and resize the title placeholder to remove extra space at the top.
   c. Change the subtitle font size to **28 pt**.

6. Add slides.
   a. Click the **New Slide** button [*Home* tab, *Slides* group] to add a new slide that automatically has the **Title and Content** layout. Type the following text for slide 2:

|  |  |
|---|---|
| *Title* | Our Services |
| *Bulleted items* | • Garden center |
| | • Tree nursery |
| | • Gift shop |
| | • Delivery and installation |
| | • Patios and irrigation systems |

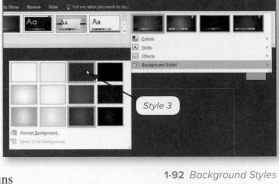

Style 3

**1-92** *Background Styles*

b. Repeat this process to create three new slides with the following text:

|  |  |
|---|---|
| *Slide 3 title* | Available Products |
| *Bulleted items* | • Shrubs, perennials, annuals |
| | • Soils and mulches |
| | • Garden décor including fountains |
| | • Shade trees and evergreen screening trees |
| | • Flowering or ornamental trees |
| | • Trees and plants for Christmas |
| *Slide 4 title* | Why Sustainable Design? |
| *Bulleted items* | • Energy efficiency increased |
| | • Water efficiency increased |
| | • Dependency on chemicals decreased |
| | • Vigor assured through native and hardy plants |
| *Slide 5 title* | We Make It Easy |
| *Bulleted items* | • We can do the entire project or we can assist |
| | • You can do as much, or as little, as you like |
| | • We will provide: |
| | • Landscape design planning or just advice |
| | • Soil testing |
| | • Low-cost delivery |
| | • Fountain set up |

c. Click the **New Slide** drop-down arrow [*Home* tab, *Slides* group] and click the **Title Slide** layout. Type this text in the placeholders:

|  |  |
|---|---|
| *Title* | Call for a Consultation |
| *Subtitle* | 615-792-8833 |

d. Increase the font size for the subtitle phone number to **32 pt**.

7. Move the slide 5 thumbnail before slide 4.

8. Apply **bold** and use the *Format Painter*.
   a. Display slide 2, select the title text, and apply **bold** [*Home* tab, *Font* group].
   b. Double-click the **Format Painter** button [*Home* tab, *Clipboard* group] so you can apply this change more than one time.
   c. Press **Page Down** and click the title text on slide 3 to apply the same change.
   d. Repeat for slides 4 and 5.
   e. Click the **Format Painter** button or press **Esc** to stop applying formatting.

9. Create a footer with the company name in the footer text.
   a. Click the **Header & Footer** button [*Insert* tab, *Text* group] to open the *Header and Footer* dialog box.
   b. On the *Slide* tab, check the following options: **Date and time** with **Update automatically**, **Slide number**, and **Footer** (Figure 1-93).

**1-93** *Header and Footer dialog box*

c. In the *Footer* text box, type **Classic Gardens and Landscaping**.

d. Select **Don't show on title slide**.

e. Click the **Apply to All** button.

10. Click the **Spelling** button [*Review* tab, *Proofing* group] and correct any spelling errors you find.

11. Format the title slide so it is more distinctive.

a. Display slide 1.

b. Select the subtitle and click the **Change Case** button [*Home* tab, *Font* group]. Select **Capitalize Each Word**.

c. Resize the title and subtitle placeholders to fit the text.

d. Click the **Insert** tab, and then click the **Pictures** button to open the *Insert Pictures* dialog box.

e. Locate your student data files.

f. Select *GardenView-01* and *CGL Logo-01*. Click **Insert**.

g. Resize the logo *Width* to **5.5"** [*Picture Tools Format* tab, *Size* group] and the *Height* will automatically adjust.

h. Align the text and pictures as shown in Figure 1-94.

12. Save and close the presentation (Figure 1-95).

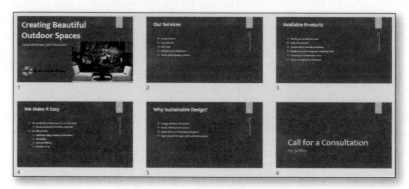

1-94 Completed title slide

1-95 PowerPoint 1-1 completed

# Guided Project 1-2

Solution Seekers, Inc., a management consulting firm, is preparing a series of brief presentations to be used in a training program for new hires. For this project, you develop a presentation about how to get better results when writing email messages.
[**Student Learning Outcomes 1.1, 1.2, 1.3, 1.6, 1.7, 1.8, 1.9**]

Files Needed: ***EmailResults-01.pptx***, ***EmailContent-01.pptx***, and ***AtSymbol-01.jpg*** (*Student data files are available in the* Library *of your SIMnet account.*)
Completed Project File Name: *[your initials] PowerPoint 1-2.pptx*

## Skills Covered in This Project

- Open a presentation.
- Change bullets.
- Reuse slides from another presentation.
- Rearrange slides.
- Check spelling.
- Adjust placeholder position.
- Insert a picture.
- Apply transitions.
- Preview a presentation.
- Change presentation properties.
- Print a handout.
- Save a presentation.

---

1. Open and resave a presentation.
   a. Click the **File** tab, select **Open**, and click **Browse**.
   b. Locate your student data files and double-click *EmailResults-01* to open the presentation.
   c. Press **F12** to open the *Save As* dialog box and save this presentation as [your initials] PowerPoint 1-2 in the appropriate location.

2. Change the bullets for additional emphasis.
   a. Display slide 2 and select the bulleted text.
   b. Click the **Bullets** drop-down arrow [*Home* tab, *Paragraph* group].
   c. Select **Bullets and Numbering**.
   d. Click the **Color** button and select **Orange, Accent 6** (Figure 1-96).
   e. Change the size to **90%** of text.
   f. Click the **Customize** button to open the *Symbol* dialog box.
   g. Change the *Subset* to **Geometric Shapes** (Figure 1-97). Select the **Black Right-Pointing Pointer** (Character code 25BA)
      - If the font **Wingdings 3** is available, select a similar symbol (Character code 117).
   h. Click **OK** to close the *Symbol* dialog box. Click **OK** again to close the *Bullets and Numbering* dialog box.

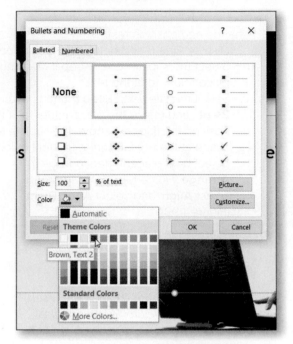

1-96 Change bullet color

3. Reuse slides from another presentation.
   a. Display slide 2. Click the **New Slide** drop-down arrow and select **Reuse Slides**.
   b. Click **Browse** on the *Reuse Slides* pane and then select **Browse file**. Locate your student data files.
   c. Select the presentation *EmailContent-01* and click **Open**. (This presentation has spelling errors that you will correct later.)
   d. Click all four slides on the *Reuse* Slides pane to insert them (Figure 1-98).
   e. Close the *Reuse Slides* pane.

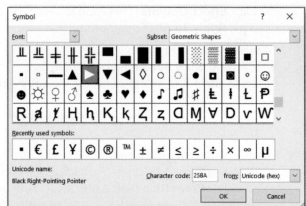

1-97 Change bullet symbol

4. Use the *Slides* pane to rearrange the six slides in this order: "Getting Results with Email," "Ask These Questions," "Why?," "Write a Meaningful Subject Line," "Organize It!," and "Keep It Short."

5. Click the **Spelling** button [*Review* tab, *Proofing* group] and correct all of the spelling errors: receive, Careless, organized, capture, response, and separate. The spelling of Email on slide 1 is correct and can be ignored.

6. Use the *Format Painter* to change bullets.
   a. Display slide 2 and select the body placeholder with the bulleted text.
   b. Double-click the **Format Painter** button [*Home* tab, *Clipboard* group] so you can apply what you have copied more than one time.
   c. Press **Page Down** and click the list on slide 3 to apply the change for the first-level bullets.
   d. Repeat for slides 4 and 5.
   e. Press **Esc** to end formatting.

7. Change and position text.
   a. Display slide 6 and delete the picture on the right.
   b. Select the subtitle text, "Keep It Meaningful," and resize the placeholder to fit the text.
   c. Select the title text, "Keep It Short," change the font size to **24 pt.**, and resize the placeholder to fit the text.
   d. Position the title text above the subtitle text on the orange shape at the right. Change the font color to **Black, Text 1**.
   e. Select both placeholders and click **Arrange** [*Home* tab, *Drawing* group], select **Align**, and select **Align Right** (Figure 1-99).

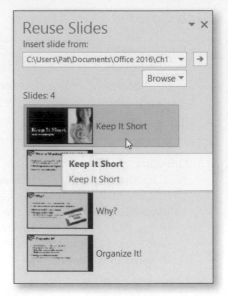

**1-98 Reuse Slides pane**

8. Insert and align a picture.
   a. Click the **Insert** tab, and then click the **Pictures** button.
   b. Locate your student data files.
   c. Select *AtSymbol-01* and click **Insert**.
   d. Click **Align** [*Picture Tools Format* tab, *Arrange* group] and select **Align Left**.

9. Apply one transition and effect option to all slides.
   a. Click the **Transitions** tab.
   b. Click the **Switch** transition from the gallery.
   c. Click **Effect Options** [*Transition to This Slide* group] and select **Left**.
   d. Click **Apply To All** [*Timing* group].

**1-99 Completed ending slide**

10. Preview the presentation.
    a. Click the **Slide Sorter** button [*Status* bar].
    b. Press **Ctrl+A** to select all slides. Click **Preview** [*Transitions* tab] to examine the movements in *Slide Sorter* view.
    c. Click the first slide and click the **Slide Show** button [*Status* bar]. Advance through the slides to see the movements in *Slide Show* view.

11. Change presentation properties.
    a. Click the **File** tab to open *Backstage* view, and then click **Info**.
    b. Click the **Properties** button and select **Advanced Properties**. Click the **Summary** tab and type this information as needed in the respective fields:

    | | |
    |---|---|
    | *Title*: | Getting Results with Email |
    | *Subject*: | Writing |
    | *Author*: | Your Name (unless it already appears) |
    | *Comments*: | This presentation is for the new hire seminar. |

    c. Click **OK** to close the *Properties* dialog box.

12. Print slides as a handout.
    a. Click the **Print** button on the left of the *Backstage* view.
    b. Select the appropriate printer.
    c. Change the following *Settings* by clicking the button list arrow for each option:

| | |
|---|---|
| *Which Slides to Print*: | **Print All Slides** |
| *What to Print*: | **Handouts, 6 Slides Horizontal, Frame Slides, Scale to Fit Paper** |
| *Print Order*: | **Collated** |
| *Orientation*: | **Portrait** |
| *Color Range*: | **Grayscale** (or **Color** if you prefer) |

    d. Click the **Print** button at the top of the *Backstage* view.

13. Save and close the presentation (Figure 1-100).

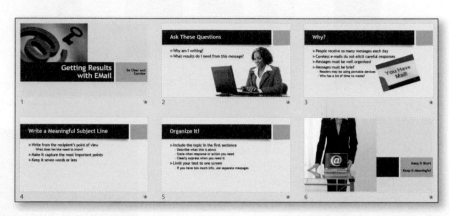

1-100 PowerPoint 1-2 completed

# Guided Project 1-3

At Placer Hills Real Estate, realtors are always thinking of ways to help sellers make their homes more marketable and help buyers find the right home. For this project, you prepare a presentation for realtors to use when they speak with individual clients to explain how sellers can provide an added-value benefit by offering a home warranty.
[**Student Learning Outcomes 1.1, 1.2, 1.5, 1.6, 1.7, 1.9**]

Files Needed: ***PHRELogo-01.png*** and ***BuyerIncentive-01.pptx*** *(Student data files are available in the Library of your SIMnet account.)*
Completed Project File Name: *[your initials] **PowerPoint 1-3.pptx***

### Skills Covered in This Project

- Create a new presentation using an online template.
- Change font size.
- Adjust picture position.
- Insert a picture.
- Reuse slides from another presentation.
- Check spelling.
- Insert a footer.
- Apply transitions.
- Change presentation properties.
- Save a presentation.

1. Create a new presentation using an online template.
    a. Click the **File** tab, and then click **New**.
    b. Type the word **marketing** in the search box and click the **Start Searching** button or press **Enter**.

c. Select the **Business sales strategy proposal presentation** (Figure 1-101) and click **Create** to download the presentation. (If you are unable to download the file, it is available as the presentation ***BusinessSalesStrategy-01*** in your student data files.)

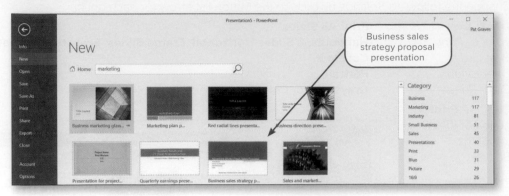

1-101 Online marketing themes and templates

d. Remove the presentation content. Select slide 1 in the *Thumbnail* pane, press **Ctrl+A** to select all slides, and press **Delete**. The slides are deleted from the presentation.

2. Click the **New Slide** button [*Home* tab, *Slides* group] and the slide that appears automatically has a *Title Slide* layout. Type the following text in the placeholders:
   *Title*: Compete with New Homes
   *Subtitle*: Angie O'Connor Sales Associate

3. Save the presentation as [your initials] PowerPoint 1-3 in the appropriate location.

1-102 Completed title slide

4. Increase the title font size to **60 pt**. and apply **bold** [*Home* tab, *Font* group].

5. Insert the PHRE company logo.
   a. Click the **Pictures** button [*Insert* tab, *Images* group] and locate your student data files.
   b. Select ***PHRELogo-01*** and click **Insert** (or double-click the file name) to insert the picture.
   c. Increase the logo size (*Width* **3"** and the *Height* automatically adjusts).
   d. Position this logo in the lower right as shown in Figure 1-102.

6. Reuse slides from another presentation.
   a. Click the **New Slide** drop-down arrow and select **Reuse Slides**.
   b. Click **Browse** on the *Reuse Slides* pane. Select **Browse file** and locate your student data files.
   c. Select the presentation ***BuyerIncentive-01*** and click **Open**.
   d. Click slides **2–6** (starting with the "Seller Needs" slide) on the *Reuse Slides* pane to insert them (Figure 1-103).
   e. Close the *Reuse Slides* pane.

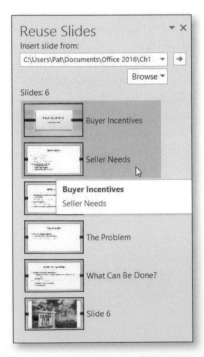

7. Click the **Spelling** button [*Review* tab, *Proofing* group] and correct the following spelling errors: Competitive, maintained, replacement, and deductible.

1-103 *Reuse Slides* pane

8. Display slide 6. Resize the picture using the center sizing handle to stretch it to the bottom of the slide.

9. Add a footer.
   a. Click the **Header & Footer** button [*Insert* tab, *Text* group].
   b. On the *Slide* tab, select **Slide number** and **Footer**.
   c. In the *Footer* text box, type Placer Hills Real Estate.
   d. Select **Don't show on title slide**.
   e. Click the **Apply to All** button. The footer appears in small text on the upper right.
   f. Delete the footer that is over the picture on slide 6.

1-104 Transition *Effect Options*

10. Apply one transition to all slides.
    a. Click the **More** button [*Transitions* tab, *Transition to This Slide* group] to open the gallery. Click the **Box** effect.
    b. Click **Effect Options** [*Transitions* tab, *Transition to This Slide* group]. Select **From Bottom** (Figure 1-104).
    c. Click **Apply To All** [*Transitions* tab, *Timing* group].
    d. Select slide 1. Click the **Slide Show** button [*Status* bar] and advance through the slides to see the movements in *Slide Show* view.

11. Change presentation properties.
    a. Click the **File** tab, then click **Info**.
    b. Click the **Properties** button and select **Advanced Properties** to open the *Properties* dialog box. Type the following information as needed in the respective fields:
       *Title*: Compete with New Homes
       *Subject*: Sales Strategies
       *Author*: Angie O'Connor
       *Comments*: Seller can offer a home warranty to encourage buyer purchase.
    c. Click the **OK** to close the *Properties* dialog box.

12. Save and close the presentation (Figure 1-105).

1-105 PowerPoint 1-3 completed

## Independent Project 1-4

Wilson Home Entertainment Systems (WHES) assists customers with everything from a single television purchase to a home network installation to the design and construction of an elaborate home theater. For this project, you work on a presentation that sales representatives can use to describe the capabilities of WHES to potential customers.
[**Student Learning Outcomes 1.1, 1.2, 1.4, 1.6, 1.7, 1.9**]

Files Needed: ***SpecialEnvironment-01.pptx***, ***WHESLogo-01.png***, ***Family-01.jpg***, and ***Theater1-01.jpg*** (*Student data files are available in the* Library *of your SIMnet account.*)
Completed Project File Name: *[your initials] **PowerPoint 1-4.pptx***

## Skills Covered in This Project

- Open a presentation.
- Add slides.
- Apply a theme.
- Change theme colors.
- Insert a picture.
- Adjust placeholders.
- Check spelling.
- Apply transitions.
- Change presentation properties.
- Save a presentation.

1. Open the presentation **SpecialEnvironment-01**.

2. Save the presentation as [your initials] PowerPoint 1-4.

3. After slide 1, insert two new slides with the *Title and Content* slide layout. Type the following text for slides 2 and 3:

   *Slide 2 title*:      Our Residential Services
   *Bulleted items*:    • Design
                        • Sales
                        • Installation
                        • Maintenance
   *Slide 3 title*:      Sales
   Bulleted items:      • Authorized dealer for the highest-quality home theater technology in the industry
                        • Televisions
                        • Projectors
                        • Blu-Ray Players
                        • Cables

1-106  Change variant

4. Apply a theme and change theme colors.
   a. Select the **Integral** theme and the third **Variant** (Figure 1-106).
   b. Select the **Orange Red** theme colors.

5. Insert different pictures.
   a. Display slide 1 and delete the popcorn picture.
   b. Delete the subtitle placeholder.
   c. Insert **Family-01** and **WHESLogo-01** from your student data files.
   d. Increase the family picture size (*Height* **5"** and *Width* **7.52"**) and align it on the top right (Figure 1-107).
   e. Align the logo on the bottom right.
   f. Change the title placeholder font color to **White, Background 1**, apply **bold**, increase the font size to **66 pt.**, and apply a **Shadow**.
   g. Resize the title placeholder so it word wraps as shown. Move it to the red area on the left.

1-107  Completed title slide

6. Click the **Spelling** button and correct the following spelling errors: cabling, television, and calibration.

7. Increase the text size and insert a picture.
   a. Display slide 2. Select the bulleted text placeholder and change the font size to **40 pt**.
   b. Insert **Theater1-01** from your student data files.
   c. Increase the picture size (*Height* **5"** and *Width* **7.52"**) and align it on the bottom right.

8. Display slide 6. Increase the picture size (*Height* **2.18"** and *Width* **9"**) and center it horizontally in the space below the text.

9. Apply one transition to all slides.
   a. Select the **Cube** transition.
   b. Apply the **From Bottom** effect option.
   c. Click **Apply To All**.

10. Open the *Properties* dialog box and insert the following presentation properties as needed on the *Summary* tab:

   | | |
   |---|---|
   | *Title*: | Create Your Special Environment |
   | *Subject*: | Residential Services |
   | *Author*: | Liam Martin |

11. Close the *Properties* dialog box.

12. Save and close the presentation (Figure 1-108).

1-108 PowerPoint 1-4 completed

# Independent Project 1-5

The Advising Offices in the Sierra Pacific Community College (SPCC) District work to assist students throughout the completion of their academic programs. Because SPCC has a large population of students who are retraining themselves for different types of employment, job-related information is especially important. For this project, you prepare a presentation about writing resumes.
[**Student Learning Outcomes 1.1, 1.2, 1.3, 1.4, 1.7, 1.8**]

Files Needed: ***ResumeUpdates-01*** and ***ResumeContent-01.pptx*** *(Student data files are available in the Library of your SIMnet account.)*
Completed Project File Name: ***[your initials] PowerPoint 1-5.pptx***

## *Skills Covered in This Project*

- Open a presentation.
- Change theme background style and fonts.
- Change case.
- Adjust sizing and alignment.
- Add slides.
- Reuse slides from another presentation.
- Check spelling.
- Apply transitions.
- Print a handout.
- Save a presentation.

1. Open the **ResumeUpdates-01** presentation from your student data files.

2. Save the presentation as [your initials] PowerPoint 1-5.

3. Change theme style and font.
   a. Change the *Background Style* to **Style 4** (Figure 1-109).
   b. Change the *Theme Fonts* to **Georgia**.

4. Adjust placeholder sizing and text.
   a. Display slide 1 and select the title placeholder. Change text alignment to **Align Left**.
   b. Resize the placeholder so the text word wraps on two lines.
   c. Select the subtitle placeholder and change text alignment to **Align Left** (Figure 1-110).

1-109 *Background Styles*

5. Insert two new slides after slide 2 with the *Title and Content* layout. Type the following text for slides 3 and 4:

| | |
|---|---|
| *Slide 3 title*: | Accomplishments, Not Duties |
| *Bulleted items*: | • Include only the most impressive details about your career |
| | • Quantify your day-to-day tasks |
| | • How many times? |
| | • What was the result? |
| | • How much money was saved? |
| *Slide 4 title*: | Proofread |
| *Bulleted items*: | • Employers take spelling and grammar errors as signs of carelessness |
| | • Ask a trusted friend or colleague to look at your resume |

1-110 **Completed title slide**

6. Reuse slides from another presentation.
   a. Move your insertion point after slide 3.
   b. Open the *Reuse Slides* pane and browse to find **ResumeContent-01** from your student data files.
   c. Insert all three slides and close the *Reuse Slides* pane.

7. Display slide 8.
   a. Select the title placeholder and change text alignment to **Align Left**. Type Success!.
   b. Resize the title placeholder to fit the text.
   c. Delete the subtitle placeholder.

8. Correct the following spelling errors: Improve, redundant, achievements, and any other errors you find.

9. Apply the **Reveal** transition with the **Through Black from Right** effect option to all slides.

10. Print slides as an outline (Figure 1-111).

11. Save and close the presentation (Figure 1-112).

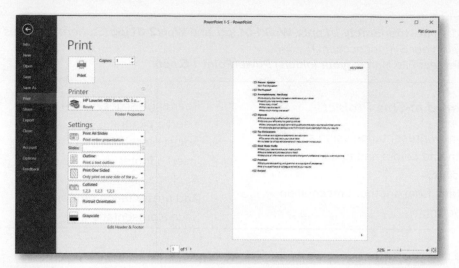

1-111 Outline

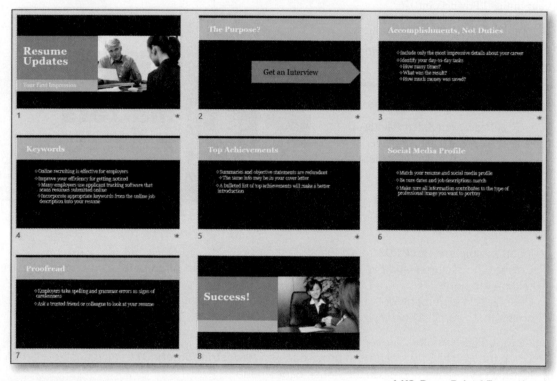

1-112 PowerPoint 1-5 completed

# Independent Project 1-6

At the Hamilton Civic Center, workshops are offered to the community to address fitness, health, and wellness issues. For this project, you develop a presentation for an upcoming series about helping families become more active.

[Student Learning Outcomes 1.1, 1.2, 1.3, 1.4, 1.5, 1.6, 1.7, 1.9]

Files Needed: ***PedestrianSafety-01.pptx***, ***Walk1-01.jpg***, and ***Walk2-01.jpg*** *(Student data files are available in the* Library *of your SIMnet account.)*
Completed Project File Name: *[your initials] **PowerPoint 1-6.pptx***

---

## *Skills Covered in This Project*

- Create a new presentation using a theme.
- Change theme colors and fonts.
- Change case.
- Reuse slides from another presentation.
- Check spelling.

- Rearrange slides.
- Insert a picture.
- Adjust placeholders.
- Insert a footer.
- Apply transitions.
- Add presentation properties.
- Save a presentation.

---

1. Create a new presentation and select the **Retrospect** theme.

2. Save the presentation as
   [your initials] PowerPoint 1-6.

3. Change the following theme options:

   | | |
   |---|---|
   | *Theme Colors*: | **Yellow Orange** |
   | *Background Styles*: | **Style 6** |
   | *Theme Fonts*: | **Arial Black-Arial** |

4. Display slide 1 and type the following text:

   | | |
   |---|---|
   | *Title*: | Pedestrian Safety Matters |
   | *Subtitle*: | Keeping That New Year's Resolution To Be More Active |

5. Select the subtitle text and change the case to **Capitalize Each Word**.

6. Insert a picture and resize the placeholders.
   a. Insert the picture ***Walk1-01*** from your student data files on slide 1.
   b. Change the picture *Height* to **7.5"** and choose **Align Top** and **Align Left** so you have room for text on the right.
   c. Change text alignment for the title and subtitle placeholders to **Align Left**. Resize the placeholders so the text wraps as shown in Figure 1-113.

7. Reuse slides from another presentation.
   a. Open the *Reuse Slides* pane and browse to find ***PedestrianSafety-01*** from your student data files.
   b. Insert all five slides and close the *Reuse Slides* pane.

8. Display slide 2. Put your insertion point in front of the word "Guard" and press **Enter** to show this text as the last item in the list.

9. Correct the following spelling errors: pedestrians, aggressive, Remember, traffic, Regardless, and cloudy.

10. Adjust slide order to match the sequence shown in Figure 1-114.

11. Add a footer with the text **Pedestrian Safety Matters**. Apply it to all slides except the title slide.

12. Insert and position a picture.
    a. Display slide 6. From your student data files, insert the picture ***Walk2-01***.
    b. Change the picture *Height* to **7.5"**.
    c. Position the picture with **Align Top** and **Align Right**.

1-113 Completed title slide

13. Apply the **Push** transition with the **From Right** effect option to all slides.

14. Preview the transitions in *Slide Show* view.

15. Open the *Properties* dialog box and insert the following presentation properties on the *Summary* tab:

   *Title*: Pedestrian Safety Matters
   *Subject*: Active Lifestyle
   *Author*: Anna Lorenzo

16. Close the *Properties* dialog box.

17. Save and close the presentation (Figure 1-115).

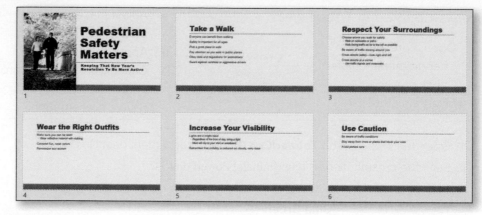

1-114 Slide order

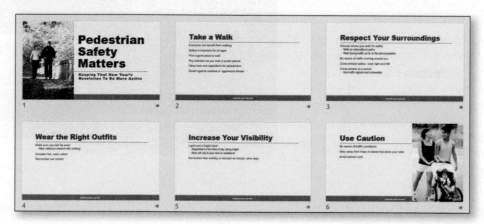

1-115 PowerPoint 1-6 completed

# Improve It Project 1-7

For this project, you revise a presentation for Margaret Jepson, insurance agent at Central Sierra Insurance. You adjust theme colors and fonts, and add other information to the slide show, including a picture.
[**Student Learning Outcomes 1.1, 1.2, 1.3, 1.4, 1.5, 1.6, 1.7, 1.8, 1.9**]

Files Needed: ***TotaledCar-01.pptx***, ***Travel-01.jpg***, and ***CSILogo-01.png*** (Student data files are available in the Library of your SIMnet account.)
Completed Project File Name: *[your initials] PowerPoint 1-7.pptx*

## Skills Covered in This Project

- Open a presentation.
- Change theme colors.
- Check spelling.
- Insert a picture.
- Adjust placeholders.
- Insert a footer.
- Apply transitions.
- Change presentation properties.
- Print a handout.
- Save a presentation.

1. Open the presentation *TotaledCar-01* from your student data files.

2. Save the presentation as [your initials] PowerPoint 1-7.

3. Change the following theme options:

   *Theme Colors*: **Blue Green**
   *Background Style*: **Style 3**
   *Theme Font*: **Trebuchet MS**

4. Format text and insert a picture logo.
   a. Display slide 1 and change the title font size to **66 pt**.
   b. Delete the subtitle placeholder.
   c. Insert the picture *CSILogo-01* from your student data files, change the *Width* to **5"**. Position the logo below the title on the shape across the bottom of the slide (Figure 1-116).

5. Change a layout and insert a picture.
   a. Display slide 5. Change the slide layout to **Section Header**.
   b. Type the following text on two lines in the placeholder near the top of the slide. The text is right aligned and this placeholder right aligns with the title placeholder below.

      780-886-2400
      Margaret Jepson

   c. Insert the picture *Travel-01*, and change the *Width* to **7"**. Position it on the left as shown in Figure 1-117.

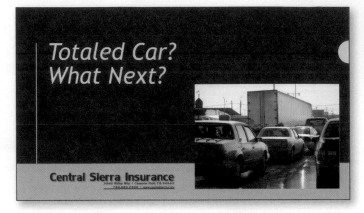

1-116 Completed title slide

6. Add footer text and slide numbering to all slides except the title slide.

   *Slide footer text*: The Totaled Car

7. Add header text and page numbering.

   *Handout header text*: Central Sierra Insurance

8. Apply and preview transitions.
   a. Select the **Clock** transition with the **Counterclockwise** effect option.
   b. Apply this transition to all slides.
   c. Preview the transitions.

9. Open the *Properties* dialog box and insert the following presentation properties as needed on the *Summary* tab.

   *Title*: Totaled Car? What Next?
   *Subject*: Accident Insurance
   *Author*: Margaret Jepson

10. Print a handout with the following options: **6 Slides Horizontal**, **Frame Slides**, and **Scale to Fit Paper** (Figure 1-117).

11. Save and close the presentation.

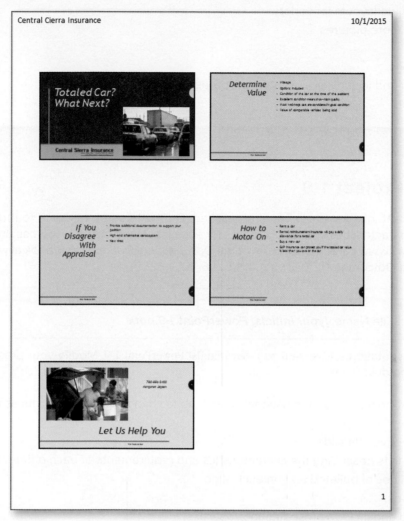

1-117 PowerPoint 1-7 completed, printed as a handout

## Challenge Project 1-8

For this project, tell the story of your favorite vacation. Create six slides that introduce the topic and describe your main points with bulleted lists. Insert photographs to illustrate locations and resize them to fit with related text.
[Student Learning Outcomes 1.1, 1.2, 1.4, 1.5, 1.6, 1.7, 1.8, 1.9]

File Needed: None
Completed Project File Name: *[your initials] PowerPoint 1-8.pptx*

Create a new presentation and save it as [your initials] PowerPoint 1-8. Modify your presentation according to the following guidelines:

- Search for an online theme that is appropriate for your topic. Apply it to your presentation.
- Use different slide layouts for variety.
- Insert three or more pictures.
- Add a footer.
- Apply transitions.
- Check spelling and include presentation properties.
- Print a handout.

## Challenge Project 1-9

Think about different jobs for which you are qualified. On the Internet, research four different jobs and identify several characteristics and requirements for each job. Many online resources provide job-related information, such as www.careerbuilder.com or the *Occupational Outlook Handbook* at www.bls.gov/ooh/. [**Student Learning Outcomes 1.1, 1.2, 1.3, 1.4, 1.5, 1.6, 1.7, 1.8, 1.9**]

File Needed: None
Completed Project File Name: *[your initials] PowerPoint 1-9.pptx*

Create a new presentation and save it as [your initials] PowerPoint 1-9. Modify your presentation according to the following guidelines:

- Select an appropriate theme and use the *Design* tab to change colors and fonts as needed for your topic.
- Create a distinctive title slide.
- Write bulleted lists describing the characteristics and requirements of each different job with no more than six lines of bulleted text on each slide.
- Apply transitions.
- Check spelling and include presentation properties.
- Print handouts with six slides on a page.

## Challenge Project 1-10

For this project, develop a presentation about how a presenter can manage nervous tendencies when presenting in front of an audience. Include information from your own experiences and refer to online resources, such as www.presentationmagazine.com. [**Student Learning Outcomes 1.1, 1.2, 1.3, 1.4, 1.5, 1.6, 1.7, 1.8, 1.9**]

File Needed: None
Completed Project File Name: *[your initials] PowerPoint 1-10.pptx*

Create a new presentation and save it as [your initials] PowerPoint 1-10. Modify your presentation according to the following guidelines:

- Select an appropriate theme and use the *Design* tab to change colors and fonts as needed for your topic.
- Create a distinctive title slide.
- Write bulleted lists describing typical causes of nervousness and suggest ways to control nervousness when presenting.
- Insert pictures to illustrate concepts.
- Apply transitions.
- Check spelling and include presentation properties.
- Print an outline of the presentation.

# Illustrating with Pictures and Information Graphics

**POWERPOINT**

## CHAPTER OVERVIEW

In our world today, we are surrounded by information graphics. We see them in television programming, web sites, and published material of all kinds. We interpret signage that helps us get from place to place and readily recognize many iconic images that help us with everyday tasks. These graphics communicate visually and can be more effective than long passages of text.

PowerPoint gives you the ability to create information graphics—to visually display information in ways that help an audience quickly grasp the concepts you are presenting. You can choose from many options, such as adding shapes or color for emphasis, pictures to illustrate, diagrams to show processes, and charts to show data relationships.

### STUDENT LEARNING OUTCOMES (SLOs)

After completing this chapter, you will be able to:

**SLO 2.1** Work with shapes, select theme colors and standard colors, and apply styles (p. P2-71).

**SLO 2.2** Create interesting and eye-catching text effects with *WordArt* styles and text effects (p. P2-80).

**SLO 2.3** Search for pictures and illustrations, modify picture appearance, and compress picture file size (p. P2-82).

**SLO 2.4** Organize information in a grid format using tables and customize the arrangement of columns and rows (p. P2-91).

**SLO 2.5** Format portions of a table by applying styles, colors, and effects (p. P2-96).

**SLO 2.6** Show processes and relationships with *SmartArt* graphics (p. P2-101).

**SLO 2.7** Improve the appearance of *SmartArt* graphics by applying styles, colors, and effects (p. P2-104).

**SLO 2.8** Create charts that show relationships between data values and emphasize data in different ways based on the chart type and chart elements (p. P2-108).

**SLO 2.9** Format a chart by applying preset styles or manually customizing individual chart elements (p. P2-113).

### CASE STUDY

Classic Gardens and Landscapes (CGL) is a landscape design company that creates beautiful and low-maintenance landscapes for outdoor living spaces. Frank and Sandra Hunter recently bought a new home from a builder. It has minimal landscaping, so they contacted Gerod Sunderland, a landscape designer for CGL, to discuss improvements.

Gerod visited the property and designed plans with several options for trees, shrubs, and plants. You have been asked to prepare a presentation illustrating his key points for his meeting with the Hunters.

***Pause & Practice 2-1:*** Add visual interest with picture enhancements and creative text designs.

***Pause & Practice 2-2:*** Prepare a table.

***Pause & Practice 2-3:*** Create an organization chart and convert text to a *SmartArt* graphic.

***Pause & Practice 2-4:*** Create column and pie charts with an enhanced appearance.

---

**SLO 2.1**

# Working with Shapes, Colors, and Styles

Shapes can emphasize key points. For example, an arrow can point to an object, or a line can connect two related objects. You can draw a variety of shapes using drawing tools from PowerPoint's **Shapes** gallery; each shape has both an outline and fill color. The **Shape Styles** galleries make it easy to apply preset colors and shape effects or you can customize shape effects as you illustrate your slides.

## Shapes and Text Boxes

The *Shapes* gallery (Figure 2-1) is on the *Home* tab [*Drawing* group], the *Insert* tab [*Illustrations* group], and the *Drawing Tools Format* tab [*Insert Shapes* group]. Shapes are grouped in the following categories:

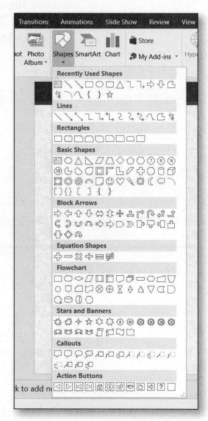

- *Recently Used Shapes*
- *Lines*
- *Rectangles*
- *Basic Shapes*
- *Block Arrows*
- *Equation Shapes*
- *Flowchart*
- *Stars and Banners*
- *Callouts*
- *Action Buttons*

To insert a shape, select the shape you want from the *Shapes* gallery and use the following features to draw and adjust your shape:

- *Crosshair:* A large plus sign used to draw the shape
- *Sizing handles:* White circles on the corners and sides of the shapes used to change shape size
- *Rotation handle:* A circular arrow on the top used to make shapes angle
- *Adjustment handle:* Yellow circles used to change curves or points

2-1 *Shapes* gallery

You can add text to shapes and format the text as you do text in a placeholder or in a text box. However, the text in shapes or in text boxes does not appear in *Outline* view.

## ▶ HOW TO: Insert a Shape

1. Click the **Insert** tab.
2. Click the **Shapes** button [*Illustrations* group] to display the *Shapes* gallery.
3. Select the shape you want and your pointer becomes a crosshair (Figure 2-2).
4. Click and drag to draw the shape in the approximate size you need (Figure 2-3). The shape appears with sizing handles and a rotation handle. It may have adjustment handles.
5. Click and drag an adjustment handle to change areas within a shape such as the tip of an arrow or star, the corners of a rounded rectangle, or the line used with a callout.
6. Add text, if needed, by typing in the selected shape as you would type in a placeholder.
7. Resize the shape if necessary and move it to the appropriate position on the slide.

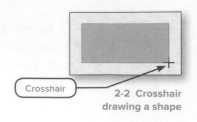

Crosshair

**2-2 Crosshair drawing a shape**

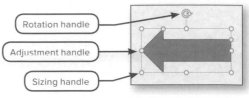

Rotation handle

Adjustment handle

Sizing handle

**2-3 Shape with handles**

> **MORE INFO**
>
> Press the **Shift** key while you drag to constrain shapes. The oval becomes round, the rectangle becomes square, and lines are straight.

When you need more than one of the same shape, you can efficiently draw them using *Lock Drawing Mode*.

## ▶ HOW TO: Insert Multiple Shapes

1. Click the **Insert** tab.
2. Click the **Shapes** button [*Illustrations* group] to display the *Shapes* gallery.
3. Right-click the shape you want, and click **Lock Drawing Mode** (Figure 2-4).
4. Draw the first shape. Repeat to draw more of the same shape.
5. Press **Esc** to turn off *Lock Drawing Mode* when you are finished.

**2-4 Lock Drawing Mode**

When you select an existing shape, the *Drawing Tools Format* tab opens and the *Shapes* gallery displays on the left in the *Insert Shapes* group. If the existing shape does not fit your purpose, you can easily change the shape.

## ▶ HOW TO: Change a Shape

1. Select the shape to be changed.
2. Click the **Edit Shape** drop-down arrow [*Drawing Tools Format* tab, *Insert Shapes* group] (Figure 2-5).

**2-5 Change Shape**

3. Select **Change Shape** and click a different shape from the *Shapes* gallery.
4. Click a blank area of the slide to deselect the shape.
5. Click **Undo** to return to your original shape.

Using **text boxes**, you can add text anywhere on a slide without using placeholders. For example, you can add notations to identify slide objects or insert brief phrases you want to emphasize. Text boxes can be sized and moved around like any other shape.

### ▶ HOW TO: Insert a Text Box

2-6 Draw a text box

1. Click the **Insert** tab.
2. Click the **Text Box** button [*Text* group] and your pointer changes to an insertion point. Create a text box using one of the following methods:
   - Click the slide background to place your insertion point where you want the text to appear. Begin typing and the text box expands as you enter text. The *Home* tab opens.
   - Click and drag to change the pointer to a crosshair and draw a text box (Figure 2-6) in the approximate width you need. The *Home* tab opens. The text box height adjusts as you type text.
3. Resize if necessary by dragging sizing handles or entering *Height* and *Width* sizes [*Drawing Tools Format* tab, *Size* group] (Figure 2-7).
4. Click and drag the text box to move it to an appropriate position on the slide.

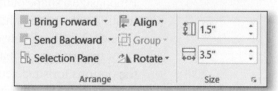

2-7 Size measurements

## Style Galleries and Effect Options

Different *Style* galleries provide collections of preset effects for shapes, pictures, or other objects. You can customize all effects using the related button such as **Shape Effects, Picture Effects**, or **Text Effects** to access drop-down galleries. You can choose from *Shadow, Reflection, Glow, Soft Edges, Bevel, 3D Rotation,* or *Transform*. These options are described in the following table. You can also apply one or more effects without first using styles from a gallery.

### Effect Options

| Effect | Options |
|--------|---------|
| Shadow | **Shadow** effects appear in three groupings. An **Outer** shadow shows behind an object from different directions. An **Inner** shadow makes part of the object looked raised. A **Perspective** shadow shows below so the object appears to float. |
| Reflection | A **Reflection** shows a mirror image below an object, like a reflection on a shiny surface or on water. You can control how close the reflection is to the object. |
| Glow | **Glow** provides a colored area around an object that fades into the background color on your slide. Glow colors by default are based on the current theme colors, but you can use other colors. The size of the *Glow* is measured in points. |

*Continued*

| Effect | Options |
|---|---|
| *Soft Edges* | Shapes and other objects have either straight edges or well-defined curves. **Soft Edges** creates a feathered edge that gradually blends into the background color. The size of the blending area is measured in points from the edge of the object inward. The larger the point size, the less you see of the object. |
| *Bevel* | **Bevel** effects add light and dark areas to create a dimensional appearance. Objects or text can look raised or inset. |
| *3D Rotation* | **3D Rotation** effects include **Parallel**, **Perspective**, and **Oblique** options that create an illusion of depth by rotating an object from front to back. |
| *Transform* | **Transform** is a *Text Effect* used to change the shape of words. It is not available for shapes or pictures. |

The width of your PowerPoint window affects how galleries are displayed on the various tabs. If you have a narrow PowerPoint window, you need to click a **Quick Style** button to open a gallery. If your window is wide, part of a gallery displays, and you click the **More** button to open the complete gallery.

## Adjust Outline Weight and Style

Emphasize a shape outline by making it wider with a contrasting color; deemphasize a shape outline by making it thinner. You can choose to show no outline or match its color to the shape to make the outline disappear. Many of the options for shape outlines also apply to lines (straight or curved) that you draw.

Select a shape or line and click the **Shape Outline** button [*Drawing Tools Format* tab, *Shape Styles* group]. Click one of the following options to choose from additional variations in a drop-down list (Figure 2-8):

2-8 *Shape Outline Weight*

- *Weight:* Displays line thickness measured in points
- *Dashes:* Displays lines made with various combinations of dots and dashes (Figure 2-9)
- *Arrows:* Displays arrowheads or other shapes for both ends of a line

At the bottom of these three drop-down lists, select **More Lines** to open the *Format Shape* pane (Figure 2-10) where you can customize the following *Line* options:

- *Color:* Provides color choices
- *Transparency:* Adjusts transparency percentages
- *Width:* Controls the thickness of lines measured in points
- *Compound type:* Provides outlines with two or more lines in different thicknesses
- *Dash type:* Displays lines made with various combinations of dots and dashes

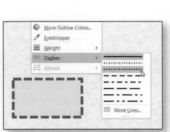

2-9 *Shape Outline Dashes*     2-10 *Format Shape pane*

- **Cap type:** Controls the look (*Square*, *Round*, or *Flat*) of the ends of lines; it is usually applied to single lines or arrows
- **Join type:** Controls the look (*Round*, *Bevel*, *Miter*) for the connection point where two lines meet (for example, at the corner of a rectangle or square)
- **Begin and End Arrow type:** Controls the shape for both ends of an arrow
- **Begin and End Arrow size:** Controls the size of the shape at both ends of an arrow

The *Format Shape* pane is a convenient place to change many options. Figure 2-10 shows the *Fill & Line* tab with *Line* options displayed because a line was selected when the pane opened. Different options appear if you have a shape selected or if you choose a *Gradient* line. Above *Line* you can select *Fill* to change shape colors. You can click the arrow in front of these options to expand or collapse each list.

Additional tabs under *Shape Options* on the *Format Shape* pane include *Effects* and *Size & Properties* with related options on each tab. Click the icons at the top of the pane to select different tabs.

> **ANOTHER WAY**
>
> Right-click a shape and then select **Format Shape** from the context menu to open the *Format Shape* pane.

## Themes and Standard Colors

As you learned in Chapter 1, each PowerPoint *Theme* starts with a set of *Theme Colors* that provide background and accent colors. When you apply *Theme Colors* for shapes and text, these colors automatically change when you select a different set of *Theme Colors*.

Consider all of the colors used throughout your presentation when you select colors because some are more appropriate than others. This section explains how colors are arranged in PowerPoint and describes different ways to "mix" custom colors. The same techniques for choosing colors apply to color fills or outline colors.

### Change Solid and Gradient Fill Colors

To change the color of a selected shape, click the **Shape Fill** button [*Drawing Tools Format* tab, *Shape Styles* group] to open the **Theme Colors** gallery (Figure 2-11). Notice the colors arranged in the first row. The first four colors represent background and text colors; however, you can use these colors for other slide objects as well. The remaining six colors represent accent colors. These colors appear when viewing gallery styles and some effect options such as *Glow*. Beneath each color on the first row is a column of lighter and darker shades (shown as percentages) of that color. When you point to any color, a *ScreenTip* shows its name.

Below the *Theme Colors* is a single row of **Standard Colors** arranged in the order of a rainbow. When standard colors are used, they remain in effect even if *Theme Colors* change.

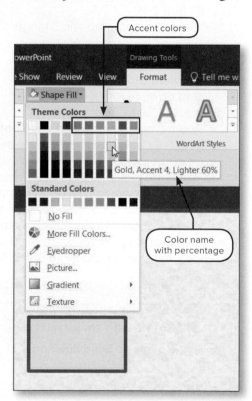

2-11 *Theme Colors* gallery

*Gradient* colors blend two or more colors together. Using the *Format Shape* pane, you can select from preset colors or customize your own gradient color by changing the colors and how they blend.

## ▶ HOW TO: Change Gradient Colors Using the Format Shape Pane

1. Select a shape and click the **Shape Fill** button [*Drawing Tools Format* tab, *Shape Styles* group].
2. Select **Gradient** to select from a gallery of light and dark variations of the current fill color that blend the colors in different directions (Figure 2-12).
3. Click **More Gradients** at the bottom of the gallery to open the *Format Shape* pane to customize the colors.
4. Choose **Gradient fill** and make selections under *Fill* options from the following:
   - *Preset gradients:* Theme color variations (Figure 2-13)
   - *Type: Linear, Radial, Rectangular,* or *Path*
   - *Direction:* Options change based on the selected *Type.*
   - *Angle:* The percentage changes with each *Type* and *Direction.*
   - *Gradient stops:* Shapes on the gradient bar that you can move to control where colors change (Figure 2-14)
5. Select a *Gradient stop* and change its settings to control color blending:
   - *Delete a stop:* Click the **Remove Gradient Stop** button or drag the stop down to remove it from the gradient bar.
   - *Add a stop:* Click the **Add Gradient Stop** button or click the gradient bar where you want the stop to appear.
   - *Color:* Select the stop, and then change the color.
   - *Position:* Enter a different percentage or drag the stop on the gradient bar to change its position.
   - *Transparency:* Click the arrows to change the percentage. When *Transparency* is 0%, the color is opaque (solid). As the percentage increases, the color becomes increasingly transparent and more of the background color shows through.
   - *Brightness:* Click the arrows to change the percentage. As the percentage decreases from 100%, the color softens.
6. Check **Rotate with shape** to maintain the color settings when a shape or text is rotated so it angles on the slide.
7. Select **No line** or **Solid line** under *Line* options to control whether or not an outline shows around a shape or text.
8. Click the **X** at the top of the pane to close the *Format Shape* pane.

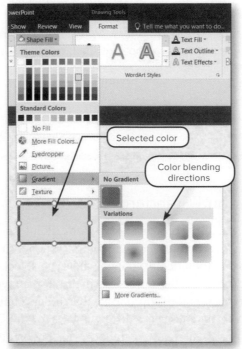

2-12 Gradient color variations for the selected color

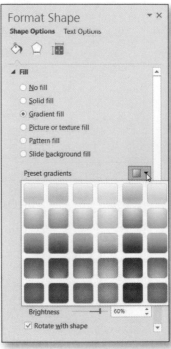

2-13 Preset gradients based on theme colors

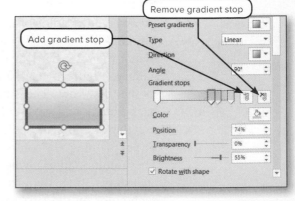

2-14 Gradient stops

### Select Custom Colors

The *Colors* dialog box provides many solid color options on two tabs so you can either pick from displayed colors or mix a custom color. The new color appears in the lower right corner so you can compare it to the original color. Custom colors are not affected by any changes made to theme colors.

▶ **HOW TO:** Use the Standard Tab to Select a Color

1. Select a shape and click the **Shape Fill** button [*Home* tab, *Drawing* group or *Drawing Tools Format* tab, *Shape Styles* group].
2. Click **More Fill Colors** to open the *Colors* dialog box.
   - Select the *Standard* tab (Figure 2-15).
   - Colors are arranged in a honeycomb shape with colors blending from white to black below.
3. Click a color to apply it and notice the *New* color that appears on the right above the *Current* color.
4. Adjust the *Transparency* as needed.
5. Click **OK** to apply the new color.

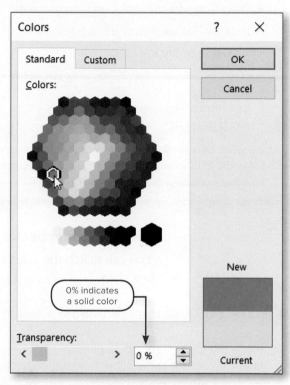

2-15 *Standard* tab in *Colors* dialog box

When you need more precision in selecting a color, use the *Custom* tab on the *Colors* dialog box. Colors are arranged like a rainbow, and you drag a crosshair to select a different color. You drag the crosshair up or down to change the color intensity and then move a slider to adjust how light or dark the color appears. Color model information is shown on the *Custom* tab also. The **RGB model** is typically used for computer displays and colors are formed by blending values of the three numbers for *Red*, *Green*, and *Blue*. Highly saturated colors at the top have higher number values (255 maximum). You can use these numbers to match colors in different shapes and in different presentations.

▶ **HOW TO:** Use the Custom Tab to Mix a Color

1. Select a shape and click the **Shape Fill** button [*Home* tab, *Drawing* group or *Drawing Tools Format* tab, *Shape Styles* group].
2. Click **More Fill Colors** to open the *Colors* dialog box.

3. Click the *Custom* tab (Figure 2-16) and a crosshair is positioned for the *Current* color.

  - Drag the crosshair horizontally to select a different color. Notice the new color that appears on the right above the *Current* color.
  - When the crosshair is at the top, colors are highly **saturated** (intense and vibrant).
  - As you move the crosshair down, colors become less saturated (duller and less intense).

4. Drag the slider on the right to adjust the **luminosity** (lightness or brightness).

  - Drag up to add white and increase the luminosity.
  - Drag down to add black and decrease the luminosity.

5. Adjust the *Transparency* as needed.

6. Click **OK** to apply the new color.

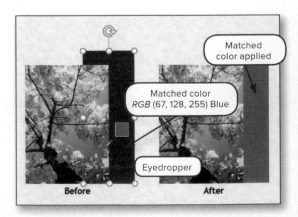

2-16 *Custom* tab in *Colors* dialog box

### MORE INFO

Use the *Custom* tab in the *Colors* dialog box if you need to enter specific RGB values to match a color such as a color used for a business or college logo.

## Use the Eyedropper for Color Matching

You can match the exact color of an object in PowerPoint with the **Eyedropper** and apply it to a shape.

### ▶ HOW TO: Use the Eyedropper

1. Place the object, such as a picture, and the shape to be changed on the same slide. Select the shape.

2. Click the **Shape Fill** button [*Home* tab, *Drawing* group or *Drawing Tools Format* tab, *Shape Styles* group] and select **Eyedropper**.

3. Move your pointer (now an Eyedropper) around in the picture and a live preview of each color appears. Pause to see a *ScreenTip* showing the *RGB* (Red Green Blue) values (Figure 2-17).

4. Click to select a color and it is applied to your selected shape.

*Or*

5. Press **Esc** to cancel the *Eyedropper* without selecting a color.

2-17 *Eyedropper* live preview and *RGB* colors

To match a color anywhere on your computer screen, left-click and hold as you drag the Eyedropper to other areas of the screen outside of PowerPoint.

### Apply Picture, Texture, or Pattern Fills

You can fill shapes with more than colors. The following options are available by clicking the **Shape Fill** button [*Drawing Tools Format* tab, *Shape Styles* group] or from the *Format Shape* pane. With *WordArt*, the *Text Fill* button [*Drawing Tools Format* tab, *WordArt Styles* group] is used.

- *Picture fill:* Fills the shape with a picture from a file or from an online search
- *Texture fill:* Applies an image such as woven fabric or wood
- *Pattern fill:* Applies a mixture of two colors in various dotted or crosshatch designs

---

### ▶ HOW TO: Apply Picture, Texture, or Pattern Fills

1. Select a shape and click the **Shape Fill** button [*Home* tab, *Drawing* group or *Drawing Tools Format* tab, *Shape Styles* group].

2. From the drop-down list, select **Picture** to open the *Insert Pictures* dialog box. Browse or search for a picture and click **Insert**. The picture fills the shape.

*Or*

3. From the drop-down list, select **Texture** to open the gallery (Figure 2-18). Click a texture to fill the shape or click **More Textures** to open the *Format Shape* pane.

   - Select **Picture or texture fill** and then click the **File** button or the **Online** button to search for textures that are saved as a picture.

*Or*

4. Select a shape and right-click. Select **Format Shape** from the callout menu to open the *Format Shape* pane.

   - Click **Fill**, if necessary, to display *Fill* options.
   - Select **Pattern fill** (Figure 2-19).
   - Click a pattern to fill the shape.
   - Change *Foreground* and *Background* colors as needed.
   - Click other patterns to see how different these colors look in different patterns.

5. Close the *Format Shape* pane.

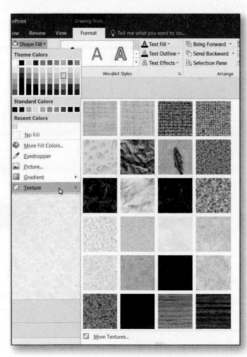

2-18 *Texture* fills

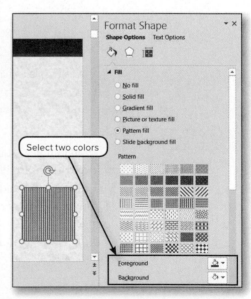

Select two colors

2-19 *Pattern* fills on the *Format Shape* pane

**SLO 2.2**

# Applying WordArt Styles and Text Effects

You can apply interesting *text effects* for many purposes. For example, you can make slide titles more attractive and easier to read, or you can provide a bold focal point on a slide. One way is to start by inserting *WordArt*.

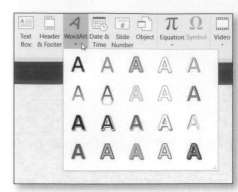

▶ **HOW TO: Apply WordArt Styles**

1. Click the **WordArt** button [*Insert* tab, *Text* group] to open the *WordArt Styles* gallery (Figure 2-20).

   • The gallery has preset text effects showing a variety of solid, gradient, and pattern fill colors.

2. Click to select a *WordArt* style.

   • A text box displays on your slide with sample text that you edit to create a *WordArt* object (Figure 2-21).

3. Use the *Font* group [*Home* tab] to apply the following character formatting:

2-20 *WordArt Styles* gallery

   • Select a different font or attribute such as bold or italic.
   • Change the font size by entering a point size or using the **Increase Font Size** and **Decrease Font Size** buttons.
   • Click the **Character Spacing** button to control the distance between letters. You can expand or condense the spacing.

2-21 *WordArt* as it first appears

---

▶ **MORE INFO**

When using text in a large size, *Tight* character spacing conserves space yet keeps the text easy to read.

---

You can also start with text in a placeholder or text box and then apply text effects. With either method, you use commands on the *WordArt Styles* group [*Drawing Tools Format* tab] (Figure 2-22) to customize your text. These commands—*Text Fill, Text Outline, and Text Effects*—are similar to the *Shape* commands.

2-22 *WordArt Styles* group

▶ **HOW TO: Apply Text Effects to Existing Text**

1. Select a *WordArt* object or text in a placeholder or text box.

   • Click the **More** button [*Drawing Tools Format* tab, *WordArt Styles* group] to open the *Styles* gallery.
   • Point to a style to see a live preview applied to your text (Figure 2-23).
   • Click a style to apply it.

2. Use the *WordArt Styles* group [*Drawing Tools Format* tab] to change colors and add special effects:
   - Click the **Text Fill** button to select **Theme** or other color options.
   - Click the **Text Outline** button to select **Theme** or other color options as well as line weight and style.
   - Click the **Text Effects** button and select from *Shadow, Reflection, Glow, Bevel, 3D Rotation,* or *Transform* effects and then choose the option you prefer.

*Or*

3. Select a *WordArt* object or text box and right-click to open the context menu. Click **Format Shape** to open the *Format Shape* pane.
   - Select **Shape Options** to change *Fill* or *Line* options.
   - Select **Text Options** to change *Text Fill* or *Text Outline* options.

2-23 *WordArt* object with a style applied

> ### MORE INFO
>
> If the *WordArt Styles* gallery is not open on your *Drawing Tools Format* tab, click the **Quick Styles** button.

Changing the text outline color and increasing line weight emphasizes the outline just as it does on shapes. Different line styles can create interesting effects. Using pictures or patterns as fill colors can add a creative touch when text is shown in a large size. A variety of different colors and effects are shown in Figure 2-24.

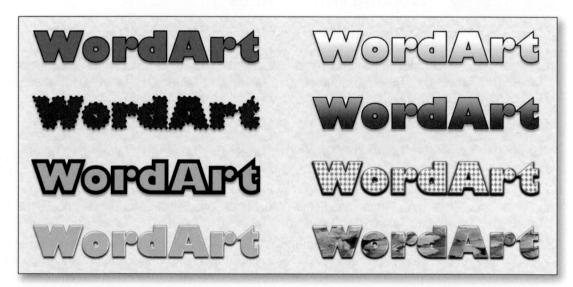

2-24 Sample fill and line effects

> ### ANOTHER WAY
>
> Select the text in a *WordArt* object and right-click. Click **Format Text Effects** from the context menu to open the *Format Shape* pane with *Text Options* listed.

*Transform* effects are unique to text and are used to warp a word or phrase to different shapes or to follow a path. For example, text can angle, flow in a circle, and arc up or down. As you point to different *Transform* effects, a live preview shows how your text will look in that shape. Once a *Transform* effect has been applied, text size is not limited to the font size because you can drag the *WordArt* sizing handles. *Transform* effects also provide one or more yellow adjustment handles that control the slant of letters or the curve of text.

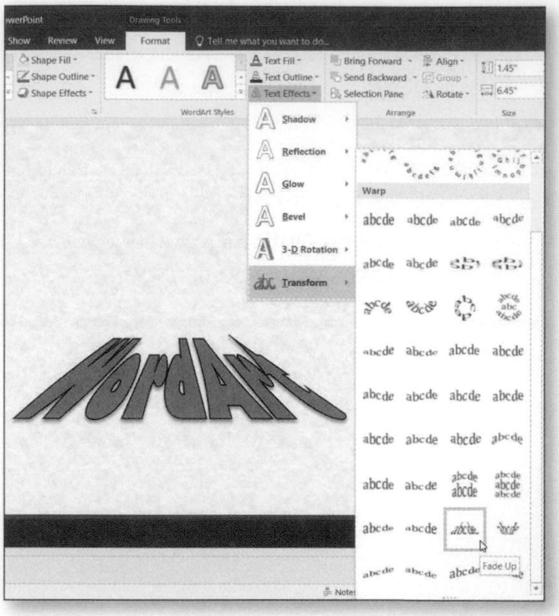

2-25 *Transform Fade Up* effect applied

### ▶ HOW TO: Apply a Transform Effect

1. Select a *WordArt* object.
2. Click the **Text Effects** button [*Format* tab, *WordArt Styles* group].
3. Select **Transform** from the drop-down list (Figure 2-25) to open the *Transform* gallery.
4. Point to an effect to see a live preview applied to your text.
5. Click an effect to apply it.
6. Adjust as needed using sizing and adjustment handles.

---

**SLO 2.3**

# Working with Pictures

In Chapter 1, you learned how to insert pictures from files, change their size, and align them on the slide. In this section, you use a variety of photo editing techniques to enhance a picture's appearance. You will also use PowerPoint's search capabilities to find images to help illustrate presentation concepts and consider various licensing requirements for the use of images available online.

## Apply Picture Styles

When you select a picture on a slide, the *Picture Tools Format* tab becomes available. Different *Styles* allow you to frame pictures, give them a 3D appearance, add a reflection, or apply other treatments. You can choose from preset options using the *Picture Effects* drop-down galleries.

When you use multiple pictures in a presentation, try to maintain consistency and use the same or a similar style for each of them. If you use different styles, be sure you have a reason for making them look different so the effects do not appear random.

### ▶ HOW TO: Apply a Picture Style

1. Select a picture and click the **Picture Tools Format** tab.
2. Click the **More** button on the gallery [*Picture Styles* group] to see the predefined effects (Figure 2-26).

P2-82

3. Drag your pointer over the styles to see a live preview applied to your picture. A *ScreenTip* showing the style name appears.
4. Click a style to apply it to your picture.
5. Change to a different style by selecting a new style from the gallery.

2-26 Picture style applied

*Picture Effects* are similar to *Shape Effects*. Each different effect has many options you can adjust.

▶ **HOW TO:** Apply or Modify Picture Effects

1. Select a picture and click the **Picture Effects** button [*Picture Tools Format* tab, *Picture Styles* group].
2. Point to each effect in the drop-down list to see a gallery (Figure 2-27) that provides many different options.
3. Select **Options** at the bottom of each gallery to open the *Format Picture* pane where you can make changes to fine-tune a specific effect.
   - Right-click the picture and select **Format Picture** from the context menu to open the *Format Picture* pane.
4. Remove a picture style by selecting the picture and clicking the **Reset Picture** button [*Picture Tools Format* tab, *Adjust* group].

2-27 Picture Effects

## Crop a Picture

You can *crop* (trim) unwanted areas of a selected picture by dragging black *cropping handles* on the corners and sides of the picture that appear when you click the **Crop** button. When you point to these handles, your pointer changes to a black shape that resembles the cropping handle. Be careful when dragging to be sure you are moving a cropping handle and not a sizing handle.

▶ **HOW TO:** Crop a Picture

1. Select a picture and click the **Crop** button [*Picture Tools Format* tab, *Size* group].
2. Drag one or more cropping handles toward the center of the picture; the area to be removed from the edges is grayed out (Figure 2-28).
3. Click the **Crop** button again to accept this change.

2-28 Cropped area of a picture

Always check your pictures and crop them as needed to be sure they have a strong focal point. Excess detail clutters a picture and does not help your viewers quickly grasp what you want them to see.

## Change Picture Colors

Pictures are digital photographs usually made up of many colors to achieve the realism that they portray. PowerPoint's *Color* feature allows you to vary picture colors. For example, you might want to make a picture look old, or fade the picture so text over the picture is easy to read.

---

▶**HOW TO:** Change Picture Colors

---

1. Select a picture you want to change.
2. Click the **Color** button [*Picture Tools Format* tab, *Adjust* group] to open a gallery showing different color options (Figure 2-29).
   - The current option within each group is highlighted.
3. Select one or more options to customize your picture colors:
   - ***Color Saturation:*** Colors are more muted as you move from the center to the left as saturation becomes lower; colors are more intense as you move from the center to the right as saturation increases.
   - ***Color Tone:*** Colors on the left have cool tones and lower temperature values; colors on the right have warm tones and higher values.
   - ***Recolor:*** Options on the first row include *Grayscale*, *Sepia*, *Washout*, and percentages of *Black and White*. The second and third rows display dark and light monotone variations of accent colors.

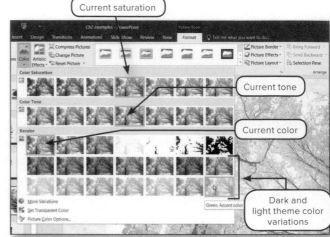

2-29 *Color* gallery

4. Click **Picture Color Options** at the bottom of the gallery to open the *Format Picture* pane with the **Picture Color** options displayed.

---

## Set a Transparent Color

An image with a white background works well on a slide with a white background (or on a typical Word document) because you see just the image. However, a white background can detract from an image if you place it on a slide background with a contrasting color.

Use the ***Set Transparent Color*** feature to remove a single-color background. Because this feature removes only one color, it does not work well for pictures that have a lot of detail and many colors.

---

▶**HOW TO:** Set a Transparent Color

---

1. Select a picture.
2. Click the **Color** button [*Picture Tools Format* tab, *Adjust* group].

3. Click **Set Transparent Color** and your pointer changes to a pen tool.

4. Point to the area of the picture you want to remove and click.

   • All of the pixels with that color value disappear, revealing what is behind the picture (Figure 2-30).

White area is removed

2-30 *Set Transparent Color* applied

## Compress Pictures

Pictures can greatly increase your presentation file size. You can *compress* single pictures or all pictures at one time to reduce the picture resolution depending on the quality you need. For print you generally need a higher resolution, and for on-screen viewing a lower resolution is usually fine. Resolution options are expressed in *pixels per inch (ppi)* and are based on *Target output* such as *Print (220 ppi)* or *Web (150 ppi)*. The ppi measurement for viewing on screen is very different from the *dots per inch (dpi)* print measurement for printing on paper. An inexpensive printer can produce 1,200 or more dpi, which produces crisp, clear letterforms that are easy to read on paper.

Deleting cropped areas of pictures removes unused information and, therefore, reduces file size. Compression only affects how the pictures display in the presentation file and not the original picture files.

▶ **HOW TO:** Compress Picture File Size

1. Select a picture.

2. Click the **Compress Picture** button [*Picture Tools Format* tab, *Adjust* group] to open the *Compress Pictures* dialog box (Figure 2-31).

3. Deselect **Apply only to this picture** if you want the compression to apply to all pictures in the presentation.

4. Select **Delete cropped areas of pictures** if you have cropped pictures.

5. Select the appropriate *Target output*. Some options will be grayed out if they are not available for your selected picture.

6. Click **OK** to close the dialog box.

2-31 *Compress Pictures* dialog box

## Insert Online Pictures and Illustrations

Click the **Picture** button [*Insert* tab, *Images* group] to open the *Insert Pictures* dialog box where you can search for pictures (digital photographs or illustrations) that you have saved in folders on your computer or any other location. Click the **Online Picture** button [*Insert* tab,

*Images* group] to open the *Insert Pictures* dialog box where you can search the web using *Bing Image Search* or search on your *OneDrive* location. Pictures you find on the web may have licensing restrictions or require fees to use them. The *Insert Pictures* dialog box does not provide a way to filter the results based on your intended use.

When the search results appear, each picture has a *ScreenTip* identifying its name and a magnifying button you can click to temporarily increase the thumbnail size.

In the lower left corner of the dialog box, the picture name, pixel size, and web source appears. A *pixel* is an abbreviated term for *picture element*, a single unit of information about color.

▶ **HOW TO:** Search for and Insert a Picture or Illustration

1. Click the **Online Pictures** button [*Insert* tab, *Images* group] (Figure 2-32) to open the *Insert Pictures* dialog box.
2. Type the search word In the *Bing Image Search* box (Figure 2-33).
3. Click the **Search** button (or press **Enter**) to activate the search.
   - Thumbnails of all the pictures that match your search word appear that are licensed under Creative Commons (Figure 2-34). **CC Only** shows in the search box.
4. Click the drop-down arrow by **CC Only** and select **All Images** to expand your search.
5. Click to select the picture you want.
6. Press **Ctrl** while you click to select more than one picture.
7. Click the **Insert** button. The picture downloads and the *Insert Pictures* dialog box closes.

2-32 *Online Pictures* button

2-33 *Insert Pictures* dialog box

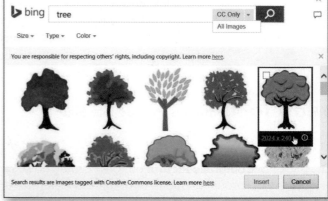

2-34 Pictures from search

> **MORE INFO**
> Open the *Insert Pictures* dialog box when creating a new slide by clicking the **Online Pictures** icon on the content placeholder.

> **MORE INFO**
> Be careful to select images that are appropriate for your topic. Some cartoon-like illustrations look amateurish and may not be appropriate for academic or business presentations.

## Creative Commons Licensing

A Creative Commons (CC) license enables the free distribution of copyrighted work when the creator wants to give people the right to copy, use, or remix by building upon the work. This right is usually for non-commercial purposes. The creator can make requirements for attribution so the creator is credited for the work. You can read more about these requirements at https://creativecommons.org.

You can activate a search on the Creative Commons site for images, music, and video using Google, Google Images, or other search engines to locate work listed with the CC license. However, the results cannot be guaranteed because no registration is required to use a CC license. You still need to contact the creator (copyright holder) directly or contact the web site where you found the content.

Another way to find images that you can save for future use is through Microsoft's *Bing* search engine at www.bing.com. Select an **Images** search, type a word in the search box, press **Enter**, and the results display. Click the link for **License** (Figure 2-35) to filter your results to one of the following criteria:

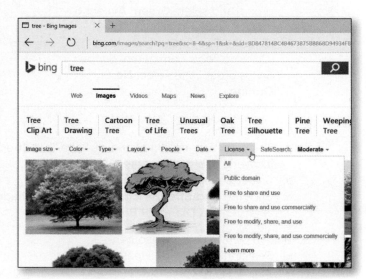

2-35 Image search at Bing.com

- Public Domain
- Free to share and use
- Free to share and use commercially
- Free to modify, share, and use
- Free to modify, share, and use commercially

*Bing* does not verify CC licensing; you still need to go to the image's web site to determine the actual licensing being used.

---

# PAUSE & PRACTICE: POWERPOINT 2-1

When Gerod Sunderland shares his landscaping proposal with homeowners, he provides detailed printed information and uses a presentation to illustrate concepts. For this project, you add pictures and other objects to his presentation and apply a variety of styles and colors to enhance the content.

---

File Needed: ***LandscapingProposal-02.pptx*** *(Student data files are available in the* Library *of your SIMnet account.)*
Completed Project File Name: ***[your initials] PP P2-1.pptx***

---

1. Open the presentation ***LandscapingProposal-02***.

2. Save the presentation as [your initials] PP P2-1.

3. Add a rectangle.
   a. Display slide 1 and click the **Shapes** button [*Insert* tab, *Illustrations* group].
   b. Select the **Rectangle** shape.
   c. Click and drag to draw a rectangle across the top of the slide.
   d. Change the rectangle *Height* to **.4"** and *Width* to **13.33"** [*Drawing Tools Format* tab, *Size* group].
   e. Click the **Shape Fill** button [*Drawing Tools Format* tab, *Shape Styles* group] and select **Green, Accent 6** (Figure 2-36).
   f. Click the **Shape Outline** button [*Drawing Tools Format* tab, *Shape Styles* group] and select **No Outline**.
   g. Position the rectangle below the orange line.

2-36  Change *Shape Fill* color

4. Add text effects.
   a. Select the title on slide 1 and click the **Text Effects** button [*Drawing Tools Format* tab, *WordArt Styles* group].
   b. Select **Bevel** and then **Circle** (Figure 2-37).
   c. Click the **Text Effects** button again, select **Shadow**, and then select **Offset Diagonal Bottom Right**.

5. Make a picture color transparent.
   a. Select the picture of a leaf on slide 1.
   b. Click **Color** [*Picture Tools Format* tab, *Adjust* group].
   c. Select **Set Transparent Color** and your pointer changes to a pen tool.
   d. Click the white area around the leaf so it becomes transparent (Figure 2-38).

2-37  Apply *Text Effects*

6. Apply effects and use the *Format Painter*.
   a. Display slide 2 and select the left list heading placeholder.
   b. Click the **Shape Fill** button [*Drawing Tools Format* tab, *Shape Styles* group] and select **Texture**.
   c. Click the **Papyrus** option (first row).
   d. Apply **Bold** [*Home* tab, *Font* group].
   e. With the placeholder still selected, click the **Format Painter** button [*Home* tab, *Clipboard* group]. Click the list heading placeholder on the right to apply the copied format.

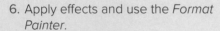

2-38  Completed slide 1

7. Add a frame shape.
   a. Display slide 3. Click the **Shape** button [*Insert* tab, *Illustrations* group] and select the **Frame** shape under the *Basic Shapes* heading.
   b. Click and drag to draw a frame.
   c. Adjust the frame size (*Height* **1"** and *Width* **3.3"**) [*Drawing Tools Format* tab, *Size* group].
   d. With the frame selected, type Allow three days.
   e. Change the font size to **24 pt**.

8. Change to a different shape and color.
   a. Select the frame shape on slide 3. Click the **Edit Shape** button [*Drawing Tools Format* tab, *Insert Shapes* group] and select **Change Shape**.
   b. Click the **Bevel** shape under the *Basic Shapes* heading.
   c. Change the *Shape Fill* [*Drawing Tools Format* tab, *Shape Styles* group] to **Gold, Accent 4**.
   d. Position this shape below the bulleted text (Figure 2-39).

9. Search for and insert an online picture on slide 3.
   a. Click the **Online Pictures** button [*Insert* tab, *Images* group] to open the *Insert Pictures* dialog box.
   b. Type the word soil in the *Bing Image Search* box.
   c. Click **Search** (or press **Enter**) to activate the search. Results will be similar to Figure 2-40.
   d. Locate a picture of a plant in soil similar to the one in Figure 2-41.
   e. Point to the picture and text appears at the bottom. Point to that area to see the picture's size information and its web address. Make a note of this web address for step 10. Click **Insert**.

10. Resize and crop a picture.
    a. Select the picture on slide 3 and change its size as needed to fit in the blank area on the right of the slide.
    b. Click the **Crop** button [*Picture Tools Format* tab, *Size* group] and crop a little space from all four edges to focus more on the plant.
    c. Click the **Crop** button again to accept the crop.
    d. Click the **More** button [*Picture Tools Format* tab, *Picture Styles* group] and select the **Rotated White** picture style.
    e. Insert a text box [*Insert tab, Text* group] and type the picture's source information.
    f. Position the text box below the picture (see Figure 2-41).

11. Compress a picture to reduce presentation file size.
    a. Select the picture on slide 3 and click **Compress Pictures** [*Picture Tools Format* tab, *Adjust* group].
    b. Deselect **Apply only to this picture**.
    c. Select **Use document resolution** for the *Target output*.
    d. Click **OK**.

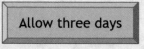
- Correct drainage problems
- Prepare soil for planting
- Plant
- Lawn installation—sod or seed

Allow three days

2-39 Text box positioned below list

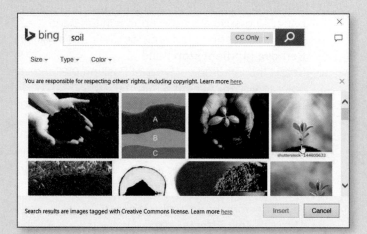

2-40 *Online Pictures* search results

2-41 Completed slide 3

12. Add *WordArt* text.
    a. Display slide 8. Click the **WordArt** button [*Insert* tab, *Text* group].
    b. Select the **Gradient Fill – Gold, Accent 4, Outline – Accent 4** style from the style gallery.
    c. Type Thank you for your business! in the *WordArt* text box.
    d. Move the *WordArt* object so it is at the top of the picture (Figure 2-42).
    e. Change the *Character Spacing* [*Home* tab, *Font* group] to **Tight**.

2-42 *WordArt* with gradient fill applied

13. Change the *WordArt* gradient fill and outline colors.
    a. Select the *WordArt* object, if necessary, and click the **Text Fill** button [*Drawing Tools Format* tab, *WordArt Styles* group]. Select **Gradient** and click **More Gradients** to open the *Format Shape* pane. All gradient options appear in the pane.
    b. Select the second gradient stop (at Position **4%**) and click the **Remove gradient stop** button.
    c. Select the left gradient stop (at Position **0%**) and change the color to **Green, Accent 6, Lighter 40%**.
    d. Select the right gradient stop and change the color to **Green, Accent 6, Darker 50%** (Figure 2-43).
    e. Close the *Format Shape* pane.
    f. Select the *WordArt* object, if necessary, and click the **Text Outline** button [*Drawing Tools Format* tab, *WordArt Styles* group]. Change the outline color to **Black, Text 1**.

14. Apply a *Transform* effect to the *WordArt*.
    a. Click the **Text Effects** button [*Drawing Tools Format* tab, *WordArt Styles* group]. From the drop-down list, select **Transform**. On the *Transform* gallery, click the **Deflate Bottom** effect (Figure 2-44).
    b. Resize the *WordArt* (*Height* **2"** and *Width* **10"**). Click **Align** [*Drawing Tools Format* tab, *Arrange* group] and click **Align Center** so the *WordArt* fits across the top of the picture (Figure 2-45).

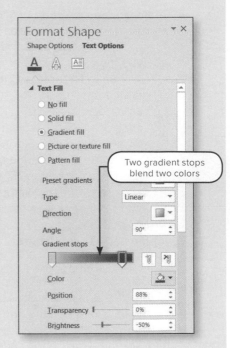

2-43 *Format Shape* pane

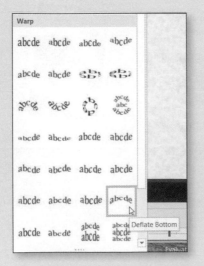

2-44 *WordArt Transform* gallery

2-45 *Deflate Bottom Transform* effect applied and adjusted

15. Save and close your presentation (Figure 2-46).

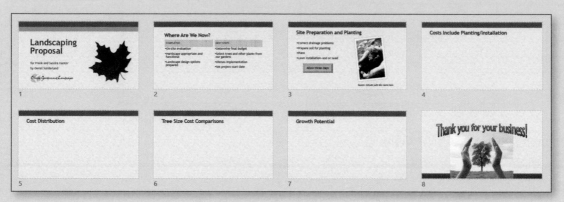

2-46 PP P2-1 completed

---

**SLO 2.4**

# Creating a Table

*Tables* show data in an organized and easy-to-read format because information is arranged in *columns* (vertical) and *rows* (horizontal). The intersection of a column and row is a *cell*. *Border* lines and *shading* show the table structure. Working with PowerPoint tables is much like working with tables in Word. You can create a table from a content placeholder when you create a new slide or by using options on the *Insert* tab.

Once you create a table, you can change its size as well as column width and row height. Use table formatting to emphasize the contents in different ways and help your audience interpret the data. If you plan to project your slides on a large screen, be sure your table information is concise so you can use a minimum font size of 20 points. If a table requires a lot of detailed information, then prepare the table as a full-page handout with body text at an 11–12 point size. You could prepare a PowerPoint slide to reference the handout as you explain the table, or perhaps show only a portion of the table on a slide.

## Insert and Draw Methods

You can create the columns and rows of a table in different ways. Click the **Table** button [*Insert* tab, *Tables* group] to visually select columns and rows by dragging over them. The table dimensions (such as *3×4 Table* meaning three columns by four rows) are shown at the top of the drop-down list. By default, columns and rows appear on the slide with even sizing, but you can adjust column width and row height as you add information.

---

▶ **HOW TO: Insert a Table and Select Columns and Rows**

1. Display the slide where you want the table.
2. Click the **Insert** tab.
3. Click the **Table** button [*Tables* group] to open the drop-down list.
4. Drag across and down to select the number of columns and rows you need (Figure 2-47).

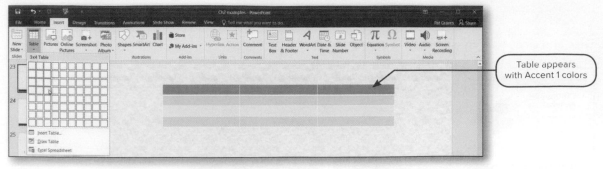

2-47 Table cells selected

5.  Release the pointer to insert the table.

Use the **Insert Table** command [*Insert* tab, *Tables* group] to create a table by entering a specific number of columns and rows.

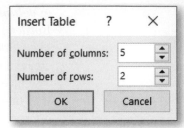

▶ **HOW TO:** Insert a Table and Enter the Number of Columns and Rows

1.  Display the slide where you want to insert the table.
2.  Click the **Insert** tab.
3.  Click the **Table** button [*Tables* group] to open the drop-down list.
4.  Click **Insert Table** and the *Insert Table* dialog box opens (Figure 2-48).
5.  Specify the number of columns and rows you need.
6.  Click **OK** to close the *Insert Table* dialog box and insert the table.

2-48 *Insert Table* dialog box

To insert a table on a new slide, click the **Table** icon in the empty content placeholder to open the *Insert Table* dialog box. Enter the number of columns and rows to create the table. Because of the placeholder size, the table width will be slightly wider than when you click the **Insert** button to create a table.

The final way to create a table is by drawing the table area and dividing it into columns and rows. This method works well when space is limited on the slide because of other content.

▶ **HOW TO:** Draw a Table

1.  Display the slide where you want the table.
2.  Click the **Insert** tab.
3.  Click the **Table** button [*Tables* group] to open the drop-down list.
4.  Click **Draw Table** and your pointer changes to a pen.
5.  Drag the pen to draw the outside border of the table in the size you want.
6.  Click the **Draw Table** button [*Table Tools Design* tab, *Draw Borders* group] to activate the pen again.

7. Drag the pen inside the table to insert horizontal and vertical lines that divide the table into rows and columns (Figure 2-49).

   • Start dragging near but not touching the outside border and the lines will expand on both ends to reach the borders.

8. Press **Esc** to turn off the pen tool.

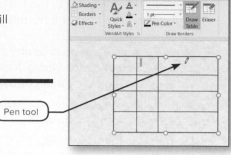

Pen tool

2-49 *Draw Table*

Regardless of the method you use to create a table, the *Table Tools Design* tab (Figure 2-50) and *Table Tools Layout* tab (Figure 2-51) are available when the table is active.

2-50 *Table Tools Design* tab

2-51 *Table Tools Layout* tab

## Move and Select

Your insertion point indicates where you are within a table to add text. To move from cell to cell, use one of the following methods:

• Press **Tab** to move to the next cell on the right (or the first cell in the next row).
• Press **Shift+Tab** to move to the previous cell on the left.
• Press arrow keys to move in different directions from the current cell.
• Click a cell to move the insertion point to that cell.

   Where you point within a table influences whether you select individual cells, columns, rows, or the entire table. Your pointer changes to a selection pointer (a black arrow that points in different directions based on what you are selecting).

▶**HOW TO:** Select Cells, Columns, Rows, and the Table

1. Select a cell by pointing inside the left border and clicking when your pointer turns into a black arrow that angles.

2. Select a column by using one of the following methods:

   • Point above the column's top border and click when your pointer turns into a downward-pointing black arrow (Figure 2-52).
   • Move your insertion point to any cell in the column. Click the **Select** button [*Table Tools Layout* tab, *Table* group] and click **Select Column.**

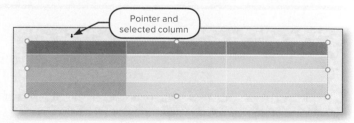

Pointer and selected column

2-52 Select table column

3. Select a row by using one of the following methods:

   - Point outside the table to the left of a row and click when your pointer turns into a right-pointing black arrow (Figure 2-53).
   - Move your insertion point to any cell in the row. Click the **Select** button [*Table Tools Layout* tab, *Table* group] and click **Select Row**.

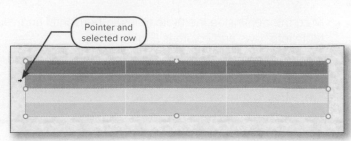

2-53 Select table row

4. Select multiple cells, columns, or rows by using one of the following methods:

   - Drag across adjacent cells.
   - Press **Shift** as you click additional adjacent cells.

5. Select an entire table by using one of the following methods:

   - Drag across all cells in the table.
   - Move your insertion point to any cell in the table. Click the **Select** button [*Table Tools Layout* tab, *Table* group] and click **Select Table**.

## Insert and Delete Rows and Columns

After you begin entering table content, you may need to add rows or columns. You can change a table's structure in several ways:

- Insert rows above or below the current row.
- Insert columns to the left or right of the current column.
- Delete rows and columns.

▶**HOW TO:** Insert and Delete Rows and Columns

1. Click inside the table.
2. Click the **Table Tools Layout** tab.
3. Insert a row or column.

   - Click a table cell next to where you want to add a column or row.
   - Click the **Insert Above** or **Insert Below** buttons [*Rows & Columns* group] to add rows.
   - Click the **Insert Left** or **Insert Right** buttons [*Rows & Columns* group] to add columns.

4. Delete a row or column.

   - Click a table cell where you want to delete a column or row.
   - Click the **Delete** button and select **Delete Columns** or **Delete Rows** [*Rows & Columns* group] (Figure 2-54).

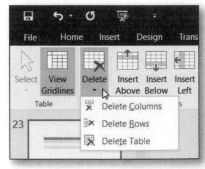

2-54 *Delete* button

▶ **ANOTHER WAY**

Right-click a row or column and insert or delete rows and columns by selecting the appropriate option from the mini toolbar.

## Merge and Split Cells

Use the *Merge Cells* command to combine two or more cells in a row or column. For example, you can merge all the cells in the top row of a table so a title will span all columns. Use the *Split Cells* command to divide any single cell into two or more cells.

### ▶ HOW TO: Merge and Split Cells

1. Select the cells to be merged.
2. Click the *Table Tools Layout* tab.
3. Click the **Merge Cells** button [*Merge* group] to combine those cells into one cell.
4. Select the cell (or cells) to be split.
5. Click the *Table Tools Layout* tab.
6. Click the **Split Cells** button [*Merge* group] to open the *Split Cells* dialog box and enter the number of columns and rows that you need.
7. Click **OK** to close the dialog box.

> **ANOTHER WAY**
>
> Click the **Eraser** button [*Table Tools Design* tab, *Draw Borders* group] and your pointer turns into an eraser. Click a border within the table to remove it and merge cells. Press **Esc** to turn off the **Eraser**.

## Adjust Sizing

You often need to resize tables to display information appropriately. Column widths will vary based on content, but row height should usually be consistent.

### ▶ HOW TO: Resize a Table, Cells, Columns, and Rows

1. Resize a table.
   - Enter sizes in the *Height* and *Width* boxes [*Table Tools Layout* tab, *Table Size* group].
   - Click and drag table sizing handles as you would to resize a shape.
2. Resize a cell, column, or row.
   - Point to a cell, column, or row border. When your pointer changes to a splitter (Figure 2-55), click and drag to increase or decrease the size of the cell, column, or row.
   - Select the cell, column, or row to change; then enter the size you want in the *Height* and *Width* boxes [*Table Tools Layout* tab, *Cell Size* group].
3. Resize a column to fit the text within it.
   - Point to a column border and double-click when your pointer changes to a splitter.
4. Distribute column width or row height evenly.
   - Select the columns or rows to be changed.
   - Click the **Distribute Rows** or **Distribute Columns** buttons [*Table Tools Layout* tab, *Cell Size* group].

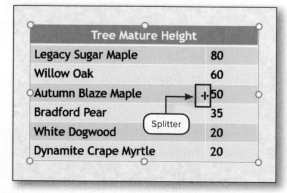

2-55 Change column width

> **MORE INFO**
>
> To maintain column width proportions, press **Shift** as you drag table sizing handles or select **Lock Aspect Ratio** [*Table Tools Layout* tab, *Table Size* group] before entering *Height* or *Width* sizes.

**SLO 2.5**

# Formatting a Table

You can format text in a table as you can any other text such as changing fonts and text effects. You can also change cell margins and text direction. While shading and borders may appear decorative, these effects can make a table easier to interpret. For example, shading on rows can make the text easier to read across rows; shading on a column can draw attention to the text displayed there. PowerPoint provides many preset styles using color combinations derived from theme colors. You can customize effects to create a unique design.

## Table Style Options and Effects

On the *Table Tools Design* tab, the **Table Styles** gallery provides options for a table's design. The first style on each row of options is shown in black and white while the other six styles are in theme accent colors. Table styles are arranged in the following categories:

- *Best Match for Document*
- *Light*
- *Medium*
- *Dark*

Each table style is influenced by the features checked for **Table Style Options** [*Table Tools Design* tab]. Fill colors that emphasize table cells vary depending on which of the following options you select:

- **Header Row** or **Total Row:** The first or last row has a darker color and has bold text in a contrasting color.
- **First Column** or **Last Column:** The first or last column has a darker color and has bold text in a contrasting color.
- **Banded Rows** or **Banded Columns:** The rows or columns have alternating colors. *Banded Rows* makes reading across the table easier. *Banded Columns* emphasizes the separate columns.

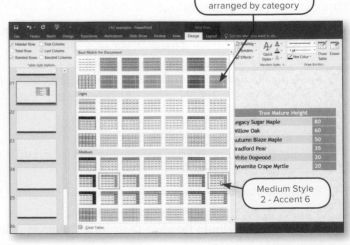

▶ **HOW TO: Apply a Table Style and Change Options**

1. Click anywhere in the table you want to change.
2. Click the **Table Tools Design** tab.
3. Click the **More** button in the *Table Styles* group to see the complete gallery (Figure 2-56). The current style is highlighted.
4. Point to a style to see a live preview. *ScreenTips* identify each style name.

2-56 *Table Styles*

5. Click a style to apply it.

6. Adjust the *Table Style Options* as needed.
   - Check **Header Row** and **Banded Rows** [*Table Style Options* group].
   - Deselect **Banded Rows** and select **Banded Columns** [*Table Style Options* group].

If you want to remove table formatting, click the **More** button [*Table Tools Design* tab, *Table Styles* group] and click **Clear Table**. To emphasize the table or cells within the table, such as a heading row, you can apply effects to selected areas.

▶ **HOW TO:** Apply Table Effects

1. Select the table, or the cells, to be changed.

2. Click the **Effects** button [*Table Tools Design* tab, *Table Styles* group (Figure 2-57).

3. Select one of the following effects:
   - **Cell Bevel**
   - **Shadow**
   - **Reflection**

4. Point to an option to see a live preview. *ScreenTips* identify each option name.

5. Click an option to apply it.

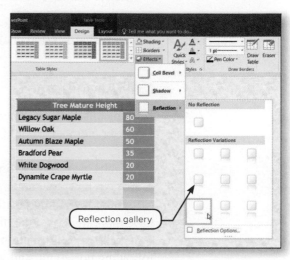

2-57 *Reflection Effects*

## Shading and Border Colors

After you apply a built-in table style, you can change colors to emphasize your content or better match other aspects of your presentation. Select the cells you want to change and use the *Shading* button [*Table Tools Design* tab, *Table Styles* group] to select a different color (Figure 2-58). The icon for this button is the same as a *Shape Fill* button.

Border lines separate cells and outline the edge of the table, but not all table styles show border lines. To add lines, use the *Borders* button [*Table Tools Design* tab, *Table Styles* group] and each available option shows where the border line will be applied when that option is selected (Figure 2-59).

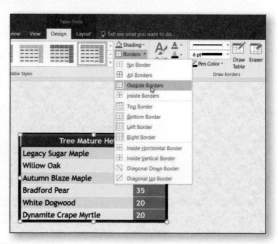

2-59 *Pen Weight* changed and *Outside Borders* applied

2-58 Shading emphasizes content

Select the appropriate area before you apply the border change. If you want the border lines thicker, increase the *Pen Weight* [*Table Tools Design* tab, *Draw Borders* group] before you apply the border change. You can remove borders from selected cells by clicking the **Borders** button and selecting **No Border**.

Also, you can apply, change, and remove borders using the *Pen* tools [*Table Tools Design* tab, *Draw Borders* group]:

- *Pen Color:* Change line color.
- *Pen Style:* Choose a different line style.
- *Pen Weight:* Change line thickness.
- *Draw Table:* Draw table area as well as column and row border lines.
- *Eraser:* Remove border lines.

It may take a little practice to use the pen to change table lines and not start a new table. Select the **Eraser** and click each border line you need to remove.

## Cell Alignment

Within cells, text is aligned on the left by default, which is appropriate for words and phrases. However, numbers should usually be right-aligned so your audience can more easily interpret values.

If cells have a single line of text, center the text vertically in the cells. If some cells contain more text than other cells, top alignment generally works best because reading is easier with a consistent beginning position. Bottom alignment works well for column headings when they have more than one line of text.

Click the **Align** buttons [*Table Tools Layout* tab, *Alignment* group] and choose from the following horizontal and vertical alignment options:

- *Horizontal alignment:* **Align Left, Center, Align Right**
- *Vertical alignment:* **Align Top, Center Vertically, Align Bottom**

## Cell Margins and Text Direction

Space is needed between the border lines of a cell and the text in the cell. The default internal margin spacing is *Normal*. You can change the spacing by clicking the **Cell Margins** button [*Table Tools Layout* tab, *Alignment* group] and choose from one of the following options (Figure 2-60):

- *Normal:* Top/Bottom **.05"** and Left/Right **.1"**
- *None:* All Sides **0"**
- *Narrow:* All Sides **0.05"**
- *Wide:* All Sides **0.15"**

Click **Custom Margins** to open the *Cell Text Layout* dialog box to enter other measurements.

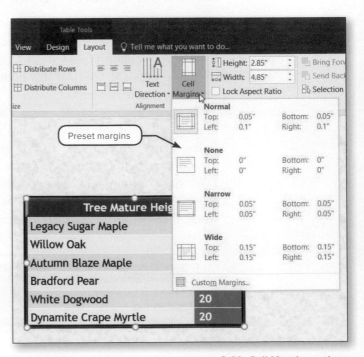

2-60 *Cell Margins* options

Text is, by default, arranged horizontally in each cell. Be careful when changing text direction because your text may not be as easy to read. Click **Text Direction** and choose one of the following four options (Figure 2-61):

- *Horizontal*
- *Rotate all text 90°*
- *Rotate all text 270°*
- *Stacked*

2-61 *Text Direction* options

## PAUSE & PRACTICE: POWERPOINT 2-2

For this project you create a table of costs, insert a row of data, and format the table to blend with other colors used in the landscaping presentation. You also add a text box to show an alternative cost.

File Needed: *[your initials] PP P2-1.pptx (Student data files are available in the* Library *of your SIMnet account.)*
Completed Project File Name: *[your initials] PP P2-2.pptx*

1. Open the presentation *[your initials] PP P2-1* and save it as [your initials] PP P2-2.

2. Create a table.
   a. Display slide 4 and click the **Insert Table** icon on the content placeholder to open the *Insert Table* dialog box.
   b. Enter 4 columns and 5 rows on the *Insert Table* dialog box. Click **OK** to close the dialog box and create the table.
   c. Type the following table text: (Note: PowerPoint does not recognize Hydroseeding, but this is the correct spelling.)

| Item | Quantity | Cost Each | Totals |
|---|---|---|---|
| Trees–shade | 3 | 500 | 1,500 |
| Trees–ornamental | 3 | 150 | 450 |
| Perennials | 30 | 12 | 360 |
| Hydroseeding sq. ft. | 8,000 | .10 | 800 |

   d. Click and drag across the table to select all cells. Change the *Font Size* to **20 pt**. [*Home* tab, *Font* group] (Figure 2-62).

3. Adjust table sizing and alignment.
   a. Adjust column width by pointing to each border separating the columns and double-clicking when your pointer changes to a splitter.
      - For the right side of the "Totals" column, the pointer will change to a splitter if you deselect the table and then point just inside the right border. Drag to make the column fit the text.

### Costs Include Planting/Installation

| Item | Quantity | Cost Each | Totals |
|---|---|---|---|
| Trees–shade | 3 | 500 | 1,500 |
| Trees–ornamental | 3 | 150 | 450 |
| Perennials | 30 | 12 | 360 |
| Hydroseeding sq. ft. | 8,000 | .10 | 800 |

2-62 Table as it first appears with font size change

b. Point above the "**Quantity**" column and click when your pointer turns into a black arrow. Drag across the "**Cost Each**" and "**Totals**" columns to select all cells in those columns. Click the **Align Right** button [*Table Tools Layout* tab, *Alignment* group].

4. Insert rows and add text.
   a. Click the "**Perennials**" cell and click the **Insert Above** button [*Table Tools Layout* tab, *Rows & Columns* group].
   b. Add the following text to the newly inserted row:
   Shrubs        10        40        400
   c. Click in the "**Hydroseeding**" cell and click the **Insert Below** button [*Table Tools Layout* tab, *Rows & Columns* group].
   d. Select the last three cells on the new row and click the **Merge Cells** button [*Table Tools Layout* tab, *Merge* group].
   e. Add the following text:
   Total        3,510

5. Select table styles, options, and shading.
   a. Click the **More** button [*Tables Tools Design* tab, *Table Styles* group] and select the **Medium Style 3, Accent 6** style.
   b. Check **Header Row, Total Row,** and **Banded Rows** [*Tables Tools Design* tab, *Table Style Options* group] if they are not already checked.
   c. Select a row with gray shading. Click the **Shading** button [*Table Tools Design* tab, *Table Styles* group] and select **Green, Accent 6, Lighter 80%**. Repeat for the remaining two gray rows.
   d. Select the last row. Click the **Shading** button and select **Green, Accent 6, Lighter 60%**.
   e. Select the first row. Click the **Effects** button [*Table Tools Design* tab, *Table Styles* group], click **Cell Bevel**, and select **Cool Slant** (Figure 2-63).

| Item | Quantity | Cost Each | Totals |
|------|----------|-----------|--------|
| Trees—shade | 3 | 500 | 1,500 |
| Trees—ornamental | 3 | 150 | 450 |
| Shrubs | 10 | 40 | 400 |
| Perennials | 30 | 12 | 360 |
| Hydroseeding sq. ft. | 8,000 | .10 | 800 |
| Total | | | 3,510 |

2-63 Style, row shading, and *Bevel* effect applied

6. Add borders and a shadow effect.
   a. Select the table.
   b. Click the **Pen Color** button [*Table Tools Design* tab, *Draw Borders* group] and select **Green, Accent 6, Darker 50%**.
   c. Click the **Pen Weight** button [*Table Tools Design* tab, *Draw Borders* group] and select **6 pt**.
   d. Click the **Borders** drop-down arrow [*Table Tools Design* tab, *Table Styles* group] and select **Outside Borders**.
   e. Select the table and click the **Effects** button [*Table Tools Design* tab, *Table Styles* group]. Click **Shadow** and select **Offset Diagonal Bottom Right** in the *Outer* category.

7. Center the table so it is centered on the slide.
   a. Click **Align** [*Table Tools Layout* tab, *Arrange* group] and select **Align Center**. Click **Align** again and select **Align Middle**.

8. Insert a text box.
   a. Click the **Text Box** button [*Insert* tab, *Text* group] and click the slide below the table to start a text box. Type the following text:
   Sod cost for 8,000 sq. ft. @ .60 = $4,800

b. Change the font size to **20 pt**. [*Home* tab, *Font* group].

c. Click the **Shape Fill** button [*Home* tab, *Drawing* group] and select **Green, Accent 6, Lighter 60%**.

d. Resize the text box as necessary so the text fits on one line. Move it to the lower right of the slide (Figure 2-64).

9. Save and close your presentation (Figure 2-65).

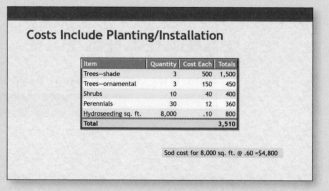

### Costs Include Planting/Installation

| Item | Quantity | Cost Each | Totals |
|---|---|---|---|
| Trees—shade | 3 | 500 | 1,500 |
| Trees—ornamental | 3 | 150 | 450 |
| Shrubs | 10 | 40 | 400 |
| Perennials | 30 | 12 | 360 |
| Hydroseeding sq. ft. | 8,000 | .10 | 800 |
| Total | | | 3,510 |

Sod cost for 8,000 sq. ft. @ .60 =$4,800

2-64 Completed table on slide 4

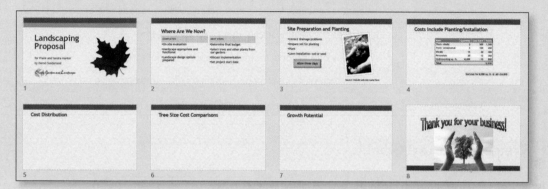

2-65 PP P2-2 completed

---

**SLO 2.6**

# Creating a SmartArt Graphic

To clearly illustrate concepts such as processes, cycles, or relationships, you can create a diagram using ***SmartArt graphics*** to help your audience see connections or sequences. This is a very important communication strategy; the shapes of the diagram are concisely labeled for each concept and the shapes are connected in various ways. For example, you can show subtopics radiating from a central topic or sequential steps in a work flow.

The *SmartArt Tools Design* tab (Figure 2-66) provides options for the overall layout and styles of the *SmartArt* graphics. You can add shapes and rearrange the order of shapes.

The *SmartArt Tools Format* tab (Figure 2-67) provides options to customize shape and text styles, fill colors, outline colors, and effects.

2-66 *SmartArt Tools Design* tab

2-67 *SmartArt Tools Format* tab

# SmartArt Layouts

*SmartArt layouts* (diagrams) are organized by type in the *Choose a SmartArt Graphic* dialog box; each type is described in the following table. When you select a layout, PowerPoint provides more information about using that specific layout.

## SmartArt Graphic Layout Types and Purposes

| Type | Purpose |
|---|---|
| *List* | Illustrates non-sequential or grouped information |
| *Process* | Illustrates sequential steps in a process or workflow |
| *Cycle* | Illustrates a continuing sequence or concepts related to a central idea |
| *Hierarchy* | Illustrates a decision tree or top-to-bottom relationship such as an organizational chart |
| *Relationship* | Illustrates concepts that are connected such as contrasting, opposing, or converging |
| *Matrix* | Illustrates the relationship of four parts to the whole |
| *Pyramid* | Illustrates proportional or interconnected relationships |
| *Picture* | Shows pictures as integral parts of many different diagrams |
| *Office.com* | Shows diagrams from layouts on Office.com |

## ▶ HOW TO: Create a SmartArt Graphic

1. Click the **Insert SmartArt Graphic** icon on the content placeholder to open the *Choose a SmartArt Graphic* dialog box.

*Or*

2. Display the slide where you want to insert the *SmartArt* graphic and click the **Insert** tab.

3. Click the **SmartArt** button [*Illustrations* group] to open the *Choose a SmartArt Graphic* dialog box.

4. Select a type from the list on the left (Figure 2-68).

5. Click a layout in the gallery to select it.

6. Click **OK** to close the dialog box. The *SmartArt* graphic appears on the slide with sample text.

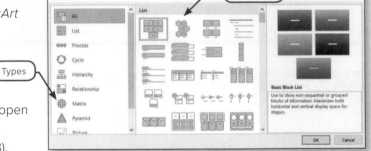

2-68 *Choose a SmartArt Graphic* dialog box

---

When you insert a *SmartArt* graphic using the *SmartArt* button on the *Insert* tab, the initial size of the *SmartArt* frame may be different than if you inserted the *SmartArt* graphic using the content placeholder on a new slide with a *Title and Content* layout. You may need to resize the frame for your content to fit appropriately on your slide.

If the layout you choose has picture placeholders on the shapes, such as the *Continuous Picture List* layout shown in Figure 2-69, click each picture icon to open the *Insert Pictures* dialog box. Locate the picture you want to use and click **Insert**. The picture is sized automatically and shaped to fit the current picture placeholder.

2-69 *SmartArt Continuous Picture List* layout

## Add Text

Click the **Text Pane** button [*SmartArt Tools Design* tab, *Create Graphic* group] to open a pane beside your layout. As you type in the pane, *SmartArt* text appears as a bulleted list and also in the *SmartArt* shapes. Text becomes smaller in the shapes as you enter more text, so it is important to use only a few words. You can resize or move the *Text pane*.

*List* layouts often work well if you have two levels of bulleted text: Level 1 (the first line) and Level 2 (text indented to a sublevel). How text is arranged when using two levels of information varies based on the selected layout. Notice in Figure 2-70 that Level 1 text is in a shape and Level 2 text is in a bulleted list below the shape.

▶ **HOW TO:** Type SmartArt Text Using the Text Pane

1. Open the *Text pane*, if necessary, by using one of the following methods:
   - Click the **Text Pane** button [*SmartArt Tools Design* tab, *Create Graphic* group].
   - Click the smaller **Text Pane** button on the left side of the *SmartArt* frame.
2. Type text after the first bullet to add Level 1 text.
3. Press **Enter** to add a new item. Another shape appears in your *SmartArt* layout, and shape sizes automatically adjust.
4. Press **Tab** to indent for Level 2 text (Figure 2-70).
5. Press **Shift** + **Tab** to go from Level 2 text to Level 1 text.
6. Use arrow keys to move through the listed items.
7. Remove a shape by deleting the related bulleted text in the *Text pane*.

   - The *Text pane* automatically closes when you click outside the *SmartArt* layout.
   - If you want to keep the current *SmartArt* layout active, click the pane's **Close** button or the **Text Pane** button to close the pane.

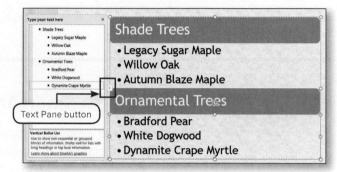

2-70 *SmartArt Text Pane*

Another way to add text is to type directly into each *SmartArt* shape so you can easily see how your text fits without becoming too small. Pressing **Tab** does not move your insertion point between shapes. You can paste copied text but you cannot drag text into a *SmartArt* shape.

▶ **HOW TO:** Type Text in SmartArt Shapes

1. Close the *Text Pane*, if open, by clicking the **Close** button in the top-right corner of the pane.
2. Click each *SmartArt* shape to select it and type your text. A dashed border appears on the shape as you type or edit your text.
3. Click outside the *SmartArt* frame, or press **Esc**, when you are finished (Figure 2-71).

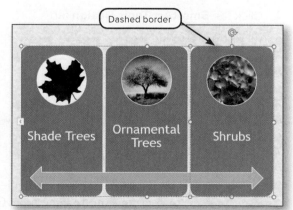

2-71 Add text in the *SmartArt Continuous Picture List* layout

If you already have listed information on your slide, you can quickly change bulleted text to a *SmartArt* graphic. The gallery layouts that first appear are designed for listed information, but you can access all of the other layouts, too.

▶ **HOW TO:** Convert Text to a SmartArt Graphic

1. Select the bulleted text placeholder or the text within the placeholder that you want to convert to a *SmartArt* graphic.
2. Click the **Home** tab.
3. Click the **Convert to SmartArt Graphic** button [*Paragraph* group] (Figure 2-72). The gallery displays layouts that are designed to show listed information.
4. Click a layout to apply it.

*Or*

5. Click **More SmartArt Graphics** to open the *Choose a SmartArt Graphic* dialog box.
6. Select from all layouts and then click **OK** to close the dialog box and insert the *SmartArt* graphic.

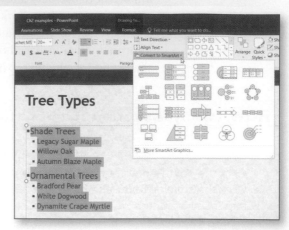

2-72 Convert to *SmartArt* graphic

---

 **SLO 2.7**

# Formatting a SmartArt Graphic

When you create a *SmartArt* graphic, by default it appears using the first accent color in the current color theme. You can customize many style options and colors using the *SmartArt Tools Design* tab as well as rearrange shape order, add shapes, or change layouts.

## SmartArt Styles

The **SmartArt Styles** gallery provides different effects for emphasizing the diagram shapes. In the **3-D** category, the styles have a dimensional effect. When choosing these styles, be sure that your diagram is not distorted or difficult to interpret.

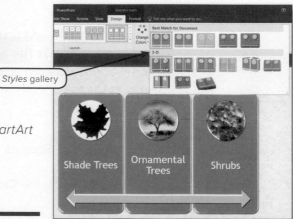

▶ **HOW TO:** Apply SmartArt Styles

1. Select the *SmartArt* graphic.
2. Click the **SmartArt Tools Design** tab.
3. Click the **More** button [*SmartArt Styles* group] to open the *SmartArt Styles* gallery (Figure 2-73).
4. Point to a style to see a live preview.
5. Click a style to apply it.

2-73 *SmartArt* graphic styles

## Change Colors

The **Change Colors** gallery provides a quick way to change all the colors in a *SmartArt* graphic at the same time. Color options are arranged in categories using theme accent colors; some show variations of the same color while others have different colors.

Individual shape colors within a *SmartArt* graphic can be changed as you would any other shape.

▶ **HOW TO:** Change SmartArt Colors

1. Select the *SmartArt* graphic.

2. Change colors for the entire diagram by clicking the **Change Colors** button [*SmartArt Tools Design* tab, *SmartArt Styles* group] and selecting a gallery option (Figure 2-74).

3. Change the color of a selected shape within a diagram by clicking the **Shape Fill** button or the **Shape Outline** button [*SmartArt Tools Format* tab, *Shape Styles* group] and choosing an appropriate color.

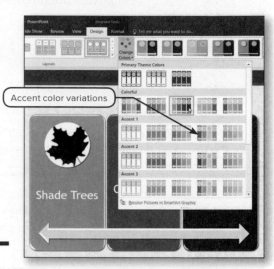

2-74 *SmartArt* graphic *Change Colors* options

## Change Layouts

You may find that the *SmartArt* graphic layout you have chosen is not appropriate for the particular process or relationship you are trying to show. Or you might need a layout that displays two levels of information.

▶ **HOW TO:** Change Layouts

1. Select the *SmartArt* graphic.

2. Click the **SmartArt Tools Design** tab, and click the **More** button [*Layouts* group] to open the *Layouts* gallery (Figure 2-75).

3. Point to a layout to see a live preview of that layout.

4. Click a layout to apply it.

*Or*

5. Click **More Layouts** to open the *Choose a SmartArt Graphic* dialog box.

6. Select from all layouts and then click **OK** to close the dialog box and apply the new layout.

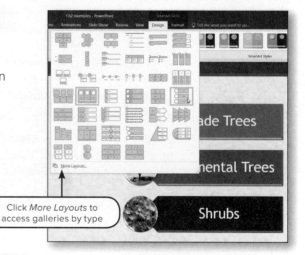

2-75 *SmartArt graphic* layouts

## Add Shapes

The ***Add Shape*** button on the *SmartArt Tools Design* tab inserts shapes in relation to the selected shape. The available options include the following:

- *Add Shape After*
- *Add Shape Before*
- *Add Shape Above*
- *Add Shape Below*
- *Add Assistant*

Being able to control where a new shape appears is important. For example, you can add shapes to an organization chart as new employees are hired. An assistant shape is only available for organization charts.

2-76 *Add Shape* options

## ▶ HOW TO: Add Shapes

1. Select the shape closest to where you want to add a shape.
2. Click the **SmartArt Tools Design** tab.
3. Click the **Add Shape** drop-down arrow [*Create Graphic* group] (Figure 2-76) and select the position where you want to add the new shape.

To change the flow of a diagram, click the **Right to Left** button [*SmartArt Tools Design* tab, *Create Graphic* group].

---

# PAUSE & PRACTICE: POWERPOINT 2-3

For this project you create an organization chart showing the CGL employees who will be managing various aspects of the landscaping for Frank and Sandra Hunter. You also convert one of the existing lists to a *SmartArt* graphic and rearrange slide objects for an interesting appearance. The *SmartArt* styles applied blend with other colors in the presentation.

File Needed: **[your initials] PP P2-2.pptx** (*Student data files are available in the* Library *of your SIMnet account.*)
Completed Project File Name: **[your initials] PP P2-3.pptx**

1. Open the presentation **[your initials] PP P2-2** and save it as [your initials] PP P2-3.
2. Create a new slide and insert a *SmartArt* graphic.

    a. Display slide 1. Click the **New Slide** drop-down arrow and select the **Title and Content** layout.
    b. Type the slide title Your CGL Team.
    c. Click the **Insert a SmartArt Graphic** icon on the content placeholder to open the *Choose a SmartArt Graphic* dialog box.
    d. Select the *Hierarchy* type from the list on the left.
    e. Click the **Organization Chart** layout and click **OK** to close the dialog box and insert the *SmartArt* graphic.

3. Insert text.
    a. Select each *SmartArt* shape and type the text displayed in Figure 2-77.

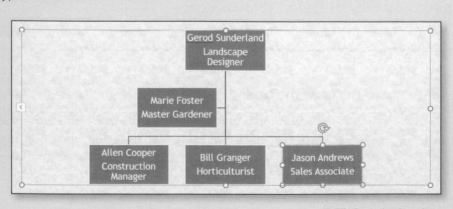

2-77 Organization chart

b. Press **Enter** after each name within a shape. Let the job titles word wrap as needed.

4. Change the organization chart using the *SmartArt Tools Design* tab.
   a. Change the flow by clicking the **Right to Left** button [*Create Graphic* group].
   b. Click the **More** button [*SmartArt Styles* group] and select the **Inset** effect (Figure 2-78).
   c. Click the **Change Colors** button [*SmartArt Styles* group] and scroll down to select **Gradient Loop, Accent 6** (Figure 2-79).

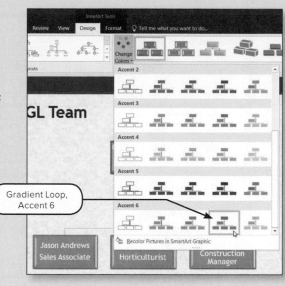

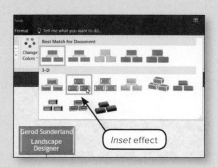

2-78 *SmartArt* graphic styles

2-79 New colors applied

5. Change bulleted text to a *SmartArt* graphic.
   a. Display slide 4. Select the bulleted text and click the **Convert to SmartArt** button [*Home* tab, *Paragraph* group].
   b. Click the **Vertical Bullet List**. The *SmartArt* list fills the slide and is too large since other objects are already on the slide (Figure 2-80).

6. Change the *SmartArt* graphic so it fits on the slide with the other objects.
   a. Press **Ctrl** while you click each *SmartArt* shape to select them all. Change the font to **24 pt**.
   b. Select the *SmartArt* frame (not individual shapes) and resize it (*Height* **3"** and *Width* **5"**) [*SmartArt Tools Format* tab, *Size* group] to better fit the text and other objects on the slide.
   c. Change the style to **Inset** [*SmartArt Tools Design* tab, *SmartArt Styles* group].
   d. Click the **Change Colors** button [*SmartArt Tools Design* tab, *SmartArt Styles* group] and select **Gradient Range – Accent 6**.
   e. Rearrange slide objects as displayed in Figure 2-81. Be careful to point to the *SmartArt* frame when moving it so the whole diagram moves and not just an individual shape within the frame.

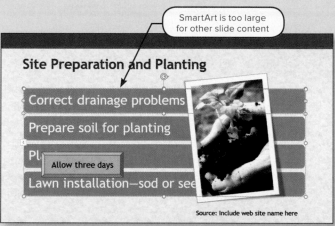

2-80 *SmartArt* graphic shapes as they originally appear

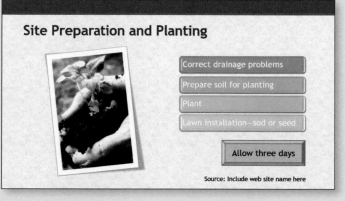

2-81 Completed slide 4

7. Save and close your presentation (Figure 2-82).

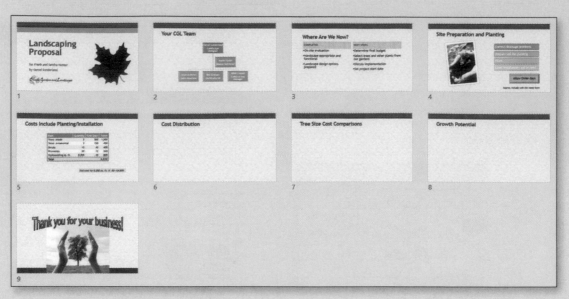

2-82 PP P-3 completed

## Creating a Chart

*Charts* help viewers interpret data and make comparisons. If you have lots of data, then create your chart in Excel and copy it to a PowerPoint slide. However, for most situations, PowerPoint's *Chart* feature will provide all the options you need.

To insert a chart in PowerPoint 2016, click the **Insert Chart** icon on a new slide content placeholder or click the **Insert** tab and click the **Chart** button [*Illustrations* group] to add a chart to an existing slide. You can choose a chart type to control how data is represented such as with columns, bars, lines, or pie slices. The following table lists chart types and describes their purposes:

### Chart Types and Purposes

| Type | Purpose |
| --- | --- |
| *Column* | Shows a comparison of values or data changes over time. Categories are shown on the horizontal axis and values are shown on the vertical axis. Columns may be clustered to show a range of values or groupings. Columns in a category may be stacked to emphasize the total category value rather than the subsections that make up the category. |
| *Line* | Shows data changes over time; works well to show trends with multiple data series plotted at even intervals. Categories are shown on the horizontal axis and values are shown on the vertical axis. Markers can indicate individual values. |
| *Pie* | Shows the values in a data series in proportional sizes that make up a whole pie. Values cannot be negative or zero values. Percentages or actual values can be displayed near or on pie slices. This category also includes *Doughnut* charts that show parts of a whole but can contain more than one data series as rings. |
| *Bar* | Similar to column charts except bars are horizontal; works well for comparison of values. Categories are shown on the vertical axis and values are shown on the horizontal axis. |

*Continued*

| Type | Purpose |
|---|---|
| Area | Shows data changes over time; emphasizes the total values across a trend. |
| X Y (Scatter) | Shows the relationships between data using values on both the X and Y axes to plot data points; works well to emphasize where data sets have similar values. This category also includes *Bubble* charts. |
| Stock | Shows fluctuation of stock prices with high, low, and close values displayed over time. |
| Surface | Shows the differences between two sets of data. Instead of values, color bands represent the same range of values as in a topographic map showing land elevations. |
| Radar | Shows the combined values of several data series with values relative to a center point. |
| Treemap | Displays categories by color arranged in a structure that helps to compare proportions within a hierarchy. |
| Sunburst | Displays data in a circular pattern of rings that create a hierarchy with the highest level in the center. With multiple categories, this chart shows how the outer rings relate to the inner rings. |
| Histogram | Shows the distribution of data grouped by frequencies. Can include a cumulative total. |
| Box & Whisker | Shows multiple data sets organized by quartiles (ranked data divided into four equal groups) and shown as proportional boxes. Variability is shown as lines above or below the boxes. Outliers are plotted as individual points. |
| Waterfall | Shows how an initial value is affected by the addition of positive and negative values with columns that reflect a running total. |
| Combo | Combines two charts such as a column chart with a line chart displayed over it. |

> **MORE INFO**
>
> Use *Help* to search for "chart types" to see examples and get tips on how to arrange data in a worksheet.

The *Chart Tools Design* tab (Figure 2-83) and the *Chart Tools Format* tab (Figure 2-84) are available when a chart is active.

2-83 *Chart Tools Design* tab

2-84 *Chart Tools Format* tab

When you insert a chart in PowerPoint, a **spreadsheet** opens with sample data in rows and columns. A group of data values from each column is a **data series**; a group of data values from each row is a **category**. You can edit the sample data by entering your own information or you could copy and paste data from Excel, Word, or Access. If you need to revise the data in Excel, click the **Excel** button in the spreadsheet title bar.

Because the spreadsheet and PowerPoint chart are linked, the changes you make to the spreadsheet are automatically reflected in the chart.

## ▶ HOW TO: Insert a Chart

1. Click the **Insert** tab; then click the **Chart** button [*Illustrations* group]. You can also click the **Insert Chart** icon on a new slide content placeholder.
   - In the *Insert Chart* dialog box (Figure 2-85), chart types are listed on the left and a variety of chart layouts for each type appear on the right.
   - A *ScreenTip* identifies chart names.
2. Click a layout to select a chart.
3. Click **OK** to close the dialog box and insert the chart.
   - A spreadsheet automatically opens showing sample data that you edit (Figure 2-86).

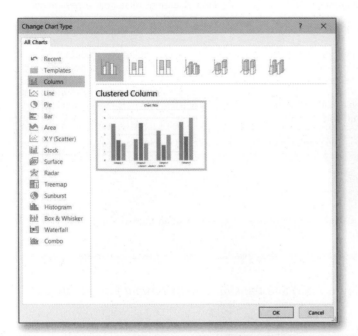

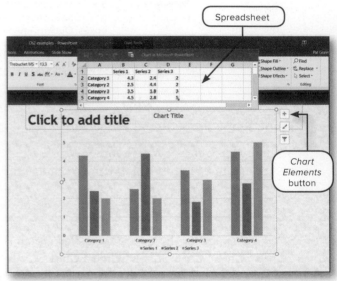

2-85 *Insert Chart* dialog box          2-86 Spreadsheet linked to a chart

> **MORE INFO**
>
> When you insert a chart using the *Insert* tab, the size of the chart frame will be different than when you insert a chart from the *Title and Content* placeholder as you create a new slide. Resize the chart frames as needed.

The chart frame displays ***chart elements,*** the objects that make up the chart. Chart elements vary based on the type of chart used. You can see which chart elements are shown by clicking the **Chart Elements** button, the top button (with a green plus sign) on the right of the chart frame. You can add or remove elements by changing selections from the list. Other chart elements appear in the drop-down list box in the *Current Selection* group on the *Chart*

*Tools Format* tab and in the *Format* pane when you are working on the chart. The following table defines chart elements:

## Chart Elements and Definitions

| Element | Definition |
|---------|-----------|
| Y-Axis (Vertical) | Also called the *Value Axis*; displayed vertically with numbers usually arranged on the left of a chart |
| X-Axis (Horizontal) | Also called the *Category Axis*; displayed horizontally with word or number labels across the bottom of the chart |
| Axis Titles | Both the Y-Axis and the X-Axis can include titles to name values or categories |
| Chart Area | The background area where the entire chart is displayed in a frame |
| Chart Title | A chart may include a title |
| Data Labels | Used to identify data series or its individual points; may include values |
| Data Markers | The graphical representation of values shown as columns, bars, slices, or data points |
| Data Table | The data that creates the chart is shown in table format below the chart |
| Error Bars | Used to show margins of error or standard deviation amounts |
| Floor | Area at the bottom of a 3-D chart that creates an illusion of depth |
| Gridlines | Lines that appear behind a chart to help the viewer judge values |
| Legend | The key that identifies each data series by color |
| Plot Area | The rectangle between the vertical and horizontal axes that appears behind the data markers |
| Tick Marks | Lines of measurement on an axis that help to interpret values on each axis |
| Trendline | Shows averages on 2-D charts that are not stacked and can extend beyond actual data to predict future values |
| Walls | Areas, including Back Walls and Side Walls, of a 3-D chart behind the data markers that help to create an illusion of depth |

## Enter Data and Edit

After you replace the spreadsheet sample data with your data, you can close the spreadsheet. If you need to revise the data as you work on the chart in PowerPoint, you can open the spreadsheet again.

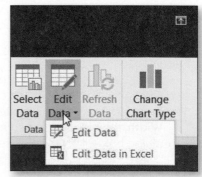

2-87 *Edit Data* button

▶ **HOW TO:** Edit Data in the Spreadsheet

1. Select the chart you want to modify.
2. Click the top of the **Edit Data** button [*Chart Tools Design* tab, *Data* group] to display the spreadsheet (Figure 2-87).
   - If you need to modify the data in Excel, click the **Edit Data** drop-down arrow and choose **Edit Data in Excel** to display the Excel worksheet.
   - You can click and drag the Excel window to a different location or resize it if more or less space is needed.

3.  Replace cell contents (Figure 2-88) by clicking in the **cell** and typing your data.
4.  Move around in the spreadsheet by clicking your pointer or using keyboard shortcuts as follows:

    -   Press **Enter** to move the insertion point down one row.
    -   Press **Shift+Enter** to move the insertion point up one row.
    -   Press **Tab** to move the insertion point to the next cell on the right.
    -   Press **Shift+Tab** to move to the previous cell on the left.
    -   Press arrow keys to move in any direction.

5.  Click the spreadsheet **Close** button to return to the PowerPoint chart.

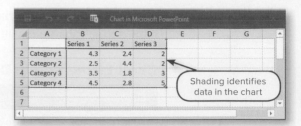

2-88 Default spreadsheet data

> **MORE INFO**
>
> Remove the sample data on the spreadsheet by clicking the **Select All** button (above the row 1 heading and to the left of the column A heading) and then pressing **Delete**.

Spreadsheet columns may need adjustments to show all data. If a cell displays number signs (#) rather than the data you entered, the cell is not wide enough to display cell contents.

-   Change column width by pointing to the top of the column and dragging the splitter or double-click the line between columns to auto fit the contents.
-   Be sure the shading of the selected rows and columns (see Figure 2-88) correctly identifies the category, series, and data cells. Drag a corner sizing handle to adjust.
-   Columns in a spreadsheet with blank cells must be deleted so the related chart displays without a blank space.
-   You can add new columns or rows in the spreadsheet or edit the spreadsheet in Excel.

## ▶ HOW TO: Modify the Spreadsheet

1.  Select the chart you want to modify.
2.  Click the top of the **Edit Data** button [*Chart Tools Design* tab, *Data* group].
3.  Adjust column width. Position your pointer on the vertical line to the right of the column heading (Figure 2-89); then use one of these methods:

    -   Drag to the correct width.
    -   Double-click and the column automatically adjusts to fit the widest data entered in that column.
    -   Right-click to open the context menu and select **Column Width**, then type the width number on the *Column Width* dialog box. Click **OK** to close the dialog box.

4.  Use Excel to modify data.

    -   Click the **Edit Data** drop-down arrow [*Chart Tools Design* tab, *Data* group] and choose **Edit Data in Excel**. The Excel window displays.

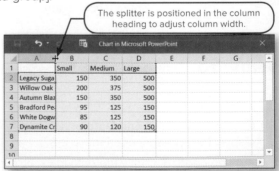

2-89 Adjust column width

- Click a cell where you need to add a cell, row, or column. Click the **Insert** drop-down arrow [*Home* tab, *Cells* group] and select the option you need.
- Adjust column width or edit titles and data values as you normally would within Excel.
- Close Excel to return to the chart on your slide.

In PowerPoint, switch the data series by clicking the **Switch Row/Column** button [*Chart Tools Design* tab, *Data* group]. In a column chart, for example, data displayed on the X-axis (bottom) and Y-axis (left) will be reversed.

### Change Chart Type

Click the **Change Chart Type** button [*Chart Tools Design* tab, *Type* group] to open the *Change Chart Type* gallery where you can choose from the many different layouts. For example, Figure 2-90 shows data in a line chart and Figure 2-91 shows the same data in a clustered column chart.

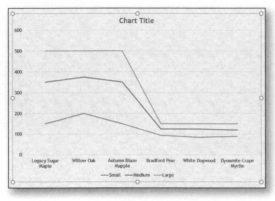

2-90 Line chart

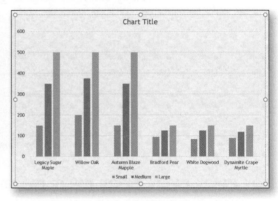

2-91 Clustered column chart

## SLO 2.9

# Formatting a Chart

You can change the look of a chart by applying preset styles or manually customizing individual chart elements.

### Chart Styles and Colors

The **Chart Styles** gallery [*Chart Tools Design* tab] provides preset effects for chart elements including the chart background. Click the **More** button to see styles arranged by number. Click a style to apply it (Figure 2-92).

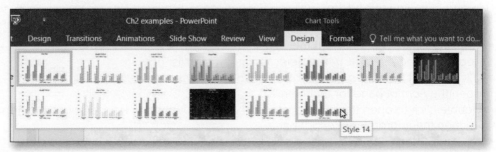

2-92 *Chart Styles* gallery

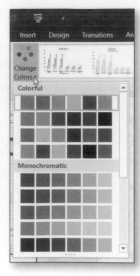

2-93 *Chart Colors* gallery

Click the **Change Colors** button [*Chart Tools Design* tab] to select **Colorful** or **Monochromatic** (shades of one color) combinations based on theme colors (Figure 2-93). The colors you choose then show in all the available chart styles. Be careful when selecting colors so the chart shapes (columns, bars, lines, or pie slices) are easy to distinguish for value comparisons. The colors also need to coordinate with your overall presentation (Figure 2-94).

If possible, avoid arranging red and green colors together. People who have difficulty recognizing different colors are most likely to have problems with red and green because they can look beige or gray.

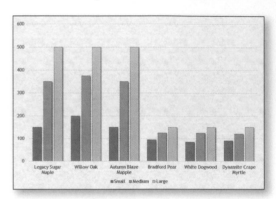

2-94 Chart style applied and colors changed

## Format Chart Elements

You can select chart elements (objects) and apply formatting in several ways.

▶**HOW TO:** Format a Chart Element

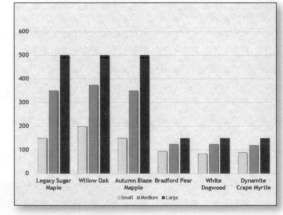

2-95 Colors changed on data series

1. Change colors and effects for a selected chart element using the Chart Tools Format tab:
   - Click the **Chart Tools Format** tab, click the **Shape Fill**, **Shape Outline**, or **Shape Effects** buttons [*Shape Styles* group] and choose appropriate colors and effects (Figure 2-95).
   - When text is selected, click the **Text Fill**, **Text Outline**, or **Text Effects** buttons [*WordArt Styles* group] and choose appropriate colors and effects.
2. Use one of these methods to open the *Format* pane (displayed on the right) and change options as needed:
   - Click the **Chart Tools Format** tab, select the element you need to change in the *Current Selection* drop-down list box. Click **Format Selection** [*Chart Tools Format* tab, *Current Selection* group] to open the *Format* pane for that element.
   - Double-click to open the appropriate *Format* pane or right-click and choose the **Format** option for that element to open the appropriate *Format* pane.
   - Click the **Chart Elements** button beside the chart and select a particular element. Click the triangle beside each element to select from different options. Click **More Options** to open the appropriate *Format* pane.

To change the chart area size, point to any sizing handle (the white circles on the chart frame) and resize by dragging. You can resize chart elements, but be careful not to distort size relationships.

You can fill elements of a chart with pictures. While a chart area picture might provide an interesting background, be careful when using pictures to avoid making the chart cluttered or the text difficult to read. The goal is always to create a chart that is easy to interpret.

In Figure 2-96, the chart area has a solid fill. The plot area has a gradient fill with the darkest color at the bottom which helps to emphasize the height of the columns. In Figure 2-97, the chart type is a *3-D Column Chart*. The column heights (especially for the shorter columns) are not as easy to compare in this chart as they are in Figure 2-96.

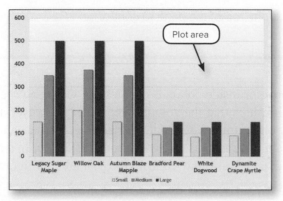

2-96 Chart plot area with gradient fill

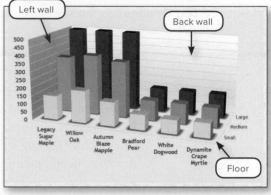

2-97 Chart with *3-D Rotation*

## Legends and Labels

The *legend* identifies each data series by color. It is usually displayed on the right, but you can move it to other positions, display it horizontally above or below the plot area, or delete it.

▶ **HOW TO:** Change Legend Position and Colors

1. Change the selected legend's position by using one of the following methods:
   - Click the **Chart Tools Format** tab, select **Legend** in the *Current Selection* drop-down list box, and click **Format Selection** [*Chart Tools Format* tab, *Current Selection* group] to open the *Format Legend* pane. Select a position. Deselect **Show the legend without overlapping the chart** if you want the legend to appear over the plot area (Figure 2-98).
   - Double-click to open the *Format Legend* pane or right-click and choose **Format Legend** to open the *Format Legend* pane. Select a position.
   - Click the **Chart Elements** button beside the chart, click the **Legend** triangle, and then select a position or choose **More Options** to open the *Format Legend* pane.
   - Select the legend and drag it to another position within the chart area. Resize it as needed.
2. Change the selected legend's colors by using one of the following methods:
   - Click the **Chart Tools Format** tab, click the **Shape Fill** or **Shape Outline** buttons, and select different colors.
   - Right-click the legend and choose **Format Legend** to open the *Format Legend* pane. Click the **Fill & Line** tab and then select appropriate fill and border colors.
3. Remove a selected legend by using one of the following methods:
   - Click the **Chart Elements** button beside the chart and deselect the **Legend**.
   - Select the legend and press **Delete**.

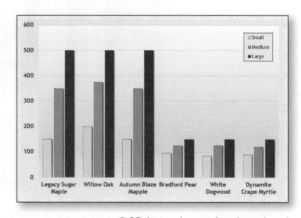

2-98 Legend moved and recolored

*Data labels* display values for each data series. These labels appear in different places based on the chart style. Use the *Format Data Labels* pane to customize labels.

## ▶ HOW TO: Display Data Labels

1. Select the chart and then click the **Chart Element** button beside the chart to open the list of *Chart Elements*.
2. Click **Data Labels** and select a position or click **More Options** to open the *Format Data Labels* pane.
   - Change *Label Options* to control the display and position of the value as well as *File & Line, Effects, Size & Properties* options.
   - Click **Text Options** and then select icons at the top of the pane to control *Text Fill & Outline* colors, apply *Text Effects,* and add a *Text Box.*

Using data labels above or inside columns enables the viewer to see the exact data value as well as the size relationships that the columns represent. However, the columns must be wide enough to display the numbers without overlapping. If the columns are too narrow (Figure 2-99), using a data table for this purpose is more effective. In a data table, the legend is automatically included, so it was removed from the plot area in Figure 2-100.

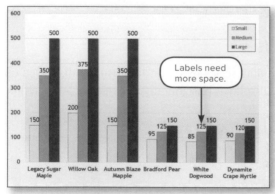

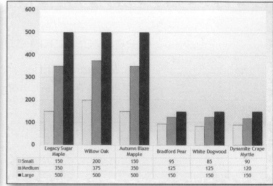

2-99 Data labels                    2-100 Data table

## ▶ HOW TO: Display a Data Table

1. Select the chart and then click the **Chart Element** button beside the chart to open the list of *Chart Elements*.
2. Deselect **Data Labels** and **Legend** if these elements are selected. They will automatically display in the table.
3. Click **Data Table** and the table appears below the chart.
4. Point to any number in the data table, right-click to open the context menu, and select **Format Data Table** to open the *Format Data Table* pane. **Table Options** are displayed with three icons at the top of the pane.
   - Change *Data Table Options* (column icon) to control table borders and the legend key (the color that identifies each data series).
   - Click the *Fill & Line* icon (paint bucket) or the *Effects* icon (pentagon) to make color and effect changes.
   - Click **Text Options** and then select icons at the top of the pane to change *Text Fill & Outline Colors,* apply *Text Effects,* or add a *Text Box.*

A pie chart has one data series. Each slice represents a value and the size of the slice illustrates its relationship to the whole. The number of slices is best limited to six or seven slices; too many slices make a pie chart difficult to interpret.

Unlike a column or line chart, a pie chart does not have axes or axes titles. Data labels are often used instead of a legend because they are easier to interpret. You have several options for where data labels appear, either on the slices or outside the slices (Figure 2-101). Be sure to select an option that makes it easy for the viewer to match the number with the related slice. Usually the label font size must be increased. The *Format Data Labels* pane has many options you can explore (Figure 2-102).

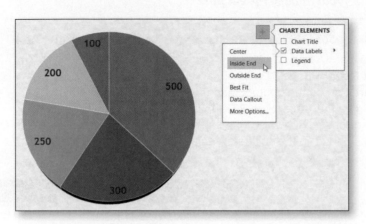

2-101 Pie chart data label positions

2-102 *Format Data Labels* pane

## Explode a Pie Slice

You can **explode** (separate) pie chart slices by dragging the pie slices away from the center. However, when all slices are separated, no single slice is emphasized. To emphasize just one slice, it is best to first design a pie chart as you want it to look and then drag that one slice away from the pie. Consider, also, how your colors are applied so the most noticeable or brightest color is used for the slice that you want to emphasize (Figure 2-103).

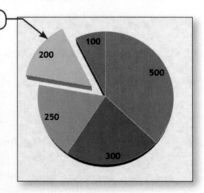

2-103 3-D pie chart with exploded slice

---

▶ **HOW TO:** Explode a Pie Slice

1. Click a pie to select the pie object.
2. Click again to select just one pie slice. Check the handles to be sure you have selected the correct slice and not a label on the slice.
3. Click and drag slightly away from the center of the pie so the slice is emphasized.

---

As you drag a pie slice away from the center, the entire pie becomes smaller. You can make the whole pie larger by resizing the plot area. Removing the legend creates more space for the pie, too.

For this project, you create a pie and two clustered column charts showing the cost distribution for CGL landscaping, cost comparisons for tree sizes, and the height of mature trees being considered for the new landscape.

Files Needed: **[your initials] PP P2-3.pptx** and **Trees-02.jpg** *(Student data files are available in the Library of your SIMnet account.)*
Completed Project File Name: **[your initials] PP 2-4.pptx**

1. Open the presentation file **[your initials] PP P2-3** and save it as [your initials] PP P2-4.
2. Create a 3-D pie chart.
   a. Select slide 6, "**Cost Distribution**."
   b. Click the **Insert Chart** icon on the content placeholder.
   c. Select the **Pie** chart type then select the **3-D Pie** layout. Click **OK**.
   d. Replace the spreadsheet sample data with the data in the following list. Point to the top of the column and then click and drag the splitter to resize columns.

|               | Cost  |
|---------------|-------|
| Trees—Shade   | 1,500 |
| Trees—Ornamental | 450 |
| Shrubs        | 400   |
| Perennials    | 360   |
| Hydroseeding sq. ft. | 800 |

3. Resize the spreadsheet window so you can proof all entries. Be sure all chart data is selected (Figure 2-104).

4. Close the spreadsheet.

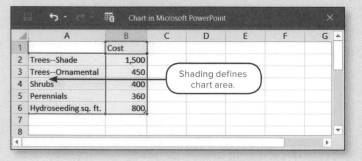

2-104 Spreadsheet linked to a chart

5. Format the 3-D pie chart.
   a. Delete the **Cost** chart title in the chart area because it duplicates the slide title.
   b. Click **Style 3** [*Chart Tools Design* tab, *Chart Styles* group].
   c. Verify that **Chart Area** [*Chart Tools Format* tab, *Current Selection* group] is selected. Click the **Shape Fill** button [*Chart Tools Format* tab, *Shape Styles* group]. Select **No Fill**.
   d. Click the **Shape Outline** button [*Chart Tools Format* tab, *Shape Styles* group] and select **No Outline**.
   e. From the drop-down list, select the **Series "Cost" Data Labels** [*Chart Tools Format* tab, *Current Selection* group]. Increase the font size to **20 pt**. [*Home* tab, *Font* group].
   f. Click the **Legend** and increase the font size to **20 pt**. [*Home* tab, *Font* group].
   g. Click and drag the legend to the upper right of the **Chart Area**.
   h. From the drop-down list, select the **Plot Area** [*Chart Tools Format* tab, *Current Selection* group]. Drag the center sizing handles to increase the plot area height so it matches the chart area height. The pie will be larger (Figure 2-105).
   i. Select the single slice for "**Trees—Ornamental**" and explode that slice by dragging it down slightly.

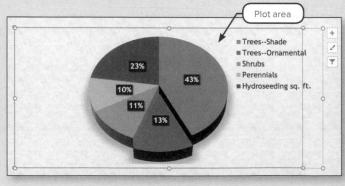

2-105 Slice exploded and legend repositioned

6. Create a clustered column chart.
   a. Select slide 7, "**Tree Size Cost Comparisons**." Click the **Insert Chart** icon on the content placeholder.
   b. Click the **Clustered Column** layout and click **OK**.
   c. Replace the spreadsheet data with the following data:

|  | Small | Medium | Large |
|---|---|---|---|
| Legacy Sugar Maple | 150 | 350 | 500 |
| Willow Oak | 200 | 375 | 500 |
| Autumn Blaze Maple | 150 | 350 | 500 |
| Bradford Pear | 95 | 125 | 150 |
| White Dogwood | 85 | 115 | 150 |
| Dynamite Crape Myrtle | 90 | 120 | 150 |

   d. Close the spreadsheet. If you need to check the data, click the **Edit Data** button [*Chart Tools Design* tab, *Data* group].
   e. Delete the chart title in the chart area.
   f. Change the chart style to **Style 8** [*Chart Tools Design* tab, *Chart Styles* group] which has a dark fill for the chart area.

7. Add chart elements.
   a. Click the **Chart Elements** button on the right side of the chart to display the list of elements (Figure 2-106).
   b. Select the following **Axes**, **Axis Titles**, **Data Table**, **Gridlines**, and **Legend** if they are not already selected.
      • The **Data Table** automatically appears below the columns.

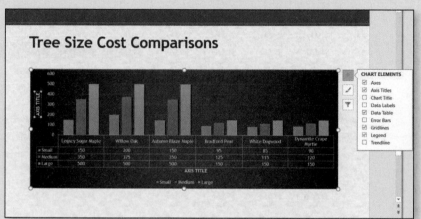

2-106  Clustered column chart with *Style 8* applied and chart elements listed on the right

8. Adjust chart formatting by selecting the following elements in the chart area. If necessary, confirm that you have the correct element selected [*Chart Tools Format* tab, *Current Selection* group].
   a. Select the *Vertical (Value) Axis Title* (rotated text on the Y-axis) and edit the text by typing Tree Cost.
   b. Select the *Horizontal (Category) Axis Title* (X-axis) below the data table and press **Delete**.
   c. Select the **Legend** and press **Delete**.
   d. Drag the chart area center sizing handle up to increase the height. Adjust the chart area size (*Height* **5"** and *Width* **11.5"**) [*Chart Tools Format* tab, *Size* group].
   e. Move the chart area up slightly so the blank space above and below the chart is even.
   f. Select each of the following chart elements and click **Shape Fill** [*Chart Tools Format* tab, *Shape Styles* group] to change the colors (Figure 2-107):
      • *Chart Area:* **Gold, Accent 4, Lighter 60%**

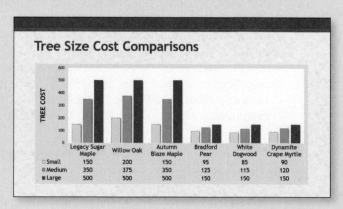

2-107  Completed chart

- *Plot Area:* **White, Background 1**
- *Large Series:* **Green, Accent 6, Darker 50%**
- *Medium Series:* **Green, Accent 6**
- *Small Series:* **Green, Accent 6, Lighter 60%**

    g.  Change text color and sizes.
- Select each text element and change the font color to **Black, Text 1**.
- Increase the font size on the axis title to **20 pt**.
- Increase the table text and axis numbers to **18 pt**.

9.  Create another clustered column chart.

    a.  Select slide 8, "**Growth Potential**." Click **Chart** [*Insert* tab, *Illustrations* group] because this slide does not have a content placeholder.

    b.  Click the **Clustered Column** layout and click **OK** to close the dialog box.

    c.  Replace the spreadsheet data with the following data:

|  | Height |
|---|---|
| Legacy Sugar Maple | 80 |
| Willow Oak | 60 |
| Autumn Blaze Maple | 50 |
| Bradford Pear | 35 |
| White Dogwood | 20 |
| Dynamite Crape Myrtle | 20 |

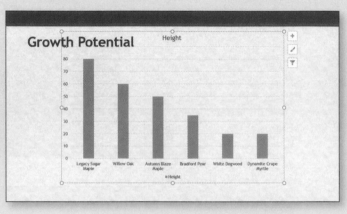

2-108 Column chart as it first appears

    d.  Delete the extra columns in the spreadsheet so the chart columns on the slide can expand in the available space (Figure 2-108).
- Select spreadsheet **Column C** and **Column D** headings and the entire columns are selected.
- Right-click, then select **Delete**. The columns are empty and the remaining columns fill the chart area.
- Verify that data is correctly selected and adjust spreadsheet borders if necessary.

    e.  Close the spreadsheet.
- The chart area is not as wide as in the previous chart because you inserted the chart directly on the slide rather than inserting it through a content placeholder that had different proportions.

10.  Format the chart.

    a.  Delete the chart title and the legend.

    b.  Resize the chart area (*Height* of **5.5"** and *Width* **10"**) [*Chart Tools Format* tab, *Size* group].

    c.  Position the chart evenly on the slide.

    d.  Click the **More** button [*Chart Tools Design* tab, *Chart Styles* group] and change the chart style to **Style 14**.

    e.  Select the columns and change the color to **Green, Accent 6**.

    f.  Change font colors and sizes as follows:
- *Vertical (Value) Axis:* **Black, Text 1, Bold**, and **20 pt**.
- *Horizontal (Category) Axis:* **Black, Text 1, Bold**, and **18 pt**.

11.  Select the *Chart Area* and apply a picture fill.

    a.  From the drop-down list, select **Chart Area** [*Chart Tools Format* tab, *Current Selection* group] and click **Format Selection** to open the *Format Chart Area* pane.

    b.  Select **Picture or texture fill**.

    c.  Click **File** and browse to your student data files. Select **Trees-02** and click **Insert**.

d. Change the *Transparency* percentage to **60%** (by dragging the slider or typing the percentage) to soften the picture's colors since it is behind the columns and text (Figure 2-109).

e. Close the Format Chart Area pane.

12. Click the **Transitions** tab and then select the **Wipe** transition with the **From Left** *Effect Options*. Click **Apply to All** [*Timing* group].

13. Save and close your presentation (Figure 2-110).

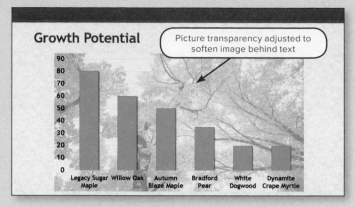

2-109 Chart resized, colors changed, and picture fill

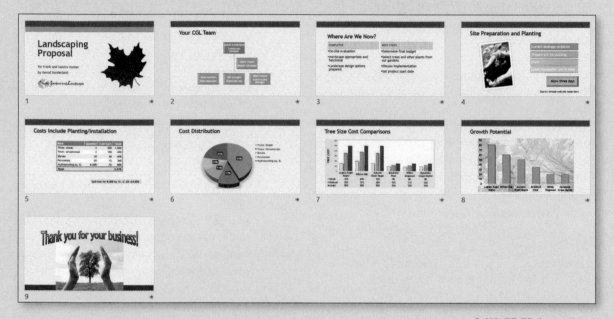

2-110 PP P2-4 completed

# Chapter Summary

**2.1** Work with shapes, select theme colors and standard colors, and apply styles (p. P2-71).

- Change shape size by entering exact height and width sizes or by dragging sizing handles.
- Use *Lock Drawing Mode* to draw the same shape multiple times.
- Use *text boxes* to position text anywhere on a slide.
- PowerPoint's various *style* galleries provide collections of preset effects for shapes, pictures, or other objects.
- Line *Weight* is the line thickness measured in points.
- *Dashes* show lines with a combination of dots and dashes.
- When you apply *Theme Colors* to shapes, the colors change when a different theme is applied.
- *Standard Colors* do not change when a different theme is applied.
- Computer screens use the *RGB model* that displays colors by blending values for *red, green,* and *blue.*
- Highly *saturated* colors are intense and vibrant; colors that are not saturated are muddy and dull.
- *Luminosity* is a measure of lightness that is adjusted by the amount of white or black in the color.
- The *Eyedropper* is used to match any color on your computer screen.

**2.2** Create interesting and eye-catching text effects with *WordArt* styles and text effects (p. P2-80).

- The *WordArt* styles gallery shows a collection of preset text effects.
- The *Transform* effect warps text into different shapes or follows a path.
- You can fill *WordArt* with solid or gradient colors, textures, patterns, or pictures.
- Use the *Line Style* option in the *Format Shape* dialog box to customize line styles.

**2.3** Search for pictures and illustrations, modify picture appearance, and compress picture file size (p. P2-82).

- Use the *Insert Pictures* dialog box to search for online pictures and illustrations.

- The *Picture Styles* gallery shows a collection of preset picture effects.
- To remove a picture style, click the *Reset Picture* button.
- Use *Crop* to trim unwanted areas of a selected picture.
- Increase *Color Saturation* to make picture colors more vibrant; decrease color saturation to make picture colors more muted.
- *Color Tone* changes a picture's cool or warm tones.
- Select *Color* and then *Recolor* to change a picture's color to a monotone color.
- The *Set Transparent Color* feature can make one color in a picture transparent. This feature works well to remove white backgrounds.
- Use *Compress Pictures* to reduce the file size of your presentation.

**2.4** Organize information in a grid format using tables and customize the arrangement of columns and rows (p. P2-91).

- You can insert and delete table *columns* and *rows.*
- *Merge* table cells to join them; *split* table cells to create multiple cells.
- Column width usually varies based on content; row height is usually a consistent size.

**2.5** Format a table by applying styles, colors, and effects (p. P2-96).

- You can apply *WordArt Styles* to table text.
- *Table Styles* provide options for a table's design using theme accent colors.
- *Table Style Options* control how columns and rows are emphasized to feature areas of the table.
- Border lines can separate cells and shading can emphasize cells.
- Horizontal cell alignment options include *Align Left, Center,* or *Align Right;* vertical cell alignment options include *Align Top, Center Vertically,* or *Align Bottom.*

**2.6** Show processes and relationships with *SmartArt* graphics (p. P2-101).

- Use *SmartArt graphics* to create diagrams that illustrate concepts such as processes, cycles, or relationships.

- **SmartArt layouts** are organized by categories.
- Each layout includes information about how you can use it or the meaning it conveys.
- Type text directly in each *SmartArt* shape or type text in the *Text Pane.*
- Change bulleted text to a *SmartArt* graphic by clicking the **Convert to SmartArt Graphic** button.

**2.7** Improve the appearance of *SmartArt* graphics by applying styles, colors, and effects (p. P2-104).

- **SmartArt Styles** provide a gallery of *Effect Options.*
- The **Change Colors** button provides a gallery of color options arranged in categories.
- The **Add Shape** button inserts shapes in relation to the selected shape.
- You can format or individually resize shapes within a *SmartArt* graphic.

**2.8** Create charts that show relationships between data values and emphasize data in different ways based on the chart type and chart elements (p. P2-108).

- Charts in PowerPoint are linked to spreadsheets where data is entered. Changes made to the data will automatically appear in the chart.

- Charts created in Excel can be edited in PowerPoint because they are linked.
- A group of data values is a **data series**.
- *Chart Layouts* are arranged in categories including *Column, Line, Pie, Bar,* and *Area.*
- The **Chart Area** displays the entire chart including all **chart elements**.
- The *Plot Area* provides a background for *Data Markers,* the columns, bars, or slices that represent data.

**2.9** Format a chart by applying preset styles or manually customizing individual chart elements (p. P2-113).

- **Chart Styles** provide a gallery of preset effects for chart elements.
- The **Legend** is a key that identifies each data series by color.
- The *Change Colors* button provides a gallery of colorful or monochromatic colors for chart elements.
- You can customize chart elements individually to enhance their appearance.
- To emphasize a pie slice, you can **explode** it by separating the slice from the rest of the pie chart.

## Check for Understanding

The SIMbook for this text (within your SIMnet account) provides the following resources for concept review:

- Multiple choice questions
- Matching exercises
- Short answer questions

## Guided Project 2-1

Guest satisfaction has always been important to the success of Paradise Lakes Resort (PLR) in Minnesota. The general manager plans to use feedback from social media to identify problems and to guide improvements at the resort. In this project you illustrate a presentation the general manager will use to explain these concepts to employees at PLR.
[Student Learning Outcomes 2.1, 2.2, 2.3, 2.6, 2.7]

File Needed: **SocialMedia-02.pptx** *(Student data files are available in the* Library *of your SIMnet account.)*
Completed Project File Name: *[your initials] **PowerPoint 2-1.pptx***

### Skills Covered in This Project

- Apply a picture style.
- Adjust size dimensions.
- Apply text effects.
- Insert a text box.
- Create a *SmartArt* graphic.
- Apply a *SmartArt* style and effects.

1. Open the presentation **SocialMedia-02**. This design theme shows slide titles at the bottom of all slides except the title slide.

2. Save the presentation as [your initials] PowerPoint 2-1.

3. Resize a picture and apply a style.
   a. Select the lake picture on slide 1.
   b. Change the picture *Width* to **6"** [*Picture Tools Format* tab, *Size* group]. The *Height* automatically adjusts.
   c. Apply the **Metal Oval** picture style [*Picture Tools Format* tab, *Picture Styles* group].
   d. Position the picture on the left (Figure 2-111).

2-111 Title slide

4. Adjust the title text to complement the wood decking shown in the picture.
   a. Select the title text "Improving Guest Satisfaction" on slide 1 and increase the font size to **60 pt**.
   b. Adjust the placeholder so it fits the text and move it down slightly.
   c. Select the title text and click the **Text Fill** button [*Drawing Tools Format* tab, *WordArt Styles* group], select **Texture**, and select **Medium Wood**.
   d. With the title text selected, click the **Text Effects** button, select **Shadow**, and select **Shadow Options**. The *Format Shape* pane opens. Change the following settings:
   *Transparency:* **20%**
   *Blur:* **5 pt**.
   *Angle:* **50°**
   *Distance:* **5 pt**.
   f. Close the *Format Shape* pane.

5. Insert a new slide with a *Title and Content* layout after slide 1.

6. Add text and a shape.
   a. Display slide 2 and type the slide title **Why Social Media?** In this theme, the title placeholder is at the bottom of the slide.
   b. Type the following bulleted text:

   Revenue
   Market Share
   Guest Satisfaction
   Guest Loyalty

   c. Resize the bulleted list placeholder so it fits the text and move the text to the right (Figure 2-112).
   d. Click the **Shapes** button [*Insert* tab, *Illustrations* group] to open the gallery. Select the **Up Arrow** shape (*Block Arrow* category).
   e. Draw an arrow (*Height* **3.5"** and *Width* **2.5"**). Then position the arrow to the left of the text.
   f. With the arrow selected, click the **More** button [*Drawing Tools Format* tab, *Shape Styles* group] and apply the **Intense Effect, Orange, Accent 1**.

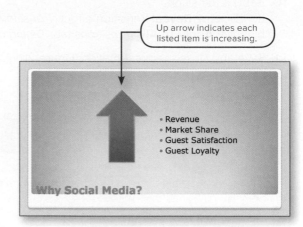

2-112 Slide 3 with a shape

7. Insert a new slide with a *Blank* layout after slide 4.

8. Create a *SmartArt* graphic and insert an additional shape on slide 5.
   a. Click the **Insert** tab.
   b. Click the **SmartArt** button and select the **Cycle** type.
   c. Select the **Continuous Cycle** layout and click **OK**.
   d. Add the following text to each shape starting with the top shape and continuing in a clockwise direction around the circle:

   More Rentals
   Rentals
   Social Media Comments
   Improvements
   Better Social Media Comments

   e. Select the "**Better Social Media Comments**" shape, click the **Add Shape** drop-down arrow [*SmartArt Tools Design* tab, *Create Graphic* group] and select **Add Shape After**.
   f. Type **Higher Ratings** in the new shape.
   g. Click the **Intense Effect** style [*SmartArt Tools Design* tab, *SmartArt Styles* group].
   h. Select all shapes with text by pressing **Ctrl** while you click each one. Change the font size to **20 pt**. and apply **bold** [*Home* tab, *Font* group].
   i. With all the shapes selected, resize the shapes horizontally (*Width* **2.75"**) so the word "Improvements" fits on one line (Figure 2-113).

9. Insert a text box.
   a. Click the **Text Box** button [*Insert* tab, *Text* group] and click inside the cycle layout.
   b. Type the following text and resize the text box so that the text wraps on two lines as shown in Figure 2-113:

   With the help of NewMediaMarketing.com

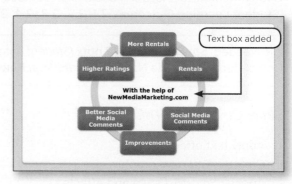

2-113 Slide 4 with *SmartArt* graphic and effects added

c. Change the font size to **20 pt.**, apply **bold**, and center the text [*Home* tab, *Font* group].

d. Adjust the text box size, if necessary, and center it in the middle of the cycle layout as shown in Figure 2-113.

10. Apply a transition.

a. Click the **Reveal** transition effect [*Transitions* tab, *Transition to This Slide* group].

b. Click **Apply To All** [*Transitions* tab, *Timing* group].

11. Save and close the presentation (Figure 2-114).

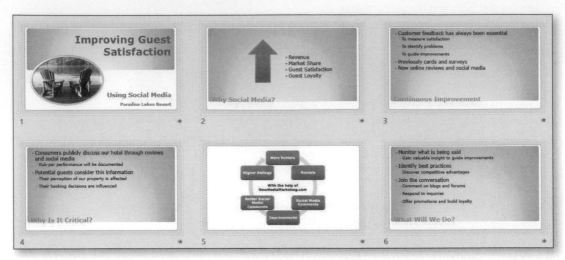

2-114 PowerPoint 2-1 completed

# Guided Project 2-2

For this project, you prepare a presentation with key points essential to maintain a healthy lifestyle and show examples of weight loss calorie requirements for men and women at different ages. The doctors at Courtyard Medical Plaza will use this presentation to encourage clients to be more active.
[**Student Learning Outcomes 2.1, 2.2, 2.3, 2.4, 2.5, 2.6, 2.7**]

File Needed: ***StayingActive-02.pptx*** (*Student data files are available in the* Library *of your SIMnet account.*)
Completed Project File Name: ***[your initials] PowerPoint 2-2.pptx***

### Skills Covered in This Project

- Apply text effects.
- Create a *SmartArt* graphic.
- Apply a *SmartArt* style and effects.
- Insert an online picture.
- Crop a picture.
- Apply a picture style.
- Adjust size dimensions.
- Insert a text box.
- Insert and format a table.

1. Open the presentation ***StayingActive-02***.

2. Save the presentation as [your initials] PowerPoint 2-2.

3. Format the presentation title.
   a. Select the title placeholder on slide 1.
   b. Click the **Text Effects** button [*Drawing Tools Format* tab, *WordArt Styles* group], click **Transform**, and select **Square** (*Square* is the first style under *Warp*). The text fills the title placeholder.
   c. Click the **Bring Forward** drop-down arrow [*Drawing Tools Format* tab, *Arrange* group], and select **Bring to Front** so the green triangle is behind the text.
   d. Click the **Text Fill** button [*Drawing Tools Format* tab, *WordArt Styles* group], select **Texture**, and click **More Textures** to open the *Format Shape* pane.
   e. Select **Pattern fill** and then choose the **Large checker board** pattern.
   f. Change the *Foreground Color* to **Aqua, Accent 1, Lighter 40%** and the *Background Color* to **White, Text 1**.
   g. Click **Text Fill** to close those options on the *Format Shape* pane. Click **Text Outline** to open outline options. Select **Solid line** and change the color to **Black, Background 1**.
   h. Click the **Text Effects** icon at the top of the pane. Select **Glow**.
   i. Change the *Color* to **Green, Accent 2, Lighter 60%** and the *Transparency* to **20%**. Verify the *Size* is **10 pt**. (Figure 2-115).
   j. Close the *Format Shape* pane.

2-115  Text Effects for presentation title

4. Insert a *SmartArt* graphic, apply a style, and change colors using the *SmartArt Tools Design* tab.
   a. Display slide 2 and click the **SmartArt** icon on the content placeholder to open the *Choose a SmartArt Graphic* dialog box.
   b. Select the **Hierarchy** type and the **Horizontal Hierarchy** layout. Click **OK** to close the dialog box and insert the SmartArt graphic.
   c. Delete the three shapes on the right.
   d. Click the **Text Pane** button on the left of the *SmartArt* frame, if necessary, to open the *Text Pane*.
   e. Type **Keep Moving** after the first bullet. Type the following items after the indented bullets:

   Moderate Intensity Activity
   Count Steps (Press **Enter** to add another bullet.)
   Combine Aerobic and Strengthening

   f. Click the *Text Pane* **Close** button.
   g. Select the **Subtle Effect** *SmartArt* style [*SmartArt Tools Design* tab, *SmartArt Styles* group].
   h. Click the **Change Colors** button [*SmartArt Tools Design* tab, *SmartArt Styles* group] and select **Colorful Range, Accent Colors 4 to 5** (Figure 2-116).

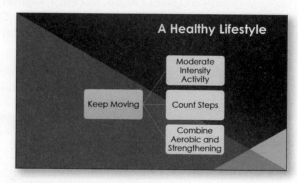

2-116  *SmartArt* graphic with style and colors changed

5. Search for a picture and apply a picture style.
   a. Display slide 3. Click the **Online Pictures** button [*Insert* tab, *Images* group] to open *the Insert Pictures* dialog box.
   b. Search for an online picture using the search word gardening.
   c. On the search results dialog box, click the list arrow by the *Search* button to select **All Images**. Select an appropriate picture and click **Insert**.
   d. Select the **Rotated White** picture style [*Picture Tools Format* tab, *Picture Styles* group].
   e. Resize the picture as needed so it fits on the right of the slide.

6. Crop a picture and apply a picture style.
   a. Display slide 5 and select the picture. Click the **Crop** button [*Picture Tools Format* tab, *Size* group] and crop the picture to focus only on the family. Click **Crop** again to accept your change.
   b. Select the **Rotated White** picture style [*Picture Tools Format* tab, *Picture Styles* group] to match the other picture.
   c. Move the picture to the right of the slide.

7. Insert a new slide after slide 6 with a *Title and Content* layout.

8. Add text.
   a. On slide 7, type the title text **Calorie Examples**.
   b. Click the **Text Box** button [*Insert* tab, *Text* group], click below the title, and type **Gaining 5 pounds a year**.
   c. Apply **Bold** and change the font size to **20 pt**. [*Home* tab, *Font* group].
   d. Resize the text box as needed. Right-align the text box and the slide title.

9. Insert a table, add text, and modify formatting.

2-117 Table with formatting changes

   a. Click the **Table** icon on the content placeholder on slide 7.
   b. Enter **6** columns and **5** rows on the *Insert Table* dialog box. Click **OK** to close the dialog box.
   c. Type the text shown in Figure 2-117.
   d. Select all cells and change the font size to **20 pt**. [*Home* tab, *Font* group]. Change to **Center** alignment [*Table Tools Layout* tab, *Alignment* group].
   e. Adjust column width by double-clicking the border line between columns. Deselect the table, if necessary, so your pointer changes to a splitter to adjust the right border of the last column so the text fits on one line. When you stop dragging, the table is selected again.
   f. Change the *Pen Color* to **Black, Background 1** and verify the *Pen Weight* is **1 pt**. [*Table Tools Design* tab, *Draw Borders* group].
   g. Click the **Borders** button, and select **All Borders** [*Table Tools Design* tab, *Table Styles* group].
   h. Select the second and third rows. Click the **Shading** button [*Table Tools Design* tab, *Table Styles* group] and select **Aqua, Accent 1, Lighter 80%**.
   i. Select the fourth and fifth rows. Click the **Shading** button [*Table Tools Design* tab, *Table Styles* group] and select **Aqua, Accent 1, Lighter 60%**.
   j. Center the table on the slide.

10. Duplicate the table and edit the text in the second table.
    a. Select the table on slide 7 and press **Ctrl+D** to duplicate it.
    b. Position the second table centered near the bottom of the slide.
    c. Edit the table content to match the text shown in Figure 2-118.

2-118 Table with text edits

11. Insert and format a shape to identify table contents on slide 7.
    a. Click the **Shapes** button [*Insert* tab, *Illustrations* group] and select the **Oval**. Draw an oval shape and adjust its size (*Height* **0.9"** and *Width* **2"**) [*Drawing Tools Format* tab, *Size* group].
    b. Click the **Shape Fill** button [*Drawing Tools Format* tab, *Shape Styles* group] and change the color to **Gold, Accent 5, Lighter 40%**.
    c. Click the **Shape Outline** button [*Drawing Tools Format* tab, *Shape Styles* group] and change the color to **Green, Accent 2**. Repeat to change the *Weight* to **3 pt**.

d. Type the word Female. Change the font color to **Black, Background 1** and apply **Bold**.

e. Click the **Edit Shape** button [*Drawing Tools Format* tab, *Insert Shapes* group] and select **Change Shape**. Select **Explosion 1** in the *Stars and Banners* category.

f. Position this shape at the left corner of the bottom table (Figure 2-119).

12. Duplicate and edit a shape.

   a. Select the "**Female**" shape and press **Ctrl+D** to duplicate it.

   b. Position the second shape at the left corner of the top table.

   c. Change the text to Male.

13. Format the table:

   a. Display slide 8 and select the table. If necessary, change the *Pen Color* to **Black, Background 1** and the *Pen Weight* to **1 pt**. [*Table Tools Design* tab, *Draw Borders* group].

   b. Click **Borders** [*Table Tools Design* tab, *Table Styles* group] and select **All Borders**.

   c. Change the font size for all text to **20 pt**.

   d. Select all cells and click the **Center Vertically** button [*Table Tools Layout* tab, *Alignment* group].

   e. Change the table size (*Height* **4.5"** and *Width* **9"**) and click the **Center** button [*Table Tools Layout* tab, *Alignment* group] to center it horizontally on the slide.

14. Apply a transition.

   a. Click the **Cube** transition effect [*Transitions* tab, *Transition to This Slide* group].

   b. Click **Apply To All** [*Transitions* tab, *Timing* group].

15. Save and close the presentation (Figure 2-120).

### Calorie Examples
Gaining 5 pounds a year

Male

| Age | Height | Weight | Maintain | Fat Loss | Extreme Fat Loss |
|-----|--------|--------|----------|----------|------------------|
| 20 | 5 ft 10 in | 200 | 2,647 | 2,118 | 1,600 |
| 25 | 5 ft 10 in | 225 | 2,769 | 2,215 | 1,800 |
| 30 | 6 ft 2 in | 240 | 2,916 | 2,333 | 1,920 |
| 35 | 6 ft 2 in | 265 | 3,038 | 2,430 | 2,120 |

Female

| Age | Height | Weight | Maintain | Fat Loss | Extreme Fat Loss |
|-----|--------|--------|----------|----------|------------------|
| 20 | 5 ft 7 in | 150 | 2,041 | 1,633 | 1,225 |
| 25 | 5 ft 7 in | 175 | 2,163 | 1,730 | 1,400 |
| 30 | 5 ft 9 in | 180 | 2,204 | 1,763 | 1,440 |
| 35 | 5 ft 9 in | 205 | 2,325 | 1,860 | 1,640 |

2-119  Slide 7 completed tables

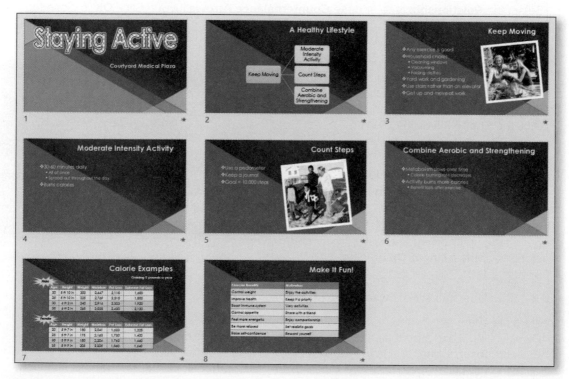

2-120  PowerPoint 2-2 completed

# Guided Project 2-3

Solution Seekers, Inc., has been asked to develop a presentation for a meeting of personnel managers about salary trends for information technology workers. For this project, you modify tables and prepare charts showing average salaries and salaries for selected jobs.
**[Student Learning Outcomes 2.1, 2.2, 2.3, 2.5, 2.6, 2.7, 2.8]**

File Needed: ***InfoTechSalaries-02.pptx*** (*Student data files are available in the* Library *of your SIMnet account.)*
Completed Project File Name: ***[your initials] PowerPoint 2-3.pptx***

### Skills Covered in This Project

- Convert text to a *SmartArt* graphic.
- Apply a *SmartArt* style and effects.
- Create a pie chart.
- Format a table.
- Create a column chart.

- Apply chart styles.
- Format chart elements.
- Insert *WordArt* and apply effects.
- Apply a picture style.
- Insert and align text boxes.

1. Open the presentation ***InfoTechSalaries-02***.

2. Save the presentation as [your initials] PowerPoint 2-3.

3. Convert bulleted text to a *SmartArt* graphic and modify the style and colors.
   a. Display slide 2. Select the bulleted text and click the **Convert to SmartArt** button [*Home* tab, *Paragraph* group].
   b. Select **More SmartArt Graphics** to open the *Choose a SmartArt Graphic* dialog box.
   c. Select the **Relationship** type and the **Counterbalance Arrows** layout. Click **OK** to close the dialog box.
   d. Apply the **Cartoon** style [*SmartArt Tools Design* tab, *SmartArt Styles* group].
   e. Select the down arrow shape pointing to "Fewer Layoffs" and click the **Shape Fill** drop-down arrow [*SmartArt Tools Format* tab, *Shape Styles* group].
   f. Select **Gradient** and under *Dark Variations,* click **Linear Down** to emphasize the downward movement.
   g. Select the up arrow and repeat step f to apply a **Linear Up** gradient (Figure 2-121).

2-121 Slide 2 *SmartArt* graphic with color changes

4. Insert a new slide after slide 2 with a *Title and Content* layout.

5. Create a pie chart.
   a. Display slide 3 and type the slide title **Employee Salary Satisfaction**.
   b. Click the **Insert Chart** icon in the content placeholder.
   c. Click the **Pie** chart type. Then select the **3-D Pie**. Click **OK** to close the dialog box and insert the chart.

d. Replace the spreadsheet data with the data shown in Figure 2-122. Close the spreadsheet.

6. Modify a pie chart.
   a. Drag the chart title "**Satisfaction%**," to the top left of the chart area. Increase the font size to **24 pt**. [*Home* tab, *Font* group].
   b. Click the **Chart Elements** button on the right side of the slide and select **Legend**. Select **Right**.
   c. Increase the font size to **20 pt**. [*Home* tab, *Font* group] and drag the legend to the bottom right of the chart area.
   d. Click the **Chart Elements** button again and select **Data Labels**. Select **Inside End**.
   e. Click the **Chart Elements** list box arrow [*Chart Tools Format* tab, *Current Selection* group] and select **Series "Satisfaction %" Data Labels**. Increase the font size to **24 pt**. and apply **Bold** [*Home* tab, *Font* group] (Figure 2-123).

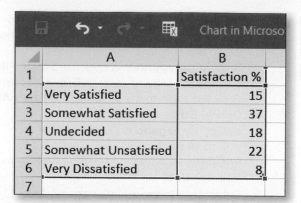

2-122 Spreadsheet linked to a chart

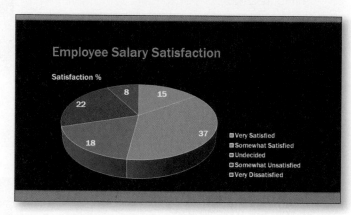

2-123 Slide 3 completed pie chart

7. Modify table formatting.
   a. Display slide 4 and select the table. Increase the font size to **20 pt**. [*Home* tab, *Font* group].
   b. Select **Header Row** and **Banded Rows** [*Table Tools Design* tab, *Table Style Options* group].
   c. Apply the **Themed Style 1, Accent 2** style [*Table Tools Design* tab, *Table Styles* group].
   d. Increase the table size (*Height* **4"**) [*Table Tools Layout* tab, *Table Size* group].
   e. Click the **Center Vertically** button [*Table Tools Layout* tab, *Alignment* group].
   f. Select columns 2–5 and click **Align Right** [*Table Tools Layout* tab, *Alignment* group].

8. After slide 4, insert a new slide with a *Title and Content* layout.

9. Create a column chart.
   a. Select slide 5 and type the slide title Salary Change, Selected Jobs.
   b. Click the **Insert Chart** button on the content placeholder.
   c. Select the **Clustered Column** chart and click **OK**.
   d. Replace the spreadsheet data with the data shown in Figure 2-124. Select **Column D**, right-click, and select **Delete**. By removing the blank column, the chart displays correctly with no blank space. Close the spreadsheet.

10. Modify a column chart.
    a. Delete the "**Chart Title**" placeholder.
    b. Click the **Chart Elements** button on the right side of the chart, select **Legend**, and then click **More Options** to open the *Format Legend* pane.

2-124 Spreadsheet linked to a chart

c. Click the **Legend Options** heading, if necessary, to open the list of options. Select **Top Right** and deselect **Show the legend without overlapping the chart**.

d. Close the *Format Chart Area* pane.

e. Select the **Legend** and click the **Shape Fill** button [*Chart Tools Format* tab, *Shape Styles* group]. Change the legend color to **Brown, Accent 2, Darker 50%**.

f. Click the chart frame to select the **Chart Area** and change the **Shape Fill** color to **Teal, Accent 1, Darker 50%**.

g. Select the **Legend** and increase the font size to **18 pt**. [*Home* tab, *Font* group]. Repeat to increase the **Vertical (Value) Axis** font size to **18 pt**.

h. Select the **Horizontal (Category) Axis** and increase the font size to **20 pt**. (Figure 2-125).

11. Select the picture on slide 6 and apply the **Moderate Frame, Black** picture style [*Picture Tools Format* tab, *Picture Styles* group].

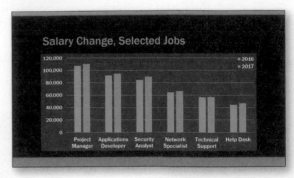

2-125  Slide 5 completed clustered column chart

12. Insert *WordArt* text on slide 6.

a. Click the **WordArt** button [*Insert* tab, *Text* group] and select the **Fill – White, Text 1, Outline – Background 1, Hard Shadow – Accent 1** style.

b. Type Employees Are Valuable in the *WordArt* placeholder and move this text above the picture.

c. With the *WordArt* placeholder selected, click the **Text Effects** button [*Drawing Tools Format* tab, *WordArt Styles* group], select **Shadow**, and click **Offset Diagonal Bottom Right**.

d. Click the **Text Outline** button [*Drawing Tools Format* tab, *WordArt Styles* group] and select **Black, Background 2**.

e. Deselect the *WordArt* text (Figure 2-126).

2-126  Slide 6 picture style, text effects, and text boxes

13. Insert text boxes on slide 6 for salary numbers.

a. Click the **Text Box** button [*Insert* tab, *Text* group], click below the picture, and type $75,270. Change the font color to **Black, Background 2**, increase the font size to **20 pt.**, and apply **Bold**.

b. Position this salary below the first person on the left in the picture.

c. With the salary text box selected, press **Ctrl+D** and position the duplicated text box below the second person in the picture. Repeat for the remaining two people in the picture.

d. Edit the text boxes to change the three duplicated salaries to $64,644, $55,340, and $49,982.

e. Select all of the salary text boxes and click the **Arrange** button [*Home* tab, *Drawing* group]. Select **Align** and click **Align Selected Objects** if necessary. Repeat to click **Align Bottom** (see Figure 2-126).

14. Apply transitions.
    a. Click the **Blinds** transition effect [*Transitions* tab, *Transition to This Slide* group].
    b. Click **Apply To All** [*Transitions* tab, *Timing* group].
    c. Apply the **Zoom** transition to slide 6.
15. Save and close the presentation (Figure 2-127).

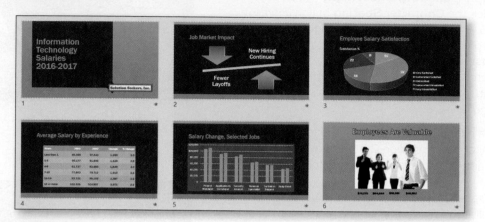

# Independent Project 2-4

At Pool & Spa Oasis, sales associates must educate new spa owners about keeping spa water safe with proper maintenance. For this project, you prepare a presentation that emphasizes the routine to follow, explains pH level numbers, and lists available products that are typically used to balance water.
[**Student Learning Outcomes 2.1, 2.2, 2.3, 2.4, 2.5, 2.6, 2.7**]

File Needed: ***Balancing-02.pptx*** (*Student data files are available in the* Library *of your SIMnet account.*)
Completed Project File Name: *[your initials]* **PowerPoint 2-4.pptx**

## Skills Covered in This Project

- Insert *WordArt* and apply effects.
- Adjust size dimensions.
- Insert an online picture.
- Apply a picture style.

- Create a *SmartArt* graphic.
- Apply a *SmartArt* style and effects.
- Insert and format a table.
- Insert a text box.
- Change solid and gradient colors.

1. Open the presentation ***Balancing-02***.
2. Save the presentation as [your initials] PowerPoint 2-4.

3. Change the title text arrangement.
   a. Display slide 1. Delete the title text "**Balancing Act**," but leave the word "**The**" as shown.
   b. Insert *WordArt* with the style **Fill – White, Outline – Accent 1, Glow – Accent 1**.
   c. Type Balancing Act.
   d. Apply a **Shadow, Offset Right** *Text Effect*.
   e. Click the **Character Spacing** button [*Home* tab, *Font* group] and choose **Tight**.
   f. Apply the *Transform* text effect of **Cascade Up**.
   g. Increase the *WordArt* size (*Height* **3"** and *Width* **9"**) and position it as shown in Figure 2-128.

2-128 Slide 1 with *WordArt*

4. Insert a picture and adjust text spacing. The bulleted list placeholder on slide 2 has a gradient fill color so it cannot be resized without distorting the slide.
   a. Display slide 2. On the first indented line in the bulleted list, place your insertion point in front of the word "correct." Press **Shift+Enter** to insert a line break so the remaining text go to the next line without starting a new paragraph. Repeat to split the next line twice: before "microorganisms" and "Bromine."
   b. Search for an online picture using the words **hot tub** and insert a picture similar to the one shown in Figure 2-129.
   c. Resize the picture as needed to fit on the right side of the slide.
   d. Apply the **Bevel Rectangle** picture style.
   e. Position the picture as shown.

2-129 Slide 2 with inserted picture and picture style

5. Insert a *SmartArt* graphic, add text, and change formatting.
   a. Display slide 4. Insert a *SmartArt* graphic from the *Process* category with the **Continuous Block Process** layout.
   b. Type Test Water, Add Necessary Products, and Enjoy! in the three shapes.
   c. Resize the *SmartArt* graphic (*Height* **5"** and *Width* **9.5"**).
   d. Apply the **Polished** *SmartArt* style.
   e. Select the **arrow** and apply **Gradient** colors. Select **More Gradient** to open the *Format Shape* pane.
   f. Select a *Preset gradient* of **Light Gradient – Accent 2**. The *Type* is **Linear** and change the *Direction* to **Linear Left**.
   g. Modify the gradient stops:
      • *First stop:* Color **Light Blue, Background 2**; Position **0%**
      • *Second stop:* Color **Light Turquoise, Accent 2, Lighter 80%**; Position **40%**; Brightness **80%**
      • *Third stop:* Remove
      • *Fourth stop:* Color **Turquoise, Accent 2, Lighter 40%**; Position **100%**; Brightness **40%**

h. Close the *Format Shape* pane.
i. Apply **Bold** to all *SmartArt* text.
j. Position the *SmartArt* graphic as shown in Figure 2-130.

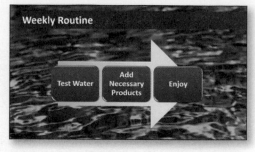

2-130 Slide 4 *SmartArt* graphic with style and color changes

6. Insert a table, add text, and change formatting.
   a. Display slide 5. Insert a table with **3** columns and **4** rows.
   b. Select **Header Row** and **Banded Rows**.
   c. Type the following text:

   | Level | Numbers | Results |
   |-------|---------|---------|
   | High | 8.0 | Alkaline, Scale |
   | Good | 7.2 – 7.6 | Ideal pH Range |
   | Low | 6.0 | Acidic, Corrosion |

   d. Change the font size to **20 pt**. for all table text.
   e. Apply the **Themed Style 1, Accent 1** table style.
   f. Select each column and adjust the *Cell Width* as follows: left column is **1.5"**, middle column is **2.8"**, and right column is **2.8"**.
   g. Change the alignment on the middle column to **Center**.
   h. Center the table on the slide.

7. Insert a text box.
   a. Insert a text box below the table on slide 5. Type Drain and replace spa water every 60-90 days.
   b. Change the font size to **20 pt**.
   c. Change the shape fill to **Turquoise, Accent 2, Lighter 80%**.
   d. Resize the text box, if necessary, so the text fits on one line. Position it below the table aligned with the right of the table.

8. Copy and format a table.
   a. Select the table on slide 5 and copy it.
   b. Display slide 6 and paste the table.
   c. Delete the middle column and size the table so it is **9"** wide.
   d. Delete the table text and add three rows.
   e. Type the following text:

   | Products | Purpose |
   |----------|---------|
   | Sanitizer | Type needed depends on sanitizer system |
   | Test Strips | Measures chemical levels |
   | Shock Treatment | Breaks down organic or unfiltered material |
   | Total Alkalinity | Increases or decreases to balance pH levels |
   | Calcium Increaser | Balances dissolved calcium |
   | Stain and Scale Prevention | Removes metallic impurities |

   f. Adjust the column width as needed to avoid word wrapping.
   g. Center the table on the slide.

9. Apply the **Ripple** transition with the **From Top-Left** effect option to all slides.

10. Save and close the presentation (Figure 2-131).

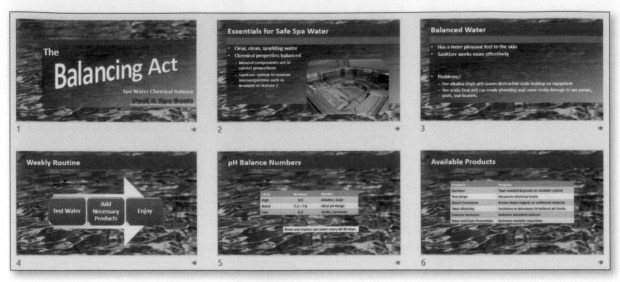

2-131 PowerPoint 2-4 completed

# Independent Project 2-5

Prospective home buyers need to understand mortgage requirements and how to prepare to apply for a mortgage. Angie O'Connor at Placer Hills Real Estate wants to use a presentation on her notebook computer to help guide her discussions about these concepts with clients. For this project, you develop the presentation.
[**Student Learning Outcomes 2.1, 2.3, 2.4, 2.5, 2.6, 2.7, 2.8**]

Files Needed: ***PreparetoBuy-02.pptx*** and ***PlacerHillsSold-02.jpg*** (*Student data files are available in the Library of your SIMnet account.*)
Completed Project File Name: *[your initials] PowerPoint 2-5.pptx*

*Skills Covered in This Project*

- Insert a picture.
- Crop a picture.
- Apply a picture style.
- Adjust size dimensions.
- Insert a chart and edit data.
- Apply chart styles.
- Format chart elements.
- Insert text boxes.
- Insert and format a table.
- Convert text to a *SmartArt* graphic.
- Apply a *SmartArt* style and effects.

1. Open the presentation ***PreparetoBuy-02***.

2. Save the presentation as [your initials] PowerPoint 2-5.

3. Insert and modify a picture.
   a. On slide 1, insert the **PlacerHillsSold-02** picture from your student data files.
   b. Crop the picture on the left and right as shown in Figure 2-132.
   c. Resize the picture (*Height* **5.5"** and the *Width* automatically adjusts).
   d. Apply the **Rounded Diagonal Corner, White** picture style.
   e. Position the picture on the right side of the slide as shown in Figure 2-132.

2-132 Slide 1 with inserted picture and picture style

4. Insert a chart showing how fixed mortgage rates have changed over time.
   a. Display slide 4. Click the **Insert Chart** button on the content placeholder.
   b. Select the **Line** chart type and then select the **Line with Markers** chart layout. Click **OK**.
   c. Replace the spreadsheet data with the data shown in Figure 2-133.
      • Be sure the selection area includes row 10 to avoid error messages.
      • Delete **Column D** so the corresponding chart area is correct with no blank space.
      • Close the spreadsheet.

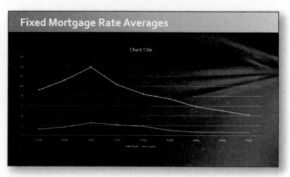

|    | A    | B     | C      |
|----|------|-------|--------|
| 1  |      | Rate  | Points |
| 2  | 1974 | 9.19  | 1.2    |
| 3  | 1979 | 11.2  | 1.6    |
| 4  | 1984 | 13.88 | 2.5    |
| 5  | 1989 | 10.32 | 2.1    |
| 6  | 1994 | 8.38  | 1.8    |
| 7  | 1999 | 7.44  | 1      |
| 8  | 2004 | 5.84  | 0.7    |
| 9  | 2009 | 5.04  | 0.7    |
| 10 | 2014 | 4.17  | 0.6    |
| 11 |      |       |        |

2-133 Spreadsheet linked to a chart

5. Examine the line chart as it first appears (Figure 2-134).
   • It is accurate, but the data series lines are too thin and data markers too small.
   • The following changes (steps 6–13) will make the chart easier to interpret.

6. Delete the chart title.

7. Change the chart area *Shape Fill* to **Brown, Background 2**.

8. Format the line and markers on the "Rate" series.
   a. Select the "Rate" line and right-click. Select **Format Data Series** to open the *Format Data Series* pane (Figure 2-135).
   b. Click the **Fill & Line** icon at the top of the pane.
   c. Click **Line** options at the top of the pane below the icons and change the *Width* to **3 pt**.
   d. Click **Marker** options below the icons and select the following:
      • *Marker Options:* **Built-in**; *Type:* **Square**, and *Size:* **15** (Figure 2-136)
      • *Fill:* **Solid fill**; *Color:* **Orange, Accent 2**

9. Format the line and markers on the "Points" series.
   a. Select the "Points" line. Click **Line** options and select the following:
      • *Line:* **Solid line**; *Color:* **Orange, Accent 4**
      • *Width:* **3 pt**.

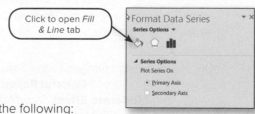

Click to open *Fill & Line* tab

2-135 *Format Data Series* pane

2-134 Line chart as it first appears

b. Select **Marker** options and select the following:
- Marker Options: **Built-in**; Type: **Diamond**; Size: **20**
- Marker Fill: **Solid fill**; Color: **Red, Accent 5**

10. Close the *Format Data Series* pane.

11. Select the *Horizontal (Category) axis* and increase the font size to **16 pt**. and apply **bold**. Repeat for the *Vertical (Value) axis*.

12. Select the **Chart Area**, change the *Width* to **11"**, and center the chart horizontally.

13. Move the chart up slightly to make room for a source notation at the bottom of the slide.
    a. Insert a text box and type the following:

    Information based on Freddie Mac survey data
    http://www.freddiemac.com/pmms/pmms30.htm

    b. Position the text box as displayed in Figure 2-137.

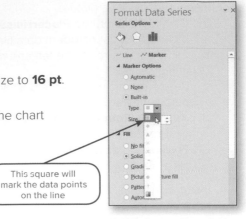

This square will mark the data points on the line

2-136 *Format Data Series* pane with *Marker* options

14. Insert and format a table:
    a. Display slide 5 and insert a table with **5** columns and **3** rows.
    b. Type the text shown in Figure 2-138.
    c. Select all text and change the font size to **24 pt**. Adjust column width as needed.
    d. Select columns **2–5** and change to **Center** alignment.
    e. Change to **Bottom** alignment in the first row and change the row *Shading* to **Gold, Accent 1, Darker 25%**.
    f. Align the table in the horizontal and vertical center on the slide.

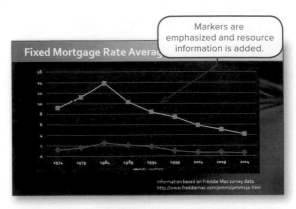

Markers are emphasized and resource information is added.

2-137 Slide 4 completed line chart

15. Insert a text box above the table on the left.
    a. Type $250,000.
    b. Change the font to **40 pt**. and **bold**.

16. Insert a text box below the table on the right.
    a. Type the following text on three lines:

    Lender rates are influenced by credit scores.
    Plan for a 20% down payment to avoid cost of points.
    Add taxes and insurance premiums.

| Loan Product | Rate | Number of Payments | Monthly Payments | Total Paid |
|---|---|---|---|---|
| 15 Year Fixed | 3.11% | 180 | $1,739.71 | $313,147.80 |
| 30 Year Fixed | 3.88% | 360 | $1,176.31 | $423,471.60 |

2-138 Table for slide 5

17. Convert a list to a *SmartArt* graphic.
    a. Display slide 6. Select the bulleted text and convert it to a *SmartArt* graphic with the **Vertical Curved List** layout.
    b. Resize the *SmartArt* frame on the right so it fits the longest line of text.

18. Apply the following changes to the *SmartArt* graphic:
    a. Change the colors to **Colorful Range, Accent Colors 2 to 3**.
    b. Apply the **Moderate Effect** *SmartArt* style.
    c. Select all of the white circles and change the *Shape Fill* to **Red, Accent 5, Darker 25%** and apply the *Bevel* effect of **Cool Slant**.
    d. Center the *SmartArt* graphic horizontally on the slide (Figure 2-139).

2-139 Slide 6 *SmartArt* graphic with style and effects changed

19. Apply the **Shape** transition with the **Out** effect option to all slides.

20. Save and close the presentation (Figure 2-140).

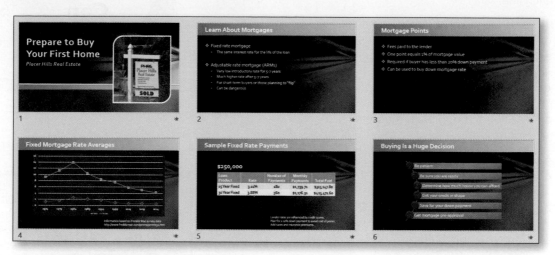

2-140 PowerPoint 2-5 completed

# Independent Project 2-6

Kathy Sung, Director of Services at Life's Animal Shelter (LAS), will talk to a luncheon group of business-people. For this project, you develop the presentation she will use to explain the needs of LAS and describe ways people can contribute through donations or by volunteering their time.
[**Student Learning Outcomes 2.1, 2.2, 2.3, 2.4, 2.5, 2.6, 2.7**]

Files Needed: ***YouCanHelp-02.pptx, CountryStroll-02.jpg, DayCare-02.jpg, Food-02.jpg, Groom-02.jpg,*** and ***RoyalTreatment-02.jpg*** (*Student data files are available in the* Library *of your SIMnet account.*)
Completed Project File Name: ***[your initials] PowerPoint 2-6.pptx***

## Skills Covered in This Project

- Apply text effects.
- Apply a picture style.
- Set transparent color.
- Recolor a picture.
- Adjust size dimensions.
- Insert a text box.
- Insert and format a table.
- Convert text to a *SmartArt* graphic.
- Create a *SmartArt* graphic with pictures.
- Apply a *SmartArt* style and effects.

1. Open the presentation ***YouCanHelp-02***.

2. Save the presentation as [your initials] PowerPoint 2-6.

3. Display slide 1. Change the title *Text Fill* color to **Dark Red, Accent 1, Darker 25%**. Apply the *Bevel* text effect of **Angle**.

4. Change the font size to **80 pt**. and resize the placeholder on the right so one word is on each line.

5. Resize a picture and remove a background color.
   a. Select the dog picture on slide 1.
   b. Increase the picture size (*Height* **5.9"** and *Width* **4.7"**).
   c. Use *Set Transparent Color* to remove the white area in the picture.
   d. Position the dog picture as shown in Figure 2-141.

2-141 Slide 1 with picture added, white background removed

6. Apply a picture style.
   a. Display slide 2 and increase the picture size (*Height* **5.84"** and *Width* **8"**).
   b. Apply the **Moderate Frame, Black** picture style.
   c. Center the picture horizontally and position it near the top of the slide.

7. Insert a text box and apply formatting:
   a. Insert a text box below the picture and type the following text:
      Our operating funds come through donations and pet adoption fees.
   b. Change the *Font Color* to **White, Background 1** and *Font Size* to **20 pt**.
   c. Resize the text box so the text wraps on two lines as shown in Figure 2-142.
   d. Change the *Shape Outline* to **White, Background 1** and the *Weight* to **3 pt**.
   e. Change the *Shape Fill* to **Black, Text 1**.
   f. Center the text box horizontally below the picture.

2-142 Slide 2 with picture and text box inserted

8. Copy and paste a slide.
   a. Select the slide 2 thumbnail and press **Ctrl+C**.
   b. Move your insertion point after slide 3 and press **Ctrl+V**.

9. Format the new slide 4.
   a. Replace the text in the text box below the picture with the words We Need Your Help!
   b. Resize the text box to fit the text and center it horizontally under the picture.
   c. Select the picture and change the *Color* to **Orange, Accent color 2 Dark** (Figure 2-143).

2-143 Slide 4 with picture recolored

10. Convert a list to a *SmartArt* graphic.
    a. Display slide 5 and convert the list to a **Vertical Bullet List** *SmartArt* graphic.
    b. Increase the *SmartArt* frame height to **4.7"** so the text size increases.
    c. Reduce the width to **9"**.
    d. Apply the **Cartoon** *SmartArt* style.

2-144 Slide 5 *SmartArt* graphic converted from bulleted text

e. Move the *SmartArt* up and center it horizontally as displayed in Figure 2-144.

11. Convert a list to a picture type *SmartArt* graphic.
   a. Display slide 6 and convert the list to a **Picture Lineup** *SmartArt* graphic.
   b. Click the **Picture** icon on each shape to open the *Insert Pictures* dialog box.
   c. Browse to locate your student data files and insert the following pictures going from left to right (Figure 2-145):

   1 *DayCare-02*
   2 *CountryStroll-02*
   3 *RoyalTreatment-02*
   4 *Food-02*
   5 *Groom-02*

   Each picture is automatically resized.

12. Insert a new slide after slide 6 with a *Title and Content* layout.
   a. Type the title Items We Need
   b. Insert a table with **3** columns and **5** rows.
   c. Type the table text shown in Figure 2-146.
   d. Increase the font size to **20 pt**.
   e. Adjust column width so each column fits the longest line of text.
   f. Center the table on the slide.

13. Apply the *Gallery* transition to all slides.

14. Save and close the presentation (Figure 2-147).

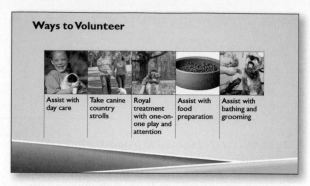

2-145 Slide 6 *SmartArt* graphic picture layout

| Cleaning | Paper Products and Bedding | Dog and Cat Play |
|----------|----------------------------|------------------|
| Bleach | Paper Towels | Dog and Cat Treats |
| Pine Sol | Paper Plates | Chewies |
| Mop Heads | Plastic Containers with Lids | Collars |
| Towels | Blankets | Leashes |

2-146 Table text

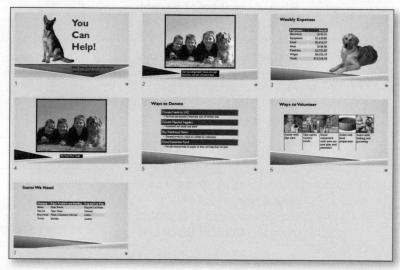

2-147 PowerPoint 2-6 completed

## Improve It Project 2-7

The Hamilton Civic Center needs a presentation to explain benefits of yoga and encourage members to join yoga classes. For this project, you revise a presentation to add pictures, create a *SmartArt* graphic and apply various styles and effects for a contemporary appearance.
[**Student Learning Outcomes 2.2, 2.3, 2.4, 2.5, 2.6, 2.7**]

File Needed: *Yoga-02.pptx* (*Student data files are available in the* Library *of your SIMnet account.*)
Completed Project File Name: *[your initials] PowerPoint 2-7.pptx*

### Skills Covered in This Project

- Apply text effects.
- Insert an online picture.
- Apply a picture style.
- Reposition slide objects.
- Convert text to a *SmartArt* graphic.
- Apply a *SmartArt* style and effects.
- Format a table.
- Compress pictures.

---

1. Open the presentation *Yoga-02* that has a *Standard* size (4:3 aspect ratio). The slide size is 10"×7.5" compared to the slide size of 13.33"×7.5" for the default Widescreen size (16:9 aspect ratio).

2. Save the presentation as [your initials] PowerPoint 2-7.

3. Format the title slide for a more dynamic appearance.
   a. Search online and insert a yoga picture similar to the one shown in Figure 2-148.
   b. Resize the picture as needed.
   c. Apply a **Bevel Rectangle** picture style.
   d. Select the title placeholder and apply the **Wave 1** *Transform text effect.*

4. Recolor the logo picture.
   a. Select the logo and change the picture *Color* to **Blue, Accent color 5 Light**. This change replaces the black with a color that matches theme colors.
   b. Use *Set Transparent Color* to remove the white so your background color shows.
   c. Change the logo *Width* to **2.5"** and the *Height* will automatically adjust.

5. Arrange title slide objects as shown in Figure 2-148.

6. Change listed text to a *SmartArt* graphic.
   a. Display slide 3 and select the bulleted list. Convert it to a *SmartArt* graphic using the **Vertical Block List** layout.
   b. Apply the **White Outline** *SmartArt* style.
   c. Apply the **Colorful Range – Accent Colors 4 to 5** *SmartArt* colors (Figure 2-149).

7. Insert, position, and compress pictures.
   a. Display slide 4. Search online and insert an appropriate yoga picture.
   b. Resize the picture if needed and position it on the right.
   c. Apply a **Bevel Rectangle** picture style.
   d. Resize the bulleted text placeholder as needed to fit with the picture.

2-148  Title slide

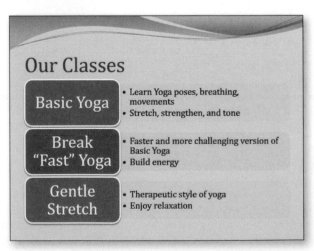

2-149  *SmartArt* graphic *Vertical Block List* layout

e. Display slide 5. Repeat steps 7a–d.

f. Select the picture, and click **Compress Pictures**. Use document resolution, delete cropped areas of pictures, and apply compression to all pictures.

8. Modify the table.

a. Display slide 6. Select the table text and increase the font size to **20 pt**.

b. Apply the **Medium Style 2 – Accent 4** table style.

c. Select the title row and apply the **Riblet** *Bevel* effect.

d. Increase the table *Height* to **2.5"**.

e. Center the text vertically in all cells.

f. Add a **1 pt**. border to all cells using the **Blue, Accent 4, Darker 50%** pen color (Figure 2-150).

g. Align the table vertically in the middle of the slide.

| Classes | Days | Hours |
|---------|------|-------|
| Basic Yoga | Mon/Wed | 4:15 – 5:15 p.m. |
| Break "Fast" Yoga | Tues/Thurs | 7:00 – 8:10 a.m. |
| Gentle Stretch | Fri | 10:00 – 11:30 a.m. |

2-150  Slide 6 table

9. Apply the **Dissolve** transition to all slides.

10. Save and close your presentation (Figure 2-151).

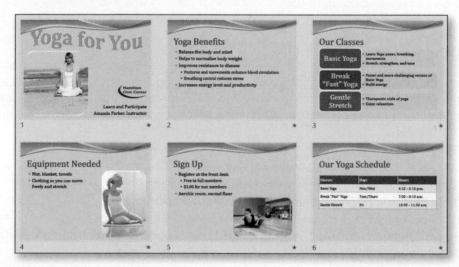

2-151  PowerPoint 2-7 completed

# Challenge Project 2-8

For this project, do online comparison shopping for items you would be likely to buy such as clothing, household products, or automotive supplies. Prepare slides describing the products and apply text effects to the slide titles. Prepare a chart that shows costs either for the same product at several web sites or similar products at the same site.

[Student Learning Outcomes 2.1, 2.2, 2.3, 2.4, 2.5, 2.6, 2.7, 2.8, 2.9]

File Needed: None
Completed Project File Name: *[your initials] PowerPoint 2-8.pptx*

Create a new presentation and save it as [your initials] PowerPoint 2-8. Modify your presentation according to the following guidelines:

- Select an appropriate theme and apply color and font changes as needed for your topic.
- Prepare a title slide and product description slides.
- Search online for a related image and insert it on the title slide.
- Add one or more shapes to emphasize a slide object.
- Insert a *SmartArt* graphic to illustrate a process or relationship.
- Create a table summarizing some of your findings.
- Create two charts to compare specific items.

## Challenge Project 2-9

Using data from the United States Department of Labor published online by the Bureau of Labor Statistics (http://www.bls.gov), prepare a presentation explaining current trends in the labor force. For example, you could show unemployment rate comparisons from different regions or wage estimates for various occupations in different states.
**Student Learning Outcomes 2.1, 2.2, 2.3, 2.4, 2.5, 2.6, 2.7, 2.8, 2.9]**

File Needed: None
Completed Project File Name: *[your initials] PowerPoint 2-9.pptx*

Create a new presentation and save it as [your initials] PowerPoint 2-9. Modify your presentation according to the following guidelines:

- Select an appropriate theme and apply color and font changes as needed for your topic.
- Create a title slide using a *Transform* text effect.
- Include several bulleted slides describing current trends.
- Search for appropriate pictures, resize as needed, and apply a picture style to each one.
- Add one or more shapes to emphasize a slide object.
- Insert a *SmartArt* graphic to illustrate a process or relationship.
- Prepare a table showing salaries for several jobs in different locations or for data changing over time.
- Prepare a chart comparing employment statistics from your state or region.

# Challenge Project 2-10

Using information from one of your favorite coffee or soft drink manufacturers, such as the facts you can find at www.thecoca-colacompany.com or www.pepsico.com, prepare a presentation comparing different products. You could show the diversity of the product line or list promotional products with pricing. From financial information provided on the sites, you could feature total revenue, total profits, or other interesting performance data in your presentation.
[Student Learning Outcomes 2.1, 2.2, 2.3, 2.4, 2.5, 2.6, 2.7, 2.8, 2.9]

File Needed: None
Completed Project File Name: *[your initials] PowerPoint 2-10.pptx*

Create a new presentation and save it as [your initials] PowerPoint 2-10. Modify your presentation according to the following guidelines:

- Select an appropriate theme and apply color and font changes as needed for your topic.
- Create a distinctive title slide using *WordArt* combined with a shape to create interest.
- Search online for appropriate pictures and insert three or more.
- Adjust picture sizes and apply picture styles.
- Prepare slides listing key factors contributing to the company's growth.
- Feature selected financial information in a table.
- Prepare a *SmartArt* graphic illustrating a specific process or relationship from historical or operational information.
- Create a chart showing comparisons for data such as net revenue, operating profit, or growth over a period of time.

# CHAPTER 3

# Preparing for Delivery and Using a Slide Presentation

**POWERPOINT**

## CHAPTER OVERVIEW

This chapter shows you how to create new theme colors customized for your topic, apply animation so selected slide objects appear just at the right time in your presentation, and link to a video from a web site. You also explore PowerPoint's rehearsal features to help you perfect your delivery timing and techniques, project your presentation more effectively, and prepare a presentation to be self-running. Finally, you learn how to save a presentation so it can be distributed on a CD.

### STUDENT LEARNING OUTCOMES (SLOs)

After completing this chapter, you will be able to:

**SLO 3.1**  Create custom theme and background colors (p. P3-147).

**SLO 3.2**  Apply animation to add interest and reinforce content (p. P3-155).

**SLO 3.3**  Link to an online video (p. P3-158).

**SLO 3.4**  Use rehearsal techniques to prepare for presentation delivery (p. P3-164).

**SLO 3.5**  Control display options for different screen sizes (p. P3-167).

**SLO 3.6**  Present effectively and professionally using projection equipment (p. P3-173).

**SLO 3.7**  Use annotation pens to highlight information and save presentation markings (p. P3-176).

**SLO 3.8**  Prepare a self-running presentation that loops (p. P3-179).

**SLO 3.9**  Use the *Package Presentation for CD* feature to prepare a slide show for display on other computers (p. P3-181).

### CASE STUDY

Specialists at Solution Seekers, Inc., frequently present to both large and small groups as they work with clients to improve business performance. Davon Washington is creating a series of seminars for new hires to help them be more productive and professional. For this project, you work with Davon to finish the presentation he has developed for a seminar on presentation planning.

**Pause & Practice 3-1:** Create custom theme and background colors. Add interest with animation and video.

**Pause & Practice 3-2:** Rehearse a presentation and prepare for a widescreen display.

**Pause & Practice 3-3:** Practice slide show delivery features.

**Pause & Practice 3-4:** Prepare a self-running presentation and package a presentation to a folder.

# Creating Custom Theme and Background Colors

Themes create a unified appearance for your presentation. When you use themes effectively, the information you present on a topic is seen by your viewers as one "package" and not a collection of random slides. You may need to match specific colors in a company logo or a school's colors, so in this section you will prepare custom theme colors that create a unique palette and help you work more efficiently. Then you will explore different ways to apply pattern, gradient, and picture fills and consider issues to keep in mind when applying these fills to slide backgrounds.

## Custom Theme Colors

As you worked with shapes, colors, and styles in previous chapters, you saw how theme colors are arranged across the top of the *Theme Colors* gallery. Recall that various percentages of each color appear below the top row colors (Figure 3-1). This section takes a closer look at where PowerPoint automatically applies theme colors to various graphics you create.

Four sample slides are shown in Figure 3-2 with the *Facet* theme and *Blue* theme colors. The white background is the *Background 1* color with decorative shapes in *Accent 1* and *Accent 2* colors.

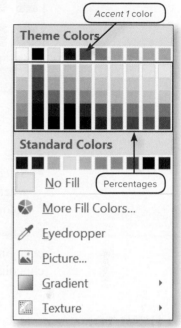

3-1 *Theme Colors* gallery

- **Slide 1**: The photograph has a border of *Text 2* color.
- **Slide 2**: The first color samples show the two sets of *Background* and *Text* colors. The second color samples show *Accent colors 1–6*.
- **Slide 3**: The bullets and the *SmartArt* shapes are shown in the *Accent 1* color.
- **Slide 4**: The table has *Accent 2* color variations. The chart shows all six *Accent* colors. They appear based on the order data is entered in the spreadsheet.

Accent colors (Figure 3-3) appear from left to right in both the *Shape Styles* gallery and the *Table Styles* gallery (Figures 3-4 and 3-5). Other galleries show options in a similar way.

You can boost productivity by creating custom theme colors because the colors you choose are available to you in the galleries as you develop your slide show. When you save custom theme colors, the colors are also available to use again in another presentation. Keep the following guidelines in mind when you create custom theme colors:

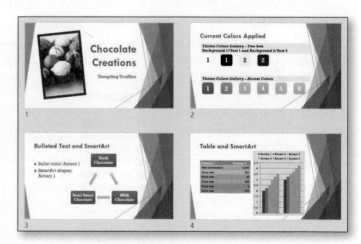

3-2 Sample slides showing graphics with *Blue* theme colors

3-3 *Blue* theme accent colors

- Select your background color first and then select other colors that work well on the background.

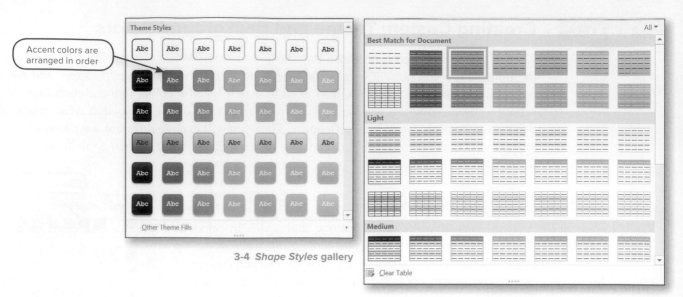

Accent colors are arranged in order

3-4 *Shape Styles* gallery

3-5 *Table Styles* gallery

- Pick a text color that has a high contrast with your background color so words are easy to read.
- Select the *Accent 1* color carefully because it will appear automatically as the fill color when you draw shapes. The *Accent 1* color is the first choice, also, in galleries that show color options.

Use the *Design* tab to quickly change theme colors. The following example illustrates changing to brown and yellow theme colors that are more appropriate for a presentation about chocolate.

## ▶ HOW TO: Create New Theme Colors

1. Start a new presentation using a design theme or open an existing presentation.
2. Click the **More** button [*Design* tab, *Variants* group].
3. Select **Colors** to open the list of built-in theme colors. The current color theme is selected (Figure 3-6).
4. Select **Customize Colors** to open the *Create New Theme Colors* dialog box (Figure 3-7).
5. Change individual colors as needed to create your custom theme (Figure 3-8). For this example, the *Text/ Background – Dark 1* and *Light 1* colors do not require a change.
   - Click the **list arrow** on a color button to open the *Themes Colors* gallery.
   - Click **More Colors** to open the *Colors* dialog box.

Current theme colors

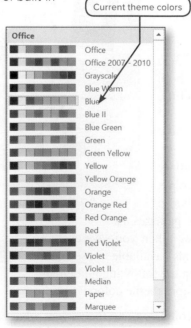

3-6 *Theme Colors* gallery

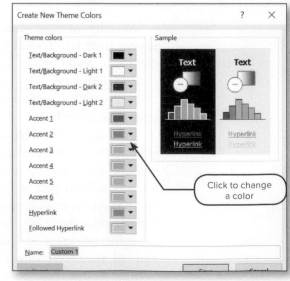

Click to change a color

3-7 *Create New Theme Colors* dialog box showing *Blue* theme colors

- Click the **Standard** or **Custom** tab, choose a color, and click **OK**.
- Repeat for each of the colors you want to change.

6. Name the new custom theme.

7. Click the **Save** button. The new custom theme is automatically applied and the name will appear in the *Custom* section of your list of available theme colors so you can use it again.

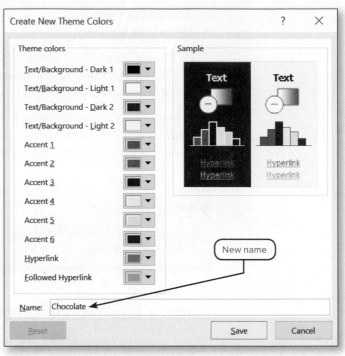

The same sample slides are shown in Figure 3-9 with the new colors. Controlling color this way is more efficient than using an existing theme and having to select a custom color each time you create various illustrations. If any slide text, such as a slide title, retains the original colors, click the **Reset** button [*Home* tab, *Slides* group] to update the colors.

3-8 *Create New Theme Colors* dialog box showing custom colors

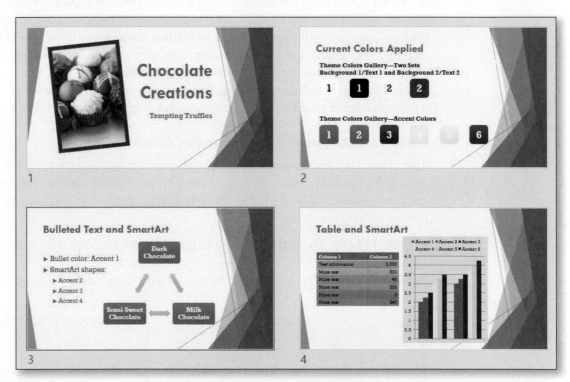

3-9 *Chocolate* theme colors applied to sample slides

Color combinations influence the tone of your presentation. Your options are endless, but you may want to consider a few of the following tonal effects:

- Varied and vibrant or similar with subtle differences
- Soothing and tranquil or lively and energetic

- Youthful or mature
- Historic or high tech

When you think about colors for your topic, consider your audience and be respectful of cultural differences. People tend to assign meaning to colors based on their cultural background and life experiences. A few examples of colors that have symbolic meaning include the following:

- *White*: Purity and cleanliness in the American culture, death in some other cultures
- *Red*: Health (red blood) in the medical field, loss (negative values) in the financial field
- *Green*: Sickness (infection) in the medical field, wealth (money) in the financial field

 **MORE INFO**

To examine this concept further, look online for information about color meaning, symbolism, or the psychology of color.

## Custom Background Colors

The *Format Background* pane has options similar to those you have used on the *Format Shape* pane (*See SLO 2.1: Working with Shapes, Colors, and Styles*). When you change background colors, text colors do not change. Also, the position of placeholders or the graphic shapes that appear on design themes do not change.

When you choose colors and creative effects for backgrounds, remember that your color choices will fill the entire slide area behind everything else you design on a slide. These changes are visible throughout the presentation if you apply them to all slides, so you should examine your changes at full screen size to be sure you are satisfied with the results.

You need to consider how your background affects text, too. If a theme or template has graphic shapes included in its design, then a solid color background fill is a good choice. Select a color that has a strong contrast from the color used for text (light on dark or dark on light).

### Format a Background with Pattern and Gradient Fills

Two colors (the *Foreground* and the *Background*) create pattern fills. Two similar colors create a subtle pattern; two contrasting colors create a more obvious pattern. Notice the difference in two title slides prepared using the *Wisp* theme and a *Dark Horizontal* background pattern fill (Figure 3-10).

- *Slide 1 (Left)*: The text is difficult to read on a background with pattern colors that have a strong contrast.
- *Slide 2 (Right)*: The text is easier to read on a background with pattern colors that are similar.

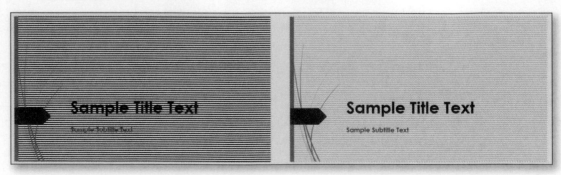

3-10 *Wisp* theme title slide with the same background pattern in different colors

## ▶ HOW TO: Add a Background Pattern Fill

1. Point to the slide background and right-click to open the context menu.
2. Click **Format Background** to open the *Format Background* pane.
3. Select the **Pattern fill** option.
4. Choose an appropriate *Foreground Color* and *Background Color*.
5. Choose one of the patterns. By default, this change is applied to the current slide only.
6. Click **Apply to All** to apply this change to the entire presentation.
7. Click **Reset Background** if you want to restore the background's original design.
8. Close the *Format Background* pane.

> ▶ **ANOTHER WAY**
>
> Open the *Format Background* pane by clicking the **Format Background** button [*Design* tab, *Customize* group]. You can also click the **Slide Master** button [*View* tab, *Master views* group], click the **Background Styles** button [*Slide Master* tab, *Background* group], and then click **Format Background**.

Preset gradient colors are based on theme colors or you can select custom colors. You first choose the *Type* of gradient that controls how the colors blend, and then you choose the *Direction* of color change. Based on these choices, gradient stops appear on the color bar. Move, delete, or add gradient stops to modify how the colors blend. The color change is more gradual with more distance between the stops. Compare the title slides of the *Wisp* design theme shown in Figures 3-11 and 3-12. These two slides started with the same preset gradient fill of *Bottom Spotlight – Accent 4* with a type of *Linear;* however, the gradient stop settings were changed differently.

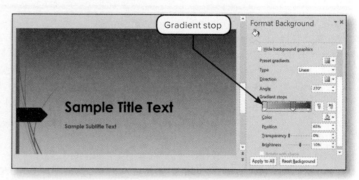

3-11 *Wisp* theme title slide with a custom background gradient fill

**Figure 3-11**

- *Linear Up* direction
- Three gradient stops are used.

**Figure 3-12**

- *Linear Diagonal – Top Left to Bottom Right* direction
- The three gradient stops on the left of the color bar are close together for a defined color change; the three right stops are spread apart for a more gradual color change.

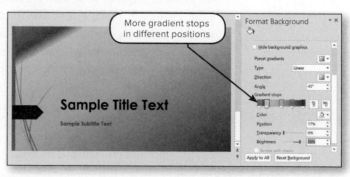

3-12 *Wisp* theme title slide with a custom background gradient fill showing different gradient stops

# ▶HOW TO: Add a Background Gradient Fill

1. Point to the slide background that you want to change and right-click to open the context menu.
2. Click **Format Background** to open the *Format Background* pane.
3. Select the **Gradient fill** option. By default, changes are applied to the current slide only.
4. Click the **Preset gradients** button and select a color such as **Light Gradient – Accent 2** or **Top Spotlight – Accent 4** from the gallery of options.
5. Click the **Type** drop-down arrow and choose one of the options: **Linear**, **Radial**, **Rectangular**, **Path**, or **Shade from title**.
6. Click the **Direction** button and choose a direction for color blending if one is available.
   - The *Angle* degree is available only for the *Linear* type, and it automatically adjusts based on the direction you choose.
   - Type a different number in the *Angle* box or click the arrows to change the number in 10 degree increments.
7. Add or remove gradient stops.
   - Click the **Add gradient stop** button to add gradient stops.
   - Click the **Remove gradient stop** button or drag the gradient stop down to remove it from the color bar.
8. Change colors by selecting a gradient stop and clicking the **Color** button. Choose a different color.
9. Change color blending by selecting the gradient stop and dragging it to a different position on the color bar.
   - Drag the stops to rearrange them if you want to change the order.
   - Change percentages for each stop position to precisely adjust the positions.
10. Adjust *Brightness* and *Transparency* as needed.
11. Click **Apply to All** to apply this background to every slide in your presentation.
12. Click **Reset Background**, if necessary, to restore the settings before you made changes.
13. Close the *Format Background* pane.

---

▶ ### ANOTHER WAY

You can access various *Background Styles* [*Design* tab, *Variants* group or *Slide Master* tab, *Background* group] that show light and dark color combinations based on theme colors.

### Format a Background with Picture and Texture Fills

Pictures help you tell your story, communicate without words, and convey emotions that are difficult to express in words. Pictures can provide a dramatic background for your presentation. However, placing text over pictures is challenging because of the many colors that are used in pictures. Textures can use many colors, too, or show a lot of detail. Pictures in a small size can be used as textures to fill a slide with many small pictures. The examples in this section show you several ways to combine background pictures and text.

# ▶HOW TO: Add a Background Picture Fill

1. Point to the slide background that you want to change and right-click to open the context menu.
2. Click **Format Background** to open the *Format Background* pane.
3. Select the **Picture or texture fill** option. By default, changes are applied to the current slide only.

4. Click the **File** button to insert a picture from your collection.

5. Click the **Online** button to search for a picture using the *Insert Picture* dialog box.
   - Type your search word and click the **Search** button or press **Enter**.
   - Select the picture you want to use and click **Insert**.

6. Use one of the following methods to soften the picture colors so text and other objects on the slide are easy to see:
   - Increase the *Transparency* percentage on the *Format Background* pane. This setting mutes the colors but the original colors are still evident.
   - Click the **Picture** icon at the top of the *Format Background* pane, and then click **Picture Color**. Click the **Presets** drop-down arrow to choose from different saturation levels or click the **Recolor** drop-down arrow to choose from dark and light accent colors for a monotone effect.
   - If you decide not to change the picture's colors, click the **Reset** button to restore the picture to its original state.

7. Click **Apply to All** to apply this background to every slide in your presentation.

8. Click **Reset Background** to restore the background to its original state.

9. Close the *Format Background* pane.

> **MORE INFO**
> You can change a slide background at any time while you are working on a presentation.

The following figures show options you can explore using the *Format Background* pane to soften background pictures or use placeholder fill colors so that text on pictures or textures is easy to read. A single flower that is almost a square image (Figure 3-13) is used differently in Figures 3-14 – 3-16. The first slide in each figure illustrates a problem while the second and third slides show possible solutions. Figure 3-17 illustrates several options for using textures as a background.

522 x 529 pixels @ 72 ppi

3-13  A flower picture used in background examples

Notice the following characteristics for the three slides shown in Figure 3-14:

- **Slide 1 (left)**: Because this picture is almost square (522×529 pixels) when it is stretched to fill the width of a widescreen display (*Height* 7.5" and *Width* 13.33"), part of the flower is cut off at the top and bottom. This is not necessarily a problem, just what happens if you use a square picture. The title text, however, is not easy to read over the dark colors of the flower. This is a problem as your slide text should be legible no matter what background designs you use.

3-14  A large square picture used as a background fill with color changes

- **Slide 2 (center)**: The title placeholder is the same width as the slide. A dark red fill is applied and the white text has a shadow so now the text is easy to read.
- **Slide 3 (right)**: The title placeholder treatment is the same as slide 2. The picture was recolored using the preset *Black and White: 25%* color. This creates a more abstract image.

Notice the following characteristics for the three slides shown in Figure 3-15:

- **Slide 4 (left)**: The large flower does not fill the slide when inserted in its original size, so now the complete flower appears. The *Tile picture as texture* option was selected with *Alignment* changed to *Center*. *Tiling* causes the picture to be repeated to fill the slide area so parts of the flower are shown around the center flower. Like slide 1 in Figure 3-14, the text is difficult to read.
- **Slide 5 (center)**: The title placeholder resembles slide 2 in Figure 3-14, but this time the fill color transparency is 30%. More of the flower shows through, yet the text is still easy to read.
- **Slide 6 (right)**: The picture was recolored with preset *Gray – 25%, Background color 2 Light*. Black text is used with no shadow to avoid making the text appear blurred.

3-15 A large square picture used as a tiled background fill with color changes

If you tile a picture or texture that is small, many images fill the screen for an effect like wallpaper. If these images still seem too large, you can adjust the *Tiling Options* and reduce the *Scale* percentage to display each image in a smaller size. *Offset* points control how much the tiled images are indented from the left (*Offset X*) and top (*Offset Y*).

Notice the following characteristics for the three slides shown in Figure 3-16:

- **Slide 7 (left)**: The *Tile picture as texture* option was selected so many of these small flower images (200 × 203 pixels) fill the screen. For an appropriate fit on the slide, *Alignment* was changed to *Top left*, then *Offset* and *Scale* were adjusted. Like slide 4 in Figure 3-15, the text is difficult to read.
- **Slide 8 (center)**: The flower picture was recolored with preset *Grayscale*. The title placeholder colors were changed to a black fill with red text. The placeholder size was increased, too, for greater emphasis.
- **Slide 9 (right)**: The repeating picture for this slide is a small rectangle (40 by 77 pixels) with a bevel effect so it looks like a real tile. The title text is left aligned and the placeholder is filled with a gold color. A rectangle was added on the right so the date would be easy to read and to help create an asymmetrical focal point with the single large flower. This flower has a transparent background rather than white as in the previous examples.

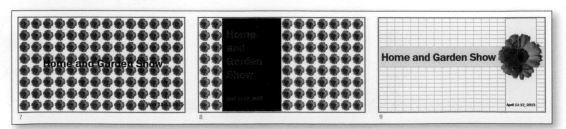

3-16 Small pictures tiled for a background fill with color changes

Textures available on the *Format Background* pane are small images, so it is generally best to tile them because the effect is more pleasing. When stretched to fill a slide, the textures may be too bold or blurred. Notice the following characteristics for the slides shown in Figure 3-17:

- **Slide 10 (left)**: The *Paper bag* texture was applied and its bold appearance dominates the slide.
- **Slide 11 (center)**: The same texture was tiled so multiple small images repeat and no other change was made.
- **Slide 12 (right)**: The same texture was tiled and the *Mirror type* changed to *Both*. This creates a pattern with horizontal and vertical mirror images.

**3-17** The same texture used as a background fill with different settings

SLO 3.2

# Applying Animation

*Animation* is the movement of objects on a slide. Animation creates a more dynamic presentation and can keep your audience focused on concepts.

Observe creative animation techniques by noticing how objects and text move in movies or in television commercials. As you decide what effects to use, try to select movements that enhance your content and support your message. Animation can be overdone when it is not used skillfully. Be sure you apply animation for the right reasons and not just for entertainment value. Use animation sparingly because too much can be distracting.

When planning movement, also consider the transitions (the movement between slides). When a presentation is supporting a speaker, you want to keep the transitions calmer and apply animation effects to draw attention to information on selected slides only.

## Add Entrance, Exit, and Emphasis Effects

Animation effects are arranged in the categories that are shown in different colors on the gallery (Figure 3-18):

- *Entrance*: A movement that occurs when an object appears on the slide (green)
- *Emphasis*: A movement that calls attention to an object that remains on the slide (yellow)
- *Exit*: A movement that occurs when an object leaves the slide (red)

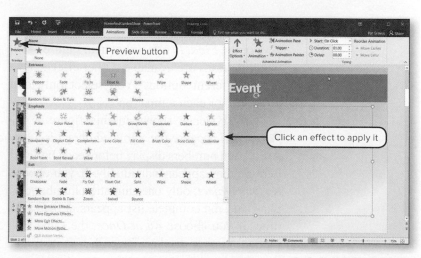

**3-18** *Animations* gallery

Note that some effects are for text only. When animating objects, those effects are gray in the gallery and are not available.

## ▶ HOW TO: Apply an Animation Effect

1. Select the text or object to animate.
2. Click the **Animations** tab.
3. Open the *Animations* gallery using one of these methods:
   - Click the **More** button on the gallery [*Animation* group].
   - Click the **Add Animation** button [*Advanced Animation* group] if the *Animations* gallery is not open because your PowerPoint window is narrow.
4. Click an effect to apply it. A number appears on the slide beside the text or object showing that it is animated.
5. Click the **Preview** button to test the animation.
6. Repeat to animate additional objects as desired. Each animated object is numbered in sequence to show animation order.
7. Remove an animation by clicking the animation number and pressing **Delete**.

> **MORE INFO**
>
> Animation numbers display only when the *Animations* tab is open.

## Effect Options, Timing, and Duration

Each different animation has ***Effect Options*** that control the direction of movement.

## ▶ HOW TO: Change Effect Options

1. Select the animated object.
2. Click the **Effect Options** button [*Animations* tab, *Animation* group].
3. Select an appropriate **Direction** and **Sequence** if it is available.

For the *Float In* effect shown in Figure 3-19, two directions are available. Other effects have many different options. You select only one direction for each animation.

The sequence shown in this figure is *By Paragraph* because the animated object is a list. Animation numbers display before each bulleted item so they appear individually. If you choose *As One Object*, only one animation number displays and the complete list appears at the same time. If you choose *All at Once*, the same animation number displays for each text item and the complete list appears at the same time.

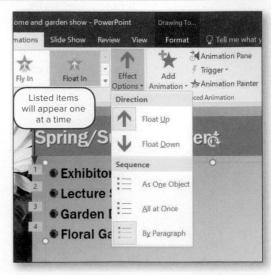

3-19 Animation and effect options applied

Some people are critical of animating text because viewers cannot read text until it stops moving. If you are going to spend significant time discussing each item in a list, adding each item as you start talking about it makes sense. However, animating a list has no value if your statements are brief or if you discuss the complete list in general terms.

You can adjust animation *Timing* using the following commands on the *Animations* tab in the *Timing* group:

- *Start*: When the *On Click* option is selected, the speaker controls when animation begins by clicking at an appropriate time. The *With Previous* or *After Previous* options cause the animation to occur automatically.
- *Duration*: By default, the time to complete each animation ranges from .50 to 2.00 seconds depending on the movement. Increasing the duration seconds extends the time an object is moving so the movement appears slower.
- *Delay*: The default setting is no delay, but you can enter seconds so the animation begins after a specified time.
- *Reorder Animation*: When multiple objects are animated, click **Move Earlier** or **Move Later** to adjust the sequence of animation.

## ▶ HOW TO:  Adjust Animation Timing and Duration

1. Select the animated object.
2. Click the *Start* drop-down arrow [*Animations* tab, *Timing* group] and select from **On Click**, **With Previous**, or **After Previous** (Figure 3-20).
3. Increase or decrease *Duration* by changing the seconds.
4. Enter seconds or click the *Delay* arrows to specify the time (in seconds) before the animation starts.
5. Click the **Preview** button [*Preview* group] to test the animation.
6. Reorder animation if necessary using the **Move Earlier** and **Move Later** buttons.

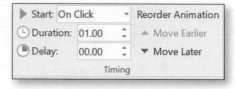

3-20 *Animations* tab, *Timing* group

When you animate several objects, check the animation numbers to be sure the sequencing is appropriate (Figure 3-21). Each number represents the mouse click on which the animation occurs. If a single object's *Start* is **With Previous** or **After Previous**, then the object's number will match the previous object's number. If either of these *Start* options is applied to all objects, then the number will display as "0".

3-21 Numbers indicate animation order

If your presentation is designed to support you as a speaker, coordinate the animation timing with your speaking. This technique usually works best in small segments only because precise timing is almost impossible to predict when you are presenting in real time to an audience. If you are designing a self-running presentation for a trade show exhibit, for example, your animation can be much more dramatic and extensive because the slide show is not dependent on a speaker's pace.

# Linking to an Online Video

Many videos are available online, but not all of them can be played within PowerPoint. When you search for a video using the *Insert Video* dialog box, the videos found from YouTube are most likely to play within PowerPoint as long as you have Internet access. You click **Insert** to put the video on your slide, but the actual video is not saved in your presentation. An image of the video appears and the necessary information to link to it is saved in your presentation.

When you search for videos, you may find a compelling interview or demonstration that will enliven your presentation, but be sure the video relates to your topic and adds value.

## ▶ HOW TO: Link a Presentation to an Online Video

1. Select the PowerPoint slide where you want to show the video. Be sure your computer has Internet access.
2. Click the **Insert** tab.
3. Click the **Video** button [*Media* group] and select **Online Video** (Figure 3-22) to open the *Insert Video* dialog box (Figure 3-23).
4. Type a word in the *YouTube* search box and click the **Search** button.
5. Available videos appear with *ScreenTips* that identify names.

   - Source information appears in the lower left corner of the dialog box (Figure 3-24).

3-22 *Video* button on the *Insert* tab

3-23 *Insert Video* dialog box showing search options

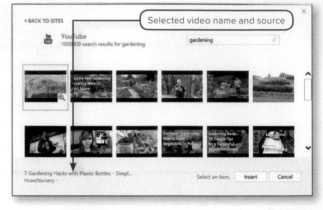

3-24 *Insert Video* dialog box showing search results

6. Click **Insert** and the video appears on your slide.
7. Add the appropriate source information as needed below the video.

> **MORE INFO**
>
> A linked video will not play in a presentation that you send by email or one that you prepare on your computer and later view on your phone through Office Online. The link that creates a path to the file is broken.

## Play the Online Video

To play an online video in PowerPoint, the computer used to display your presentation must have Internet access.

The clarity you see in playback depends on the resolution of the original video and how it was compressed for online distribution. Resolution is expressed in pixel width and height. With more pixels, image clarity and detail improves.

As with all computer technology, video capabilities continue to improve and many videos can be played at full-screen size from their online source. However, video sharing sites often provide video in the standard definition size (640 × 480 pixels) or even smaller. Be careful when increasing the size of a video object on your slide to avoid reducing image quality. Test how the video plays before you use it in your presentation. You can drag the video object to reposition it on the slide just as you would a picture or shape.

## ▶ HOW TO: Resize and Play an Online Video

3-25 *Format Video* pane

1. Select *Normal* view, if necessary, and select the video object.
2. Increase the size of the video by using one of the following methods:
   - Drag handles.
   - Enter specific *Height* and *Width* measurements [*Video Tools Format* tab, *Size* group].
   - Click the **Size** launcher to open the *Format Video* pane (Figure 3-25). Click the **Size & Properties** icon at the top of the pane. Adjust size by changing *Height* and *Width* measurements or changing the *Scale Height* and *Scale Width* percentages.
3. Maintain video dimensions as you resize. Right-click the video object and select **Format Video** to open the **Format Video** pane, if necessary.
   - Check **Lock aspect ratio** and **Relative to original picture size** to maintain dimensions as your resize.
   - Check **Best scale for slide show** to select a different resolution.
4. Reposition the video object as needed.
5. Play the video in *Normal* view.
   - Click the **Play** button [*Video Tools Playback* tab, *Preview* group] to start the video.
   - If the video can play within PowerPoint, a timeline will appear below the video with playback controls you can use to play, pause, mute, and access other options (Figure 3-26).
   - Click the **Play** button on the video to play it.
   - Notice the clarity of the video as you play it. If the image is degraded after resizing, click the **Reset Design** drop-down arrow [*Video Tools Format* tab, *Adjust* group] and click **Reset Design & Size** to restore the video to its original dimensions.

3-26 Video playing in *Normal* view

6. Play the video in *Slide Show* view.
   - Select **Play Full Screen** [*Video Tools Playback* tab, *Video Options* group] if the video can be played at full screen size.
   - Click the **Slide Show** button [*Status* bar] to start your slide show on the current slide.
   - Click the **Play** button in the middle of the video.
   - The same timeline described in step 7 appears at the bottom of the video as it plays.
   - Press **Esc** to stop the slide show and return to *Normal* view.
7. Make the video start automatically in *Slide Show* view.
   - Click the **Start** list box [*Video Tools Playback* tab, *Video Options* group] and select **Automatically**.
   - Click the **Slide Show** tab and the **From Beginning** button [*Start Slide Show* group]. Advance to the slide with the video to test that it begins playing automatically.
8. Move your pointer so it does not appear on the video while it is playing.
9. Advance to the next slide when the video playback ends.

## Obtain Permission

Linking to a video for classroom purposes falls under the guidelines of *fair use* for education and crediting the source may be sufficient. However, business use is different. Just like television programming or movies in a theater, videos are copyrighted by the creator. You need permission before you link to, display, or distribute video that is copyrighted. Obtaining permission is time consuming and can be expensive. If the creator does not give you permission, you must find another video and start the process again.

 **HOW TO:** Obtain Permission to Use an Online Video

1. Go to the web site where the video is posted and identify the user name of the creator.
2. Click a link to go to more profile information or, in some cases, another web site.
3. Look for terms of use and find contact information.
4. Send an email message explaining the following:
   - How you want to use the video
   - What portion of the video you will use
   - When you will use the video
   - How you will show credits on the slide where the video is displayed.
   - Your contact information for the creator's response

With the dynamic nature of the web, a video you find may be available for only a limited time. You may need to request a high resolution copy of the video and the creator may charge you for this service.

## PAUSE & PRACTICE: POWERPOINT 3-1

Davon Washington has almost finished the slide show for his seminar on presentation planning. For this project, you create custom theme colors that better match the Solution Seekers, Inc. logo, modify a background style, animate several slide objects, and link to a video on a web site.

File Needed: ***PresentationPlanning-03.pptx*** *(Student data files are available in the* Library *of your* SIMnet *account)*
Completed Project File Name: ***[your initials] PP P3-1.pptx***

1. Open the presentation ***PresentationPlanning-03***.

2. Save the presentation as [your initials] PP P3-1.

3. Create new theme colors.
   a. Click the **More** button [*Design* tab, *Variants* group].
   b. Click **Colors** and select **Customize Colors** to open the *Create New Theme Colors* dialog box (Figure 3-27).
   c. Change four colors. For each change, click the color drop-down arrow and select **More Colors** to open the *Colors* dialog box. Click the **Custom** tab and enter the numbers for *Red*, *Green*, and *Blue* from the following table:

3-27 Original theme colors

| | Text/Back-ground – Light 2 | Accent 1 | Accent 2 | Accent 3 |
|---|---|---|---|---|
| *Red* | 234 | 3 | 102 | 181 |
| *Green* | 214 | 110 | 0 | 139 |
| *Blue* | 184 | 131 | 51 | 128 |

   d. Name the new custom theme Planning (Figure 3-28).
   e. Click the **Save** button. The new custom theme is saved in the **Custom** section of your list of available theme colors.

4. Apply a gradient fill as shown in Figure 3-29.
   a. Display slide 1.
   b. Point to the slide background and right-click. Select **Format Background** to open the *Format Background* pane.
   c. Select the **Gradient fill** option.
   d. Click the **Type** drop-down arrow and choose **Linear** if it is not selected.
   e. Click the **Direction** drop-down arrow and choose **Linear Diagonal – Top Right to Bottom Left**. The *Angle* percentage automatically adjusts to 135%.
   f. Click the **Add gradient stop** button, if necessary, so you have four gradient stops.
   g. Click each gradient stop from left to right (Figure 3-30) and adjust the *Color*, *Position*, *Brightness*, and *Transparency* values as needed to match values in the following table:

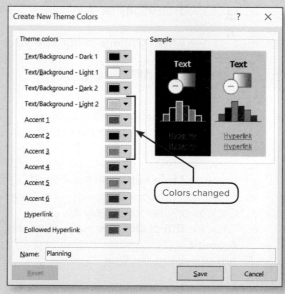

3-28 *Planning* theme colors

3-29 Title slide background gradient fill

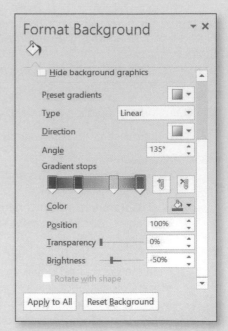

3-30 Gradient stops adjusted

| Gradient Stops | Stop 1 | Stop 2 | Stop 3 | Stop 4 |
|---|---|---|---|---|
| Color | Dark Teal, Accent 1 | Dark Teal, Accent 1, Lighter 60% | Tan, Text 2 | Tan, Text 2, Darker 50% |
| Position | 0% | 30% | 70% | 100% |
| Transparency | 0% | 50% | 0% | 0% |
| Brightness | 0% | 0% | 0% | −50% |

5. Create a *Picture fill* background.
   a. Display slide 2. On the *Format Background* pane, select **Picture or texture fill** and click the **File** button to open the *Insert Picture* dialog box.
   b. Locate your student data files, select ***Presenter-03***, and click **Insert**.
   c. Click the **Picture** icon at the top of the *Format Background* pane and then click **Picture Color**.
   d. Click the **Recolor** drop-down arrow and choose **Tan, Background color 2 Light** (Figure 3-31).
   e. Close the *Format Background* pane.

6. Apply a transition.
   a. Click the **Transitions** tab and apply the **Wipe** transition.
   b. Click the **Effect Options** button and select **From Left**.
   c. Click **Apply to All** [*Timing* group].

3-31 Background picture fill recolored

7. Apply animation.
   a. Click the **Animations** tab and repeat steps b–g for each object in the following table.
   b. Select the text or object to be animated.
   c. Click the **More** button on the *Animation* gallery or click the **Add Animation** button [*Advanced Animation* group] if the gallery is not open.
   d. Click an animation to apply it.
   e. Click the **Effect Options** button and select the **Direction** and **Sequence** or **Amount**.
   f. Adjust settings for *Start*, *Duration*, and *Delay*. Some of the settings will appear by default.
   g. Click the **Preview** button [*Preview* group] or **Slide Show** button [*Status* bar] to test the animation.

| Slide | Object | Animation Effect | Effect Options | Start | Duration | Delay |
|-------|--------|------------------|----------------|-------|----------|-------|
| 4 | Down arrow and possible body sequences text box | *Wipe* (Entrance) | *From Top* | *On Click* | *02.00* | None |
| 5 | First impression text | *Wave* (Emphasis) | *By Paragraph* | *After Previous* | *00.50* | None |
| 7 | Quoted text | *Bounce* (Entrance) | *As One Object* | *After Previous* | *02.00* | *01:00* |
| 8 | Road picture | *Grow & Turn* (Entrance) | None | *With Previous* | *02.00* | *01:00* |
| 14 | Heart | *Spin* (Emphasis) | *Clockwise, Two Spins* | *With Previous* | *02.00* | None |

8. Insert a new blank slide after slide 14.

9. Insert an online video, adjust its size, and add source information.
    a. Display slide 15. Click the **Video** button [*Insert* tab, *Media* group] and select **Online Video** to open the *Insert Video* dialog box.
    b. Type the words **presentation skills** in the *YouTube Search* box and click **Search**.
    c. Select an appropriate video from the search results and click **Insert**.
    d. Increase the size so the width is approximately 7" wide.
    e. Center the video on the slide.
    f. Click the **Play** button [*Video Tools Playback* tab, *Preview* group] to activate the video.
    g. Click the **Play** button on the video to test it.
    h. Reduce the size of the video for a clear image if necessary.
    i. Add a text box below the video with source information.

10. Test all of your transitions and animations in your presentation.

11. Save and close the presentation (Figure 3-32).

3-32 PP P3-1 completed

**SLO 3.4**    # Using Rehearsal Techniques

Everyone, no matter how experienced, can benefit from rehearsing a presentation. Practicing your delivery ensures that each slide's information supports what you are saying. Practice builds confidence, too.

## Speaker Notes

*Speaker notes* help you remember what you need to say in your presentation, but they should never include text that would tempt you to read to your audience. Notes should be your personal reminders, such as items to emphasize or terminology to define. Notes should not be a script for everything you are going to say. For example, you could include statistics you want to mention, a quote you want to say but not show on a slide, a list of upcoming events, or additional resources for your audience. Even if you don't use the speaker notes you prepare, having them available while you present can be comforting and help to reduce nervousness.

As you think about what to include in your notes, plan for smooth and logical transitions between the various topics of your presentation. You can compose your notes using the *Notes* pane in *Normal* view or you can change to *Notes Page* view.

▶ **HOW TO:** Use the Notes Pane in Normal View

1. Click the **Notes** button [*View* tab, *Show* group] or the **Normal** button [*View* tab, *Presentation Views* group] to show the *Notes* pane.
2. Expand the *Notes* pane by dragging the border up (Figure 3-33).
3. Remove the **Notes** pane by dragging the border down. Click the **Notes** button or the **Normal** button to restore it.

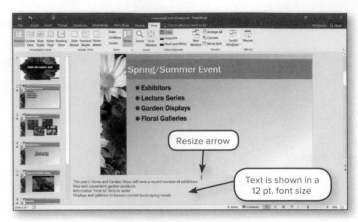

3-33 Increased *Notes* pane size

The *Notes Page* view provides much more space to type text than you have when using the *Notes* pane in *Normal* view.

▶ **HOW TO:** Use Notes Page View

1. Click the **Notes Page** button [*View* tab, *Presentation Views* group] to show the slide at the top of a page with a large text box below.
2. Type your notes in the text box (Figure 3-34).

You may want to increase the font size before you print the pages because large text is easier for you to see on a lectern or podium while you are speaking. You will need your notes to be visible even if overhead lighting is dimmed so slide colors display better on the projection screen.

3-34 *Notes Page* view with slide and text

P3-164

## ▶ HOW TO: Print Notes Pages

1. Click the **File** tab and click **Print**.
2. For *Print Layout*, choose **Notes Pages** and check **Scale to Fit Paper** to make the slide images larger (Figure 3-35).
3. Omit the **Frame Slide** option for *Notes Pages*. A single-line border around the entire page is unnecessary.
4. Click the **Print** button.

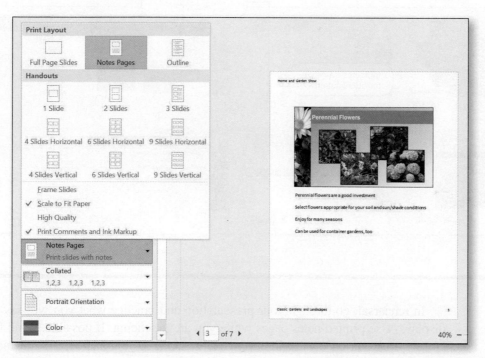

**3-35** Print settings for *Notes Pages*

## Rehearse Timings

PowerPoint's **Rehearse Timings** feature makes it easy to judge the pace of your presentation. When you use this feature to rehearse, the time you spend on each slide is recorded as you move through the presentation. The timings that you save from rehearsing appear below each slide in *Slide Sorter* view. This view enables you to see the "big picture" aspect of your presentation. You can compare the time spent on each slide and consider spending less time on certain slides and more time on other slides where the content takes longer to explain. You can save the timings to automate the presentation so it is self-running. If you are presenting to an audience, remove the timings so you can control when the slides advance.

## ▶HOW TO: Rehearse Timings

1. Click the **Rehearse Timings** button [*Slide Show* tab, *Set Up* group] and your slide show will start.

   3-36 Current slide time and total elapsed time

   - A *Recording* dialog box appears in the upper left corner (Figure 3-36). It shows the time each slide is displayed and the total elapsed time.
   - Click the **Next Slide** button (or press the **spacebar**) to advance.
   - Click the **Pause** or **Repeat** buttons as needed.
   - When you reach the end of your presentation, a message will ask if you want to save your timings.

2. Click **Yes** and the timings, in seconds, will display below each slide in *Slide Sorter* view (Figure 3-37). (The seconds shown in this example are brief because they were recorded when testing the presentation. The times may be much longer in an actual presentation.)

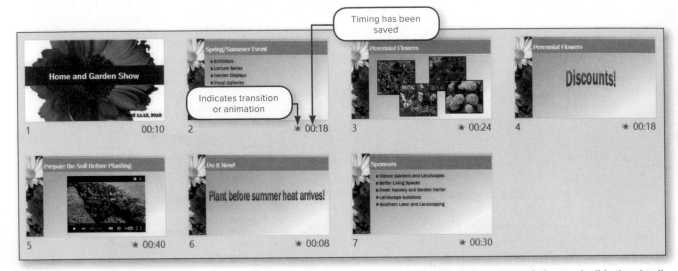

3-37 Slide timings appear below each slide thumbnail.

In rehearsal, go through your presentation and practice what you will say while each slide displays. Use printed notes pages while you are practicing. If possible, stand to replicate more closely the experience you will have when speaking to your audience. Knowing how and where to stand in relation to the keyboard and monitor you are using takes a little practice. Your body posture is important. Good posture makes you appear confident and it positively affects how your voice projects. If possible, rehearse with the equipment you will use to deliver the presentation.

## Set Timings Manually

You can enter all timings manually, but it is quicker to rehearse your presentation, save the timings, and adjust the time as needed for individual slides.

## ▶HOW TO: Modify Timings

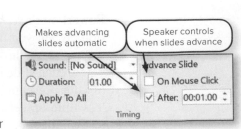

3-38 *Transitions* tab, *Timings* group

1. Click the **Transitions** tab and be sure the **After** option is selected [*Transitions* tab, *Timing* group] and second numbers are showing (Figure 3-38).

2. Change the number of seconds for each slide, as needed, to increase or decrease the amount of time the slide is displayed.

3. Deselect the **On Mouse Click** option if you want the slides to advance automatically.

4. Remove timings by clicking the **Record Slide Show** button [*Slide Show* tab, *Set Up* group], select **Clear**, and then select **Clear Timing on Current Slide** or **Clear Timings on All Slides** (Figure 3-39).

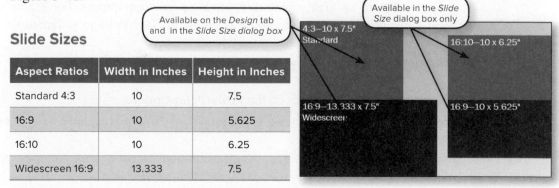

3-39 *Clear Timings* options

### Prepare for Mishaps

Be sure you have backup copies of your presentation in case you experience equipment failure and you need to switch to a different computer. In a worst-case situation, where both your computer and projector have malfunctioned, you can present using your handouts to support what you say. All experienced presenters encounter such problems at some time during their careers.

## SLO 3.5   Controlling Display Options

As you learned in Chapter 1, online themes and templates are available in different sizes called *Standard* and *Widescreen*. The default size for PowerPoint 2016 is *Widescreen;* the default size before PowerPoint 2013 was *Standard*. Therefore, you may encounter files that require updating to fit your current screen size, or you may need to adjust the size of your presentation to fit an older projection screen in a room where you will deliver your presentation.

### Adjust Slide Size

Today widescreen computers (like television screens) use a 16:9 or 16:10 aspect ratio (the ratio of width to height). A slide show designed in the 16:9 aspect ratio takes advantage of this wide horizontal space because it fills the screen. A slide show designed in the 4:3 aspect ratio (more square) and displayed on a widescreen will be positioned in the center of the screen with black areas on both sides. Both of these slide sizes are available on the *Design* tab in the *Customize* group and you can change from one to the other by clicking the **Slide Size** button and choosing **Standard (4:3)** or **Widescreen (16:9)**. Two other sizes are available on the *Slide Size* dialog box and you can create a custom size if necessary. These sizes are listed in the following table and illustrated as blue and green thumbnails in Figure 3-40:

### Slide Sizes

| Aspect Ratios | Width in Inches | Height in Inches |
|---|---|---|
| Standard 4:3 | 10 | 7.5 |
| 16:9 | 10 | 5.625 |
| 16:10 | 10 | 6.25 |
| Widescreen 16:9 | 13.333 | 7.5 |

Available on the *Design* tab and in the *Slide Size dialog box*

Available in the *Slide Size* dialog box only

4:3—10 x 7.5"
Standard

16:10—10 x 6.25"

16:9—13.333 x 7.5"
Widescreen

16:9—10 x 5.625"

3-40 Slide sizes illustrated

The two wide sizes available in the *Slide Size* dialog box (illustrated in Figure 3-40 on the right) look smaller because their width is 10", the same as the Standard 4:3 width. On your computer screen they will look almost the same as the *Widescreen* size, but ruler measurements and object sizes will be different because of the difference in width and height.

Changing between slide show sizes is a simple process, but necessary adjustments after the change can be time consuming. You need to consider how the change affects the text and graphics on your slide. Both *Standard* and *Widescreen* sizes have the same vertical measurement, so the width is what changes. Adjustments are usually needed so slide objects fit on the slides.

If you change from 4:3 to 16:9 or 16:10, the vertical size is reduced which compresses the slide vertically. Pictures or text in placeholders may not fit appropriately.

Be aware of these height and width differences when changing slide sizes. If you think you may need to change back to your original size, save the original presentation as a separate file before you begin making changes for the new size. By doing this, you can avoid all the resizing changes that would be necessary to return to the original size.

## ▶ HOW TO: Change the Aspect Ratio

1. Click the **Design** tab.
2. Click the **Slide Size** button [*Customize* group], and then click either **Standard (4:3)** or **Widescreen (16:9)** to select a different size.
3. From the dialog box that appears, select either **Maximize** or **Ensure Fit** for the best scaling option.
4. Click **Custom Slide Size** to open the *Slide Size* dialog box. Sizes for printing and four sizes for on-screen viewing are available. You can choose from the following:
   - *On-screen Show (4:3):* 10" × 7.5" (Standard)
   - *On-screen Show (16:9):* 10" × 5.625"
   - *On-screen Show (16:10):* 10" × 6.25"
   - *Widescreen (16:9):* 13.333" × 7.5"
5. Click **OK** (Figure 3-41). If necessary, select either **Maximize** or **Ensure Fit**.

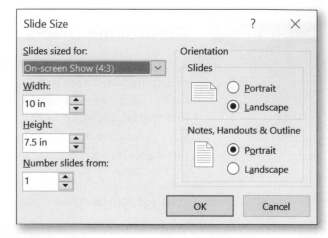

3-41 *Slide Size* dialog box

## Presenter View

*Presenter View* allows you to display your presentation on the screens of two monitors. For example, you could use a tablet or laptop and a large screen television. Or in a presentation room with built-in equipment, you might use a desktop computer with a ceiling-mounted projector and a large screen. The computer you are using must support the use of multiple monitors.

Setting up your monitors depends on your equipment. For example, if you are using a tablet or laptop, you can choose an option in PowerPoint to automatically extend your display.

## ▶ HOW TO: Modify Display Settings to Extend a Tablet or Laptop

1. Click the **File** tab and select **Options** to open the **PowerPoint Options** dialog box.
2. Select **Advanced**. In the *Display* category, select **Automatically extend display when presenting on a laptop or tablet**. Click **OK**.
3. Insert a wireless display adapter into a television HDMI port and then connect a laptop or tablet to the television through that adapter. Specific instructions will vary depending on your equipment.

If you have two monitors connected to one computer, you need to modify your computer's display settings to extend to the second monitor. This is a *Microsoft Windows* function.

**▶ HOW TO:** Modify Display Settings for Two Monitors

1. Click the *Windows* **Start** button and select **Settings** to open the *Settings* dialog box.
2. Click **System** and then select **Display**. Under *Customize your display*, two monitors will appear (Figure 3-42).
3. Click **Identify** and numbers appear on each monitor.
   - The *Orientation* should automatically be set for **Landscape**.
4. Click the **Multiple Displays** list box arrow and select **Extend these displays**.
5. Select **Monitor 1** and choose **Make this my main display**.
6. Click **Apply**.
7. Select **Advanced display settings** to make additional changes such as resolution or color calibration for both monitors.
8. Close the *Settings* dialog box.

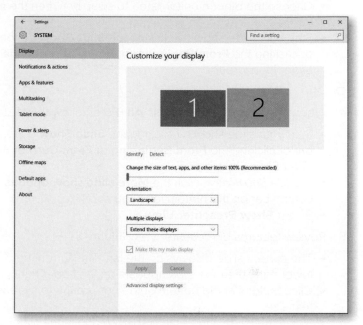

3-42 Customize display settings using Windows 10

These settings also can be made from the *Control Panel* [*Windows System* folder]. Select **Appearance and Personalization**, **Display**, and then **Change display settings**.

PowerPoint can automatically detect when two monitors are connected and will recognize one monitor as your primary monitor for *Presenter View* that shows your view of the presentation and includes the displayed slide, the navigation tools, the next slide, and an area for notes. The second monitor (or projector) displays the full-size slide show for your audience. Using *Presenter View* is helpful because while you are speaking you can:

- View the current slide and see the next slide in your presentation.
- Use convenient navigation tools.
- Have speaker notes available on the monitor for easy reading instead of needing printed notes.
- View thumbnails for all slides in the presentation and click thumbnails to display slides out of sequence.
- Zoom in to sections of a slide.
- Use pen tools without the audience seeing how you select pen options.
- Make the screen that's visible to your audience black yet still have speaker notes available to you.

To practice your presentation, it is possible to use *Presenter View* with only one monitor.

## ▶HOW TO: Use Presenter View

1. Click the **Slide Show** tab.

2. Select **Use Presenter View** [*Monitors* group] (Figure 3-43).

*3-43 Use Presenter View option on the Slide Show tab*

3. Follow these steps when using two monitors:

   - Click the **Monitor** drop-down arrow [*Monitors* group] to select the monitor used for audience viewing of your full-size slide show.
   - Choose the other monitor listed to swap between the monitors used for *Presenter View* and audience viewing.
   - Start your slide show by clicking the **Slide Show** button [*Status* bar] or clicking the **From Beginning** or **From Current Slide** buttons [*Start Slide Show* group].

*Or*

4. When using one monitor, press **Alt+F5** or follow these steps:

   - Start your slide show by clicking the **Slide Show** button on the *Status* bar or clicking the **From Beginning** or **From Current Slide** buttons [*Start Slide Show* group].
   - In *Slide Show* view, click the **More slide show options** button on the control bar on the bottom left (Figure 3-44).
   - Select **Show Presenter View**.

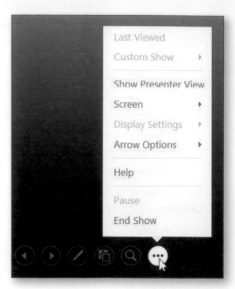

5. Review features of *Presenter View* (Figure 3-45).

   - The current slide displays on the left. The current notes appear on the lower right; the next slide appears on the upper right.
   - Click buttons at the bottom of the notes pane to increase or decrease text size.
   - Notice the slide show time displayed above the slide. Click **Pause the timer** to stop the seconds from increasing, but this change does not affect automatic transitions. Click **Resume the timer** to continue the time.
   - Click **Restart the timer** to set the time back to **0:00:00**.
   - Options above the slide include **Show Taskbar** so you can easily switch to other applications, **Display Settings** to swap monitors or duplicate a slide show, or **End Slide Show**.
   - Click the **Advance to next slide** button in the navigation area below the slide to move forward through your slides or click the **Return to the previous slide** button to move back.

*3-44 Control bar in Slide Show view and More slide show options*

*3-45 Presenter View window*

6. Review the control bar options in *Presenter View* (Figure 3-46).

   - Click the **Pen and laser pointer tools** button to select options for marking on your slide.
   - Click the **See all slides** button to show slide thumbnails. Click a thumbnail to jump to a different slide out of sequence.
   - Click the **Zoom into the slide** button, drag the selection area over an object or text you want to magnify so you can show detail, and then click. That section of the screen is displayed for your audience. Click the same button again (now **Zoom out**) to return to normal screen size.

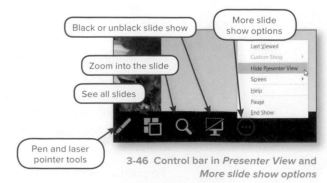

*3-46 Control bar in Presenter View and More slide show options*

- Click the **Black or unblack** button to make your second monitor appear blank and temporarily hide your current slide.
- Click **More slide show options** to choose other options such as **Hide Presenter View** so PowerPoint displays on your primary monitor.
- Press **Esc** or click **End Slide Show** to exit the slide show.

For this project, you add speaker notes, print notes pages, and rehearse a presentation. You will use *Presenter View* to display your slide show.

File Needed: *[your initials] PP P3-1.pptx*
Completed Project File Name: *[your initials] PP P3-2.pptx*

1. Open the *[your initials] PP P3-1* presentation completed in *Pause & Practice 3-1*.

2. Save the presentation as [your initials] PP P3-2.

3. Create a visual transition between topics.
   a. Insert a new slide with the *Section Header* layout after slides 3, 9, and 15.
   b. Delete the subtitle placeholder on each new slide and type the title text as follows:
      - Slide 4 title: Presentation Structure (Figure 3-47)
      - Slide 10 title: Presentation Practice
      - Slide 16 title: Summary

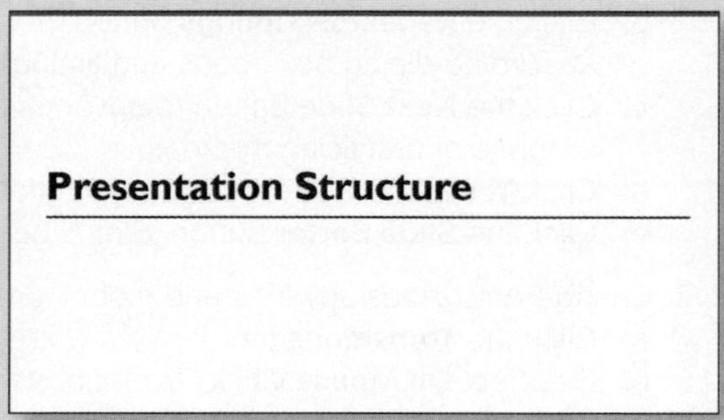

**Presentation Structure**

3-47 *Section Header* slide layout

4. Prepare speaker notes for two slides that do not have notes.
   a. Display slide 11, "Prepare Speaker Notes," and click the **Notes Page** button [*View* tab, *Presentation Views* group].
   b. Click the **Zoom In** button several times to increase the percentage to **120%** so you can easily see the text you will add.
   c. Type the following bulleted text [*Home* tab, *Paragraph* group] with a blank space between items for easy reading (Figure 3-48):
      - Print slide with discussion points below
        - Make notes brief (like cue cards)
        - Keep text large so it is easy to read
      - Can be a "safety net" (builds confidence)
      - Use to rehearse a presentation
      - Do not read during a presentation

- Print slides with discussion points below
  - Make notes brief (like cue cards)
  - Keep text large so it is easy to read
- Can be a "safety net" (builds confidence)
- Use to rehearse a presentation
- Do not read during a presentation

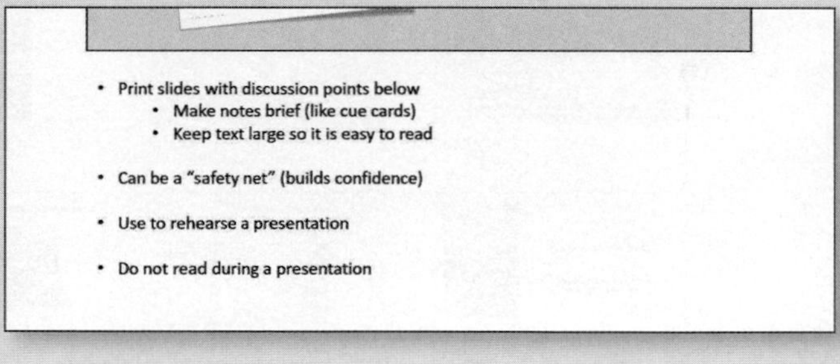

3-48 *Notes Page* view with text

   d. Click the **Next Slide** button [*Scroll* bar] or press **Page Down** to display the *Notes Page* for slide 12. Add the following text:
      - Experience is the best teacher
      - Identify strengths and develop them

- Identify weaknesses and work to overcome them
- Reduce tendency to be nervous

e. Click the **Normal** button [*View* tab, *Presentation Views* group].

5. Print notes pages for slides 11 and 12.
   a. Click the **File** tab and click **Print**.
   b. Select the appropriate printer and make sure that you are printing just one copy.
   c. For *Slides*, type 11-12 to print a *Custom Range*.
   d. For *Print Layout*, choose **Notes Pages** and select **Scale to Fit Paper** (Figure 3-49).
   e. Click the **Print** button.

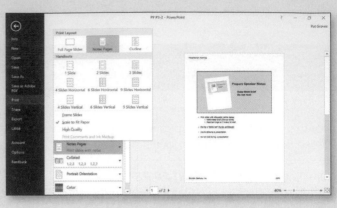

6. Rehearse your presentation and save timings.

**3-49** Print settings for *Notes Pages*

   a. Click the **Slide Show** tab.
   b. Click the **Rehearse Timings** button [*Set Up* group]. The *Recording* dialog box opens and timing begins.
   c. Click the **Next Slide** button to advance each slide after approximately 3–5 seconds (for the purpose of practicing this feature).
   d. Click **Yes** at the end of your presentation to save your timings.
   e. Click the **Slide Sorter** button [*Status* bar] to see the timings displayed below each slide.

7. Change how slides advance and modify presentation timings.
   a. Click the **Transitions** tab.
   b. Deselect **On Mouse Click** [*Transitions* tab, *Timing* group].
   c. Change the *After* timing to **3** seconds.
   d. Click the **Apply To All** button.
   e. Change the *After* timing on the *Section Header* slides (slides 4, 10, and 16) to **1** second (shown as **00:01**) (Figure 3-50).

**3-50** PP P3-2 completed

8. Review your presentation using *Presenter View*.
   a. Click the **Slide Show** tab.
   b. Click **Use Presenter View** [*Monitors* group].
   c. Review your slides.
      • If you have two monitors, click the **From Beginning** button [*Start Slide Show* group].
      • If you have one monitor, start your slide show. Click the **More slide show options** button on the control bar at the bottom left and select **Show Presenter View**.

9. Save and close the presentation.

# Presenting Using Projection Equipment

When you look at the front of a presentation room from where people are seated, the ideal location for a speaker is to the left of the projection screen. People are conditioned to read from left to right, so it is natural for the audience to first look at the speaker and then at the projection screen. Many situations are less than ideal, however, so be flexible when you cannot control the speaker area. Keep the following guidelines in mind:

• Become familiar with your equipment so you won't feel awkward using it.
• Be sure the computer or other device you are using has an adequate battery charge if you are using a wireless system to project your slide show.
• If possible, load your slide show before the audience enters the room so you are not seen scrambling around with preliminary preparations. Arrive early and test your presentation to be sure all content works correctly.
• Allow time to relax before your presentation starts. Almost everyone feels nervous before a presentation begins. This reaction is normal and just shows you are respectful of the situation. Harness your nervous energy in a positive way.
• Have your title slide displayed as people enter the room.
• If possible, greet people to make them feel welcome. Let people know that you are glad to have the opportunity to share with them.

## Position Equipment

Using a computer while you speak can create challenges. If you are using a desktop or notebook computer, you must see the computer screen when facing the audience and be able to access the computer to advance slides. Controlling your slide show using a tablet computer or even a smart phone makes it easy to advance slides using a touch screen, but these devices must work with your projector or a television if you are using a wireless display adapter.

In presentation rooms, you may need to place your computer on a table. A podium (or lectern) may be available to hold your computer or printed notes pages. Be careful, however, that the podium does not create a barrier between you and the audience. Move away from it when you can.

Even if your computer has a wireless Internet connection and is running on battery power, you may need to manage power cords for other equipment. Connections may not be convenient. Be sure to keep cables and cords away from the area where you and audience members will be walking or tape cords to the floor.

## Navigate in a Slide Show

You have advanced through a slide show by pressing the spacebar or clicking a slide. You can use other methods to advance, to go to specific slides, or to end a slide show.

During a slide show, navigation buttons are on the lower left of each slide (Figure 3-51). They are barely noticeable unless you point to that area.

- *Previous* or *Next*: Move between slides.
- *Pen and laser pointer tools*: Shows the menu for pen options.
- *See all slides*: Displays slide thumbnails; click a thumbnail to jump to that slide. Click the **Back** button to return to your previous slide.
- *Zoom into the slide*: Provides a selection area you can drag over your slide to magnify a section of the screen so you can show detail. You can drag the magnified area to show other portions of the screen in the large size. Right-click or press **Esc** to return to the current slide.
- *More slide show options*: Shows the menu for presentation options. For example, you can make the screen go black, change to *Presenter View*, or end a slide show.

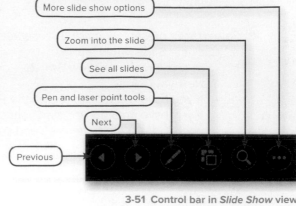

3-51 Control bar in *Slide Show* view

## Control Slide Display

The audience needs to focus on you, the speaker. Slides support your message, but you may not want a slide displayed all the time. Also, going from a blank screen to your next slide can seem dramatic.

### Blank Slides

If you know in advance that you need to discuss a topic unrelated to your slides, then plan ahead and place one or more slides with a black background in specific places in your slide show. During a presentation, you can blank the screen by pressing **B** on your keyboard to display an empty black screen or **W** to display an empty white screen. Be careful about using the white option, however, because an all-white screen can create glare that will be unpleasant for your audience. In the on-screen navigation, you can click a button to blank your screen to black then click it again to display your slide.

### Hide and Reveal Slides

Hiding a slide is helpful when you have information that is not essential to your presentation, but you want to have that slide available if you need it depending on time and audience interest. For example, you could hide slides containing information such as:

- References
- Additional pictures
- Additional details about a topic
- Optional charts, diagrams, or tables

Select one or more slides and click the **Hide Slide** button [*Slide Show* tab, *Set Up* group] (Figure 3-52). In *Normal* and *Slide Sorter* views, the slide thumbnail for a hidden slide appears grayed out with a diagonal line through the slide number.

During a slide show, you can display a hidden slide by typing the slide number and pressing **Enter**.

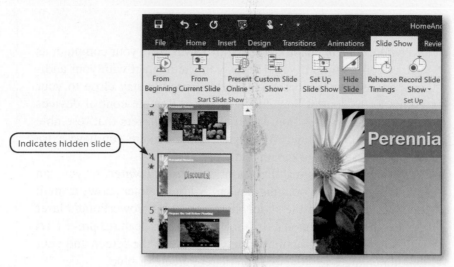

Indicates hidden slide

3-52 *Hide Slide* button and hidden slide 12

---

**MORE INFO**

You can print hidden slides. Click the **File** tab, then select **Print**. Click the **Print All Slides** option and select **Print Hidden Slides**.

---

### Use Keyboard Shortcuts

Keyboard shortcuts are convenient if you have easy access to your keyboard while speaking.

### Slide Show Navigation Shortcuts

| Press | Action |
| --- | --- |
| **N**, spacebar, right arrow, down arrow, **Enter**, or **Page Down** | Advance to the next slide. |
| **P**, **Backspace**, left arrow, up arrow, or **Page Up** | Go to the previous slide. |
| Slide number, then **Enter** | Go to a particular slide. |
| **Ctrl+S** | Open *All slides* dialog box, select slide, and click **Go To**. |
| **B** or period | Blanks the screen to black. |
| **W** or comma | Blanks the screen to white. |
| **S** | Stop or restart an automatic show. |
| Plus sign | Zoom in. |
| Minus sign | Zoom out. |
| **H** or slide number, then **Enter** | Go to a hidden slide. |

The presentation context menu is available during a slide show by right-clicking when you point anywhere on a slide (Figure 3-53).

## Remote Control and Laser Pointer

A *remote control* enables you to move away from your computer as you are presenting. If you do this, you can interact with your audience more naturally because you don't need to stay close to your computer to control how slides advance. Remote control devices come in many styles from small clickers to clickers that resemble pens with USB storage. When presenting, be sure you have extra batteries available for the remote control.

Remote controls may have a built-in *laser pointer*, or you can purchase a separate pointing device. A laser pointer shows a small dot (usually red) on the slide where you point. PowerPoint's laser pointer feature resembles this dot. To use this feature, press **Ctrl** and your left mouse button while you point on the screen and your pointer changes to a dot that can be red, green, or blue.

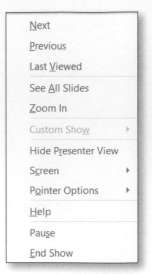

3-53 Presentation context menu

### ▶ HOW TO: Change Laser Pointer Color

1. Click the *Set Up Slide Show* button [*Slide Show* tab, *Set Up* group] to open the *Set Up Show* dialog box (Figure 3-54).
2. Click the **Laser pointer color** list box arrow and select **green** or **blue**.
3. Click **OK**.

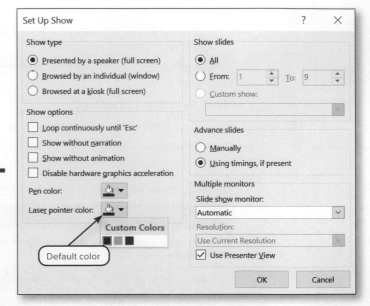

3-54 Change laser pointer color in the *Set Up Show* dialog box

A dot on the screen directs audience attention to a particular location. Be sure you show the dot long enough for your audience to find it and keep the dot steady. Do not bounce it around on the screen with random movements because this distracts viewers. A very small pointer movement on your computer screen creates a large movement on a projection screen.

### SLO 3.7 — Using Annotation Pens

You can call attention to information by writing or drawing on slides during a presentation. These markings are called *ink annotations*. While controlling the pointer to write with a hand-held mouse is a little awkward, using a stylus or your finger to draw on a tablet is more natural. You can record audience feedback and make simple drawings on slides. When you reach the end of your presentation, you can save ink annotations. All markings, even if you draw a rectangle, are saved as lines and not as shapes.

To write or draw on a slide, use the *Pen*. To add a color overlay on text, use the *Highlighter* just as you would mark text to highlight information on paper. When you change *Ink Color*, be sure the color you select contrasts with the slide background so it is easy to see.

## ▶ HOW TO: Use the Pen and Highlighter

1. Start a slide show and go to the slide you want to annotate.
2. Select the *Pen* or *Highlighter* using one of the following methods:
   - Click the **Pen** button in the navigation area (Figure 3-55) to open the context menu. Select an option as desired.
   - Right-click anywhere on the slide to open the context menu and select **Pointer Options**. Select an option as desired (Figure 3-56).
3. Begin writing or drawing on one or more slides.
4. Remove markings. Right-click, select **Pointer Options** from the context menu, and select **Eraser**. Click markings to delete each continuous pen stroke.
5. Change ink color. Right-click, select **Pointer Options** from the context menu, and select the **Ink Color** option. Select a different color (Figure 3-57).
6. Click **Keep** at the end of a presentation to save ink annotations. The markings are saved as lines that you can edit.

3-55 Pen and laser pointer tools

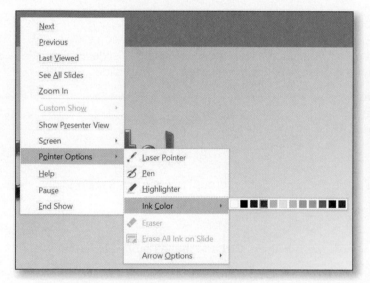

3-56 Change *Ink Color* for the *Pen* or *Highlighter*

3-57 Ink annotations and the *Eraser* tool

Pen tools are available in *Presenter View*, also. You can also control many of these options using keyboard shortcuts summarized in the following table:

### Ink Markup Shortcuts

| Press | Action |
| --- | --- |
| **Ctrl+P** | Changes the pointer to a pen |
| **Ctrl+A** | Changes the pointer to an arrow |
| **Ctrl+E** | Changes the pointer to an eraser |
| **Ctrl+M** | Shows or hides ink markup |
| **E** | Erases markings on the screen |

# PAUSE & PRACTICE: POWERPOINT 3-3

For this project, you use PowerPoint features to present more effectively. You hide and reveal slides, blank slides, practice with the laser pointer, change pen colors, use the pen and highlighter, and save annotations.

File Needed: *[your initials] PP P3-2.pptx*
Completed Project File Name: *[your initials] PP P3-3.pptx*

1. Open the *[your initials] PP P3-2* presentation completed in *Pause & Practice 3-2*.

2. Save the presentation as [your initials] PP P3-3.

3. Click the **Transitions** tab and change the slide transitions.
   a. Select **On Mouse Click** and deselect **After** [*Timing* group].
   b. Click **Apply To All** [*Timing* group].

4. Select slide 4 and click the **Hide Slide** button [*Slide Show* tab, *Set Up* group].
   a. Click the **From Beginning** button [*Slide Show* tab, *Start Slide Show* group] to start a slide show and advance through slides to confirm that you automatically go from slide 3 to slide 5.
   b. Display slide 6 in *Slide Show* view, type 4, and press **Enter** to show the hidden slide.

5. Practice blanking slides in *Slide Show* view.
   a. Press **B** to blank a slide to black. Press **B** to return to the slide.
   b. Press **W** to blank a slide to white. Press **W** to return to the slide.
   c. Press **Esc** to exit *Slide Show* view.

6. Change the laser pointer color.
   a. Click the **Set Up Slide Show** button [*Slide Show* tab, *Set Up* group] to open the *Set Up Show* dialog box.
   b. Click the **Laser pointer color** list box arrow and select **Blue**.
   c. Click **OK**.
   d. Practice using the laser pointer in *Slide Show* view. Press **Ctrl** and the left mouse button as you move the pointer on your slide.

7. Use the pen and highlighter.
   a. Go to slide 7 in *Slide Show* view.
   b. Right-click to open the context menu, select **Pointer Options**, and then repeat for each of the following actions:
      - Select **Ink Color** and select the color **Blue**.
      - Select the **Pen**. Draw a circle around the shape with the word "How" (Figure 3-58).
      - Select the **Highlighter**.
      - Select **Ink Color** and select the color **Light Blue**.
      - Draw a line twice to highlight the word "involved."

3-58 Pen color changed

   c. Type 13 and press **Enter** to go to slide 13. Use the **Highlighter** to highlight the words "Get help" and "feedback."
   d. Type 17 and press **Enter** to go to slide 17. Use the **Highlighter** to highlight the words "how an audience," "accepts," "heart," "what an audience," and "remembers."
   e. Right-click to open the context menu, select **Pointer Options**, and then select **Eraser**. Click to remove the highlights from the words "how an audience" and "what an audience."
   f. Advance to the end of the presentation and click **Keep** to save your annotations.

8. Save and close your presentation (Figure 3-59).

3-59 PP P3-3 completed

# Preparing a Self-Running Presentation

A self-running slide show, also referred to as a *kiosk presentation*, can be set up to run continuously without someone being present to advance the slides of the presentation. This type of presentation works well for trade shows or open house events where people walk up to a computer screen and watch the slide show. For example, self-running presentations can be used for marketing products to customers or to educate patients in medical office waiting rooms. You can record narration to accompany the slides. You can also set up the slide show to *loop* so it will automatically repeat and cycle continuously from beginning to end.

## Record a Slide Show with Narration

To record voice narration for your presentation, your computer must have a microphone and sound card. Like rehearsal, you can use this feature to practice what you will say during a presentation and evaluate your vocal qualities. You can also make a narrated slide show available as a complete presentation to distribute on CDs or DVDs or to post online for viewers.

Prepare carefully to decide what you will say as each slide displays. Use notes pages or other resources as references.

## ▶ HOW TO: Record Narration

1. Click the **Slide Show** tab.
2. Click the **Record Slide Show** drop-down arrow [*Set Up* group] and then select **Start Recording from Beginning** or **Start Recording from Current Slide** to open the *Record Slide Show* dialog box.
3. Select **Slide and animation timings** if it is not already selected.
4. Select **Narrations, ink, and laser pointer**. (This option is available only if your computer has a microphone.)
5. Click **Start Recording** (Figure 3-60).
   - A *Recording* box appears in the top left corner of the screen.
   - You can advance, pause, or resume recording in the same way you do when you rehearse a presentation (see *SLO 3.4: Using Rehearsal Techniques*).
6. Speak clearly into your microphone as each slide displays.
   - At the end of the presentation, the narration and slide timings will automatically be saved.
   - Separate audio files are recorded on each slide and an audio icon appears in the lower right of each slide thumbnail. Review your slide show and listen to your narration.
7. Save your presentation.

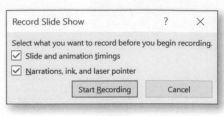

3-60 *Record Slide Show* dialog box

Press **Esc** if you need to end the slide show before reaching the last slide. You can clear timing or narration on the current slide or all slides. When you play back a narration, the recording is synchronized with the presentation.

## ▶ HOW TO: Clear Timings or Narration

1. Click the **Slide Show** tab.
2. Click the **Record Slide Show** drop-down arrow [*Set Up* group] and then select **Clear**.
3. Select from these options:

   **Clear Timing on Current Slide**
   **Clear Timing on All Slides**
   **Clear Narration on Current Slide**
   **Clear Narration on All Slides**

If you need to display the slide show without narration, click the **Set Up Show** button [*Slide Show* tab, *Set Up* group]. Select **Show without narration** and click **OK**.

## Set Up a Kiosk Presentation with Looping

Depending on how you plan to use it, a kiosk presentation may need different design guidelines than a slide show that is shown by a presenter. While other presentations provide minimal text because the slides support the speaker's message, a kiosk presentation may contain more information because it is a stand-alone product. If your kiosk presentation is displayed in a public place with a lot of distractions, then splashy graphics can be used to grab attention. On the other hand, if your kiosk presentation is for educational purposes in a quiet setting such as a doctor's office, the slides might be designed more like pages in a book with smaller text and more detailed information.

## ▶ HOW TO: Set Up a Kiosk Presentation

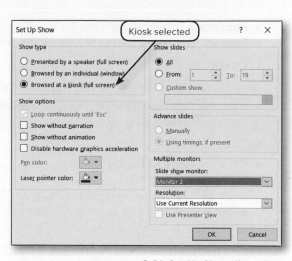

3-61 *Set Up Show* dialog box

1. Click the **Slide Show** tab.
2. Click the **Set Up Slide Show** button [*Set Up* group] to open the *Set Up Show* dialog box (Figure 3-61).
3. Choose the following settings:
   - *Show type*: **Browsed at a kiosk (full screen)**.
   - *Show options*: **Loop continuously until 'Esc'** is automatically selected and grayed out because you chose a kiosk.
   - *Show slides*: **All** or enter the first and last slide numbers you want to display.
   - *Advance slides*: **Use timings, if present** is automatically selected for a kiosk.
   - *Slide show monitor*: If you are using more than one monitor, select the appropriate monitor for the slide show.
   - *Resolution*: **Use Current Resolution** or the highest resolution possible for your equipment.
   - **Use Presenter View** is not available for a kiosk presentation.
4. Click **OK**.
5. Save the presentation with these changes.

---

**SLO 3.9**

# Packaging a Presentation to a CD or Folder

The *Package Presentation for CD* feature allows you to easily transport one or more presentations for use on another computer. You can copy your presentation file and any linked files to a blank CD (CD-R, recordable or CD-RW, rewritable) or to a folder on your computer, network location, or removable drive.

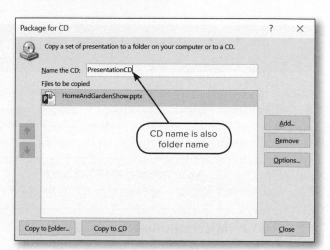

3-62 *Package for CD* dialog box

## ▶ HOW TO: Save a Presentation to a CD or Folder

1. Insert a CD in your CD/DVD drive if you are saving to that location.
2. Click the **File** tab and select **Export**.
3. Select **Package Presentation for CD**. Click the **Package for CD** button to open the *Package for CD* dialog box.
4. Type a name for the CD (Figure 3-62).
5. Click the **Options** button to open the *Options* dialog box (Figure 3-63) and choose from the following options:
   - **Linked Files:** Preserves links and copies any external files such as audio or video files.
   - **Embedded TrueType fonts**: Assures that the fonts used in your presentation are available on the playback computer.

3-63 *Options* dialog box

- **Password**: Enhances security for opening or modifying a presentation.
- **Inspect**: Checks for inappropriate or private information.

6. Click **OK**.

7. Save the presentation using one of the following methods:
   - Click the **Copy to CD** button and click **Yes** to verify that you want to include linked files.

   *Or*

   - Click the **Copy to Folder** button to open the *Copy to Folder* dialog box (Figure 3-64). Type a name for the folder and browse for the location to save the presentation. Select the option to **Open folder when complete** if you want to see all the files that are copied. Click **OK**.

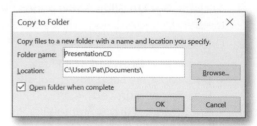

3-64 *Copy to Folder* dialog box

8. Click **No** when the packaging process is complete to indicate that you don't need to make another copy. Click **Close**.

9. Test the presentation by loading it from the folder or from the CD.

---

> ### MORE INFO
> If file size requirements exceed the storage capacity of a CD, you can convert your slide show to a video and then use DVD burning software to save the files to a DVD. PowerPoint does not support direct burning to DVDs.

## PAUSE & PRACTICE: POWERPOINT 3-4

This project consists of two parts. You record a presentation with audio if you have a microphone connected to your computer in Part A. In Part B, you prepare a kiosk presentation, set it up to loop so it is self-running, and then use the *Package Presentation for CD* feature to save it to a folder.

File Needed: ***[your initials] PP P3-2.pptx***
Completed Project File Name: ***[your initials] PP P3-4a.pptx* and *[your initials] PP P3-4b.pptx***

### Part A (Microphone Required)

1. Open the ***[your initials] PP P3-2*** presentation completed in *Pause & Practice 3-2*.

2. Save the presentation as [your initials] PP P3-4a and change to *Slide Sorter* view.

3. Delete slides 6–19. For this project, you need only slides 1–5.

4. Remove the timings.
   a. Click the **Record Slide Show** button [*Slide Show* tab, *Set Up* group] and select **Clear**.
   b. Select **Clear Timings on All Slides** (Figure 3-65).

3-65 Clear timings on all slides

5. Click the **Notes Page** button [*View* tab, *Presentation Views* group] and add notes to two slides.
   a. Display the *Notes Page* for slide 2. Add four items after the first line of text and add bullets [*Home* tab, *Paragraph* group]:
      - What is their background?
      - What is their educational level?
      - How familiar are they with your topic?
      - Are they likely to be accepting of your ideas or resistant?
   b. Display the *Notes Page* for slide 3. Add two more bulleted items at the end of the bulleted text:
      - Overall cleanliness and organization of the room
      - Temperature level for comfort
   c. Print the notes pages for slides 1-3 and 5 to use as a reference when recording the slide show.

6. Click the **Record Slide Show** drop-down arrow [*Slide Show* tab, *Set Up* group] and select **Start Recording from Beginning**.
   a. Select **Slide and animation timings** and **Narrations, ink, and laser pointer** (Figure 3-66).
   b. Click **Start Recording**.
   c. Speak clearly into your microphone as you go through the slide show. If you don't have a microphone, go through the slide show to practice. Your timings will be saved and sound icons will appear even if no sound was recorded.

3-66 *Record Slide Show* dialog box

7. Review the presentation and listen to the narration.

8. Save and close the presentation.

## Part B

1. Open the presentation **[your initials] PP P3-2** again.

2. Save the presentation as [your initials] PP P3-4b.

3. Apply timing so slides change rapidly.
   a. Confirm that **On Mouse Click** [*Transitions* tab, *Timing* group] is not selected.
   b. Change *Duration* to **01.00** and *After* to **00:02:00**.
   c. Click **Apply to All** (Figure 3-67).

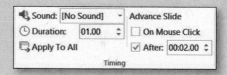

3-67 *Timing* group on the *Transitions* tab

4. Click the **Set Up Slide Show** button [*Slide Show* tab, *Set Up* group] to open the *Set Up Show* dialog box.
   a. Select the following settings (Figure 3-68):
      - *Show type*: **Browsed at a kiosk (full screen)**.
      - *Show options*: **Loop continuously until 'Esc'** is automatically checked for a kiosk.
      - *Show slides*: **All**.
      - *Advance slides*: **Use timings, if present** is automatically checked for a kiosk.
      - *Slide show monitor*: Select the appropriate monitor.
      - **Use Presenter View** is not available because you selected a kiosk presentation.
   b. Click **OK**.

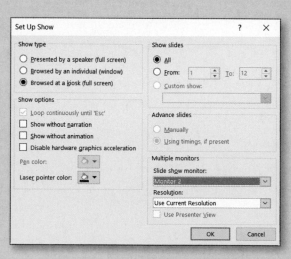

3-68 *Set Up Show* dialog box

5. Use the *Package Presentation for CD* feature to save a presentation to a folder.
   a. Click the **File** tab and select **Export**.
   b. Click **Package Presentation for CD** and click the **Package for CD** button to open the *Package for CD* dialog box.
   c. Type Planning for the name of the CD.

6. Click the **Options** button to open the *Options* dialog box and select the following:
   a. Choose **Linked Files** to preserve links and copy any external files such as audio or video files.
   b. Choose **Embedded TrueType fonts** to assure that the fonts you use in your presentation are available on the playback computer.
   c. Click **OK** and the dialog box closes.

7. Click the **Copy to Folder** button to open the *Copy to Folder* dialog box. The name you typed for the CD automatically appears.
   a. Click **Browse** to open the *Choose Location* dialog box and find the place where you want to save the presentation. Click **Select**.
   b. Select the option to **Open folder when complete**.
   c. Click **OK** and the dialog box closes.
   d. Click **Yes** if you receive a message about including linked files.

      • A *File Explorer* window opens showing the files in the open *Planning* folder (Figure 3-69).

8. Move the *File Explorer* window so you can close the *Package for CD* dialog box.

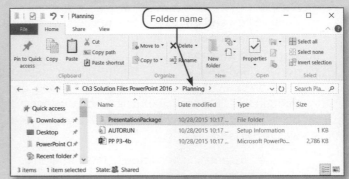

3-69 Folder for completed slide show

9. Close your original *[your initials] PP P3-4b* presentation.

10. Test the saved presentation by opening it from the *Planning* folder. Double click the *[your initials] PP P3-4b* file name.

11. Close the presentation and folder.

# Chapter Summary

**3.1** Create custom theme colors and background fills (p. P3-147).

- Design themes create a unified appearance for your presentation.
- The *Accent 1* theme color is the color that appears, by default, each time you draw a shape.
- Create custom theme colors by selecting different colors for background, text, and accent colors. Select the background color first and then select other colors that work well on that background.
- Modify backgrounds using the *Format Background* dialog box to apply a custom pattern, gradient, or picture fill.
- Carefully control how text is placed over background pictures and other fills so text is easy to read.

**3.2** Apply animation to add interest and reinforce content (p. P3-155).

- **Animation** adds movement to slide objects and text.
- Animation is applied through **Entrance**, **Exit**, and **Emphasis** effects.
- If more than one animation is used, each animation is numbered in sequence.
- **Effect Options** control the direction and sequence of movement.
- Animation **Start** options include *On Click*, *With Previous*, or *After Previous*.
- **Duration** is the time that it takes to complete an animation.

**3.3** Link to an online video (p. P3-158).

- Search for an online video using the *Insert Video* dialog box.
- You need Internet access and a video must currently be available online if you want to link to it during a PowerPoint presentation.
- Some videos cannot be played effectively at full screen size because the resolution is too low.
- Playback controls appear at the bottom of the video.

**3.4** Use rehearsal techniques to prepare for presentation delivery (p. P3-164).

- Type **speaker notes** using the *Notes* pane or *Notes Page* view.
- Print speaker notes for reference during a presentation.
- Use **Rehearse Timings** to practice and judge the pace of your presentation.

- You can manually adjust timings to increase or decrease the time a slide is displayed.
- Prepare backup copies of your presentation and your notes.

**3.5** Control display options for different screen sizes (p. P3-167).

- The dimensions of your slides vary based on the aspect ratio (the ratio of width to height) you use.
- PowerPoint's default aspect ratio is **Widescreen** *16:9;* the **Standard** *4:3* is available.
- *Presenter View* displays the current slide, next slide, notes, and navigation controls on one monitor, while the slide show displays on a second monitor or projection screen.
- *Presenter View* can be used with one monitor or multiple monitors/devices.

**3.6** Present effectively and professionally using projection equipment (p. P3-173).

- Use the slide show toolbar, context menu, or keyboard shortcuts to navigate to different slides in a presentation.
- To blank a slide to black, press **B;** to blank a slide to white, press **W**.
- When you hide a slide, it is still in the presentation but will not display during a slide show unless you go to that specific slide by typing its number and pressing **Enter**.
- Use a **remote control** to advance slides so you can move away from your computer.
- Use PowerPoint's **laser pointer** to temporarily display a dot on the slide during a slide show.

**3.7** Use annotation pens to highlight information and save presentation markings (p. P3-176).

- Use the **Pen** or **Highlighter** to mark or draw on a slide during a slide show.
- Use the **Eraser** to remove markings during a slide show.
- These markings, called **ink annotations**, can be saved at the end of the presentation.

**3.8** Prepare a self-running presentation that loops (p. P3-179).

- If your computer has a microphone, you can include narration in a presentation.
- A self-running presentation, a **kiosk presentation**, is set to automatically **loop** so it runs continuously.
- Use the *Set Up Show* dialog box to choose options for a kiosk presentation.

**3.9** Use the *Package Presentation for CD* feature to prepare a slide show for display on other computers (p. P3-181).

- The ***Package Presentation for CD*** feature saves linked files to a CD or other location.
- To assure that the fonts you used to create your presentation are available on the computer you will use to display your presentation, select ***Embedded TrueType Fonts***.

## Check for Understanding

The SIMbook for this text (within your SIMnet account) provides the following resources for concept review:

- Multiple choice questions
- Matching exercises
- Short answer questions

## Guided Project 3-1

One of the community colleges in the Sierra Pacific Community College District has finished construction of a new building for their business program. A dedication ceremony and open house is planned. For this project, you finalize the presentation for this special program.
[**Student Learning Outcomes 3.1, 3.2, 3.4, 3.5, 3.6, 3.8**]

Files Needed: ***Dedication-03.pptx*** and ***Building-03.jpg*** (*Student data files are available in the* Library *of your SIMnet account.*)
Completed Project File Names: ***[your initials] PowerPoint 3-1.pptx***

### Skills Covered in This Project

- Apply a background picture fill.
- Apply animation and effect options.
- Create and print notes pages.
- Rehearse a presentation and save timings.
- Use *Presenter View.*
- Use slide show navigation tools, keyboard shortcuts, and insert blank slides.

1. Open the ***Dedication-03*** presentation from your student data files.
2. Save the presentation as [your initials] PowerPoint 3-1.
3. Apply a background picture fill with a softened effect to all slides.
   a. Display slide 1. Point to the slide background and right-click to open the context menu. Click **Format Background** to open the *Format Background* pane.
   b. Select the **Picture or texture fill** option.
   c. Click the **File** button to open the *Insert Pictures* dialog box.
   d. Locate your student data files, select the ***Building-03*** picture, and click the **Insert** button.
   e. Click the **Picture** button at the top of the pane and then click **Picture Color**. Click the **Recolor** drop-down list and select **Blue, Accent color 2 Dark** (Figure 3-70).

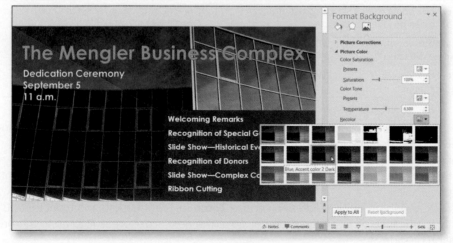

3-70 Picture background with *Recolor* options

   f. Click **Apply to All** so this picture is used as the background for all slides.

4. Restore the background picture to its original color on two slides.
   a. Display slide 1. On the *Format Background* pane under *Picture Color,* click the **Reset** button.
   b. Display slide 2 and click the **Reset** button again.

5. Prepare a black slide so the speaker can talk for a few moments with no slide displayed.
   a. Display slide 6. On the *Format Background* pane, click **Fill** at the top of the pane if it is not selected. Select the **Solid fill** option.
   b. Click the **Color** drop-down arrow and select **Black, Background 1**.
   c. Close the *Format Background* pane.

6. Apply a transition to all slides.
   a. Click the **Transitions** tab and apply the **Shape** transition.
   b. Click the **Effect Options** button [*Animation* group] and select **Diamond**.
   c. Click **Apply to All** [*Timing* group] (Figure 3-71).

3-71 *Transition Effect Options*

7. Apply animation and effect options using the settings shown in the following table.
   a. Select the text or object to be animated.
   b. Click the **More** button on the gallery [*Animation* group] or click the **Add Animation** button [*Animations* tab, *Advanced Animation* group] if the *Animation* gallery is not displayed.
   c. Click an animation effect to apply it.
   d. Click the **Effects Options** button [*Animation* group] to apply *Direction, Sequence,* or *Amount* settings. Some settings will appear by default.
   e. Adjust settings for *Start* and *Duration* [*Timing* group] as needed.
   f. Click the **Preview** button [*Preview* group] or **Slide Show** button [*Status* bar] to test the animation.

| Slide | Object | Animation Effect | Effect Options | Start | Duration |
|-------|--------|------------------|----------------|-------|----------|
| 1 | Text box for the agenda on the right | *Wipe* (Entrance) | *From Bottom, By Paragraph* | On Click | 00.50 |
| 3 | Picture | *Shape* (Entrance) | *Out, Diamond* | *After Previous* | 02:00 |
| 7 | Text box about space design | *Zoom* (Entrance) | *Object Center, As One Object* | On Click | 00:50 |
| 7 | Text box about wireless access | *Zoom* (Entrance) | *Object Center, As One Object* | On Click | 00:50 |
| 8 | Text box with donor names | *Wipe* (Entrance) | *From Bottom, All At Once* | *After Previous* | 01:00 |

8. Use *Slide Show* view to practice use of navigation tools, keyboard shortcuts, and blanking slides.
   a. Display slide 1 and click the **Slide Show** button [*Status* bar].
   b. Click the **Next** button in the control bar to advance slides.
   c. Click the **See all slides** button in the control bar to see slide thumbnails; click a thumbnail to jump to a specific slide.
   d. Right-click anywhere on the slide and choose **Zoom In**. Right-click to zoom out to regular slide size.
   e. Press **N** to advance through animation or go to the next slide; press **P** to go to the previous animation or slide.
   f. Type 5 and press **Enter** to go to slide 5.
   g. Press **B** to blank a slide; press **B** to view the slide again.
   h. Press **Esc** to exit *Slide Show* view.

9. Prepare speaker notes on two slides.
   a. Select slide 1. Click the **Notes Page** button [*View* tab, *Presentation Views* group].
   b. Click the **Zoom** button on the *Notes Page* and increase the *Percent* to **150%** so you can more easily see the text. Click **OK**.
   c. Add the following text with a blank line between each item (Figure 3-72):

3-72 *Notes Page* view showing speaker notes

   *Slide 1*: Welcome the audience
            Review today's agenda—go through animation

   *Slide 5*: Fostered business innovation and involvement
            Developed the Business Development Institute
            Expanded internship opportunities

   d. Click the **Normal** button [*View* tab, *Presentation Views* group] to return to *Normal* view.

10. Print notes pages for slides 4 and 5.
    a. Click the **File** tab and click **Print**.
    b. Select the appropriate printer and make sure that you are printing just one copy.
    c. For *Slides*, type 4–5 to print a *Custom Range*.
    d. For *Print Layout*, choose **Notes Pages** and check **Scale to Fit Paper** (Figure 3-73).
    e. Click the **Print** button.

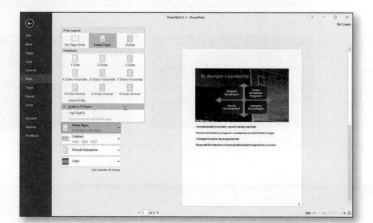

3-73 Print view of *Notes Page*

11. Rehearse and save timings.
    a. Click the **Rehearse Timings** button [*Slide Show* tab, *Set Up* group] to open the *Recording* dialog box and start timing.
    b. Click the **Next Slide** button to advance each slide and animation effect after approximately 3–5 seconds.
    c. Click **Yes** at the end of your presentation to save your timings. The timings are displayed below each slide in *Slide Sorter* view.

12. Use *Presenter View* to review your presentation.
    a. Click the **Slide Show** tab.
    b. Deselect **Use Timings** [*Set Up* group].
    c. Click **Use Presenter View** [*Monitors* group].
    d. Click the **From Beginning** button [*Start Slide Show* group].
       • If you have one monitor, right-click and select **Show Presenter View**.
    e. Click the **Advance to next slide** button to review your slides.
    f. Click the **Zoom into the slide** button to magnify a section of the slide. Click **Zoom Out** (the same button) to return to the normal slide size (Figure 3-74).

3-74 *Presenter View*

g. Click the **See all slides** button to view thumbnails of all slides. Click to display different slides.

h. Press **Esc** to exit *Presenter View.*

13. Save and close the presentation (Figure 3-75).

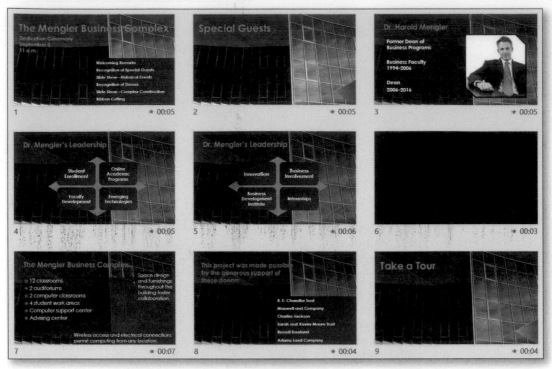

3-75 PowerPoint 3-1 completed

## Guided Project 3-2

For the second training session for new hires on presenting effectively, Davon Washington, management consultant at Solution Seekers, Inc., is preparing guidelines for designing slides and developing content in a visual way. For this project, you finish the presentation that Davon has prepared and save it on a CD so participants can refer to it after the session.
[**Student Learning Outcomes 3.1, 3.2, 3.3, 3.4, 3.7, 3.9**]

Files Needed: *SlideShowDevelopment-03.pptx, Background-03.jpg*, and *Applause-03.jpg* (*Student data files are available in the* Library *of your SIMnet account.*)
Completed Project File Names: *[your initials] PowerPoint 3-2.pptx* and folder *Develop Slides*

### Skills Covered in This Project

- Apply a background picture fill.
- Create custom theme colors.
- Apply animation and effect options.
- Print notes pages.
- Add ink annotations.
- Use the *Package Presentation for CD* feature.

1. Open the **SlideShowDevelopment-03** presentation from your student data files.

2. Save the presentation as [your initials] PowerPoint 3-2.

3. Apply a background picture fill to all slides.
   a. Point to the background and right-click. Select **Format Background** to open the *Format Background* pane.
   b. Select the **Picture or texture fill** option.
   c. Click the **File** button to open the *Insert Pictures* dialog box.
   d. Locate your student data files, select **Background-03,** and click **Insert** (Figure 3-76).
   e. Click **Apply to All** so this picture is the background for all slides.

3-76 Title slide with new background picture fill

4. Display slide 12. Repeat step 3 to apply a different background picture, **Applause-03,** for this slide only.
   a. Change the *Offset left* to **−9%** and the *Offset top* to **−5%** for better picture positioning on the slide. (*Offset right* is 0% and *Offset bottom* is −9%.)
   b. Close the *Format Background* pane.

5. Prepare a new custom color theme to blend with the background picture.
   a. Click the **More** button [*Design* tab, *Variants* group].
   b. Click **Colors** and click **Customize Colors** to open the *Create New Theme Colors* dialog box.
   c. Change five accent colors according to the following table.
      • For each change, click the color drop-down arrow and select **More Colors** to open the *Colors* dialog box.
      • Click the **Custom** tab and enter the numbers for *Red, Green,* and *Blue.*

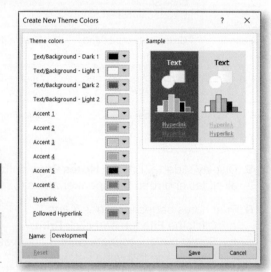

|       | Accent 1 | Accent 2 | Accent 3 | Accent 4 | Accent 5 |
|-------|----------|----------|----------|----------|----------|
| *Red*   | 255 | 157 | 255 | 38  | 95 |
| *Green* | 247 | 175 | 217 | 203 | 30 |
| *Blue*  | 220 | 210 | 82  | 236 | 60 |

   d. Name the new custom theme Development (Figure 3-77).
   e. Click the **Save** button.

3-77 New theme colors

6. Select the following slides and adjust text and object colors:
   a. *Slide 7*: Select the *SmartArt* graphic. Click the **Change Colors** button [*SmartArt Tools Design* tab, *SmartArt Styles* group] and select the **Colored Fill – Accent 5** style in the *Accent 5* category (Figure 3-78).
   b. *Slide 12*: Select the text box. Click the **Shape Fill** button [*Home* tab, *Drawing* group] and select **Plum, Accent 5**.

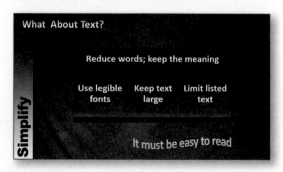

3-78 *SmartArt* recolored

7. Apply a transition to all slides.
   a. Click the **Transitions** tab and apply the **Reveal** transition.
   b. Click the **Effect Options** button [*Transition to this Slide* group] and select **Smoothly from Right**.
   c. Change the *Duration* to **02:00** [*Timing* group].
   d. Click **Apply to All**.

8. Apply animation on four slides and change effect options as shown in the following table.
   a. Select the text or object to be animated.
   b. Click the **Animations** tab and click the **More** button on the *Animation* gallery. (Click the **Add Animation** button [*Advanced Animation* group] if the gallery is not open.)
   c. Click an effect to apply it.
   d. Click the **Effects Options** button [*Animation* group] to apply *Direction, Sequence,* or *Amount* settings.
   e. Adjust settings for *Start and Duration* [*Timing* group] as needed to match the table. Some settings will appear by default.
   f. Click the **Preview** button [*Preview* group] or **Slide Show** button [*Status* bar] to test the animation.

| Slide | Object | Animation Effect | Effect Options | Start | Duration |
|-------|--------|------------------|----------------|-------|----------|
| 2 | Ducks | *Fly In* (Entrance) | *From Left* | *On Click* | 02.00 |
| 2 | Slide Show Development text box | *Bounce* (Entrance) | None | *After Previous* | 02.00 |
| 4 and 5 | Grouped text box and up arrow | *Float In* (Entrance) | *Float Up* | *After Previous* | 01.00 |
| 4 and 5 | Grouped text box and down arrow | *Float In* (Entrance) | *Float Down* | *After Previous* | 01.00 |
| 6 | Color wheel | *Spin* (Emphasis) | *Clockwise, Two Spins* | *After Previous* | 03.00 |

9. Display slide 1. Click the **Notes Page** button [*View* tab, *Presentation Views* group]. Advance through all slides and read the speaker notes to review tips for slide design.

10. Print notes pages for slides 7 and 11.
    a. Click the **File** tab and click **Print**.
    b. Select the appropriate printer and make sure that you are printing just one copy.
    c. Choose the following settings:
       - *Slides*: 7, 11 for a *Custom Range*.
       - *Print Layout*: **Notes Pages** and **Scale to Fit Paper** (Figure 3-79).
    d. Click the **Print** button.

11. Add ink annotations on slides 4, 5, and 7.
    a. Display slide 4. Click the **Slide Show** button [*Status* bar] to start your slide show on this slide.
    b. Right-click to open the context menu, select **Pointer Options** and **Highlighter**. Highlight the word "**organization**" in the text box.
    c. Display slide 5, repeat step 11b and highlight the words "**creative thinking**" in the text box.
    d. Display slide 7, right-click to open the context menu. Select **Pointer Options** and **Pen**. Circle the words "**Reduce words**" and "**keep the meaning**."
    e. Advance to the end of the presentation and click **Keep** to save your ink annotations.

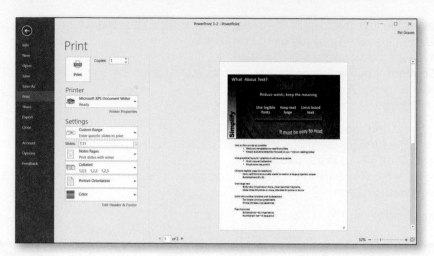

**3-79 Print Notes Pages**

12. Save the presentation (Figure 3-80).

**3-80 PowerPoint 3-2 completed**

13. Use the *Package Presentation for CD* feature to save the presentation to a folder.
    a. Click the **File** tab and select **Export**.
    b. Click **Package Presentation for CD** and click the **Package for CD** button to open the *Package for CD* dialog box.
    c. Type Develop Slides to name the CD.
    d. Click the **Options** button to open the *Options* dialog box and select **Linked Files** and **Embedded TrueType fonts** (Figure 3-81).
    e. Click **OK**.
    f. Click the **Copy to Folder** button to open the *Copy to Folder* dialog box. The folder name appears and is the same name you typed for the CD. Deselect the **Open folder when complete** option.

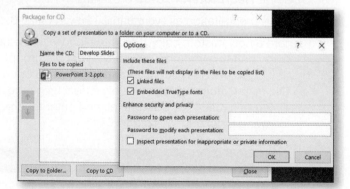

**3-81 *Package for CD* and *Copy to Folder* dialog boxes**

P3-193

g. Browse for the location to save the presentation and click the **Select** button.

h. Click **OK** to close the *Copy to Folder* dialog box.

i. Click **Yes** when a message appears asking if you want to include linked files.

j. Click **Continue** when another message appears about comments and annotations.

k. Close the *Package for CD* dialog box.

l. Close the presentation.

14. Open the "packaged" presentation.

a. Open the *Develop Slides* folder where you "packaged" the presentation. Notice that additional files have been saved in this folder.

b. Double-click the file name in the folder to open the presentation. If you receive a security warning, click the **Enable** button.

15. Test the presentation and then close it.

# Guided Project 3-3

At an upcoming meeting of the American River Cycling Club, Eric Salinas is giving a presentation about the importance of knowing your target heart rate and exercising with your heart rate at an appropriate target level. For this project, you finalize the presentation.
[Student Learning Outcomes 3.1, 3.3, 3.4, 3.5, 3.8]

Files Needed: ***HeartRateARCC-03.pptx*** and ***RiderAir.jpg*** *(Student data files are available in the Library of your SIMnet account.)*
Completed Project File Name: *[your initials] PowerPoint 3-3.pptx*

### Skills Covered in This Project

- Create custom theme colors.
- Apply a background picture fill.
- Link to a video on a web site.
- Use *Presenter View.*
- Create and print notes pages.
- Record a presentation with narration.
- Prepare a kiosk presentation.

1. Open the ***HeartRateARCC-03*** presentation from your student data files.

2. Save the presentation as [your initials] PowerPoint 3-3.

3. Prepare a new custom color theme to blend with the heart picture on slide 3.

a. Click the **More** button [*Design* tab, *Variants* group].

b. Select **Colors** and click **Customize Colors** to open the *Create New Theme Colors* dialog box.

c. Click the **Color** drop-down arrow for each change, and select **More Colors** to open the *Colors* dialog box. Click the **Custom** tab and enter the *Red, Green,* and *Blue* numbers shown in the following table for four colors.

| | Text/Background – Dark 2 | Accent 1 | Accent 2 | Accent 3 |
|---|---|---|---|---|
| Red | 24 | 36 | 204 | 227 |
| Green | 66 | 99 | 0 | 108 |
| Blue | 77 | 116 | 0 | 9 |

d. Name the new custom theme **ARCC** (Figure 3-82).
e. Click the **Save** button and the new colors will automatically be applied to all slides.

4. Format the title slide by adding a background picture fill.
   a. Display slide 1. Point to the background, right-click, and select **Format Background** to open the *Format Background* pane.
   b. Select the **Picture or texture fill** option.
   c. Click the **File** button to open the *Insert Pictures* dialog box.
   d. Locate your student data files, select *RiderAir-03,* and click **Insert**.
   e. Click **Picture** at the top of the pane and select **Picture Color**. Click the **Recolor** button and select **Black and White**: **25%** (Figure 3-83).
   f. Close the *Format Background* pane.

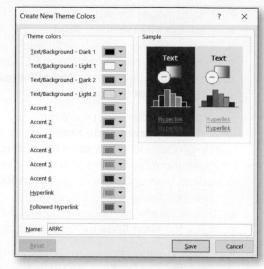

3-82 New ARCC color theme

5. Increase the subtitle font size on the title slide to **36 pt**. and resize the placeholder so one word fits on each line.

6. Find and insert an online video.
   a. Display slide 5 and click the **Insert** tab.
   b. Click the **Video** button [*Media* group] and select **Online Video** to open the *Insert Video* dialog box.
   c. Type the words Col de la Madone in the *YouTube* search box and click the **Search** button. Select an appropriate video. Click **Insert**.
   d. Position the video to the left of the picture and resize it (*Width* **5.5"**), if necessary. Be sure the video quality remains acceptable.
   e. Below the video, add the appropriate source information in a text box.
   f. Play the video in *Slide Show* view by clicking the **Start** button in the middle of the video.

3-83 Completed title slide

7. Apply a transition. Choose **Cube** [*Transitions* tab, *Transition to This Slide* group] with the **From Right** effect options. Click **Apply To All**.

8. Use *Presenter View* to review your presentation.
   a. Click the **Slide Show** tab.
   b. Click **Use Presenter View** [*Monitors* group].
   c. Click the **From Beginning** button [*Start Slide Show* group] to start your presentation.
      - If you have one monitor, right-click and select **Show Presenter View**.
   d. Click the **Advance to the next slide** button to advance slides as you review them.
   e. At the bottom of the Notes pane, click the **Make the text larger** button to increase the text size for notes on all slides. Scroll to read the text on slide 3 (Figure 3-84).
   f. Press **Esc** to end the slide show.

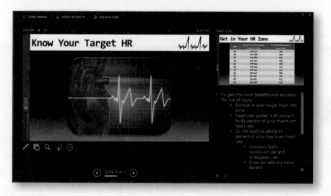

3-84 *Presenter View*

9. Print notes pages for slides 3 and 4.
   a. Click the **File** tab. Click **Print**.
   b. Select the appropriate printer and make sure that you are printing just one copy.
   c. For *Slides,* type 3-4 to choose a *Custom Range.*
   d. For *Print Layout,* choose **Notes Pages** and select **Scale to Fit Paper**.
   e. Click the **Print** button.

10. Record a slide show with narration.
   a. Click the **Record Slide Show** button [*Slide Show* tab, *Set Up* group] and select **Start Recording from Beginning** to open the *Record Slide Show* dialog box.
   b. Select both options and click **Start Recording** (Figure 3-85). The *Recording* dialog box appears.
   c. Speak clearly into your microphone as each slide is displayed.
   d. Click the **Next Slide** navigation button to advance each slide.

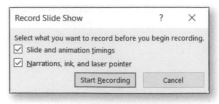

3-85 *Record Slide Show* dialog box

11. Prepare a kiosk presentation with looping.
   a. Click the **Set Up Slide Show** button [*Slide Show* tab, *Set Up* group] to open the *Set Up Show* dialog box.
   b. Select the *Show type* **Browsed at a kiosk (full screen)**.
   c. For *Show slides* select **All**.
   d. Select the **Primary Monitor**.
   e. Click **OK**.

12. Save and close your presentation (Figure 3-86).

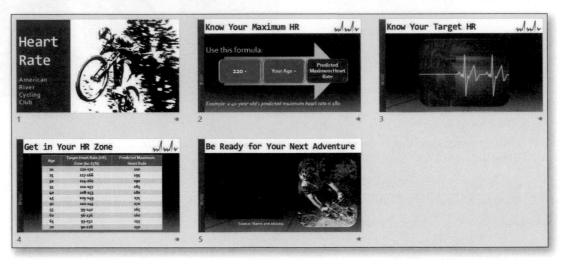

3-86 PowerPoint 3-3 completed

## Independent Project 3-4

The sales representatives at Wilson Home Entertainment Systems review acceptable viewing distances when talking with clients who are in the early stages of planning a home theater or media room. They discuss options for televisions or projection systems for the spaces being planned. For this project, you complete a presentation to prepare clients for an in-home consultation.
[**Student Learning Outcomes 3.1, 3.2, 3.4, 3.6, 3.7, 3.8**]

Files Needed: ***ScreenSizes-03.pptx***, ***TVCabinet-03.jpg***, ***TVWallMount-03.jpg***, and ***Projector-03.jpg***
*(Student data files are available in the* Library *of your SIMnet account.)*
Completed Project File Name: ***[your initials] PowerPoint 3-4.pptx***

## Skills Covered in This Project

- Change slide size.
- Apply a background picture fill.
- Apply animation and effect options.
- Rehearse a presentation and save timings.

- Use slide show navigation tools, keyboard shortcuts, and blank slides.
- Hide and reveal slides.
- Use the laser pointer feature.
- Use annotation pens.
- Prepare a kiosk presentation.

1. Open the ***ScreenSizes-03*** presentation from your student data files. This presentation is saved in the **Standard (4:3)** format.

2. Click the **Slide Size** button [*Design* tab, *Customize* group] and click **Widescreen (16:9)** (Figure 3-87). The slide size has changed from 10" to 13.33" wide.

3. Save the presentation in the widescreen size as [your initials] PowerPoint 3-4.

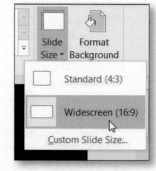

3-87 *Slide Size*

4. Open the *Format Background* pane and change the background to a picture fill on three slides. Locate your student data files and insert the following pictures:
   a. *Slide 5*: **TVCabinet-03**
   b. *Slide 6*: **TVWallMount-03**
   c. *Slide 7*: **Projector-03**

5. Close the *Format Background* pane.

6. Right-align the text boxes at the bottom of slides 5, 6, and 7 to better fit the widescreen size (Figure 3-88).

7. Right-align the WHES logo on slides 1 and 8.

8. Apply the **Vortex** transition with the **From Bottom** effect option. Change the *Duration* to **3.00**. Apply these settings to all slides (Figure 3-89).

3-88 Background picture fill

9. Apply animation on four slides and change settings as needed to match the following table.

| Slide | Object | Animation Effect | Effect Options | Start | Duration |
|-------|--------|------------------|----------------|-------|----------|
| 2 | Question mark | *Spin* (Emphasis) | *Counterclockwise, Two Spins* | *After Previous* | *02.00* |
| 5, 6, 7 | Text box | *Fly In* (Entrance) | *From Top-Left, As One Object* | *After Previous* | *00.50* |

10. Rehearse the presentation and save timings.

11. Modify the timings to advance each slide after 5 seconds.

12. Hide slide 4.

13. Use the *Set Up Show* dialog box to change *Advance Slides* to **Manually**. Click **OK**.

14. Practice the following slide show features in *Slide Show* view:
    a. Use the control bar buttons to move to the next slide.
    b. Press **B** to blank a slide. Press **B** to display the slide again.
    c. Right-click to open the context menu, select **Pointer Options,** and change the *Laser Pointer* color.
    d. Go to the hidden slide 4.
    e. Point to slide objects (Height, Lighting, and Viewing Angle) with the laser pointer.
    f. Use keyboard shortcuts. Type 2 and press **Enter** to go to slide 2.

15. Add annotations on slides 3 and 4 using the **Pen** with **Red** ink and keep annotations. Use *Presenter View* and practice making annotations on the presenter slide.
    a. *Slide 3*: Circle the "**55-60**" and "**100**" screen sizes.
    b. *Slide 4*: Go to this hidden slide and circle the following phrases in the bulleted items: "**level with the middle,**""**reduce color clarity,**" and "**visibility at all seats.**"
    c. Keep ink annotations

16. Prepare a kiosk presentation with looping.
    a. Select **Use Timings** on the *Slide Show* tab.
    b. Click the **Set Up Slide Show** button to open the *Set Up Show* dialog box.
    c. For *Show Slides,* select **All**.
    d. For *Advance Slides,* select **Use timings, if present**.
    e. Select **Browsed at a kiosk (full screen)** (Figure 3-90).
    f. Select the appropriate monitor.
    g. Click **OK**.

17. Save and close the presentation (Figure 3-91).

3-89 *Vortex* transition effect options

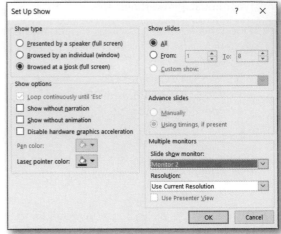

3-90 *Set Up Show* dialog box

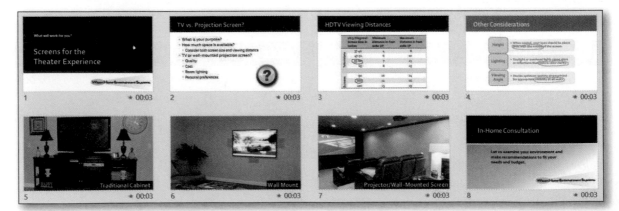

3-91 PowerPoint 3-4 completed

# Independent Project 3-5

For the third training session for new hires on presenting effectively, Davon Washington, management consultant at Solution Seekers, Inc., is preparing guidelines for delivering a presentation with projection equipment. For this project, you finish the presentation that Davon has prepared.
[Student Learning Outcomes 3.1, 3.2, 3.4, 3.5, 3.7, 3.8]

---

File Needed: ***PresentationDelivery-03.pptx*** *(Student data files are available in the* Library *of your SIMnet account.)*
Completed Project File Name: *[your initials]* **PowerPoint 3-5.pptx**

---

## Skills Covered in This Project

- Apply a background picture fill.
- Apply animation and effect options.
- Create and print notes pages.
- Hide and reveal slides.
- Rehearse a presentation and save timings.
- Use *Presenter View.*
- Use ink annotation pens.
- Record a presentation with narration.

---

1. Open the ***PresentationDelivery-03*** presentation from your student data files.

2. Save the presentation as [your initials] PowerPoint 3-5.

3. Apply the **Fade** transition with the **Smoothly** effect option. Change the *Duration* to **01.00**. Click **Apply To All**.

4. Apply animation on five slides and change effect options, start, and duration settings as shown in the following table. Some of these settings will appear by default.

| Slide | Object | Animation Effect | Effect Options | Start | Duration |
|-------|--------|------------------|----------------|-------|----------|
| 2 | Text "You get only one . . ." | *Bounce* (Entrance) | *As One Object* | *After Previous* | *02.00* |
| 5 | Butterfly image | *Grow & Turn* (Entrance) | *None* | *After Previous* | *02.00* |
| 7 | Graphic | *Wipe* (Entrance) | *From Left* | *After Previous* | *02.50* |
| 11 | Text "Make it memorable" | *Bounce* (Entrance) | *As One Object* | *After Previous* | *02.00* |
| 12 | Success shape | *Grow/Shrink* (Emphasis) | *Both, Larger* | *After Previous* | *02.50* |

5. Prepare speaker notes on two slides. In the notes for slide 9, apply bullets and indent the bulleted text (Figure 3-92).

   a. *Slide 2*: Never underestimate the importance of a first impression
      If possible, welcome people as they arrive for your presentation

   b. Slide *9*: Be careful with how you use humor
      - Use humor only if it is appropriate
      - Avoid jokes—you could unintentionally offend someone
      Humor works best when it fits the presentation and seems natural
      - Break the ice

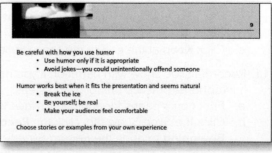

3-92 Notes with bullets and indents

- Be yourself; be real
- Make your audience feel comfortable

Choose stories or examples from your own experience

6. Print notes pages for slides 5, 6, and 7.

7. Hide slide 8.

8. Review the presentation to check transitions and animations.
   a. Select the *Transitions* tab and deselect **On Mouse Click**.
   b. Change *After* to **00:03:00** seconds.
   c. Click **Apply To All**.
   d. Start your slide show from the beginning and review all slide movements.

9. Use *Presenter View* to review your presentation.
   a. Deselect **Use Timings** [*Slide Show* tab, *Set Up* group] so you can advance through the slides at your own pace.
   b. Select **Use Presenter View**.
   c. Begin the presentation. If you have one monitor, right-click and select **Show Presenter View**.
   d. Navigate through slides using the **Advance to the next slide** and **Return to the previous slide** buttons.
   e. Click the **See all slides** button and click thumbnails to move to different slides.

10. Use *Presenter View* to add annotations on the following slides using the **Pen** with **Blue** ink. If you are not satisfied with your markings, then use the **Eraser** to remove them and try again.
    a. *Slide 2*: Circle the words "**Be professional**."
    b. *Slide 4*: Draw a rectangle around the words "**Eye Contact**" and "**Smile**" (Figure 3-93).

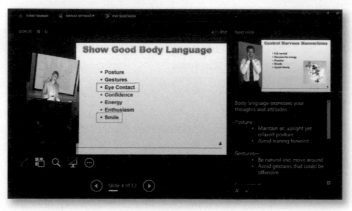

3-93 *Presenter View* showing ink annotations

    c. *Slide 7*: Circle the words "**Avoid monotone**."
    d. *Slide 10*: Circle "**End on time**."
    e. Click **Keep** at the end of the presentation to save annotations.

11. Record a slide show with narration if you have a microphone on your computer. If you don't have a microphone, practice the following steps.
    a. Print notes pages for additional slides where you need reminders about what to discuss.
    b. Click the *Slide Show* tab, click the **Record Slide Show** list arrow and select **Start Recording from Beginning** to open the *Record Slide Show* dialog box.
    c. Select both **Slide and animation timings** and **Narrations, ink, and laser pointer**. Click **Start Recording**.
    d. Speak clearly into your microphone as each slide displayed.
    e. Save and close your presentation (Figure 3-94).

3-94 PowerPoint 3-5 completed

# Independent Project 3-6

At the Hamilton Civic Center (HCC), classes are offered for a variety of fitness activities. For this project, you complete a presentation to promote the water aerobics classes at several community events. It will also be used as a self-running presentation at the HCC front desk.
[Student Learning Outcomes 3.1, 3.2, 3.3, 3.4, 3.5, 3.6, 3.8]

File Needed: *WaterAerobics-03.pptx (Student data files are available in the* Library *of your SIMnet account.)*
Completed Project File Name: *[your initials] PowerPoint 3-6.pptx*

### Skills Covered in This Project

- Create custom theme colors.
- Modify background fill colors.
- Change object colors on selected slides.
- Apply animation and effect options.
- Change to a widescreen slide size.
- Hide and reveal a slide.
- Use slide show navigation tools, keyboard shortcuts, and blank slides.
- Link to an online video.
- Prepare a kiosk presentation.

1. Open the **WaterAerobics-03** presentation from your student data files. This presentation is saved in the **Standard (4:3)** format (Figure 3-95).

2. Click the **Slide Size** button [*Design* tab, *Customize* group] and click **Widescreen (16:9)**. The slide size has changed from 10" to 13.33" wide.

3. Save the presentation as [your initials] PowerPoint 3-6.

4. Adjust objects to better fit the widescreen format:
   a. *Slide 1*: Increase the picture size (*Height*  **4"** and *Width*  **6"**).
   b. *Slide 4*: Resize the text box on the right so the text fits on four lines (Figure 3-96). Align it to the slide on the right.

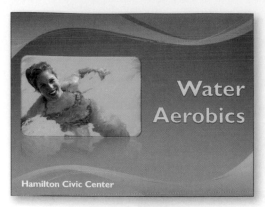

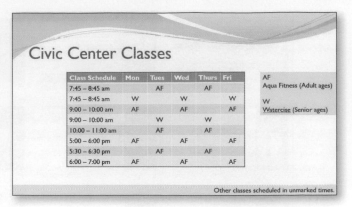

**3-95** Title slide in standard slide size

**3-96** Text boxes adjusted

c. *Slide 4*: Right align the text box at the bottom of the slide then extend the left end of the box to fit across the bottom of the slide.

d. *Slide 5*: Repeat the same alignment and size increase process for the text box at the bottom of the slide.

5. Use the *Create New Theme Colors* dialog box (Figure 3-97) to create a custom theme. Change four colors according to the *Red, Green*, and *Blue* numbers shown in the following table. Name the custom theme **Water** and save it.

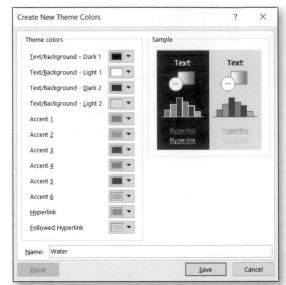

**3-97** *Water* theme colors

|  | Text/ Background - Dark 2 | Accent 1 | Accent 3 | Accent 5 |
|---|---|---|---|---|
| *Red* | 7 | 53 | 16 | 255 |
| *Green* | 55 | 151 | 89 | 51 |
| *Blue* | 99 | 241 | 100 | 153 |

6. Change the background colors.
   a. Click the **More** button [*Design* tab, *Variants* group] and select **Background Styles**. Click **Style 2** so a light blue is applied to the background of all slides in the presentation.
   b. Select slide 1. Use the *Format Background* pane to change the background fill. Select **Solid Fill** and choose **Dark Blue, Text 2**.
   c. Change the font color for "Hamilton Civic Center" to **White, Background 1** (Figure 3-98).
   d. Select slide 8 and change to the same background and text colors (steps 6 b – c).

**3-98** Title slide in widescreen slide size and *Water* theme colors

7. Change the color for the following two objects to **Pink, Accent 5**.
   a. *Slide 3*: *Text Fill for* "Fun"
   b. *Slide 4*: *Shading* for the table heading row

8. Apply the **Ripple** transition with the **From Top-Left** effect option. Apply this transition to all slides.

9. Apply animation on three slides and change options as shown in the following table. Some settings will appear by default.

| Slide | Object | Animation Effect | Effect Options | Start | Duration |
|---|---|---|---|---|---|
| 2 | Bulleted list | *Fly In* (Entrance) | *From Bottom-Right, By Paragraph* | *After Previous* | *01.00* |
| 3 | Bulleted list | *Fly In* (Entrance) | *From Bottom, As One Object* | *After Previous* | *01.00* |
| 3 | *WordArt* "Fun" | *Bounce* (Entrance) | *As One Object* | *After Previous* | *02.50* |

10. Hide slide 6.

11. Practice the following features using *Slide Show* view:
    a. Click **Next** and **Previous** in the control bar to change slides.
    b. Click the **See all slides** button in the control bar to see slide thumbnails; click a thumbnail to go to a different slide.
    c. Click the **Zoom into the slide** button in the control bar to magnify the "To Wear" list on slide 8.
    d. Click the **More slide show options** button in the control bar, select **Screen,** and then select **Black Screen**. Click the screen to return to the same slide.
    e. Go to the hidden slide 6.

12. Use the *Insert Video* dialog box to find and insert an online video.
    a. Display slide 5. Use the search words **water aerobics exercises** and select an appropriate video. For referencing purposes, write down the name of the video and online source from the lower left of the dialog box. Click **Insert**.
    b. Increase the video size if the quality remains acceptable.
    c. Below the video, insert a text box for a source note with the name of the video and online address.
    d. Test the video in *Slide Show* view to be sure it plays correctly.

13. Use *Presenter View* to review the presentation.
    a. Select **Presenter View** on the *Slide Show* tab.
    b. Select slide 1 and begin the presentation. If you have one monitor, right-click and select **Show Presenter View**.
    c. Advance through the presentation and review the speaker notes that appear in *Presenter View*.

14. Apply timings to advance each slide after 5 seconds.

15. Use the *Set Up Show* dialog box to select the following settings for a kiosk presentation.
    a. *Show type*: **Browsed at a kiosk (full screen)**
    b. *Show options*: **Loop continuously until 'Esc'** (automatically selected)
    c. *Show slides*: **All**
    d. *Advance slides*: **Use timings, if present** (automatically selected)

16. Save and close the presentation (Figure 3-99).

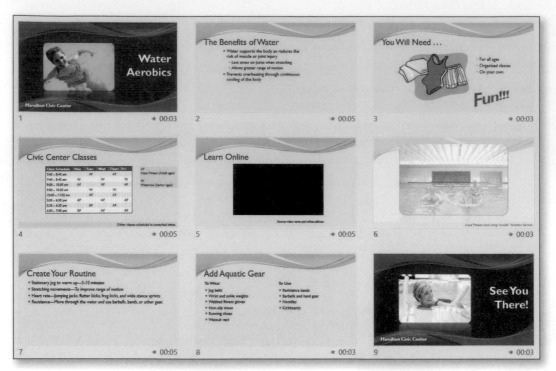

3-99 PowerPoint 3-6 completed

# Improve It Project 3-7

Delivering news that employees may perceive as bad news is a difficult task. Olivia Hudson with Solution Seekers has been working to convert a formerly text-only presentation to one that is more visual. She is using pictures with brief text and transferring listed information to notes pages she will use during her presentation. She has asked you to complete a notes page, convert a list to a *SmartArt* graphic, apply custom theme colors, and add animation.
**[Student Learning Outcomes 3.1, 3.2, 3.4, 3.8]**

File Needed: ***Announcement-03.pptx*** *(Student data files are available in the* Library *of your SIMnet account.)*
Completed Project File Name: *[your initials]* ***PowerPoint 3-7.pptx***

## *Skills Covered in This Project*

- Create custom theme colors.
- Modify slide content with *SmartArt*.
- Create and print notes pages.
- Apply appropriate transitions.
- Apply animation and effect options.
- Use *Presenter View*.
- Prepare a kiosk presentation.

1. Open the **Announcement-03** presentation from your student data files.
2. Save the presentation as [your initials] PowerPoint 3-7.
3. Create custom theme colors using the name Announce. Change five colors as shown in the following table.

|  | Text/Background - Dark 2 | Text/Background - Light 2 | Accent 1 | Accent 2 | Accent 3 |
|---|---|---|---|---|---|
| *Red* | 38 | 255 | 255 | 124 | 204 |
| *Green* | 19 | 230 | 153 | 26 | 236 |
| *Blue* | 0 | 193 | 0 | 26 | 255 |

4. Make the title slide text more distinctive.
   a. Display slide 1 and apply bold to the title and subtitle.
   b. Increase the title font size to **66 pt**. and "Big" to **96 pt**.
   c. Change the title font color to **Orange, Accent 1, Lighter 40%**.
   d. Increase the subtitle text to **32 pt**. and "You" to **48 pt**.
   e. Resize the subtitle placeholder on the left so the text fits on one line (Figure 3-100).

3-100 **Revised title slide**

5. Use the existing bulleted text to create a notes page.
   a. Display slide 2. If the *Notes* pane is not available below the slide in *Normal* view, click the **Notes** button on the *Status* bar. Increase the size of the *Notes* pane so you can work in both panes.
   b. Copy the existing bulleted text on the slide and paste it in the *Notes* pane. Arrange this text neatly (Figure 3-101).
   c. Click the **Notes** button again to hide the *Notes* pane.

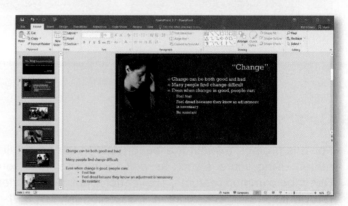

3-101 *Notes* pane expanded

6. On slide 2, modify and reposition the bulleted text.
   a. Replace the bulleted text with three words:
      - Fear
      - Dread
      - Resistance.
   b. Resize the body placeholder and move it to the lower right.

7. Insert a *SmartArt* graphic to show that "change" can be perceived as both good and bad.
   a. Insert the **Opposing Arrows** layout from the *Relationship* category.
   b. Type the text Good and Bad.
   c. Apply the **Inset** *SmartArt* Style.
   d. Resize *SmartArt* objects and position them as shown (Figure 3-102).

3-102 **Slide 2 revised**

8. Animate a text box on slides 3-5.
   a. Display slide 3. Select the "**Do**" text box.
   b. Apply the **Wipe** animation with the **From Left** effect option.
   c. Repeat this animation for the "**Do**" text boxes on slides 4 and 5.

9. Apply the **Gallery** transition to all slides.

10. Review the presentation and speaker notes using *Presenter View*.

11. Modify the transitions by entering 00:03:00 for *After* seconds and apply the change to all slides.

12. Set up the slide show for a kiosk presentation.

13. Save and close the presentation (Figure 3-103).

3-103 PowerPoint 3-7 completed

## Challenge Project 3-8

For this project, explain the benefits of tablet computing and factors to consider when purchasing a tablet. Using sources such as www.pcmag.com, list some of the top-rated products and their prices. Describe common features, applications, and accessories.
**[Student Learning Outcomes 3.1, 3.2, 3.3, 3.4, 3.5, 3.9]**

File Needed: None
Completed Project File Name: *[your initials] PowerPoint 3-8.pptx*

Create a new presentation and save it as [your initials] PowerPoint 3-8. Modify your presentation according to the following guidelines:

- Select an appropriate theme and create custom theme colors for a high-tech appearance.
- Change to a widescreen format, if necessary.
- Include pictures from www.pcmag.com or other sources and credit the source below each picture.
- Animate approximately three objects for emphasis and apply appropriate effects.
- Rehearse the presentation and save timings.
- Link to an online video.
- Prepare a slide listing your references and include it as the last slide in your presentation.
- Use *Package Presentation for CD* to save the presentation to a folder.

## Challenge Project 3-9

Prepare a presentation to promote a student or civic organization. Use pictures and very brief text to convey the purpose of the organization. Consider using an organization chart to illustrate the officer or committee structure. Apply styles and text treatments consistently.
[Student Learning Outcomes 3.1, 3.2, 3.3, 3.4, 3.6, 3.9]

File Needed: None
Completed Project File Name: *[your initials] PowerPoint 3-9.pptx*

Create a new presentation and save it as [your initials] PowerPoint 3-9. Modify your presentation according to the following guidelines:

- Select an appropriate theme then prepare custom theme colors for your topic.
- Modify backgrounds by applying a gradient fill to all slides and a picture fill to one slide.
- Design slides with a variety of illustration techniques and minimal text.
- Add transitions and animations with appropriate effects.
- Create and print notes pages.
- Include an online video if one is available and credit your source.
- Prepare a slide listing your references and include it as the last slide in your presentation.
- Rehearse the presentation and use a variety of navigation techniques.
- Use *Package Presentation for CD* to save your presentation to a folder.

## Challenge Project 3-10

Create a presentation about living green. Focus on ways to conserve water and other resources. Use references such as www.mygreenside.org and others. Prepare a slide listing your references and include it as the last slide in your presentation.
[Student Learning Outcomes 3.1, 3.2, 3.3, 3.4, 3.6, 3.7, 3.8]

File Needed: None
Completed Project File Name: *[your initials] PowerPoint 3-10.pptx*

Create a new presentation and save it as [your initials] PowerPoint 3-10. Modify your presentation according to the following guidelines:

- Select an appropriate theme then prepare custom theme colors that fit the "green" topic.
- Modify backgrounds and use at least one picture fill.
- Design slides with a variety of illustration techniques and minimal text.
- Add transitions and animations with appropriate effects.
- Create and print notes pages.
- Include an online video about "green" living and credit your source.
- Hide one or more slides.
- Rehearse the presentation, use the pen to circle key points, and save timings
- Modify timings as needed for a kiosk presentation.
- Prepare a kiosk presentation with looping.

# Customizing Images, Illustrations, and Themes

**POWERPOINT**

## CHAPTER OVERVIEW

This chapter focuses on PowerPoint's illustration features to customize shapes, images, and illustrations. You will apply these features to create an original theme and template design using *Slide Masters*. You will capture screen images and edit pictures to improve their appearance, apply artistic effects, and create photo albums. Finally, you will use PowerPoint's new *Designer* feature to quickly select attractive slide layouts for picture content.

## STUDENT LEARNING OUTCOMES (SLOs)

After completing this chapter, you will be able to:

**SLO 4.1**  Customize and work with shapes (p. P4-210).

**SLO 4.2**  Work with objects to align, distribute, and group; convert *SmartArt* to text or shapes (p. P4-215).

**SLO 4.3**  Use *Slide Masters* to create a custom theme with new colors, fonts, and background graphics (p. P4-228).

**SLO 4.4**  Capture screen images with a screenshot or a screen clipping (p. P4-238).

**SLO 4.5**  Edit pictures to apply photo corrections, choose artistic effects, and remove backgrounds; recolor illustrated images (p. P4-240).

**SLO 4.6**  Create a photo album and adjust picture order, layout, and captions; apply and customize a photo album theme (p. P4-249).

**SLO 4.7**  Create and use a custom template (p. P4-252).

**SLO 4.8**  Use *PowerPoint Designer* to select slide layouts for picture content. (p. P4-258).

## Case Study

Paradise Lakes Resort (PLR) is a vacation company with four resorts located throughout northern Minnesota. To increase awareness of the natural resources of this area and promote bookings, the resort managers are preparing a tourism presentation entitled "PLR in the Land of 10,000 Lakes."

**Pause & Practice 4-1:** Create original graphics including a business logo.

**Pause & Practice 4-2:** Use *Slide Masters* to create a unique theme with original graphics and custom colors.

**Pause & Practice 4-3:** Modify pictures and apply interesting effects.

**Pause & Practice 4-4:** Create a photo album presentation with a custom design theme and save the presentation as a template.

**Pause & Practice 4-5:** Apply *Designer* layouts.

# Customizing Shapes

In Chapter 2, you worked with several simple shapes. The *Shapes* gallery displays shapes in 10 different groups and you customize shapes by using the *Drawing Tools Format* tab and the *Format Shape* pane. When drawing shapes, press **Shift** or **Ctrl** as you drag to *constrain* the shape. Constraining keeps your lines straight, your circles round, and your rectangles square. When you resize shapes, press **Shift** and **Ctrl** while you drag sizing handles to constrain shapes in the following ways:

- **Shift** preserves height and width proportions.
- **Ctrl** keeps the center in the same place.
- **Ctrl+Shift** keeps the center of the shape in the same place and maintains height and width proportions.

## Adjust Text and Spacing within Text Boxes and Shapes

The same alignment and direction adjustments apply to both text boxes and shapes with text; however, the default settings vary. For example, *Vertical alignment* for a shape is *Middle* with *Do not Autofit* selected; *Vertical alignment* for a text box is *Top* with *Resize shape to fit text* selected.

Text arranged horizontally is easy to read, but you may want to arrange text in different directions for special purposes.

---

▶ **HOW TO:** Change Text Direction and Vertical Alignment

1. Select a text box or shape that contains text.

2. Click the **Text Direction** button [*Home* tab, *Paragraph* group] and select from the following options (Figure 4-1):

   - *Horizontal:* The default direction.
   - *Rotate all text 90°:* Text reads from the top down.
   - *Rotate all text 270°:* Text reads from the bottom up.
   - *Stacked:* Text is arranged in a one-letter column.

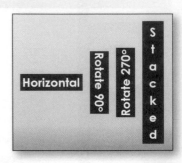

3. Click the **Align Text** button [*Home* tab, *Paragraph* group] and select from the following options that vary based on the selected text direction:

4-1 Text direction examples

   - *Horizontal:* Top, Middle, or Bottom
   - *Rotate all text 90°:* Right, Center, or Left
   - *Rotate all text 270°:* Left, Center, or Right
   - *Stacked:* Left, Center, or Right

4. Click **More Options** from the *Text Direction* or the *Align Text* options lists to open the *Format Shape* pane.

   - Figure 4-2 illustrates the settings for the horizontal text box in Figure 4-1.

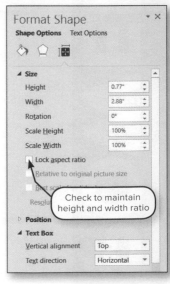

Alternatively, you can right-click a text object and select **Format Shape** from the context menu to open the *Format Shape* pane. Additional options on this pane allow you to control how text fits in the text box or shape. For example, you can increase the space between the text and the edge of the shape or you can arrange the text in columns.

4-2 Text box size options

▶ **HOW TO:** Control Text Resizing, Margins, Wrapping, and Columns

1. Select a text box or shape, right-click, and select **Format Shape** from the context menu to open the *Format Shape* pane.

2. Click **Text Options** at the top of the pane then click the **Textbox** button. Click the **Text Box** heading to expand the list if necessary.

3. Verify that *Text direction* is **Horizontal**.

4. Choose one of the following options if you have too much text to fit in a text box or shape. An example of each option is shown in Figure 4-3.

   - *Do not Autofit:* Text size remains the same and text extends beyond the text box or shape.
   - *Shrink text on overflow:* Text size is reduced so all text displays in the text box or shape.
   - *Resize shape to fit text:* Text size remains the same but the text box or shape size increases to contain all text.

5. Enter **Left Margin**, **Right Margin**, **Top Margin**, and **Bottom Margin** in inches.

   - Space is inserted around the text so it is not too close to the border of a text box or shape (Figure 4-4).
   - This option works well when the *Resize shape to fit text* option is selected.
   - You can enter numbers in points, but PowerPoint converts those numbers to inches. One inch contains 72 points.

6. Select **Wrap text in shape** to maintain the width of a text box or shape.

   - The height increases as you enter more text.

7. Click the **Columns** button to arrange the text in two or more columns with space between columns.

   - Text fills the first column from top to bottom then wraps to the top of the second column (Figure 4-5).
   - The settings for the sample in Figure 4-5 are entered at the bottom of the *Format Shape* pane (Figure 4-6).

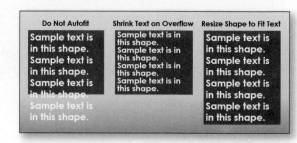

4-3 Text resizing examples

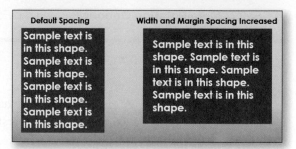

4-4 Margin spacing examples

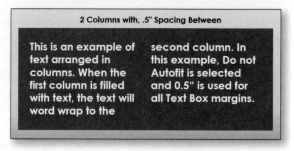

4-5 Column example with word wrap

4-6 Margin size options

▶ MORE INFO

By default, the width of a text box is one column. When you change to two or more columns, be sure text remains easy to read. The number of columns and spacing between the columns affects readability. You may need to make your text box wider.

## Flip and Rotate Shapes

The *Flip* and *Rotate* commands work with many PowerPoint objects. For example, you can point an arrow in a different direction, angle a shape on the slide, or create a mirror image of a picture. The *rotation handle* provides quick movements; you can enter precise rotation degrees by using the *Format Shape* pane.

1. Select a shape.
2. Click and drag the **rotation handle** to angle the shape.
3. Click the **Rotate** button [*Drawing Tools Format* tab, *Arrange* group] and choose from one of the following options (Figure 4-7):

   - *Rotate Right 90°*
   - *Rotate Left 90°*
   - *Flip Vertical*
   - *Flip Horizontal*

4. Select **More Rotation Options** to open the *Format Shape* pane and enter specific rotation values.

4-7 Rotation options

A creative way to rotate individual letters of a word on a title slide is shown in Figure 4-8.

## Shape Adjustment Handles

Several shapes, such as arrows or stars, have *adjustment handles* (yellow circles) that you drag to change the shape dimension. Shapes can have more than one adjustment handle, too. Even the shape of text can be changed using adjustment handles if the *Transform* text effect has been applied.

Figure 4-9 shows two variations of a 16-point star. The example on the left is the original shape with the adjustment handle in the default position at the top. On the right, the adjustment handle has been moved toward the center, and the star looks quite different with long, narrow points.

4-8 Individual letters rotated

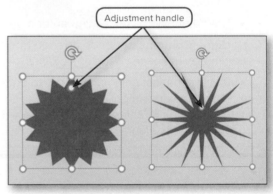

4-9 Star shape changed using the adjustment handle

## Edit Shape Points

Although you can't see them when drawing, all shapes that you draw have small black squares called *points* that control where lines curve or change direction such as in the corners of a diamond shape. A point is also called a *vertex*. More points are used when lines curve compared to straight lines.

These points appear on the border of a shape when you use the *Edit Points* command. You can drag the points to move the border and alter the shape.

When you click a point, two lines appear that are attached to the point with white squares on each end to create *direction handles*. Dragging the direction handles changes the curve of the line between two points. Direction handles are used in many graphics programs and practice is required to use them skillfully. Both the length of the handle and the distance of movement affect the curve that is made.

## ▶HOW TO: Edit Points

1. Draw a shape.

2. Click the **Edit Shape** button [*Drawing Tools Format* tab, *Insert Shapes* group] and click **Edit Points** (Figure 4-10).

3. Click a black point and drag. For example, elongate a diamond shape by dragging the top point up and bottom point down (Figure 4-11).

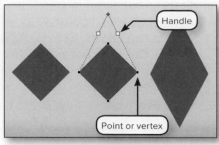

4. Press **Ctrl** and click a line to add a point.

5. Press **Ctrl** and click a point to remove it. When you press **Ctrl** and click to remove a point, the pointer displays an "x".

   - You can also right-click a point to open the context menu and click **Delete Point**.

6. Use direction handles to change the curve of the line between two points.

   - Click a point to display direction handles with white squares at the end of each line.
   - Click a white square and drag the handle to change the curve. A heart shape is shown in Figure 4-12.
   - Drag the white square to adjust the direction handle line length because the direction handle length affects how the line curves.

7. Press **Esc** or click off the line to turn off *Edit Points*.

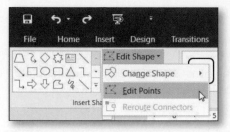

4-10 *Edit Points* command

4-11 Drag points to change a shape

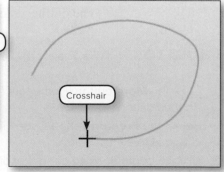

4-12 Drag a direction handle to change the curve between points

---

## Curved Lines and Freeform Shapes

The *Shapes* gallery has three line tools for drawing curved lines and freeform shapes and each of them work differently. With the **Curve** line, your pointer changes to a crosshair. You click to begin drawing the line and continue clicking as you extend the line. The line automatically curves as you change direction and will draw with smooth curves. An edit point is added each time the direction changes.

---

## ▶HOW TO: Draw Curved Lines

1. Click the **Shapes** button [*Insert* tab, *Illustrations* group] to open the *Shapes* gallery.

   - The *Shapes* gallery is also available on the *Home* tab [*Drawing* group] and the *Drawing Tools Format* tab [*Insert Shapes* group].
   - Click the **More** button on each of these galleries to open the complete gallery.

2. Select the **Curve** line (Figure 4-13).

3. Click to begin drawing with the crosshair pointer. Click again to extend the line or to change direction (Figure 4-14).

4. Press **Esc** or double-click to end the line.

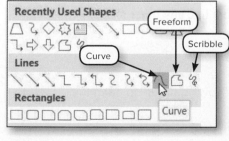

4-13 The *Lines* group in the *Shapes* gallery

4-14 Curved line with smooth curves

5. Click the **Edit Shape** button [*Drawing Tools Format* tab, *Insert Shapes* group] and select **Edit Points** to adjust the curves using the points and direction handles (Figure 4-15).
   - Drag points to move the line.
   - Press **Ctrl** and click the line to add a point.
   - Press **Ctrl** and click a point to remove it.
   - Select a point, right-click to open the context menu, select **Smooth Point** to make the curve more even, or click **Delete Points** to remove the point.
6. Press **Esc** or click off the line to turn off *Edit Points*.

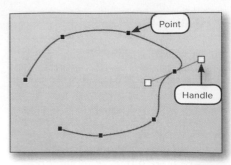

4-15 Drag points and direction handles on points to adjust a curved line

With the *Scribble* line, your pointer changes to a pen. Click to begin drawing and drag the pointer as though you are writing on paper to create a continuous line. This tool is easier to use with a tablet pen or stylus than with a mouse. Many edit points are added because the line direction changes so many times.

### ▶ HOW TO: Draw Scribble Lines

1. Click the **More** button [*Home* tab, *Drawing* group] to open the *Shapes* gallery.
2. Select the **Scribble** line (see Figure 4-13) and your pointer changes to a pen.
3. Click and hold the left mouse button to begin drawing and drag the pointer. Release the button to end the line.
4. Click the **Edit Points** button [*Drawing Tools Format* tab, *Insert Shapes* group] and select **Edit Points**.
   - Many points will appear based on how curved your line is; it may be difficult to adjust the curves using points and direction handles (Figure 4-16).
   - Drag points to move the line.
   - Press **Ctrl** and click the line to add a point.
   - Press **Ctrl** and click a point to remove it.
   - Select a point, right-click to open the context menu, select **Smooth Point** to make the curve more even, or click **Delete Points** to remove the point.
5. Press **Esc** or click off the line to turn off *Edit Points*.

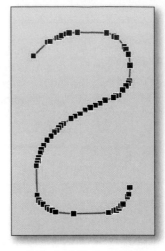

4-16 *Scribble* line showing points

With the *Freeform* line, your pointer changes to a crosshair to draw both straight and curved lines. When you drag the crosshair, the line will curve like the *Scribble* tool. You can click to draw straight lines between points and to change directions with the line as you draw. An edit point is added each time you click. When the end of the line you are drawing touches the beginning of the line, a shape is created using your *Accent 1* fill color. You can change fill and outline colors like any other shape.

### ▶ HOW TO: Draw a Freeform Shape

1. Click the **More** button [*Home* tab, *Drawing* group] to open the *Shapes* gallery.
2. Select the **Freeform** shape (see Figure 4-13) and your pointer changes to a crosshair.
3. Click to begin drawing curved or straight lines.
   - Press **Shift** to keep the line straight or change direction (Figure 4-17).
   - Press the left mouse button while you move the crosshair to draw a scribble line.

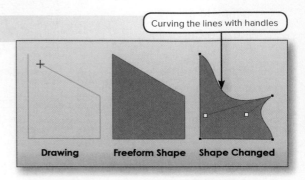

4-17 Freeform shapes

4. Touch the beginning point with your crosshair to create a shape.

   - You can change fill and outline options.

5. Click the **Edit Shape** button [*Drawing Tools Format* tab, *Insert Shapes* group] and select **Edit Points** to adjust the position of points or use direction handles to adjust the curves between points.

   - Drag points to move the line.
   - Press **Ctrl** and click the line to add a point.
   - Press **Ctrl** and click a point to remove it.
   - Select a point, right-click to open the context menu, select **Smooth Point** to make the curve more even, or click **Delete Points** to remove the point.

6. Press **Esc** or click off the line to turn off *Edit Points*.

---

## SLO 4.2    Working with Multiple Objects

In this section, you combine objects in interesting ways and learn to efficiently align and position objects. The following list previews these drawing concepts:

- Align multiple objects and evenly distribute the space between them.
- Use gridlines and guides to align objects.
- Layer objects and adjust their stacking order.
- Group, ungroup, and regroup shapes.
- Save grouped objects as a picture.
- Merge shapes to create an original shape.
- Convert *SmartArt* graphics to text and shapes that you can use in different ways.
- Use connector lines to create unique diagrams.

You can select multiple objects in several ways. Always confirm that objects show sizing handles to be sure your selection is complete.

### ▶ HOW TO:  Select Multiple Objects

1. Use one of the following methods to select multiple objects:

   - Select the first object and press **Shift** (to select adjacent objects) or **Ctrl** (to select nonadjacent objects) as you click additional objects.
   - Click and drag to draw a selection rectangle over multiple objects and release your left mouse button (Figure 4-18).
   - Click the **Select** button on the *Home* tab [*Editing* group] and choose from *Select All*, *Select Objects*, or *Selection Pane*.
   - Click the **Selection Pane** button [*Drawing Tools Format* tab, *Arrange* group] to open the *Selection* pane (Figure 4-19). Press **Ctrl** to select multiple objects in the list and to highlight their names.

2. Remove an individual object from a selection of multiple objects by pressing **Ctrl** as you click the object.

4-18 Selection rectangle over multiple shapes

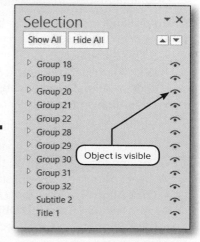

4-19 *Selection* pane

---

In the *Selection* pane, an "eye" icon (see Figure 4-19) beside each object name means that you can see it on the slide. If you click the eye, that object is still on the slide but is no longer visible.

### Align and Distribute Objects

All objects on a slide should align with other objects or with the slide to show logical groupings. Using similar alignment techniques throughout a presentation provides consistency; however, alignment should accommodate specific content and design variety can be good if it is used in a purposeful way.

## ▶ HOW TO: Align Multiple Objects

1. Select multiple objects.
2. Align the objects with each other.
   - Click the **Align** button [*Drawing Tools Format* tab, *Arrange* group] or click the **Arrange** button [*Home* tab, *Drawing* group] and then click **Align**.
3. Select one of the following options on the drop-down list:
   - *Align to Slide:* Objects are aligned in the space of the entire slide.
   - *Align Selected Objects:* Objects are aligned with each other.
4. Click the **Align** button again and then select one of the following alignment options:
   - *Align Left*
   - *Align Center*
   - *Align Right*
   - *Align Top*
   - *Align Middle*
   - *Align Bottom* (Figure 4-20).

4-20 Multiple objects aligned with each other

The ***Distribute*** feature creates even spacing between multiple slide objects. You can distribute space vertically or horizontally on the entire slide or between the objects. When you distribute selected objects vertically, you must first position the top and bottom objects. When you distribute horizontally, you must first position the left and right objects. Then space is distributed evenly between all selected objects.

## ▶ HOW TO: Distribute Multiple Objects

1. Select multiple objects.
2. Distribute selected objects on the slide.
   - Click **Align** [*Drawing Tools Format* tab, *Arrange* group] and choose **Align to Slide**.
   - Click **Align** again and select **Distribute Horizontally** or **Distribute Vertically**.
3. Distribute objects to each other horizontally.
   - Position the first object on the left.
   - Position the last object on the right.
   - Select all objects to be distributed.
   - Click **Align** [*Drawing Tools Format* tab, *Arrange* group] and choose **Align Selected Objects**.
   - Click **Align** again and select **Distribute Horizontally** (Figure 4-21).
4. Distribute objects to each other vertically.
   - Position the first object on the top.
   - Position the last object on the bottom.
   - Select all objects to be distributed.
   - Click **Align** [*Drawing Tools Format* tab, *Arrange* group] and choose **Align Selected Objects**.
   - Click **Align** again and select **Distribute Vertically**.

4-21 Multiple aligned objects with space distributed evenly

# Use Gridlines and Guides

*Gridlines* are evenly spaced vertical and horizontal lines that aid in object alignment. *Guides* have one vertical and one horizontal line in the middle of the slide. You can move guides to a specific position as an aid to consistently align objects across several slides. *Gridlines* and *Guides* are not visible in *Slide Show* view.

*Smart Guides* are temporary lines that appear when your objects are aligned or spaced evenly. *Smart Guides* are not affected by *Gridlines or Guides*.

▶ **HOW TO:** Display and Customize Guides and Gridlines

1. Select **Guides** [*View* tab, *Show* group] (Figure 4-22).

   - One dashed vertical and horizontal line appears at the center of the slide (Figure 4-23).
   - Point to one of the lines and your pointer changes to a splitter. Drag to reposition the line.
   - The number that appears on the guide indicates the distance away from the horizontal or vertical center (Figure 4-24).
   - Remove guides from the slide area by deselecting **Guides** [*View* tab, *Show* group].

2. Select **Gridlines** [*View* tab, *Show* group].

   - Dotted vertical and horizontal lines appear on the slide (Figure 4-25).
   - *Smart Guides* temporarily appear when objects are aligned and when objects are spaced evenly.
   - Remove *Gridlines* from the slide area by deselecting **Gridlines** [*View* tab, *Show* group].

4-22  *View* tab with *Guides* selected

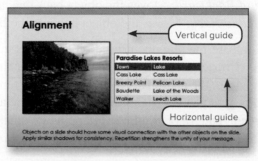

4-23  *Guides* displayed as vertical and horizontal lines

4-24  *Guide* position changed

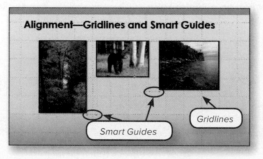

4-25  *Gridlines* and *Smart Guides*

4-26  *Grid and Guides* dialog box

3. Customize *Grid* and *Guide* settings. Click the **launcher** [*View* tab, *Show* group] to open the *Grid and Guides* dialog box (Figure 4-26). Select from the following options:

   - ***Snap to:*** An object automatically moves from dot-to-dot (Figure 4-27) on the *Gridlines* as you drag it. You can see this movement better when your view is zoomed at 100% or more. To move an object smoothly and position it between grid dots, press **Alt** as you drag.
   - ***Grid settings:*** Enter different spacing amounts for the grid dots and select **Display grid on screen**.
   - ***Guide settings:*** Select **Display drawing guides on screen** to show the guides. Select **Display smart guides when shapes are aligned** to see the temporary guides that help you align vertically and horizontally with other objects on the slide.

4. Click **OK** to close the *Grids and Guides* dialog box.

4-27  Top of shapes aligned to the grid

## Layer Objects and Adjust Stacking Order

When working with multiple shapes and objects, you can combine them in interesting ways by layering one object on top of another object. This layering is also called *stacking*. Use the *Selection* pane or click the *Bring Forward* or *Send Backward* commands [*Drawing Tools Format* tab, *Arrange* group] to rearrange the stacking order.

- ***Bring Forward:*** Moves the object up one layer at a time.
- ***Bring to Front:*** Moves the object in front of all other objects.
- ***Send Backward:*** Moves the object back one layer at a time.
- ***Send to Back:*** Moves the object behind all other objects.

Compare the alignment used on the slides in Figures 4-28 and 4-29. Figure 4-28 shows two text boxes aligned with their edges touching the picture in an asymmetrical way. In Figure 4-29, the text boxes overlap the picture and seem more connected. The technique that looks best to you is a matter of personal preference. Aim for consistency and repeat the same alignment pattern or similar overlapping on other slides in your presentation. Notice how the shadows on the text boxes match the *Drop Shadow Rectangle* picture style.

4-28 Text boxes touch picture

4-29 Text boxes overlap picture

When multiple objects are layered, it can be difficult to select one object within the stack especially if a larger object covers a smaller object. Use the *Selection* pane to choose from the objects on the slide. You can also select any object and press **Tab** several times to cycle through each object until the object you want is selected. Then you can move it or adjust its stacking order.

## Group, Ungroup, and Regroup Objects

The ***Group*** command is available on several tabs. When you group two or more shapes or other objects such as pictures, they are connected as one object. Sizing handles appear around the group and not the individual objects unless you click an object within the group. Colors, sizes, and effects can change for individual objects or all objects in a group. The ***Ungroup*** command separates objects so you can modify them independently. The ***Regroup*** command connects the objects again.

## ▶HOW TO: Group, Ungroup, and Regroup

1. Select the objects you want to group. Sizing handles appear around all of the individual shapes (see the example on the left in Figure 4-30).
2. Combine multiple objects so one set of sizing handles appears around the entire group (the example on the right in Figure 4-30). Use one of these methods:
   - Click the **Group** button [*Drawing Tools Format* tab, *Arrange* group] and select **Group**.
   - Click the **Arrange** button [*Home* tab, *Drawing* group] and select **Group**.
   - Click the **Group** button [*Picture Tools Format* tab, *Arrange* group] and select **Group** when you are working with pictures.
3. Resize the group by dragging the sizing handles.
4. Change an object within a group.
   - Select an individual object within the group.
   - Resize the individual object, change its color, or adjust its position.
5. Click the **Group** button [*Drawing Tools Format* tab, *Arrange* group] and select **Ungroup** to separate the objects and modify individual objects independently.
   - Change colors or sizing as needed and click **Regroup** to reconnect objects.
   - Click **Group** to reconnect objects if you change the layering of grouped objects.

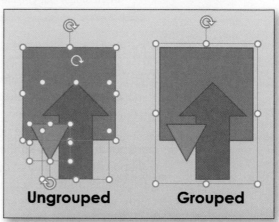

**Ungrouped**        **Grouped**

4-30 Three shapes ungrouped and grouped

## Save Grouped Objects as a Picture

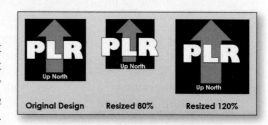

Original Design     Resized 80%     Resized 120%

4-31 Grouped logo is distorted with resizing

When text is included in a grouped object, it is not always easy to get good results when you attempt to resize the group. Text sizes do not change by dragging unless you have applied the *Transform* text effect. Resizing the group affects text alignment. In Figure 4-31, a company logo is shown in the original size on the left. The center logo is resized by 80%; the letters extend beyond the background shape and text is not centered below the arrow. The right logo is resized by 120%; the large letters no longer fill the background shape and the text below the arrow is not centered.

To prevent this problem, save your grouped objects as a picture so you can resize the picture without distortion. A picture file also helps to maintain color consistency. For example, if you use theme colors to design a logo with grouped objects and later use this logo in a different presentation with different theme colors, the logo colors will change. But if you save the logo as a picture, all the colors will remain the same.

## ▶HOW TO: Save Grouped Objects as a Picture

1. Select the grouped objects and right-click to open the context menu.
2. Click **Save as Picture** to open the *Save as Picture* dialog box.
3. Select the appropriate location to save the file.
4. Type your file name.
5. Select an appropriate file type. The *PNG Portable Network Graphics Format* (.png) or *JPEG File Interchange Format* (.jpg) file types generally work well in presentations.
6. Click **Save** to save the picture file and close the dialog box.

## Merge Shapes

The ***Merge Shapes*** command combines two or more shapes. Unlike grouping where the shapes are merely connected and can be moved or recolored within the group, merging creates a completely new shape.

Merging is possible when shapes do not touch, but not all merge options will work. Usually shapes are stacked so they overlap. When merged, the top shape color is applied to the new shape with most merge options.

Shapes must be selected to be merged, but they cannot be grouped. Also, merging works only with shapes; you cannot merge shapes with pictures or other objects.

▶ **HOW TO:** Merge Shapes

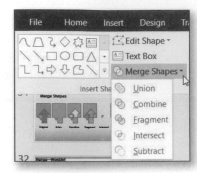

1. Select two or more shapes that overlap.

2. Click the **Merge Shapes** button [*Drawing Tools Format* tab, *Insert Shapes* group (Figure 4-32).

3. Choose from one of the following options to join multiple selected shapes into a new shape. An example of each option is shown in Figure 4-33.

   - ***Union:*** All shapes are combined as one (top shape color).
   - ***Combine:*** The joined shape has transparent areas where the separate shapes originally overlapped. Individual shape outlines are retained (top shape color).
   - ***Fragment:*** The joined shape shows individual shape outlines (top shape color). The shape is sliced into pieces where the shapes originally overlapped. The pieces can be removed or recolored.
   - ***Intersect:*** Only the shape where all original shapes overlapped remains (top shape color).
   - ***Subtract:*** The joined shape (bottom shape color) has transparent areas indicating the places where the other shapes overlapped the bottom shape.

4-32 *Merge Shapes* button

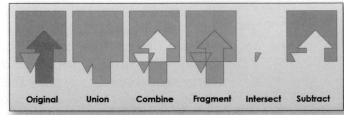

4-33 Original shapes and *Merge Shapes* options

If you arrange *WordArt* text over a shape and apply the *Combine* or *Subtract* merge option, the text becomes transparent and looks cut out because the background shows in the letters (Figure 4-34). Be careful to size your shape to fit the text appropriately before merging; once merged, the text is no longer editable and resizing the shape distorts the text.

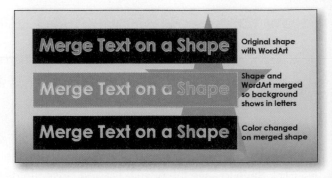

4-34 Merged shape and *WordArt* text showing a cut out effect

After shapes are merged, even if they are spaced apart, you can edit points to modify the new shape.

## Connector Lines

In the *Shapes* gallery, ***Connector Lines*** are available in a variety of shapes: *Straight Connectors*, *Elbow Connectors* (90° angle), or *Curved Connectors*. You can use these lines to connect two or more shapes for custom diagrams. Several connector lines have arrowheads on the ends.

> ### ▶ HOW TO: Connect Shapes

1. Draw two or more shapes.
2. Click the **More** button [*Home* tab, *Drawing* group] to open the *Shapes* gallery.
3. Select a connector line such as the *Elbow Connector* or the *Curved Arrow Connector* (Figure 4-35). Your pointer changes to a crosshair.
4. Point to the first shape to be connected.

   - Small gray circles appear on the shape indicating connection sites where the shape and the connector line can be joined.

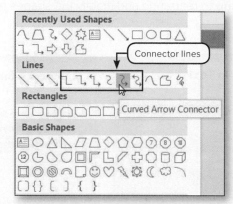

4-35 Connector lines in the *Lines* group of the *Shapes* gallery

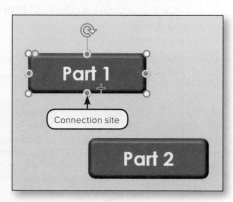

4-36 Connection sites on a shape

5. Click the connection site on the first shape where the connector line will start (Figure 4-36) and continue pressing your left mouse button as you drag.

   - A line forms as you move the crosshair.
   - Click a connection site on the next shape and the connection site circle changes to green.
   - Click the line and green circles appear on both ends of the line when the shapes are connected.
   - Click one of the connected shapes and the connection site reverts to its original color until you click the line again.

6. Move connected shapes as needed and the line between them remains attached.

   - The connection sites will remain connected until you separate the line from the shape.

7. Drag an adjustment handle (yellow circle) to change line curves or angles (Figure 4-37).
8. Increase the line width and color so the line is more obvious (Figure 4-38).
9. Change how the lines are connected to shapes by clicking **Edit Shape** [*Drawing Tools Format* tab, *Insert Shapes* group] and selecting **Reroute Connections**. Click a green circle and move it to the connection site on a different shape.

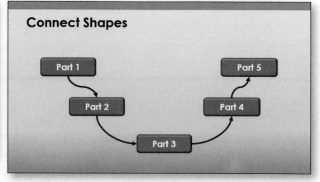

4-37 Line connects shapes

4-38 Line color and width changed

# Convert a SmartArt Graphic to Text or to Shapes

You can change a *SmartArt* graphic to bulleted text or to a group of individual shapes.

1. Select the *SmartArt* graphic you want to change (Figure 4-39).
2. Click the **Convert** button [*SmartArt Tools Design* tab, *Reset* group].
3. Choose one of the following options:
   - *Convert to Text:* *SmartArt* text is changed to a bulleted list (Figure 4-40). Edit the text as needed.
   - *Convert to Shapes:* *SmartArt* shapes are changed to a group of shapes. Click **Arrange** [*Home* tab, *Drawing* group] then select **Ungroup** to rearrange and modify the shapes individually (Figures 4-41 and 4-42).

4-39 *SmartArt* graphic original design

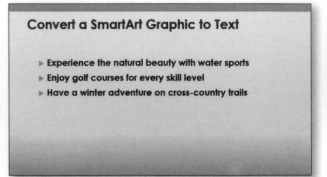

4-40 *SmartArt* graphic converted to text

4-41 *SmartArt* graphic shapes rearranged

4-42 *SmartArt* graphic shapes changed and rearranged

In Figure 4-41 the shapes are staggered evenly and made slightly longer, and the pictures are moved to the right of each shape. Figure 4-42 emphasizes the pictures more by making them bigger; the shapes fill the slide in a staggered arrangement. The shapes are changed to rounded rectangles and the text wraps around each picture.

For this project, you work with shapes to create interesting designs for a presentation promoting Paradise Lakes Resort. You change text direction, use adjustment handles, and adjust layering. You flip, ungroup, and merge shapes and group a series of shapes. You also add connector lines to reinforce the flow of ideas, and convert *SmartArt* graphics to text and to shapes. Finally, you create a business logo for PLR.

---

**File Needed: *PLRPromotion-04.pptx*** *(student data files are available in the Library of your SIMnet account)*
**Completed Project File Names: *[your initials] PP P4-1.pptx*** and ***PLR-Logo2.png***

---

1. Open the ***PLRPromotion-04*** presentation from your student data files.

2. Save this presentation as [your initials] PP P4-1.

3. Change text direction and alignment in a text box.
    a. Display slide 1. Select the "Minnesota" text box.
    b. Click the **Text Direction** button [*Home* tab, *Paragraph* group] and select **Rotate all text 270°**.
    c. Click the **Arrange** button [*Home* tab, *Drawing* group], select **Align**, and select **Align to Slide** if it is not already selected
    d. Click the **Arrange** button again, select **Align** and select **Align Left**. Repeat to select **Align Bottom** (Figure 4-43).

**4-43** Text direction rotated

4. Create a shape and modify it using adjustment handles.
    a. Display slide 2. Click the **More** button [*Home* tab, *Drawing* group] (Figure 4-44) to open the *Shapes* gallery.
    b. Select the **24-Point Star** (*Stars and Banners* group) and draw a star shape (*Height* **1.5"** and *Width* **2"**) [*Drawing Tools Format* tab, *Size* group] on a blank area of the slide.
    c. Drag the adjustment handle toward the center to make the star points longer.
    d. Change the *Shape Fill* to **Blue, Accent 4** [*Drawing Tools Format* tab, *Shape Styles* group].
    e. Change the *Shape Outline* to **No Outline** [*Drawing Tools Format* tab, *Shape Styles* group].

**4-44** *Stars and Banners* group in the *Shapes* gallery

5. Change shape alignment and stacking order.
    a. Select **Gridlines** [*View* tab, *Show* group].
    b. Move the list placeholder down so the top border is even with the third horizontal grid line.
    c. Click the first bulleted line and click the **Bullets** button to remove the bullet.
    d. Press **Enter** to add blank space after the first line.
    e. Move the star shape over "PLR" and click **Send Backward** twice [*Drawing Tools Format* tab, *Arrange* group] to move the shape behind the text.
    f. Adjust the shape position as necessary (Figure 4-45) and deselect **Gridlines** [*View* tab, *Show* group].

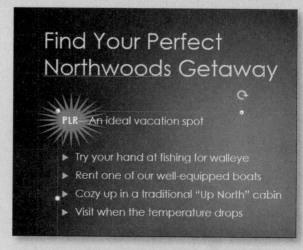

**4-45** *Gridlines* displayed and the shape is behind text

6. Change shapes.
   a. Display slide 3. Select the four location name shapes.
   b. Click the **Edit Shape** button [*Drawing Tools Format* tab, *Insert Shapes* group] and select **Change Shape** to open the gallery.
   c. Select the **Line Callout 1** shape (Figure 4-46).
      • A line appears to the left of each text box.
      • The line is part of the shape, but it looks better when it touches the shape outline.

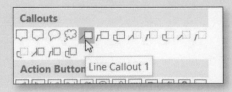

4-46 *Callouts* group in the *Shapes* gallery

   d. Click the **Zoom** button on the *Status* bar to increase your viewing percentage to **150%** so detailed positioning is easier.
   e. Adjust callout lines.
      • Select the "Baudette" shape. Drag the yellow adjustment handle on the right side of the line so it touches the left middle handle on the shape.
      • Repeat for "Breezy Point" and "Cass Lake."
      • Select the "Walker" shape and change the line. Drag the line's adjustment handle that touches the left side of the shape so it touches the right side of the shape. Drag the line's other adjustment handle so it points away from the shape on the right (Figure 4-47).

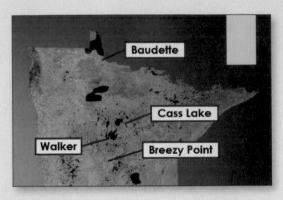

4-47 Shapes adjusted

   f. Drag the shapes to the right so they are on top of the Minnesota map.
   g. Position each name as shown in Figure 4-48 and extend the lines as necessary to point to the specific locations.

7. Modify, flip, ungroup, and merge shapes.
   a. Display slide 4 and select the oval only.
   b. Click **Edit Shape** [*Drawing Tools Format* tab, *Insert Shapes* group], select **Change Shape**, and select **Rectangle**.
   c. Select the fish only. Click the **Rotate** button [*Drawing Tools Format* tab, *Arrange* group] and select **Flip Horizontal**.
   d. Click **Group** [*Drawing Tools Format* tab, *Arrange* group] and select **Ungroup** (Figure 4-49).
   e. Press **Shift** and click the rectangle to add it to the selection.
      • If you have deselected the fish shapes, draw a selection rectangle to select all the shapes again.
   f. Click the **Merge Shapes** button [*Drawing Tools Format* tab, *Insert Shapes* group] and select **Combine** (Figure 4-50).
      • The new shape adopts the top color. Change the *Shape Fill* to **Blue, Accent 4** and the *Shape Outline* to **No Outline** [*Drawing Tools Format* tab, *Shape Styles* group].

4-48 Shapes positioned on the map

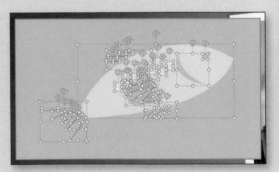

4-49 Ungrouped shapes                    4-50 Merged shape

g. Click the **Size Launcher** [*Drawing Tools Format* tab, *Size* group] to open the *Format Shape* pane.
   - Select **Lock aspect ratio** so the shape resizes proportionally.
   - Decrease the *Height* to **1"** and the width automatically changes.

8. Close the *Format Shape* pane and click the **Fit slide to current window** button [*Status* bar].

9. Duplicate, align, and distribute shapes.
   a. Select the merged shape on slide 4 and press **Ctrl+D**.
      - Position the duplicated shape, if necessary, to overlap the first shape.
   b. Press **Ctrl+D** six more times to create eight shapes.
      - Each new shape is automatically positioned as the second shape was positioned.
   c. Select all eight shapes (Figure 4-51). Click **Align** [*Drawing Tools Format* tab, *Arrange* group] and select **Align to Slide**.
      - Repeat this step to select **Align Left** and to select **Distribute Vertically** (Figure 4-52).
   d. Click **Group** [*Drawing Tools Format* tab, *Arrange* group] and select **Group**.

10. Apply connector lines.
    a. Move the picture on slide 4 to the left and position the text boxes as shown in Figure 4.53.
    b. Click the **More** button [*Drawing Tools Format* tab, *Insert Shapes* group] to open the shapes gallery and select the **Curved Arrow Connector** [*Lines* group].
    c. Click the right side connection site on the "Fishing" text box and drag the crosshair to the "Family" text box and click the top connection site.
       - The connection site on the "Family" text box turns green showing it is connected.
    d. Repeat to connect the bottom of the "Family" text box to the top of the "Fun!" text box.
       - As you draw the connector line, draw over the picture so the line has a curve with an adjustment handle.
       - Adjust the curve of the line if necessary.
    e. Select both connector lines, click the **Shape Outline** button [*Drawing Tools Format* tab, *Shape Styles* group], and change the *Weight* to **6 pt**.

11. Resize a shape to fit text and adjust text box spacing for two columns.
    a. Display slide 7. Right-click the text placeholder and select **Format Shape** to open the *Format Shape* pane.
    b. Click **Text Options** at the top of the pane if it is not already selected and click the **Textbox** button (Figure 4-54).

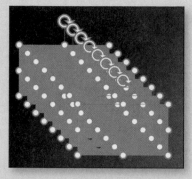

4-51 Duplicated shapes

4-53 Shapes with connector lines

4-52 Aligned and distributed shapes

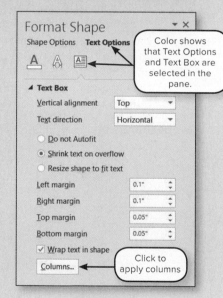

Color shows that Text Options and Text Box are selected in the pane.

Click to apply columns

4-54 *Format Shape* pane

c. Select **Resize shape to fit text**. The text box extends below the slide.

d. Click the **Columns** button to open the *Columns* dialog box. Select **2** columns with **.3"** spacing. Click **OK**.

e. Resize the text box (*Height* **5"** and *Width* **8.5"**) [*Drawing Tools Format* tab, *Size* group] (Figure 4-55).

f. Close the *Format Shape* pane.

12. Convert a *SmartArt* graphic to text.

a. Display slide 11. Select the *SmartArt* graphic on the left (Figure 4-56).

b. Click the **Convert** button [*SmartArt Tools Design* tab, *Reset* group].

c. Select **Convert to Text** to change text to a bulleted list.

d. Increase the font size to **20 pt**. [*Home* tab, *Font* group].

13. Convert a *SmartArt* graphic to shapes.

a. Display slide 6. Select the *SmartArt* graphic.

b. Click the **Convert** button [*SmartArt Tools Design* tab, *Reset* group].

c. Click **Convert to Shapes** to change to grouped shapes (Figure 4-57). Click the **Arrange** button [*Home* tab, *Drawing* group] and select **Ungroup**.

d. Click the slide background to deselect the shapes.

14. Rearrange ungrouped *SmartArt* shapes.

a. Select the "Seasonal Rates" shape within the graphic on slide 6 and press **Delete**.

b. Select the "Fall" and "Winter" shapes and press the down arrow 10 times.

c. Select the black rectangle with white text and position it between the shapes (Figure 4-58).

15. Add a shape, layer, and change color.

a. Display slide 13. Draw a rectangle (*Height* **3.5"** and *Width* **4"**) [*Drawing Tools Format* tab, *Size* group].

b. Move the rectangle over "Paradise Lakes Resort" (the three words are in separate text boxes).

   • Click **Send Backward** and select **Send to Back** [*Drawing Tools Format* tab, *Arrange* group].

c. Change the *Shape Fill* to **Blue, Accent 4, Darker 25%** and the *Shape Outline* to **No Outline** [*Drawing Tools Format* tab, *Shape Styles* group].

4-55 Text box with columns

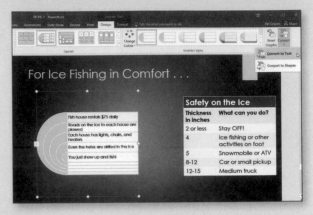

4-56 Convert a *SmartArt* graphic to text

4-57 *SmartArt* graphic converted to shapes and ungrouped

4-58 *SmartArt* graphic shapes adjusted

16. Edit shape points and apply a shape effect.
   a. Click the **Edit Shape** button [*Drawing Tools Format* tab, *Insert Shapes* group] and select **Edit Points**. The four corners now have black square edit points.
      - Click the center of the top border to add a point.
      - Click again in the middle of the right border to add a point.
   b. Click a corner edit point so its direction handles appear.
      - Direction handles are straight lines extending from the black edit point ending in a white square Figure 4-59.
   c. Change the curves so the shape behind "Paradise Lakes Resort" resembles the irregular shape of a lake.
      - Drag the white squares at the end of direction handles on each point to control the curve of the line between two points.
      - Drag the black edit point on the line to change the position of where the curve begins and ends.
      - Right-click points and select **Smooth Points** from the context menu.
      - Press **Esc** to turn off points.
   d. Select the shape. Click **Shape Effects** [*Drawing Tools Format* tab, *Shape Styles* group], select **Bevel**, and click **Cool Slant**.

4-59 Edit points to change the shape

17. Group objects and save the group as a picture to create a business logo.
   a. Select all text boxes (three words) on slide 13 and the shape. Click **Group** [*Drawing Tools Format* tab, *Arrange* group] and select **Group** from the drop-down list.
   b. Right-click the group to open the context menu and select **Save as picture** (Figure 4-60).
   c. Select the location to save the logo. For *Save as type*, select **PNG Portable Network Graphics Format** so the area around the logo remains transparent.
   d. Name the picture PLR-Logo2 and click **Save**.

4-60 Shape and text are grouped before saving as a picture

18. Insert the logo picture.
   a. Display slide 12. Click **Pictures** [*Insert* tab, *Images* group] and locate the ***PLR-Logo2*** picture.
   b. Click **Insert**. Position the logo on the lower right overlapping the picture.

19. Copy and paste the logo.
   a. Copy the ***PLR-Logo2*** on slide 12.
   b. Display slide 1. Paste the ***PLR-Logo2***.
   c. Resize the logo (*Height* approximately **1.9"**) and position it on the lower left of the picture.

20. Use *Gridlines* and *Guides* to check placeholder alignment and adjust as needed.

21. Delete slide 13 that contains only the grouped logo.

22. Save and close the presentation (Figure 4-61).

4-61 PP P4-1 completed

# Using Slide Masters to Create a Custom Theme

In *SLO 1.4: Changing Theme Colors and Fonts*, you learned to create custom theme colors using the *Slide Master*. Design features for each theme appear automatically when you develop slides and are controlled by the *Slide Master*. You can modify background graphics, customize layouts, and change theme fonts to create a unique theme. Changes made to *Slide Master* layouts display on all slides that use those layouts. Therefore, you can work more efficiently by making changes one time rather than repeating the same change on multiple slides.

## Change Background Graphics

PowerPoint themes often have graphic accents such as shapes with different fill colors. Using the *Slide Master*, you can customize a background with graphics chosen to support your message. If you have a text-only presentation, you may want your background to be more decorative. If your presentation has a lot of graphic content, you will want to keep the background simple so it does not compete with your content.

Because PowerPoint's *Eyedropper* enables you to precisely match colors, you can choose an original combination for custom theme colors based on an important picture or a graphic image of a particular product you are promoting. Once you have made your initial choice, you can add shapes colored in different ways to emphasize the slide title area or divide the slide content.

> **MORE INFO**
>
> Some online themes cannot easily be changed because of the way they are designed. Use *Slide Master* view to determine if the theme can be changed.

To illustrate the concepts of this section, five slides from another presentation (Figure 4-62) are used to create a separate summer promotion for PLR. The presentation has custom theme colors based on the PLR logo and the picture of a family in a canoe (Figure 4-63).

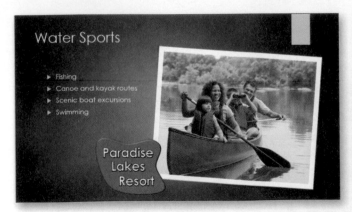

4-62 Original *Ion* theme colors

4-63 *Summer* custom theme colors

Shapes on the *Slide Master* change the background design. Placeholders are adjusted to fit the new shapes, and the PLR logo is positioned so it displays on all slides.

## ▶ HOW TO: Add Background Shapes

1. Open your presentation and click the **Slide Master** button [*View* tab, *Master Views* group] to open the *Slide Master* tab.
   - The thumbnail pane contains layouts for the current theme.
   - When you point to a layout, a *ScreenTip* identifies it and indicates which slides use that layout.

2. Scroll to the top of the layouts and select the first one.
   - Figure 4-64 shows the *Slide Master* and layouts for PowerPoint's *Ion* theme.
   - When you point to the first layout, a *ScreenTip* shows the theme name.
   - In this example, the *ScreenTip* shows *Ion Slide Master: used by slide(s) 1-5*.

4-64 *Ion Slide Master: used by slide(s) 1-5*

3. Modify or delete existing shapes.
   - Figure 4-65 shows the blue shape behind the slide number placeholder stretched across the top of the slide.
   - Another rectangle added on the left has a fill color slightly lighter than the slide background to define that area for bulleted text.

4. Select the shapes that you added and click **Send Backward** [*Drawing Tools Format* tab, *Arrange* group] so the shapes are behind all text placeholders.

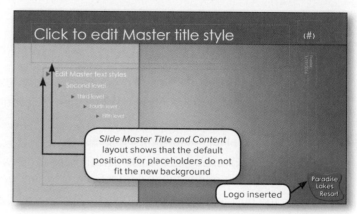

4-65 Shapes added behind text placeholders on the *Slide Master*

   - The shapes in Figure 4-65 are behind the title and the bulleted text placeholders.
   - If appropriate, you can add a business logo or other picture to the first layout so it appears on all slides.
   - Add shapes to other layouts as needed.

5. Click the **Close Master View** button [*Slide Master* tab, *Close* group]. The changes you have made appear on your slides.

> **MORE INFO**
>
> Remember to save frequently as you are working.

## Adjust Slide Layout Placeholders

As you develop PowerPoint presentations, you use slide layouts that control what is placed on a slide and where various objects are positioned. As discussed in the *Add Slides and Choose Layouts* section in *SLO 1.2: Working with Slides, Layouts, Placeholders, and Text*, the most common layouts include the following:

- *Title Slide*
- *Title and Content*
- *Section Header*

- *Two Content*
- *Comparison*
- *Title Only*
- *Blank*

In *Slide Master* view, these layouts display under the first layout, which you use to make global changes that affect the entire presentation. Other layouts (not listed above) display, too. When you customize your *Slide Master*, delete layouts that you do not plan to use.

Placeholders on the *Slide Master* layouts are positioned based on a theme's background design. Therefore, as you change the background by adding shapes or pictures, you must adjust placeholder positioning. Evaluate how your changes affect the text and objects on your slides. You may need to adjust shape sizing or adjust text placeholder sizing to better fit your shapes.

## ▶ HOW TO: Adjust Placeholder Positions

1. Click the **Slide Master** button [*View* tab, *Master Views* group] to open the *Slide Master* tab.
2. Scroll to the top of your layouts and select the first layout. Notice the *ScreenTip* that shows the current theme name.
3. Modify the title placeholder size, if necessary.
   - An example for changing the title placeholder size is when a longer title wraps to a second line and needs more space to prevent the text from becoming smaller.
4. Change the bulleted text placeholder size, if necessary, and position it to fit appropriately with shapes.
5. Adjust text color as needed.
   - A revised *Slide Master* layout is shown in Figure 4-66.
   - The text placeholders are adjusted to fit within the shapes.
   - Compare Figure 4-66 to the default positions shown in Figure 4-65.
6. Click the **Close Master View** button [*Slide Master* tab, *Close* group].
7. Look at each slide in *Normal* view to check the new layouts.
   - Text automatically adjusts to the new placeholder changes.
   - Figure 4-67 shows slide 2 after placeholder size and positions were changed on the *Slide Master*.
8. Adjust slide content if you need slight changes for the new layouts. If you notice a problem, revise your layouts on the *Slide Master*.

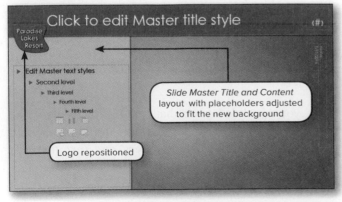

4-66 *Slide Master* placeholders adjusted

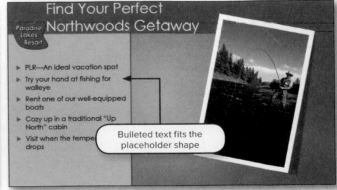

4-67 Slide 2 content after *Slide Master* changes

## Create New Theme Fonts

In *SLO 1.4: Changing Theme Colors and Fonts*, you changed theme fonts using built-in font pairs on the *Design* tab and the *Slide Master* tab. Several font pairs use the same font for headings and for body (bulleted text and text box default fonts). Others use two different fonts that work well together. You can create your own theme fonts as well.

The two major categories of fonts are **serif** (which include details at the ends of letter strokes) and **sans serif** (which do not include details at the ends of letter strokes) (Figure 4-68). For presentation slides, a sans serif font usually works well because the letters are easier to read from a distance. This becomes very important when lighting conditions in a presentation room are less than ideal.

Certain fonts can appear larger than others even when the same point size is used, because of the way letters are designed. You might choose a font with very thick characters for short heading text or choose a more decorative font that appears like handwriting or printing. Examples of different fonts are shown in Figures 4-69 and 4-70. The examples all have the same point size and line spacing.

Notice the differences in the horizontal space these fonts use even though they are all the same size. As you select fonts for a new theme, consider both the size differences and how easy-to-read they will be when projected on a large screen. Fonts that are suitable for printing purposes may not work well for slides. Also consider the tone a font creates. A whimsical font might not be appropriate for a serious business presentation, for example. When using two fonts, be sure they blend well together.

4-68 Font categories

4-69 Fonts available in the *Theme Fonts* list and commonly used for slides

| Serif fonts | Sample text | Times New Roman |
| | Sample text | Cambria |
| | Sample text | Georgia |
| | Sample text | Palatino Linotype |
| | Sample text | Century Schoolbook |
| Sans serif fonts | Sample text | Calibri |
| | Sample text | Franklin Gothic Book |
| | Sample text | Arial |
| | Sample text | Trebuchet |
| | Sample text | Verdana |

4-70 Fonts for special uses

| Bold fonts | Sample text | Kozuka Gothic Pro B |
| | Sample text | Cooper Black |
| | Sample text | Arial Black |
| | Sample text | Rockwell Extra Bold |
| | Sample text | Gill Sans Ultra Bold |
| Decorative fonts | Sample text | Freestyle Script |
| | Sample text | Bradley Hand ITC |
| | Sample text | Maiandra GD |
| | Sample text | Papyrus |
| | Sample text | MV Boli |

---

▶ **HOW TO: Create New Theme Fonts**

1. Click the **Design** tab.
   - You can also change theme fonts using options in the *Background* group on the *Slide Master* tab.
2. Click the **More** button [*Variants* group].

3. Select **Fonts** and choose **Customize Fonts** from the drop-down list to open the *Create New Theme Fonts* dialog box.

4. Select a *Heading font* and select a *Body font*; then name your font pair (Figure 4-71). Click **Save** and the dialog box closes.

   - This new theme font is saved in the *Custom* category of your *Theme Fonts* list.

5. Check your slides and adjust text if necessary.

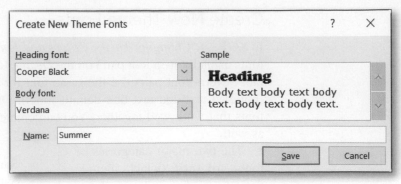

4-71 *Create New Theme Fonts* dialog box

## Apply Text Effects

Consistent font treatments for color, effects, and size can create a hierarchy of importance that will help your audience understand and prioritize your content. The most important text should be emphasized the most. Slide titles should be larger than body text, and they could also have a shadow or bevel effect to emphasize them more. A shadow effect can help to define letters and improve the contrast between the text color and the slide background color. Always strive to make text easy to read. For consistency across multiple slides in your presentation, apply text effects using the *Slide Master*.

### ▶ HOW TO: Apply Text Effects on the Slide Master

1. Click the **Slide Master** button [*View* tab, *Master Views* group] to open the *Slide Master* tab.

2. Scroll up to select the first layout so your changes affect all slide layouts.

3. Select the title text placeholder and click the **Text Effects** button [*Drawing Tools Format* tab, *WordArt Styles* group].

4. Apply appropriate effects and adjust effect options.

   - Change font size and color as needed [*Home* tab, *Font* group].
   - Change case if necessary [*Home* tab, *Font* group].
   - The title text on all slide layouts automatically changes.

5. Select other slide layouts and change text effects as needed.

6. Click the **Close Master View** button [*Slide Master* tab, *Close* group].

7. Check your slides and adjust text as necessary.

## Change List Bullets and List Indent

In the *Change List Bullet Symbols* section of *SLO 1.2: Working with Slides, Layouts, Placeholders, and Text*, you changed list bullets by selecting different characters and adjusting the character color and size. You can also apply picture bullets from online sources or insert your own picture file. A picture bullet can add a creative accent to support the topic of your presentation. Although you could use an actual photograph in a tiny size, most likely it would not be recognizable. A simple line art image usually works best, and you may want it to be larger than your text size.

You can change the bullet for one or more indent levels by selecting those items within the bulleted text placeholder; you can change the bullet for all indent levels if you select the bulleted text placeholder. Changing bullets on the *Slide Master* is more efficient than changing bullets on multiple slides.

## ▶ HOW TO:  Change Bullets to Pictures

1. Click the **Slide Master** button [*View* tab, *Master Views* group] to open the *Slide Master* tab.

2. Scroll up to select the first layout.

3. Select the bulleted text placeholder.

4. Click the **Bullets** drop-down arrow [*Home* tab, *Paragraph* group].

5. Click **Bullets and Numbering** to open the *Bullets and Numbering* dialog box (Figure 4-72).

6. Change the bullet *Size* to a percentage that is appropriate for your picture.

7. Click the **Picture** button to open the *Insert Pictures* dialog box.

8. Browse to find a picture you have saved, or search for an appropriate picture.

9. Select a picture and click **Insert**.

   - The bullet is inserted and the *Bullets and Numbering* dialog box closes.

10. Click the **Close Master View** button [*Slide Master* tab, *Close* group].

11. Check your slides with bulleted text to see if text word wraps correctly under text and not under the picture.

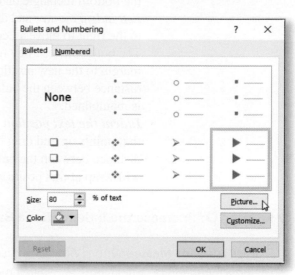

4-72 *Bullets and Numbering* dialog box

A picture bullet is often larger than a character bullet, so you may need to change the distance between the bullet and the text so the text aligns correctly (Figure 4-73). Change bullets on the *Slide Master* when multiple slides are affected.

When you select the ***Ruler*** on the *View* tab, a ruler displays above the slide and on the left side. If no text is selected, ruler numbering begins at the center and extends to the edge of the slide. Default ***tab stops*** are spaced every one-half inch which causes your insertion point to indent one-half inch to the right when you press **Tab**.

When your insertion point is in a text placeholder, the ruler adjusts and the slide area not used is grayed out. Two markers on the ruler show the current margin and indent. The *First-line indent marker* is most commonly used for paragraph indentions because only the indent on the first line changes when you drag the triangle pointing down to the right. All other text continues to wrap at the margin.

> PLR—An ideal vacation spot
>
> Try your hand at fishing for walleye
>
> Rent one of our well-equipped boats
>
> Cozy up in a traditional "Up North" cabin
>
> Visit when the temperature drops

4-73 Incorrect word wrap under the bullet

The *Left indent marker* (with two parts) can be used for paragraphs, too, but is commonly used for bulleted and numbered text. It works differently depending on which part you move (Figure 4-74).

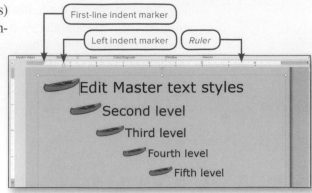

4-74 Bulleted text placeholder on the *Slide Master* before indent changes

- ***Indent the entire list***—Click the bottom rectangle on the *Left indent marker* and drag it to the right to move all content. The bullet moves away from the margin to the new position and the distance between the bullet and text is maintained.

- ***Indent the text position following a bullet***—Click the triangle on the *Left indent marker* that points up and drag it to the right. The bullet will remain at the left margin and the distance between the bullet and text is increased. Because this is a hanging indent, text will wrap at this position.

▶ **HOW TO:** Increase the Indent after a Bullet

1. Click the **Slide Master** button [*View* tab, *Master Views* group] to open the *Slide Master* tab.
2. Scroll to the top of your layouts and select the first layout.
3. Click the **Ruler** button [*View* tab, *Show* group] and the ruler displays.
4. Drag the **Zoom** slider [*Status* bar] to **200%** so working with the ruler is easier.
   - Drag the slide scroll boxes below the slide or on the right so you can see the bulleted text close to the ruler above.

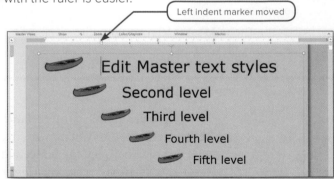

4-75 The indent markers are moved to add space and to wrap text evenly

5. Click to position your insertion point before the first word in the first line of bulleted text.
   - Indent markers appear on the horizontal ruler.
6. Drag the **Left indent marker** (triangle at the top) to the right. (The **1"** position on the *Ruler* is shown in Figure 4-75.)
   - You may need less or more space, depending on the size of your picture bullet, to achieve even alignment for all the text that follows a bullet.
   - The bullet picture size in Figure 4-74 and 4-75 was increased to **130%** for the first line of bulleted text. The other bullet sizes are smaller in proportion to their indent level.
7. Repeat steps 5–6 for second-level bullets or other list levels that you may use.
8. Click the **Close Master View** button [*Slide Master* tab, *Close* group].
9. Click the **Fit slide to current window** button [*Status* bar].
10. Adjust placeholder size on individual slides if needed (Figure 4-76).

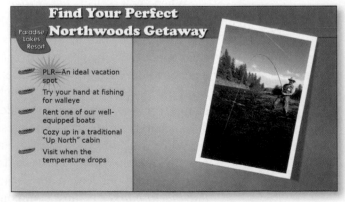

4-76 Slide 2 with corrected indent

## The Handout Master

The *Handout* feature is a printing option that allows you to share a paper copy of your presentation with your audience. It displays several slides on each page in fixed positions based on the number of slides you select. The *Handout Master* is used to rearrange header and footer placeholders or to change fonts or add graphics.

It works well to include a design element from the presentation in the handout. Handouts provide a convenient place for people to take notes during a presentation and can be a useful resource for them after the presentation.

▶ **HOW TO:** Customize the Handout Master

1. Click the **View** tab and click the **Handout Master** button [*Master Views* group] to open the *Handout Master* tab.
2. Click buttons in the *Page Setup* group (Figure 4-77) to change the following:
   - **Handout Orientation:** *Portrait* (default) or *Landscape* orientation.
   - **Slide Size:** *Widescreen* (default) or *Standard* slide size. Be very careful when changing slide size. The miniature slides in standard size may fit the handout better than widescreen size, but a change here also affects the slide show. You may not want the slide show changed especially if extensive editing is required so that slide content fits the different slide size.
   - **Slides Per Page:** *1, 2, 3, 4, 6, 9 Slides* or the *Slide Outline* can be shown. Lines for writing notes appear beside each slide if you choose three slides.
3. Select options from the *Placeholders* group to appear on the *Handout* page.
   - Remove placeholders by deselecting the checkbox or by deleting them on the page.
4. Click the **Colors**, **Fonts**, **Effects**, or **Background Styles** buttons [*Handout Master* tab, *Background* group] to choose options from the available galleries.
   - Click the **Background Styles** button and select **Format Background** to open the *Format Background* pane where you can change fill options.
   - Do not click the **Apply to All** button. If you do, the changes you make for the handout will affect your slide show.
   - While color backgrounds may look attractive on handouts, printing full-color pages can be expensive and note taking on the pages may be more difficult. A plain page background is usually effective.
5. Select each placeholder and edit it using one or more of the following techniques. Increase the **Zoom** as needed to work with detailed areas of the page.
   - Change the font, apply text effects, or change alignment [*Home* tab].
   - Insert text in a placeholder or replace the data that is displayed.
   - Resize a placeholder.
   - Drag a placeholder to a different position.
6. Click the **Insert** tab to add a picture, such as a company logo, or other objects that you want to appear on all printed pages (Figure 4-78).
7. Click the **Close Master View** button [*Handout Master* tab].

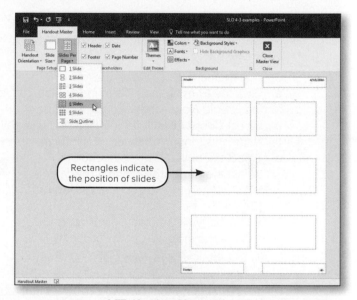

Rectangles indicate the position of slides

4-77 *Handout Master* tab and page placeholders

4-78 Handout master changed

To create a PLR summer promotion presentation, you use the *Slide Master* to add background shapes and the PLR logo. The current theme colors have already been customized. You adjust placeholder positioning, customize fonts, and insert a picture bullet for a unique theme.

Files Needed: ***PLRPromotionSummer-04.pptx*** *(student data files are available in the* Library *of your SIMnet account)* and ***PLRLogo2.png*** *(created in* Pause & Practice: PowerPoint 4-1*)*
Completed Project File Name: *[your initials] PP P4-2.pptx*

1. Open the ***PLRPromotionSummer-04*** presentation from your student data files.
2. Save the presentation as [your initials] PP P4-2.
3. Click the **Slide Master** button [*View* tab, *Master Views* group] to open the *Slide Master* tab.
4. Scroll to the top of your thumbnail layouts on the left and select the first layout, *Ion Slide Master, used by slide(s) 1-5*.
5. Change theme fonts.
   a. Click the **Fonts** button [*Slide Master* tab, *Background* group] and select **Customize Fonts** to open the *Create New Theme Fonts* dialog box.
   b. Select **Cooper Black** for the *Heading* font. Select **Verdana** for the *Body* font.
   c. Name this font pair **Summer**. Click **Save**.
   d. Select the bulleted text placeholder. Select the **Font** drop-down arrow [*Home* tab, *Font* group] and choose **Verdana (Body)** (Figure 4-79).
      • The body placeholders on all other *Slide Master* layouts will update accordingly.

4-79 Applying the correct *Theme Fonts* style

6. Apply a shadow style to title text.
   a. Select the title placeholder and click the **Text Effects** button [*Drawing Tools Format* tab, *WordArt Styles* group]. Select **Shadow** and click **Shadow Options** to open the *Format Shape* pane.
   b. Click **Presets** and select **Offset Diagonal Bottom Right** (in the *Outer* group).
   c. Reduce the shadow *Transparency* to **30%**. Increase the *Blur* to **6 pt**. and the *Distance* to **6 pt**.
   d. Close the *Format Shape* pane.
7. Modify and insert background shapes.
   a. Select the blue rectangle at the top of the slide and stretch it on the left and right to the width of the slide (**13.33"**).
   b. Click the **Rectangle** tool [*Drawing Tools Format* tab, *Insert Shapes* group]. Draw a second rectangle (*Height* **7.5"** and *Width* **5"**) anywhere on the slide.
   c. Click the **Shape Fill** button [*Drawing Tools Format* tab, *Shape Styles* group] and change the fill color to **Olive Green, Background 2, Lighter 40%**.
   d. Click the **Shape Outline** button [*Drawing Tools Format* tab, *Shape Styles* group] and choose **No Outline**.
   e. Click the **Shape Effects** button [*Drawing Tools Format* tab, *Shape Styles* group], select **Shadow**, and **Offset Right** (in the *Outer* group).
   f. Click the **Send Backward** drop-down arrow [*Drawing Tools Format* tab, *Arrange* group] and choose **Send to Back**.
   g. Click the **Align** button [*Drawing Tools Format* tab, *Arrange* group] and choose **Align Left**. Repeat to choose **Align Top**.
8. Insert a logo.
   a. Click the **Pictures** button [*Insert* tab, *Images* group] and locate your saved files.

b. Select the **PLRLogo2** that you created in *Pause & Practice: PowerPoint 4-1* and insert the logo.

c. Resize the logo (*Height* approximately **1.2"**).

d. Move it to the upper left of the *Slide Master* layout partially over the blue rectangle.

9. Adjust placeholder positions.

   a. Position the title placeholder on the blue rectangle at the top of the slide beside the PLR logo.

     • Resize the title placeholder so it has the same height as the blue rectangle.

     • Click the **Align Text** button [*Home* tab, *Paragraph* group] and choose **Middle** so the text will be centered vertically in the title placeholder.

   b. Move the bulleted text placeholder to the left and resize it so all text fits on the rectangle with the lighter olive green color.

   c. Select the text and change the font color to **Black, Background 1** (Figure 4-80).

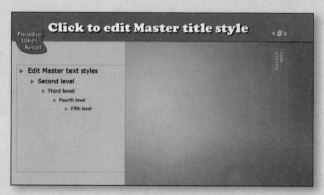

10. Add a picture bullet and adjust the indent.

   a. Select the bulleted text placeholder. Click the **Bullets** button [*Home* tab, *Paragraph* group] and click **Bullets and Numbering**.

   b. Click the **Pictures** button and browse to your student data files. Select **CanoeBlue-04** and click **Insert**.

   c. Select the **Ruler** [*View* tab, *Show* group].

   d. Drag the **Zoom** slider to **150%**. Adjust your slide position so you can see the top of the bulleted placeholder.

4-80 Inserted logo resized and moved near the title

   e. Click to position your insertion point at the beginning of the first bulleted item.

   f. Drag the left indent marker (triangle) (Figure 4-81) to the **0.5"** position (the first-line indent marker does not change).

   g. Click to position your insertion point at the beginning of the second bulleted item.

   h. Drag the left indent marker (triangle) to the **1"** position. Deselect the **Ruler**.

   i. Click the **Fit Slide to Current Window** button [*Status* bar].

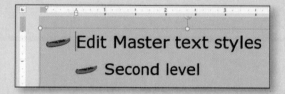

4-81 The bullet indent is adjusted using the *Ruler*

11. Move placeholders and adjust text.

   a. Select the *Title Slide* layout.

   b. Move the footer and date placeholders to the right of the slide.

   c. Resize the title placeholder to fit on the darker green area.

   d. Select the subtitle placeholder.

     • Click the **Change Case** button [*Home* tab, *Font* group] and select **Capitalize Each Word**.

     • Increase the font size to **28 pt**. and apply **bold**.

     • Resize the subtitle placeholder to fit the text.

     • Move the subtitle placeholder to the darker green area below the title placeholder.

12. Insert the PLR logo on the *Title Slide* layout.

   a. Click the **Pictures** button [*Insert* tab] and locate your student data files.

   b. Select the **PLRLogo2** that you created in *Pause & Practice: PowerPoint 4-1* and insert the logo.

   c. Move the logo to the upper left to cover the smaller logo behind it.

   d. Increase the logo size to be as wide as the rectangle that it is over (Figure 4-82).

4-82 Completed title slide

13. Click the **Slide Master** tab and click the **Close Master View** button.

14. Display slide 1. If necessary, click the **Reset** button [*Home* tab, *Slides* group] to apply the *Slide Master* changes.

15. Check each slide to be sure that all slide objects fit appropriately and adjust if necessary.

16. Save and close the presentation (Figure 4-83).

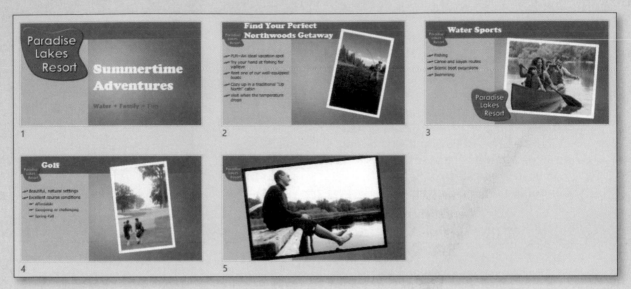

4-83 PP P4-2 completed

## Capturing a Screenshot or Screen Clipping

When you need an image of your computer screen, you can capture it using PowerPoint's *Screenshot* feature to copy the entire application window or the *Screen Clipping* feature to copy a portion of the window. These features are very useful, especially if you need to reference a web page during a presentation when no Internet access is available. The document or web page you want to capture must be open while you are working on your PowerPoint presentation.

4-84 *Screenshot* button and available windows

### ▶HOW TO: Insert a Screenshot

1. Open the document or web page you want to capture.

2. Open PowerPoint and go to the slide where you want the captured image to appear.

3. Click the **Screenshot** button [*Insert* tab, *Images* group] and a gallery appears showing all available (open) windows (Figure 4-84).

P4-238

4. Click the window you want to show in PowerPoint and the entire window of the application or web page displays on the current slide as a picture. It will automatically be sized to the vertical size of your slide (Figure 4-85).

5. Use the *Picture Tools Format* tab to customize the picture by cropping or applying picture effects.

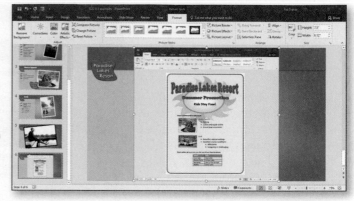

4-85 Screenshot inserted showing full application window

### ANOTHER WAY

You can capture a screen image with other methods, too, based on what keys are available on your keyboard. For example, press **Print Screen** and a copy of your computer screen is placed on the *Clipboard*. Press **Alt+Print Screen** to copy only the current window. In both cases, press **Ctrl+V** to paste these images from the *Clipboard*. They will appear on the slide at full size.

Windows tablets, such as a Microsoft Surface, don't have the *Print Screen* button. To capture the full screen, press **FN+Space** or the **Windows** button and the **Volume Down** hardware button on the side of the tablet. Press **Alt+FN+Space** to capture the current window. Press **Ctrl+V** to paste these images.

In the gallery of available windows that appears when you click the *Screenshot* button, the first window on the left is the most recently opened window. It is the one from which a *screen clipping* can be made. Therefore, you should view the document or web page you plan to capture right before moving to the slide in PowerPoint where you intend to place the screen clipping. Then when you select *Screen Clipping* at the bottom of the *Screenshot* gallery, that window will appear and be grayed out. You select the area to capture by dragging a crosshair across the screen.

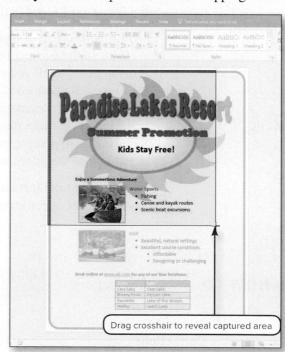

4-86 The screen area to be captured is revealed for a *Screen Clipping*

### ▶ HOW TO: Insert a Screen Clipping

1. Open the document or web page that contains the information you want to capture.

2. Open PowerPoint and go to the slide where you want the image to appear.

3. Click the **Screenshot** button [*Insert* tab, *Images* group] and click **Screen Clipping**.

4. Your screen becomes gray and displays the window showing your last open document or web page.
   - Your pointer changes to a crosshair.

5. Click and drag to reveal the screen area you want to capture (Figure 4-86).

G. Release the mouse button and your screen clipping displays on your slide as a picture such as the one shown on the left in Figure 4-87.

- The screen clipping on the right in Figure 4-87 has the *Bevel Rectangle* picture style which rounds the corners to better match the image and makes the border looked raised.
- An *Offset Diagonal Bottom Right* shadow was applied with settings adjusted to better define the image.

4-87 Screen clipping inserted and shown with picture effects applied

 **Editing Pictures**

PowerPoint provides many photo editing features that allow you to improve your pictures or arrange them in creative and artistic ways.

## Make Corrections

If a picture lacks detail because it is too dark or if colors are washed out from bright sunshine, you can improve the picture using *Corrections*. The *Corrections* gallery opens with the current image positioned in the middle of available options.

- **Sharpen/Soften:** *Sharpen* makes picture details more evident; *Soften* creates a blending effect. In the *Corrections* gallery, the options change in 25 percent increments; softer colors are on the left and sharper colors are on the right.
- **Contrast/Brightness:** *Contrast* affects the difference between the picture's lightest and darkest colors. Increasing *Brightness* lightens a picture by adding white while decreasing *Brightness* darkens the picture by adding black. In the *Corrections* gallery, the options change in 20 percent increments for both adjustments. Darker variations are on the left and lighter variations are on the right.

If these percentages create bigger changes than you want, you can open the *Format Picture* pane to choose specific percentages using **Picture Corrections** options.

▶ **HOW TO:** Make Corrections

1. Select the picture you want to change.
2. Click the **Corrections** button [*Picture Tools Format* tab, *Adjust* group] to open the gallery.
3. Point to various effects in the *Sharpen/Soften* category or in the *Brightness/Contrast* category to see the live preview of the effect on your picture.

4. Click an effect to apply it.
   - Figure 4-88 shows the original picture and the one on the right has **Sharpen: 50%** applied.
   - Figure 4-89 shows the original picture and the one on the right has **Brightness: 0% (Normal) Contrast:+40%** applied.

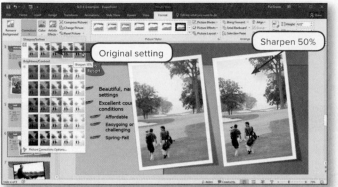

4-88 Original picture and picture with *Sharpen* effect applied

4-89 Original picture and picture with *Contrast* effect applied

5. Click the **Reset Picture** button [*Picture Tools Format* tab, *Adjust* group] to restore the picture to its original colors.

## Artistic Effects

With the ***Artistic Effects*** gallery, you can transform your picture using various effects that resemble painting techniques. The effects include *Pencil Sketch, Line Drawing, Watercolor Sponge, Glass, Plastic Wrap*, and many others. These effects lessen the realism of a picture, but the results can be beautiful in a creative way. Consider using these effects for special situations.

### ▶ HOW TO: Apply Artistic Effects

1. Select the picture you want to change.

2. Click the **Artistic Effects** button [*Picture Tools Format* tab, *Adjust* group].

3. Point to various effects. Observe the name of the effect and the live preview of that effect on your picture.

4. Click an effect to apply it.
   - Figure 4-90 shows the original picture and the one on the right has the *Cutout* effect applied.

5. Click the **Reset Picture** button [*Picture Tools Format* tab, *Adjust* group] to restore the picture to its original appearance.

4-90 Original picture and picture with *Artistic* effect applied

## Crop a Picture to a Shape or an Aspect Ratio

As you learned in *SLO 2.3: Working with Pictures,* you crop a picture by dragging the cropping handles from the edge of the picture. You can also crop a picture to a shape from the *Shape* gallery or to a specific aspect ratio.

### ▶ HOW TO: Crop a Picture to a Shape or Aspect Ratio

1. Select the picture you want to change.
2. Click the **Crop** button list arrow [*Picture Tools Format* tab, *Size* group].
3. Select **Crop to Shape** to open the *Shapes* gallery and click a shape for the picture such as the *7-Point Star* shown in Figure 4-91.

   - The picture is centered in the shape. To reposition the picture, right-click and select **Format Picture** to open the *Format Picture* pane.
   - Click the **Picture** icon at the top of the pane and click **Crop**.
   - Enter negative values for *Offset X* to move the picture left; enter positive values to move the picture right.
   - Enter negative values for *Offset Y* to move the picture up; enter positive values to move the picture down.
   - Close the *Format Picture* pane.

*Or*

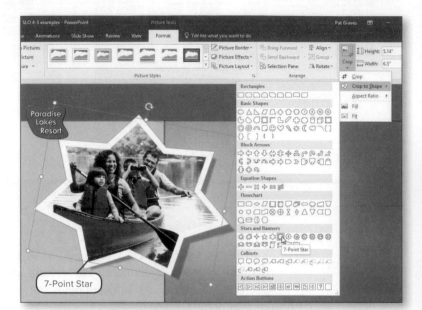

4-91 Picture is cropped to a shape from the *Shapes* gallery

4. Select **Aspect Ratio** from the *Crop* menu to open a list of sizes organized by orientation: *Square, Portrait,* and *Landscape*.
5. Click an *Aspect Ratio* size to apply it.

   - The first number is the horizontal ratio; the second number is the vertical ratio.
   - The picture is centered with each different aspect ratio while areas from the edges of the picture are removed to achieve that particular size (Figure 4-92).
   - Click and drag the picture to reposition it as needed within the crop area.
6. Click the **Crop** button.

### ▶ MORE INFO

Changing the fill on a shape to a picture fill results in the same appearance as cropping a picture to a shape.

4-92 *Aspect Ratio* of 5:3 crops from the picture's middle

## Change a Picture

The ***Change Picture*** command replaces one picture with another. It works with an inserted picture even when the picture is cropped. It does not work if you use a picture as a shape fill.

---

**▶HOW TO: Change a Picture**

1. Select a picture and click the **Change Picture** button [*Picture Tools Format* tab, *Adjust* group] (Figure 4-93) to open the *Insert Pictures* dialog box.
2. Click **Browse** to search in your files for the picture you need.
3. Select a picture and click **Insert**.
   - The new picture replaces the original picture but retains the same styles that were applied to the original picture.
   - You will notice a change in size if one picture has a portrait orientation and the other one has a landscape orientation because the width remains the same.
   - You can also right-click a picture and select **Change Picture** from the context menu.

4-93 *Change Picture* button

---

## Apply a SmartArt Picture Layout

When a picture is selected, you can apply a *SmartArt* layout. Click the **Picture Layout** button [*Picture Tools Format* tab, *Picture Styles* group] (Figure 4-94). The *SmartArt* layouts that appear all have pictures in them.

## Remove a Picture Background

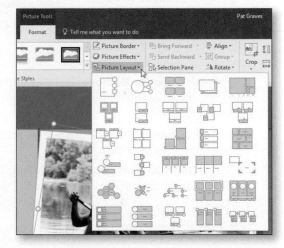

As you learned in *SLO 2.3: Working with Pictures*, it is easy to remove the background that is a solid fill by using the *Set Transparent Color* feature. You can also remove detailed areas of a background to focus on just one element of the picture. Click the **Remove Background** button [*Picture Tools Format* tab, *Adjust* group] and use the following commands on the *Background Removal* tab.

4-94 *SmartArt* layouts available for pictures

- ***Mark Areas to Keep:*** Selects colors to keep and places a small circle with a plus sign on that area.
- ***Mark Areas to Remove:*** Selects colors to remove and places a small circle with a minus sign on that area.
- ***Delete Mark:*** Removes keep or remove marks.
- ***Discard All Changes:*** Restores the picture to its original colors.
- ***Keep Changes:*** Accepts all changes you have marked.

The area removed appears transparent on the slide. Depending on the complexity of the picture, it may take more than one attempt to get good results.

Your original picture file is not affected by removing the background in PowerPoint. However, if you want to use the modified picture again, save it using a different name and the appropriate file type. The .png file type will preserve the transparent area that you removed. The .jpg file type does not support transparency and the removed area will be displayed as white.

## ▶ HOW TO: Remove a Picture Background

1. Select the picture you want to change.
2. Click the **Remove Background** button [*Picture Tools Format* tab, *Adjust* group].

   - The *Background Removal* tab opens with editing tools (Figure 4-95).
   - A rectangle on the picture suggests the area you may want to keep with part of it shown in color.
   - The rest of the picture has a magenta color that indicates the area to be removed (Figure 4-96).

4-95  *Background Removal* tab

3. Adjust the selection rectangle (Figure 4-97).

   - Increase the **Zoom** percentage so you can work more easily with details.
   - Click the rectangle border and drag to move the area. Drag sizing handles to select only the area you want to keep.

4. Click **Mark Areas to Keep** [*Background Removal* tab, *Refine* group] and click areas of the picture currently being removed that you want to keep.

4-96  *Background Removal* showing the selected area before editing

4-97  *Background Removal* area is changed and areas to keep are marked

5. Click **Mark Areas to Remove** [*Background Removal* tab, *Refine* group] and click areas of the picture that are currently displayed but should be removed.
6. Click **Keep Changes** to accept your selections and remove the background (Figure 4-98).
7. Click the **Remove Background** button again if you are not satisfied with the result and mark more areas.

   - You can continue to mark changes on the picture until you save your presentation.
   - Only the modified picture remains when you open the presentation again.

8. Save the modified picture.

   - Right-click to open the context menu and select **Save As Picture**.
   - Select the location to save the file.
   - Rename the picture with a different file name.
   - Select the .png file type to preserve the transparent area that you removed.
   - Click **Save**.

4-98  The background is removed

## Ungroup Illustrations and Recolor

While illustrations created with drawing programs do not have the realism of photographic images, they can range from very simple drawings to extremely complex and beautiful designs. Drawing programs use *vector* graphics (based on angles and points). You learned to edit points using PowerPoint shapes in *SLO 4.1: Customizing Shapes* in the *Edit Shape Points* section. Common vector file formats are .eps (Encapsulated Postscript), .wmf (Windows Metafile) or .emf (Enhanced Metafile). Vector graphics can be resized without becoming distorted.

Once an illustration is designed, it is often saved in its original vector file format for possible future editing. Then the file is resaved as a .jpg or .png file to reduce the file size, maintain color accuracy, and make it compatible for many different software applications. Therefore, you can use functions on the *Picture Tools Format* tab for illustrations when they are saved using these file formats.

It can be difficult to determine this file format difference when searching for images unless you can see the file extension (for example, .wmf) that denotes a vector graphic. When this type of image is ungrouped, it becomes a PowerPoint drawing. When you ungroup it again, you can select individual parts of the image to change fill and outline colors, delete parts, or combine parts in different ways to create a new image. You can use functions on the *Drawing Tools Format* tab for illustrations using these vector graphic file formats.

So depending on how an illustration is saved, you may be able to modify the illustration using the techniques described in this section.

> ### MORE INFO
> If an illustration cannot be ungrouped, you will receive an error message when you try to ungroup it.

In *SLO 4.1 Customizing Shapes* in the *Save Grouped Objects as a Picture* section, you used the .png file format to preserve colors and text sizing. However, if you create a drawing in PowerPoint that you may want to modify in the future, choose the *Windows Metafile* file type when you save the image. Then when you insert this image into another presentation, it can be ungrouped so you can modify the individual parts or rearrange them.

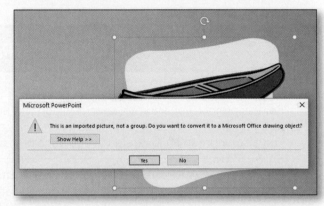

4-99 Warning message that appears when ungrouping an illustrated image

## ▶ HOW TO: Ungroup an Illustration and Recolor

1. Select an illustrated image in a vector graphic format (such as .wmf).

2. Change the **Zoom** percentage so you can see the image in a larger size to work in detail.

3. Click **Group** [*Picture Tools Format* tab, *Arrange* group] and select **Ungroup**.

   - A dialog box asks if you want to convert this picture to a Microsoft Office drawing object (Figure 4-99).
   - Click **Yes**. The *Drawing Tools Format* tab opens instead of the *Picture Tools Format* tab.
   - One set of handles appears around the illustration.

4. Click the **Group** button [*Drawing Tools Format* tab, *Arrange* group] and click **Ungroup** again.

   - Selection handles appear on the many shapes in the illustrated image (Figure 4-100).
   - These shapes may have a blank shape behind them that should be removed if you are deleting part of the image to be used in a different way.

5. Click anywhere on the slide to turn off handles.

   - Now you can select individual parts of the image and delete parts you do not want, change fill or line colors, or rearrange shapes.

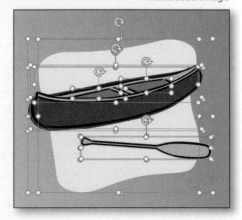

4-100 Ungrouped image showing handles for multiple shapes

6. If you are deleting a large area with multiple parts, draw a selection rectangle so more parts are selected at once. Press **Delete**.

7. Select all of the remaining shapes when your changes are complete.
   - Click the **Group** button [*Drawing Tools Format* tab, *Arrange* group] again and click **Regroup**.
   - The modified image is shown in Figure 4-101.

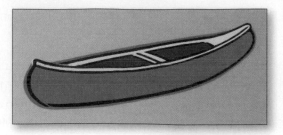

4-101 Modified image

> **ANOTHER WAY**
>
> If you have difficulty selecting individual shapes in a detailed illustration that you have ungrouped, select one shape and press **Tab** several times to move between the shapes.

> **MORE INFO**
>
> After ungrouping a picture, you may find a section of the picture that is grouped because the designer created subgroups before assembling the entire image. Therefore, you would need to ungroup that section again to modify those shapes.

## PAUSE & PRACTICE: POWERPOINT 4-3

For this project, you improve several images for a PLR winter promotion by making picture corrections and applying artistic effects. You change picture shapes by cropping to a shape and removing a background. You also ungroup an illustrated image, recolor it, and regroup the image.

Files Needed: ***PLRPromotionWinter-04.pptx***, ***SnowBackground1-04.jpg***, ***Minnesota-04.wmf***, and ***SnowBranch-04.jpg*** (*student data files are available in the* Library *of your SIMnet account*)
Completed Project File Name: ***[your initials] PP P4-3.pptx***

1. Open the ***PLRPromotionWinter-04*** presentation.

2. Save the presentation as [your initials] PP P4-3.

3. Select the snowflake on slide 1 and press **Ctrl+C** to copy it.

4. Use the *Slide Master* to add a picture background and change the font.
   a. Click the **View** tab and click the **Slide Master** button [*Master Views* group].
   b. Select the first *Slide Master* layout (*Office Theme Slide Master: used by slides 1–6*).
   c. Insert a background picture fill.
      - Click the **Background Styles** drop-down arrow [*Slide Master* tab, *Background* group] and choose **Format Background** to open the *Format Background* pane.
      - Select **Picture or texture fill** and click **File**. Locate your student files and select ***SnowBackground1-04***. Click **Insert**.

**PowerPoint 2016** Chapter 4 Customizing Images, Illustrations, and Themes

d. Change the font.
  - Click the **Fonts** drop-down arrow [*Slide Master* tab, *Background* group], scroll down, and choose the **Arial Black, Arial** theme font.
  - Select both the slide title and bulleted text placeholders and change the font color to **White, Background 1** [*Home* tab, *Font* group] and click the **Shadow** button.

5. Arrange three snowflakes on the first *Slide Master* layout.
  a. Click the **Clipboard Launcher** button [*Home* tab, *Clipboard* group].
    - The snowflake image you copied displays in the *Clipboard* pane.
  b. Click the snowflake image in the *Clipboard* pane three times.
    - Change each snowflake to a different size (*Height* **2"**, **1"**, and **3"**; *Width* will change automatically).
    - Arrange the snowflakes on the right with the top and bottom snowflakes extending slightly off the edge of the slide.
    - Rotate the snowflakes so they are not aligned in the same way (Figure 4-102.

4-102 *Slide Master* view showing background picture fill and snowflakes

  c. Close the *Clipboard* pane.
  d. Click the **Close Master View** button [*Slide Master* tab].
  e. Delete the original snowflake image on slide 1.

6. Insert an illustrated image on slide 1 and modify it as follows.
  a. Click the **Pictures** button [*Insert* tab, *Images* group] to open the *Insert Picture* dialog box and locate your student data files.
  b. Select **Minnesota-04** and click **Insert**.
  c. Resize the Minnesota map (*Height* **7"**) [*Picture Tools Format* tab, *Size* group]. Ensure proportions are maintained.
  d. Click the **Group** button [*Picture Tools Format* tab, *Arrange* group] and choose **Ungroup**.
    - Click **Yes** to convert this image to a drawing object.
    - Click the **Group** button again and choose **Ungroup**.
    - Now many handles appear on all the shapes that create the drawing object (Figure 4-103).

4-103 Ungrouped shape

  e. Click the slide background to turn off shape handles.
  f. Select the small blue and black circles on the map and press **Delete**.
  g. Select the black shape that looks like a shadow behind the map and press **Delete**.
  h. Click just below the map to select the transparent shape that is behind the map and press **Delete**. Only one shape of the Minnesota map remains.

7. Move the map on slide 1 and apply a picture fill.
   a. Select the map and move it to the left side of the slide.
   b. Click **Fill** on the *Format Shape* pane if options are not displayed.
   c. Select **Picture or texture fill** and click the **File** button. Locate your student files and select the file *SnowBranch-04.jpg* and click **Insert**.
   d. Change *Offset left* to **−12%** and *Offset bottom to* **−6%"** so the branch is more centered in the shape.
   e. Close the *Format Picture* pane.
   f. Click the **Shape Outline** button [*Drawing Tools Format* tab, *Shape Styles* group] and select **Black, Text 1**. Repeat to select **Weight** and **3 pt**.
   g. Click the **Shape Effects** button [*Drawing Tools Format* tab, *Shape Styles* group], select **Shadow**, and select **Offset Diagonal Bottom Right** (in the *Outer* group).

8. Modify the text on slide 1.
   a. Change the title font size to **66 pt**. and resize the title placeholder so the text appears as shown in Figure 4-104.
   b. Change the subtitle font to **White, Background 1**, **bold**, and **36 pt**. Align the subtitle with the bottom of the slide.

4-104 Title slide completed

9. Modify three pictures [*Picture Tools Format* tab, *Adjust* group] as shown in the following list:

| Slide 3 | **Snowmobile** | **Corrections** | **Sharpen: 50%** |
| Slide 4 | **Girl/Snowboard** | **Corrections** | **Brightness: 0% (Normal) Contrast: −20% Sharpen: 50%.** |
| Slide 6 | **Snowman** | **Artistic Effects** | **Cutout** |

10. Review the slide show.

11. Save and close the presentation (Figure 4-105).

4-105 PP P4-3 completed

# Creating a Photo Album

To create a presentation consisting mainly of pictures, use the **Photo Album** feature. In a photo album, one or more pictures appear on as many slides as you need to display them. You can set up many options for display when creating the photo album, and you can edit the photo album later to change settings. The following options are controlled using the *Photo Album* dialog box:

- Select pictures and adjust picture order.
- Select a caption text box for each picture.
- Adjust brightness, contrast, and rotation.
- Insert text boxes to create a text placeholder between pictures.
- Use special layout options.
- Apply a theme and customize *Slide Masters*.

## Select Pictures

Pictures for an album can come from any storage location, but it is best to place all pictures in one file folder before creating a photo album. A new presentation is created when you start a photo album.

---

### ▶ HOW TO: Select Pictures, Adjust Picture Order, and Edit Pictures

1. Open PowerPoint and start a new, blank presentation so you can access the *Insert tab*.
2. Click the **Photo Album** drop-down arrow [*Insert* tab, *Images* group] and select **New Photo Album** to open the *Photo Album* dialog box.
3. Click the **File/Disk** button to open the *Insert New Pictures* dialog box.
4. Locate your first picture and select its file name. Press **Ctrl** while you click additional file names to select them or press **Ctrl+A** to select all pictures at once.
5. Click **Insert**. All the names for the selected pictures appear in the picture list (Figure 4-106).
6. Click the check box in front of each picture to select it for individual changes.
   - Reorder the pictures as needed using the *Up* and *Down* arrows below the picture list (Figure 4-107).
   - Click **Remove** when a picture is highlighted to remove it from the album.

4-106 *Photo Album* dialog box with pictures listed

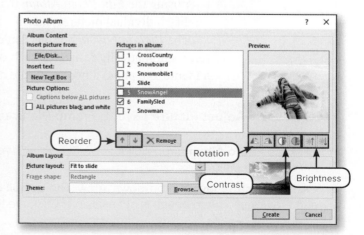

4-107 Pictures reordered

7. Below the *Preview* image for each selected picture, click to use the following editing functions:
   - *Rotate Left* or *Rotate Right*
   - *Contrast Up* or *Contrast Down*
   - *Brightness Up* or *Brightness Down*

8. Click **Create** and a new presentation is created with a title slide and each of your pictures on separate slides (Figure 4-108).
   - The default *Picture layout* of *Fit to slide* resizes each picture to the height of the slide.

4-108  Photo album created

9. Save the photo album.

## Adjust Album Layout, Frame Pictures, and Apply a Theme

Choosing the appropriate options for a photo album can save editing time because options apply to all pictures in the album. You can select options when you create a photo album or later using the *Edit Photo Album* dialog box. If you need to make additional changes, you can modify individual pictures later.

The *Picture Layout* options can display *Fit to slide*, *1*, *2*, or *4* pictures on a slide. The pictures automatically resize for each option. Just as with any other presentation, you can apply a theme to a photo album to create a consistent background.

▶**HOW TO:** Adjust Picture Layout, Frame Pictures, and Apply a Theme

1. Click the **Photo Album** drop-down arrow [*Insert* tab, *Images* group] and click **Edit Photo Album** to open the *Edit Photo Album* dialog box.

2. Click the **Picture layout** drop-down arrow. The default option is **Fit to slide** so each picture fills your slide height and the *Frame shape* option is not available. Click the list box arrow to choose from these options:
   - *1 picture, 2 pictures,* or *4 pictures*
   - *1 picture, 2 pictures,* or *4 pictures with titles* (a slide title)

3. Select a *Frame shape*. The default option is *Rectangle*; this shape works for many situations. Click the list box arrow to see other options such as the following:

- **Rounded Rectangle**
- **Simple Frame, White**
- **Simple Frame, Black**
- **Compound Frame, Black**
- **Center Shadow Rectangle**
- **Soft Edge Rectangle**

4. Select a *Theme*. Click the **Browse** button to open the **Choose Theme** dialog box. Select a presentation theme and click **Select** (Figure 4-109). The theme name appears in the *Theme* list box (Figure 4-110).

4-109 *Choose Theme* dialog box

4-110 *Edit Photo Album* dialog box with changes

5. Click **Update** to apply these settings.

> **ANOTHER WAY**
>
> Apply a theme using the *Design* tab after you have created the photo album.

## Add Photo Album Text

Use the *Edit Photo Album* dialog box to add text placeholders to your photo album in two ways: as text boxes or as captions below each picture. If you want to add captions, you must use a picture layout other than *Fit to slide* so space is available for caption text. Text boxes will appear beside a picture or on separate slides depending on how many pictures are on each slide. *Picture Options* can also display pictures in black and white.

## ▶ HOW TO: Add Captions and Text Boxes

1. Click the **Photo Album** drop-down arrow [*Insert* tab, *Images* group] and click **Edit Photo Album** to open the *Edit Photo Album* dialog box.

2. Add text boxes on separate slides.

- Select the check box for a picture name where you would like to add a text box. If you have two or four pictures on a slide, the text box fits in the space of a picture. If you have one picture on a slide, the text box appears on a separate slide.
- Click the **New Text Box** button and a new slide appears in the *Pictures in album* list. Repeat as needed.
- When you click **Update**, separate text boxes are inserted.

3.  Add captions.
    - Select **Captions below ALL pictures**. This option is not available if the *Picture Layout* is *Fit to slide*.
    - When you click **Update**, the file name appears in a text box below each picture. Edit that text on each slide and change the font as needed (Figure 4-111).

4-111 *Album Layout* options adjusted, text box added, captions added

Plan ahead to work efficiently when making changes to the entire photo album or to individual slides. First create and edit the album before making changes on individual slides. Once the album settings are complete, then you can modify and reposition the pictures just as you do in any other presentation. Add other content, animation, or transitions as needed.

## SLO 4.7

## Creating and Using a Custom Template

You can save any presentation as a ***template*** to make its design available to use again. For example, you might develop a presentation that contains graphics, such as your company logo, or text that may be appropriate for many different situations. A template can make developing a presentation more efficient and provides design consistency for multiple presentations.

In *SLO 4.3: Using Slide Masters to Create a Custom Theme*, you learned to customize background shapes and fonts for your presentation. You can customize existing layouts by deleting or adding placeholders. Click the **Insert Placeholder** button [*Slide Master* tab, *Master Layout* group] to add placeholders for the type of slides that you need. Delete any unused layouts to streamline the available options. You also can include sample content that will help other people who may use your template.

### Save a Presentation as a Template

To create a template, choose the **PowerPoint Template** file format when saving your presentation. The file is automatically saved on your computer in the folder called *Custom Office Templates*, in the *Documents* folder. Saving your templates in this way means they will be easy to access when you start a new presentation. However, you can save a template in any location, such as on your *OneDrive* or a removable drive if you are working away from your own computer. A template file has a .potx file extension instead of the .pptx file extension for a presentation file.

▶ **HOW TO:** Save a Presentation as a Template

1.  Complete all changes to your presentation and save it as a presentation file (.pptx file extension) in case you want to change the presentation file in the future.

2.  Resave the presentation as a template. Click the **File** tab and click **Save As**. Click the **Browse** button to open the *Save As* dialog box.

3. Type an appropriate name in the *File Name* box.

4. Choose **PowerPoint Template** in the *Save As Type* list box (Figure 4-112).

   - The default path to Microsoft's *Custom Office Template* folder appears.
   - You can save the file in this location so it is easily available and all templates are together.
   - You can browse to save it in a different file location.

5. Click **Save** and the presentation is saved as a template (.potx file extension).

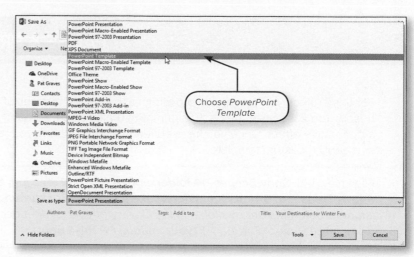

4-112 *Save As* dialog box, *Save as type* selected

## Apply a Template

If you save a template to the default storage location, the *Custom Office Templates* folder, the files are available on the *Backstage* view when you start a new presentation. Select **Personal** to see thumbnails for the templates you have saved.

---

▶ **HOW TO:** Apply a Custom Template to a New or Existing Presentation

1. Apply a custom template to a new presentation.

   - Click **File** and click **New**.
   - At the top of the *Featured* thumbnails, click **Personal** (Figure 4-113).
   - Select your template and click **Create**.

2. Apply a custom template to an existing presentation.

   - Open the presentation.
   - Click the **More** button [*Design* tab, *Themes* group] and click **Browse for Themes** to open the *Choose Theme or Themed Document* folder.
   - Double-click **Custom Office Templates** to open the folder (or browse to locate your file if you have saved the template in a different location).
   - Select the template and click **Apply**.

4-113 *Personal* themes saved in *Custom Office Templates* folder

---

When you start a presentation using a template, save the presentation with a different name to avoid modifying your template file.

For this project, you create a photo album using seven pictures of snow scenes for Paradise Lakes Resort. You customize the photo album with a picture background and modify an illustrated image for a decorative effect. Once you have edited the photo album, you resave the presentation as a template and apply a custom template.

Files Needed: *SnowScenes-04 folder: Forest.jpg, IcyTrees.jpg, SnowScene1.jpg, SnowScene2.jpg, SnowyTrees.jpg, Stream.jpg, WinterLake.jpg; SnowBackground2-04.jpg*, and *Snowflake2-04.jpg* (*student data files are available in the* Library *of your SIMnet account*)
Completed Project File Name: *[your initials] PP P4-4.pptx*

1. Select pictures for a photo album.
   a. Open PowerPoint, select **New**, and click **Blank Presentation**.
   b. Click the **Insert** tab and click the **Photo Album** button to open the *Photo Album* dialog box.
   c. Click the **File/Disk** button, locate your student files, and open the folder *SnowScenes-04*.
   d. Press **Ctrl+A** to select all of the pictures. Click **Insert**.
      • The file names are listed (Figure 4-114).
   e. Click **Create**.
      • The default setting of *Fit to slide* sizes each picture as large as possible with the height the same as the slide height.
      • The default slide background is black.

4-114 Pictures added to photo album list

2. Save the presentation as [your initials] PP P4-4.

3. Edit the photo album to reorder slide sequence, adjust contrast, and adjust brightness.
   a. Click the **Photo Album** drop-down arrow [*Insert* tab, *Images* group] and select **Edit Photo Album** to open the *Edit Photo Album* dialog box.
   b. Click the **SnowScene1** check box to place a check in the box that precedes the slide number and name.
      • Click the up arrow twice to move this picture to the top of the list.
      • Deselect this picture (Figure 4-115).
   c. Select the **SnowyTrees** picture.
      • Click the up arrow one time.
      • Deselect this picture.

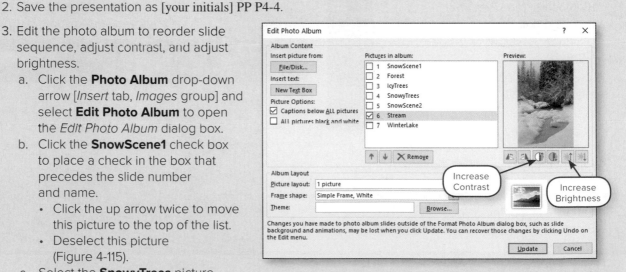

4-115 Photo album edits complete

d. Select the **Stream** picture.
   - Click the **Increase Contrast** button six times.
   - Click the **Increase Brightness** button six times.
4. Continue editing the photo album to select *Album Layout* options.
   a. Click the **Picture layout** drop-down arrow under *Album Layout*, and select **1 picture**.
   b. Click the drop-down arrow for *Frame Shape* and select **Center Shadow Rectangle**.
   c. Select **Captions below ALL pictures** under *Picture Options*.
   d. Click **Update**. (This completes changes to the photo album editing.)
      - The pictures now appear in a smaller size with the file names shown as captions below each picture.
      - The picture and captions are grouped.
      - The shadow you applied is not yet evident because the background is black.
5. Edit each of the captions as follows to change the text or add a space between words:

   Slide 2    The Road to PLR
   Slide 3    A Quiet Forest
   Slide 4    Icy Trees
   Slide 5    Snowy Trees
   Slide 6    New Snow
   Slide 7    Woodland Stream
   Slide 8    Winter Lake

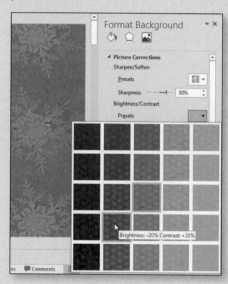

4-116 Adjust *Brightness* and *Contrast*

6. Insert and format a picture background.
   a. Select slide 1. Point to the background, right-click and choose **Format Background** to open the *Format Background* pane.
   b. Select **Picture or texture fill**. Click the **File** button.
      - Locate your student data files, select **SnowBackground2-04**, and click **Insert**.
   c. Click the **Picture** icon at the top of the *Format Background* pane.
      - Click **Picture Color** to access those options.
      - Click the **Recolor** button and select **Blue, Accent color 5 Dark**.
   d. Click **Picture Corrections** to apply the following options:
      - Click the **Sharpen/Soften Presets** button and choose **Sharpen: 50%**.
      - Click the **Brightness/Contrast Presets** button and choose **Brightness: −20% Contrast: +20%** (Figure 4-116).
   e. Click **Apply to All**.
   f. Close the *Format Background* pane.

7. Change the font for slide titles on the *Slide Master*.
   a. Click the **Slide Master** button [*View* tab, *Master Views* group].
   b. Select the first *Slide Master* layout.
      - Select the title placeholder and change the font to **Arial Black** [*Home* tab, *Font* group].
      - Select the body text placeholder and change the font to **Arial**. Click the **Shadow** button.
   c. Select the *Title Slide* layout.
      - Change the title font size to **66 pt**. [*Home* tab, *Font* group] and choose **Align Left** [*Home* tab, *Paragraph* group].
      - Change the subtitle placeholder font size to **40 pt**. and choose **Align Left**. Click the **Bold** and the **Shadow** buttons.
   d. Select **Gridlines** [*View* tab, *Show* group].

e. Resize the title and subtitle placeholders and align them on the gridlines as shown in Figure 4-117.

8. Insert a snowflake picture on the right side of the *Title Slide* layout. Remove the picture background.
   a. Click the **Pictures** button [*Insert tab, Images* group] and locate your student files.
   b. Select ***Snowflake2-04***. Click **Insert**.
   c. Click the **Remove Background** button [*Picture Tools Format* tab, *Adjust* group].
   d. Resize the selection area so the entire snowflake is shown.
   e. Click the **Zoom In** button on the *Status* bar several times for **200%** so you can easily see the detail.
   f. Click the **Mark Areas to Remove** button [*Background Removal* tab, *Refine* group] and delete blue areas within the snowflake that should not appear (Figure 4-118).
   g. Click the **Keep Changes** button [*Background Removal* tab, *Close* group].
   h. Click the **Fit slide to current window** button on the *Status* bar.
   i. Resize the snowflake to approximately **6.5"** square. Move the snowflake to the right.
   j. Click the **Close Master View** button [*Slide Master* tab, *Close* group].

4-117 *Slide Master, Title Slide* layout

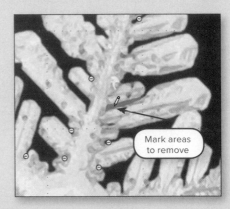

4-118 Removing the background

9. Insert the following text on slide 1:
   Title        Dressed in White
   Subtitle     Paradise Lakes Resort

10. Select the slide 1 thumbnail and press **Ctrl+C**. Select slide 8 and press **Ctrl+V**.

11. Edit the text on slide 9 as follows:
    Title        Paradise Lakes Resort
    Subtitle     1256 Raymond Drive
                 Cass Lake, MN 56633
                 218-339-5551

12. Display slide 9. Resize the subtitle placeholder so the font size remains at **40 pt**. (Figure 4-119).
    a. Verify that the title font size remains at **66 pt**.

4-119 Slide 9 with snowflake and revised text

13. Deselect **Gridlines** [*View* tab, *Show* group].

14. Apply a transition.
    a. Click the *Transitions* tab and apply the **Glitter** transition with the **Diamonds from Top** effect options.
    b. Change the *Duration* to **03.00**.

c. Click **Apply to All**.

d. Review the transitions.

15. Save the presentation (Figure 4-121).

16. Resave the presentation as a template.

    a. Click the **File** tab and click **Save As**.

    b. Select **This PC** and click **Browse**.

    c. Type the file name Winter.

    d. Select **PowerPoint template** for the *Save as type*.

       • The default folder *Custom Office Templates* will open unless you have selected a particular location (Figure 4-120).

    e. Click **Save**.

    f. Close the template but keep PowerPoint open.

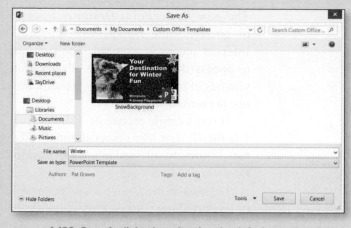

4-120 *Save As* dialog box showing the default template folder

17. Apply a custom template.

    a. Click the **File** tab and click **New**.

    b. Click **Personal** and files saved in the *Custom Office Templates* folder appear.

       • Find your template file if you saved it in another location.

    c. Select the **Winter** theme.

    d. Click the **Create** button.

       • Now you have the option of replacing the pictures, adding new content, and revising the text to create a different presentation.

    e. Close the presentation without saving.

4-121 PP P4-4 completed

# Using PowerPoint Designer for Slide Layouts

The new *PowerPoint Designer* feature, available with Office 365, provides a quick way to arrange slide layouts with pictures when using any of Microsoft's built-in themes. Internet access is required. The first time you use *Designer*, you must provide permission to access the online Office service that provides design ideas. You can use *Designer* as you begin to develop a new presentation or at any time while you are working on an existing presentation.

Insert a single picture on a slide using the *Title Slide* layout or the *Title and Content* layout and the *Design Ideas* pane automatically opens. To use this feature for a slide where the picture is already inserted, click the **Design Ideas** button [*Design* tab, *Designer* group] to open the *Design Ideas* pane.

Layouts in the *Design Ideas* pane will vary based on the theme you are using. Thumbnails of layouts show your picture with different effects and sizes. The layouts combine the picture and text placeholders differently, too. Options vary based on the particular theme and layout you are using. If you change to a different theme, then click the **Design Ideas** button to refresh the pane with different layouts.

You can insert multiple pictures on a slide, but other shapes or objects will prevent the *Designer* from showing layout options. Once the layout is applied, you can add other objects as needed or adjust the pictures with different styles and effects. Microsoft will continue to add new capabilities to the *Designer* feature.

The picture aspect ratio can change with different *Designer* layouts. Check the image to be sure cropping, if applied, is acceptable for your needs.

## ▶ HOW TO: Use PowerPoint Designer

1. Start a new presentation using one of PowerPoint's built-in themes or open a presentation using a theme.
2. Select a slide using a *Title Slide* or *Title and Content* layout.
3. Click the **Pictures** button [*Insert* tab, *Images* group] to open the *Insert Picture* dialog box.
4. Search for and select a picture. Click **Insert** and the *Design Ideas* pane automatically opens.
   - When you use *Designer* for the first time, a message appears asking if you want to try *Design Ideas* because you are using an online *Office* service (Figure 4-122). Click **Let's Go**.
   - Slide thumbnails appear showing different layouts (Figure 4-123).
   - Layouts vary based on the presentation's theme.
   - Scroll down to see all the available layouts in this pane. Some emphasize the picture more than others.
5. Click a layout to apply it to your slide. Repeat to change to another layout.
6. Check the picture in each layout to be sure important portions of the picture have not been removed through cropping.

4-122 *Design Ideas* permission request

4-123 *Design Ideas* pane

- The image in Figure 4-124 has been cropped on the left and right.

7. Select a picture on a slide and click the **Design Ideas** button [*Design* tab, *Designer* group] to open the *Design Ideas* pane showing layout options.

8. Close the *Design Ideas* pane when you are satisfied with your selection.

4-124 Different slide layout is selected

*PowerPoint Designer* must be enabled on your computer. If the *Design Ideas* pane does not open automatically, click the **File** tab. Read your *Office Updates* information to confirm that your software is current. If updates are available, click **Office Updates** and select **Update Now**. Once this process is complete, click the **File** tab again and click **Options** to open the *PowerPoint Options* dialog box. On the *General* tab, select **Enable PowerPoint Designer** and click **OK**.

You can apply a different theme so your background, fonts, and placeholder positions will be different. The previously selected *Designer* layouts may still work, but you might need to adjust formatting and layout. With a picture selected, click the **Design Ideas** button again and select from layouts on the *Design Ideas* pane for the different theme.

## PAUSE & PRACTICE: POWERPOINT 4-5

For this project, you use the Office 365 *PowerPoint Designer* feature to modify a presentation for Paradise Lakes Resort. You insert a picture and select a layout from the *Design Ideas* pane then consider layouts for other pictures in the presentation. You change to a different theme and finalize layouts. If your software does not have *PowerPoint Designer*, then skip this project.

Files Needed: ***MinnesotaMemories-04.pptx***, ***Relax-04***, and ***SnowScene2.jpg*** in the ***SnowScenes-04*** folder *(student data files are available in the* Library *of your SIMnet account)*
Completed Project File Name: ***[your initials] PP P4-5.pptx***

1. Open the ***MinnesotaMemories-04*** presentation from your student data files.

2. Save this presentation as [your initials] PP P4-5.

3. Select a layout for the title slide.
   a. Display slide 1 which has a *Title Slide* layout.
   b. Click **Pictures** [*Insert* tab, *Images* group] to open the *Insert Picture* dialog box.
   c. Browse to locate your student data files, open the **SnowScenes-04** folder, and select ***SnowScene2***. Click **Insert**.
      - If you are using *Designer* for the first time and the permission message appears, click **Let's Go**.
      - If you have used *Designer* before, the *Design Ideas* pane opens with a variety of picture layouts.
      - If *Designer* does not automatically open, click the **Design Ideas** button [*Design* tab, *Designer* group].

4. Click the layout that displays the picture expanded to fill the slide behind text and shapes (Figure 4-125).

4-125 New layout for the title slide

a. Notice that the picture is on the slide and is not arranged as a background picture fill.
b. Your layouts may appear in a different sequence.

5. Display slide 2 with a *Title and Content* layout.
   a. Click the **Design Ideas** button [*Design* tab, *Designer* group] to open the *Design Ideas* pane if it is not already open.
   b. Click the layout that aligns the picture on the right of the slide (Figure 4-126).

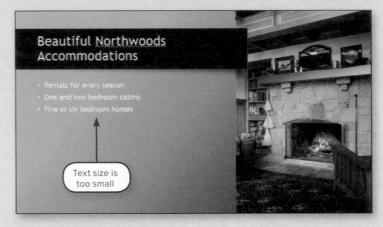

4-126 New layout for slide 2

6. Display slide 4 with a *Title and Content* layout.
   a. Click the **Pictures** button [*Insert* tab, *Images* group] to open the *Insert Picture* dialog box.
   b. Browse to locate your student data files and select ***Relax-04***.
   c. Click **Insert** and the *Design Ideas* pane opens.
   d. Click the layout with blue rectangles (fourth from the top of the pane) (Figure 4-127).

7. Adjust text size on three slides. The new layouts have made body text too small.

4-127 New layout for slide 3

a. Select the bulleted list placeholder on slide 2 and increase the font size so the first-level text is **24 pt**.

b. Repeat for slides 4 and 5.

8. Review the slides in *Slide Show* view.

9. Save and close the presentation (Figure 4-128).

4-128 PP P4-5 completed

# Chapter Summary

**4.1** Customize and work with shapes (p. P4-210).

- Press **Shift** to preserve a shape's proportions as you resize. Press **Shift** when drawing to make a rectangle square, an oval round, or lines straight.
- You can rotate or stack text in a text box.
- Use the *rotation handle* to angle objects.
- Use the *adjustment handle* to change the dimension of a shape.
- Use *Edit Points* to move lines, alter line curves and points, and create original shapes.
- With the **Curve** line tool, a line forms each time you click; the line curves as you change direction.
- With the **Scribble** line tool, a line is formed as you drag your pointer similar to writing.
- With the **Freeform** line tool, a solid fill is applied when the end point of your line touches the beginning point.

**4.2** Work with objects to align, distribute, and group; convert *SmartArt* to text or shapes (p. P4-215).

- Select multiple objects by pressing **Shift** as you click, drawing a selection rectangle, or using the *Selection* pane.
- You can align objects to each other or to the slide.
- Use *Distribute* to create even spacing between multiple slide objects.
- *Gridlines* are evenly spaced vertical and horizontal lines that aid in object alignment.
- *Guides* are one horizontal and one vertical line in the middle of the slide that you can move to check for consistent alignment.
- Adjust the stacking order of layered objects by clicking *Bring Forward*, *Bring to Front*, *Send Backward*, or *Send to Back* options.
- The *Group* command enables you to connect multiple shapes or other objects. Shapes within a group can be recolored or resized.
- Save grouped shapes as a picture to maintain accurate sizing and colors.
- Use the **Merge Shapes** command to create a new shape from two or more overlapping shapes.

- *Connector lines* connect two or more shapes for custom diagrams.
- You can convert a *SmartArt* graphic to bulleted text or to grouped shapes.

**4.3** Use *Slide Masters* to create a custom theme with new colors, fonts, and background graphics (p. P4-228).

- Background graphics added on the *Slide Master* can affect placeholder positioning on side layouts.
- Change *Theme Colors* and *Theme Fonts* on the *Slide Master* tab or the *Design* tab.
- Changes made to *Slide Master* layouts affect all slides in the presentation that use those layouts.
- Small pictures can be used as list bullets.
- For presentation consistency, use design elements from the *Slide Master* on your *Handout Master*.

**4.4** Capture screen images with a screenshot or a screen clipping (p. P4-238).

- The **Screenshot** feature copies an entire application window and displays it on a slide.
- The **Screen Clipping** feature copies the portion of an application window that you select and displays it on a slide.

**4.5** Edit pictures to apply photo corrections, choose artistic effects, and remove backgrounds; recolor illustrated images (p. P4-240).

- *Sharpen* is a picture correction option that makes details more evident; *Soften* is a picture correction option that creates a blending effect.
- Adjusting the *Contrast* picture correction affects the difference between a picture's lightest and darkest colors.
- *Brightness* lightens a picture by adding white and darkens a picture by adding black.
- The *Artistic Effects* gallery provides many options to apply creative effects.
- Crop a picture to a shape from the *Shapes* gallery.

- The **Change Picture** command enables you to replace one picture with another while retaining the same size and effects.
- The **Remove Background** feature deletes portions of a picture on a slide without affecting the original picture. The areas you remove become transparent; save the picture using the .png format to preserve the transparent area for future use.
- Line drawings or simple illustrations can be ungrouped and modified if they are saved in a vector file format.

**4.6** Create a photo album and adjust picture order, layout, and captions; apply and customize a photo album theme (p. P4-249).

- Use the **Photo Album** command to prepare a presentation featuring pictures.
- After selecting pictures for a photo album, you can adjust their order and rotation as well as change contrast and brightness.
- A photo album can include text captions under pictures and text-only slides between picture slides.
- Various picture layout options are available for a photo album.
- You can apply a PowerPoint theme to a photo album.

**4.7** Create and use a custom template (p. P4-252).

- Use the *Save As* dialog box to save a presentation as a template.

- A presentation template has the file extension of .potx.
- Start a new presentation from a template, or apply a template to an existing presentation.
- When you start a presentation using a template, resave the presentation with a different name to avoid modifying your template file.

**4.8** Use *PowerPoint Designer* to select slide layouts for picture content (p. P4-258).

- **PowerPoint Designer** provides layout options in the *Design Ideas* pane for slides that include pictures.
- PowerPoint's built-in themes and *Title Slide* or *Title and Content* layouts are required to use *PowerPoint Designer*.
- Suggested layouts can arrange multiple pictures, but other graphic objects on a slide will prevent *PowerPoint Designer* from working.
- Internet access is required to use *PowerPoint Designer*.

## Check for Understanding

The SIMbook for this text (within your SIMnet account) provides the following resources for concept review.

- Multiple choice questions
- Matching exercises
- Short answer questions

## Guided Project 4-1

A presentation about services at the Livingood Income Tax and Accounting firm needs improvement. For this project, you will customize the *Slide Master* and create an original diagram to highlight the firm's ethical standards, change a *SmartArt* graphic to feature specialties, and prepare listed information to show the firm's business services.
[**Student Learning Outcomes 4.1, 4.2, 4.3, 4.8**]

---

File Needed: ***AccountingServices-04.pptx***
Completed Project File Name: ***[your initials] PowerPoint 4-1.pptx***

---

### Skills Covered in This Project

- Use text box columns.
- Flip and rotate a shape.
- Use adjustment handles.
- Select and distribute multiple objects.
- Ungroup objects.
- Convert a *SmartArt* graphic to text.
- Convert a *SmartArt* graphic to shapes.
- Use the *Slide Master* to change background shapes and slide layouts.
- Apply an artistic effect to a picture.
- Apply and adjust a *Designer* layout.

---

1. Open the presentation ***AccountingServices-04***. Save the presentation as [your initials] PowerPoint 4-1.

2. Customize the first *Slide Master* layout.
   a. Click the **Slide Master** button [*View* tab, *Master Views*] group.
   b. Select the first layout, *Office Theme Slide Master: used by slides 1-6*.
   c. Select the brown rectangle below the title placeholder.
   d. Click the **Align** button [*Drawing Tools Format* tab, *Arrange* group] and select **Align Bottom**.
   e. Click the **Send Backward** drop-down arrow [*Drawing Tools Format* tab, *Arrange* group] and choose **Send to Back** so the rectangle is behind the slide footer placeholders.
   f. Select the title placeholder and change the font to **Cooper Black** at **44 pt**. [*Home* tab, *Font* group]. Change the *Font Color* to **Orange, Accent 6**.
   g. Click the first line of the bulleted text placeholder.
   h. Click the **Bullets** drop-down arrow [*Home* tab, *Paragraph* group] and select **Bullets and Numbering** to open the *Bullets and Numbering* dialog box.
   i. Change the bullet color to **Orange, Accent 6** and click **OK** (Figure 4-129).

4-129 First *Slide Master* layout complete

3. Customize the *Title and Content* layout on the *Slide Master*.
   a. Select the *Title and Content* layout (third layout).
   b. Select the group of shapes below the title placeholder, click **Group** [*Drawing Tools Format* tab, *Arrange* group] and then choose **Ungroup**.
   c. Select the top rectangle below the title and change the following:
      - Change the *Height* to **1.5"** and *Width* to **13.33"** [*Drawing Tools Format* tab, *Size* group].
      - Click the **Align** button [*Drawing Tools Format* tab, *Arrange* group] and choose **Align Top**. Repeat to select **Align Center**.
      - Change the *Shape Fill* [*Drawing Tools Format* tab, *Shape Styles* group] to **Brown, Accent 5, Lighter 60%**.
      - Click the **Send Backward** drop-down arrow [*Drawing Tools Format* tab, *Arrange* group] and choose **Send to Back** so the rectangle is behind the title placeholder.
   d. Select the brown square and change the following:
      - Change the *Height* and *Width* to **1.5"** [*Drawing Tools Format* tab, *Size* group].
      - Click the **Align** button [*Drawing Tools Format* tab, *Arrange* group] and choose **Align Top**. Repeat to select **Align Left**.
   e. Resize the title placeholder on the left so it does not overlap the brown square.
   f. Select the thin rectangle and change the following:
      - Change the *Height* to **.1"** and *Width* to **13.33"** [*Drawing Tools Format* tab, *Size* group].
      - Center this thin rectangle at the bottom of the title area.
      - Click **Bring Forward** so it displays over the brown square (Figure 4-130).

4. Customize the *Title Slide* layout on the *Slide Master*.
   a. Select the *Title Slide* layout (second layout).
   b. Select the grouped squares and change the following:
      - Change the *Height* to **7.5"** and *Width* to **2.5"** [*Drawing Tools Format* tab, *Size* group].
      - Click the **Align** button [*Drawing Tools Format* tab, *Arrange* group] and choose **Align Left**.
      - Click the **Send Backward** drop-down arrow [*Drawing Tools Format* tab, *Arrange* group] and choose **Send to Back** so the grouped squares are behind the picture.
   c. Select the picture and click the **Artistic Effects** button [*Picture Tools Format* tab, *Adjust* group] and choose the **Cutout** effect (first column, last row) as shown in Figure 4-131.

5. Click the **Slide Master** tab and click **Close Master View**.

6. Display slide 1 and select the text box "We build relationships." Change the *Font Color* to **Light Yellow, Text 2**.

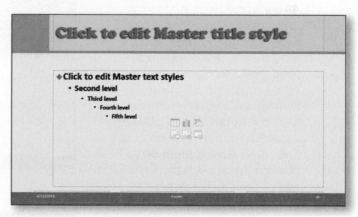

4-130 *Slide Master Title and Content* layout complete

4-131 *Slide Master Title Slide* layout complete

7. Convert a *SmartArt* graphic to shapes and rearrange shapes.
    a. Display slide 2. Select the *SmartArt* graphic and click the **Convert** button [*SmartArt Tools Design* tab, *Reset* group]. Choose **Convert to Shapes** and the shapes are grouped and selected.
    b. Click **Group** [*Drawing Tools Format* tab, *Arrange* group] and then choose **Ungroup**.
        • Now handles appear around each shape.
    c. Select the three shapes with text and change the following:
        • Click the **Edit Shape** button [*Drawing Tools Format* tab, *Insert Shapes* group]. Choose **Change Shape** and select the **Rectangle**.
        • Change the *Shape Fill* [*Drawing Tools Format* tab, *Shape Styles* group] to **Brown, Accent 5, Darker 25%**.
        • Resize the shapes so the bulleted text fits on one line. The shape lengths will vary.
        • Change the *Height* to **1.2"** [*Drawing Tools Format* tab, *Size* group].
    d. Position the "Professionalism" rectangle on the left of the slide (Figure 4-132).
    e. Position the "Quality" rectangle on the lower right of the slide.
    f. Select the circular arrow and press **Delete**.
    g. Select the "Responsiveness" rectangle and click the **Align** button [*Drawing Tools Format* tab, *Arrange* group], and select **Align Center**.
    h. Select all three rectangles, click the **Align** button [*Drawing Tools Format* tab, *Arrange* group], and select **Align Selected Objects**. Repeat to select **Distribute Vertically**.

8. Add shapes to show the connection between concepts.
    a. Click the *Shapes* gallery **More** button [*Home* tab, *Drawing* group] on slide 2 and choose the **Left-Up Arrow** (in the *Block Arrows* category).
    b. Draw an arrow and adjust the size [*Drawing Tools Format* tab, *Size* group] (*Height* and *Width* **1.5"**).
    c. Drag the adjustment handle on the inside corner where the arrows join to make the arrow more thin.
    d. Click the **Rotate** button [*Drawing Tools Format* tab, *Arrange* group] and select **Rotate Right 90°**.
    e. Position this arrow between the first and second rectangles.
    f. Press **Ctrl+D** to duplicate this arrow and position the duplicated arrow between the second and third rectangles.
    g. Refer to Figure 4-132 for placement.

4-132 Custom diagram

9. Change a *SmartArt* graphic to a different layout.
    a. Display slide 3. Select the *SmartArt* graphic and click the **More** button [*SmartArt Tools Design* tab, *Layouts* group].
    b. Choose **Bending Picture Caption List** because it better fits the content.
    c. Click the **Change Colors** button [*SmartArt Tools Design* tab, *SmartArt Styles* group] and select the **Colored Fill – Accent 5** (Figure 4-133).

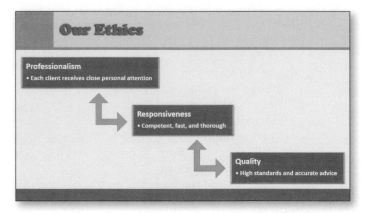

4-133 *SmartArt* graphic layout changed

10. Convert a *SmartArt* graphic to text and reformat text.
   a. Display slide 4. Select the *SmartArt* graphic and click the **Convert** button [*SmartArt Tools Design* tab, *Reset* group] and choose **Convert to Text**. Now the text appears in a placeholder.
   b. Resize the placeholder (*Width* **11"**) [*Drawing Tools Format* tab, *Size* group].
   c. Select the text and increase the font size to **28 pt**. [*Home* tab, *Font* group].
   d. Click the **Bullets** button [*Home* tab, *Paragraph* group] and select **None** to remove the bullets.
   e. Click the **Columns** button [*Home* tab, *Paragraph* group] and select **Two Columns**.
   f. Resize the placeholder from the bottom until the columns are more even with 5-6 items in each column.

11. Apply a *Designer* layout. If *PowerPoint* Designer is not available in your software, skip steps 11a-b and create a similar background design using shapes.
   a. Display slide 6. Click the **Design Ideas** button [*Design* tab, *Designer* group] to open the *Design Ideas* pane.
   b. Scroll down and select the layout that is second from the bottom (Figure 4-134) or a similar layout.

4-134  Slide 6 with new layout

   c. Select each object and adjust sizes:
      • Company name and address: Change the font size to **24 pt**. and resize the placeholder to fit the text.
      • "We can help" text: Resize the placeholder so the first line word wraps after "the."
      • Picture: Increase the *Width* to **6"**.
   d. Adjust object positions as shown in Figure 4-135.
12. Save and close your presentation (Figure 4-136).

4-135  Slide 6 with new layout adjusted

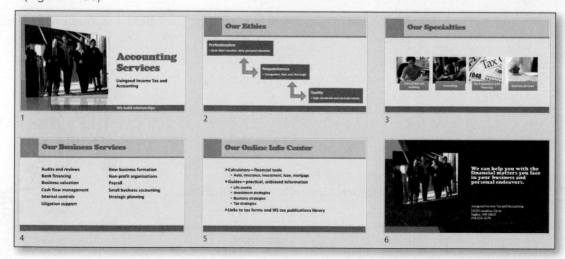

4-136  PowerPoint 4-1 completed

# Guided Project 4-2

At the four colleges of the Sierra Pacific Community College District, outdoor summer concerts are performed by music students and alumni. For this presentation, you use the *Slide Master* to prepare an elegant background using decorative graphics and fonts for a concert of love songs from well-known movies to be held at American River College. Once your background is prepared, you modify other slide elements to blend with this new design.
[Student Learning Outcomes 4.1, 4.2, 4.3, 4.5, 4.7]

---

Files Needed: ***LoveSongs-04.pptx***, ***Vine1-04.wmf***, ***Vine2-04.wmf***, ***Note-04.png***, and ***Violin-04.jpg***
Completed Project File Names: *[your initials] **PowerPoint 4-2.pptx*** and *[your initials]*
***PowerPoint 4-2.potx***

---

## Skills Covered in This Project

- Flip and rotate a shape.
- Align objects with *Gridlines*.
- Layer objects and adjust stacking order.
- Use the *Slide Master* to change background shapes and slide layouts.
- Use the *Slide Master* to change theme fonts and text effects.
- Apply picture bullets.
- Remove a picture background.
- Save a presentation as a template.

1. Open the presentation ***LoveSongs-04***. Save the presentation as [your initials] PowerPoint 4-2.

2. Click the **Slide Master** button [*View* tab, *Master Views* group]. For this project you will change four layouts.

3. Align placeholders with *Gridlines*, then change size, color, and fonts.
   a. Select the first layout, *Office Theme Slide Master: used by slides 1-5*.
   b. Select **Gridlines** [*View* tab, *Show* group].
   c. Select the title placeholder and press the down arrow several times so the top of it is even with the first horizontal grid line.
   d. Change the title placeholder size [*Drawing Tools Format* tab, *Size* group] (*Height* **1"** and *Width* **13.33"**).
   e. Click the **Align** button [*Drawing Tools Format* tab, *Arrange* group] and choose **Align Center**.
   f. Change the *Shape Fill* to **Dark Red, Accent 6, Darker 50%** [*Drawing Tools Format* tab, *Shape Styles* group].
   g. Change the font to **Gabriola** [*Home* tab, *Font* group] at **60 pt**. Click **Bold** and **Shadow**. Change *Character Spacing* to **Loose**.

4. Insert and rotate a decorative image.
   a. Click the **Pictures** button [*Insert* tab, *Images* group] on the first layout to open the *Insert Picture* dialog box.
   b. Browse to your student data files and select ***Vine1-04*** (Figure 4-137). Click **Insert**.
   c. Increase the decorative image size (*Height* **4.5"** and the *Width* automatically adjusts).
   d. Click the **Rotate** button [*Picture Tools Format* tab, *Arrange* group] and choose **Flip Horizontal**. Repeat to choose **Rotate Left 90°**.
   e. Click the **Align** button [*Picture Tools Format* tab, *Arrange* group] and choose **Align Top**. Repeat to choose **Align Right**.

4-137 *Vine1-04* picture

f. Click the **Bring Forward** drop-down arrow [*Picture Tools Format* tab, *Arrange* group] and select **Bring to Front**. (Figure 4-138).

5. Add a rectangle and adjust stacking order.
   a. Select the *Title Slide* layout (the second layout).
   b. Click the **Shapes** button, select the **Rectangle** tool [*Home* tab, *Drawing* group], and draw a rectangle (*Height* **4.5"** and *Width* **13.33"**) [*Drawing Tools Format* tab, *Size* group].
   c. Click the **Align** button [*Drawing Tools Format* tab, *Arrange* group] and select **Align Top**. Repeat to select **Align Center**.
   d. Change the *Shape Fill* [*Drawing Tools Format* tab, *Shape Styles* group] to **Black, Background 1**.
   e. Change the *Shape Outline* [*Drawing Tools Format* tab, *Shape Styles* group] to **No Outline**.
   f. Click the **Send Backward** drop-down arrow [*Drawing Tools Format* tab, *Arrange* group] and select **Send to Back**.

4-138 First *Slide Master* layout completed

6. Adjust placeholders.
   a. Select the title placeholder on the *Title Slide* layout and change the font size to **80 pt**. [*Home* tab, *Font* group].
   b. Change the title placeholder *Width* to **9"** [*Drawing Tools Format* tab, *Arrange* group].
   c. Click the **Align** button [*Drawing Tools Format* tab, *Arrange* group]. Select **Align Top**. Repeat to select **Align Center**.
   d. Change the *Shape Fill* [*Drawing Tools Format* tab, *Shape Styles* group] to **No Fill**.
   e. Select the subtitle placeholder and click the **Bring Forward** drop-down arrow [*Drawing Tools Format* tab, *Arrange* group]. Select **Bring to Front**.

7. Insert a decorative image and use *Gridlines*.
   a. Click the **Pictures** button [*Insert* tab, *Images* group] on the *Title Slide* layout to open the *Insert Picture* dialog box.
   b. Browse to your student data files and select **Vine2-04**. Click **Insert**. Drag this image down so you can see it on the gray area.
   c. Click the **launcher** button [*Picture Tools Format* tab, *Size* group] to open the *Format Picture* pane.
   d. Deselect **Lock aspect ratio**. Increase the vine image size (*Height* **2.5"** and *Width* **11"**).
   e. Close the *Format Picture* pane.
   f. Using the gridlines to judge spacing, move the vine image to the center of the gray area at the bottom of the slide. Because the vine has extra space on the left, the handles will not appear centered (Figure 4-139).

4-139 *Title Slide* layout completed

8. Apply a *Picture* bullet.
   a. Select the *Title and Content* layout.
   b. Select the first two bulleted items.
   c. Click the **Bullets** drop-down arrow [*Home* tab, *Paragraph* group] and choose **Bullets and Numbering**.
   d. Click the **Picture** button to open the *Insert Picture* dialog box.
   e. Click **Browse** and locate your student data files. Select **Note-04** and click **Insert**.

9. Use *Gridlines*, align placeholders, and change text.
   a. Select the *Section Header* layout.
   b. Select the *Title* placeholder and change the following:
      • Change its size (*Height* **3.5"** and *Width* **9.65"**).
      • Click the **Align** button [*Drawing Tools Format* tab, *Arrange* group] and select **Align Right**.
      • Move the title placeholder up so the top is even with the second horizontal gridline.
      • Change the font size to **44 pt**. [*Home* tab, *Font* group] and click **Shadow**.
      • Click the **Align Text** button [*Home* tab, *Paragraph* group] and select **Middle**.
   c. Select the *Subtitle* placeholder and change the following:
      • Change the font to **Gabriola** at **36 pt**. [*Home* tab, *Font* group]. Click **Bold** and **Shadow**.
      • Click the **Align Text** button [*Home* tab, *Paragraph* group] and select **Middle**.
      • Resize the subtitle placeholder and align it on the *Gridlines* as shown in Figure 4-140.
   d. Click the *Rectangle* tool [*Home* tab, *Drawing* group] and draw a rectangle (*Height* **.3"** and *Width* **13.33"**).
      • Click the **Align** button [*Drawing Tools Format* tab, *Arrange* group] and select **Align Center**.
      • Change the *Shape Fill* [*Drawing Tools Format* tab, *Shape Styles* group] to **Black, Background 1**. Repeat to change the *Shape Outline* to **No Outline**.
      • Move this shape above the title placeholder.

10. Copy an image from a *Slide Master* layout and paste it on a slide.
    a. On first layout, select the vine shape and press **Ctrl+C** to copy.
    b. Select the *Section Header* layout. Press **Ctrl+V** to paste.
    c. Using the rotation handle, rotate the image. Refer to Figure 4-140 for placement on the left.

11. Click the **Slide Master** tab and click the **Close Master View** button.

12. Display slide 1 and move the subtitle up until the date is on the dark red shape.

4-140 *Section Header* layout completed

13. Display slide 2. This slide is complete with changes made on the *Slide Master*. Notice the round note picture bullets.

14. Display slide 3. Select the *SmartArt* graphic. Click the **Change Colors** button [*SmartArt Tools Design* tab, *SmartArt Styles* group] and select **Dark 2 Fill** in the *Primary Theme Colors* category. Apply the **Intense Effect** [*SmartArt Tools Design* tab, *Styles* group].

15. Modify a table.
    a. Display slide 4. Select the table and click the **More** button [*Table Tools Design* tab, *Table Styles* group]. Select **Medium Style 2**.

b. Select the table text and change the font to **Gabriola** [*Home* tab, *Font* group] and the font size to **24 pt**. Apply **Bold**.

c. Resize the table slightly to align with the *Gridlines* as shown in Figure 4-141.

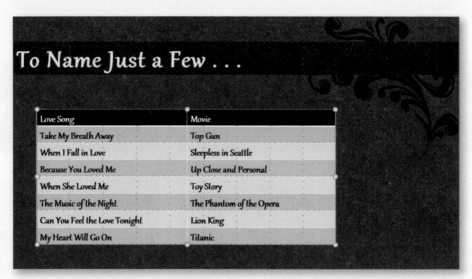

4-141 Table aligned on the *Gridlines*

16. Deselect the **Gridlines** [*View* tab, *Show* group].

17. Insert and align a picture.
    a. Click the **New Slide** drop-down arrow and select the **Title Only** layout.
    b. Type the slide title **Enjoy the Show!** on slide 5.
    c. Click the **Pictures** button [*Insert* tab, *Images* group] to open the *Insert Picture* dialog box.
    d. Click **Browse** and locate your student data files. Select **Violin-04** and click **Insert**.
    e. Resize the violin (*Height* **5.75"** and *Width* automatically changes to **3.83"**).
    f. Click the **Align** button [*Picture Tools Format* tab, *Arrange* group] and choose **Align Left**. Repeat to choose **Align Bottom**.

18. Remove the picture background.
    a. Select the violin picture on slide 5.
    b. Click the **Remove Background** button [*Picture Tools Format* tab, *Adjust* group] and the selection area shows a magenta color over all the area to be removed.
    c. Increase the selection area size by dragging the handles to the edge of the photograph so the violin retains its original size.
    d. Click the **Mark Areas to Keep** button and click the violin areas until all of the violin displays in color. The background on the right will be removed.
    e. Click the **Mark Areas to Remove** button and click the small area on the left of the violin until the background shows a magenta color so it will be removed, too.
    f. Click **Keep Changes** (Figure 4-142).

4-142 Picture with background removed

19. Review all slides and make adjustments if necessary.

20. Save the presentation (Figure 4-143).

21. Resave the presentation as a template and close the template file.

4-143 PowerPoint 4-2 completed

## Guided Project 4-3

Creative Gardens and Landscaping maintains a woodland area to showcase natural and seasonal plantings. In the spring, plantings of tulips and other spring flowers are featured. This woodland area is open to the public daily. In this project, you create a photo album using pictures of tulips to illustrate the annual Tulip Extravaganza.
[**Student Learning Outcomes 4.1, 4.3, 4.5, 4.6, 4.7**]

Files Needed: ***TulipPictures-04 folder: CandyCane.jpg, CGL-Logo.png, DynastyPink.jpg, GardenParty.jpg, PinkWhite.jpg, RedRhapsody.jpg, SunshineFire.jpg, Tulip1.jpg, Tulip2.jpg,*** and ***Watermelon.jpg***
Completed Project File Names: ***[your initials] PowerPoint 4-3.pptx*** and ***[your initials] PowerPoint 4-3.potx***

### Skills Covered in This Project

- Rotate a picture.
- Use the *Slide Master* to add a background shape and adjust placeholders.
- Use the *Slide Master* to change theme fonts and text effects.

- Remove a picture background.
- Select pictures to create a photo album.
- Edit photo album settings to change order and add captions.
- Save a presentation as a template.

1. Open PowerPoint, select **New**, and click **Blank Presentation**.

2. Select pictures for a photo album.
   a. Click the **Insert** tab and click the **Photo Album** button [*Images* group].
   b. Click the **File/Disk** button, locate your student files, and open the folder *TulipPictures-04*.
   c. Press **Ctrl+A** to select all of the pictures and click **Insert**.

3. Adjust picture order and select photo album options.
   a. Select the **Tulip1**, **Tulip2**, and **CGL-Logo** picture check boxes in the *Pictures in album* list and click the **Remove** button.
   b. Select the **SunshineFire** picture check box and click the up arrow four times until it is the second picture. Deselect this picture.
   c. Select the **RedRhapsody** picture check box and click the down arrow once.
   d. Click the **Picture layout** drop-down arrow under *Album Layout* and select **1 picture**.
   e. Click the **Frame Shape** drop-down arrow and select **Center Shadow Rectangle**.
   f. Select **Captions below ALL pictures** under *Picture Options* (Figure 4-144). Click **Create**.
      • This completes the photo album set up. If you need to recheck your settings, select **Edit Photo Album** to change settings.
      • The pictures now appear with the file names as captions below each picture. The picture and file names are grouped.

4-144 Picture names in album and options selected

4. Save the presentation as [your initials] PowerPoint 4-3.

5. Adjust picture captions.
   a. Click the **Align Right** button [*Home* tab, *Paragraph* group] for each picture caption.
   b. Revise each of the picture captions as follows and verify that the font color is **White, Text 1**:
      Slide 2   Candy Cane
      Slide 3   Sunshine and Fire
      Slide 4   Dynasty Pink
      Slide 5   Garden Party
      Slide 6   Purity and Romance
      Slide 7   Watermelon
      Slide 8   Red Rhapsody

6. Click the **Slide Master** button [*View* tab, *Master Views* group].

7. Adjust the *Slide Master* background and text effects
   a. Select the first layout, *Office Theme Slide Master: used by slides 1-8*.
   b. Click the **Colors** button [*Slide Master* tab, *Background* group] and select the **Paper** theme colors.
   c. Click the **Background Styles** button [*Slide Master* tab, *Background* group] and select **Style 3**.
   d. Select the title placeholder, change the font to **Pristina** [*Home* tab, *Font* group] at **44 pt**. Click **Bold** and **Shadow**.
   e. Select both the title and body text placeholders and change the font color to **Light Yellow, Text 2** [*Home* tab, *Font* group].

8. Add a shape and adjust placeholder text.
   a. Select the *Title Slide* layout (second layout). Click the **Rectangle** tool [*Home* tab, *Drawing* group] and draw a rectangle (*Height* **2"** and *Width* **13.33"**).
   b. Click the **Align** button [*Drawing Tools Format* tab, *Arrange* group] and select **Align Center**.
   c. Change the **Shape Fill** [*Drawing Tools Format* tab, *Shape Styles* group] to **Light Yellow, Text 2**.
   d. Change the **Shape Outline** [*Drawing Tools Format* tab, *Shape Styles* group] to **No Outline**.
   e. Click the **Send Backward** drop-down arrow [*Drawing Tools Format* tab, *Arrange* group] and select **Send to Back**. Arrange the rectangle evenly behind the title placeholder.
   f. Select the title placeholder and change the font color to **Dark Green, Background 2** and the font size to **66 pt**. [*Home* tab, *Font* group]. Resize the placeholder to fit the text. Click the **Align Left** button [*Home* tab, *Paragraph* group].
   g. Move the subtitle down slightly and increase the font size to **32 pt**. Click the **Align Right** button [*Home* tab, *Paragraph* group]. Resize the placeholder to fit the text.

9. Insert and resize a picture.
   a. Click the **Pictures** button [*Insert* tab, *Images* group] on the *Title Slide* layout and open the ***TulipPictures-04*** folder in your student files.
   b. Select the **Tulip1** picture and click **Insert**.
   c. Increase the picture height to **6"** [*Picture Tools Format* tab, *Size* group].
   d. Increase the **Zoom** to **100%** [*Status* bar] so you can more easily work with the detailed areas.

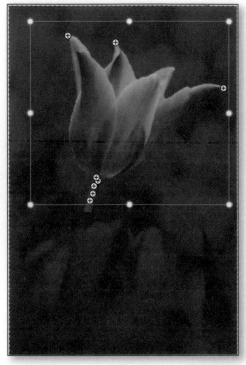

10. Remove a picture background and crop a picture.
    a. Click the **Remove Background** button [*Picture Tools Format* tab, *Adjust* group].
    b. Adjust the selection area size by dragging the handles to fit the single tulip and the stem only (Figure 4-145).
       • Click the **Mark Areas to Keep** button and click the tips of the petals and the stem.
       • Click **Keep Changes**.
    c. Click the top of the **Crop** button [*Picture Tools Format* tab, *Size* group] and resize the picture area to better fit the tulip. Click the **Crop** button again.
    d. Click the **Fit slide to current window** button [*Status* bar].
    e. Position the **Tulip1** picture on the left side of the yellow rectangle.
       • Move the title placeholder near the **Tulip1** picture.

4-145 Background removed

11. Repeat steps 9 and 10 to insert the **Tulip2** picture and remove the background. No cropping or size change is needed. Align the **Tulip2** picture on the right.

12. Insert a logo.
    a. On the *Title Slide* layout, click the **Pictures** button [*Insert* tab, *Images* group] and locate your student files.
    b. Select **CGL-Logo** and click **Insert**.
    c. Position the logo below the title placeholder.
    d. Resize the subtitle placeholder to fit the text (Figure 4-146).

4-146 *Slide Master Title Slide* layout completed

13. Copy, paste, and arrange pictures.
    a. Select the **Tulip1** image on the *Title Slide* layout and press **Ctrl+C**.
    b. Scroll down the layouts and select the **Blank Slide** layout (notice the *ScreenTips* that name layouts) and press **Ctrl+V**.
    c. Move the tulip to the lower left of the slide extending slightly off the slide.
    d. Press **Ctrl+D** and move the duplicated tulip to the upper right. Rotate this picture and extend it slightly off the slide (Figure 4-147).

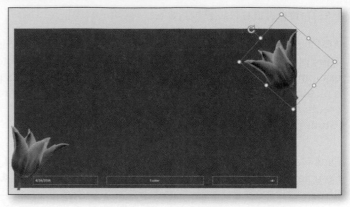

4-147 *Slide Master Blank Slide* **layout completed**

14. Click the **Slide Master** tab and click the **Close Master View** button.

15. Edit text on slide 1.
    a. Select the title placeholder and change the text to Tulip Extravaganza.
    b. Change the subtitle text to Tour Our Woodland Gardens.

16. Copy and paste a slide, then edit text.
    a. Select the slide 1 thumbnail and press **Ctrl+C**.
    b. Click after slide 8 and press **Ctrl+V**.
    c. Change the subtitle font size to **24 pt**. [*Home* tab, *Font* group] on slide 9. Click **Align Left** [*Home* tab, *Paragraph* group].
    d. Increase the subtitle placeholder size as needed and edit the text as follows:

       Subtitle:    400 Powell Avenue
                    Brentwood, TN 38522
                    615-792-8833

17. Click the **Transitions** tab and apply the **Wind** transition with the **Right** effect options. Click **Apply to All**. Review the transitions in *Slide Show* view.

18. Save the presentation (Figure 4-148).

19. Resave the presentation as a template and close the template file.

4-148 **PowerPoint 4-3 completed**

# Independent Project 4-4

At Wilson Home Entertainment Systems, employees help homeowners design home theater spaces. They plan features that work well with large-screen projected images, storage space for the necessary equipment, and durable furniture for family needs. For this project, you create a seating plan, remove a picture background to feature an equipment rack, and prepare a creative title slide design. You also create a new Wilson logo using the *Merge* feature.
[Student Learning Outcomes 4.1, 4.2, 4.3, 4.5]

Files Needed: *HomeTheater-04.pptx*, *EquipmentRack-04.jpg*, and *Family-04.jpg*
Completed Project File Names: *[your initials] PowerPoint 4-4.pptx*, *WHESLogo2.png* and *WHESLogo2.wmf*

## Skills Covered in This Project

- Rotate a shape.
- Align multiple objects.
- Layer objects and adjust stacking order.
- Group, ungroup, and regroup objects.

- Merge shapes.
- Save grouped shapes as a picture.
- Use the *Slide Master* to add background shapes.
- Remove a picture background.
- Ungroup an illustration and recolor.

1. Open the presentation **HomeTheater-04**. Save the presentation as [your initials] PowerPoint 4-4.

2. Add background shapes on a *Slide Master* layout.
   a. Click the **Slide Master** button and select the **Title and Content** layout (third).
   b. Draw a rectangle (*Height* **1.5"** and *Width* **13.33"**). Align it with the slide top and center. Change the *Shape Fill* to **Black** with no outline.
   c. Click the **Send Backward** drop-down arrow and select **Send to Back** so this rectangle is behind the title placeholder.
   d. Draw a horizontal line (*Width* **13.33"**). Change the *Shape Outline* to standard **Dark Red** and *Weight* to **6 pt**. Center this line on the slide and position it at the bottom of the black rectangle.
   e. Close *Slide Master* view.

3. Add a background shape for a theater room seating arrangement and duplicate a shape.
   a. Display slide 7. Draw a rectangle (*Height* **6"** and *Width* **10"**) that represents the size of a room.
   b. Change the **Shape Fill** to **Tan, Accent 2, Lighter 40%**.
   c. Click the **Send Backward** drop-down arrow and select **Send to Back**. Align this rectangle with the slide by clicking **Align Bottom** and **Align Center**.
   d. Select the chair (one seat with a cup holder on both sides) and duplicate the chair.

4. Add, layer, group, and position shapes.
   a. Prepare a rectangle on slide 7 to represent a raised platform for the back row of seating.
   b. Draw a rectangle (*Height* **1.5"** and *Width* **6"**) and position it near the bottom and center it in the room area.
   c. Change the *Shape Fill* to **Gray, Accent 1, Darker 25%**.
   d. Select the row of four seats and click the **Bring Forward** drop-down arrow and select **Bring to Front**. Position this group of seats on the "raised platform."
   e. Adjust the seating objects with the chairs rotated as shown in Figure 4-149.
   f. Group the seating arrangement including the platform.

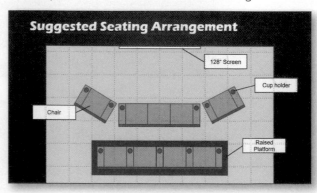

4-149 Room arrangement with theater seating

5. Add, duplicate, and position shapes.
   a. Draw a thin rectangle (*Height* **.1"** and *Width* **3.6"**) on slide 7 representing the projection screen. Change the *Shape Fill* to **White, Text 1** and position it at the top of the room area.
   b. Select the cupholder callout box. Click **Bring Forward** and select **Bring to Front**. Move this callout to point to the cupholder on the right chair.
   c. Duplicate this callout three times and edit the text on the duplicated callouts as follows: 128" Screen, Chair, and Raised Platform.
   d. Adjust the callout positions and where the line points to label these objects (See Figure 4-149).

6. Insert a picture and remove the background.
   a. Display slide 6. Insert the ***EquipmentRack-04*** picture from your student files.
   b. Select the picture and click the **Remove Background** button [*Picture Tools Format* tab]. Resize the selection area to fit the black equipment rack.
   c. Use the **Mark Areas to Remove** button to delete the area around the equipment rack. Click **Keep Changes**.
   d. Crop the picture to remove blank space. Apply a **Simple Frame, White** picture style so the image can be seen on the black background. Change the height to **6.5"** and position the rack on the right side of the slide.

7. Draw, layer, merge, and recolor shapes.
   a. Display slide 8. Text is grouped for a logo. Increase your **Zoom** to about **150%** so you can work in detail.
   b. Select the **Flow Chart: Merge** shape (in the *Flowchart* category) and draw a triangle (*Height* and *Width* **1.5"**).
   c. Draw a rectangle shape (*Height* **.5"** and *Width* **2.8"**). Overlap these shapes. The outline around the rectangle shape is evident.
   d. Select the triangle and the rectangle and click **Send Backward**. Position the shapes behind the grouped text as shown in Figure 4-150.
   e. Select the triangle and rectangle only (not the text), click the **Merge Shapes** button [*Drawing Tools Format* tab, *Insert Shape* group] and select **Union**.
   f. Change the *Shape Fill* to the standard **Dark Red**. Change the *Shape Outline* to **Black, Background 1**.
      • Compare how the line now appears around the single merged shape rather than around two separate shapes (Figure 4-151).
   g. Draw another rectangle shape (*Height* **.5"** and *Width* **2.8"**). Change the *Shape Fill* to **Black, Background 1** with **No Outline**.
   h. Click the **Send Backward** drop-down arrow and select **Send to Back**. Position this rectangle behind "Home Entertainment Systems."
   i. Check alignment and adjust shapes if needed (see Figure 4-151).
   j. Select all shapes and text in the logo and group.

4-150 Logo shapes behind text

4-151 Shapes merged and logo complete

8. Save the grouped logo as a picture using two file types.
   a. Point to any shape in the grouped logo and right-click to open the context menu. Choose **Save as Picture**.
   b. Name the logo WHESLogo2 (WHESLogo2.png). Save using the .png file type. Click **Save**.
   c. Repeat to save the logo again with the name WHESLogo2wm (WHESLogo2wm.wmf). Select the *Windows Metafile* file type so the shapes that make up the logo could be modified in the future. Click **Save**.

9. Click the **Fit slide to current window** button.

10. Delete slide 8 since you used it only to create the logo.

11. Ungroup and recolor an illustrated image then layer images and text for a concluding slide.

    a. Display slide 8, the final slide, with two images and text. Resize the theater screen image (*Height* **6.5"** and *Width* **9.35"**).

    b. Ungroup the image to convert it to a drawing object. Ungroup it again.

    c. Select the shapes on the bottom half of the image that represent rows of seats and delete them.

    d. Select all other lines that are around the center screen and change the *Fill Color* to **Black, Background 1**.

    e. Change the color of the three background shapes to these three colors going from left to right: **Gray, Accent 1; Light Gray, Text 2;** and **Tan, Accent 3**.

    f. Regroup all of the theater screen shapes.

    g. Resize the movies image (*Height* and *Width* **1.5"**). Click the **Bring Forward** drop-down arrow and then select **Bring to Front**.

    h. Position the movies image on the theater screen.

    i. Select the text, "Family Night," click the **Bring Forward** drop-down arrow, and then select **Bring to Front**. Move it to the bottom of the theater image (Figure 4-152).

4-152 Illustrated image recolored

12. Create a picture fill with an artistic effect. Insert a picture and remove a background.

    a. Display slide 1. Right-click and select **Format Background** to open the *Format Background* pane. Select **Picture or texture fill** and click the **File** button. Locate your student files, choose *Family-04*, and click **Insert**.

    b. Click the **Pictures** button [*Insert* tab, *Images* group] and select the **Family-04** again. Click **Insert**.

    c. Resize this picture to fit the height of the slide (**7.5"**).

    d. Click the **Crop** button and crop the picture on all four sides as shown in Figure 4-153. Click **Crop**.

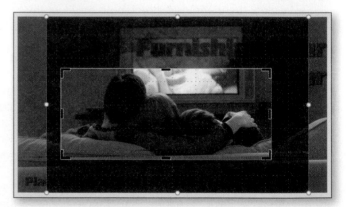

4-153 Inserted family picture cropped

    e. Resize the picture again until it fits over the background image and aligns with that image.

    f. Click **Remove Background** and adjust the selection area to fit the family.

       • Mark areas to keep or remove as needed (Figure 4-154).

       • Click **Keep Changes**.

       • Deselect the picture.

    g. Open the *Format Background* pane again. Click the **Effects** icon at the top of the pane and change the following:

       • Click the **Artistic Effects** drop-down arrow and choose the **Line Drawing** effect (first row, last effect).

4-154 Background removed on family picture

- Change the **Pencil Size** to **10** (Figure 4-155).
  - Now the background has a decorative effect while the family remains in focus.
  h. Close the *Format Background* pane.
  i. Insert the **WHESLogo2.png** file that you saved.
  - Resize the logo (*Height* **1.5"** and the *Width* automatically changes).
  - Position it on the lower right.

13. Check the slides that you changed to be sure spacing is appropriate.

14. Select the **Fall Over** transition and apply it to all slides.

15. Save and close the presentation (Figure 4-156).

4-155  Title slide completed

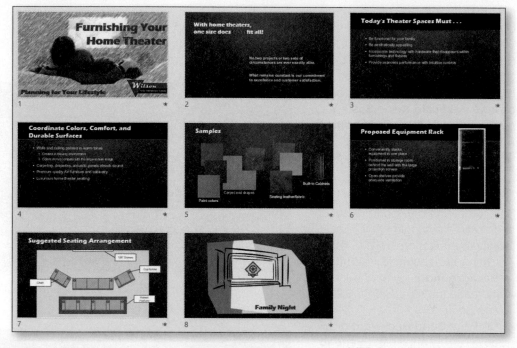

4-156  PowerPoint 4-4 completed

# Independent Project 4-5

Life's Animal Shelter rescues dogs and cats, provides medical services, and finds both foster care and forever homes. For this project, you prepare a presentation to be shown at the shelter and at other local sites to promote pet adoption.
[Student Learning Outcomes 4.1, 4.2, 4.3, 4.4, 4.5, 4.8]

Files Needed: **PetAdoption-04.pptx**, **PawPrintBackground-04.jpg**, **PawPrint-04.jpg**, **AdoptionApplication-04.docx**, and **Gabriel-04.jpg**
Completed Project File Name: **[your initials] PowerPoint 4-5.pptx**

## Skills Covered in This Project

- Change text direction.
- Use adjustment handles.
- Work with layered objects.
- Convert a *SmartArt* graphic to text.
- Use the *Slide Master* to create a custom theme with a tiled background picture and adjusted layouts.

- Apply a picture bullet.
- Apply a *Designer* layout.
- Crop a picture to a shape.
- Apply artistic effects to a picture.

1. Open the presentation ***PetAdoption-04***. Save the presentation as [your initials] PowerPoint 4-5.

2. Insert a tiled background picture on the *Slide Master*.
   a. Click the **Slide Master** button to open *Slide Master* view and select the first *Slide Master* layout.
   b. Select the large, tan rectangle and delete it. Repeat to delete the rectangle that has a thin black outline with no fill.
   c. Click **Background Styles** and select **Format Background** to open the *Format Background* pane.
   d. Select **Picture or texture fill**. Click the **File** button, locate your student files, and select ***PawPrintBackground-04***. Click **Insert**.
   e. Check **Tile picture as texture** on the *Format Background* pane and change the **Scale X** and **Scale Y** percentages to **40%**. Click **Apply to All** (Figure 4-157).
   f. Close the *Format Background* pane.

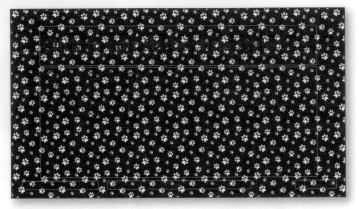

4-157 Background picture tiled and scaled to 40%

3. Add and copy a shape then apply a picture bullet.
   a. Select the *Title and Content* layout and draw a rectangle.
   b. Modify the rectangle.
      - Change rectangle fill to **White, Background 1**.
      - Increase the size (*Height* **6.7"** and *Width* **11.3"**).
      - Click the **Send Backward** drop-down arrow and select **Send to Back**.
      - Click **Align** then select **Align Bottom** and **Align Right** on the slide.
   c. Resize both text placeholders and move them to the right to fit on the white rectangle (Figure 4-158).
   d. Select the first line of text in the bulleted text placeholder and apply **Bold**.
   e. Change the bullet.
      - Click the **Bullets** drop-down arrow and select **Bullets and Numbering**.
      - Change the *Size % of text* to **150**.
      - Click the **Picture** button and browse to your student files.
      - Select ***PawPrint-04*** and click **Insert**.

4-158 *Slide Master Title and Content* layout complete

4. Delete three *Slide Master* layouts that you are not using in this presentation: *Section Header Layout*, *Two Content Layout*, and *Comparison Layout* (Figure 4-159).

5. Paste a shape and change text direction.
   a. Select the *Title and Content* layout and select the white rectangle only. Press **Ctrl+C**.
   b. Select the *Title Only* layout and press **Ctrl+V** to paste the white rectangle that you copied from the *Title and Content* layout.
   c. Click **Send to Back** and align the rectangle on the slide bottom and right.
   d. Select the title placeholder and change the following:
      • Click the **Text Direction** button [*Home* tab, *Paragraph* group], and choose **Rotate all text 270°**.
      • Resize the placeholder (*Height* **6.5"** and *Width* **1.5"**) move the placeholder to align on the left side of the white rectangle.
      • Change the font to **40 pt**.
      • Click **Align Text** and choose **Left**.

6. Modify text; then adjust placeholders.
   a. Select the *Title Slide* layout.
   b. Select the title placeholder and change the font size to **66 pt.**, **Bold**, and **Align Left**.
   c. Select the subtitle and change the font size to **28 pt.**, **Bold**, and **Align Left**.
   d. Keep the title, subtitle, and white rectangle on this slide. Delete all other objects, including a transparent picture over the slide background.
   e. Resize the white rectangle (*Height* **4.5"** and *Width* **10.5"**) and click **Align Left**.
   f. Resize the title and subtitle placeholders and position them as shown on Figure 4-160.

7. Close *Slide Master* view.

8. Display slide 1. Click the **Reset** button [*Home* tab, *Slides* group].

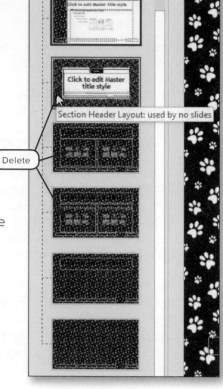

4-159 Unused *Slide Master* layouts to delete

4-160 *Slide Master Title Slide* layout completed

9. Display slide 2. Drag the *SmartArt* graphic center sizing handle down so it is below the title.

10. Display slide 3. Convert the *SmartArt* graphic to a listed text using the **Convert** button on the *SmartArt Tools Design* tab.

11. Change fonts, shape size, and adjust alignment.
    a. Display slide 4. Move the bottom arrow down slightly so it is positioned evenly behind the description text.
       • Resize the arrows on other slides as needed.
       • When more space is needed, keep the arrow point size the same and adjust the arrow height using the adjustment handle.
    b. Align objects on the right with the right side of the slide. Align other objects with each other on the left.

c. Arrange pet names in varied ways with each of the pictures (Figure 4-161).

d. Repeat steps a–c for slides 5–7.

12. Insert a screen clipping from a Word document.

a. Display slide 8.

b. Open **Microsoft Word**. Open the **AdoptionApplication-04** for Life's Animal Shelter.

- Only the first page of the application is shown in this file.
- Adjust the *View* size to **100%**.
- Click text in the bottom table to place your insertion point in a part of the document that will not be captured.
- Scroll up so the top of the document is displayed.

c. Return to slide 8 in PowerPoint.

d. Click the **Screenshot** button [*Insert* tab] and select **Screen Clipping**. Capture the top portion of this application form including the contact information section.

e. The *Design Ideas* pane opens. Click the first layout. If *PowerPoint* Designer is not available in your software, modify this step to create a text box on the right similar to the one shown in Figure 4-162.

- Delete the content placeholder on the right so only the text at the top displays (Figure 4-162).
- Select the text on the right and change the font size to **44 pt**.
- Click the **Change Case** button and select **Capitalize Each Word**. Change the word "An" to lowercase.

f. Close Word.

13. Crop a picture to a shape.

a. Display slide 9. Select the picture, click the **Crop** drop-down arrow, and select **Crop To Shape**. Choose the **Heart** shape in the *Basic Shapes* category.

b. Click the **Picture Border** drop-down arrow and select the color **Dark Red** and *Weight* **6 pt**. (Figure 4-163).

14. Resize the bulleted text placeholder on slide 9 so it fits the text.

a. Move the bulleted text down beside the picture.

b. Move the title text below the bulleted text.

15. Change a picture and apply an artistic effect.

a. Display slide 1. Select the picture and click the **Change Picture** button. Locate your student files and select the picture **Gabriel-04**. Click **Insert**.

b. Resize the width to **7.5"** and click **Align Top** and **Align Right**.

4-161 Pet pictures and text arrangement

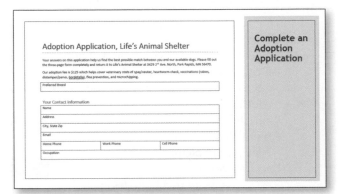

4-162 *Screen Clipping* inserted

4-163 Picture cropped to a shape

c.  Stretch the picture on the bottom so it ends evenly with the white rectangle.
d.  Click the **Artistic Effects** button and choose **Pencil Sketch**.

16. Save and close the presentation (Figure 4-164).

4-164  PowerPoint 4-5 completed

## Independent Project 4-6

At Placer Hills Real Estate, a screen is set up in the lobby displaying news, available property listings, and promotional events for visitors. In this project you create a photo album presentation featuring four homes in an upcoming open house event.
[**Student Learning Outcomes 4.2, 4.3, 4.6, 4.7, 4.8**]

Files Needed: *RealEstatePictures-04 folder: House 1-04.jpg, House 2-04.jpg, House 3-04.jpg, House 4-04.jpg, OpenHouse-04.jpg, PlacerHillsSold-04.jpg,  and Sold-04.jpg; and PHRELogo.png*
Completed Project File Names: *[your initials] PowerPoint 4-6.pptx and [your initials] PowerPoint 4-6.potx*

### Skills Covered in This Project

- Layer objects and adjust stacking order.
- Select pictures to create a photo album.
- Edit photo album settings.

- Apply a theme and use the *Slide Master* to customize a theme.
- Apply a *Designer* layout.
- Save a presentation as a template.

1. Open PowerPoint, select **New**, and click **Blank Presentation**.

2. Click the **Photo Album** button on the *Insert* tab.

3. Add pictures to a photo album.
   a. On the *Photo Album* dialog box, click the **File/Disk** button.
   b. Locate your student files and open the ***RealEstatePictures-04*** folder. Select the four "House" pictures. Click **Insert**.
      • The pictures are numbered 1–4 in the album because the *Picture layout* is currently *Fit to slide* which show one picture on each slide.

4. Select photo album options so each slide will contain a picture and a text box.
   a. Click the box before **House1-04** and a check shows it is selected.
   b. Click the **New Text Box** button four times.
   c. Click the down arrow so a text box is the first item in the list and **House1-04** is the second item. Deselect this picture.
   d. Move **House2-04** up so it follows the second text box. Deselect this picture. Repeat for **House3-04** so it follows the third text box.
      • The list has eight items (representing eight slides) starting with a text box and alternating between text boxes and pictures.
   e. Click the **Picture layout** drop-down arrow under *Album Layout* and select **2 pictures**.
      • The list has changed showing four slides.
      • Because each text box precedes each picture, they will appear on the left and the picture will be on the right of the slide.
   f. Click the drop-down arrow for *Frame Shape* and select **Simple Frame, White**.
   g. Select **Captions below ALL pictures** under *Picture Options* (Figure 4-165). Click **Create**.

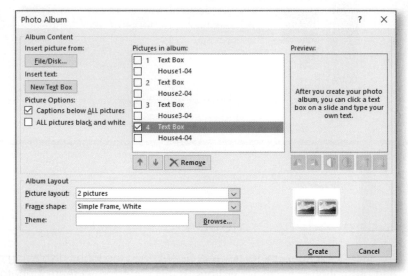

4-165 *Photo Album* pictures and options selected

5. Save the presentation as [your initials] PowerPoint 4-6.

6. Apply the **Frame** theme and **Office** theme colors.

7. Open the *Format Background* pane, choose **Picture or texture fill**.
   a. Click **Texture** and choose **Denim**.
   b. Click **Apply to All**.

8. Customize a *Slide Master* layout with shapes, a logo, and font changes.
   a. Click the **Slide Master** button and select the first *Slide Master* layout.
   b. Select the narrow rectangle on the right, resize it (*Height* **0.83"** and *Width* **13.33"**), and reposition it to align at the top and center of the slide.
      • Change the *Shape Fill* to **Blue, Accent 5, Darker 50%** with no outline.
      • Leave the *Transparency* setting at **50%** as shown.
   c. Select the rectangle behind the title placeholder on the left. Change the *Shape Fill* to **Blue, Accent 1, Lighter 40%** with no outline.
   d. Click the **Fonts** button and choose the **TrebuchetMS** font pair.

e. Select the title placeholder and change the font size to **28 pt**.
   - Change the placeholder *Width* to **3.5"**.
   - Center it on the light blue rectangle.
f. Draw a rectangle (*Height* **0.9"** and *Width* **3.77"**).
   - Align it to the slide on the bottom and left below the title placeholder.
   - Change the *Shape Fill* to **White, Background 1** with no outline.
g. Insert the ***PHRELogo-04*** from your student files. Decrease the logo size (*Height* **0.7"**) and position it on the white rectangle (Figure 4-166).

9. Close the *Slide Master* tab.

10. Revise text and add a picture to the title slide.
   a. Display slide 1. Replace the title with **Open House**.
   b. Type the following text for the subtitle:

   Sunday 1-4 p.m.
   Placer Hills Real Estate

4-166 First *Slide Master* layout completed

   c. Insert the picture **OpenHouse-04** from the *RealEstatePictures-04* folder in your student data files. The *Design Ideas* pane opens. If *PowerPoint* Designer is not available in your software, modify step 12d to make the picture fit the slide and create a blue rectangle on the left behind text as shown in Figure 4-167.
   d. Select the third layout with the picture background and blue rectangle on the left behind text.
   e. Change the title font size to **72 pt.**; apply **Bold** and **Shadow**.
   f. Change the subtitle font size to **28 pt.**; apply **Bold** and **Shadow**.
   g. Position the text as shown in Figure 4-167.

4-167 Title slide completed

11. Adjust slide layouts.
   a. Delete the *Text Box* placeholder on slide 2 (*House 1-04*), and change the *Slide Layout* to **Title Only**.
      - The text box served the purpose of controlling the size and spacing for two objects on the slide.
      - Using the *Title Only* layout provides the title placeholder so it fits on the background shape.
   b. Increase the picture caption font size to **28 pt.** and apply **Bold**.
   c. Move the caption down slightly so that it does not overlap the picture.

12. Repeat step 11 on slides 3–5 to prepare the slides for text.

13. Insert the following text on slides 2–5.
    a. Replace the caption (file name) under each picture with the city name and adjust the caption alignment by alternating between right and left as shown.
    b. Type the listing information in the title placeholder on the left. Resize this placeholder, if necessary, so each street address fits on one line.

| Slide | Picture Caption | Listing Information |
| --- | --- | --- |
| 2 | Lincoln (Align Right) | 615 Silver Hill Court 1,600 sq ft 3 br, 2 ba $339,600 |
| 3 | Roseville (Align Left) | 1720 Grey Owl Circle 2,182 sq ft 3 br, 2 ba $389,900 |
| 4 | Roseville (Align Right) | 1917 Oak Crest Drive 2,397 sq ft 4 br, 3 ba $368,505 |
| 5 | Auburn (Align Left) | 863 Holly Hills Drive 2,367 sq ft 3 br, 2 ba $349,900 |

14. Insert, color, size, and layer a shape.
    a. Display slide 2. Insert a diamond shape (*Height* and *Width* **7"**).
    b. Apply a *Shape Fill* of **Blue, Accent 5, Darker 50%** and no outline.
    c. Click the **Send Backward** button and select **Send to Back**.
    d. Adjust the shape and picture positions as shown in Figure 4-168 to feature the city names that alternate between right and left alignment.

4-168 Slide 2 completed

15. Copy and position a shape on multiple slides.
    a. Copy the diamond shape on slide 2 and paste it on slides 3–5.
    b. Click **Send to Back** on each slide.
    c. The city names alternate between left and right alignment below each picture. Position the diamond so it fits behind the picture on the other side.

16. Add a slide, insert a picture, and apply a picture style.
    a. Display slide 5. Insert a new slide with the *Title and Content* layout.
    b. Insert **PlacerHillsSold-04** from your student data files.
    c. Change the *Width* to **6"** and the *Height* automatically changes.
    d. Apply the **Rotated, White** picture style.
    e. Center the picture on the slide by selecting **Align Center** and **Align Middle**.

17. Apply an automatic transition and loop the presentation.
    a. Select the **Gallery** transition on the *Transitions* tab.

b. Type 00:03.00 for *After*. Click **Apply To All**.
c. On the *Slide Show* tab, click the **Set Up Slide Show** button and select **Browsed at a kiosk (full screen)** so the presentation will loop continuously.
d. Select **Show all slides** and select the appropriate monitor. Click **OK**.

18. Save the presentation (Figure 4-169).

19. Resave the presentation as a template and close the template.

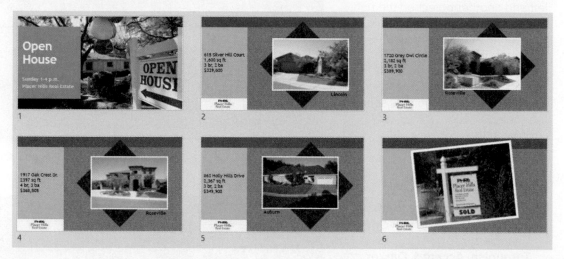

4-169 PowerPoint 4-6 completed

# Improve It Project 4-7

At Courtyard Medical Plaza, nurse practitioners frequently provide educational seminars for patients as part of the CMP Women's Wellness Program. In this project, you enhance a presentation about three important fitness requirements for women.
**[Student Learning Outcomes 4.1, 4.2, 4.5]**

Files Needed: ***BalancedFitness-04.pptx***, ***Fitness1-04***, and ***Fitness2-04***
Completed Project File Name: ***[your initials] PowerPoint 4-7.pptx***

### Skills Covered in This Project

- Edit shape points.
- Align and distribute multiple objects.
- Layer objects and adjust stacking order.
- Make sharpen, contrast, and brightness picture corrections.
- Remove a picture background.
- Group, ungroup, and regroup.

1. Open the presentation ***BalancedFitness-04***. Save the presentation as [your initials] PowerPoint 4-7.

2. Ungroup, modify, regroup, duplicate, and align an illustrated image.
   a. Display slide 1. Select the heart rate image.
   b. Increase your **Zoom** to about **150%** so you can work in detail.
   c. Click **Ungroup** to change this image to a drawing object; click **Ungroup** again so you can work with individual shapes.

d. Delete all shapes in the object except the three white shapes that represent a heartbeat. **Regroup** them.

e. Click the **Fit slide to current window** button so you can see the entire slide again.

f. Increase the size of the grouped object (*Height* **2.35"** and *Width* **4.2"**).

g. Duplicate the grouped object two times. Position one object on the left and another object on the right.

h. Select all three objects. Align them on the top and distribute them horizontally. If you notice an overlap, resize one or more of the objects horizontally and redistribute them until the three objects span the slide.

i. Group the three objects (Figure 4-170).

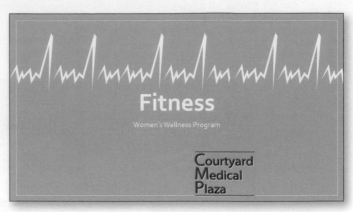

4-170 Heart rate image modified

3. Apply text effects and group.
   a. Insert a text box and type 3.
      • Increase the font size to **96 pt**. and apply **Bold**.
      • Change the *Text Fill* to **Turquoise, Accent 1, Darker 25%**.
   b. Click the **Text Effects** button, select **Transform**, and choose the **Square** effect (*Warp* category).
   c. Resize the number (*Height* **6.5"** and *Width* **6"**) and position it evenly on the slide (refer to Figure 4-171).
   d. Group the heart rate group and the large **3**.

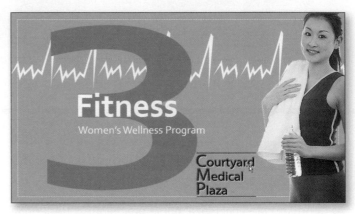

4-171 Title slide completed

4. Layer title placeholders and adjust text size.
   a. Select the title placeholder and click **Bring Forward** and select **Bring to Front**.
   b. Increase the font size to **96 pt**. Adjust the placeholder size to better fit the text.
   c. Position the text in the middle of the large **3**.
   d. Select the subtitle placeholder and click **Bring to Front**.
   e. Increase the font size to **32 pt**. Adjust the placeholder to fit the text.
   f. Position the text below the word **Fitness**.

5. Insert a picture, make corrections, and remove the background.
   a. Insert the **Fitness1-04** picture from your student files on slide 1. Align it on the right.
   b. Click **Corrections** and select **Sharpen: 50%**.
   c. Repeat to select **Brightness: 0% (Normal) Contrast**: **+20%**.
   d. Click **Remove Background**. Adjust the selection area and mark areas to keep or remove. Keep changes.

6. Adjust the position of the Courtyard Medical Plaza logo, if necessary, so it does not overlap other slide objects.

7. Draw a shape and edit shape points.
   a. Display slide 3. Draw a heart shape (*Height* **2.5"** and *Width* **3"**).
   b. Change the *Shape Fill* to **Dark Red** and the *ShapeOutline* to **Dark Teal, Text 2**.
   c. Edit shape points to stretch the heart vertically and make it narrower.
   d. Position the heart in the upper right corner of the slide (Figure 4-172).

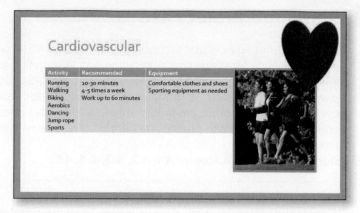

4-172 Heart with points edited

8. Insert a picture, make corrections, crop, and remove the background.
   a. Select slide 7. Insert the **Fitness2-04** picture from your student files and align it on the right.
   b. Click **Corrections** and select **Sharpen: 50%**.
   c. Repeat to select **Brightness: +20% Contrast: +20%**.
   d. Crop the picture to include only the woman in the middle.
   e. Click **Remove Background**. Adjust the selection area and mark areas to keep or remove. Use **Zoom** to work in detail. Keep changes.
   f. Click the **Rotate** button and choose **Flip Horizontal**.
   g. Position the picture on the right side of the slide.

9. Save and close the presentation (Figure 4-173).

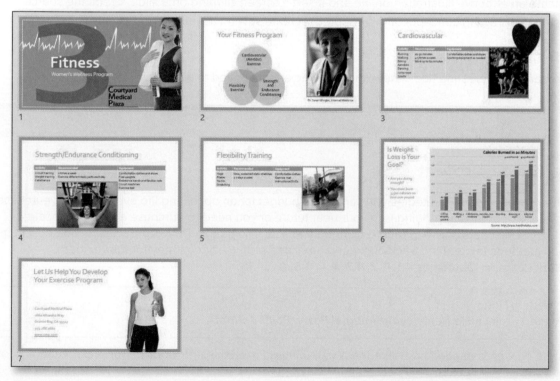

4-173 PowerPoint 4-7 completed

## Challenge Project 4-8

Today's Internet and cellular technology have made visual content accessible to the masses. Explore emerging trends for visual communication and information graphics. These topics are quite broad, so look online for a specific idea that interests you. Consider topics such as why information graphics matter, what makes information graphics successful, tips for design, ethical representation of information, or how information graphics are impacting marketing strategies. Show how some of these concepts can be applied in PowerPoint to present content in a visual way that is pleasing to the eye and more interesting than plain text.
[Student Learning Outcomes 4.1, 4.2, 4.3, 4.4, 4.5]

File Needed: None
Completed Project File Name: *[your initials] PowerPoint 4-8.pptx*

Create a new presentation and save it as [your initials] PowerPoint 4-8. Modify your presentation according to the following guidelines:

- Customize a theme using *Slide Master* layouts to create a unique background. Add simple shapes that are layered and have subtle color differences. Select a title font with a bold appearance such as Arial Black for slide titles and Arial for body text.
- Provide text content for necessary definitions. Limit use of bulleted text.
- Create one *SmartArt* graphic that you convert to shapes. Design your own diagram.
- Design a timeline showing several key dates as information graphics continues to evolve.
- Locate an effective illustration online and insert a screen clipping on a slide. Credit the source.
- Using the drawing concepts of this chapter, recreate several aspects of this illustration on one or more slides.
- Create a merged shape.
- Prepare an interesting title slide with an artistic effect applied to a picture.

## Challenge Project 4-9

For this project, identify strategies you can use to budget for an upcoming life event or major purchase. For example, perhaps a wedding is in your near future or you need to purchase a new car. Locate a variety of worksheets online to record planned and actual spending. Develop a presentation describing various methods for keeping track of expenditures and setting aside money for future needs.
[Student Learning Outcomes 4.1, 4.2, 4.3, 4.4, 4.5, 4.7, 4.8]

File Needed: None
Completed Project File Name: *[your initials] PowerPoint 4-9.pptx*

Create a new presentation and save it as [your initials] PowerPoint 4-9. Modify your presentation according to the following guidelines:

- Create a custom theme that reflects a goal-oriented approach to saving money.
- Use *Slide Master* layouts and include background images or shapes. Use *Gridlines* to control alignment consistency. Arrange rotated text as part of the design with a color that blends with the background.

- Apply a modern-looking font for slide titles and apply appropriate text effects. Apply a simple font for body text. Be sure all text is easy to read.
- Insert a picture to represent the upcoming event or major purchase for which you are saving and select a *Designer* layout.
- Locate two budget worksheets online and insert a screen clipping of each one on its own slide.
- Compare the differences in what the worksheets track or how they work. Prepare a comparison slide or table listing similarities or differences. Credit the sources.
- Save the presentation as a template.

## Challenge Project 4-10

Prepare a photo album presentation featuring pictures you have from an event such as a wedding, family reunion, or organization activity. Design an appropriate custom background for this topic that helps to communicate the mood of the presentation. Add captions and text boxes as well as illustrations to design the presentation like a scrapbook that can be viewed on a tablet or notebook computer. **[Student Learning Outcomes 4.1, 4.2, 4.3, 4.4, 4.5, 4.6]**

File Needed: None
Completed Project File Name: *[your initials] PowerPoint 4-10.pptx*

Create a new presentation and save it as [your initials] PowerPoint 4-10. Modify your presentation according to the following guidelines:

- Create a photo album with six or more pictures. Include captions for each picture and text boxes inserted as needed. Adjust the album order and select a picture layout. Edit the photo album if necessary before other changes are made to individual slides.
- Create a custom theme appropriate for your topic. Use *Slide Master* layouts to design background graphics and colors. Using the drawing concepts of this chapter, include creative elements for a unique design.
- Use *Gridlines* to assure alignment consistency.
- Insert additional slides to provide supporting information such as a text box with a list of brief terms or statements that are arranged in columns.
- Insert a screen clipping from a related document or a web site that has appropriate information. Credit the source.
- Check each picture and make corrections as needed.
- Select one picture to feature in a creative way using artistic effects.
- Crop one picture to a shape.

# Working with Advanced Animation, Hyperlinks, and Rich Media

POWERPOINT

## CHAPTER OVERVIEW

With PowerPoint 2016, you can integrate many forms of media into your presentations. The term *rich media*, also called *multimedia*, encompasses a broad range of digital media that includes text, pictures, audio, and video combined with dynamic motion and interactivity. This chapter explores how to work with audio and video content, add motion through complex animations, and provide interactivity with hyperlinks. You will learn how to arrange and link content in your presentations to actively engage your audience.

### STUDENT LEARNING OUTCOMES (SLOs)

After completing this chapter, you will be able to:

**SLO 5.1** Apply animation with multiple effects and complex sequences including *Morph* transitions (p. P5-293).

**SLO 5.2** Add hyperlinks and action buttons to create navigation and to link to other sources (p. P5-310).

**SLO 5.3** Insert audio and video content (p. P5-316).

**SLO 5.4** Adjust audio and video playback settings using bookmark, trim, and fade options (p. P5-319).

**SLO 5.5** Record audio and add sound to animation (p. P5-324).

**SLO 5.6** Format, optimize, and compress media (p. P5-325).

**SLO 5.7** Integrate rich media effectively (p. P5-327).

### Case Study

Allen Wilson, owner of Wilson Home Entertainment Systems (WHES), was recently asked to speak to the "Leaders Under 40" annual recognition ceremony about the success of his family-owned business and the services WHES provides. In the Pause & Practice projects in Chapter 5, you apply the concepts of the chapter to complete his presentation.

**Pause & Practice 5-1:** Apply animation to multiple slide objects and create complex animations.

**Pause & Practice 5-2:** Create a menu of presentation topics with hyperlinks and action buttons to control navigation; link to other sources.

**Pause & Practice 5-3:** Insert video and audio files, adjust playback settings, and record audio.

# Applying Advanced Animation

Animation in your presentation helps to tell your story. Using animation, you can break a concept into small increments that you *build* on a slide at just the right time to focus attention. Building can help your audience see the connections between concepts as you progressively reveal them. Animation also works well for comparison situations such as showing before and after pictures one at a time, or presenting two lists independently. You can control animation timing as you present or set up animation to occur automatically.

In *SLO 3.2: Applying Animation*, you explored animation with *Entrance* effects that display an object, *Emphasis* effects that apply a movement or color change to call attention to an object, or *Exit* effects that make an object leave the slide. In this chapter, you will work with animations that are more complex with multiple effects, synchronized timings, and sound effects. Be sure you save your presentations frequently while you are working.

*Motion Path* animation allows you to vary the direction of movement. As with other types of animation, PowerPoint provides many *Motion Path* effects in the gallery, or you can click **More Motion Paths** to access additional effects or even draw a path using the *Custom Path* option.

PowerPoint's new *Morph* transition provides another way to add movement and other changes to slide objects including blending text effects in interesting ways. These effects require two or more slides since the transition from one slide to another is where the change occurs.

Animation effects should not be used simply to attract attention. Animation quickly loses its novelty when you overuse it. A little goes a long way. Remember that presentations are for sharing information; they are usually not intended to be entertainment events. Judge carefully what is best to include in each individual presentation situation. Object movements should match what you say and appear naturally to aid meaning.

Animation can be effective for the following:

- Progressively introducing content.
- Featuring or emphasizing content.
- Reinforcing or supporting content.
- Showing change.
- Illustrating dynamic concepts or objects in motion.

## Animate a List and Dim Text

You can add movement and control animation settings for selected objects with commands on the *Animations* tab. Recall from *SLO 3.2: Applying Animation* that an **animation tag**, a small numbered box, appears on the slide next to an animated object when the *Animations* tab is active. If you want to remove an animation, delete this animation tag. The **Animation Pane** offers additional options you can use to fine tune settings or coordinate complex sequences.

Remember that audience members won't read text until it stops moving. People may find constant movement distracting, so animate text sparingly. When animating lists, consider choosing a color to dim text for the items you have already presented. This text is still readable but not emphasized as much as the new text that you are introducing.

---

▶ **HOW TO:** Animate a List and Dim Text

1. Select the bulleted list to be animated.
2. Click the **More** button [*Animations* tab, *Animation* group] to open the *Animation* gallery (Figure 5-1), or click the **Add Animation** button [*Animations* tab, *Advanced Animation* group].

3. Click an **Animation** effect to apply it or click one of the options at the bottom of the gallery to open a dialog box with more effects for each animation type. *Entrance* effects are shown in Figure 5-2.

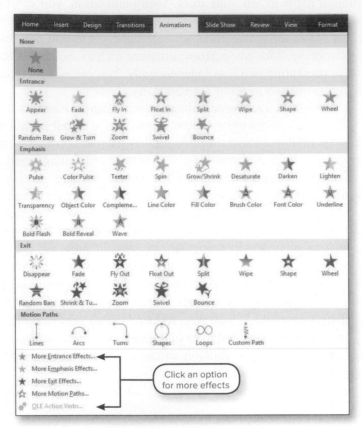

5-2 More *Entrance* effects

5-1 *Animation* gallery

4. Click the **Effect Options** button [*Animations* tab, *Animation* group] once an animation is applied to control options such as *Direction* or *Sequence*. The options vary based on the selected animation effect. Choose from one of the following for *Sequence* options (Figure 5-3):

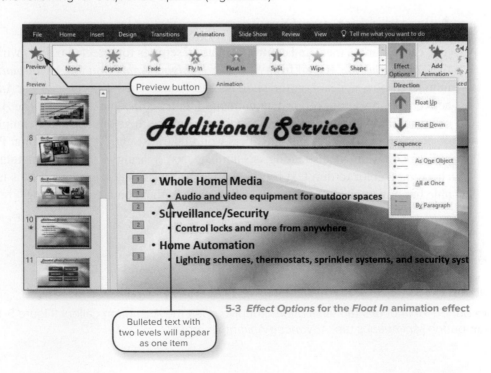

5-3 *Effect Options* for the *Float In* animation effect

- **As One Object:** All text appears at one time.
- **All at Once:** All text appears at once but the animation effect is applied to each part individually.
  - **By Paragraph:** Each bulleted item and related subpoints appear together.

5. Click the **Preview** button [*Animations* tab, *Preview* group] to test the animation.

6. Click the launcher [*Animations* tab, *Animation* group] to open a dialog box with additional effect options that vary based on the selected animation.

   - The animation effect name appears in the dialog box title bar (Figure 5-4).

7. Click the **After Animation** drop-down list arrow to select a different color for the text after it has been animated.

   - Select a color that keeps the text readable but deemphasizes it compared to the color used for the new text.

8. Click the **Animate text** drop-down list arrow and choose from **All at once**, **By word**, or **By letter**.

9. Click **OK** to close the dialog box.

10. Remove an animation by deleting the animation tag or select **None** in the *Animations* gallery.

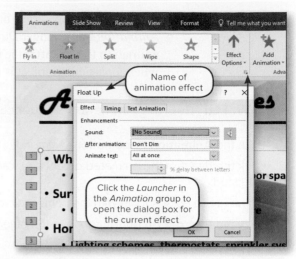

5-4 *Float Up* dialog box

You can use the same keyboard shortcuts (described in the following table) to move between animations that you use for moving to the next or previous slides.

### Animation Keyboard Shortcuts

| Press | Action |
| --- | --- |
| **N**, **Enter**, **Page Down**, right arrow, down arrow, or spacebar | Start the next animation. |
| **P**, **Page Up**, left arrow, up arrow, or **Backspace** | Start the previous animation. |

## The Animation Pane

You can control most animation effects on the *Animations* tab. However, the *Animation Pane* shows all of the animation on one slide, and it is useful when you are preparing animation for multiple objects and multiple effects. Typically, one animation effect occurs after another. By default, animation occurs with the *Start* option of *On Click* so the speaker activates the animation. To have animation appear automatically, the *Start* option is *After Previous* or *With Previous*.

Each animation effect has a slightly different duration time. Recall from *SLO 3.2: Applying Animation* that a longer *Duration* time creates a slower movement. The *Delay* time causes the animation to start after the number of seconds you enter. You can also create a ***trigger*** so that when a particular object is clicked, the animation starts.

▶ **HOW TO:** Reorder Animation Sequence and Create a Trigger

1. Click the **Animation Pane** button [*Animations* tab, *Advanced Animation* group] to open the *Animation Pane*.

2. Click the name of the animated object you want to reorder in the *Animation Pane* where multiple animations are listed.
   - The green color shown with the name indicates an *Entrance* effect; yellow indicates an *Emphasis* effect.

3. Click the **Reorder up** button to move the object up in the list. Click the **Reorder down** button to move the object down in the list (Figure 5-5).

4. Test your animation by clicking the **Play** button in the *Animation Pane*. Its name changes based on what is selected (Figures 5-6), so click one of the following buttons:
   - ***Play Selected*** when an animated object is selected on the slide.
   - ***Play From*** when an animated object is selected in the animation list.
   - ***Play All*** when no object is selected.

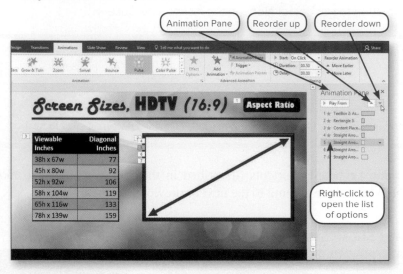
5-5 Reorder animation effects in the *Animation Pane* list

5-6 Open the *Animation Effect* dialog box from the *Animation Pane* list

5. Right-click the effect in the *Animation Pane* (or click the down triangle) and select **Effect Options** (Figure 5-6) or **Timing**.
   - A dialog box opens with two or three tabs (depending on what is animated) where you can control more settings at once.

6. Click the *Timing* tab to adjust these options:
   - Select **Start**, **Delay**, and **Duration** options.
   - Click the **Repeat** list box arrow and choose an appropriate number.
   - Select **Rewind when done playing**, if appropriate.
   - Click the **Triggers** button and choose **Start effect on click of** to select a particular object on your slide to begin the animation (Figure 5-7). By default, the animation being applied is considered part of an animation sequence.
   - The option **Start effect on play of** is available only when a video or audio object is on a slide.

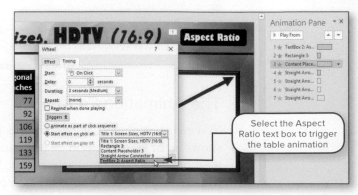
5-7 Choose a trigger

7. Click **OK** to close the dialog box.

8. Click the **Play From** button to test animation.

   - On the *Animation Pane*, the colored bar following each object name reflects the duration for that animation effect (Figure 5-8).
   - Animation effects that start *On Click* begin at the same position; those that start *After Previous* will begin after the previous duration ends.
   - At the bottom of the pane, the elapsed seconds show while the animation plays.

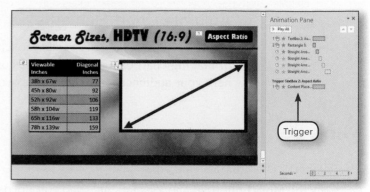

5-8 Trigger assigned and other timing adjusted

When working with complex animations, increase the width of the *Animation Pane* to see when each animation begins and ends. You can resize the pane after you finish making changes. When you close the *Animation Pane* and then open it again, the size will be the same as when you closed it.

If a chevron icon pointing down appears below an animation name, then that animation has multiple parts. Click the chevron pointing down to expand the list. When the list is expanded, click the chevron pointing up to collapse the list.

## The Animation Painter

The ***Animation Painter*** copies animation settings and applies them to another object in the same way the *Format Painter* copies format settings. Using *Animation Painter* is especially helpful when you have created a complex animation sequence and you want to apply those settings again.

▶**HOW TO:** Use Animation Painter

1. Select the object with the animation you need.

2. Click the **Animation Painter** button [*Animations* tab, *Advanced Animation* group] to copy the animation settings (Figure 5-9).

5-9 *Animation Painter* button

   - Click another object to apply this animation.
   ***Or***

3. Double-click the **Animation Painter** button and it will remain active.

   - Click more than one object to apply this animation.
   - Press **Page Down** to display a different slide and then click another object to apply this animation.

4. Press **Esc** to turn off the *Animation Painter*.

When you animate an object, selection handles are replaced with an animation tag. The color of the animation tag changes when the object is selected. To add a second animation to a selected object, you must click the **Add Animation** button to open the gallery and select another effect. If you simply choose a different effect from the open gallery, the previous effect is replaced with the current effect. You can click anywhere on the slide background to deselect the animated object.

# Animate Chart Elements

Animation effects for charts add movement by making the entire chart appear as one object or making chart data appear by series or category. Chart animation can be a powerful way to help your audience absorb content as you gradually introduce comparison data.

## ▶HOW TO: Animate Chart Elements

1. Select the chart to be animated.
2. Click the **More** button [*Animations* tab, *Animation* group] or click the **Add Animation** button [*Animations* tab, *Advanced Animation* group] to open the gallery.
3. Choose an animation effect or click one of the **More** options at the bottom of the gallery to select from additional effects.
4. Click the **Effect Options** button [*Animations* tab, *Animation* group] once an animation effect is applied and choose a particular sequence for how your chart will build (Figures 5-10 and 5-11).

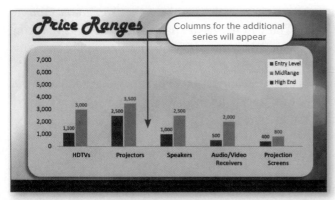

5-10  **Chart being animated** *By Series*

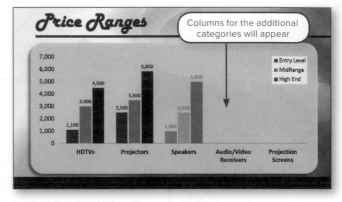

5-11  **Chart being animated** *By Category*

5. Change the default *Start* option of *On Click* to *After Previous* with an appropriate time for *Delay* to better focus on either the series or the categories as they appear.
6. Click the **Animations Pane** button [*Animations* tab, *Advanced Animation* group].
   - Click the **chevron** icon below an item name on the *Animation Pane* to expand the animation list and show the multiple parts such as series data displayed in columns with different colors (Figure 5-12).
   - Adjust individual items in the expanded list (Figure 5-13). Click the **chevron** again to collapse the list.
7. Select the chart object in the *Animation Pane* list.
8. Right-click and choose **Effect Options** to open the dialog box for the animation effect you chose.
   - Click the **Chart Animation** tab (Figure 5-14).
   - For the *Group Chart* option, note that the same *Effect Options* are available.

5-12  **Expand animation list**

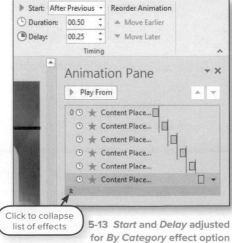

5-13  ***Start*** and ***Delay*** adjusted for *By Category* effect option

- Deselect the option for **Start animation by drawing the chart background**. The chart background will appear at the time the slide appears.
  - Options in the *Group Chart* list box are not available with all animation effects.

9. Click **OK**.

10. Test your animation by clicking the **Play** button in the *Animation Pane*. Its name changes based on what is selected (see Figures 5-12 and 5-13), so click one of the following buttons:
    - *Play Selected* when an animated object is selected on the slide.
    - *Play From* when an animated object is selected in the animation list.
    - *Play All* when no object is selected.

11. Click **Effect Options** [*Animations* tab, *Animation* group] once an animation has been applied, and then choose a different sequence to consider.
    - Select a sequence that displays your chart in the most logical order for what you need to show.

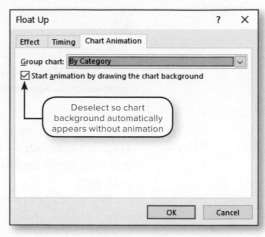

5-14 *Float Up* dialog box

---

## Animate a SmartArt Graphic

When you apply animation to a *SmartArt* graphic, you can control the direction and the sequence so shapes appear in phases. Use the *Timing* group options [*Animations* tab] or the *Animation Pane* to control other settings for how the animation starts and the timings for duration and delay.

---

▶**HOW TO:** Animate a SmartArt Graphic

1. Select the *SmartArt* graphic you want to animate. Be sure you select the *SmartArt* frame so the entire *SmartArt* graphic is selected and not an individual shape within the frame.

2. Click the **More** button [*Animations* tab, *Animation* group] or click the **Add Animation** button [*Animations* tab, *Advanced Animation* group] to open the gallery.

3. Choose an animation effect or click one of the **More** options at the bottom of the gallery to select from additional effects.

4. Click the **Effect Options** button [*Animations* tab, *Animation* group] once an animation effect is applied. Choose a *Direction*, a *Sequence*, or one of the other options that are available based on the selected animation.
   - The *Effect Options* of **One by One** builds the *SmartArt* graphic one shape at a time. Figure 5-15, which was captured during the animation, shows how each shape and related picture swivel together.
   - When animating *SmartArt* graphics, animation effects that grow or rotate will look quite different using the *One by One* versus the *As One Object* sequence.

5. Test the animation by clicking the **Preview** button [*Animations* tab], the **Play Selected** button [*Animation Pane*], or view the slide in *Slide Show* view.

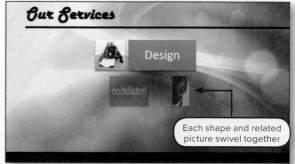

5-15 *Swivel* animation with *One by One* sequence

To create a more complex animation sequence, first show the completed *SmartArt* graphic to provide an overview, apply an exit animation so the *SmartArt* graphic disappears, and then apply an *Entrance* effect so the *SmartArt* graphic appears in stages as you discuss each part.

Not all diagrams benefit from animation. But if you need more control over how the individual shapes appear, convert the *SmartArt* graphic to shapes. Then regroup the shapes as needed and animate them in a way that works best for your message.

## Create Motion Path Animation

With a *Motion Path* animation, you control how an object moves from one position to another following a predesigned path. PowerPoint provides many different *Motion Path* effects, or you can select **Custom Path** to draw your own.

A *Motion Path* animation effect has a green triangle marker for the beginning point, and most of the effects have a red triangle marker for the ending point. Drag these markers to adjust their positions and use sizing handles to change the area that contains the movement. Change curves of a path by modifying ***editing points***. Place the object outside the slide for its start position to make an object begin movement off the slide and then enter the slide. The end position after movement can be on the slide or outside the slide to create an exit effect.

### ▶ HOW TO: Apply a Motion Path Animation

1. Change your *Zoom* to **50%** so you can use the blank area around your slide for object placement.
2. Select the object you want to animate and move it to its start position.
   - The object's position is where the animation starts or where it ends depending on the effect you choose.
   - If you want the object to move onto the slide, drag the object off the slide for its start position on the blank area outside the slide. Then select the animation effect.
3. Select the object and click the **Add Animation** button [*Animations* tab, *Advanced Animation* group] to open the gallery.
4. Select from the following options in the *Motion Paths* category (Figure 5-16):

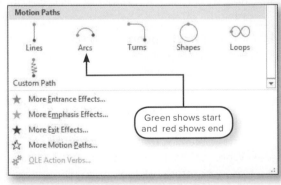

   - Choose one of the six animation effects shown.
   - Click the **Custom Path** to draw the path an object will follow.
   - Choose **More Motion Paths** to open the *Change Motion Path* dialog box and view more options (Figure 5-17). Select an animation from one of the three categories: *Basic*, *Lines-Curves*, or *Special*. Click **OK**.
5. Drag a sizing handle and observe how the line that connects your object changes.

5-16 *Motion Path* effects in the *Animation* gallery

   - The shape of the line varies based on the particular path you selected.
   - A green triangle marker in the center of the object indicates the start point of the *Motion Path* animation.
   - The center of your object will move along the path.

5-17 *Change Motion Path* dialog box

5-18 *Motion Path Swoosh* effect as it first appears

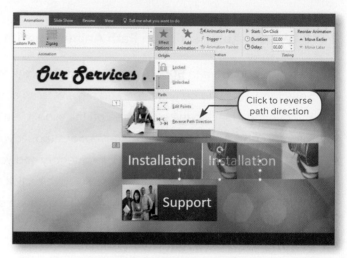

5-19 *Motion Path Zigzag* effect as it first appears

6.  Click **Preview** [*Animations* tab, *Preview* group] to test your animation.

    •  A *Swoosh Motion Path* effect (*Special* category) applied to the first grouped object is shown in Figure 5-18. This effect begins and ends in the same position.
    •  Drag the sizing handles to increase the size of the movement area.

7.  Change the direction of movement.

    •  Depending on which *Motion Path* effect you choose, the effect may have a red marker that indicates the ending point of the *Motion Path* animation.
    •  A *Zigzag Motion Path* effect (*Lines-Curves* category) is applied to the second grouped object (Figure 5-19). The red marker is on the left and the green marker is on the right showing movement from left to right.
    •  Click the **Effect Options** button [*Animations* tab, *Animation* group] and choose **Reverse Path Direction**. Now the second object moves from right to left so the final position of this object aligns with the first object on the slide.

8.  Move an object's start or end position.

    •  Point to the marker for the object you want to move.
    •  When your pointer changes to a four-tipped arrow, drag the marker to a different position.
    •  The object you are moving shows in a transparent color while you move it.

9.  Adjust the animation sequence so an object with motion path animation is invisible until the motion starts.

    •  Select the animated object.
    •  Click the **Add Animation** button [*Animations* tab, *Advanced Animation* group] and apply an **Entrance** effect.
    •  In the *Animation Pane*, move the **Entrance** effect above the **Motion Path** effect.
    •  Change the *Start* option on the **Motion Path** effect to **With Previous** so the entrance and movement happen together.
    •  Click **Preview** [*Animations* tab] to test each movement.

10. Test the animation by clicking the **Preview** button [*Animations* tab], the **Play Selected** button [*Animation Pane*], or view the slide in *Slide Show* view.

    •  If movements seem too rapid, increase *Duration* so the movements occur more slowly.

Prepare a *Custom Path* animation when you want an object to follow a particular path that you draw as shown in Figure 5-20. A car is in its start position outside the slide on the right, the custom path the car will follow is drawn to match the curve of the road, and the car end position is by the stop sign on the left. When this animation is played, the car enters the slide and moves along the road.

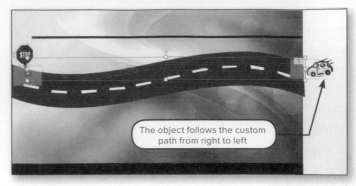

The object follows the custom path from right to left

5-20 *Motion Path Custom Path* effect

▶ **HOW TO:** Apply a Motion Path Animation with a Custom Path

1. Change your *Zoom* to **50%** so you can use the blank area outside the slide.
2. Select the object to be animated and move it to an appropriate start position.
   - Move the object to the blank area off the slide if you want it to enter the slide during animation.
3. Click the **Add Animation** button [*Animations* tab, *Advanced Animation* group].
4. Click **Custom Path** in the *Motion Path* category and your pointer changes to a crosshair.
5. Draw the line that your object will follow. Double-click at the end of the line.
   - When drawing a custom path so an object exits the slide during animation, the end position must be in the blank area outside the slide.
6. Adjust the animation area or line as needed.
   - Drag the start and end markers to change their positions.
   - Resize the animation area.
   - Adjust the curve of the line. Select the animated object, right click and select **Edit Points**, then drag points or use direction handles to change curves.
7. Click **Preview** [*Animations* tab] to test the movement.
8. Adjust *Duration* as needed.

When working with complex animations, increase the size of the *Animation Pane* so you can see the color bars showing when each animation plays. Test each portion of the animation and adjust as necessary before working on the next part. If your sequence becomes lengthy, you may want to work in stages by duplicating your slide and adding additional animation to the duplicated slide. Then you can always go back to the previous slide and start again if you have problems getting the sequences and timing to work as you need. Save your presentation frequently.

Test the animation on the computer used for delivery. You may need to adjust timings if the computer you are using to project the presentation has a different processing speed from the computer you use to develop the presentation.

## Animate with the Morph Transition

The *Morph* transition is a new PowerPoint feature (available with an *Office 365* subscription) that provides another way to animate. The term "morph" means to change from one image to another using small, gradual steps so the change is smooth. Software such as Photoshop can morph one picture into a different picture, but PowerPoint's *Morph* works a little differently. *Morph* can handle many types of changes, but at least one object must be the same object on two slides. You simply prepare one slide showing these objects before changes and a second slide that shows the final design. Then with the *Morph* transition, the changes happen seamlessly. *Effect Options* for *Morph* include: *Objects*, *Words*, and *Characters*.

When planning your slides, think in terms of "before" and "after." For example, you could create your final slide design and then duplicate that slide to create the beginning design. Move the duplicate slide before the final one and change color, size, or repositioning on the before slide. Select the after slide and apply the *Morph* transition that will blend from the before slide to the after slide. In some cases, however, it will be easier to start with the beginning slide and then create the final slide with all your changes. As you get more experienced, you'll learn which method to use in different situations. And you may want to increase the duration to slow the changes.

A few examples for using *Morph* include the following:

- **Text:** Start with text in a regular font treatment and morph into a much larger size with a different font and dramatic text effects. The color, position, and rotation of the text can change. The *Effect Options* of *Word* and *Character* cause text to move in different ways.
- **Objects:** Much like *Motion Path* animation, you can position an object in the area off a slide to create an entrance effect. The object can rotate into the final position or you can create a zoom effect by making the sizes or the shape of an object different on the before and after slides. By using adjustment handles or edit points, you can change one shape into a very different shape. Even a *SmartArt* graphic can be changed if it is converted to shapes and ungrouped.
- **Pictures:** As with objects, sizing and movement options can change. By using *Picture Styles*, a picture can morph from a plain picture into one that is framed or has a different shape. You can start with one of the *Artistic Effects* or a monochrome color that changes so a picture comes into focus. Or add motion to a cropping effect to emphasize just a portion of a picture.

In this first example, text is arranged on one slide (Figure 5-21) and that slide is duplicated. The second slide (Figure 5-22) is redesigned to become the final slide.

---

▶**HOW TO:** Use the Morph Transition to Animate Words and Characters

1. Prepare two slides for a *Morph* transition.
   - Display the "before" slide using any layout.
   - Type the text in placeholders or in a text box (see Figure 5-21).
   - Select the slide thumbnail and press **Ctrl+D**. The duplicate thumbnail follows the original slide, and it will be the "after" slide.
2. Display the "after" slide, change text, to create your final design, and apply the *Morph* transition.
   - Change font, font size, style, color, text effects, or rotation as needed.
   - Move text objects into their final position (see Figure 5-22).

5-21 *Morph* transition "before" slide

- Click **Morph** [*Transitions* tab, *Transition to This Slide* group], click **Effect Options**, and then select **Words**.
- Click **Preview** [*Transitions* tab, *Preview* group] to test the changes.
- Click **Effect Options** [*Transitions* tab, *Transition to This Slide* group] again and select **Characters**. Click **Preview** again to see if this setting creates better results.
- Increase **Duration** [*Transitions* tab, *Timing* group] to slow the movements.
- Adjust the before and after slides as needed and test the changes again.
- Start with the before slide and test the *Morph* transition to the after slide in *Slide Show* view.

5-22 *Morph* transition "after" slide

3. Apply a *Morph* transition between two slides with limited matching text.

- Display a slide with bulleted text such as in the previous before slide.
- Display the next slide with shapes that includes a few of the same words on both the before and after slides.
- Click **Morph** [*Transitions* tab, *Transition to This Slide* group] on the after slide and select the **Characters** *Effect Options*.
- Click **Preview** [*Transitions* tab, *Preview* group] and the text from the before slide will separate leaving only the text that flows into position for the after slide (Figure 5-23).
- Start with the before slide and test the *Morph* transition to the after slide in *Slide Show* view.

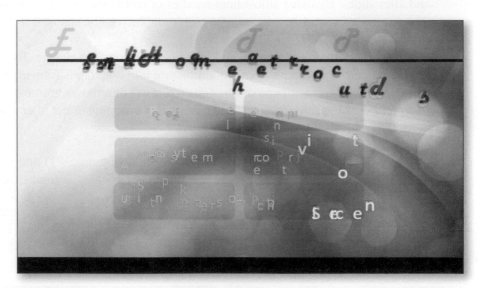

5-23 *Morph* transition as the *Character Effect* causes letters to float from one position into another

In this second example, the completed slide (Figure 5-24) is first designed with shapes and pictures for the after slide. That slide is duplicated and the new thumbnail is moved before the original slide. Then objects are moved and other changes made to create the before slide (Figure 5-25).

## ▶ HOW TO: Use the Morph Transition to Animate Objects

1. Prepare two slides for a *Morph* transition.
   - Display the "after" slide and complete its design using a combination of text, shapes, and photographs as needed.
   - Select the slide thumbnail and press **Ctrl+D**. In this case, the duplicate thumbnail is moved before the "after" slide (see Figure 5-24).
2. Display the "before" slide and complete your choice of the following changes.
   - Change shape color, styles, shape effects, picture effects, or rotation as needed.
3. Move objects into their start positions which may be outside the slide (see Figure 5-25).

5-24 *Morph* transition "after" slide

5-25 *Morph* transition "before" slide with object start positions outside the slide and size, color, and rotation changes

4. Select the "after" slide.
5. Click **Morph** [*Transitions* tab, *Transition to This Slide* group], click **Effect Options**, and select **Objects**.
   - Click **Preview** [*Transitions* tab, *Preview* group] to test the changes (Figure 5-26).
   - Adjust the before and after slides as needed and test the changes again.
6. Start with the before slide and test the *Morph* transition to the after slide in *Slide Show* view.

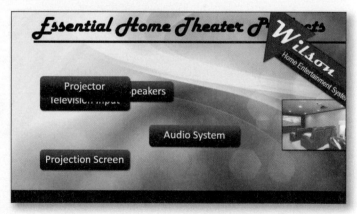

5-26 *Morph* transition *Objects* effect option causes shapes to float from one position into another

Since all slide changes occur at the same time with the *Morph* transition, complex animation sequences will require several slides to control when movement or other changes occur. You can add animation effects that appear after the *Morph* transition changes are complete. Do not add animation prior to applying the *Morph* transition because the transition may not work correctly. Also, remember that not all slide objects must change.

## PAUSE AND PRACTICE: POWERPOINT 5-1

For the "Leaders Under 40" annual recognition ceremony, Allen Wilson has prepared a slide show about the success and services of his family-owned business, Wilson Home Entertainment Systems. The presentation features a theater-like, countdown effect leading to a red curtain that opens as a transition to the title slide. For this project, you create complex animations with multiple slide objects and the *Morph* transition.

File Needed: ***BringingHollywoodHome-05.pptx***
Completed Project File Name: ***[your initials] PP P5-1.pptx***

1. Open the ***BringingHollywoodHome-05*** presentation and resave it as [your initials] PP P5-1.

2. Animate a list and dim text.
   a. Display slide 5 and, select the bulleted list placeholder.
   b. Click the **Add Animation** button [*Animations* tab, *Advanced Animation* group] to open the gallery. Choose the **Float In** *Entrance* effect.
   c. Click the **Effect Options** button [*Animations* tab, *Animation* group] and note that **By Paragraph** is already selected. Each bulleted item and related subpoints will appear together.
   d. Click the **launcher** [*Animations* tab, *Animation* group] to open the *Float Up* dialog box.
   e. Click the **After Animation** drop-down list arrow and select the **dark gray** color (Figure 5-27).
   f. Click **OK** to close the dialog box.

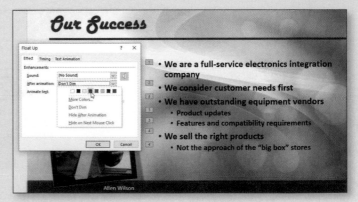

5-27 Text color will dim to the selected color after animation

3. Use the *Animation Painter*.
   a. Select the animated list on slide 5 and click the **Animation Painter** button [*Animations* tab, *Advanced Animation* group].
   b. Press **Page Down** so the *Animation Painter* remains active as you move to another slide.
   c. Display slide 6 and click the list to apply this animation.

4. Rearrange animation order using the *Animation Pane* for a countdown shape on slide 1. Ten boxes have large numbers that are stacked in the center of the slide on a circular shape. One box with no numbers is on top.

a. Display slide 1 and click the **Animation Pane** button [*Animations* tab, *Advanced Animation* group].
b. Increase the *Animation Pane* width so you can see the names for the eleven text boxes.
   • The names in the *Animation Pane* list each item as a "TextBox" followed by two numbers.
   • The first number was assigned as each text box was created.
   • After the colon, the second number shows the text in each box, which is also a number.
   • *TextBox13* is a black box only and it has no numbers.
   • The timing has been set to create a countdown sequence as each number fades in the *Exit* animation.
      • The numbers are not in the correct order.
c. Select **TextBox13** in the *Animation Pane* list and click the **Reorder Up** button to move it to the top of the list.
d. Click the **Reorder Up** and **Reorder Down** buttons as necessary to rearrange the remaining animated items in descending order (**TextBox11:10** to **TextBox 2:1**) below *TextBox13* (Figure 5-28).
e. Select **TextBox13** again and click the **Preview** button [*Animations* tab, *Preview* group] to test the animation.

5. Create a trigger to start the animation sequence.
   a. Select **TextBox13** in the *Animation Pane* list. Right-click and choose **Timing** to open the *Fade* dialog box.
   b. Click the **Triggers** button. By default, **Animate as part of click sequence** is applied.
   c. Click the **Start effect on click of** drop-down list arrow and scroll down to select the **5-Point Star 12** (Figure 5-29).
   d. Click **OK** to close the dialog box.
      • Select **TextBox 11:10** in the *Animation Pane* list and change *Delay* to 04:00 [*Animations* tab, *Timing* group].
   e. Click the **Slide Show** button [*Status* bar]. Test the animation by clicking the star on the lower left of the slide.
      • Press **Esc** to exit *Slide Show* view.

6. Animate chart elements.
   a. Display slide 7 and select the area chart.
      • This chart has one data series and the area for that series is filled with a picture.
   b. Click the **Add Animation** button [*Animations* tab, *Advanced Animation* group] to open the gallery. Select the **Wipe** *Entrance* effect.
   c. Click the **Effect Options** button [*Animations* tab, *Animation* group] and choose the *Direction* **From Bottom**. Click the **Effect Options** button again and choose the *Sequence* of **By Series**.
      • This option displays the chart background elements before the data series area.
   d. Change *Duration* to **5.00** seconds [*Animations* tab, *Timing* group].
   e. Select the arrow on the chart. Click the **Add Animation** button, select the **Wipe** *Entrance* effect, and the **From Left** *Effect Option*. Change the *Start* option to **After Previous**.

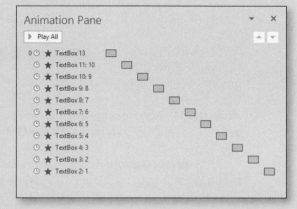

5-28 Animated objects are arranged in descending order

5-29 The *Trigger* is the *5-Point Star 12*

f. Select the arrow, if necessary, and repeat step 6e to apply the **Teeter** *Emphasis* effect (Figure 5-30).

g. Click **Preview** [*Animations* tab] to test the animation.

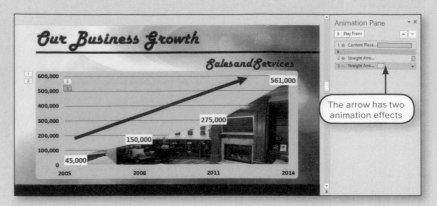

5-30 Completed chart animation

7. Animate a *SmartArt* graphic.

a. Display slide 9 and select the **SmartArt** graphic.

b. Click the **Add Animation** button [*Animations* tab, *Advanced Animation* group] to open the gallery. Select the **Grow & Turn** *Entrance* effect.

c. Click the **Effect Options** button [*Animations* tab, *Animation* group] and choose the *Sequence* of **One by One**.

d. Click **Preview** [*Animations* tab] to test the animation.

8. Apply two animation effects that display together on one shape.

a. Display slide 10 and select the "**Receiver**" shape. Click the **Add Animation** button [*Animations* tab, *Advanced Animation* group] to open the gallery. Select the **Grow & Turn** *Entrance* effect.

b. Change *Start* to **After Previous** [*Animations* tab, *Timing* group].

c. Click the **Add Animation** button again and choose **More Motion Paths** to open the *Change Motion Path* dialog box. Select the **Arc Down** *Motion Path* effect [*Lines-Curves* category] (Figure 5-31). Click **OK**.

d. Change *Start* to **With Previous**.

- A line appears with a green triangle marker indicating the beginning point of the *Motion Path* animation (its start position).
- A red triangle marker indicates the ending point of the *Motion Path* animation (moving from left to right).

e. Click the **Effect Options** button [*Animations* tab, *Animation* group] and choose **Reverse Path Direction** (moving from right to left).

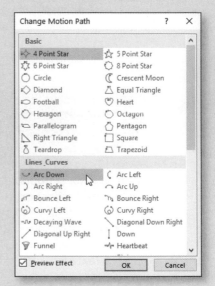

5-31 *Change Motion Path* dialog box

9. Use the *Animation Painter* to create an animation sequence.

a. Select the animated shape and double-click the **Animation Painter** button.

b. Click all other shapes to apply the same animation effects. Each shape moves as you apply the animation to it (Figure 5-32).

c. Press **Esc** to turn off the *Animation Painter*.

10. Create an animated sequence including a custom path.

a. Display slide 13. Select the text on the right (Figure 5-33) and click the **Add Animation** button [*Animations* tab, *Advanced Animation* group]. Select the **Grow & Turn** *Entrance* effect.

b. Select the **red oval** positioned over "Peoria" on the map.

- Click the **Add Animation** button and select the **Appear** *Entrance* effect. Change *Start* to **After Previous**.
- Click the **Add Animation** button again and select the **Spin** *Emphasis* effect. Click the **Effect Options** button [*Animations* tab, *Animation* group] and choose **Two Spins**. Change *Start* to **With Previous**, *Duration* to 03.00 and *Delay* to 01.00.

5-32 The animation sequence plays automatically

c. Select the **car** and move it near "Waukegan" at the top of the map.
- Click the **Add Animation** button and select the **Appear** *Entrance* effect. Change *Start* to **After Previous**.
- Click the **Add Animation** button again, scroll down the gallery, and select the **Custom Path** *Motion Paths* effect.
- Draw a path going left to "De Kalb" and then down to the oval around "Peoria" and double click to stop drawing the path (see Figure 5-33). Change *Start* to **With Previous** and *Delay* to **05.00**.
- Close the *Animation Pane*.

5-33 Animation sequence with a custom motion path

11. Use a *Morph* transition to animate.
(If *Morph* is not available with your software, skip step 11.)
   a. Display slide 14. Select the slide thumbnail and press **Ctrl+D**. The new slide 15 will be the "after" slide.
   b. Select the "Feature Presentation" image on slide 14 and change the following:
   - Click the **Rotate** button [*Picture Tools Format* tab, *Arrange* group] and select **More Rotation Options** to open the *Format Picture* pane. Rotate it – **180°**.
   - Change the *Height* to **1"** and the *Width* automatically changes.
   - Close the *Format Picture* pane.
   - Drag this image to the lower left outside the slide.
   c. Display slide 15. Click **Morph** [*Transitions* tab, *Transition to This Slide* group], click **Effect Options**, and then select **Objects**.
   d. Click **Preview** [*Transitions* tab, *Preview* group] to test the changes (Figure 5-34).

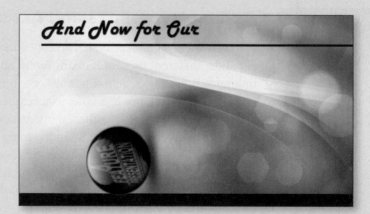

5-34 *Morph* transition with movement, rotation, and size change

12. Test the animation in *Slide Show* view.

13. Save and close the presentation (Figure 5-35).

5-35 PP P5-1 completed

# Adding Hyperlinks and Action Buttons

A *hyperlink* is a connection between two locations. It enables you to move quickly to a different slide, different presentation, different application, or even a web site. You can assign the linking action to text, action buttons, or objects.

Use a hyperlink, for example, to access a series of slides that you plan to show during a presentation only if there is audience interest or if time permits. Hyperlinks enable interactivity for either the presenter or for an individual viewing a slide show independently.

This feature is especially valuable for kiosk presentations where an individual user controls how the presentation is viewed. For example, you can create a slide with a table of contents or list of presentation topics using text or shapes. Then assign a hyperlink action to each of the items to create a menu of choices. When a user clicks one of these items during the presentation, the user is taken directly to the series of slides for that topic. At the end of the slides for that topic, a hyperlink can return the user to the menu slide where he or she can choose another topic. This navigation ability of returning to the main menu is available throughout the presentation by creating a hyperlink on the *Slide Master*.

## Create Text Hyperlinks

You can create a text hyperlink from one word or several words. During the slide show, a user clicks this text to jump to the destination. With text hyperlinks, the linked text automatically has an underline and the text displays in a different color than other text. After a user clicks a text hyperlink, the text color changes again because the text is a "followed hyperlink." You cannot change hyperlink colors directly on the slide. Use the *Create New Theme Colors* dialog box to change colors for the *Hyperlink* and *Followed Hyperlink* options.

### ▶ HOW TO: Create and Use Text Hyperlinks

1. Select the text for your link and click the **Hyperlink** button [*Insert* tab, *Links* group] (or press **Ctrl+K**) to open the *Insert Hyperlink* dialog box.

2. Choose **Place in this document** under *Link to* on the left side (Figure 5-36) so the *Select a place in this document* list box displays the current slide numbers and names.

3. Choose the slide number and title to which you want to link. Click **OK**.

   - The linked text on the slide is underlined and displays in a different color.
   - If you are creating a table of contents or menu slide, repeat this process for each item in your list.

4. Test each link in *Slide Show* view to be sure the correct slide displays.

5. Type the slide number for your menu slide and press **Enter** to return to that slide.

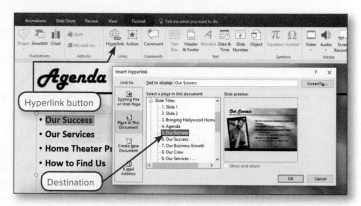

5-36 *Insert Hyperlink* dialog box

## Create Object Hyperlinks with ScreenTips

You can also hyperlink shapes or pictures. For example, you can create a series of shapes with identifying text to serve as a table of contents or a menu for your topics. Each shape or object can include hyperlinks to the appropriate slides in your presentation.

You can also add a *ScreenTip* to a hyperlink. A *ScreenTip* is text that displays when the user points to a hyperlink. A *ScreenTip* can provide more information than the shape displays or indicate where the link will go. Grouped objects cannot be hyperlinked.

### ▶ HOW TO: Hyperlink from Objects and Display ScreenTips

1. Select the first shape or picture to be linked. Click the **Hyperlink** button [*Insert* tab, *Links* group] or press **Ctrl+K** to open the *Insert Hyperlink* dialog box.

2. Choose **Place in This document** under *Link to* on the left side.

   - The *Select a place in this document* list box displays the current slide numbers and names.

3. Choose the slide number and title to which you want to link.

4. Click the **ScreenTip** button in the upper right corner of the dialog box.

   • The *Set Hyperlink ScreenTip* dialog box opens (Figure 5-37).

5. Type appropriate text in the *ScreenTip* box.

   • This text will appear when you point to the hyperlink during a slide show (Figure 5-38).

6. Click **OK** to close the *Set Hyperlink ScreenTip* dialog box; click **OK** again to close the *Insert Hyperlink* dialog box.

7. Repeat steps 1–5 for each shape that should link in your presentation.

8. Test each link in *Slide Show* view to be sure the correct slide opens.

9. Type the slide number in *Slide Show* view for your menu slide and press **Enter** to return to your menu slide to test another link.

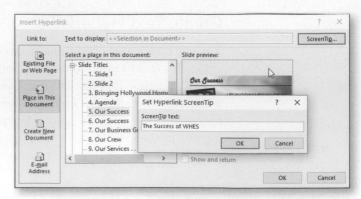

5-37  *Set Hyperlink ScreenTip* dialog box

5-38  *ScreenTip* example

## Create Action Buttons

The *Shapes* gallery includes a category of shapes called ***Action Buttons***. You can draw and format these shapes as you would any other shape, but usually action buttons are shown in a small size. As soon as you draw one of these shapes, the *Action Settings* dialog box automatically opens with a suggested hyperlink destination such as *Previous*, *Next*, *Beginning*, *Home*, and others. You can customize these options and control what happens during a slide show if the shape is clicked (called *Mouse Click)* or if you just point to the shape (called *Mouse Over.*)

A common use for action buttons is to provide a way to move quickly back to a menu where a user can select another topic. You can place the buttons on the last slide in a series, or you could place them on a *Slide Master* layout, where they are visible throughout a presentation.

▶ **HOW TO:** Create Action Buttons

1. Select the slide where you want to create an action button.

2. Click the **Shapes** button [*Insert* tab, *Illustrations* group] to open the *Shapes* gallery. Select a shape from the *Action Buttons* category (Figure 5-39).

5-39  *Action Buttons* in the *Shapes* gallery

3. Draw a small rectangle such as the *Home* shape shown in Figure 5-40. The *Action Settings* dialog box automatically opens.

   • Select **Hyperlink to:** on the *Mouse Click* tab and click the list box arrow. Choose **Slide** to open the *Hyperlink to Slide* dialog box (Figure 5-41).

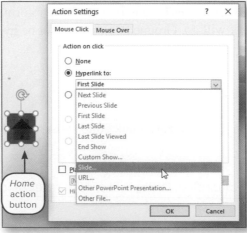

5-40  *Action Settings* dialog box

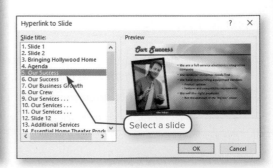

5-41  *Hyperlink to Slide* dialog box

- Select the slide for your link.
- Click **OK**.

4. Click **OK** after options are selected to close the *Action Settings* dialog box.

5. Provide navigation back to the menu slide from other slides as needed.

- If you have several slides to link, copy the action button and paste it on each slide.
- If you want navigation options throughout a slide show, create the action buttons on the appropriate *Slide Master* layout.

6. View your slide show and check the links to be sure they function correctly.

- If you need to change the action button on your slide, select it and then click the **Action** button [*Insert* tab, *Links* group] to open the *Action Settings* dialog box.

## Link to Other Sources

Your slide show can link to other sources such as a different presentation, files from another application, or a web page.

▶ **HOW TO:** Link to Other Sources

1. Display the slide where you need a link and select the text or shape for your hyperlink.

2. Click the **Hyperlink** button [*Insert* tab, *Links* group] or press **Ctrl+K**. The *Insert Hyperlink* dialog box opens.

3. Choose **Existing File or Web Page** under the *Link to* heading on the left (Figure 5-42).

4. Link to a file by following these steps:

- In the *Look in* box, navigate to the file location and select the file you want to open.
- The file name is added to your list. Note that the application icon precedes the file name.

*Or*

5. Link to a web page by following these steps:

- Copy the entire web address for the page to which you want to link.
- Paste the web address in the *Address* list box on the *Insert Hyperlink* dialog box.

5-42 *Insert Hyperlink* dialog box

6. Click the **ScreenTip** button and type appropriate text.

7. Click **OK** to close the *Set Hyperlink ScreenTip* dialog box. Click **OK** again to close the *Insert Hyperlink* dialog box.

8. View your slide show and check the links to be sure that they work correctly and the appropriate files or web pages open.

9. Click the PowerPoint button on the *Taskbar* to return to your slide show after working in a different file or web page.

If you display your presentation on a different computer, links can be broken. It is a good idea to save all presentation files in the same folder. Then you can copy the entire folder for use on a different computer. If you are linking to other application files or to web pages, you need to reestablish the links after you open your slide show on the different computer.

## PAUSE & PRACTICE: POWERPOINT 5-2

For this Pause & Practice project, you continue to work with the Wilson Home Entertainment Systems (WHES) presentation and create a menu of presentation topics with object hyperlinks to the appropriate slides, add action buttons on the *Slide Master* to control navigation, and include a text hyperlink to a web page.

File Needed: *[your initials] PP P5-1.pptx*
Completed Project File Name: *[your initials] PP P5-2.pptx*

1. Open the *[your initials] PP P5-1* presentation and save it as [your initials] PP P5-2.

2. Display slide 4. Assign hyperlinks to shapes to create a menu of presentation topics on the "Agenda" slide. Be sure to select each shape and not just the text on the shape.
   a. Select the "Our Success" shape and click the **Hyperlink** button [*Insert* tab, *Links* group] or press **Ctrl+K** to open the *Insert Hyperlink* dialog box.
   b. Choose **Place in This Document** under *Link to* on the left side so the *Select a place in this document* list box displays the current slide numbers and names. Choose slide title **5. Our Success**. Click **OK**.
   c. Repeat steps 2a–b to hyperlink each of the remaining menu shapes on slide 4 to its respective slide in the presentation (Figure 5-43):

5-43 *Insert Hyperlink* dialog box

| Menu Shape | Hyperlink to Slide |
|---|---|
| Our Services | 9. Our Services . . . |
| Home Theater Products | 10. Essential Home Theater Products |
| How to Find Us | 13. Slide 13 |

   d. Click each menu shape in *Slide Show* view to be sure the link opens the correct slide. From each of these slides, type **4** and press **Enter** to return to the slide menu.

3. Create navigation controls with action buttons on the *Slide Master*.
   a. Click the **Slide Master** button [*View* tab, *Master Views* group].
   b. Select the first *Slide Master* layout, *Office Theme Slide Master: used by slide(s) 1-16*.
   c. Click the **Shapes** button [*Insert* tab, *Illustrations* group] to open the *Shapes* gallery.
      • Select the **Forward or Next** action button (Figure 5-44).
      • Draw a small rectangle anywhere on the slide. You will move it into position later.

5-44 *Forward or Next Action Button in* the *Shapes* gallery

- The *Action Settings* dialog box automatically opens with the *Mouse Click* tab displayed.
- The **Hyperlink to**: list box automatically shows **Next Slide** because you selected that shape.
- Click **OK** to close the *Action Settings* dialog box.

d. Repeat step 3c for the following two additional action buttons:

| Action Button | Hyperlink to |
| --- | --- |
| *Previous* | Previous Slide |
| *Home* | Slide . . ., and then choose 4. Agenda |

e. Select the three action buttons and change their size (*Height* **.5"** and *Width* **.5"**).

f. Move the three action buttons to the bottom of the slide and arrange them evenly on the right (Figure 5-45).

g. Click the **Close Master View** button [*Slide Master* tab, *Close* group].

h. View your slide show and check the links to be sure that movements are correct.

5-45 *Action Buttons* arranged on the *Slide Master* layout

4. Create a text hyperlink with a *ScreenTip* to link to a web page.

a. Display slide 6. Select the text "**CEDIA (Custom Electronic Design and Installation Association)**."

b. Click the **Hyperlink** button [*Insert* tab, *Links* group]. Select **Existing File or Web Page**.

c. Type http://www.cedia.org/ in the *Address* box.

d. Click the **ScreenTip** button in the upper right corner of the dialog box. The *Set Hyperlink ScreenTip* dialog box opens.

e. Type Link to CEDIA @ http://www.cedia.org in the *ScreenTip* text box.

f. Click **OK** to close the *Set Hyperlink ScreenTip* dialog box. Click **OK** again to close the *Insert Hyperlink* dialog box.

g. Test the *ScreenTip* and the hyperlink to the CEDIA web page in *Slide Show* view.

5. Save and close the presentation (Figure 5-46).

5-46 PP P5-2 completed

# Inserting Audio and Video Content

Including an audio recording in your presentation can be an effective way to share a speech, a testimony, or discussion from an expert. Or you may want to play music before your presentation as people enter the room.

Seeing a video may be the best way for your audience to understand your message. Video is effective for showing time-based and situation-based conditions. Video can also convey non-verbal information that is impossible to portray in a text-only presentation. Video combines both audio and visual components, and it can appeal to emotions and stimulate responses.

When you use video, avoid visual clutter with a simple slide design. Use text to label and credit sources when appropriate. Any formatting you apply should work well with your background graphics and other consistently used elements in your presentation.

Your computer system must have a sound card and speakers to present audio or video content. Audio and video files greatly increase your presentation file size. Digital video is made of individual frames (like pictures) that are played back rapidly to create the illusion of real-time motion. (You may have noticed these frames on YouTube videos when the slider at the bottom of the video is dragged.) Both digital audio and video are encoded to standardize data for storage and transmission. The files are compressed to reduce file size and various formats are used for different purposes.

The online playback rate has been 30 frames per second (fps) for many years, but video and web technologies continue to evolve. Today 60 fps is possible to record video with a high definition camcorder and view with playback devices such as HDTVs, computer monitors, tablets, and phones. This faster rate creates a more lifelike video. However, 60 fps is difficult to achieve for streaming online because of limitations in transfer rates and network bandwidth.

PowerPoint supports many audio and video file formats, which are listed in the following table. For best results, use *.m4a* audio files and *.mp4* videos files. If you use a file conversion program, you can convert audio and video files from a different format to one that will play in PowerPoint. Problems can occur if the required *codec* (compressor/decompressor) is not installed on your computer or if a file is not recognized by your version of Microsoft Windows. In *SLO 5.6: Formatting, Optimizing, and Compressing Media*, you learn about PowerPoint features to improve playback.

## Supported Audio and Video File Formats

| File Format | Extension | More Information and Common Uses |
|---|---|---|
| **Audio** | | |
| MPEG-4 file | .m4a, .mp4 | Moving Pictures Expert Group, encoded with Advanced Audio Coding. |
| MP3 file | .mp3 | MPEG Audio Layer 3. Files are compressed. |
| WAV file | .wav | Windows Audio File. Audio is saved as sound waves and file sizes can vary significantly. |
| WMA file | .wma | Windows Media Audio. Files are compressed with Microsoft Windows Media Audio codec; commonly used to distribute recorded music on the web. |
| MIDI file | .mid or .midi | Musical Instrument Digital Interface. Standard format used for musical instruments, synthesizers, and computers. |
| AIFF file | .aiff | Audio Interchange File Format. Files are not compressed so file sizes are large. |
| AU file | .au | Audio UNIX. Used for UNIX computers and the web. |

| Video | | | |
|---|---|---|---|
| MP4 file | .mp4, .m4v, .mov | Video file, encoded with H.264 compression and Advanced Audio Coding audio (MPEG-4 AVC). Commonly used format. | |
| Movie file | .mpg or .mpeg | Moving Picture Experts Group. An evolving set of standards for video and audio compression. | |
| Windows Media file | .asf | Advanced Streaming Format. Stores synchronized data used to stream audio and video content. | |
| Windows Media Video file | .wmv | Windows Media Video. Uses a codec to compress audio and video content requiring minimal storage space. | |
| Windows Video file | .avi | Audio Video Interleave. Common format that compresses audio and video content with a wide variety of codecs | |
| Adobe Flash file | .swf | Adobe Flash Media file. Common format for web graphics with animations and interactivity. | |

## Insert an Audio or Video File

The methods for inserting digital audio and video are very similar. When you insert audio or video files, they become objects in your presentation and are saved with the presentation. Audio and video objects can play automatically when a slide appears or a user can activate them with a click.

## ▶ HOW TO: Insert an Audio or Video File

1. Select the slide where you want to insert audio or video.

2. Click the **Audio** or **Video** button [*Insert* tab, *Media* group] and choose *Audio on My PC* or *Video on My PC*.

3. Locate the audio or video file on your computer, select the file, and click **Insert**.

   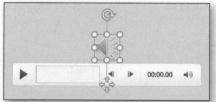
   5-47 Audio object with media controls

   5-48 Video object with media controls

   - *Audio:* An icon that looks like a speaker appears on your slide. When the speaker icon is selected, media controls display (Figure 5-47).
   - *Video:* The first frame or a black fill displays in a rectangle on your slide. When the rectangle is selected, media controls display (Figure 5-48). The size and shape of the rectangle will vary depending on the resolution and aspect ratio of the video.

4. Drag the audio or video object to an appropriate position on the slide.

5. Adjust video size as needed. Depending on how a video was made, you may be able to increase its size without too much distortion. Experiment until you are satisfied with the results.

If you want to hide media controls during your presentation, deselect the **Show Media Controls** checkbox [*Slide Show* tab, *Set Up* group].

## Insert a Video Using the Embed Code

Recall that in *SLO 3.3: Linking to an Online Video* you learned how to search for and link to files from YouTube using the *Insert Video* dialog box. You can also link to files on your *OneDrive* or paste ***embed code*** from YouTube videos. The actual video is not saved in your presentation. The embed code saves information necessary to play the video—its location, name, and playback instructions.

YouTube displays embed codes through a link below a video. You can copy the embed code and paste it in the *Insert Video* dialog box in PowerPoint. Or perhaps you found a video at a time when you were not using PowerPoint. Then you could copy and save the embed code and then paste it in the *Insert Video* dialog box later. This technique provides a convenient way to save the video information for future use. The video will play in PowerPoint as long as it is still available online.

---

### ▶ HOW TO: Insert a YouTube Video Using Embed Codes

1. Open the www.youtube.com site with the video you want to use in your presentation.

2. Below the video, click **Share** (Figure 5-49) and then click **Embed**.

5-49 *YouTube Share*

3. Control how the video will playback before copying the embed code.

   - Below the video, select from the available video sizes.
   - Choose other options as appropriate (Figure 5-50) and the instructions are added to the embed code.
   - Click the *Embed* text box and press **Ctrl+A** to select all of the code (Figure 5-51). Press **Ctrl+C** to copy the code.

5-50 **Select playback options**

4. Open PowerPoint and display the slide where you want to insert the video.

5. Click the **Video** button [*Insert* tab, *Media* group] and select **Online Video**. The *Insert Video* dialog box opens.

5-51 **Copy embed code**

6. Paste the embed code in the *From a Video Embed Code* box (Figure 5-52) and click the **right arrow** (or press **Enter**).

7. Test the video playback.

   - In *Normal* view, click the **Play** button [*Video Tools Format* tab, *Preview* group] and then press the **Play** button on the video.
   - In *Slide Show* view, click the **Play** button on the video.

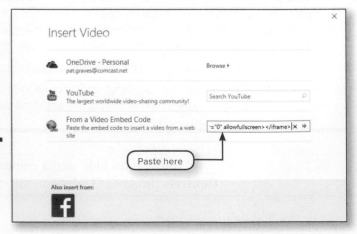

5-52 **Paste copied embed code**

# Adjusting Audio and Video Playback Settings

By default, audio and video files play in *Slide Show* view when you click them on the slide or click the **Play** button on a linked video. Therefore, the audio or video object must be visible on the slide. When you point to these objects during your slide show, the ***media controls*** become visible. Options are slightly different between inserted and linked videos. This section will focus on inserted video and audio files. Media controls display a timeline with *Play/Pause*, *Move Back*, *Move Forward*, and *Mute/Unmute* buttons. The elapsed time appears, also.

With both audio and video objects, two tabs become available for editing. The *Audio Tools Format* tab and the *Video Tools Format* tab provide options that are similar to the *Picture Tools Format* tab. Both the *Audio Tools Playback* tab and the *Video Tools Playback* tab provide unique options for customizing how the audio and video objects play on a slide. Editing options for both audio and video objects include the following:

- Specify *Automatic* or *On Click* playback.
- Bookmark to designate specific locations.
- Trim to reduce playback time.
- Fade so the video object gradually appears or disappears.
- Adjust or mute volume.
- Hide the object in *Reading* view or *Slide Show* view when it is not playing.
- Play in full screen size if that option is available.
- Select loop or rewind options.

With video files, playback at full-screen size may be possible. Video clarity depends on how the video was created and its resolution. If an audio or video object is used in conjunction with animation effects, you can adjust the playback sequence on the *Animation Pane*.

## Add and Remove Bookmarks

You can add a ***bookmark*** to an audio or video object at a specific location on the media controls timeline so you can jump to a point of interest to focus on that content rather than starting playback at the beginning. A bookmark can also activate animation effects.

---

▶**HOW TO:** Add and Remove Bookmarks

1. Select the audio or video object and the *Audio Tools Playback* tab or the *Video Tools Playback* tab (Figure 5-53) becomes available.

5-53 *Video Tools Playback* tab

2. Move your pointer over the media controls timeline without clicking and you can see how the timing seconds change (Figure 5-54).
3. Click the timeline to advance the audio or video object to that position (Figure 5-55).
   - To the left of where you click, the timeline becomes gray.
   - If you click the **Play** button, the audio or video will begin playing from this position.

5-54 Timeline showing the video seconds from the start

5-55 *Timeline* showing the seconds at the current position where the video is stopped

4. Click the **Move Back** or **Move Forward** buttons on the media controls to adjust the stopped position of the audio or video object.

   • These buttons move the stopped position in increments of .25 seconds.

5. Click the **Add Bookmark** button [*Audio Tools Playback* tab or *Video Tools Playback* tab, *Bookmarks* group] and a bookmark circle appears on the timeline.

   • Yellow shows the bookmark is selected (Figures 5-56 and 5-57).
   • You can also add a bookmark while the audio or video is playing.
   • The audio or video object stops when you click the **Add Bookmark** button.

5-56 *Timeline* showing a video bookmark

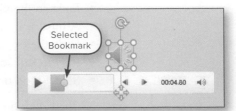

5-57 *Timeline* showing an audio bookmark

6. Repeat if you want to add a second bookmark. Bookmarks are numbered in sequence.

7. To remove a bookmark, select the bookmark and click the **Remove Bookmark** button [*Audio Tools Playback* tab or *Video Tools Playback* tab, *Bookmarks* group].

A trigger starts an animation sequence. A trigger is either an object on the slide that is clicked or a bookmark. For example, if you create two bookmarks on a video, the first one can trigger an object's entrance effect during playback and a second bookmark can trigger the object's exit effect. The object, or text, enters and leaves the video at preplanned times. You can use this technique to call attention to key parts of the video.

▶ **HOW TO:** Trigger an Animation with a Video Bookmark

1. Create one or more animation effects on the slide where you display your video.

2. Create a bookmark on the timeline where you want the animation effect to begin and a second one if you want the animation to end at a specific timeline position.

3. Click the **Animation Pane** button [*Animations* tab, *Advanced Animation* group] to open the *Animation Pane*.

4. Move the video to the top of the list in the *Animation Pane* (Figure 5-58).

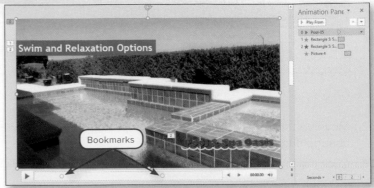

5-58 Slide and *Animation Pane* list before adding triggers

- In *Slide Show* view, these settings would play the entire video first and then the text box and logo would appear.

5. Select the animation effect that you want to start when the video playback reaches the first bookmark.

6. Click the **Trigger** button [*Animations* tab, *Advanced Animation* group], select **On Bookmark**, and select the bookmark that will start the animation (Figure 5-59).

   - The *Start* option changes to **On Click** because the trigger controls the animation.

7. Test the animation trigger by playing the video.

   - The *Animation Pane* list in Figure 5-60 shows that the pool video starts automatically, the text box enters at *Bookmark 1* and then exits at *Bookmark 2* when the company logo appears.

8. Add an animation exit effect triggered with another bookmark so the animation ends before the video ends.

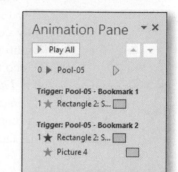

5-59 *Bookmark 1* is the animation trigger

5-60 *Triggers* control animation

The procedure just described will trigger animation sequences with bookmarks on audio objects.

When you create several bookmarks to control entrance and exit animations, the bookmarks may get out of sequence. The bookmark numbering does not matter as long as the bookmark for the beginning and ending positions correctly match each entrance and exit effect.

Selecting **Play Full Screen** [*Video Tools Playback* tab, *Video Options* group] will cause shapes that overlay the video to not display. Therefore, to achieve the effect of the animated shapes in Figure 5-61 where the text box and logo appear over the pool video at full-screen size, simply stretch the inserted video to fill the slide.

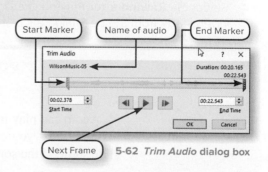

5-61 Video object stretched to fill the slide

## Trim and Fade

The ***Trim Audio*** and ***Trim Video*** features enable you to shorten playback time by removing seconds from the beginning or end of an audio or video object. You cannot trim seconds from within an audio or video object. Trimming only affects the way an object plays in your slide show; the original object file is not affected.

### ▶ HOW TO: Trim Audio and Video

1. Select the audio or video object you want to edit and click the **Trim** button [*Audio Tools Playback* tab or *Video Tools Playback* tab, *Editing* group] to open the *Trim Audio* dialog box (Figure 5-62) or *Trim Video* dialog box (Figure 5-63).

2. Adjust the green start marker or the red end marker on the timeline to remove seconds. Use one of the following methods:

   - Drag the start or end marker on the timeline (Figures 5-62 and 5-63).

5-62 *Trim Audio* dialog box

- Type the specific number of seconds (or click the arrows) in the *Start Time* or *End Time* boxes.
- Select the marker and click the *Previous Frame* or *Next Frame* buttons.

5-63 *Trim Video* dialog box

*Fade In* causes an audio to gradually reach full volume or a video to gradually come into focus. *Fade Out* causes an audio to gradually decrease in volume or a video to gradually blur out. Enter a number for *Fade In* or *Fade Out* duration seconds [*Video Tools Playback* tab, *Editing* group]. A longer duration time creates a more gradual fade.

## Playback Options

Additional options on the *Audio Tools Playback* tab and the *Video Tools Playback* tab control volume and determine if audio and video objects start automatically when the slide appears or on click so that you can start playback by clicking the audio or video object during the presentation. Both audio and video objects can loop until stopped or rewind after playing.

The following examples first illustrate the commands that apply to both tabs, then the commands that are unique to each tab.

▶ **HOW TO:** Control Volume, Start, and Rewind Options

1. Select the audio or video object.
2. Choose options as needed [*Audio Tools Playback* tab, *Audio Options* group or *Video Tools Playback* tab, *Video Options* group] (Figure 5-64):
   - **Volume:** *Low, Medium, High,* or *Mute.*
   - **Start:** *On Click* or *Automatically.*
3. Select the **Loop until Stopped** checkbox and the audio or video will replay as long as the current slide displays.
4. Select the **Rewind after Playing** checkbox and the audio or video starts from the beginning each time it is played.

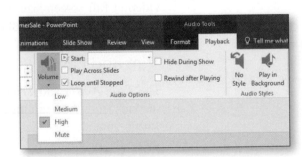

5-64 *Audio Options*

Audio can play in the background while several slides change. If you set the audio to play automatically, you can hide the sound icon so it does not appear on the screen during your slide show. If the sound icon is hidden, then you must create a trigger to start playback.

You can hide video while it is not playing or expand video to play at full screen size during playback. Always check the video playback at full screen size. If the resolution of the video file is too low, the video may seem distorted or blurry when displayed in the larger screen size.

▶ **HOW TO: Control Play and Hide Options**

1. Select the audio object.
2. Choose options as needed [*Audio Tools Playback* tab, *Audio Options* group]:
   - **Play Across Slides:** Audio plays throughout the presentation as slides advance. This option has the same effect as *Play in Background* [*Audio Tools Playback* tab, *Audio Styles* group].
   - **Hide During Show:** The audio icon is invisible in *Reading* view or *Slide Show* view. When using this option, you should have the audio play automatically.
3. Select the video object.
4. Choose options as needed [*Video Tools Playback* tab, *Video Options* group]:
   - **Play Full Screen:** Video expands to fill the screen.
   - **Hide During Show:** The video object is invisible in *Reading* view or *Slide Show* view. When using this option, you should have the video play automatically.

If you need audio to play only while a specific sequence of slides displays, click the launcher [*Animations* tab, *Animation* group] to open the *Play Audio* dialog box (Figure 5-65). Control when the audio stops playing by selecting from *On click*, *After current slide*, or *After* where you enter the specific number of slides to show before the audio stops. The *Start* default setting is *From beginning*, but you could enter the specific number of seconds to play only a portion of your audio from that position.

The shortcuts listed in the following table work with an inserted video file but not with an online video file.

5-65 *Play Audio* dialog box

## Audio and Video Shortcuts

| Press | Action |
|---|---|
| **Alt+Q** | Stop playback |
| **Alt+P** | Play or pause |
| **Alt+End** | Go to the next bookmark |
| **Alt+Home** | Go to the previous bookmark |
| **Alt+Shift+Page Down** | Seek forward |
| **Alt+Shift+Page Up** | Seek backward |
| **Alt+Up** | Increase sound volume |
| **Alt+Down** | Decrease sound volume |
| **Alt+U** | Mute sound |

## Recording Audio and Adding Sound to Animation

SLO 5.5

Your computer must have a sound card, microphone, and speakers installed to record and test audio. You will need external speakers to amplify the audio in a large room.

### Record Audio on a Slide

If you have a microphone with your computer, you can use *Record Audio* to create an audio clip of your own voice that is saved in the presentation.

▶ **HOW TO:** Record Audio

1. Select the slide where you want to insert the audio.
2. Click the **Audio** button [*Insert* tab, *Media* group] and select **Record Audio** to open the *Record Sound* dialog box (Figure 5-66).
3. Type a name for your audio clip in the *Name* box.
4. Click the **Record** button to begin recording and speak into the microphone.
5. Click **OK** when your recording is complete. The audio object appears on your slide.
6. Click the **Play** button to review your recording.
7. Test the audio in *Slide Show* view by clicking the audio object.

5-66 *Record Sound* dialog box

### Add Sound to an Animation

In the dialog box for each animation effect, you can name an audio file to play with the animation effect. When audio is included with an animated object, the audio playback is controlled by how the object is animated such as to begin playing when the animated object appears on the slide. An audio object does not show on the slide and the audio does not show as a separate object in the *Animation Pane* list.

▶ **HOW TO:** Add Sound to an Animation

1. Select the object to be animated.
2. Click an animation effect from the gallery or click the **Add Animation** button [*Animations* tab, *Advanced Animation* group] and choose an effect.
3. Click the **launcher** [*Animations* tab, *Animations* group] to open a dialog box for the particular animation effect that you chose (Figure 5-67).
   - The available options can vary.
4. Click the **Sound** list arrow on the *Effect* tab and scroll down the list to select one of the default sounds.
   - Click **Other Sound** at the bottom of the list to open the *Add Audio* dialog box (Figure 5-68).
   - By default, the file type is *Audio Files* and all file formats in your collection may not be shown. Change the file type to *All Files* (Figure 5-69).

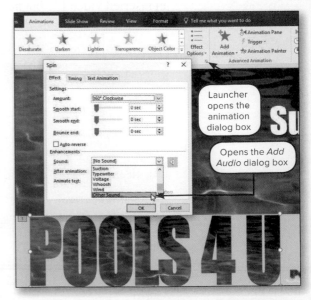

5-67 *Spin Animation* dialog box

5-68 *Add Audio* dialog box showing *.wav* files only

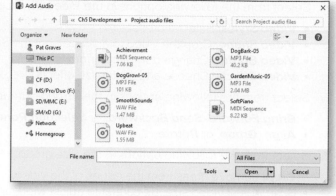

5-69 *Add Audio* dialog box showing all files

5. Locate and select the file you want to use.
6. Check the volume level by clicking the **Volume** button beside the audio name and adjust it if necessary.
7. Adjust other options as needed for *Settings* or *Timing*. Click **OK** to close the dialog box.
8. Test your animation to make sure your sound plays appropriately.

# SLO 5.6

## Formatting, Optimizing, and Compressing Media

Formatting options for audio and video objects are similar to options for pictures. When your presentation is complete, you optimize media to avoid playback issues and assure compatibility with other devices. Then you compress the media to reduce the file size of your presentation.

### Format an Audio and Video Object

The *Audio Tools Format* tab and the *Video Tools Format* tab have commands to change the appearance of audio and video objects like those on the *Picture Tools Format* tab. You can change colors, styles, borders, shapes, and cropping.

Audio objects are usually small, so changes to them may be less obvious. However, you can substitute a different picture for the default speaker icon to feature the audio in an interesting way. A video can have a ***poster frame***, which is a picture displayed at the beginning of the video.

---

### ▶ HOW TO: Format a Video

1. Select the video object you want to format.
2. Select the *Video Tools Format* tab.
3. Select from the following options from the *Adjust* group:
   - ***Corrections:*** Change contrast and brightness.
   - ***Color:*** Change to a monotone shade of theme colors.
   - ***Poster Frame:*** Insert a picture that will display as a preview image of the video before it plays (Figure 5-70).
   - ***Reset Design:*** Remove changes to the video by restoring it to its original design.

5-70 Select an image for a video poster frame

4. Select from the following options in the *Video Styles* group:
   - **Video Styles:** Select a preset style.
   - **Video Shape:** Crop the video to a shape from the *Shapes* gallery.
   - **Video Border:** Change border color or weight.
   - **Video Effects:** Choose and customize effects.

5. Select from the following options in the *Arrange* group:
   - **Bring Forward**, **Send Backward**, or **Selection Pane**
   - **Align**, **Group**, or **Rotate**

6. Select from the following options in the *Size* group:
   - **Crop:** Remove areas from the edges of the video.
   - **Size:** Adjust video size. Be careful to adjust width and height in accurate proportions to maintain the original aspect ratio.

## Optimize Media Compatibility

When you use audio and video in your presentation, you may face problems if you change computers to deliver your presentation. To avoid playback issues, you can optimize the media files for compatibility.

▶ **HOW TO:** Optimize Media Compatibility

1. Click the **File** tab and select **Info**.
   - The *Optimize Media Compatibility* option appears when files can be optimized.
   - It shows a summary of files that can be optimized (Figure 5-71).

2. Click the **Optimize Compatibility** button.
   - When optimization is complete, a summary is provided (Figure 5-72).

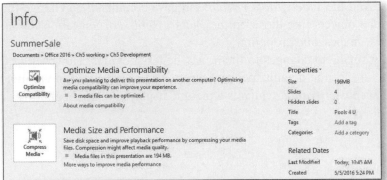

5-71 *Optimize Compatibility* and *Compress Media* options

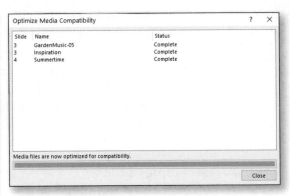

5-72 *Optimize Media Compatibility* dialog box showing results

3. Click **Close**.

## Compress Media

Audio and video files greatly increase the file size of your presentation. Compress the files to improve playback performance and to reduce presentation file size. Different levels of quality are available.

## ▶HOW TO: Compress Media

1. Create a copy of your original file before you perform a compression in case you are not satisfied with the result of a compression.
2. Click the **File** tab and select **Info**.
   - If files can be compressed, the **Compress Media** option appears showing the total media file size and how compression could be helpful (see Figure 5-71).
   - The way you plan to present and display your slide show dictates the level of compression you should choose.
3. Click the **Compress Media** button and choose from the following options (Figure 5-73):
   - ● *Presentation Quality*
   - ● *Internet Quality*
   - ● *Low Quality*
4. Review the summary of compression results.
   - In the example shown in Figure 5-74, the media file size was 176 MB.
   - Media file size was reduced 99.8 MB using *Presentation Quality*.
   - Although not shown, other options reduced more (*Internet Quality* reduced 142.7 MB; *Low Quality* reduced 147.8 MB).
5. Click **Close**.
6. Test your presentation to determine if the clarity of your slides is satisfactory for the way you plan to display them.
   - If you are not satisfied, click the **Undo** option.
   - You can also close the presentation without saving and return to your original file.

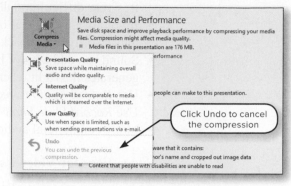

5-73 *Compress Media* options

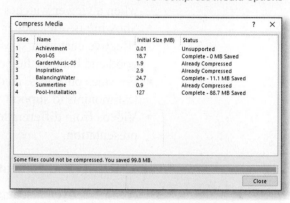

5-74 *Compress Media* dialog box

---

SLO 5.7

# Integrating Rich Media

Sounds and images can enrich a presentation. Animation can reinforce content through movement and timing. The first step in using media effectively in PowerPoint is carefully selecting content specifically for your presentation. You may find online content to use at no cost, or you may need to purchase suitable content. For some situations, you may want to create your own content. If you are preparing an educational or informative presentation designed for a single user, you could incorporate interactivity so the user can choose which content to view and in what order as well as link to other related sources.

The following lists provide ideas for using rich media in your presentations, guidelines to consider if you capture your own video content, and suggestions for effectively introducing video content during a presentation.

### Suggestions for Audio Use

- Recorded sound must be loud enough for your audience to hear. Therefore, the effective use of sound in a presentation depends on a number of factors. For example, you use sound differently when you are presenting to a large group in a conference room and when you are speaking to an individual using your tablet or notebook computer.

- Use music to energize or to create a relaxing mood.
- Usually, it is best to only use music when you are not speaking during your presentation. It is very difficult to talk over music.
- If you include a series of images displayed as a photo album, you might choose to play music softly in the background as the slides change.
- Sound can add a bit of humor. Carefully consider what you use, however, so that it generates the right reaction.
- Use *Record Audio* to record your voice, or a colleague's voice, to be played on one slide. Use *Record Slide Show* to include audio for every slide in the presentation.
- Many commercial audio file collections are available online.

### Suggestions for Video Use

- A situation too complicated to explain in words can sometimes be instantly understood when a viewer watches a video.
- Showing is often better than simply telling. For example, when training employees about effective customer service practices, a series of video clips of transaction examples, both good and bad, would be helpful.
- For sales purposes, record a video displaying product information or customer testimonials to support your product.
- Videos from different locations can be sent electronically and inserted in your presentation.

### Interactivity and Animation

- An interactive presentation is set up to respond to user input.
- A menu with hyperlinks and other navigation options allows users to have control for how they view the content.
- Interaction can help users to learn because they are actively engaged with the presentation content.
- Animation should be logical, intuitive, and not disorienting.

### Video Quality

- The quality of a video depends on the hardware, software, and type of compression used to capture the video.
- Video files are recorded at different pixel resolutions and commonly play at a rate of approximately 30 frames per second to show smooth, realistic movement. Depending on how the video is recorded, it may or may not be clear when displayed at full-screen size.
- Be sure the video displays in a large enough size for the entire audience to see.
- The video should contain enough information for the audience to understand the point that you are making without showing unnecessary information.
- Limit the length of your video. If you need to show a longer video, consider breaking it into multiple parts that you can integrate into your discussion.

### Delivery Techniques When Using a Video

- Unless you are using a video for its surprise factor, introduce the video to your audience before you play it.
- Be sure that you face your audience when you introduce a video. Let your audience know what to look for in a video. Point out highlights or a change you want them to observe.
- Always have your playback settings prepared so the video begins playing from the correct location and ends appropriately.

- Move your pointer away from the video so the pointer is not on screen while the video plays.
- Refrain from looking at the projection screen when the video is playing. It's better for you to watch the response of your audience so you can react to this when the video is finished.
- After the video is finished, review what your audience should have seen. Be sure your audience understands why you played the video. Engage the audience in discussion about the video.

## PAUSE & PRACTICE: POWERPOINT 5-3

For *Pause & Practice 5-3*, you insert a video file that was created *from Pause & Practice: PowerPoint 4-4* into the Wilson Home Entertainment Systems (WHES) presentation and position it on a theater screen picture. You insert an audio file and adjust playback settings then bookmark the video and make the bookmark a trigger for the audio. You also record audio on a slide and add sound to an animation.

Files Needed: *[your initials] PP P5-2.pptx*, *Furnishing-05.mp4*, *WilsonMusic-05.mp3*, and *WHES-Start-05.jpg*
Completed Project File Name: *[your initials] PP P5-3.pptx*

1. Open the file *[your initials] PP P5-2* and save it as [your initials] PP P5-3.

2. Insert a video.
   a. Display slide 16. Click the **Video** button [*Insert* tab, *Media* group] and choose **Video on My PC**.
   b. Locate your student data files, select **Furnishing-05**, and click **Insert**.
      - This video is 32.47 seconds long.
      - It was recorded in low quality because it will be displayed in a small size.
   c. Decrease the video's size (*Height* **3.06"**).
   d. Drag the video object over the white area of the projection screen in the picture.
   e. Drag a sizing handle on the side to stretch the video (*Width* approximately **6.16"**) so it covers the white area (Figure 5-75).

5-75  Video inserted and resized

3. Format the video object with a poster frame.
   a. Select the **Furnishing-05** video object.
   b. Click the **Poster Frame** button [*Video Tools Format* tab, *Adjust* group] and click **Image from file**.
   c. Locate your student data files, select **WHES-Start-05**, and click **Insert** (Figure 5-76).
   d. View the slide in *Slide Show* view and click the **Play** button on the video timeline to test the video.

5-76  Video with a poster frame

4. Insert an audio file to play while the video plays.
   a. Select slide 16 and click the **Audio** button [*Insert* tab, *Media* group]. Select **Audio on My PC** and the *Insert Audio* dialog box opens.
   b. Locate your student files and select ***WilsonMusic-05.mp3*** that is 23.00 seconds long. Click **Insert**.
   c. Select **Loop until Stopped** and **Hide During Show** [*Audio Tools Playback* tab, *Audio Options* group].

5. Trim the audio on slide 16 to remove time at the end.
   a. Click the **Trim Audio** button [*Audio Tools Playback* tab, *Editing* group].
   b. Change the **End Time** to 00:16.600. Click **OK**.
      • The music will play twice during the video playback.
   c. Move the audio object to the right side of the slide.

6. Add a bookmark to the video.
   a. Select the video object on slide 16 and click the **Video Tools Playback** tab.
   b. Move your pointer on the media controls timeline to approximately 02.00 seconds and click to stop the video in that position.
      • Click the **Move Back** or **Move Forward** buttons if necessary.
   c. Click the **Add Bookmark** button [*Audio Tools Playback* tab or *Video Tools Playback* tab, *Bookmarks* group] and a bookmark circle appears on the timeline.
   d. Repeat this step to put another bookmark at the end of the video.

7. Trigger the audio to play and stop when the video playback reaches the bookmarks.

5-77 *Trigger*

   a. Click the **Animation Pane** button [*Animations* tab, *Advanced Animation* group] to open the *Animation Pane*.
   b. Select the audio object.
   c. Click the **Trigger** button [*Animations* tab, *Advanced Animation* group], select **On Bookmark**, and then select **Bookmark 1** (Figure 5-77).
   d. Click the **Add Animation** button [*Animations* tab, *Advanced Animation* group] and select **Stop** and a second "WilsonMusic" name appears in the *Animation Pane* list.
   e. Select this audio object, click the **Trigger** button, select **On Bookmark**, and select **Bookmark 2**.
   f. Test the audio trigger by clicking the **Preview** button [*Animations* tab, *Preview* group].

8. Start the video automatically, rewind, and fade out.
   a. Select the video object on slide 16. For the *Start* option [*Video Tools Playback* tab, *Video Options* group], choose **Automatically** and then click **Rewind after Playing**.
   b. Click the **Fade Out** spin box up arrow so *Duration* is 02.00 [*Video Tools Playback* tab, *Editing* group].
   c. Test the video by clicking the **Preview** button [*Animations* tab, *Preview* group].
      • The video ends with the poster frame because it rewinds after playing.

9. Record an audio clip. (Skip this step if your computer cannot record sound.)
   a. Display slide 8. Click the **Audio** button [*Insert* tab, *Media* group] and select **Record Audio** to open the *Record Sound* dialog box.
   b. Delete the text in the *Name* box and type Dream.
   c. Click the **Record** button and speak into your microphone as you read the quoted text on the slide.
   d. Click **OK** when your recording is complete. The audio object appears on your slide.

e. Click the **Play** button [*Audio Tools Playback* tab, *Preview* group] to review your recording.

f. Change the *Start* option to **Automatically** [*Audio Tools Playback* tab, *Audio Options* group] and select **Hide During Show**.

g. Select slide 7 and click the **Slide Show** button [*Status* bar] and advance to slide 8 to confirm that the audio starts automatically and that the audio object is hidden. Press **Esc**.

10. Animate text to appear after the audio plays.

a. Select the "**If you can dream it . . .**" text box on slide 8.

b. Click the **Wipe** *Entrance* effect [*Animations* tab, *Animation* group].

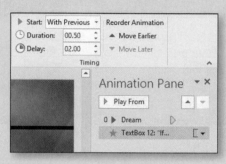

* Click **Effect Options** and choose **From Left**.
* Change *Start* to **With Previous** [*Animations* tab, *Timing* group].
* Change *Delay* to 02.00.

c. Click the **Animation Pane** button [*Animations* tab, *Advanced Animation* group] if the pane is not open.

* Verify that the *Dream* audio effect is above the *TextBox* in the *Animation Pane* list (Figure 5-78).

d. Test your animation in *Slide Show* view to make sure your sound plays appropriately.

5-78 Animation settings for the recorded audio

e. Close the *Animation Pane*.

11. Optimize and compress the media.

a. Click the **File** tab and select **Info**.

* The *Optimize Compatibility* option shows a summary of files that can be optimized (Figure 5-79).

b. Click the **Optimize Compatibility** button.

* When optimization is complete, a summary is provided.
* Click **Close**.

c. Click the **Compress Media** button and select the **Presentation Quality** option.

* When compression is complete, a summary of the results is provided (Figure 5-80).
* Click **Close**.

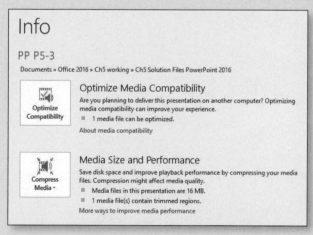

5-79 *Optimize Compatibility* and *Compress Media* options

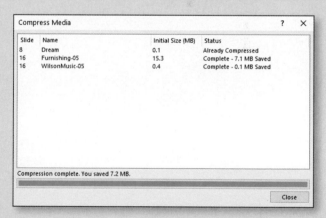

5-80 *Compress Media* dialog box showing results

12. Save and close the presentation (Figure 5-81).

5-81  PP P5-3 completed

# Chapter Summary

**5.1** Apply animation with multiple effects and complex sequences including *Morph* transitions (p. P5-293).

- You can apply multiple animation effects and synchronize their timing.
- Dialog boxes for each animation effect provide additional options not available on the *Animations* tab.
- Adjust animation sequence using the **Animation Pane**.
- When applied to an object, a **trigger** starts an animation.
- The **Animation Painter** copies animation settings and applies them to another object.
- Animate chart elements by series or by category.
- Animate *SmartArt* graphics so the shapes appear in phases.
- With **Motion Path** animation, you apply a predesigned path or a custom path to move an object from one position to another.
- A **Custom Path** is a Motion Path animation option that enables you to draw the path that an animated object will follow.
- Use the **Morph** transition effect on multiple slides to create animation.

**5.2** Add hyperlinks and action buttons to create navigation and to link to other sources (p. P5-310).

- A **hyperlink** is a connection between two locations. In PowerPoint, you can hyperlink to another slide, presentation, application, or web page.
- Both text and objects such as shapes or pictures can hyperlink.
- A menu or table of contents created with text or shapes and hyperlinks makes a presentation interactive by giving the viewer control over how the presentation is viewed.
- A **ScreenTip** provides text information that appears when you point to a hyperlink.
- **Action buttons** have preset hyperlinks that you can customize.
- When you click a PowerPoint hyperlink to a web page, the default browser opens and the web page appears. Click the **PowerPoint** button on the *Taskbar* to return to PowerPoint.

- Hyperlinks to external sources will be broken if you move your presentation to a different computer.

**5.3** Insert audio and video content (p. P5-316).

- PowerPoint supports a variety of audio and video file formats.
- Inserted audio or video files become objects in your presentation and are saved with the presentation.
- Online videos are linked to the online source; only the linking information is saved with the presentation.
- If an online video owner has made the **embed code** public, you can copy the code and paste it in the *Insert Video* dialog box to create a link to that video.

**5.4** Adjust audio and video playback settings using bookmark, trim, and fade options (p. P5-319).

- By default, audio and video files play when clicked but can be made to play automatically.
- You can **bookmark** a video to designate specific locations for start times or to trigger an animation sequence during playback.
- Use the **Trim Audio** or **Trim Video** feature to reduces playback time by removing seconds from the beginning or ends of the file.
- Use the **Fade In** or **Fade Out** features to cause audio and video files to gradually appear or disappear during playback.
- Playback changes made for an audio or video file do not affect the original file.

**5.5** Record audio and add sound to animation (p. P5-324).

- Your computer must have a sound card, microphone, and speakers installed to record and test sounds.
- Record your voice in a presentation with **Record Audio**.
- When you create an audio recording, an audio icon appears on the slide.
- Add sound to animation by using the dialog box for each different animation effect. An audio object does not display on the slide.

P5-333

**5.6** Format, optimize, and compress media (p. P5-325).

- Formatting options for video and audio are similar to the options for formatting pictures.
- A *poster frame* provides a preview image for a video.
- Crop video objects to remove unneeded areas or crop to a shape.
- To change the appearance of a video, use *video styles* and change the border and effects as needed.
- Use *Optimize Media Compatibility* to avoid playback issues if you change computers.
- Use *Compress Media* to reduce media size and, therefore, presentation file size.

**5.7** Integrate rich media effectively (p. P5-327).

- Carefully select audio and video content to enhance and add value to your presentation message.
- Add interactive elements when designing for user control.
- Apply animation effects that are logical and aid meaning.

## Check for Understanding

The SIMbook for this text (within your SIMnet account) provides the following resources for concept review.

- Multiple choice questions
- Matching exercises
- Short answer questions

## Guided Project 5-1

An associate at Central Sierra Insurance is giving a talk to a student organization about common disasters and what individuals can do to prepare themselves. For this presentation, you work with animation effects and timings as well as insert and format an audio file. You include hyperlinks to other sources and optimize and compress the revised presentation.
[Student Learning Outcomes 5.1, 5.2, 5.3, 5.4, 5.6, 5.7]

---

Files Needed: *DisastersHappen-05.pptx*, *Wind-05.mp3*, and *Storm-05.png*
Completed Project File Name: *[your initials] PowerPoint 5-1.pptx*

---

### Skills Covered in This Project

- Animate a list and dim text.
- Reorder an animation sequence.
- Create a trigger.
- Use the *Animation Painter*.
- Create a hyperlink.
- Create an action button.
- Hyperlink to another source.

- Apply a *Morph* transition.
- Insert an audio.
- Trim, fade, and bookmark an audio object.
- Format an audio object.
- Optimize media compatibility.
- Compress media.

---

1. Open the presentation *DisastersHappen-05*. Save the presentation as [your initials] PowerPoint 5-1.

2. Apply two animation effects that display together.
   a. Display slide 2. Select the "**Will you be prepared?**" text.
   b. Click the **Add Animation** button [*Animations* tab, *Advanced Animation* group] to open the gallery.
   c. Click **More Entrance Effects** and select the **Flip** effect [*Exciting* group]. Click **OK**.
      - No change is required for *Effect Options*.
      - Change *Start* to **With Previous** [*Animations* tab, *Timing* group].
      - Verify that *Duration* is **01.00**.
   d. Select the same text again. Click the **Add Animation** button again and choose the **Font Color** *Emphasis* effect.
      - Change *Start* to **With Previous**.
      - Change *Duration* time to 01.00 and the *Delay* to 02.00 so the color change is more gradual.
   e. Click the **Preview** button [*Animations* tab, *Preview* group] to test the animation.

3. Animate a list and dim text.
   a. Display slide 6 and select the **bulleted list** placeholder.
   b. Click the **More** button [*Animations* tab, *Animation* group] to open the *Animation* gallery. Choose the **Random Bars** effect.
      - No change is required for *Effect Options*.
   c. Click the **Animation Effect** launcher [*Animations* tab, *Animation* group] to open the *Random Bars* dialog box (Figure 5-82).

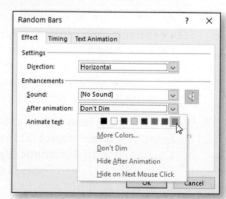

5-82 *Random Bars* dialog box

d. Click the **After Animation** drop-down arrow and select the **orange** color (last color on the right).

e. Click **OK** to close the dialog box and the color change appears.

f. Click the **Preview** button [*Animations* tab, *Preview* group] to test the animation.

4. Use the *Animation Painter*.

a. Select the **animated list** placeholder on slide 6.

b. Double-click the **Animation Painter** button [*Animations* tab, *Advanced Animation* group].

c. Press **Page Down** so the *Animation Painter* remains active and click the list on slide 7.

d. Continue to press **Page Down** and apply the animation to the lists on slides 8 and 9.

e. Press **Esc** to turn off the *Animation Painter*.

5. Fade and trim an audio file.

a. Display slide 3 and select the audio object (an alarm) on the left.

b. Change the *Fade In* and *Fade Out* times to 02.50 [*Audio Tools Playback* tab, *Editing* group].

c. Click **Trim Audio** [*Audio Tools Playback* tab, *Editing* group] to open the *Trim Audio* dialog box.

   • Drag the *End* marker to 00:08.00 on the audio timeline or type 00.08 (Figure 5-83).

   • Click **OK** to close the dialog box.

d. Click the **Play** button [*Audio Tools Playback* tab, *Preview* group] to test the audio.

5-83 *Trim Audio* dialog box

6. Insert an audio clip.

a. Display slide 5.

   • The design of slide 5 matches the design of slides 3 and 4.

   • Pictures and rotated text are grouped.

   • Pictures are aligned with slide edges, so the picture frame extends beyond the slide.

   • The two groups are animated separately using the *Blinds* animation effect.

b. Click the **Audio** button [*Insert* tab, *Media* group] and select **Audio on My PC**. The *Insert Audio* dialog box opens.

   • Locate your student files and select **Wind-05.mp3**. Click **Insert**.

   • Move the audio object to the left of the slide.

7. Set the start time, fade, trim, and bookmark an audio object.

a. Select the **audio object** on slide 5.

b. Change *Start* to **Automatically** [*Audio Tools Playback* tab, *Audio Options* group].

c. Change *Fade In* and *Fade Out* to 03.00 [*Audio Tools Playback* tab, *Editing* group].

d. Click **Trim Audio** [*Audio Tools Playback* tab, *Editing* group] to open the *Trim Audio* dialog box.

   • Drag the **End** marker to 00:16.00 on the audio timeline or type 00:16.

   • Click **OK** to close the dialog box.

e. Point to the audio object timeline and click at approximately 00:08.00 (Figure 5-84).

f. Click the **Add Bookmark** button [*Audio Tools Playback* tab, *Bookmark* group].

g. Click the **Play** button [*Audio Tools Playback* tab, *Preview* group] to test the audio.

8. Rearrange animation order and apply a trigger.

a. Click the **Animation Pane** button [*Animations* tab, *Advanced Animation* group] to open the *Animation Pane*.

b. Select **Group 8** in the animation list (left group on the slide).
   - Click the **Reorder Up** button so it is above *Group 5*.
   - Change *Start* to **With Previous** [*Animations* tab, *Timing* group].

c. Select **Wind-05** (the audio object).
   - Click the **Reorder Up** button twice so it is at the top of the animation list.
   - Change *Start* to **With Previous**.

d. Right-click **Group 5** in the *Animation Pane* list and select **Timing** to open the *Blinds* dialog box.
   - Verify that *Start* is **On Click**.
   - Click the **Triggers** button to display trigger options.
   - Select **Start effect on play of**, and **Wind-05 - Bookmark 1.** The name of the audio object automatically appears (Figure 5-85).
   - Click **OK** to close the dialog box.

e. Close the *Animation Pane*.

f. Click the **Slide Show** button on the *Status* bar to test the animation in *Slide Show* view.
   - Audio plays through the animation of both groups.

9. Format an audio object.

a. Select the **audio object** on slide 5.

b. Click **Change Picture** [*Audio Tools Format* tab, *Adjust* group] to open the *Insert Pictures* dialog box.

c. Browse to locate your student data files and select **Storm-05.** Click **Insert**.

d. Increase the audio object size (*Height* and *Width* **1"**) and position the object in the black area on the left of the slide (Figure 5-86).

10. Create a text hyperlink with a *ScreenTip* to link to a web page.

a. Select the text "**Federal Emergency Management Agency**" on slide 10.

b. Click the **Hyperlink** button [*Insert* tab, *Links* group].
   - The **Existing File or Web Page** option is selected.
   - Type http://www.fema.gov in the *Address* box.

c. Click the **ScreenTip** button in the upper right corner of the dialog box. The *Set Hyperlink ScreenTip* dialog box opens.
   - Type Link to FEMA @ http://www.fema.gov in the *ScreenTip* text box (Figure 5-87).
   - Click **OK** to close the *Set Hyperlink ScreenTip* dialog box

d. Click **OK** again to close the *Insert Hyperlink* dialog box.

11. Select the text "**American Red Cross**" and repeat steps 10b-d.

5-84 Bookmark position for the audio object

5-85 The *Trigger* controls when animation starts

5-86 Formatted audio object

P5-337

Address:    http://www.redcross.org
ScreenTip:  Link to American Red
                Cross @ http://www.
                redcross.org

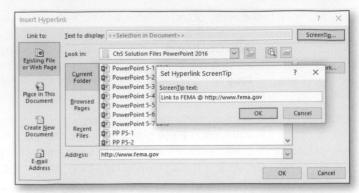

5-87 *Insert Hyperlink* **dialog box**

12. Test the *ScreenTip* and the hyperlink to both web pages in *Slide Show* view.

13. Assign hyperlinks to shapes to create links to presentation topics.
   a. Select the "**Disasters**" shape on slide 2. Click the **Hyperlink** button [*Insert* tab, *Links* group] or press **Ctrl+K** to open the *Insert Hyperlink* dialog box.
   b. Choose **Place in This Document** under *Link to* on the left side. Choose **Slide 3** in the *Select a place in this document* list box. Click **OK**.
   c. Repeat steps 13a–b to hyperlink the "Preparedness" shape to **Slide 6. Food Supplies**.
   d. Test each link in *Slide Show* view to be sure the correct slide opens. Type 2 and press **Enter** to return to the menu slide.

14. Insert an action button on the *Slide Master*.
   a. Click the **Slide Master** button [*View* tab, *Master Views* group].
   b. Select the first *Slide Master* layout.
   c. Click the **Shapes** button [*Insert* tab, *Illustrations* group] to open the *Shapes* gallery.
   d. Select the **Home** action button and draw a small rectangle (Figure 5-88). The *Action Settings* dialog box automatically opens.
      - Select **Slide . . .** in the *Hyperlink to* list box on the *Mouse Click* tab.
      - Select **Slide 2** In the *Hyperlink to Slide* dialog box (see Figure 5-88).
      - Click **OK** to close each dialog box.
   e. Change the action button size (*Height* and *Width* **.5"**).
   f. Move the action button to the lower left beside the footer placeholder.
   g. Click the **Close Master View** button [*Slide Master* tab, *Close* group].
   h. View your slide show and check the links to be sure that movements are correct.

5-88 *Action Settings* **to hyperlink**

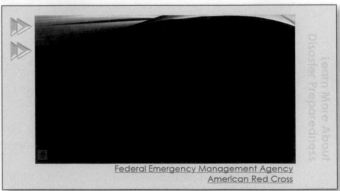

5-89 **Object positions for** *Morph* **transition**

15. Prepare slides for movement and apply the *Morph* transition. (If *Morph* is not available with your software, skip step 15.)
   a. Select slide 10 and press **Ctrl+D** to duplicate.
   b. Change the *Zoom* to **60%** so you can move objects off the slide.
   c. Select slide 10 and prepare it as the before slide (Figure 5-89).

- Select the **title**. Click the **Rotate** button [*Drawing Tools Format* tab, *Arrange* group] and select **Rotate Right 90°**. Move the title off the slide on the right.
- Move the two hyperlinked text boxes below the slide on the lower right.
- Move the two red shapes off the slide on the left near the top of the slide.
- Change the *Fill Color* [*Drawing Tools Format* tab, *Shape Styles* group] for the shapes to **Gold, Accent 3**.

d. Select slide 11, the after slide, and apply the transition.
- Click **Morph** [*Transitions* tab, *Transition to This Slide* group].
- Change *Duration* [*Transitions* tab, *Timing* group] to 03.00.

e. Test the transition in *Slide Show* view starting with slide 10.

16. Optimize and compress the media.
    a. Click the **File** tab and select **Info**.
       - The **Optimize Compatibility** option shows a summary of files that can be optimized (Figure 5-90).
    b. Click the **Optimize Compatibility** button.
       - When optimization is complete, a summary appears.
       - Click **Close**.
    c. Click the **Compress Media** button and select the **Presentation Quality** option.
       - When compression is complete, a summary of the results appears (Figure 5-91).
       - Click **Close**.

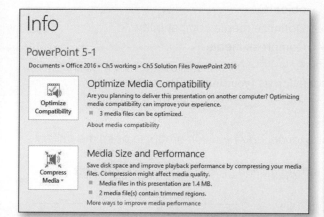

5-90 *Optimize* and *Media Size* information

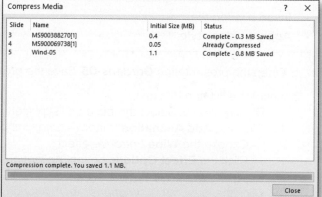

5-91 *Compress Media* dialog box with results

17. Save and close the presentation (Figure 5-92).

5-92 PowerPoint 5-1 completed

## Guided Project 5-2

Classic Gardens and Landscaping (CGL) has prepared a presentation about designing and installing custom gardens for a CGL exhibit at a home improvement show. The presentation includes pictures of gardens CGL has installed and features a scale drawing, a photo imaging plan, and a video of installed plantings. You use a variety of animation effects to display pictures and text, insert and format a video, and add music to the video playback.
[Student Learning Outcomes 5.1, 5.3, 5.4, 5.6, 5-7]

Files Needed: **Gardens-05.pptx**, **GardenPanorama-05.mp4**, and **GardenMusic-05.mp3**
Completed Project File Name: **[your initials] PowerPoint 5-2.pptx**

### Skills Covered in This Project

- Animate a list and dim text.
- Create an animation sequence and rearrange order.
- Use the *Animation Painter*.
- Animate a *SmartArt* graphic.
- Insert a video file.
- Apply a video style.

- Trim, fade, and bookmark a video object.
- Create a trigger.
- Insert an audio file.
- Hide, loop, and rewind video and audio objects.
- Optimize media compatibility.
- Compress media.

1. Open the presentation **Gardens-05**. Save the presentation as [your initials] PowerPoint 5-2.

2. Animate a list and dim text.
   a. Display slide 9. Select the bulleted list placeholder.
   b. Click the **Add Animation** button [*Animations* tab, *Advanced Animation* group] to open the gallery.
      - Choose the **Wipe** *Entrance* effect.
      - Click the **Effect Options** button [*Animations* tab, *Animation* group] and select **From Left** (*By Paragraph* is already selected).
   c. Click the launcher [*Animations* tab, *Animation* group] to open the *Wipe* dialog box.
      - Click the **After Animation** drop-down arrow and select the **dark red** color (Figure 5-93).
      - Click **OK** to close the dialog box.
   d. Adjust timing.
      - Change *Start* to **After Previous**.
      - Change *Duration* to 01.00.
      - Change *Delay* to 01.00.

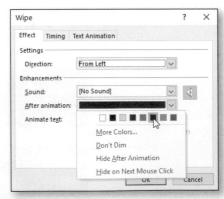

5-93 Dim text color

3. Apply multiple animation effects.
   a. Display slide 2. Select the picture on the left.
   b. Click the **Add Animation** button [*Animations* tab, *Advanced Animation* group] to open the gallery.
      - Select the **Fade** *Entrance* effect.
      - Change *Start* to **After Previous** [*Animations* tab, *Timing* group].
      - Change *Duration* to 02.00.
   c. Click the **Add Animation** button again.
      - Select the **Fade** *Exit* effect.
      - Change *Start* to **After Previous**.
      - Change *Duration* to 02.00.

- Change *Delay* to 02.00.
- Click the picture again so the *Animation Painter* becomes available.
  d. Double-click the **Animation Painter** button.
    - Click the middle picture and then the right picture to apply the same animation effects.
    - Press **Esc** to turn off the *Animation Painter*.
  e. Click the **Animation Pane** button and increase its size to see the timeline for all entrance and exit effects for this entire sequence (Figure 5-94).
  f. Select the **Picture 3** *Exit* effect (with a red star) in the *Animation Pane* list and press **Delete** so that picture remains on the slide until you advance to the next slide.

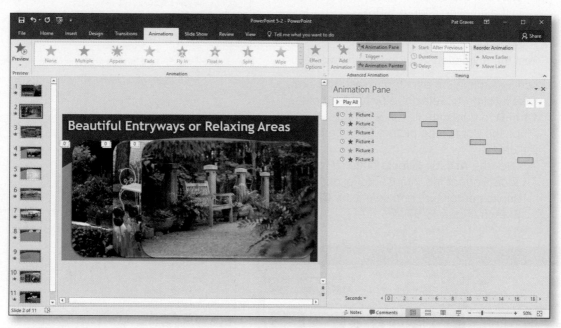

5-94 *Animation Pane* **expanded to show duration times for all effects**

4. Animate a *SmartArt* graphic.
  a. Display slide 10 and select the *SmartArt* graphic
  b. Click the **Add Animation** button [*Animations* tab, *Advanced Animation* group] to open the gallery.
    - Select the **Pulse** *Emphasis* effect.
    - Click the **Effect Options** button [*Animations* tab, *Animation* group] and choose the *Sequence* of **Level One by One**.
    - Change *Start* to **After Previous**.
    - Click **Preview** [*Animations* tab] to test the animation.

5. Apply animation effects and rearrange order.
  a. Select the larger picture on slide 10 behind the picture with red flowers.
  b. Click the **Add Animation** button [*Animations* tab, *Advanced Animation*].
    - Select the **Fade** *Entrance* effect.
    - Change *Start* to **After Previous** [*Animations* tab, *Timing* group].
    - Change *Duration* to 02.00.
    - Click the picture (greenhouse) again so the *Animation Painter* becomes available.
  c. Click the **Animation Painter** button to copy these settings and then click the top picture (woman with flower basket).
  d. Select the **Picture 2** *Entrance* effect in the *Animation Pane* list.
    - Click **Reorder Up** to move it above the *Diagram* effect.

e. Select **Picture 2** and click the **Add Animation** button.
- Select the **Fade** *Exit* effect.
- Change *Start* to **After Previous** [*Animations* tab, *Timing* group].
- Change *Duration* to 02.00.
- Click **Reorder Up** to move *Picture 2* above *Picture 3* (Figure 5-95).

f. Click the **chevron** icon to expand the "Diagram" animation.
- Review the contents to see how each shape in the *SmartArt* graphic appears in the timeline (Figure 5-96).
- Click the **chevron** icon again to collapse the list.

g. Test the animation in *Slide Show* view.

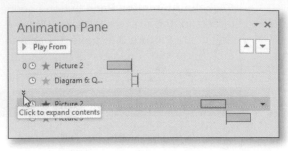

5-95 *Animation Pane* showing duration times and a collapsed list

6. Add an *Exit* animation effect to reveal a picture.

a. Display slide 11. Select the picture and press **Ctrl+D** to duplicate it.

b. Place the duplicated picture over the original picture.
- Click the **Artistic Effects** button [*Picture Tools Format* tab, *Adjust* group] on the duplicated picture and select the **Chalk Sketch** (Figure 5-97).

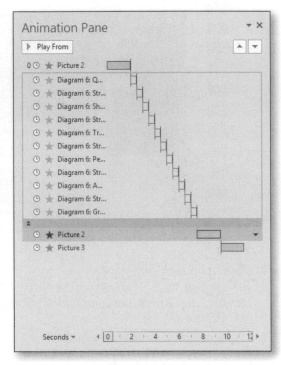

5-96 *Animation Pane* showing duration times and an expanded list

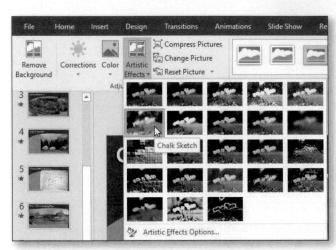

5-97 *Artistic Effects* gallery

c. Click the **Add Animation** button [*Animations* tab, *Advanced Animation* group].
- Select the **Fade** *Exit* effect.
- Change *Start* to **After Previous** [*Animations* tab, *Timing* group].
- Change *Duration* to 03.00.

d. Click **Preview** [*Animations* tab] to test the animation.
- The "Chalk Sketch" picture in grayscale gradually fades away revealing the original color picture.

7. Reposition pictures with animation.

a. Display slide 7. Select the four overlapping pictures that are animated.

b. Click the **Align** button [*Picture Tools Format* tab, *Arrange* group] and select **Align Center**.

c. Repeat to select **Align Middle**.

d. Move the four selected pictures up slightly and position them evenly on the slide.
e. Check the *Animation Pane* list and verify that the pictures are arranged in ascending order from *Picture 2* to *Picture 5*.
f. Click **Preview** [*Animations* tab] to test the animation.
g. Close the *Animation Pane*.

8. Insert a video and apply a video style.
   a. Display slide 8. Click the **Video** button [*Insert* tab, *Media* group] and choose **Video on My PC**.
   b. Locate your student data files, select **GardenPanorama-05**, and click **Insert**.
      - Decrease the video's size (*Height* **6"** and the *Width* will automatically adjust) [*Video Tools Format* tab, *Size* group].
      - Move the video down below the slide title.
   c. Click the **More** button on the *Video Styles* gallery [*Video Tools Format* tab, *Video Styles* group] and click the **Beveled Rounded Rectangle** style (*Moderate* category).

9. Adjust video playback options.
   a. Click the **Trim Video** button [*Video Tools Playback* tab, *Editing* group] (Figure 5-98).
      - Drag the *Start* marker or type **00:03.00** seconds.
      - Drag the *End* marker or type **00:30.00** seconds
      - This trim reduces the video from almost 35 seconds to 27 seconds.
      - Click **OK**.
   b. Type **03.00** for both *Fade In* and *Fade Out*.
   c. Change *Start* to **Automatically**.
   d. Select **Rewind after Playing**.
   e. Click **Send Backward** [*Video Tools Format* tab, *Arrange* group] and select **Send to Back** so the video is behind the two "cloud" shapes.
   f. View the video in *Slide Show* view.

10. Add bookmarks and trigger animated shapes.
    a. Click the timeline on the video object on slide 8 at approximately **05:00** seconds.
       - Click the **Add Bookmark** button [*Video Tools Playback* tab, *Bookmarks* group].
       - Repeat to add three more bookmarks at approximately **10.00**, **14.00**, and **20.00** seconds (Figure 5-99).
    b. Select the "cloud" shape on the left with the text, "Video captured in August."
    c. Click the **Add Animation** button [*Animations* tab, *Advanced Animation* group].
       - Select the **Fade** *Entrance* effect.
       - Click the **Trigger** button [*Animations* tab, *Advanced Animation* group], select **On Bookmark**, and select **Bookmark 1**.

5-98 Trimming the video to remove 8 seconds

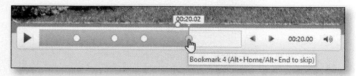

5-99 Four bookmarks added to the video timeline

d. Click the **Add Animation** button again.
   - Select the **Fade** *Exit* effect.
   - Click the **Trigger** button, select **On Bookmark**, and select **Bookmark 2**.
e. Repeat steps 10c–d for the "cloud" shape on the right with the text, "Different colors for every season."
   - Apply the **Fade** *Entrance* and *Exit* effects that are triggered by *Bookmark 3* and *Bookmark 4* (Figure 5-100).
f. Close the *Animation Pane*.

5-100 *Fade entrance and exit effects are triggered by bookmarks*

11. Insert an audio file to play while the presentation plays.
    a. Display slide 1. Click the **Audio** button [*Insert* tab, *Media* group] and select **Audio on My PC**. The *Insert Audio* dialog box opens.
    b. Locate your student files and select **GardenMusic-05.mp3**. Click **Insert**.
       - This audio file is 60.00 seconds long.
       - Change *Start* to **Automatically**.
       - Click the **Volume** button to change the volume level if necessary [*Audio Tools Playback* tab, *Audio Options* group].
       - Select **Play Across Slides**, **Loop until Stopped**, **Hide During Show**, and **Rewind after Playing** [*Audio Tools Playback* tab, *Audio Options* group] (Figure 5-101).

5-101 *Audio Options*

12. Adjust transition timings and change show type to a kiosk presentation.
    a. Click the *Transitions* tab.
    b. Deselect **On Mouse Click**. Select **After** and type 03.00 [*Transitions* tab, *Timing* group]. Click **Apply To All**.
    c. Select slide 9 and change the *After* time to 00:08.00. Repeat to apply the same time to slide 11.
    d. Click the **Set Up Slide Show** button [*Slide Show* tab, *Set Up* group] to open the *Set Up Show* dialog box.
    e. Select **Browsed at a kiosk (full screen)**. Click **OK** to close the dialog box.

13. Test all transitions and animations.
    a. Review the presentation in *Slide Show* view to be sure all settings are working correctly.
    b. Adjust timings as needed.
       • Speeds can vary on different computers, so you may need to increase or decrease some animation or transition timings.

14. Optimize and compress the media if options are available.
    a. Click the **File** tab and select **Info**.
    b. Click the **Optimize Compatibility** button.
       • When optimization is complete, a summary appears.
       • Click **Close**.
    c. Click the **Compress Media** button and select the **Presentation Quality** option.
       • When compression is complete, a summary appears.
       • Click **Close**.

15. Save and close the presentation (Figure 5-102).

5-102 PowerPoint 5-2 completed

# Guided Project 5-3

American River Cycling Club has many events and racing opportunities that are appropriate for members with different skill and ability levels. This presentation describes racing opportunities and team options. It includes a variety of animation effects and a formatted video.
[Student Learning Outcomes 5.1, 5.2, 5.3, 5.4, 5.6, 5.7]

Files Needed: ***ARCCPromotion-05.pptx*** and ***StartYoung-05.mov***
Completed Project File Name: ***[your initials] PowerPoint 5-3.pptx***

## Skills Covered in This Project

- Animate a list and dim text.
- Reorder an animation sequence.
- Create a trigger.
- Animate a *SmartArt* graphic.
- Create motion path animation.
- Hyperlink to another source.

- Insert a video file.
- Hide, loop, and rewind a video.
- Apply a video style.
- Optimize media compatibility.
- Compress media.

1. Open the presentation ***ARCCPromotion-05***. Save the presentation as [your initials] PowerPoint 5-3.

2. Animate a list and dim text.
   a. Display slide 2 and select the bulleted list placeholder.
   b. Click the **Add Animation** button [*Animations* tab, *Advanced Animation* group] to open the gallery.
      - Choose the **Zoom** *Entrance* effect.
      - Click the **Effect Options** button [*Animations* tab, *Animation* group] and choose **Slide Center**.
      - Verify that the **By Paragraph** option is already selected.
   c. Click the **launcher** [*Animations* tab, *Animation* group] to open the *Zoom* dialog box.
      - Click the **After animation** drop-down arrow and select the **blue** color.
      - Click **OK** to close the dialog box.

3. Apply multiple animation effects and adjust their sequence and timing.
   a. Display slide 5. Select the five groups that each contains a picture and a text box.
      - Since the pictures overlap, draw a selection rectangle or use the *Selection* pane [*Drawing Tools Format* tab, *Arrange* group] to select all five groups.
   b. Click the **Add Animation** button.
      - Select the **Wheel** *Entrance* effect.
      - Change *Start* to **After Previous**.
      - Change *Duration* to 02.50.
      - Animation tags appear with each grouped picture and this indicates the grouped pictures are still selected.
   c. Click the **Add Animation** button again.
      - Select the **Shrink and Turn** *Exit* effect.
      - Verify that *Start* is **After Previous**.
      - Change *Duration* to 01.50.
      - Change *Delay* to 3.00.
   d. Click the **Animation Pane** button [*Animations* tab, *Advanced Animation* group].

- The *Exit* effects appear below the *Entrance* effects (Figure 5-103).

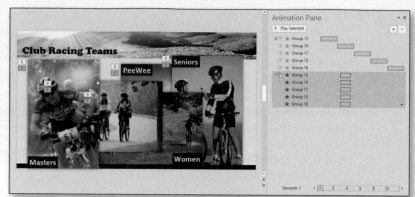

e. Select each *Exit* effect and click the **Reorder Up** button to rearrange the animations in ascending order with each group's *Exit* effect following the *Entrance* effect.
  - If you wish, resize the *Animation Pane* to see the duration for each effect (Figure 5-104), then resize the pane to its regular size.

5-103 *Exit* effects are after *Entrance* effects

f. Select the first group in the list and click the **Preview** button [*Animations* tab] to test the animation.

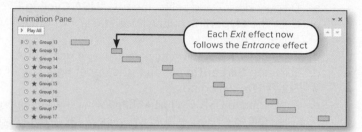

g. Close the *Animation Pane*.

5-104 Animation sequence changed

4. Animate a *SmartArt* graphic.
   a. Display slide 6 and select the *SmartArt* graphic.
      - Be sure you have selected the entire *SmartArt* graphic and not an individual shape within the *SmartArt* graphic frame.
   b. Click the **Add Animation** button [*Animations* tab, *Advanced Animation* group] to open the gallery.
      - Select the **Wipe** *Entrance* effect.
      - Click the **Effect Options** button [*Animations* tab, *Animation* group]. Select the *Direction* **From Top** and the *Sequence* of **One by One**.
      - Change *Start* to **After Previous**.
      - Change *Duration* to 01.00.
   c. Click the **Preview** button [*Animations* tab] to test the animation.

5. Apply multiple animation effects that display together on the same object.
   a. Display slide 1 and select the rider picture.
   b. Apply three effects as shown in the following table by clicking the **Add Animation** button [*Animations* tab, *Advanced Animation* group] each time to open the gallery and select an effect.
   c. For the third animation, click **More Motion Paths** and select the **S Curve 2** in the *Lines-Curves* category.
   d. Adjust *Timing* options for each effect as shown in the following table:

| Animation Effect | Effect Options | Start | Duration | Delay |
|---|---|---|---|---|
| Appear *(Entrance)* | | *After Previous* | 01.00 | 00.50 |
| Zoom *(Entrance)* | *Object Center* | *With Previous* | 10.00 | 00.00 |
| S Curve 2 *(Motion Path)* | | *With Previous* | 10.00 | 00.00 |

   e. Adjust marker positions.
      - Select the animated rider. Move the green triangle marker (the beginning point) of the *Motion Path* animation to the left of the slide.

- Move the red marker (the ending point) to the middle of the slide so the rider movement ends beside the title (Figure 5-105).

f. Click **Preview** [*Animations* tab] to test the animation.
   - Adjust the beginning and ending positions if necessary so it looks like the rider is approaching from the distant hill.

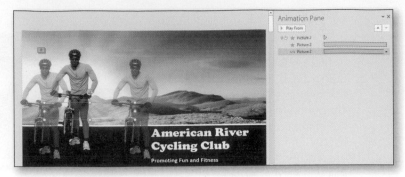

5-105 *Motion Path* beginning and ending positions

6. Create a text hyperlink with a *ScreenTip* to link to a web page.
   a. Display slide 7 and select the text **"USA Cycling."**
   b. Click the **Hyperlink** button [*Insert* tab, *Links* group]. Verify that the **Existing File or Web Page** option is selected.
   c. Type http://www.usacycling.org in the *Address* box.
   d. Click the **ScreenTip** button in the upper right corner of the dialog box to open the *Set Hyperlink ScreenTip* dialog box.
   e. Type Link to USA Cycling @ http://www.usacycling.org in the *ScreenTip* text box.
   f. Click **OK** to close the *Set Hyperlink ScreenTip* dialog box. Click **OK** again to close the *Insert Hyperlink* dialog box.
   g. Test the *ScreenTip* and the hyperlink to the USA Cycling web page in *Slide Show* view.

7. Insert a video and apply a style.
   a. Display slide 8. Click the **Video** button [*Insert* tab, *Media* group] and choose **Video on My PC**.
   b. Locate your student data files, select *StartYoung-05*, and click **Insert**.
   c. Position the video on the right side of the slide.
   d. Click the **Crop** button [*Video Tools Format* tab, *Size* group] and remove the black area at the top and bottom of the video.
   e. Increase the video's size (*Height* **3.5"** and *Width* will automatically adjust) [*Video Tools Format* tab, *Size* group].
   f. Click the **Drop Shadow Rectangle** [*Video Tools Format* tab, *Video Styles* group] (in the *Subtle* group) (Figure 5-106).
   g. View the slide in *Slide Show* view and click the **Play** button on the video timeline to test the video.

5-106 Video inserted, cropped, resized, and style applied

8. Add a trigger to play the video when the title is clicked.
   a. Select the **video object** on slide 8.
      - Select **Hide While Not Playing** [*Video Tools Playback* tab, *Video Options* group].
      - Verify that *Start* is **On Click**.
   b. Click the **Trigger** button [*Animations* tab, *Advanced Animation* group], select **On Click of**, and then select **Title 1**.
      - Change *Delay* to 00.50.
      - View the slide in *Slide Show* view. When the title animation ends, click the title to test that the trigger starts the video.

9. Review the entire presentation in *Slide Show* view to check all animation sequences. Make any necessary adjustments.
10. Optimize and compress the media.
    a. Click the **File** tab and select **Info**.
    b. Click the **Optimize Compatibility** button. When optimization is complete, a summary appears. Click **Close**.
    c. Click the **Compress Media** button and select the **Presentation Quality** option. When compression is complete, a summary appears. Click **Close**.
11. Save and close the presentation (Figure 5-107).

5-107 PowerPoint 5-3 completed

# Independent Project 5-4

At Life's Animal Shelter, training sessions are given for adopted dogs and their owners. For this project, you work on a presentation for an introductory training session that includes a variety of animation effects and two brief formatted videos. You also optimize media compatibility and compress media to reduce the presentation's file size.
[Student Learning Outcomes 5.1, 5.2, 5.3, 5.4, 5.6, 5.7]

---

Files Needed: *DogTraining-05.pptx*, *PillowPup-05.mov*, *Sit-05.mov*, *DogGrowl-05*, and *DogBark-05*
Completed Project File Name: *[your initials] PowerPoint 5-4.pptx*

---

## Skills Covered in This Project

- Animate a list and dim text.
- Reorder an animation sequence.
- Use the *Animation Painter*.
- Create a motion path animation.
- Hyperlink to another source.
- Apply a *Morph* transition.

- Insert a video file.
- Insert an audio file.
- Format a video object.
- Optimize media compatibility.
- Compress media.

---

1. Open the presentation **DogTraining-05**. Save the presentation as [your initials] PowerPoint 5-4.

2. Prepare slides for movement and apply a *Morph* transition (If *Morph* is not available with your software, skip step 2.).
   a. Display slide 1 and press **Ctrl+D** to duplicate.
      - Slide 1 will be the before slide as shown.
   b. Display slide 2 and prepare it as the after slide (Figure 5-108).
      - Select the title. Apply **Bold** and **Shadow** [*Home* tab, *Font* group] and increase the font size to **72 pt**.
      - Move the title placeholder up to the top right of the slide.
      - Click the **Text Outline** button [*Drawing Tools Format* tab, *WordArt Styles* group] and select **Black, Background 1**.
      - Select the subtitle. Change the font color to **White, Text 1** [*Home* tab, *Font* group] and increase the font size to **36 pt**. Resize the placeholder vertically so it fits the text.
      - Move the subtitle placeholder over the black rectangle.
   c. Apply the transition on slide 2.
      - Click **Morph** [*Transitions* tab, *Transition to This Slide* group].
   d. Display slide 1 and adjust the timing so the transition to slide 2 occurs automatically.
      - Change the *Duration* [*Transitions* tab, *Timing* group] to 03.00.
      - Deselect **On Mouse Click** [*Transitions* tab, *Timing* group] and enter **After** time of 00:01.00.
   e. Test the transition in *Slide Show* view starting with slide 1.

3. Animate a list and dim text.
   a. Display slide 5 and select the bulleted list placeholder.
      - Apply the **Float In** *Entrance* effect.
      - Verify that *Effect Options* are **Float Up** and **By Paragraph**.
   b. Click the **launcher** to open the *Float Up* dialog box.
      - Change the *After Animation* effect to a **light blue** color, the last one on the right.
      - Click **OK** to close the dialog box.
   c. Use the *Animation Painter* to copy this animation and apply it to the lists on slides 6 and 7.

4. Create an animated sequence including a motion path.
   a. Display slide 4. Select the red "**Name**" shape which is in its final position.
   b. Click the **Add Animation** button.
      - Click **More Motion Paths** to open the *Add Motion Path* dialog box.
      - Select the **Spiral Right** *Motion Path* effect (in the *Lines-Curves* category) and click **OK**.
   c. Click the **Effect Options** button.
      - Select **Reverse Path Direction**.

5-108 Final positions for objects after the *Morph* transition

- Change *Start* to **After Previous**.
- Change *Duration* to 04.00.

d. Resize the animation area to almost fill the slide.
   - The center of the animated object moves on the line.
   - Be sure to keep the animated shape's start position above the beginning of the sentence text (Figure 5-109).

e. Preview the animation to be sure it moves around the slide and ends in its original position.

f. Select the text box "**Should be the first**" and apply the **Wipe** *Entrance* effect.
   - Change *Effect Options* to **From Left**.
   - Change *Start* to **After Previous**.
   - Change *Duration* to 01.50.
   - Change *Delay* to 01.00.

g. Test the animations in *Slide Show* view.

5. Apply animation and color changes.
   a. Display slide 8 and select the first arrow on the left.
      - Apply a **Wipe** *Entrance* effect.
      - Change *Direction* to **From Left**.
   b. Use the *Animation Painter* to apply the same effect to the second and third arrow.
   c. Select the first star shape on the right and click the **Add Animation** button.
      - Apply the **Appear** *Entrance* effect.
      - Change *Start* to **After Previous**.
      - Verify that *Duration* is **Auto**.
   d. Click the **Add Animation** button again.
      - Apply the **Fill Color** *Emphasis* effect.
      - Change *Effect Options* to **Red, Accent 5, Darker 25%** (second column from the right; second color from the bottom).
      - Change *Start* to **With Previous**.
      - Verify that *Duration* is 02.00.
   e. Use the *Animation Painter* to apply the same effect to the second and third star shapes.

6. Insert audio files and adjust animation timing.
   a. Insert the audio file **DogGrowl-05.mp3** from your student data files.
      - Change *Start* to **Automatically**.
      - Select the **Hide During Show** option.
   b. Insert the audio file **DogBark-05.mp3** from your student data files.
      - Apply the same options as you did in 6a.
   c. Position both audio objects on their related arrows (Figure 5-110).
   d. Adjust the animation sequence as shown in Figure 5-111.

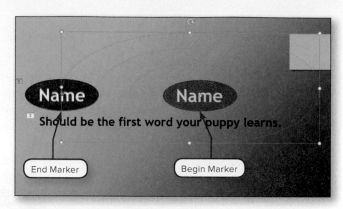

5-109 *Spiral Right Motion Path* **animation with direction reversed**

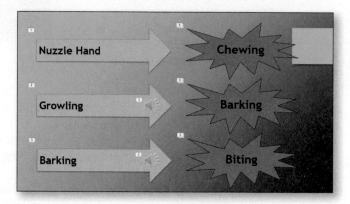

5-110 **Animation applied and audio inserted**

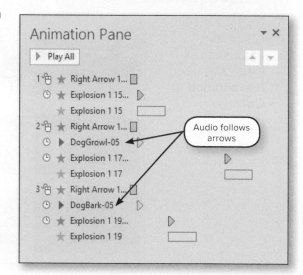

5-111 **Animation sequence changed with audio and emphasis effects shown**

- The arrows appear when clicked.
- Other effects are sequenced to appear in order.

7. Create a hyperlink to a web page.
   a. Display slide 12. Select the text "**Cesar's Way**" and prepare a hyperlink to http://www.Cesarsway.com. Add the *ScreenTip* Cesar's Way @ http://www.Cesarsway.com.
   b. Select the text "**Dog Training Central**" and prepare a hyperlink to http://www.dog-obedience-training-review.com. Add the *ScreenTip* Dog Training Central @ http://www.dog-obedience-training-review.com.

8. Insert two video files.
   a. Display slide 3. Insert the **PillowPup-05** video from your student data files.
      - Crop the black border lines from the top and bottom of the video.
      - Change the video size (*Height* **4.5"** and *Width* automatically adjusts).
      - Add the **Moderate Frame, Black** video style.
      - Position the video as shown in Figure 5-112.
      - Change *Start* [*Video Options* group] to **Automatically**.
      - Select **Rewind after Playing**.

5-112 Video inserted, cropped, resized, and style applied

   b. Display slide 5. Insert the **Sit-05** video from your student data files.
      - Change the video size (*Height* **3.6"** and *Width* automatically adjusts).
      - Add the **Moderate Frame, Black** video style.
      - Position the video on the right so it does not overlap text.
      - Change *Start* [*Video Tools Format* tab, *Video Options* group] to **Automatically**.
      - Select **Hide While Not Playing**.
      - Change *Animation Start* [*Animations* tab, *Timing* group] to **After Previous**.

9. Review the entire presentation in *Slide Show* view to check all animation sequences. Make any needed adjustments.

10. Optimize media compatibility and compress media size using **Presentation Quality**.

11. Save and close the presentation (Figure 5-113).

5-113 PowerPoint 5-4 completed

# Independent Project 5-5

The doctors at Courtyard Medical Plaza visit schools to talk to classes and student organizations. One of their goals is to reduce the number of young people who start smoking; therefore, they have developed a presentation to discuss some of the long-range effects of smoking. For this project you add animation and create hyperlinks for a menu slide and navigation. You also insert and format a video.
[**Student Learning Outcomes 5.1, 5.2, 5.3, 5.4, 5.5, 5.6, 5.7**]

Files Needed: ***TeenSmoking-05.pptx***, ***Smoking05.mov***, and ***Lungs-05.png***
Completed Project File Name: ***[your initials] PowerPoint 5-5.pptx***

## *Skills Covered in This Project*

- Create an animation sequence.
- Use the *Animation Painter*.
- Animate chart elements.
- Create a hyperlink.
- Create an action button.
- Apply a *Morph* transition.

- Insert a video file.
- Format a video object.
- Record an audio clip.
- Optimize media compatibility.
- Compress media.

1. Open the presentation ***TeenSmoking-05***. Save the presentation as [your initials] PowerPoint 5-5.

2. Create an animated sequence.
   a. Display slide 2. Select the text box with "90%" and apply the **Grow & Turn** *Entrance* effect.
      - Change *Start* to **After Previous**.
   b. Select the callout shape with "**13**" and apply the **Zoom** *Entrance* effect.
      - Change *Start* to **After Previous**.
      - Change *Duration* to 01.00.
      - Change *Delay* to 00.75.
   c. Use the *Animation Painter* to apply this animation to the callout with "12".
      - Change *Delay* to 00.25.
   d. Use the *Animation Painter* to apply this animation to the remaining callouts continuing in a clockwise order (Figure 5-114).
   e. Test the animation in *Slide Show* view.

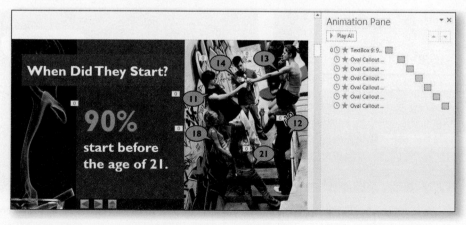

5-114 Animation sequence

3. Create an animated sequence including a chart.
  a. Display slide 3. Select the pie chart and apply the **Wheel** *Entrance* effect.
    - Change the *Effect Options* to **By Category** (Figure 5-115)
    - Change *Start* to **After Previous**.
    - Change *Duration* to 01.50.
  b. Select the text box on the left.
    - Apply the **Grow & Turn** *Entrance* effect.
    - Change *Start* setting to **After Previous**.
  c. Select the text box on the bottom right.
    - Apply the **Grow & Turn** *Entrance* effect.
    - Change *Start* to **After Previous**.
    - Change *Delay* to 1.00.
  d. Test the animation in *Slide Show* view.

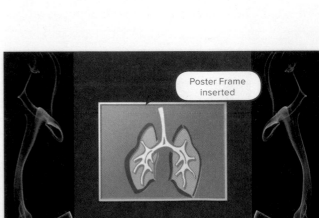

5-115 *By Category Effect Options*

4. Apply two animation effects that display together.
  a. Display slide 5. Select the "**Cool**" shape and click the **Add Animation** button.
    - Apply the **Fade** *Entrance* effect.
    - Change *Start* to **After Previous**.
    - Change *Duration* to 03.00.
  b. Click the **Add Animation** button again and apply the **Bounce** *Entrance* effects.
    - Change *Start* to **With Previous**.
    - Change *Duration* to 03.00 so both effects last the same amount of time.

5. Insert, resize, and format a video.
  a. Display slide 9. Insert the video ***Smoking-05*** from your student data files.
    - This video is 1:27 minutes long and its size is very small (Figure 5-116).
  b. Increase the size of the video (*Height* **4"** and *Width* automatically adjusts).
    - The video quality is not high enough to display well at a larger size without too much distortion.
  c. Move the video to the center of the slide.
  d. Click the **Poster Frame** button [*Video Tools Format* tab, *Adjust* group] and click **Image from file**.
    - Locate your student data files, select ***Lungs-05***, and click **Insert**.
    - Apply the **Beveled Frame**, **Gradient** video style [*Subtle* group] (Figure 5-117).
    - Select **Rewind after Playing**.
  e. Test the video in *Slide Show* view.

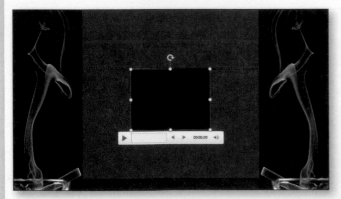

5-116  *Video inserted*

5-117  *Video with a poster frame and video style*

6. Prepare a menu slide with hyperlinked shapes.
   a. Insert a new slide with a *Blank* layout after slide 1.
   b. Draw a rounded rectangle and type **Early Smoking Is Dangerous**.
      - Increase the font size to **28 pt**. and apply **bold**.
      - Apply the **Intense Effect – Black, Dark 1** *Shape Style*. (Figure 5-118).
      - Resize the shape to fit the text
      - Move the shape so it is below the horizontal blue line.
   c. Press **Ctrl+D** to duplicate this shape and align the second shape below the first one.
      - Edit this text so it reads **Smoking-Related Diseases**.
      - Position both shapes below the horizontal line on the slide.
   d. Select the first shape and hyperlink it to **Slide 3. When Did They Start**.
   e. Select the second shape and hyperlink it to **Slide 7. Smoking-Related Diseases**.

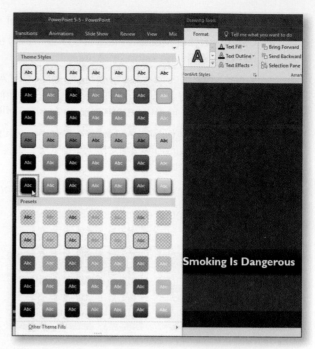

5-118 Shape styles

7. Create action buttons on the *Slide Master* to provide navigation.
   a. Change to *Slide Master* view and select the first *Slide Master* layout.
   b. Select the **Forward or Next** shape in the *Shapes* gallery and draw this shape on the slide.
      - Make it link to the **Next** slide.
      - Resize it (*Height* and *Width* **.4"**).
      - Repeat this step to draw the **Back or Previous** shape linked to the **Previous** slide.
      - Repeat this step to draw the **Home** shape linked to **Slide 2**.
   c. Select the three shapes and apply the **Intense Effect – Aqua**, **Accent 4** *Shape Style*.
      - Position the three shapes at the bottom of the slide near the cigarette (Figure 5-119).
   d. Close *Slide Master* view.

5-119 Action buttons

8. Display slide 11 and apply an exit animation effect.
   a. Select the rounded rectangle shape and apply the **Shrink & Turn** *Exit* effect to reveal the CMP logo.
   b. Change *Start* to **After Previous**.
   c. Change *Delay* to 4:00.
   d. Preview this change.

9. Record an audio clip. (Skip this step if your computer cannot record sound.)
   a. Display slide 11. Click the **Audio** button [*Insert* tab, *Media* group] and select **Record Audio** to open the *Record Sound* dialog box.
   b. Name the audio clip by typing **Help** in the *Name* box (Figure 5-120).

5-120 *Record Sound* dialog box

c. Click the **Record** button and speak into your microphone as you read the following text:

Call Courtyard Medical Plaza at 559-288-1600 to set up a consultation appointment. We will help you customize a plan to stop smoking.

d. When your recording is complete, click **OK**. An audio object appears on your slide.
e. Click the **Play** button to review your recording [*Audio Tools Playback* tab, *Preview* group].
f. Change *Start* to **Automatically** and select **Hide During Show**.

10. Display slide 12. Apply the **Morph** transition with the **By Characters** *Effect Option*. (If *Morph* is not available with your software, skip step 10.)
    a. Preview this change.

11. Optimize and compress the media using *Presentation Quality*.

12. Save and close the presentation (Figure 5-121).

5-121 PowerPoint 5-5 completed

# Independent Project 5-6

A community college in the Sierra Community College District is hosting a training camp for track athletes in grades 6–12. The college will distribute a presentation to coaches so they can share it with students before the registration deadline. For this project you add animation sequences, record audio, and insert a video. You also customize video playback options to control audio and animated text with bookmarks.
[Student Learning Outcomes 5.1, 5.3, 5.4, 5.5, 5.6]

---

Files Needed: *TrainingCamp-05.pptx*, *RunningRace-05.m4v*, and *RaceWin-05.mp3*
Completed Project File Name: *[your initials] PowerPoint 5-6.pptx*

---

## Skills Covered in This Project

- Animate a list.
- Use the *Animation Painter*.
- Animate a *SmartArt* graphic.
- Create a motion path animation.
- Insert a video file.
- Insert an audio file.

- Add bookmarks.
- Create a trigger.
- Record an audio clip.
- Format a video object.
- Optimize media compatibility.
- Compress media.

1. Open the presentation **TrainingCamp-05**. Save the presentation as [your initials] PowerPoint 5-6.

2. Animate a *SmartArt* graphic.
   a. Display slide 4. Select the *SmartArt* graphic showing application and camp registration information.
   b. Click the **Add Animation** button, select **More Entrance Effects**, and select the **Curve Up** *Entrance* effect (in the *Exciting* category on the *Add Entrance Effect* dialog box).
      - Change *Effect Options* to **One by One**.
      - Change *Start* to **After Previous**.
      - Change *Duration* to 02.00.

3. Create an animation sequence using the objects and animation settings listed in the following table.
   a. Display slide 5 and select the first object, the bulleted list.
   b. Click the **Add Animation** button and select the *Animation Effect*. Apply the *Effect Option* and settings for *Start*, *Duration*, and *Delay*.
   c. Repeat for each remaining object.
      - The coach picture has two effects that display together.
      - Open the *Animation Pane* and click **Play All** to test the animation sequence (Figure 5-122).

| Object | Animation Effect | Effect Options | Start | Duration | Delay |
|---|---|---|---|---|---|
| Bulleted list | Fly In (Entrance) | From Right | After Previous | 1.00 | 00.00 |
| Coach picture | Spiral In (Entrance) | None | After Previous | 3.00 | 00.00 |
| Coach picture | Dissolve In (Entrance) | None | With Previous | 3.00 | 00.00 |
| Other Coaches text box | Dissolve In (Entrance) | As One Object | After Previous | 2.00 | 00.00 |

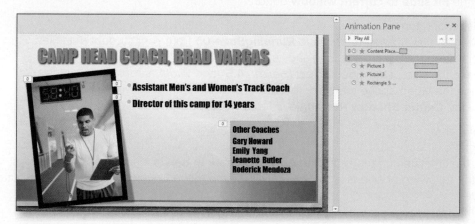

5-122 Animation sequence

4. Create an animated sequence to build a custom diagram.
   a. Display slide 3. Select the "**Nutrition**" shape and apply the **Fly In** animation effect.

- Change *Effect Options* to **From Top-Right**.
- Change *Start* to **After Previous**.
- Change *Duration* to 01.00.
- Double-click the **Animation Painter** button.

   b. Click the other shapes going across the bottom row and then up to apply the same effects to the other shapes.

   c. Click the **Effect Options** button and change the *Direction* on three shapes as follows:

| | |
|---|---|
| Running Mechanics | **From Top** |
| Racing Tactics | **From Top-Left** |
| Motivation | **From Top-Left** |

   d. Click **Preview** to test the animation.

5. Close the *Animation Pane*.

6. Apply a motion-path animation.
   a. Display slide 1.
   b. Change the **Zoom** to about **50%** so you can use the area around the slide.
   c. Select the runner shape and move it off the slide on the left.
   d. Click the **Add Animation** button and select **More Motion Paths**. Select the **Right** effect [*Lines-Curves* group].

- Change *Start* setting to **After Previous**.
- Change *Duration* to 03.00.
- Check the *Start* and *End* positions and adjust if necessary so the animation path aligns with the angle of the green rectangle on the slide (Figure 5-123).

5-123 *Motion Path* animation beginning and ending positions

   e. Select the star shape, click the **Add Animation** button and apply the **Spin** *Emphasis* effects.
- Change *Effect Options* to **Two Spins**.
- Change *Start* to **After Previous**.
- Change *Duration* to 02.50.

   f. Test the animation in *Slide Show* view.
   g. Click the **Fit slide to current window** button.

7. Insert, resize, and format a video.
   a. Display slide 10 and insert the video ***RunningRace-05*** from your student data files.
- This video is 1:28 minutes long and its size is small.

   b. Increase the size of the video object (*Height* **4.5"** and *Width* automatically adjusts).
   c. Position the video above the black text about the Championship winner.
   d. Apply the **Center Shadow Rectangle** video style [*Subtle* group].

8. Add bookmarks.
   a. Select the video.
   b. Click the timeline and then click the **Add Bookmark** button to insert seven bookmarks.
   c. Use the following positions (approximately). Use the *Move Back* and *Move Forward* buttons as needed.

| | |
|---|---|
| • 00:05.00 | • 00:50.00 |
| • 00:15.00 | • 01:02.00 |
| • 00:26.00 | • 01:25.00 |
| • 00:39.00 | |

9. Trigger animation with bookmarks to control start and end times.
   a. Select the video and click **Send to Back** so text boxes can be positioned over the video.
   b. Move the four text boxes at the bottom of the slide over the video.
      • Position each text box as shown in Figure 5-124.
      • These positions were planned to fit appropriately on the video as it plays.
   c. Select the "Sydney moves to the inside lane" text box and apply the animation effects:
      • Apply the **Appear** *Entrance* effect.
      • Click the **Trigger** button and select *Bookmark 1*.
      • Click the **Add Animation** button and apply the **Fade** *Exit* effect.
      • Click the **Trigger** button and select *Bookmark 2*.
   d. Repeat step 9c for each of the remaining text boxes with the effects and bookmarks in the following table.

5-124  Text in position to appear with video *Triggers*

| Text Box | Appear Entrance Effect Trigger | Fade Exit Effect Trigger |
|---|---|---|
| She's in the lead | Bookmark 3 | Bookmark 4 |
| No competition | Bookmark 5 | Bookmark 6 |
| The winner is Sydney | Bookmark 7 | None |

10. Adjust video playback settings.
    a. Use the default *Start* of **On Click**.
    b. Select **Rewind after Playing**.
    c. Test the video in *Slide Show* view.

11. Insert an audio file to play while the video plays.
    a. Display slide 10. Click the **Audio** button and select **Audio on My PC**. The *Insert Audio* dialog box opens.
    b. Locate your student files and select **RaceWin-05.mp3**. Click **Insert**.
    c. Reduce the playback time. Trim the audio file by changing the *Start Time* to $00:10$ seconds and the *End Time* to $01:40$ seconds. Click **OK**.
    d. Select **Hide During Show** [*Audio Tools Playback* tab, *Audio Options* group].
    e. Click the **Trigger** button [*Animations* tab, *Advanced Animation* group], click **On Bookmark**, and select **Bookmark 1**.
    f. Move the audio object to the bottom of the slide (Figure 5-125).
    g. Test the audio and video in *Slide Show* view.

5-125  Text boxes and audio clip are triggered with bookmarks

12. Record an audio clip. (Skip this step if your computer cannot record sound.)
    a. Display slide 2. Click the **Audio** button [*Insert* tab, *Media* group] and select **Record Audio** to open the *Record Sound* dialog box.
    b. Type Goal in the *Name* box.
    c. Click the **Record** button and speak into your microphone as you read the following text:

    Our goal is for campers to leave the camp as more knowledgeable, motivated, and team-oriented runners than when they arrived.

    d. When your recording is complete, click **OK**. An audio object appears on your slide.
    e. Click the **Play** button to review your recording.
    f. Change *Start* to **Automatically** and select **Hide During Show**.

13. Optimize and compress the media using *Presentation Quality*.

14. Save and close the presentation (Figure 5-126).

5-126  PowerPoint 5-6 completed

## Improve It Project 5-7

For this project, you update a presentation for Placer Hills Real Estate about preparing to buy a new home. You apply animation effects, add hyperlinks, and record audio. Then you adjust the animation effects and timing settings as appropriate.
[**Student Learning Outcomes 5.1, 5.2, 5.5, 5.6, 5.7**]

File Needed: *PreparetoBuy-05.pptx*
Completed Project File Name: *[your initials] PowerPoint 5-7.pptx*

## Skills Covered in This Project

- Create an animation sequence.
- Animate a list.
- Use the *Animation Painter*.
- Animate chart elements.
- Animate a *SmartArt* graphic.

- Hyperlink to another source.
- Record an audio clip.
- Apply a *Morph* transition.
- Compress media.

---

1. Open the presentation **PreparetoBuy-05**. Save it as [your initials] PowerPoint 5-7.

2. Animate a list.
   a. Display slide 2 and select the bulleted text.
      - Apply a **Wipe** *Entrance* effect with **From Left** *Effect Options*.
      - Verify that the default **By Paragraph** option is selected.
      - Change *Start* to **After Previous**.
   b. Use the **Animation Painter** to apply these effects to the list on slide 3.

3. Animate chart elements.
   a. Display slide 4 and select the chart.
      - Apply a **Wipe** *Entrance* effect with **From Left** *Effect Options*.
      - Select the **By Series** option.
      - Change *Start* to **After Previous**.
      - Change *Duration* to 01.00.
   b. Select the source text below the chart and animate it to appear after the chart.
      - Apply a **Wipe** *Entrance* effect with **From Right** *Effect Options*.
      - Change *Start* to **After Previous**.
      - Change *Duration* to 01.00.

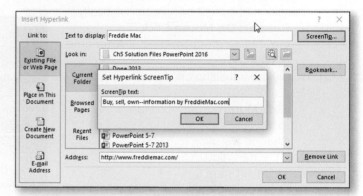

5-127 *Insert Hyperlink* and *Set Hyperlink ScreenTip* dialog boxes

4. Apply a hyperlink.
   a. Select the text **Freddie Mac** on slide 4.
   b. Prepare a hyperlink to the web site http://www.freddiemac.com and include the *ScreenTip* Buy, sell, own—information by FreddieMac.com (Figure 5-127).

5. Animate a *SmartArt* graphic.
   a. Display slide 6 and select the *SmartArt* graphic.
      - Apply the **Rise Up** *Entrance* effect (in the *Moderate* category on the *Change Entrance Effect* dialog box).
      - Select the **One by One** *Effect Options*.
   b. Select the picture on slide 6.
      - Apply the **Dissolve In** *Entrance* effect (in the *Basic* category on the *Change Entrance Effect* dialog box).
      - Change *Start* to **After Previous**.
      - Change *Duration* to 02.00.

6. Record audio. (Skip this step if your computer cannot record sound.)
   a. Display slide 5. Click the **Audio** button and select **Record Audio**.
      - Name the recording Loan costs.
      - Read the text at the bottom of the slide as you record.
      - Change *Start* to **Automatically**.
      - Select **Hide During Show**.
   b. Test the audio and make adjustments if needed.

7. Prepare slides and apply a *Morph* transition. (If *Morph* is not available with your software, skip step 7.)
   a. Display slide 1 and press **Ctrl+D** to duplicate.
      • Slide 2 will be the after slide as shown.
   b. Display slide 1 and prepare it as the before slide (Figure 5-128).
      • Change the *Zoom* to **50%** so you can use the area outside the slide.
      • Select the title. Change the font size to **16 pt**.
      • Select the subtitle and drag it below the slide.
      • Select the picture. Change the color to **Sepia** and the *Height* to **2"**. Drag the picture below the slide.
   c. Adjust the timing on slide 1 so the transition to slide 2 occurs automatically.
      • Deselect **On Mouse Click** [*Transitions* tab, *Timing* group] and enter **After** time of 00:01.00.
   d. Apply the transition on slide 2 (Figure 5-129).
      • Click **Morph** [*Transitions* tab, *Transition to This Slide* group].
      • Change *Duration* to 05.00.
   e. Test the transition in *Slide Show* view starting with slide 1.

8. Display slide 8. Select the **Fade** transition. Change the *Duration* to 03:00.

9. Use *Compress Media* using *Presentation Quality* to reduce the file size.

10. Save and close the presentation (Figure 5-130).

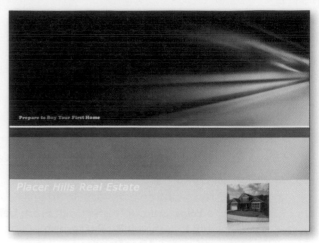

5-128 Object positions for the *Morph* transition

5-129 Completed title slide after the *Morph* transition

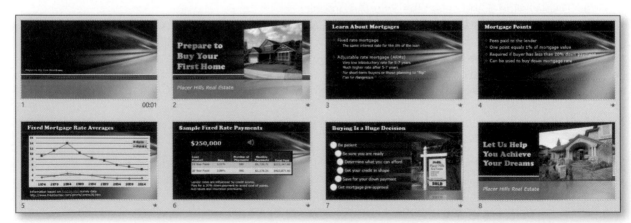

5-130 PowerPoint 5-7 completed

## Challenge Project 5-8

For this project, you develop a kiosk presentation to promote an event at a zoo. Using sources such as www.nashvillezoo.org, research typical zoo events and learning activities to get ideas. Search online to find suitable animal pictures and sounds to add interest. Create complex animations and adjust timings so sequences are timed appropriately.
[Student Learning Outcomes 5.1, 5.2, 5.3, 5.4, 5.5, 5.6, 5.7]

File Needed: None
Completed Project File Name: *[your initials] PowerPoint 5-8.pptx*

Create a new presentation and save it as [your initials] PowerPoint 5-8. Modify your presentation according to the following guidelines:

- Select an appropriate theme and colors for an outdoor environment.
- Prepare a distinctive title slide to announce the event.
- Tell the story with pictures and brief text to develop interesting slides.
- Create animation sequences including audio files of animal sounds.
- Include a chart or *SmartArt* graphic that is animated.
- Provide a hyperlink to the Association of Zoos & Aquariums at http://www.aza.org.
- Insert a picture of a zoo employee and record an audio file to play while the picture displays.
- Select an appropriate transition and check all animation and transition timings.
- Optimize compatibility and compress media.
- Save as a kiosk presentation with automatic looping.
- Credit sources that you use.

## Challenge Project 5-9

Prepare a presentation about your favorite musical artist or group. Research information about their history, current news, albums, and upcoming shows and include pictures and brief text to tell their story. Prepare a *SmartArt* graphic with several show dates and locations. Create complex animations and add navigation with hyperlinks and action buttons. If a video performance is available, include a link to it in your presentation.
[Student Learning Outcomes 5.1, 5.2, 5.3, 5.4. 5.5, 5.6, 5.7]

File Needed: None
Completed Project File Name: *[your initials] PowerPoint 5-9.pptx*

Create a new presentation and save it as [your initials] PowerPoint 5-9. Modify your presentation according to the following guidelines:

- Select an appropriate theme and colors for the artist or group.
- Prepare a distinctive title slide.
- Tell the story with pictures and brief text to develop interesting slides.
- Create animation sequences with pictures and text boxes.
- Prepare a table of contents or menu slide to link to the major topics of the presentation.

- Include action buttons on the *Slide Master* for navigation.
- Link to or insert a video performance.
- Select an appropriate transition and check all animation and transition timings.
- Optimize compatibility and compress media.
- Credit sources that you use.

## Challenge Project 5-10

For this project, assume you work for a property management company that handles rental property. Develop a kiosk presentation to advertise the availability of an apartment or home. Use pictures and descriptions of your own residence or pictures you find online of another residence. Prepare complex animations with at least one motion path animation. If possible, record a brief video showing a feature of interest in your residence that a prospective renter would find interesting. Include soft music that plays in the background as slides automatically advance.
[Student Learning Outcomes 5.1, 5.3, 5.4, 5.6, 5.7]

File Needed: None
Completed Project File Name: *[your initials] PowerPoint 5-10.pptx*

Create a new presentation and save it as [your initials] PowerPoint 5-10. Modify your presentation according to the following guidelines:

- Select an appropriate theme and colors for a property management company.
- Prepare a distinctive title slide to announce the availability of a residence.
- Include pictures and brief text to illustrate the residence's features.
- Create animation sequences such as clicking the name of a room to make descriptive text appear.
- Include a chart showing estimated utility costs and other fees.
- Select an appropriate transition and check all animation and transition timings.
- Insert a soft-sounding music clip and have it play while the entire slide show displays.
- Set up the slide show as a kiosk presentation with automatic looping.
- Optimize compatibility and compress media.
- Credit sources that you use.

# Integrating, Reviewing, and Collaborating

## CHAPTER OVERVIEW

Microsoft PowerPoint has many powerful tools to make presentation preparation easy and effective. For example, you can integrate materials into your presentation from applications such as an Excel chart, a Word document, or other objects. When a presentation becomes lengthy, you can divide it into sections to gain easy access to each topic. Custom shows create a presentation within a presentation and enable you to show only selected slides. Proofing tools help you locate errors, select good word choices, and even translate when necessary.

Incorporating comments and suggestions to refine presentation content enables you to collaborate with other people. Before you share your presentation with others, you may want to remove personal information or edit your presentation so it meets accessibility standards. You can also control the security of your content by marking a presentation as final so it cannot be accidentally changed or by requiring a password to open the presentation.

### STUDENT LEARNING OUTCOMES (SLOs)

After completing this chapter, you will be able to:

**SLO 6.1** Add content from other sources and work with multiple open windows (p. P6-366).

**SLO 6.2** Add sections to organize presentation slides (p. P6-377).

**SLO 6.3** Use proofing tools to correct errors, improve word choices, and translate content (p. P6-383).

**SLO 6.4** Create a custom slide show of selected slides within a presentation (p. P6-389).

**SLO 6.5** Insert, edit, and review comments, compare presentations, and consider reviewer feedback (p. P6-395).

**SLO 6.6** Prepare to share a presentation by removing personal information, checking for accessibility issues, checking compatibility, marking as final, and adding a password (p. P6-403).

**SLO 6.7** Save and export a presentation by creating different file types and by creating a video (p. P6-413).

### CASE STUDY

For the Pause & Practice projects in this chapter, you improve a presentation to promote the Hope Run, an annual fundraising event sponsored by the Hamilton Civic Center. People who participate can select a charity to receive the funds they raise. Kamala Graham is the event coordinator.

You use various methods to edit and organize the presentation, prepare it for sharing, and export it in different file formats.

**Pause & Practice 6-1:** Create presentation slides from a Word outline, insert content from other sources, and add sections.

**Pause & Practice 6-2:** Use proofing tools and create custom shows within a presentation.

**Pause & Practice 6-3:** Review a presentation and revise using comments.

**Pause & Practice 6-4:** Remove personal information, check for accessibility issues, check compatibility, add a password, and mark as final.

**Pause & Practice 6-5:** Export a presentation to create a slide picture, a PDF version of a presentation, a presentation video, and a handout in Word.

---

SLO 6.1

## Adding Content from Other Sources

PowerPoint can integrate information between the different Office applications. For example, you can create a presentation from a Word outline, insert a document as an image, or link to an Excel worksheet. Using multiple open windows makes it easy to copy slides and other content from one presentation or document and paste them into your current presentation.

### Use a Word Outline to Create Slides

If you want to create slides with bulleted text using a Microsoft Word document, the document must be formatted as an outline with heading styles applied to the text. PowerPoint interprets heading styles as follows:

- **Heading 1 style:** The text becomes slide titles.
- **Heading 2 style:** The text becomes first-level bulleted text.
- **Heading 3 style:** The text becomes second-level bulleted text.

You can use documents from other word processing programs, too, if heading styles are supported and the text is in outline form. If no heading styles are used, PowerPoint creates an outline based on paragraphs in the document and your results may not be optimal. PowerPoint interprets every item as a slide title, so too many slides may be created.

To efficiently create a Word outline to be used in PowerPoint, type each slide title and bulleted text on a separate line (Figure 6-1) and apply heading styles. If you have a lot of bulleted text, first select all the text and apply a *Heading 2* style since that style applies to listed text. Then apply *Heading 1* or *Heading 3* styles as needed for slide titles and bulleted subpoints (Figure 6-2). Save the document and close it. Use the outline to create slides in a new presentation or to add slides to an existing presentation.

Presentation Title
Presentation Subtitle
Slide 2 Title
Listed item 1
Listed item 2
Listed item 3
Slide 3 Title
Listed item 1
Listed item 1a
Listed item 1b
Listed item 2
Slide 4 Title
Listed item 1
Listed item 2
Listed item 2a
Listed item 2b

6-1 Text for slides in Microsoft Word

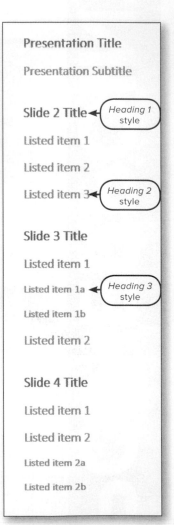

6-2 Text for slides in Microsoft Word with heading styles applied

## ▶ HOW TO: Create Slides from a Word Outline

1. Start a new presentation or select the slide in an existing presentation that you want the new slides to follow.
2. Click the **New Slide** drop-down arrow [*Home* tab, *Slides* group] and select **Slides from Outline** (Figure 6-3) to open the *Insert Outline* dialog box.

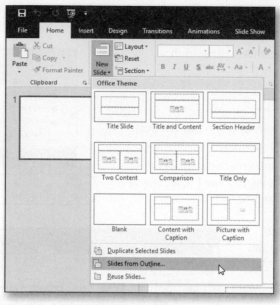

6-3 Create slides from a Word outline

3. Locate the Word file you want to use for slide text.
4. Click **Insert**.
   - All inserted slides use the *Title and Content* layout. The new slides will appear in the current theme (Figure 6-4).
   - You may have a blank slide at the beginning depending on which slide was selected when you created the new slides. Delete this slide if you do not need it.
   - If your first slide is a title slide, select the *Title Slide* layout [*Home* tab, *Slides* group].
   - Apply a theme and other formatting as needed.
5. Save your presentation.

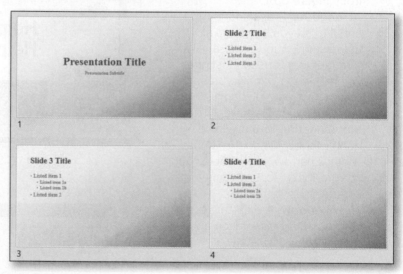

6-4 Slides created from a Word outline

## Work with Multiple Open Windows

In Chapter 1, you learned two ways to reuse and edit slides in the *Reuse Slides from Another Presentation* section in *SLO 1.2: Working with Slides, Layouts, Placeholders, and Text* and in the *Copy, Paste, and Duplicate Slides* section in *SLO 1.3: Navigating between Slides and Organizing Content*. The *Reuse Slides* feature requires that you have access to the second presentation, but you do not need to open it. For many situations, however, it is helpful to see more than one presentation at the same time to determine which slides you want to use again.

Arrange multiple windows using *Switch*, *Cascade*, or *Arrange All*. These options work differently depending on whether PowerPoint is maximized to fill your screen or if PowerPoint is used with a floating window.

## ▶ HOW TO: Work with Multiple PowerPoint Windows

1. Open two presentations or start a new presentation and open an existing one.

2. Click the **Maximize** button [*Title* bar] so PowerPoint fills the screen.

3. Click the **View** tab in either presentation. In the *Window* group, click one of the following options:

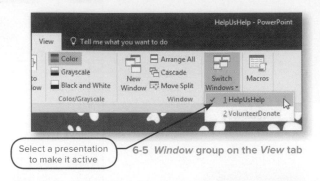

Select a presentation to make it active

6-5 *Window* group on the *View* tab

   - **Switch Windows:** Only one presentation displays at a time. Select the presentation that you want to be active from the drop-down list (Figure 6-5).

   - **Cascade:** Each presentation displays in a separate window with its own *Ribbon*. The windows are layered with the presentation name in each *Title* bar. Click a *Title* bar to activate that presentation and bring it to the front (Figure 6-6).

   - **Arrange All:** Presentation windows are tiled so you see them all at the same time. A side-by-side arrangement is used most often when working with two presentations. However, you can tile more than two windows. All *Ribbon* options are available with each window. When the window width is narrow, you must expand the groups to access commands (Figure 6-7).

   - **New Window:** A duplicate presentation of the active presentation opens in a new window.

6-6 *Cascade* layers all open presentation windows

6-7 *Arrange All* shows all open presentation windows

With multiple open windows, it is easy to move back and forth between presentations. Copy slide content or slide thumbnails in one active presentation, activate the other presentation, and paste. By default, a pasted slide uses the theme of the slide that precedes it. *Format Painter* works between presentations, too.

## ▶ HOW TO: Copy Slides from Another Presentation

1. Open the current presentation you are developing, and open the one from which you want to copy slides.

2. Click **Arrange All** [*View* tab, *Window* group].
   - Your current presentation appears on the left and the second presentation is on the right.
   - Move between presentations by clicking the *Title* bar or anywhere in a window to activate a presentation.

3. Change to *Slide Sorter* view in both presentations and adjust the *Zoom* to **50%**.

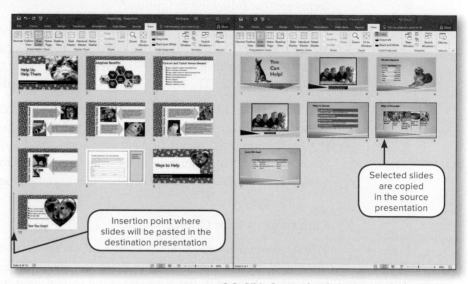

6-8 *Slide Sorter* view in both open presentations

4. Select one or more slides in the presentation on the right that you want to paste in your current presentation (Figure 6-8) and press **Ctrl+C**.

5. Click the *Title* bar on your current presentation to activate it.

6. Click to move your insertion point to the location where you want to paste the copied slides.

7. Press **Ctrl+V** to paste the slides in this position.

8. Rearrange slide order if necessary (Figure 6-9).

9. Save your current presentation when all slides that you need are copied.

10. Close the second presentation.

11. Edit the new slides as needed. *Paste Options* are discussed in the *Paste Options and Paste Special* section in *SLO 6.1: Adding Content from Other Sources*.

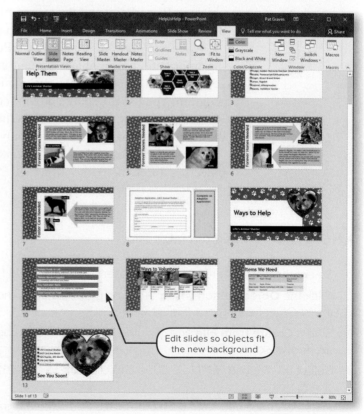

6-9 Slides are pasted

If you want to copy content from another application such as an Excel worksheet or a Word document, display both PowerPoint and the other application window by resizing them.

## Link and Embed Office Objects

*Object linking and embedding* (*OLE*) is a technology developed by Microsoft to share objects between different Microsoft Office applications. For example, you can insert an Excel worksheet into your PowerPoint presentation. When you do this, it is important to know these terms and the following definitions:

- *Source program:* The Office application where the object was created
- *Source file:* The file where the original content is stored
- *Destination program:* The Office application where the object is inserted
- *Destination file:* The file where the object is inserted

For example, if you want to place an Excel worksheet in your presentation, the worksheet is the object. Excel is the source program and the worksheet is the source file. PowerPoint is the destination program and the presentation is the destination file. When you insert content from another Office application, the way you modify the object within the PowerPoint presentation differs based on whether the object is embedded or linked.

### Embed or Link an Object

When you *embed* an object, PowerPoint creates a connection to the source program and the object retains the formatting from the source program. When you activate the object by double-clicking it, the *Ribbon* for the source program becomes available for editing and replaces the PowerPoint *Ribbon*. Even though you can edit the object using this *Ribbon*, the object in PowerPoint and the source file are independent of each other. Any changes made to the object displayed in PowerPoint do not affect the original file in the source program.

When you *link* an object, PowerPoint displays a representation of the object with linking information. The object content and formatting is stored in the source file. When you activate the object by double-clicking it, the object opens in a separate window for the source program. You use the source program to make changes and those changes are reflected in the PowerPoint object. When you edit a linked object from either the object file in PowerPoint or the source file, changes are stored only in the source file.

The process for embedding or linking is essentially the same, but the way you edit the objects is different.

---

### ▶ HOW TO: Embed or Link a File

1. Select the slide where you want to insert the embedded file.

2. Click the **Object** button [*Insert* tab, *Text* group] to open the *Insert Object* dialog box (Figure 6-10).

3. Select **Create from File** and click the **Browse** button to open the *Browse* dialog box.

4. Select the file you want to embed and click **OK** to close the dialog box.

   - Select **Link** if you want to link the file to its source program.
   - Click **Display as icon** to show the link in a small size rather than as a full-size image.

6-10 *Insert Object* dialog box

5. Click **OK** to close the *Insert Object* dialog box and embed or link the file.

- If you embed the file, a copy of it appears on your slide (Figure 6-11).
- If you link the file, a representation of it (a picture) appears on your slide.

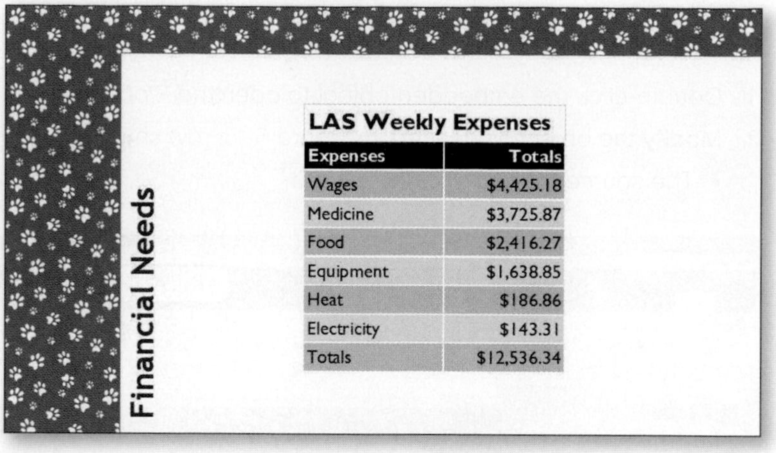

**Financial Needs**

| LAS Weekly Expenses | |
|---|---|
| Expenses | Totals |
| Wages | $4,425.18 |
| Medicine | $3,725.87 |
| Food | $2,416.27 |
| Equipment | $1,638.85 |
| Heat | $186.86 |
| Electricity | $143.31 |
| Totals | $12,536.34 |

6-11 Embedded Excel object with its size increased

> **ANOTHER WAY**
>
> Use the *Paste Special* command to embed or link an object from another application. This technique is discussed in the next section.

The *Insert Object* dialog box enables you to create a new file that will be embedded using another program from within PowerPoint. Click the **Create new** option to open the source program and create the object. When the object is complete, click outside the object to close the source program.

Embedded objects increase your presentation file size because PowerPoint stores not only the entire object but the information about how to access the source program. A smaller PowerPoint file generally results when objects are linked because only the data needed to display the information is saved.

Use embedding when the source and destination files do not need to remain the same. For example, if you are showing sales data in Excel for a past time period, embedding is a good choice because the data is not expected to change. It is best to keep permanent changes in the source file and update your presentation as needed. However, if you are showing projected sales data in Excel, linking is a better option because the information will likely change as time goes by.

> **MORE INFO**
>
> If you no longer need an object to be embedded, ungroup the object and regroup it. This step removes the OLE data and the remaining picture can be compressed and your presentation file size reduced.

### Modify Embedded and Linked Objects

The file type you select when you insert an object determines how the object is edited. For certain embedded file types, such as a picture or Microsoft Office Object, you edit the object using PowerPoint tabs. When you double-click an inserted object with a different file type, the source program *Ribbon* and tabs open. You use these tabs to modify the embedded object. Any changes made to the object in PowerPoint do not affect the original file.

## HOW TO: Modify an Embedded Object

1. Double-click the embedded object to open the *Ribbon* from the source program (Figure 6-12).
2. Modify the object as desired. In Figure 6-13, row shading colors are changed and the table is sorted.
   - The source file remains unchanged.

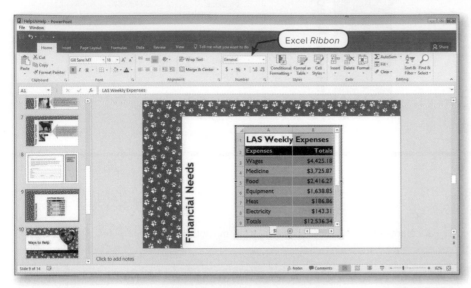

6-12 Editing a selected object within PowerPoint using the source program *Ribbon*

6-13 Object embedded in PowerPoint and edited

3. Click outside the object or press **Esc** to deselect it.

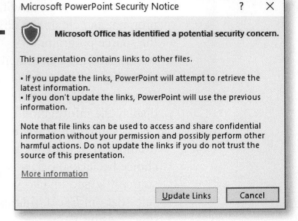

6-14 Security notice about updating links

When you open a presentation containing one or more links, a dialog box opens telling you that Microsoft Office has identified a security concern because the presentation has links to other files. You are asked if you want to update the links (Figure 6-14). If you are comfortable with the source of the files, click **Update Links**. The dialog box closes and your links are updated.

When you edit the linked object, the source file opens. After you change and resave the source file, update the linked object to reflect the current data from the source file.

## HOW TO: Modify a Linked Object

1. Double-click the linked object to open the source program and file.
   - Alternatively, right-click the linked object, select the **Linked Document Object** or **Linked Worksheet Object**, and select **Edit** or **Open** (Figure 6-15) to open the source program and file.

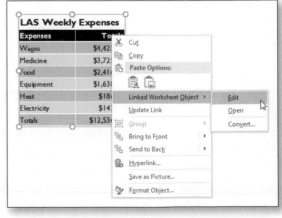

6-15 Use the context menu to edit a linked object

2. Select the source file.
   - Because both files are open, the linked object in PowerPoint is updated (Figure 6-16).
   - If the linked object does not update, right-click the linked object and select **Update Link** from the context menu.

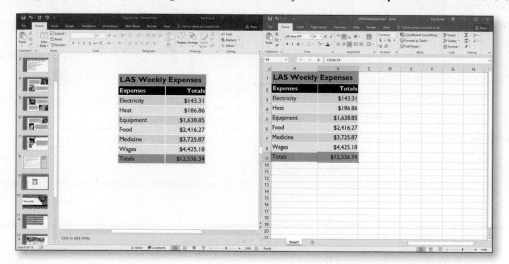

6-16 Changes in the Excel worksheet automatically appear in the PowerPoint linked object

3. Save and close the source file.

If changes are made to the source file when the destination file is not open, the next time you open the destination file you will be prompted to update the linked objects in the presentation.

### Modify a Link to an Object

If the location of a source or a destination file with a linked object changes, the link is broken. The instructions saved by PowerPoint to connect the source and destination files are no longer valid. Reestablish the link to a file using the *Links* dialog box.

▶ **HOW TO:** Modify a Link

1. Open the destination file. When you are prompted to update links in the presentation, click **Update Links**.
2. Click **OK** to close the dialog box if you are notified that links could not be found.
3. Click the **File** tab to open the *Backstage* view.
4. Click the **Info** button on the left.
5. Click **Edit Links to Files** at the bottom of the *Properties* list on the right side of *Backstage* view (Figure 6-17) to open the *Links* dialog box (Figure 6-18).

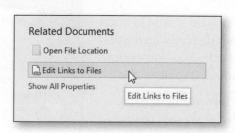

6-17 *Edit Links to Files* on the *Backstage* view

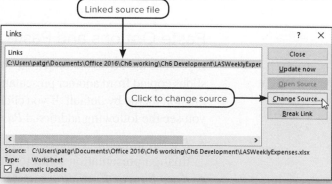

6-18 The *Links* dialog box

- In the *Links* area, source files used in the presentation are listed.
  - Select the source file you need to change if more than one is listed.

6. Click the **Change Source** button to open the *Change Source* dialog box (Figure 6-19).

7. Select the source file for the linked objects and click **Open** to modify the link and close the *Change Source* dialog box.

8. Click **Close** to close the *Links* dialog box.

9. Click the **Back** arrow to return to your presentation.

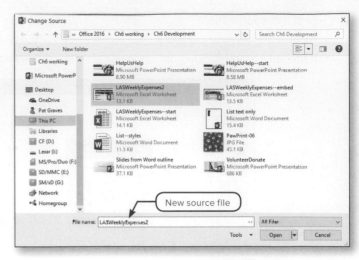

6-19 *Change Source* dialog box

---

### Break a Link to an Object

If you no longer want a linked object connected to the source file, then break the link between them. The linked object is converted to an embedded object and can be modified independently of the source file.

> **MORE INFO**
>
> A file must be saved in order to see the *Edit Links to Files* below *Properties* on the *Backstage* view.

---

▶ **HOW TO:** Break a Link

1. Open the destination file containing the linked object. When you are prompted to update links in the presentation, click **Cancel**.

2. Click the **File** tab to open the *Backstage* view.

3. Click the **Info** button on the left.

4. Click **Edit Links to Files** (see Figure 6-17) on the right at the bottom of the *Properties* list. The *Links* dialog box opens.

5. Select the source file of the linked object in the *Source file* area.

6. Click the **Break Link** button (see Figure 6-18) and the source file name is removed automatically.

7. Click **Close** to close the *Links* dialog box.

8. Click the **Back** arrow to return to your presentation.

---

## Paste Options and Paste Special

If you use the *Paste* button [*Home* tab, *Clipboard* group] to insert slides copied from another presentation, they display with the destination theme by default. If you click the *Paste* drop-down arrow, you see the following additional *Paste Options* (Figure 6-20):

- *Use Destination Theme:* Applies the formatting of the destination presentation styles to the material you are pasting.
- *Keep Source Formatting:* Retains theme formatting from the source document (the presentation where the slides were copied) in the material you are pasting.

6-20 *Paste Options*

Context-specific paste options vary based on what you are pasting. For example, you may have options for embedding, retaining styles, or one of the following options:

- *Picture:* Pastes an object, even text, as a picture rather than editable text.
- *Keep Text Only:* Pastes unformatted text.

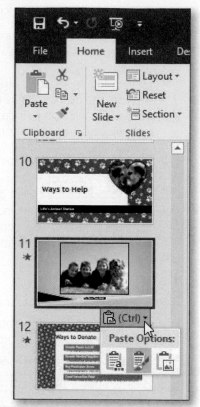

> **MORE INFO**
>
> If you have trouble with the format of pasted text, try pasting the text using *Keep Text Only,* and format the text *after* you have pasted it into the presentation.

After a slide is pasted in a new location, the *Paste Options* button (Figure 6-21) automatically appears near the pasted slide thumbnail in *Normal* view so you can select a different option. If you don't see the button, right-click a slide thumbnail and select a paste option from the context menu.

To paste objects from other programs on a slide, use the **Paste Special** command. Given the space constraints on a slide, you often will want to show just a portion of an object rather than embedding the entire file. For example, you may need just a chart from an Excel worksheet rather than the entire worksheet. Copy the portion of the source file you want to show in PowerPoint and use the *Paste Special* dialog box to select the file format of the object. Choose **Paste** to embed the object and choose **Paste link** to link to the object.

6-21 *Paste Options* after a slide is pasted

---

▶ **HOW TO:** Use Paste Special

1. Open the source file in your source program.
2. Select and copy the portion of this file you want to display in PowerPoint.
3. Open your presentation (the destination file) in PowerPoint.
4. Select the slide where you want to insert the copied object.
5. Click the **Paste** drop-down arrow [*Home* tab, *Clipboard* group] and select **Paste Special** (Figure 6-22) to open the *Paste Special* dialog box (Figure 6-23).

6-22 Open the *Paste Special* dialog box

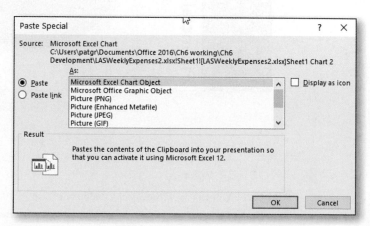

6-23 *Paste Special* dialog box with *Paste* options

6. Select **Paste** to embed the object.
  - In the *As* area, select the appropriate format such as *Microsoft Excel Chart Object*.
  - If you select the source program file type, the object retains the connection with the source program, and you edit the object from within PowerPoint.
  - If you choose a different file type, such as a *Picture* or *Microsoft Office Graphic Object*, the object does not retain connection with the source program. In PowerPoint, you edit this type of embedded object as you would a picture.

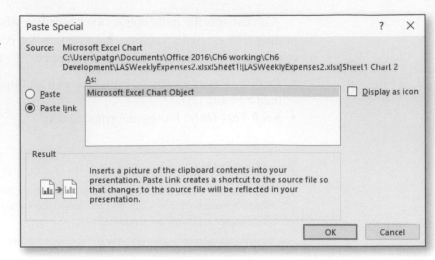

6-24 *Paste Special* dialog box with *Paste link* options

*Or*

7. Select **Paste link** to link to the object.
  - In the *As* area, only the appropriate format for the object will display (Figure 6-24).
  - Changes made in the source file are also made in the linked destination file.
8. Click **OK** to close the *Paste Special* dialog box and a copy of the object appears in the destination file.
9. Close the source file and program when you are satisfied with how the object looks.

Regardless of the pasting method used (embedding or pasting the link), the object will look the same on the slide, such as the pie chart shown in Figure 6-25.

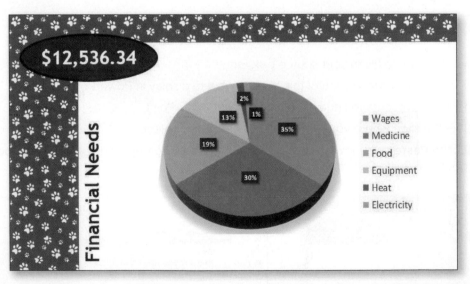

6-25 Excel chart object embedded in PowerPoint using *Paste Special*

> **ANOTHER WAY**
> **Alt+Ctrl+V** opens the *Paste Special* dialog box.

# Adding Sections to Organize a Presentation

Organize your slides into *Sections* to group related slides or to divide a lengthy presentation. Collapse sections and focus on one section at a time as you develop slides so the entire presentation is easier to manage. Sections do not interrupt the flow of your presentation during a slide show because they are not visible to your audience.

## Add and Rename a Section

Add a section in *Normal* view using the *Slides* pane as well as in *Slide Sorter* view. Once the section is in place, give it a logical name. It is generally easier to work in *Slide Sorter* view, which allows you to see the slides in multiple sections at one time.

---

### ▶ HOW TO: Add and Rename a Section

1. Click between slide thumbnails where you want to add a section.
2. Add a section using one of these methods:
   - Click the **Section** button [*Home* tab, *Slides* group] and select **Add Section** (Figure 6-26).
   - Press **Ctrl+comma**.
   - Right-click and select **Add Section** from the context menu (Figure 6-27).

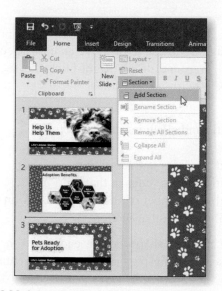

6-26 Select *Add Section* using the *Home* tab

6-27 Select *Add Section* from the context menu

3. Point to the **Untitled Section** name that appears and right-click.
   - Slides below the name are automatically selected.
4. Select **Rename Section** to open the *Rename Section* dialog box (Figure 6-28).
5. Type the name for your section and click **Rename**.

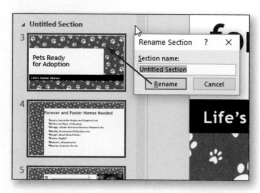

6-28 Rename the *Untitled Section*

---

## Edit Sections

As noted earlier, *Slide Sorter* view generally works best when you are revising slide order or adjusting sections. Reduce the *Zoom* percentage, if necessary, to see more slides at one time. Note that slide thumbnails are grouped following each section name (Figure 6-29).

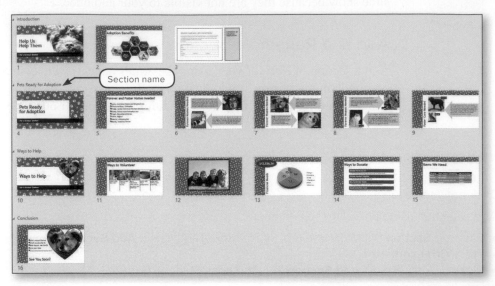

6-29 Sections in *Slide Sorter* view

Move a slide from one section to another by dragging the slide or move an entire section by dragging the section name to its new position (drag and drop). Right-click the section name and choose from one of the following options to rearrange sections:

- *Remove Section:* Deletes the section title
- *Remove Section & Slides:* Deletes the section title and all slides in that section
- *Remove All Sections:* Deletes all section titles
- *Move Section Up:* Moves up the section title and all slides in that section
- *Move Section Down:* Moves down the section title and all slides in that section
- *Collapse All:* Displays only the section titles with the number of slides in that section
- *Expand All:* Displays the slide thumbnails for all slides in that section

Collapse and expand sections by clicking the triangle shape beside each section title (Figure 6-30). Collapsing the titles can help you see the "big picture" of your presentation

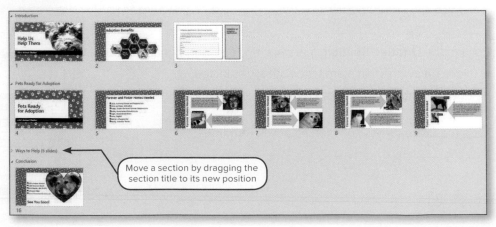

6-30 A section is collapsed

by focusing on major topics. Seeing only the section titles makes it easy to examine topic order and rearrange sections by dragging (Figure 6-31). When you are ready to develop detailed information, expand sections one at a time to focus on each topic individually.

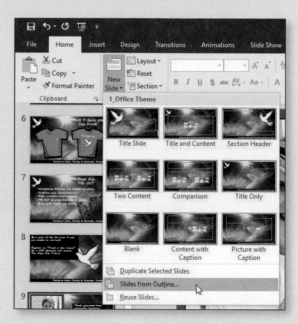

> Introduction (3 slides)

**Ways to Help (6)**

> Pets Ready for Adoption (6 slides)

> Conclusion (1 slide)

6-31 Rearranging collapsed sections

# PAUSE & PRACTICE: POWERPOINT 6-1

For this project, you add content from a variety of sources to the Hope Run presentation. You create slides from a Word outline, work with multiple windows, copy and paste slides, and embed and link objects. You also organize a presentation into logical groups by inserting sections and rearranging sections and slide order.

---

Files Needed: ***HopeRun-06.pptx, HopeRunInfo-06.docx, PrepareToRun-06.pptx, PledgeForm-06.docx***, and ***HopeRunSchedule-06.png*** (student data files are available in the Library of your SIMnet account)
Completed Project File Name: ***[your initials] PP P6-1.pptx***

---

1. Open the ***HopeRun-06*** presentation and save it as [your initials] PP P6-1.

2. Add slides from a Word outline.
   a. Display slide 9. Click the **New Slide** drop-down arrow [*Home* tab, *Slides* group] and select **Slides from Outline** (Figure 6-32) to open the *Insert Outline* dialog box.
   b. Locate your student data files and select ***HopeRunInfo-06***.
   c. Click **Insert**. Two slides are inserted.
   d. Select slide 10 and click the **Reset** button [*Home* tab, *Slides* group] to change the font to the theme font.
   e. Repeat step 2d for slide 11.

3. Arrange two PowerPoint windows side-by-side.
   a. Click the **Maximize** button [*Title* bar] if your window is not already maximized so PowerPoint fills the screen.
   b. Open the ***PrepareToRun-06*** presentation.
   c. Click the **Switch Windows** button [*View* tab, *Window* group] and select ***[your initials] PP P6-1*** to activate it.
   d. Click **Arrange All** [*View* tab, *Window* group].
      • Your current presentation (destination) is on the left and the second presentation (source) is on the right.

6-32 Create slides from a Word outline

4. Copy slides from the source presentation and paste them in the destination presentation.
   a. Change to *Slide Sorter* view in both presentations and adjust the *Zoom* to approximately **60%**.
   b. Select slides 3–6 (Figure 6-33) in the ***Prepare to Run-06*** presentation (source) on the right and press **Ctrl+C**.

6-33 Two presentation windows displayed using *Arrange All*

   c. Activate the ***[your initials] PP P6-1*** presentation (destination) and click after slide 12.
   d. Press **Ctrl+V** to insert the slides in this position.
      • The new slides are automatically formatted for the current theme.
   e. Save your current presentation with the new slides and close the ***PrepareToRun-06*** presentation.
   f. Maximize your PowerPoint window or restore it to the size you prefer.

5. Embed a Word file and modify the embedded object.
   a. Double-click slide 4 to open it in *Normal* view.
   b. Click the **Object** button [*Insert* tab, *Text* group] to open the *Insert Object* dialog box.
   c. Select **Create from File** and click the **Browse** button to open the *Browse* dialog box.
      • Locate your student data files and select ***PledgeForm-06***.
      • Click **OK** to close the *Browse* dialog box.
   d. Click **OK** to close the *Insert Object* dialog box (Figure 6-34) and embed the file.
      • It currently displays with a transparent background.

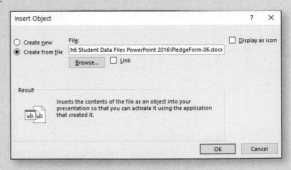

6-34 *Insert Object* dialog box

   e. Click the **Shape Fill** button [*Drawing Tools Format* tab, *Shape Styles* group] and select **White, Background 1**.
   f. Move the object to the right.
   g. Double-click the embedded object to open the *Ribbon* from the source program.

- Change the form title to **The Hope Run Donation Pledge** (Figure 6-35).
- Click outside the object or press **Esc** to deselect it.
- The source program *Ribbon* closes.

6. Use *Paste Special* to link to an object.
   a. Open Excel. Click **File** and then click **Open**.
   b. Locate your student data files and select ***HopeRunSchedule-06***.
   c. Click **Open** to open the worksheet and close the dialog box.
   d. Select the table cells **A3:B10** and press **Ctrl+C**.
   e. Switch to PowerPoint and display slide 3.
   f. Click the **Paste** drop-down arrow [*Home* tab, *Clipboard* group] and select **Paste Special** to open the *Paste Special* dialog box (Figure 6-36).
      - Select **Paste link**.
      - In the *As* area, select **Microsoft Excel Worksheet Object**.
      - Click **OK** to close the *Paste Special* dialog box and the object appears on your slide.
   g. Double-click the worksheet to open it in Excel.
      - Change the times on Excel row 4 to 7:15 and on Excel row 8 to 10:15.
      - Save and close the worksheet.
      - Close Excel.
   h. Increase the size of the linked worksheet on slide 3 (*Height* **4"**) so the text is easy to read and position it as shown in Figure 6-37.

7. Break the link to an object.
   a. Click the **File** tab to open the *Backstage* view.
   b. Click the **Info** button on the left.
   c. Click **Edit Links to Files** at the bottom of the *Properties* list.
      - The *Links* dialog box opens.
      - Select the source file of the linked object in the *Links* area (Figure 6-38).
      - Click the **Break Link** button, and the source file name is removed.
      - Click **Close** to close the *Links* dialog box.
   d. Click the **Back** arrow to return to your presentation.

6-35 Embedded Word file revised

6-36 *Paste Special* dialog box

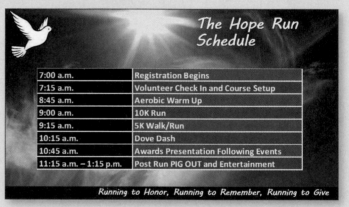

6-37 Linked Excel object revised

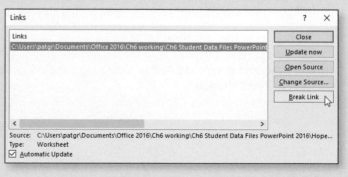

6-38 *Links* dialog box

8. Add and rename sections.
   a. Click the **Slide Sorter** button [*Status* bar] and adjust your *Zoom* percentage to approximately **60%**.
   b. Click after slide 8.
   c. Click the **Section** button [*Home* tab, *Slides* group] and select **Add Section**.
      • The **Untitled Section** name appears and the slides below the name are selected.
   d. Point to the **Untitled Section** name and right-click (Figure 6-39).
   e. Select **Rename Section** to open the *Rename Section* dialog box.

6-39 *Rename Section* in *Slide Sorter* view

   f. Type Donations and Volunteer Positions (Figure 6-40) and click **Rename**.
   g. Click after slide 11. Repeat steps 8c–f and rename the section Tips to Prepare.
   h. Rename the *Default Section* before slide 1 Event Details.

9. Rearrange slides between sections.
   a. Select slide 4 in the *Event Details* section.
   b. Drag and drop slide 4 after slide 10 in the *Donations and Volunteer Positions* section.

6-40 *Rename Section* dialog box

10. Save and close the presentation (Figure 6-41).

6-41 PP P6-1 completed

## SLO 6.3

# Using Proofing Tools

PowerPoint has many built-in features to automatically catch common spelling and typing mistakes. For example, if you type "teh," it is automatically changed to "the." If you type "ANalyze," the word is automatically changed to "Analyze." Similarly, some punctuation marks are changed to characters used in printing for a more modern text appearance.

## AutoCorrect and AutoFormat

The *AutoCorrect* feature recognizes and corrects commonly misspelled words and corrects the following:

- Eliminates two initial capitals in a word
- Capitalizes the first letter of a sentence
- Capitalizes the first letter of table cells
- Capitalizes the names of days
- Resolves accidental usage of the **Caps Lock** key
- Replaces incorrectly spelled words with the correct spelling

The *AutoFormat* feature applies the following replacements and formatting as you type:

- Changes the keyboard "straight quotes" to "smart quotes"
- Converts fractions (such as 3/4) with a fraction character such as ¾

- Applies superscript to ordinal numbers such as $1^{st}$, $2^{nd}$, $3^{rd}$, etc.
- Converts two hyphens (--) with no space on both sides to an em dash (—)
- Converts a single hyphen with a space on both sides (-) to an en dash (–)
- Displays URLs (web addresses) as hyperlinks
- Adds bullets or numbers to listed text in the body text placeholder
- *AutoFits* text in title and body text placeholders

Customize these options in the *AutoCorrect* dialog box. Click **File** and select **Options** to open the *PowerPoint Options* dialog box. Select **Proofing** and then click the **AutoCorrect Options** button to open the *AutoCorrect* dialog box. Deselect options on the *AutoCorrect* tab or click the **Exceptions** button to list words or spelling that you do not want *AutoCorrect* to change.

The *AutoCorrect* tab has two parallel word lists with the wrong spelling on the left and the correct spelling on the right that is used for the correction. This list also includes a few symbols such as the copyright notation "(c)" that automatically changes to "©." Add words to this list that you frequently misspell, or add an abbreviation that you will later change to a complete name.

This same list is used in all of your Office applications; therefore, changes in PowerPoint will affect other Office applications as well.

> **HOW TO:** Add a Custom AutoCorrect Entry

1. Click the **File** tab to open the *Backstage* view.
2. Choose the **Options** button to open the *PowerPoint Options* dialog box.
3. Select **Proofing** on the left (Figure 6-42).
4. Click the **AutoCorrect Options** button to open the *AutoCorrect* dialog box.
5. Type the misspelled word or abbreviation you want PowerPoint to recognize in the *Replace* box.
6. Type the word(s) to replace the original text in the *With* box (Figure 6-43).

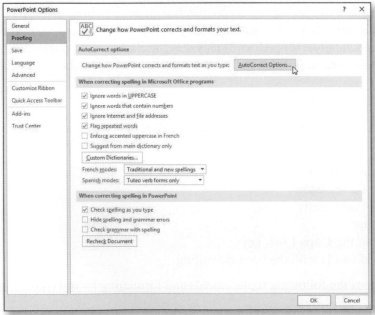

6-42 *Proofing Options* in the *PowerPoint Options* dialog box

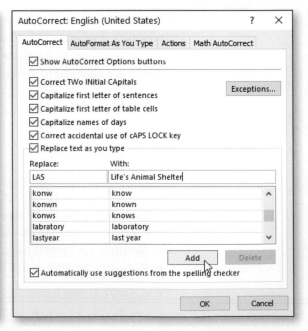

6-43 *AutoCorrect* dialog box

7. Click **Add**. This pair of words is added to the *AutoCorrect* list.
8. Click **OK** to close the *AutoCorrect* dialog box.
9. Click **OK** to close the *PowerPoint Options* dialog box.

▶ MORE INFO

In the *AutoCorrect* dialog box, click the **AutoFormat As You Type** tab to customize selections.

When PowerPoint automatically corrects or changes formatting, you may not notice that a change has been made. A very subtle mark, a short bar, appears below the corrected word. If you keep typing, the change is accepted. If you click the short line, a list button appears with several options depending on the correction that was made. For example, when the misspelled word "independant" is typed as the first word in a text box, it is corrected to "Independent." These options (Figure 6-44) appear:

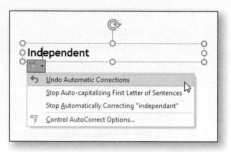

6-44 *AutoCorrect* options

- *Undo Automatic Corrections*
- *Stop Auto-capitalizing First Letter of Sentences*
- *Stop Automatically Correcting "independant"*
- *Control AutoCorrect Options*

Click one of the options to undo or prevent a correction. Click **Control Auto Correct Options** to open the *AutoCorrect* dialog box.

▶ ANOTHER WAY

Press **Ctrl+Z** or click *Undo* to reverse an automatic correction.

## Find and Replace

Use the ***Find*** feature to search for and locate a word, part of a word, or a phrase. Use *Find*, also, to locate occurrences matching a specific case. You can restrict the search to whole words only such as the, them, there, or therapy rather than locating occurrences within longer words. The ***Replace*** feature enables you to change the words that match your specifications. The *Find* dialog box also has a *Replace* button to change words. Searches begin on the currently selected slide.

▶ **HOW TO:** Use Find and Replace

1. Select the first slide in your presentation.
2. Click the **Find** button [*Home* tab, *Editing* group] or press **Ctrl+F** to open the *Find* dialog box (Figure 6-45).

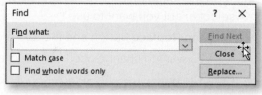

6-45 *Find* dialog box

3. Type the word you want to locate in the *Find what* box.

   - Select **Match case** and only words matching the capitalization of the word you type will be found.
   - Select **Find whole words only** if you do not want PowerPoint to find matches for the word you type within a longer word.

4. Click the **Find Next** button.

   - If the text is in your presentation, PowerPoint will highlight the first occurrence of the matching text (Figure 6-46).

5. Edit the highlighted word if you want to change it.

6. Continue clicking the **Find Next** button to move through each matching occurrence in the presentation.

7. Click the **Replace** button (in the *Find* dialog box or on the *Home* tab) or press **Ctrl+H** to open the *Replace* dialog box (Figure 6-47).

   - Type the alternative word in the *Replace with* box.
   - Click the **Find Next** button to locate the next word without making a change.
   - Click the **Replace** button to change only the highlighted word.
   - Click the **Replace All** button to change all occurrences of the word.
   - When the matching process is complete, a dialog box opens identifying the last match.

8. Click **OK** to close the dialog box.

9. Click **Close** to close the *Find* or the *Replace* dialog box.

6-46 Select *Find whole words only*

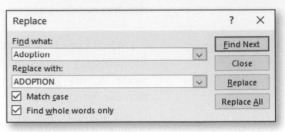

6-47 *Replace* dialog box

> **MORE INFO**
>
> It is a good idea to use *Match Case* when replacing acronyms (an abbreviation formed from initials—usually capital letters) with words so the replaced words will not be all uppercase.

Use the *Replace* feature to replace one font with another. In the *Replace* box, only the fonts used in your current presentation are listed. After you change fonts, check each slide because text box sizing and alignment with other slide objects may need adjustment.

### ▶ HOW TO: Use Replace to Change Fonts

1. Display any slide in your presentation.

2. Click the **Replace** drop-down arrow [*Home* tab, *Editing* group] and select **Replace Fonts**.

   - The *Replace Font* dialog box opens (Figure 6-48).

3. Click the arrow in the *Replace* box to select from the fonts used in the current presentation.

4. Type the name of the font or click the arrow in the *With* box to select a font you want to use.

5. Click the **Replace** button and the text is changed.

   - If you want to change another font, change both the *Replace* and *With* font names and click **Replace** again.

6. Click **Close** to close the *Replace Font* dialog box.

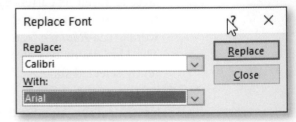

6-48 *Replace Font* dialog box

## Smart Lookup

The **Smart Lookup** pane is a new feature in PowerPoint 2016 that uses Bing, an Internet search engine, to provide information about a selected word or words. The *Smart Lookup* pane displays dictionary definitions and provides links to other online information without leaving PowerPoint.

---

▶ **HOW TO:** Use Smart Lookup

1. Click the word you want to check.
   - If you need to check a phrase, then select the words.
2. Click the **Smart Lookup** button [*Review* tab, *Insights* group] (Figure 6-49) to open the *Smart Lookup* pane.
   - You may see a message about Microsoft's privacy statement (Figure 6-50) if this is the first time *Smart Lookup* is used on your computer.
   - Click **Got it** to use this feature.
3. View the results in the *Smart Lookup* pane (Figure 6-51).
   - At the top of the pane, **Explore** is selected by default.
   - Pronunciation for the word, a brief definition, example of use, and synonyms are shown. Images may appear.
   - Scroll down the pane to see additional links to Wikipedia or other sites on the web.
   - Click the link, which appears as a title, and that web site opens in a new window.
4. Click **Define** at the top of the pane to read a more detailed definition with synonyms.
5. Click a different word in PowerPoint and then click the **Smart Lookup** button again to see different search results.
6. Close the *Smart Lookup* pane.

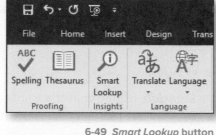

6-49 *Smart Lookup* button

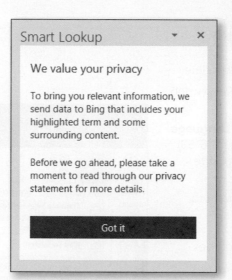

6-50 *Smart Lookup* privacy note

6-51 *Smart Lookup* pane

---

## Change Proofing Language

If you change the **proofing language** in PowerPoint, the spell checking and grammar rules for that language are applied automatically as you type.

## ▶HOW TO: Change Proofing Language

1. Select any text object. Click the **Language** button [*Review* tab, *Language* group].

2. Select **Set Proofing Language** and select a language (Figure 6-52). Click **OK**.

3. Type a word or phrase in the English language and the words will be marked as spelling errors since they are not in the language dictionary you selected.

4. Type a word in the proofing language you selected.
   - No spelling errors are noted.

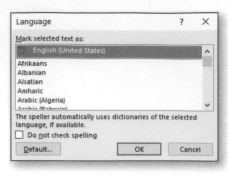

6-52 *Language* dialog box

## Translate Words

PowerPoint's **Translate** feature converts words or phrases to a different language. This translation works best for short passages and is not intended to translate an entire presentation.

## ▶HOW TO: Translate Words

1. Click the word you want to translate.

2. Click the **Translate** button [*Review* tab, *Language* group].

3. Select **Choose Translation Language** from the drop-down list (Figure 6-53) to open the *Translation Language Options* dialog box.
   - Select the language you want to use from the drop-down list (Figure 6-54).
   - Click **OK** to close the dialog box.

4. Click the **Translate** button [*Review* tab, *Language* group] again and select **Translate Selected Text**.
   - If you are using *Translate* for the first time, you will receive a message asking your permission to proceed since information is sent over the Internet. Click **Yes** to use this feature.
   - The *Research* pane (Figure 6-55) opens showing the *Bilingual Dictionary* definition.
   - Use this pane to look up a different word or change languages and search again.

6-53 Select *Choose Translation Language*

6-54 *Translation Language Options* dialog box

6-55 *Research* pane

*Or*

5. Click the **Translate** button and choose **Mini Translator**.

6. Point to the word you want to translate and the *Bilingual Dictionary* displays.
   - If you want to insert the translated word, click the **Copy** button on the *Mini Translator*, move to where you want the new word, and click **Paste**. Editing may be required.
   - Click the **Expand** button on the *Mini Translator* to open the *Research* pane where you select different languages.

7. Click the **Translate** button and click **Mini Translator** to turn off the translation feature.

> **ANOTHER WAY**
>
> Click the **Translate** button and select **Translate Selected Text**. Click **Yes** to proceed and the *Research* pane opens. Enter the language you want to use for translation.

## SLO 6.4 Creating Custom Slide Shows

The *Custom Slide Show* feature creates a presentation within a presentation. For example, if you have a lengthy presentation, you could prepare custom slide shows for each topic. Or perhaps slides from one presentation could be combined in different ways for two different audiences. Then a menu slide with hyperlinks will give you quick access to each custom slide show.

### Create, Edit, and Show a Custom Slide Show

To create a custom slide show, you start with an open presentation. The *Define Custom Show* dialog box identifies all slides in your presentation listed by number and slide title. You select which slides you want in your custom show and arrange their order.

### ▶ HOW TO: Create a Custom Slide Show

1. Open the presentation that contains the slides you want to use in your custom slide show.
2. Click the **Slide Show** tab.
3. Click the **Custom Slide Show** button [*Start Slide Show* group], and choose **Custom Shows** (Figure 6-56) to open the *Custom Shows* dialog box (Figure 6-57).

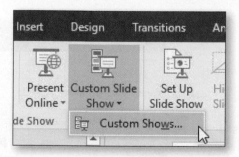

6-56 Select *Custom Shows*

6-57 *Custom Shows* dialog box

4. Click the **New** button to open the *Define Custom Show* dialog box (Figure 6-58).
   - On the left, all slides in the original presentation are listed under *Slides in presentation*.

5. Type a name for the custom show.

6. Select the check box next to each slide you want to include in the custom show.

7. Click the **Add** button and the slides you have selected are listed on the right under *Slides in custom show* (Figure 6-59).

   - Change the slide order, if necessary, by selecting a slide name and clicking the **Up** and **Down** buttons.
   - Delete a slide from your list by selecting the slide name and clicking the **Remove** button.
   - When you delete a slide from the custom show, your original presentation is not affected.

8. Click **OK** when your list of slides is complete and in the order you want.

9. Choose from the following options in the *Custom Shows* dialog box:

   - **New:** Create another custom show
   - **Edit:** Revise the selected custom show
   - **Remove:** Delete a custom show
   - **Copy:** Copy a custom show
   - **Show:** Display a slide show starting with the first slide of the custom show
   - **Close:** Close the *Define Custom Show* dialog box

10. Save your presentation so the custom shows are saved within it.

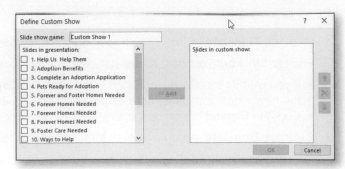

6-58 Define *Custom Show* dialog box

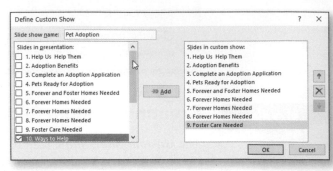

6-59 Slides added to the custom show

> **MORE INFO**
>
> If a presentation being used for custom shows has sections, the section names do not appear in the sequential list of slides in the *Define Custom Show* dialog box.

Once a show is created, you can view it using the *Custom Slide Show* button.

### ▶HOW TO: Show a Custom Slide Show

1. Open a presentation that includes one or more custom shows.

2. Click the **Slide Show** tab.

3. Click the **Custom Slide Show** button [*Start Slide Show* group] and select the name of your custom show (Figure 6-60).

   - The slide show automatically begins.

4. Test the custom show from beginning to end to verify that the correct slides display in the correct sequence.

6-60 Select a custom show

## Hyperlink Custom Slide Shows

To make it easy to access custom slide shows within a presentation, create a table of contents or menu slide with hyperlinks from text or shapes to link to the custom shows. For more on hyperlinks, see *SLO 5.2: Adding Hyperlinks and Action Buttons.*

### ▸ HOW TO: Hyperlink to a Custom Show

1. Open a presentation that includes one or more custom shows.
2. Type text or prepare shapes with text labels to identify the custom shows and serve as your hyperlink.
3. Select the text or shape for the first show.
4. Click the **Hyperlink** button [*Insert* tab, *Links* group] to open the *Insert Hyperlinks* dialog box.
   - Under *Link to*, click **Place in This Document**.
   - In the *Select a place in this document* list, select the custom show you want to link to (Figure 6-61).
   - Select the **Show and return** check box. Click **OK**.
5. Repeat steps 2–4 to link to additional custom shows.
6. Test the hyperlinks in *Slide Show* view to be sure each custom show opens, advances correctly, and returns to the linked slide.

6-61 Prepare a hyperlink to a custom show

If you want a subtle approach for your link to custom shows, create action buttons designed to be less noticeable on the slide. See the *Create Action Buttons* section in *SLO 5.2: Adding Hyperlinks and Action Buttons.*

For this project, you continue to work on the Hope Run presentation. You use proofing tools and create custom shows within the presentation.

File Needed: **PP P6-1.pptx**
Completed Project File Name: **[your initials] PP P6-2.pptx**

1. Open the **[your initials] PP P6-1** presentation and save it as [your initials] PP P6-2.

2. Remove sections.
   a. Click the **Section** button [*Home* tab, *Slides* group].
   b. Select **Remove All Sections**.

3. Add a custom *AutoCorrect* entry.
   a. Click the **File** tab to open the *Backstage* view.
   b. Choose the **Options** button to open the *PowerPoint Options* dialog box.
   c. Click the **Proofing** button on the left.
   d. Select the **AutoCorrect Options** button. The *AutoCorrect* dialog box opens.
      • In the *Replace* box, type Kamila.
      • In the *With* box, type Kamela (Figure 6-62).
      • Click **Add**. This pair of words is added to the *AutoCorrect* lists.
      • Click **OK** to close the *AutoCorrect* dialog box.
   e. Click **OK** to close the *PowerPoint Options* dialog box.

6-62 *AutoCorrect* dialog box

4. Test the new *AutoCorrect* entry.
   a. Display slide 8 and select the text **Mrs** below the picture.
   b. Type Kamila and space once. Notice that the spelling automatically changes to **Kamela**.

5. Use *Find* and *Replace*.
   a. Display slide 1 and click the **Find** button [*Home* tab, *Editing* group] or press **Ctrl+F**. The *Find* dialog box opens.
      • Delete text if any letters remain from a previous search.
      • Type Honor in the *Find what* box.
      • Select **Match case** and **Find whole words only**.
   b. Click the **Replace** button to change to the *Replace* dialog box (Figure 6-63).
      • Type HONOR in the *Replace with* box.
      • Click the **Replace All** button to change all occurrences of the word.
      • Click **OK** to close the dialog box indicating the replacements were made.
   c. Repeat steps 5a–b to change the words Remember to REMEMBER and Give to GIVE.
      • Press **Tab** to quickly move from the *Find what*: text box to the *Replace with*: text box.
   d. Click **Close** to close the *Replace* dialog box.

6-63 *Replace* dialog box

6. Use the *Smart Lookup* pane.
   a. Display slide 13 and click the word "**camaraderie**" to place your insertion point in the word.
   b. Click the **Smart Lookup** button [*Review* tab, *Insights* group] to open the *Smart Lookup* pane (Figure 6-64).
      • An Internet connection is required to use this feature so you may be asked to accept Microsoft's privacy statement. Click **Yes**.
      • Consider the definition shown.
      • Click one of the links to open a browser window with additional information.
      • Close the browser window.
   c. Close the *Smart Lookup* pane.

7. Create two custom slide shows.
   a. Click the **Slide Show** tab.
   b. Click the **Custom Slide Show** button [*Start Slide Show* group], and select **Custom Shows** to open the *Custom Shows* dialog box.
   c. Click the **New** button to open the *Define Custom Show* dialog box.
      • Select the default text in the *Slide show name* text box and type Event Information.
      • Click slides 2–11 on the left to select them (Figure 6-65).
      • Click the **Add** button so these slides are also listed on the right under *Slides in custom show*.
      • Click **OK** to close the *Define Custom Show* dialog box.
   d. Repeat step 6c using the *Slide show name* Tips to Prepare and select slides 12–16.
   e. Click **OK** to close the *Define Custom Show* dialog box.
   f. Click **Close** to close the *Custom Show* dialog box.

8. Hyperlink to the two custom shows.
   a. Display slide 1. Insert two rectangle shapes (*Height* **.5"**) with the word Event on one and Prepare on the other to identify the custom shows.
      • Apply **Bold** and change the font color (if necessary) to **White, Background 1** [*Home* tab, *Font* group].
      • Position these shapes on the lower left (Figure 6-66).
   b. Select the *Event* shape.
   c. Click the **Hyperlink** button [*Insert* tab, *Links* group] to open the *Insert Hyperlink* dialog box.

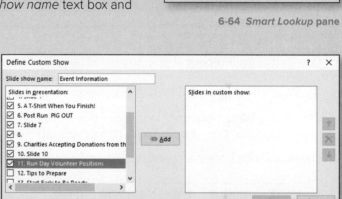

6-64 *Smart Lookup* pane

6-65 Slides selected for the custom show

6-66 Shapes for hyperlinks to custom shows

- Click **Place in This Document** under *Link to*.
- Select the **Event Information** custom show in the *Select a place in this document* list (Figure 6-67).
- Select the **Show and return** check box. Click **OK**.

6-67 Prepare a hyperlink to a custom show

d. Select the **Prepare** shape and repeat step 8c to create a hyperlink for the **Tips to Prepare** custom show.

e. Test the hyperlinks in *Slide Show* view to verify that each custom show opens and advances correctly.

9. Select the **Wipe** transition [*Transitions* tab, *Transition to This Slide* group] and apply the **From Left** *Effect Options*. Click **Apply To All** [*Transitions* tab, *Timing* group].

10. Save and close the presentation (Figure 6-68).

6-68 PP P6-2 completed

# Adding and Reviewing Comments

The **Comments** feature provides a way to enter notes about presentation content without affecting the design of slides. Comments are attached to text, objects, or the slide itself. While developing a presentation, use comments to write notes to yourself about revisions or where additional information is needed. If you plan to collaborate with another person, you can ask questions or comment on specific slides and the person reviewing the presentation can respond with his or her own comments.

When your presentation is ready for review, be sure to save the original. Then share a copy of your presentation as an email attachment or by posting it on a shared location. The person reviewing the presentation can make changes and add comments and return or repost it. Use PowerPoint's **Compare** feature to merge the reviewed presentation with your original version so you view all the changes and comments at one time and consider edits and suggestions. Once you decide which advice to heed, accept or reject any changes that were made.

## Insert Comments

When you insert a comment, a comment icon appears on the slide and the *Comments* pane opens. A text box showing your name is available where you type your comment. The time when the comment is made is automatically recorded and updated.

---

▶**HOW TO:** Insert a Comment

---

1. Select the text or object on the slide that you want to reference.

2. Click the **New Comment** button [*Review* tab, *Comments* group] (Figure 6-69).

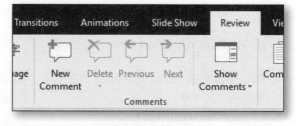

6-69 *New Comment* button

   - The comment icon appears near the selected object. If no object is selected, the comment icon appears in the upper left corner of the slide.
   - The *Comments* pane opens showing your name and an empty text box.
   - Type your comment in the text box (Figure 6-70).

6-70 Comment typed in the *Comments* pane

   - The comment time displays first as seconds; it is automatically updated to minutes or hours as time progresses. If the comment was created more than 24 hours ago, the date displays.
   - Press **Enter** or click outside the comment box when you have finished entering your comment.

3. Click the *New Comment* button [*Review* tab, *Comments* group] or the *New* button at the top of the *Comments* pane to insert another comment.

4. Close the *Comments* pane when all comments are complete.

---

If you are working on a presentation with multiple comments, click the **Next** or **Previous** button in the *Comments* group on the *Review* tab (Figure 6-71) to move between comments. Scroll through comments by clicking the up or down arrows at the top of the *Comments* pane.

When you close the *Comments* pane, the comment icons remain on the slide. If you want to hide comments, click the **Show Comments** button and deselect **Show Markup** (see Figure 6-71).

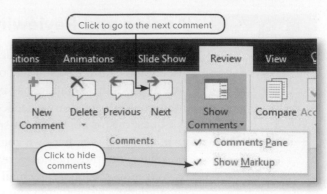

6-71 Move to the next comment

## Change User Name

Comments are identified by the user name and initials specified in the *PowerPoint Options* dialog box. When you initially install Microsoft Office on your computer, you are prompted to enter your ***user name*** and ***initials***. Office stores this information to personalize Office on your computer. As a result, your user name appears as the ***author*** of each new presentation you create. Similarly, each comment made in PowerPoint is attributed to the user name stored in Office.

On a public computer, such as in a computer lab on your college campus, a generic user name is assigned to Office. Change your user name and initials so your comments are attributed to you.

▶ **HOW TO:** Change User Name

1. Click the **File** tab to open the *Backstage* view.

2. Choose the **Options** button to open the *PowerPoint Options* dialog box.

3. Click the **General** button on the left (Figure 6-72).

4. Type your name in the *User name* text box.

5. Type your initials in the *Initials* text box.

6. Click **OK** to close the *PowerPoint Options* dialog box.

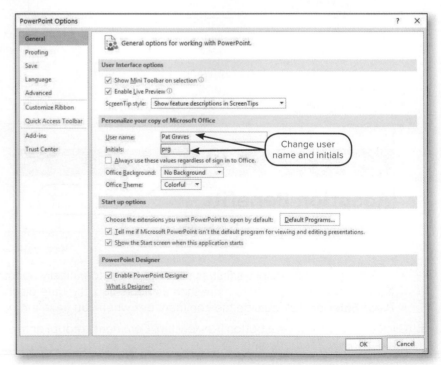

6-72 Change user name in the *PowerPoint Options* dialog box

## Edit and Reply to a Comment

If the *Comment* pane is not open, double-click the comment icon. Edit a comment by clicking the *Comment* pane text box and making revisions. Below each comment is a *Reply* box where you can add a related comment. Using the *Reply* box creates a "discussion thread" about that concept (Figure 6-73).

## Compare Presentations

*Compare* is a collaboration feature that combines two versions of a presentation. This feature is very useful when you want to consider the feedback from someone who has reviewed the presentation. You can consider all comments and changes and accept or reject the revisions. Be sure you have your original presentation saved in case you need to go back to that version. When you use *Compare*, the revised presentation is merged with the original presentation so you can save it with a different name.

More than one reviewer can provide feedback on a presentation as long as all the presentations with reviewer comments are compared to your same presentation file.

6-73 Reply to a comment

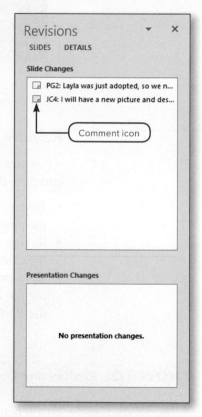

6-74 *Revisions* pane

▶**HOW TO:** Compare Presentations

1. Open your original presentation. Click the **Compare** button [*Review* tab, *Compare* group] to open the *Choose File to Merge with Current Presentation* dialog box.

2. Browse to locate the reviewer presentation, select it, and click **Merge**.

   • The two presentations are combined and the *Revisions* pane automatically opens (Figure 6-74).

3. Save this merged version with a different file name so you still have the original presentation.

   • If the *Revisions* pane closes, reopen it by clicking the **Reviewing Pane** button in the *Compare* group on the *Review* tab (Figure 6-75).

At the top of the *Revisions* pane, the *Details* tab is selected showing *Slide Changes* as you review each slide. In the *Revisions* pane, comments are shown in an abbreviated form and include the initials of the person making the comment. An icon also appears before the comment in a different color for each person. These comments are the same ones you see when you review them in the *Comments* pane.

6-75 *Reviewing Pane* button

If you want to read all of the text for a comment, click the icon or the **Show Comments** button [*Review* tab, *Comments* group] to open the *Comments* pane. Changes made to content placeholders or slide objects are listed with a different icon and a brief explanation for what changed. Click the icon in the *Revisions* pane or on the slide to see the reviewer's changes (Figure 6-76). Consider each change and comment in a presentation and accept, reject, or skip the changes.

6-76 Changes were made to a placeholder by the reviewer

## Review Comments and Accept or Reject Changes

After you have compared presentations and you are working with the merged presentation, complete the review process using one of these methods:

- Review each comment individually and delete them one-by-one or delete all comments in the presentation when you have finished.
- Review proposed changes and either accept or reject each item individually or accept all the changes at one time.
- View only the slides that have either a comment or change. Move to those slides by clicking the *Previous* or *Next* buttons in either the *Comments* group or the *Compare* group on the *Review* tab.

---

▶ **HOW TO:** Review and Delete Comments

1. Begin your review on the first slide of the presentation.
2. Click the first comment if it is on this slide or click the **Next** button [*Review* tab, *Comments* group] to go to the first comment.
3. Click the comment icon to open the *Comments* pane.
   - If you already have the *Revisions* pane open, the *Comments* pane opens beside it.
   - Comments appear on both panes.
   - To focus on just comments now, close the *Revisions* pane.
4. Consider the comment and then use one of the following methods to delete it:
   - Select the comment in the *Comments* pane and click the black **X** (Figure 6-77) or press **Delete**.

6-77 *Delete* in the *Comments* pane

- Right-click a comment icon on the slide and select **Delete Comment** from the context menu.
- Select a comment icon and click the top half of the **Delete** button [*Review* tab, *Comments* group] (Figure 6-78).
- Click the **Delete** drop-down arrow [*Review* tab, *Comments* group] and select **Delete All Comments and Ink on This Slide** or **Delete All Comments and Ink in This Presentation**.

6-78 *Delete* options

When you accept an editing or formatting change, the change is applied to the slide, and the change icon is marked. When you reject an editing or formatting change, the text and formatting remain in their original form.

▶ **HOW TO:** Accept or Reject Changes

1. Begin your review on the first slide of the presentation. If no changes are on this slide, click the **Next** button [*Review* tab, *Compare* group] to go to the first change.
2. Click the first change icon on the slide or in the *Revisions* pane to view the change.
3. Click the **Accept** or **Reject** button [*Review* tab, *Compare* group] to accept or reject the change.

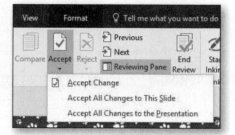

6-79 *Accept* options

   - If you click the **Accept** drop-down arrow, you may then choose *Accept Change*, *Accept All Changes to This Slide*, or *Accept All Changes to the Presentation* (Figure 6-79).
   - If you click the **Reject** drop-down arrow, you may then choose *Reject Change*, *Reject All Changes to This Slide*, or *Reject All Changes to the Presentation*.
   - Click the **Next** button to skip a comment or revision in the document.
4. Click the **Next** button when you have completed the changes on a slide to go to the next change.
5. Click one or more check boxes on a placeholder with multiple changes before accepting or rejecting.

   - Click the change icon to see the entire list of changes.
   - Check the box at the top of the list to select all changes (Figure 6-80).
   - Check the box for each item listed that you want to accept or reject.

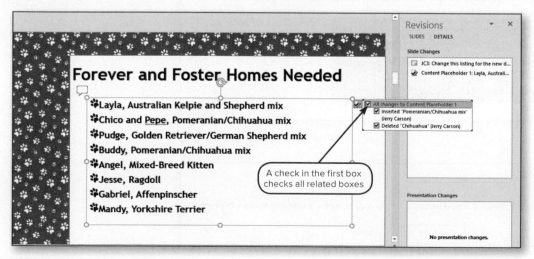

6-80 Select changes to accept or reject

6. Click the change icon and check the box for a reviewer's inserted object (Figure 6-81) to add the object to the slide (Figure 6-82).

- If a reviewer changed an object such as a table, you first see the original version on the slide (Figure 6-83). Check the change icon to see the reviewer's changes (Figure 6-84).

After you accept or reject the last change in the presentation, a dialog box opens confirming the last change and asking if you want to continue reviewing from the beginning. Click **Cancel** (Figure 6-85) to close the dialog box.

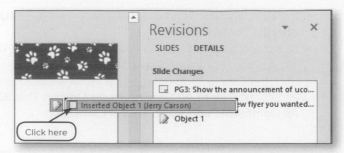

6-81 Click the change icon check box to insert the object

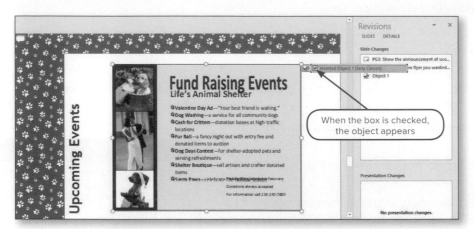

6-82 Reviewer's object inserted

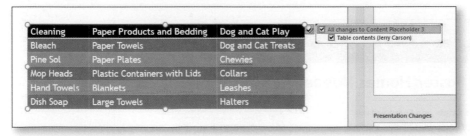

6-83 Table before reviewer's changes

6-84 Table with reviewer's changes

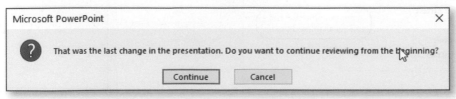

6-85 Dialog box that appears after reviewing the presentation

For this project, you insert comments for Kamela Graham and then compare the original and a reviewed presentation. You consider and delete comments and accept or reject changes made by the reviewer.

Files Needed: **[your initials] PP P6-2.pptx** and **HopeRunReview-06.pptx** (student data files are available in the Library of your SIMnet account)
Completed Project File Names: **[your initials] PP P6-3a.pptx** and **[your initials] PP P6-3b.pptx**

1. Open the **[your initials] PP P6-2** presentation and save it as [your initials] PP P6-3a.

2. Change the user name if necessary.
   a. Click the **File** tab to open the Backstage view.
   b. Choose the **Options** button to open the PowerPoint Options dialog box.
      - Click the **General** button on the left (Figure 6-86).
      - Type your name in the User name text box.
      - Type your initials in the Initials text box.
   c. Click **OK** to close the PowerPoint Options dialog box.

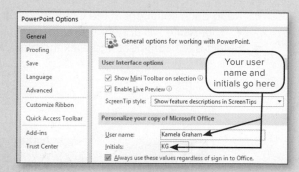

6-86 Change user name in *PowerPoint Options*

3. Insert comments.
   a. Display slide 3. Click the **New Comment** button [Review tab, Comments group] to open the Comments pane.
      - Type Have you verified that these times are all correct? (Figure 6-87).
      - Move the comment icon above the times in the table.

6-87 Comment inserted

   b. Display slide 9. Click the **New** button at the top of the Comments pane.
      - Type Please check this list to be sure all charities we are using are listed.
      - Move the comment icon near the list.
   c. Display slide 10. Click the **New** button in the Comments pane again.
      - Type Be sure we have printed enough copies of this form.
      - Move the comment icon near the form.
   d. Close the Comments pane.
   e. Save the presentation.
      - Assume this presentation was distributed to Travis Alano for his feedback.
      - The remaining steps will compare presentations and you will consider his comments and changes.

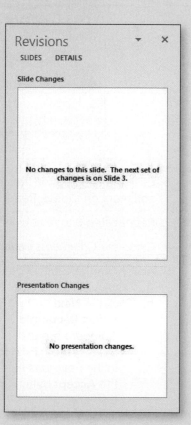

6-88 *Revisions* pane showing no changes on slide 1

4. Compare presentations.
   a. With *[your initials] PP P6-3a* open, click the **Compare** button [*Review* tab, *Compare* group]. The *Choose File to Merge with Current Presentation* dialog box opens.
   b. Browse to locate your student data files, select ***HopeRunReview-06***, and click **Merge**.
      - The two presentations are combined and the *Revisions* pane automatically opens.
      - Display slide 1 and notice no changes are on this slide (Figure 6-88).
   c. Save this merged version as *[your initials] PP P6-3b*.

5. Review and delete comments.
   a. Display slide 3, the first slide with a comment.
   b. Click one of the comment icons to open the *Comments* pane.
   c. Read each comment in the *Comments* pane (Figure 6-89).
      - Your name will appear rather than Kamela Graham. The dates and times will be different.
   d. Select each comment and click the black **X** that appears to delete the comment.

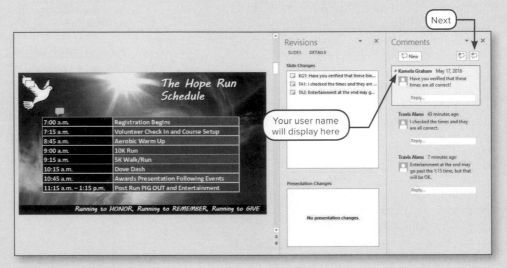

6-89 *Comments* pane with comments on slide 3

6. Click the **Next** button [*Review* tab, *Comments* group or on the *Comments* pane] to go to the next comment on slide 5. Read and delete the comment.

7. Repeat step 6 to review and delete the remaining comments on slides 9 and 10.

8. Close the *Comments* pane.

9. Accept and reject changes.
   a. Display slide 1 to begin your review.
   b. Click the **Next** button [*Review* tab, *Compare* group] to go to the first reviewer change on slide 6.
      - Select **Rectangle 7** in the *Revisions* pane and click the **Accept** button [*Review* tab, *Compare* group].
      - Select **Title2: Post Run PIG OUT** in the *Revisions* pane and click the **Accept** button [*Review* tab, *Compare* group] (Figure 6-90).
      - Notice that the icons for these items are checked in the *Revisions* pane and on the slide.

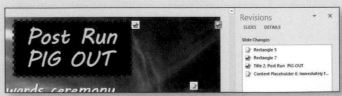

6-90 Accepting changes

- Check the revision icon on the right of the slide (**Content Placeholder** in the *Revisions* pane) so you can see the change of yellow text. Click the **Reject** button [*Review* tab, *Compare* group].
- Check the revision icon beside "PIG OUT" (**Rectangle 5** in the *Revisions* pane) so you can see the change of a rectangle. Click the **Reject** button [*Review* tab, *Compare* group].
- Notice that the icons for these rejected items are still visible but are not checked.

c. Click the **Next** button [*Review* tab, *Compare* group] to go to slide **11**. Accept the changes by checking the icon or clicking the **Accept** button. Repeat to accept changes on each of the remaining slides (12, 13, and 14) with reviewer changes.
- Slide 11: Title 1 wordwrap changes and yellow is applied to text in the content placeholder.
- Slide 12: Title 2 is revised.
- Slide 13: Title 2 wordwrap changes.
- Slide 14: Text is revised in the content placeholder.

d. Click the **Next** button after slide 14 and a dialog box opens indicating the last change has been made.
- Click **Cancel** to avoid reviewing again from the beginning.

e. Click the **End Review** button [*Review* tab, *Compare* group] because you have read and deleted all comments and accepted or rejected all changes.

f. Click **Yes** to close the dialog box about ending the review.
- The changes are made and icons removed. The *Revisions* pane closes.

10. Save and close the presentation (Figure 6-91).

6-91 PP P6-3b completed

## Preparing to Share a Presentation

PowerPoint can alert you to potential problems when preparing your presentation to be shared with and modified by multiple users. You may want to protect your content so it cannot be modified by other users or restrict who can view the presentation by adding a password. All of these inspecting and protecting features are available on the *Backstage* view in the *Info* section.

## Inspect Presentation

The **Inspect Presentation** feature looks for hidden content, properties, or personal information that you may not want to share. When you use the *Inspect Presentation* feature, PowerPoint generates a report and allows you to choose to remove properties or hidden information from your presentation before sharing it with other users.

Once information is removed using the *Document Inspector* dialog box, you may not be able to restore the removed information if you later need it. Therefore, create a copy of your presentation before removing the information.

### ▶ HOW TO: Inspect a Presentation

1. Click the **File** tab to open the *Backstage* view, *Info* section (Figure 6-92).
2. Click the **Check for Issues** button and select **Inspect Document** to open the *Document Inspector* dialog box (Figure 6-93).
   - Most listed items are already selected.
   - Deselect any item that you do not want to inspect.

6-92 *Check for Issues* options

6-93 *Document Inspector* dialog box

3. Click **Inspect**.
   - The inspection results appear in the *Document Inspector* dialog box (Figure 6-94).
4. Click the **Remove All** button for each area that contains content you want to remove from your presentation.
   - If you want to inspect the presentation again after you remove content, click the **Reinspect** button.
5. Click the **Close** button to close the *Document Inspector* dialog box.

6-94 Document inspection results

## Check Accessibility

When a presentation with audio recordings is distributed for independent viewing, people with hearing impairments will be limited because this content cannot be heard. Graphic information such as pictures, charts, and *SmartArt* that add visual appeal and contribute to a sighted person's understanding cannot be seen by people with visual impairments.

A variety of assistive technologies help with these problems. For example, screen reader software can convert text to audio. An individual can start a PowerPoint slide show in *Reading* view and will hear the text content of slides as they advance. While converting text to audio works well for many PowerPoint slides, pictures and graphics, such as *SmartArt* or other illustrations, cannot be read. Background themes may contain graphics and artwork, but those items are not read on the individual slides.

PowerPoint's **Check Accessibility** feature identifies potential issues that users with disabilities may have with your presentation. The *Accessibility Checker* pane displays what is found as errors or warnings and provides tips about other items you might need to check. As you click each item in the list, additional information displays for each issue and a possible fix is suggested.

▶ **HOW TO:** Check Accessibility

1. Click the **File** tab to open the *Backstage* view, *Info* section.
2. Click the **Check for Issues** button and select **Check Accessibility** to open the *Accessibility Checker* pane (Figure 6-95).
3. Select one of the results in the *Inspection Results* area.
   - In the *Additional Information* area, details on why and how to fix accessibility issues display.
   - If a list is collapsed, a white arrow appears before the item name and a number in parentheses follows the item name showing the number of errors (Figure 6-96).
4. Click the **X** in the upper right corner to close the *Accessibility Checker* pane.

6-95 *Accessibility Checker* pane with expanded and collapsed lists

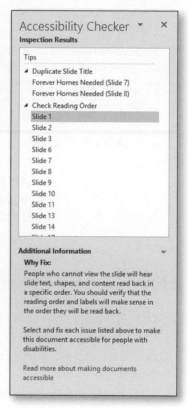

6-96 *Accessibility Checker* pane showing a suggestion

Not everything displayed in the list must change. For example, you may have the same title on more than one slide if you intentionally duplicated the slide and changed content but not the title.

Solutions for accessibility issues may be as simple as revising the reading order for slide content. When a screen reader is used, a slide title is heard before bulleted text. If you have a slide with other content, you may need to specify the reading order so content makes sense to someone who is only hearing the text rather than seeing the slide. Reading order is changed using the *Selection* pane.

## ▶HOW TO: Change Reading Order

1. Use the inspection results in the *Accessibility Checker* pane as your guide to select a slide where reading order may be an issue.

2. Click the **Home** tab, click the **Select** button [*Editing* group], and then choose **Selection Pane.**

3. Select an object name in the *Selection* pane and that object is also selected on the slide.

   - Consider the order shown for the names of slide objects (Figure 6-97).
   - With a screen reader, objects are read starting at the bottom of the list and ending with the top object.

4. Select an object name that is not in the correct order and click the **Bring Forward** or **Send Backward** arrows as needed to move the object up or down in the list.

   - In this example, *TextBox 6* should move below *TextBox 5* so the *Pet Adoption* shape is read before the *Ways to Help* shape.

5. Repeat as needed to address other items listed in the *Accessibility Checker* pane.

6. Close the *Accessibility Checker* and the *Selection* panes when the order is correct.

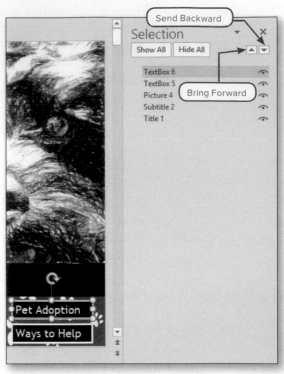

6-97 *Selection* pane

*Alt Text* (Alternative text) is text describing pictures or other graphic objects on a slide. With a screen reader, the description text is read so a person who cannot see the slide can still understand the content of the picture or object.

## ▶HOW TO: Add Alt Text

1. Use the inspection results in the *Accessibility Checker* pane as your guide to select a slide missing *Alt Text*.

2. Select a picture or shape, right-click, and choose *Format Picture* or *Format Shape*.

3. Click the **Size & Properties** button and click **Alt Text**.

4. Type an appropriate description and title (Figure 6-98).

   - Once you enter *Alt Text*, the item is no longer listed on the *Accessibility Checker* pane.
   - In this example, the text on *SmartArt* graphic shapes is typed as *Alt Text*.

5. Repeat as needed to address other items listed in the *Accessibility Checker* pane.

6. Close the *Accessibility Checker* and the *Format Shape* panes when all the *Alt Text* is added.

6-98 Add *Alt Text* for a *SmartArt* graphic

> **MORE INFO**
>
> When preparing slides that you want to be as accessible as possible, enter all text using slide placeholders. Reading is better during playback. Omit footer or header information that would be redundant when read on every slide.

## Check Compatibility

The *Check Compatibility* feature looks for compatibility issues between the current version of PowerPoint and versions before 2007. This feature is useful if you share presentations with others who are using these earlier versions of PowerPoint.

### ▶ HOW TO: Check Compatibility

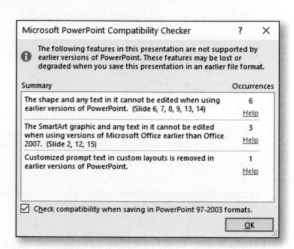

1. Click the **File** tab to open the *Backstage* view, *Info* section.
2. Click the **Check for Issues** button and select **Check Compatibility** to open the *Microsoft PowerPoint Compatibility Checker* dialog box (Figure 6-99).
   - The *Summary* area displays potential compatibility issues.
   - Based on the summary, change your presentation as needed.
3. Click **OK** to close the dialog box.

6-99 *Microsoft PowerPoint Compatibility Checker dialog box*

Conversions between PowerPoint 2016 and 2013, 2010, or 2007 should work well. However, new features such as transition effects, styles, or video capabilities are not supported in these earlier versions and will display differently. If you convert from the current software to the 97-2003 version, additional changes will be evident. For example, *SmartArt* and tables are converted to pictures and soft shadows are converted to solid-color shadows. The appearance of these objects on the slide may be acceptable, but the features cannot be edited in the older software.

When you open an earlier presentation file in PowerPoint 2016, it opens in compatibility mode. Many software features are disabled if you continue to work on the presentation in compatibility mode. Resave it as a 2016 presentation to take advantage of all current software features.

## Mark as Final

*Mark as Final* creates a read-only file. This action protects a presentation from being accidentally altered. When a user opens a presentation that is marked as final, the *Info* bar displays a notification message and a *Mark as Final* icon displays in the *Status* bar.

### ▶ HOW TO: Mark a Presentation as Final

1. Save the presentation before marking it as final.
2. Click the **File** tab to open the *Backstage* view, *Info* section.

3. Click the **Protect Presentation** button (Figure 6-100) and select **Mark as Final**.

- A dialog box opens to inform you that the presentation will be marked as final and saved (Figure 6-101).
- Click **OK**.

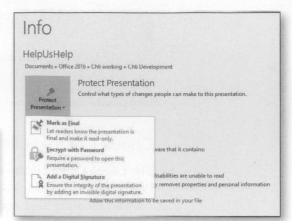

6-100 *Protect Presentation* options

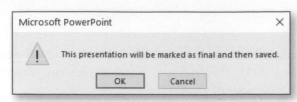

6-101 Dialog box confirms choice to mark as final

- Another dialog box opens to provide information about the final version (Figure 6-102).

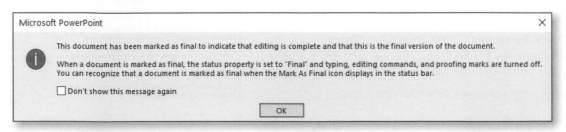

6-102 Marked as final informational dialog box

- Check the **Don't show this message again** box if you don't want this informational dialog box to appear again.
- Click **OK**.

4. Read the *Info* bar notation between the *Ribbon* and the *Ruler*. It indicates that the presentation has been marked as final (Figure 6-103).

6-103 *Marked as Final* notation in the *Info* bar

- The *Ribbon* is collapsed and the presentation is protected from editing.
- A *Mark as Final* icon displays near slide numbers on the *Status* bar.
- On the *Backstage* view, a notation stating the presentation has been marked as final appears in the *Protect Presentation* area (Figure 6-104).

6-104 *Marked as Final* notation on the *Backstage* view

---

*Mark as Final* is not considered a security feature because users can still edit the presentation by turning off *Mark as Final*. You can turn off *Mark as Final* in two ways:

- Click the **Edit Anyway** button in the *Info* bar (see Figure 6-103).
- Click the **File** tab to open the *Backstage* view, click the **Protect Presentation** button, and then select **Mark as Final**.

# Encrypt with Password

Protect a presentation with the ***Encrypt with Password*** feature so it can only be opened if a user enters the authorized password when prompted. You must apply this feature before marking a presentation as final.

> ### HOW TO: Encrypt a Presentation with a Password

1. Click the **File** tab to open the *Backstage* view, *Info* section.
2. Click the **Protect Presentation** button and select **Encrypt with Password** to open the *Encrypt Document* dialog box (Figure 6-105).
3. Type a password in the *Password* text box.
   - Passwords are case sensitive.
   - Verify that **Caps Lock** is turned off when you type your password.
4. Click **OK**. The *Confirm Password* dialog box opens.
5. Type the password in the *Reenter password* text box and click **OK**.
   - On the *Backstage* view, a notation stating that a password is required to open the presentation appears in the *Protect Presentation* area (Figure 6-106).
6. Click the **Back** button to close the *Backstage* view and return to the presentation.

6-105 *Encrypt Document* dialog box

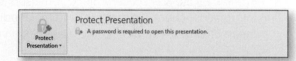

6-106 Password notation on the *Backstage* view

> ### MORE INFO
> Be sure to store presentation passwords in a secure location. If you lose your password, you will not be able to open your own file.

After you save and close your password-encrypted presentation, you must enter the password to reopen it. Type the password in the dialog box (Figure 6-107) and click **OK** to open the presentation.

Once you have opened a presentation that is encrypted with a password, you can remove the password.

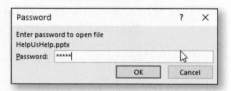

6-107 *Password* dialog box

> ### HOW TO: Remove a Presentation Password

1. Open the password-encrypted presentation using the authorized password.
2. Click the **File** tab to open the *Backstage* view, *Info* section.
3. Click the **Protect Presentation** button and select **Encrypt with Password**.
   - The *Encrypt Document* dialog box opens.
4. Delete the password in the *Password* text box and leave the box blank.
5. Click **OK** to close the dialog box and remove the password.
6. Click the **Back** button to close the *Backstage* view and return to the presentation.

## Digital Signature

A digital signature, or digital ID, is used to sign documents electronically. It confirms identity of the signer and assures that the document where it is applied has not been altered. A digital signature has become important because of the migration from paper to digital documents. You obtain a digital signature from a certification authority such as *DocuSign* or *Comodo*. A signature is usually valid for one year and then must be renewed.

The **Add a Digital Signature** feature [*Backstage* view, *Info* section] helps ensure the integrity of a presentation. The presentation is marked as final and becomes a read-only presentation. Signed presentations display a *Signatures* button on the *Status* bar.

## PAUSE & PRACTICE: POWERPOINT 6-4

For this Pause & Practice project, you inspect the revised Hope Run presentation and remove personal information, check accessibility and make adjustments, and check compatibility. After you have made these changes, you protect the presentation by encrypting it with a password and marking it as final.

File Needed: *[your initials] PP P6-3b.pptx*
Completed Project File Name: *[your initials] PP P6-4.pptx*

1. Open the presentation *[your initials] PP P6-3b* and save it as [your initials] PP P6-4.

2. Inspect the presentation.
   a. Click the **File** tab to open the *Backstage* view, *Info* section.
   b. Click the **Check for Issues** button and select **Inspect Document** to open the *Document Inspector* dialog box.
   c. Deselect the **Document Properties and Personal Information** check box.
   d. Click **Inspect**. The *Document Inspector* dialog box opens with the inspection results displayed (Figure 6-108).
      - Click **Remove All** in the *Comments and Annotations* area if any comments were found.
      - The embedded document cannot be removed from this dialog box. Leave as shown.
   e. Click **Close**.
   f. Save the presentation.

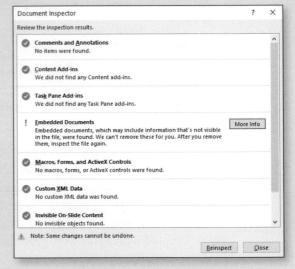

6-108 *Document Inspector* with inspection results displayed

3. Check accessibility and add *Alt Text* on three slides.
   a. Click the **File** tab to open the *Backstage* view, *Info* section.
   b. Click the **Check for Issues** button and select **Check Accessibility** to open the *Accessibility Checker* pane.

c. Select **Picture 8 (Slide 4)** under *Missing Alt Text* (Figure 6-109).
   - Slide 8 automatically displays.
d. Right-click the picture of a woman running and choose **Format Picture**.
   - The *Format Picture* pane opens on the left of the *Accessibility Checker* pane.
   - Click the **Size & Properties** icon and click **Alt Text** (Figure 6-110).
e. Locate the text for this item in the first row of the following table.
   - Type the title and the description text under *Alt Text* in the *Format Picture* pane.
   - As you add *Alt Text*, the item is removed from the list.
f. Select **Picture 1 (Slide 5)**.
   - The slide displays and the T-shirt on the left is automatically selected.
   - Type the title and description text in the second row of the following table.
g. Repeat step 3f for the remaining items listed in the following table.

6-109 *Accessibility Checker* with results displayed

6-110 *Alt Text* added

| Item | Title Text | Description Text |
|---|---|---|
| Picture 8 (Slide 4) | Woman runner | A picture of a woman runner. |
| Picture 1 (Slide 5) | T-shirt front | The Hope Run T-shirt has a small dove on the front. |
| Picture 3 (Slide 5) | T-shirt back | The Hope Run T-shirt has a large dove on the back. |
| Picture 1 (Slide 10) | Dove | A dove is the symbol of the Hope Run. |
| Object 3 (Slide 10) | Pledge form | The Hope Run Donation Pledge form is featured. |

h. Close the *Format Object* pane.
4. Adjust reading order for one slide listed in the *Accessibility Checker* pane.
   a. Select **Slide 1** in the list under *Check Reading Order*.
   b. Click the **Home** tab, click the **Select** button [*Editing* group], and choose **Selection Pane**.
   c. Click the **eye** icon for *Rectangle 6*, *Rectangle 4*, and *Rectangle 8*.
      - A straight line replaces the eye showing that these shapes will not be visible on the slide.
      - In this case, a person using a screen reader will advance through all slides in sequence rather than using custom shows.
   d. Select **Subtitle 2** and click the **Bring Forward** button (Figure 6-111).
      - A screen reader will read from the bottom of the list and go up: the title, sponsored by text, then the subtitle.
   e. Close the *Accessibility Checker* and the *Selection* panes.
   f. Save the presentation.

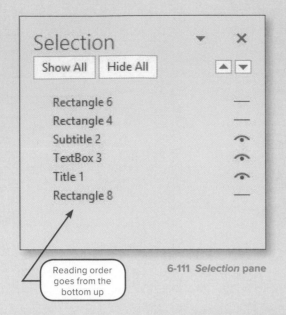

6-111 *Selection* pane

Reading order goes from the bottom up

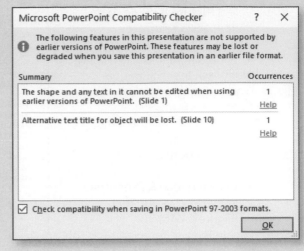

6-112 *Microsoft PowerPoint Compatibility Checker* dialog box

5. Check compatibility of the presentation with 97-2003 software.
   a. Click the **File** tab to open the *Backstage* view, *Info* section.
   b. Click the **Check for Issues** button and select **Check Compatibility**.
   c. Note the summary on the *Microsoft PowerPoint Compatibility Checker* dialog box (Figure 6-112).
   d. Click **OK** to close the dialog box.

6. Encrypt the presentation with a password.
   a. Click the **File** tab to open the *Backstage* view, *Info* section.
   b. Click the **Protect Presentation** button and select **Encrypt with Password** to open the *Encrypt Document* dialog box (Figure 6-113).
   c. Type the password Dove1 and click **OK** to open the *Confirm Password* dialog box.
   d. Type Dove1 in the *Reenter password to confirm* text box.
   e. Click **OK** to close the dialog box.

7. Mark the presentation as final.
   a. Click the **Protect Presentation** button [*File* tab, *Info* section] and select **Mark as Final**.
      • A dialog box opens with the marked as final message.
   b. Click **OK**.
      • Another dialog box opens with the final version message.
      • The message will not appear if you previously selected the *Don't show this message again* check box.
   c. Click **OK**.
      • The presentation is automatically saved.

6-113 *Encrypt Document* dialog box

8. Close the presentation (Figure 6-114).

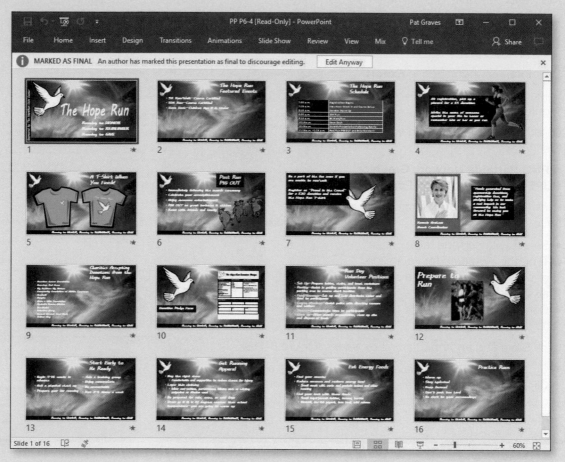

6-114 PP P6-4 completed

## Saving and Exporting in Different File Types

Save individual slides as pictures to use the content in different ways such as in a flyer or a report. Create a PDF file or save your presentation as a video file so people can view your presentation if PowerPoint is not available. Create handouts using Microsoft Word to choose from several layouts not available in PowerPoint.

### Save a Slide as a Picture

When you save slides in a picture format, you have the option to save all the slides in the presentation as separate pictures or to save only selected slides.

You can use these individual slides within other documents, or you could use them to create posters. For example, if you sent your slide picture to a photo printing company, you could have a large poster-size print made. Even large canvas prints can be made.

1. Open the presentation with the slides you want to save as one or more pictures.

   • If you want to save just one slide, select the slide.

2. Click **File** and then choose **Export**.

3. Select **Change File Type** (Figure 6-115).

4. Select one of the following *Image File Types:*

   • **PNG Portable Network Graphics**
   • **JPEG File Interchange Format**

5. Click the **Save As** button to open the *Save As* dialog box.

   • Select your storage location.
   • Type the file name for your slide or presentation if you are saving all slides.
   • Confirm the *Save as type* is the one you want (*PNG* or *JPEG*).

6. Click **Save** and another dialog box opens (Figure 6-116),

   • Click **Just This One** to save the current slide as a picture.
   • Click **All Slides** to save every slide in the presentation as a picture. Pictures will be saved in a folder and individually named and numbered beginning with *Slide 1.*

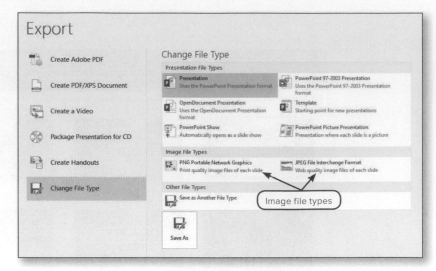

6-115 Export a presentation by changing the file type

6-116 Export one slide or all slides as pictures

▶ **ANOTHER WAY**

Select a slide and choose the **Save As** option from the *File* tab and name the file. In the *Save as type* box, select *PNG* or *JPEG* from the available options. Click **Save**.

## Create PDF/XPS Documents

When your presentation is finished, save it in a PDF or XPS format. PDF (Portable Document Format) is an Adobe format that is viewed using Adobe Reader (available at no cost) or Adobe Acrobat. XPS (XML Paper Specification) is a document format developed by Microsoft.

These PDF and XPS formats create copies of a presentation that can be viewed or printed without PowerPoint. This content is more secure than it is when viewed in PowerPoint because it is not editable. These formats also significantly reduce file size, so electronic distribution is easier. You can create a PDF or XPS file from individual slides, handouts, or notes pages.

## ▶HOW TO: Save a Presentation as a PDF File

1. Open the presentation you want to save as a PDF file.
2. Click **File** and choose **Export**.
3. Select **Create PDF/XPS Document** and click the **Create PDF/XPS** button (Figure 6-117) to open the *Publish as PDF or XPS* dialog box.
4. Select your storage location.
5. Type the file name for your presentation.
6. Confirm the *Save as type* is **PDF** (Figure 6-118).
7. Select **Open file after publishing** if you want to open the file in its new format.
   - The file will open in *Acrobat Reader* if that program is installed on your computer.
8. Verify that the default *Optimize* option for **Standard (publishing online and printing)** is selected.
   - This option results in higher print quality.
   - Select **Minimum size (publishing online)** to create a smaller file size that makes electronic distribution easier.
9. Click the **Options** button to open the *Options* dialog box (Figure 6-119).
   - For *Range*, select **All**, **Current slide**, or **Selection**.
   - For *Publish what*, select **Slides**, **Handouts**, **Notes pages**, or **Outline view**.
   - Select other options as needed.
10. Click **OK** to close the *Options* dialog box.
11. Click **Publish**.
    - A presentation exported as a handout is shown in *Adobe Reader* (Figure 6-120).

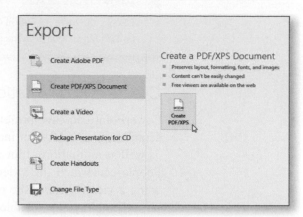

6-117  Export as PDF or XPS document

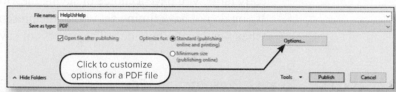

Click to customize options for a PDF file

6-118  File type, *Optimize* choices, and *Options* in the *Save As* dialog box

6-119 *Options* dialog box for creating a PDF file

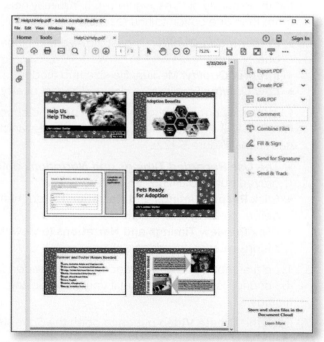

6-120  Exported presentation as a PDF handout shown in *Adobe Reader*

## Create a Presentation Video

PowerPoint can save presentations as video files. When you create a video from your presentation, the video can include all recorded timings, narrations, and laser pointer gestures as well as animations, transitions, and media. All of these elements are saved with the slides. People can watch the video on their computers without PowerPoint if you share it online using a video sharing site or *OneDrive*. With a DVD burner and burning software, you can burn the video to a writable DVD.

Video files are created using the Windows media video format. Because file sizes are typically large, you have a choice of saving the video at different resolutions based on your needs. If you do not have timing set within the presentation, then control how fast the slides advance when you create the video. The process of saving as a video can take quite a bit of time.

### ▶ HOW TO: Create a Presentation Video

1. Open the presentation you want to save as a video.
2. Click the **File** tab and then choose **Export**.
3. Select **Create a Video**.
4. Click the list arrow on the first list box and choose one of the three quality options (Figure 6-121). You may need to test more than one option to find results that meet your needs.
   - *Presentation Quality:* Largest file size and highest quality
   - *Internet Quality:* Medium file size and moderate quality
   - *Low Quality:* Smallest file size and lowest quality
5. Click the list arrow on the second list box and choose whether you want to include recorded timings and narrations (Figure 6-122).
   - The *Use Recorded Timings and Narrations* option is grayed out if no timings are entered.
   - Click **Record Timings and Narration** to add them before creating the video.
   - Click **Preview Timings and Narrations** to view them before creating the video.
6. Type a number for *Seconds spent on each slide* (5 seconds is the default time) if you are not using timings.
7. Click the **Create Video** button to open the *Save As* dialog box.
   - Select your storage location.
   - Type the file name for your video.
   - For *Save as type*, select *MPEG-4 Video* or *Windows Media Video*.
   - Click **Save**.

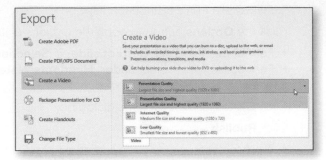

6-121 Select an appropriate video quality

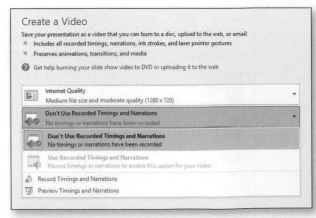

6-122 Select timings and narrations

Test your video by adding a blank slide in PowerPoint and inserting your video. Play the video to be sure it plays correctly (Figure 6-123). If you need to change transitions for selected slides, make the changes, resave your presentation, and then export the video again.

## Create Handouts in Word

If you would like more control over formatting when you create handouts than is available in PowerPoint, use Word to revise and print handouts.

6-123 Test the video in PowerPoint

---

### ▶ HOW TO: Create Handouts in Word

1. Open the presentation you want to use to create handouts.
2. On the *File* tab, choose **Export** and select **Create Handouts** (Figure 6-124).
3. Click the **Create Handouts** button to open the *Send to Microsoft Word* dialog box (Figure 6-125).
4. Choose from one of the following page layouts:
   - **Notes next to slides**
   - **Blank lines next to slides**
   - **Notes below slides**
   - **Blank lines below slides**
   - **Outline only**
5. Select one of the following paste options:
   - **Paste** embeds the slides and the Word Document will remain unchanged if the presentation changes.
   - **Paste link** allows changes made to the presentation to be reflected in the Word document.
6. Click **OK** and Word opens with the slides arranged as you selected.
   - This process takes a few moments as slides are converted to images and arranged in Word.
7. Edit the Word document as needed and save it using an appropriate name.

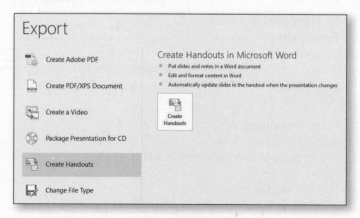

6-124 Export a presentation to create handouts in Microsoft Word

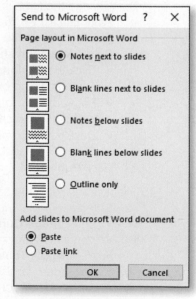

6-125 Page layouts in Word

For this Pause & Practice project, you work on additional presentation materials for the Hope Run event. You export a presentation to create a slide picture, a PDF version of a presentation, a presentation video, and a handout in Word.

---

File Needed: *[your initials] PP P6-4.pptx*
Completed Project File Names: *[your initials] PP P6-5a.jpg*, *[your initials] PP P6-5b.pdf*, *[your initials] PP P6-5c.pptx*, *[your initials] PP P6-5d.mp4*, and *[your initials] PP P6-5e.docx*

---

1. Open the presentation *[your initials] PP P6-4* using the password Dove1.

2. Click the **Edit Anyway** button to remove the *Marked as Final* notation.

3. Save a slide as a picture.
   a. Select slide 1.
   b. Click the **File** tab, choose **Export**, and select **Change File Type**.
   c. Select **JPEG File Interchange Format** (Figure 6-126).
   d. Click the **Save As** button to open the *Save As* dialog box.
      • Type the file name [your initials] PP P6-5a.
      • Click **Save** and a dialog box opens.
      • Click **Just This One**.

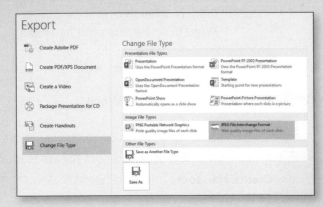

6-126 Export with the JPEG file format

4. Create a PDF file.
   a. Click the **File** tab, choose **Export**, and select **Create PDF/XPS Document**.
   b. Click the **Create PDF/XPS** button to open the *Publish as PDF or XPS* dialog box.
   c. Change the file name that appears to [your initials] PP P6-5b.
   d. Deselect **Open file after publishing**.
   e. Select **Minimum size (publishing online)**.
      • Click the **Options** button to open the *Options* dialog box.
      • For *Publish what*, select **Handouts** (**6** slides per page) and check **Frame slides**.
      • Deselect **Document Properties** (Figure 6-127).
      • Click **OK** to close the dialog box.
   f. Click **Publish**.

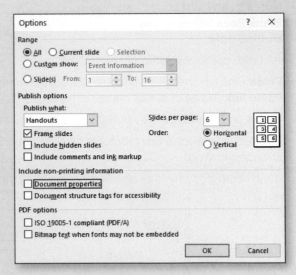

6-127 *Options* dialog box for saving a PDF file

5. Apply transitions and save the presentation.
   a. Select any slide and click the **Transitions** tab.
      • Select **Page Curl** [*Transition to This Slide* group].
      • Verify that *Effect Options* is **Double Left** [*Transition to This Slide* group]
      • Click **Apply To All** [*Timing* group].
   b. Select slides 1 and 2. Select the **Vortex** transition.
      • Select the *Effect Options* **From Right** [*Transition to This Slide* group].
   c. Save the presentation as [your initials] PP P6-5c.

6. Create a presentation video.
   a. Click the **File** tab, choose **Export**, and select **Create a Video**.
   b. Click the list arrow in the first box and choose the **Low Quality** option.
   c. Use the default setting on the second box for **Don't Use Recorded Timings and Narrations**.
   d. Type 3:00 seconds for *Seconds to spend on each slide* (Figure 6-128).
   e. Click **Create Video** to open the *Save As* dialog box.
   f. Change the file name that appears to [your initials] PP P6-5d.
   g. Select **MPEG-4 Video** for *Save as type*.
   h. Click **Save**.

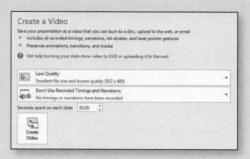

6-128 Options for exporting a video

7. Create a handout in Word.
   a. Prepare a sample of slides from this presentation to create a smaller file size. (Creating a document with slides as currently shown creates a Word file size over 69 MB.)
      • Click the **Slide Sorter** button. Select slides 6–16 and press **Delete**.
      • Double-click slide 1 to open it in *Normal* view.
      • Right-click the background and select **Format Background** to open the *Format Background* pane.
      • Select **Solid fill** and change the *Color* to **Blue, Accent 1** if necessary.
      • Click **Apply to All** in the *Format Background* pane.
   b. Click the **File** tab, choose **Export**, and select **Create Handouts**.
   c. Click the **Create Handouts** button to open the *Send to Microsoft Word* dialog box.
      • Select the page layout **Blank lines next to slides**.
      • Select **Paste** (Figure 6-129).
   d. Click **OK** and Word opens with the slides arranged as you selected.
      • If Word is minimized on the task bar, click the task bar Word button to open the Word window.

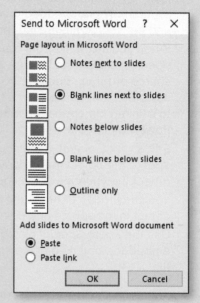

6-129 Options for exporting to Word

8. Compress pictures and save the document.
   a. Click **File** and choose **Save As** to open the *Save As* dialog box.
      • Locate where you need to save the file.
      • Type the file name [your initials] PP P6-5e.
      • Click the **Tools** drop-down arrow and select **Compress Pictures**.
      • Select **E-mail (96 ppi): minimize document size for sharing**. Click **OK**.
      • Click **Save**.
   b. Close the document and close Word.

9. Close the *[your initials] PP P6-5c* presentation without saving.

# Chapter Summary

**6.1** Add content from other sources and work with multiple open windows (p. P6-366).

- Create slides from a Word outline with heading styles.
- *Arrange All* enables you to see all open PowerPoint windows at one time.
- *Object linking and embedding (OLE)* allows users to integrate information from other Office applications into PowerPoint.
- When you *embed* a file from a source program, edit the embedded object in PowerPoint using the *Ribbon* from the source program. The embedded object in PowerPoint and the source file are independent.
- When you *link* a file from a source program, it opens in a separate window for editing in the source program. Because PowerPoint retains its connection to the source file, changes to a linked file appear in both the object in PowerPoint and the source file.
- Edit a linked object in the source file and update the object in the destination file to reflect the changes in the source file.
- You can modify or break the link between an object in the source and destination files.
- Use the *Paste Special* dialog box to paste an embedded or linked object into the destination file.

**6.2** Add sections to organize presentation slides (p. P6-377).

- *Sections* divide slides into groups which is helpful for a lengthy presentation.
- Add and rename sections in *Normal* view or *Slide Sorter* view.
- Edit and rearrange sections in *Slide Sorter* view.
- Move sections or move slides between sections.
- When you collapse sections, only section titles are visible.

**6.3** Use proofing tools to correct errors, improve word choices, and translate content (p. P6-383).

- The *AutoCorrect* feature recognizes and corrects commonly misspelled words and other errors.

- The *AutoFormat* feature makes punctuation corrections and other replacements.
- Add or delete *AutoCorrect* entries to customize proofing options.
- The *Find* feature allows you to search for a word, part of a word, or a phrase.
- The *Replace* feature allows you to search for a word, part of a word, or a phrase and replace it with other information. You can use the *Replace* feature to replace one font with another.
- The *Research* pane is useful for finding dictionary definitions, synonyms, and language translation.
- Change PowerPoint's *Proofing Language* to take advantage of spell checking and grammar rules for that language.
- The *Translate* feature converts words or phrases to a different language.

**6.4** Create a custom slide show of selected slides within a presentation (p. P6-389).

- A *Custom Slide Show* is a list of slides you choose within a presentation that displays in the order you determine.
- A presentation can contain more than one custom show.
- A hyperlink provides a convenient way to start a custom show.

**6.5** Insert, edit, and review comments, compare presentations, and consider reviewer feedback (p. P6-395).

- *Comments* allow you to write notes or provide feedback in a presentation without changing the design of slides.
- Add, edit, reply to, or delete comments. *Comments* appear in the *Comments* pane with a corresponding comment icon on the slide.
- Comments are associated with a Microsoft Office *user name* and *initials*, which can be changed in the *PowerPoint Options* dialog box.
- Use the *Previous* and *Next* buttons to review comments in a presentation. Delete comments individually or delete all comments in the presentation at the same time.

- **Compare** enables you to merge two versions of a presentation and review comments and changes to obtain reviewer feedback.
- The *Revisions* pane displays all of the changes in the presentation. Icon color and user initials distinguish changes made by different reviewers.
- Use the *Previous* and *Next* buttons to review changes in the merged presentation.
- Accept or reject changes individually or accept or reject all of the changes in the merged presentation at once.

**6.6** Prepare to share a presentation by removing personal information, checking for accessibility issues, checking compatibility, marking as final, and adding a password (p. P6-403).

- The **Inspect Presentation** feature targets hidden content, properties, or personal information that you may not want to share.
- The **Check Accessibility** feature identifies potential issues in a presentation that may cause problems for users with disabilities.
- **Alt Text** identifies graphic objects for assistive technologies such as screen readers.
- The **Check Compatibility** feature identifies potential problems when a current presentation is saved in a version before 2007.

- **Mark as Final** creates a read-only file and prevents the file from being accidentally edited.
- **Encrypt with Password** prevents a document from being opened without a password.

**6.7** Save and export a presentation by creating different file types and by creating a video (p. P6-413).

- When you change to an image file type, you can save one slide or all slides as separate pictures in a PNG or JPG format.
- PDF (Portable Document Format) or XPS (XML Paper Specification) files create copies of a presentation that can be viewed or printed without PowerPoint. Both formats create small file sizes.
- When you save a presentation as a video, all recorded timings, narrations, laser pointer gestures, and animations can be included. Video file sizes are usually large.
- Exporting a presentation to create handouts in Word provides additional layout options.

## Check for Understanding

The SIMbook for this text (within your SIMnet account) provides the following resources for concept review.

- Multiple choice questions
- Matching exercises
- Short answer questions

## Guided Project 6-1

For this project, you create a presentation for Margaret Jepson, insurance agent at Central Sierra Insurance, about home safety for her clients. You add content from different sources, make revisions, set up custom shows for each topic, and prepare the presentation for sharing.
[Student Learning Outcomes 6.1, 6.3, 6.4, 6.6]

Files Needed: **HomeSafety-06.pptx**, **FiresFalls-06.docx**, and **AccidentInjury-06.xlsx** (student data files are available in the Library of your SIMnet account)
Completed Project File Name: **[your initials] PowerPoint 6-1.pptx**

### Skills Covered in This Project

- Create slides from a Word outline.
- Embed a file.
- Use *Replace*.
- Create a custom slide show.

- Hyperlink a custom slide show.
- Inspect a presentation.
- Check accessibility issues.
- Add *Alt Text* and adjust reading order.

1. Open the presentation **HomeSafety-06** and save it as [your initials] PowerPoint 6-1.

2. Create slides from a Word outline.
   a. Display slide 3. Click the **New Slide** drop-down arrow [*Home* tab, *Slides* group] and select **Slides from Outline** to open the *Insert Outline* dialog box.
   b. Locate your student data files and select **FiresFalls-06**.
   c. Click **Insert**.

3. Update slide layouts.
   a. Click the **Maximize** button [*Title* bar] if your window is not already maximized so PowerPoint fills the screen.
   b. Change to *Slide Sorter* view and adjust the *Zoom* percentage so you can see all 18 slides (Figure 6-130).
   c. Select slides 4–9. Click the **Layout** button [*Home* tab, *Slides* group] and select the **Title and Content** layout.
   d. Click the **Reset** button to update the font.

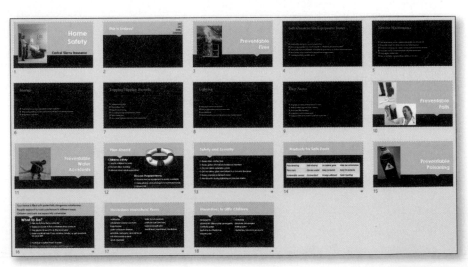

6-130 Slides inserted from a Word outline

4. Select slide 10, "Preventable Falls" (*Section Header* layout) and move it before slide 7 (Figure 6-131).

5. Save your presentation with the new slides. Restore your window or change it to a size you prefer.

6. Embed an Excel worksheet and modify the embedded object.

   a. Double-click slide 2 to display it in *Normal* view.

   b. Click the **Object** button [*Insert* tab, *Text* group] to open the *Insert Object* dialog box.

   c. Select **Create from File** and click the **Browse** button to open the *Browse* dialog box.
      - Locate your student data files and select *AccidentInjury-06*.
      - Click **OK** to close the *Browse* dialog box.

   d. Click **OK** to close the *Insert Object* dialog box and insert the worksheet.

   e. Increase the object size (approximate *Height* **4.5"**) and center it horizontally on the slide.

   f. Double-click the embedded object to open the *Ribbon* from the source program.

   g. Change the worksheet title to Accidental Deaths (Figure 6-132).

   h. Click outside the object to deselect it.

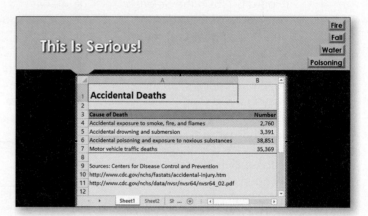

6-131 Slides with *Title and Content* layout applied

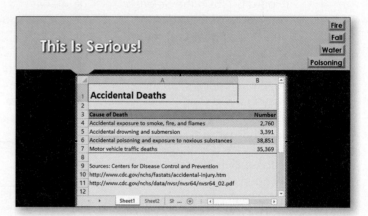

6-132 Embedded Excel file revised in PowerPoint

7. Use *Replace*.

   a. Display the first slide and click the **Replace** button [*Home* tab, *Editing* group] to open the *Replace* dialog box.
      - In the *Find what* box, type Preventable.
      - In the *Replace with* box, type Prevent.
      - Select **Match case** and **Find whole words only** (Figure 6-133).
      - Click the **Replace All** button to change all occurrences of the word.

   b. Click **OK** to close the dialog box indicating the number of replacements.

   c. Click **Close** to close the *Replace* dialog box.

8. Create four custom slide shows.

   a. Click the **Slide Show** tab.

   b. Click the **Custom Slide Show** button [*Start Slide Show* group] and select **Custom Shows** to open the *Custom Shows* dialog box.

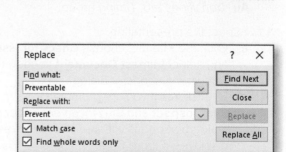

6-133 *Replace* dialog box

c. Click the **New** button to open the *Define Custom Show* dialog box.
  • For the *Slide show name*, type Fire.
  • Click slides 3–6 on the left to select them.
  • Click the **Add** button so these slides are also listed on the right under *Slides in custom show* (Figure 6-134).
  • Click **OK**.
d. Repeat step 8c for three more shows:

| Slide show name | Slides |
| --- | --- |
| Fall | 7–10 |
| Water | 11–14 |
| Poisoning | 15–18 |

e. Click **Close**.

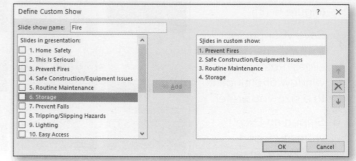

6-134 Slides added to the custom show

9. Hyperlink to the four custom shows.
  a. Display slide 2. Select the shape on the upper right corner with the word "Fire."
     • Be careful to select the shape and not the text only.
  b. Click the **Hyperlink** button [*Insert* tab, *Links* group] to open the *Insert Hyperlink* dialog box.
     • Under *Link to*, click **Place in This Document**.
     • Select the **Fire** custom show (Figure 6-135) in the *Select a place in this document* list.
     • Select the **Show and return** check box.
     • Click **OK**.
  c. Repeat to hyperlink from the remaining three shapes (*Fall, Water,* and *Poisoning*) to their respective custom shows.
  d. Test the hyperlinks in *Slide Show* view to verify that each custom show opens and advances correctly.

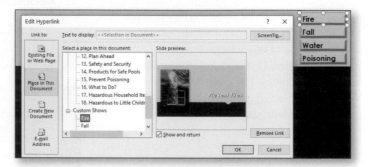

6-135 Hyperlink to a custom show

10. Select the **Fracture** transition [*Transitions* tab, *Transition to This Slide* group] and click **Apply To All** [*Transitions* tab, *Timing* group].

11. Inspect the presentation.
  a. Click the **File** tab, choose **Check for Issues**, and select **Inspect Document** to open the *Document Inspector* dialog box.
     • Click **Yes** if you are prompted to save the file.
  b. Click **Inspect** and the *Document Inspector* dialog box opens with the inspection results displayed (Figure 6-136).
  c. Click **Remove All** in the *Document Properties and Personal Information* area.
  d. Click **Close** to close the dialog box.

6-136 *Document Inspector* with inspection results displayed

12. Check presentation accessibility and add *Alt Text*.
  a. Click the **File** tab, click the **Check for Issues** button, and select **Check Accessibility**.
  b. Select **Object 1 (Slide 2)** in the *Accessibility Checker* pane under *Missing Alt Text*. The worksheet is selected on the slide.

c. Right-click the worksheet and choose **Format Object** to open the *Format Object* pane.
d. Click the **Size & Properties** button and click **Alt Text** (Figure 6-137).

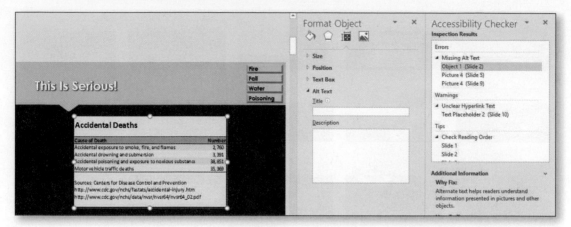

6-137 Add *Alt Text* to describe an object

e. Type the title and the description text for this item. Repeat for the two other items listed under *Missing Alt Text* in the *Accessibility Checker* pane as shown horizontally in the following table. The items are removed from the list as the *Alt Text* is entered.

| Item | Title Text | Description Text |
|---|---|---|
| Content Object 1 (Slide 2) | Accidental deaths | This table shows statistics in four categories of accidental deaths. |
| Picture 4 (Slide 11) | Swimming lesson | An adult is teaching a young girl to swim. |
| Picture 4 (Slide 15) | Poison | This picture shows a bottle of poison. |

f. Close the *Format Object* pane.

13. Adjust the reading order for two items listed in the *Accessibility Checker* pane.
    a. Select **Slide 2** under *Check Reading Order*.
    b. Click the **Home** tab, click the **Select** button [*Editing* group] and choose **Selection Pane**.
    c. Click the *Bring Forward* or *Send Backward* arrow so the content is in the order shown in the following table. (A screen reader reads from the bottom up.)
    d. Repeat for **Slide 12**.

| Slide 2 | | Slide 12 | |
|---|---|---|---|
| *Selection Pane* | *Description* | *Selection Pane* | *Description* |
| Object 1 | Inserted worksheet | Content Placeholder 6 | Rescue Preparedness |
| TextBox 10 | Poisoning | Picture 7 | Flotation |
| TextBox 9 | Water | Content Placeholder 2 | Children Safety |
| TextBox 11 | Fall | Title 1 | Plan Ahead |
| TextBox 12 | Fire | | |
| Title 3 | This is Serious! | | |

e. Close the *Accessibility Checker* and the *Selection* panes.

14. Save and close the presentation (Figure 6-138).

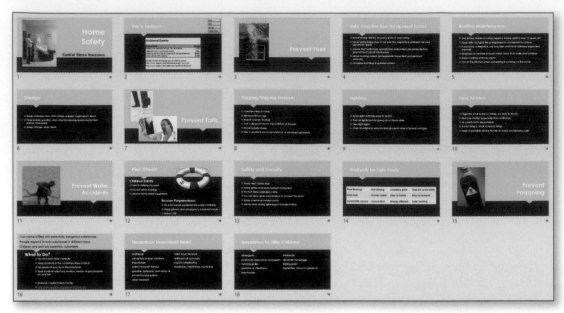

6-138 PowerPoint 6-1 completed

## Guided Project 6-2

Business faculty from the colleges within the Sierra Pacific Community College District are working together to create promotional presentations about available careers in different fields of business. For this project, you highlight several information technology careers with content from other sources and divide the presentation into sections.

**[Student Learning Outcomes 6.1, 6.2, 6.3, 6.5, 6.6]**

Files Needed: ***ITCareers-06.pptx***, ***ITCertifications-06.docx***, and ***ITSalaryChanges-06.xlsx*** *(student data files are available in the* Library *of your SIMnet account)*
Completed Project File Names: *[your initials]* ***PowerPoint 6-2a.pptx*** and *[your initials]*
***PowerPoint 6-2b.jpg***

### *Skills Covered in This Project*

- Embed a Word object.
- Use *Paste Special* to link to an Excel object.
- Break a link to an object.
- Add and rename sections.

- Use *Replace*.
- Insert comments.
- Add a password.
- Export a slide as a picture.

1. Open the presentation ***ITCareers-06*** and save it as [your initials] PowerPoint 6-2a.

2. Embed an object from a Word file.

a. Display slide 10. Click the **Object** button [*Insert* tab, *Text* group] to open the *Insert Object* dialog box.

b. Select **Create from File** and click the **Browse** button to open the *Browse* dialog box.
   - Locate your student data files and select **ITCertifications-06** (Figure 6-139).
   - Click **OK** to close the dialog box.

c. Click **OK** to close the *Insert Object* dialog box and embed the object.
   - A list of certifications with a texture fill and black outline appears.

d. Position the list on the right as shown in Figure 6-140.

e. Click outside the object or press **Esc** to deselect it.

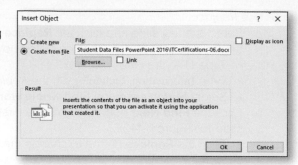

6-139 *Insert Object* dialog box

3. Use *Paste Special* to link to an object.
   a. Open Excel. Click **File** and **Open**.
      - Locate your student data files and select **ITSalaryChanges-06**.
      - Click **Open** to open the worksheet and close the dialog box.
   b. Select the chart and press **Ctrl+C**.
   c. Go to PowerPoint and display slide 12.
   d. Click the **Paste** drop-down arrow [*Home* tab, *Clipboard* group] and select **Paste Special** to open the *Paste Special* dialog box.
      - Select **Paste link**. In the *As* area, select **Microsoft Excel Chart Object**.
      - Click **OK** to close the *Paste Special* dialog box and the object appears on your slide.
   e. Increase the chart size (approximate *Height* **4.5"** and *Width* **7"**).
   f. Move the chart to the right side of the slide (Figure 6-141).
   g. Press **Esc** to turn off the copy selection.
   h. Close the worksheet and close Excel.

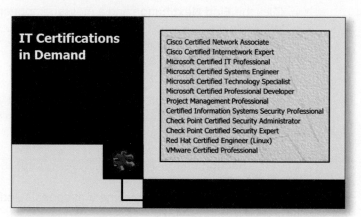

6-140 Word file embedded in PowerPoint

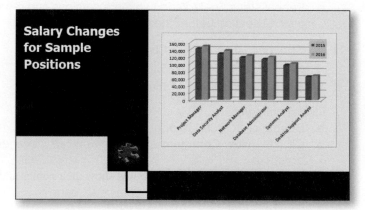

6-141 Linked Excel chart in PowerPoint

4. Break the link to an object.
   a. Click the **File** tab to open the *Backstage* view.
   b. Click the **Info** button on the left.
   c. Click **Edit Links to Files** at the bottom of the *Properties* list to open the *Links* dialog box.
      - Select the source file of the linked object in the *Links* area.
      - Click the **Break Link** button and the source file name is removed automatically.
      - Click **Close** to close the *Links* dialog box.
   d. Click the **Back** arrow to return to your presentation.

5. Use *Replace*.
   a. Select the first slide and click the **Replace** button [*Home* tab, *Editing* group]. The *Replace* dialog box opens.
      - Type **IT** in the *Find what* box.
      - Type **Information Technology** in the *Replace with* box.
      - Select **Match case** and **Find whole words only**.
   b. Click the **Find Next** button to go to the first occurrence on slide 10 (Figure 6-142).
      - Click the **Replace** button to change the highlighted word.
      - Resize the text placeholder on the right side so "in Demand" is on the last line of text.
      - Deselect the placeholder.
      - Click the **Find Next** button and a message appears indicating that this was the last match.
      - Click **OK** to close the message.
   c. Click **Close** to close the *Replace* dialog box.

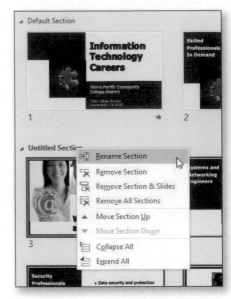

6-142 *Replace* dialog box

6. Add and rename sections.
   a. Click the **Slide Sorter** button [*Status* bar] and adjust your *Zoom* percentage to approximately **70%** so you can see all slides.
   b. Click after slide 2.
   c. Click the **Section** button [*Home* tab, *Slides* group] and select **Add Section**.
   d. Point to the **Untitled Section** name that appears and right-click (Figure 6-143).
   e. Select **Rename Section** to open the *Rename Section* dialog box.
   f. Type **Skills** and click **Rename**.
   g. Repeat steps 6c–f to add two more sections and rename the first section before the first slide:

   | | |
   |---|---|
   | *Click after slide 8* | Certifications |
   | *Click after slide 10* | Salaries |
   | *Default Section* | Introduction |

7. Insert comments.
   a. Double-click slide 1 to open it in *Normal* view.
   b. Click the **New Comment** button [*Review* tab, *Comments* group].
   c. Type **Colleges in the District could show their names and addresses on this slide.** in the *Comments* pane (Figure 6-144).
   d. Display slide 12. Click the **New** button at the top of the *Comments* pane.
   e. Type **Please verify this data for our area.**
      - Move the comment icon near the top of the chart.
   f. Close the *Comments* pane.

8. Save a slide as a picture.
   a. Display slide 1.
   b. Click the **File** tab, choose **Export**, and select **Change File Type**.

6-143 *Rename Section* in *Slide Sorter* view

6-144 Comment inserted

c. Select **JPEG File Interchange Format** (Figure 6-145).

d. Click the **Save As** button.

e. Type the file name [your initials] PowerPoint P6-2b in the *Save As* dialog box.

f. Click **Save**. In the dialog box that opens, click **Just This One**.

9. Select the **Gallery** transition [*Transitions* tab, *Transition to This Slide* group] and click **Apply To All** [*Transitions* tab, *Timing* group].

10. Encrypt a presentation with a password.

a. Click the **File** tab, click the **Protect Presentation** button, and select **Encrypt with Password** to open the *Encrypt Document* dialog box.

b. Type the password PP6-2a (Figure 6-146) then click **OK** to open the *Confirm Password* dialog box.

c. Type PP6-2a in the *Reenter password to confirm* text box.

d. Click **OK** to close the dialog box.

11. Save and close the presentation (Figure 6-147).

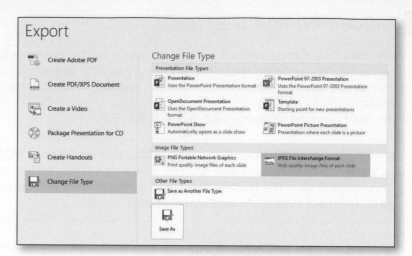

6-145 Export with the JPEG file format

6-146 *Encrypt Document* dialog box

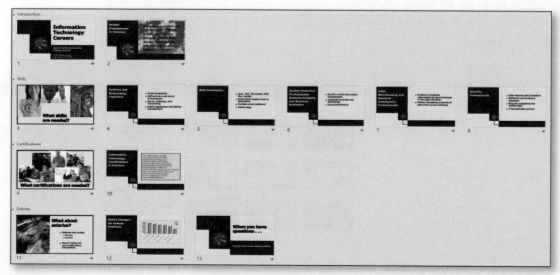

6-147 PowerPoint 6-2a completed with inserted sections in *Slide Sorter* view

# Guided Project 6-3

Hamilton Civic Center offers a summer day camp for children ages 6–12. For this project, you will complete a presentation about the day camp including information on fees, activities, and regulations. You add content from other sources, create custom shows, consider reviewer comments, and mark the presentation as final.
**[Student Learning Outcomes 6.1, 6.3, 6.5, 6.6, 6.7]**

Files Needed: ***HCCDayCamp-06.pptx***, ***HCCListedInfo-06.pptx***, ***HCC-SoccerClub-06.pdf***, and ***HCCDayCampReview-06.pptx*** (*student data files are available in the* Library *of your SIMnet account*)
Completed Project File Names: *[your initials] PowerPoint 6-3a.pptx*, *[your initials] PowerPoint 6-3b. pptx*, and *[your initials] PowerPoint 6-3c.mp4*

## Skills Covered in This Project

- Work with multiple PowerPoint windows.
- Copy slides from one presentation to another.
- Embed a file.
- Insert comments.

- Compare presentations.
- Accept or reject changes.
- Inspect a presentation.
- Create a video.
- Mark as final.

### `Part A

1. Open the presentation ***HCCDayCamp-06*** and save it as [your initials] PowerPoint 6-3a.

2. If your window is not already maximized, click the **Maximize** button [*Title* bar] so PowerPoint fills the screen.

3. Open a second presentation and arrange two PowerPoint windows side-by-side.
   a. Open the ***HCCListedInfo-06*** presentation.
   b. Click the **Switch Windows** button [*View t*ab, *Window* group] and select **[your initials] PowerPoint 6-3a** to active it.
   c. Click **Arrange All** [*View t*ab, *Window* group].
      - Your current presentation (destination) is on the left and the second presentation (source) is on the right.
      - Change to *Slide Sorter* view in both presentations.
      - Change the *Zoom* in each presentation to approximately **80%** so you can see all slides.

4. Copy and paste slides from the source presentation.
   a. Select slides 2–4 (Figure 6-148) in the source presentation on the right and press **Ctrl+C**.
   b. Select your current presentation (destination presentation) to make it active and click after slide 8.

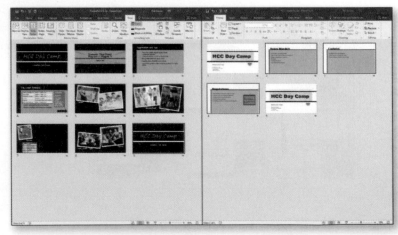

6-148 Two presentation windows displayed using *Arrange All*

   c. Press **Ctrl+V** to paste the slides.

   d. Save your *[your initials] PowerPoint 6-3a* presentation with the new slides and close the *HCCListedInfo-06* presentation.

   e. Maximize your PowerPoint window or restore it to the size you prefer.

5. Adjust placeholders.

   a. Double-click slide 11 to open it in *Normal* view.

   b. Select the bulleted placeholder and drag the right sizing handle to change the *Width* to **7"**.

6. Embed a PDF file.

   a. Display slide 7 and click the **Object** button [*Insert* tab, *Text* group] to open the *Insert Object* dialog box.

   b. Select **Create from File** and click the **Browse** button to open the *Browse* dialog box.

     • Locate your student data files and select *HCCSoccerClub-06*.

     • Click **OK** to close the dialog box.

   c. Click **OK** to close the *Insert Object* dialog box.

   d. Change the object size (*Height* **5.5"**) [*Drawing Tools Format* tab, *Size* group] and position it on the right.

   e. Click outside the object to deselect it (Figure 6-149).

6-149 **PDF object embedded in PowerPoint**

7. Change the user name if necessary.

   a. Click the **File** tab to open the *Backstage* view.

   b. Choose the **Options** button to open the *PowerPoint Options* dialog box.

   c. Click the **General** button on the left.

   d. Type your name in the *User name* text box.

   e. Type your initials in the *Initials* text box.

   f. Click **OK** to close the *PowerPoint Options* dialog box.

8. Insert comments.

   a. Display slide 2. Click the **New Comment** button [*Review* tab, *Comments* group] to open the *Comments* pane.

     • Type Please find an appropriate picture from last year to fit on the bottom of this slide. (Figure 6-150).

   b. Display slide 4. Click the **New** button at the top of the *Comments* pane.

     • Type Breakfast is new this year. Should we emphasize it more?

     • Click the **New** button again and type Please provide additional feedback.

   c. Close the *Comments* pane.

6-150 **Comment inserted**

9. Save the *[your initials] PowerPoint 6-3a* presentation and keep it open.

## Part B

10. Compare the current presentation with a reviewer presentation.
    a. With *[your initials] PowerPoint 6-3a* open, click the **Compare** button [*Review* tab, *Compare* group] to open the *Choose File to Merge with Current Presentation* dialog box.
       * Browse to locate your student data files and select **HCCDayCampReview-06**.
       * Click **Merge** to combine the two presentations.
       * The *Revisions* pane automatically opens.
    b. Save this merged presentation as [your initials] PowerPoint 6-3b.

11. Review and delete comments.
    a. Display slide 2, the first slide with a comment.
    b. Click one of the comment icons to open the *Comments* pane.
    c. Read the comments in the *Comments* pane and click the black **X** (Figure 6-151) to delete each comment.
    d. Click the **Next** button [*Review* tab, *Comments* group or on the *Comments* pane] to go to the next comment on slide 4. Read and delete the comments.

    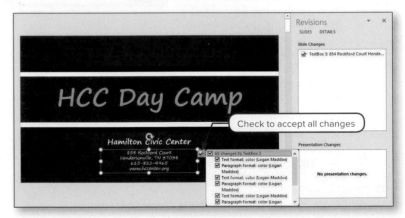

    6-151 *Revisions* and *Comments* panes on slide 2

    e. The *Comments* pane indicates that no additional comments remain in the presentation.
    f. Close the *Comments* pane.

12. Accept reviewer changes by checking the change icons displayed on each slide with changes.
    a. Display slide 1. Select the change icon and check **All Changes to TextBox 3** (Figure 6-152).
    b. Click the **Next** button [*Review* tab, *Compare* group] to go to the next change on slide 2.
    c. Select the change icon and check **Inserted Picture 3**.

    6-152 Accept multiple changes to one object

    d. Repeat steps 12b–c to go to each remaining slide with changes and accept all changes:
       * Slide 3, two changes
       * Slide 4, four changes
       * Slide 7, one change
       * Slide 11, two changes
       * Slide 12, one change
    e. Click **End Review** [*Review* tab, *Compare* group].

f. Click **Yes** when asked to confirm ending the review.
- The *Revisions* pane closes and all change icons are removed.

g. Select "Discipline Problems" on slide 11 and change the font size to **28 pt**. and apply **Bold**.

13. Save your presentation.

14. Select the **Wipe** transition [*Transitions* tab, *Transition to This Slide* group] and **From Left** effect options.
    a. Click **Apply To All** [*Transitions* tab, *Timing* group].
    b. Review the presentation in *Slide Show* view to be sure all slides are corrected and advance appropriately.

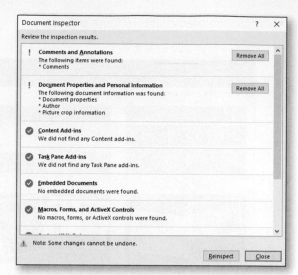
6-153 *Document Inspector* with inspection results displayed

15. Inspect the presentation.
    a. Click the **File** tab, choose **Check for Issues**, and select **Inspect Document**.
    b. Click **Yes** if a warning message appears about saving your presentation.
    c. Verify that all check boxes are selected on the *Document Inspector* dialog box.
    d. Click **Inspect** and results display (Figure 6-153).
    e. Click **Remove All** after *Document Properties and Personal Information*.
    f. Click **Close** to close the dialog box.
    g. Save the presentation.

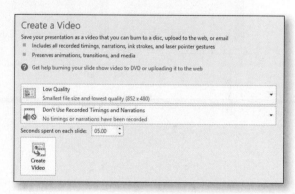
6-154 Options for exporting a video

16. Create a presentation video.
    a. Click **File** and choose **Export** [*Backstage* view] and select **Create a Video**.
    b. On the first box, click the list arrow and choose the **Low Quality** option (Figure 6-154).
    c. Verify that **Don't Use Recorded Timings and Narrations** is selected.
    d. Type 3:00 for *Seconds to spend on each slide*.
    e. Click **Create Video** to open the *Save As* dialog box.
    f. Change the file name that appears to [your initials] PowerPoint 6-3c.
    g. For *Save as type*, verify that **MPEG-4 Video** is selected.
    h. Click **Save**.

17. Mark the presentation as final.
    a. Click **File**, **Info**, **Protect Presentation**, and select **Mark as Final**.
    - A message box opens.
    b. Click **OK**.
    - Another dialog box opens with the final version message.
    - This dialog box will not appear if you previously checked **Don't show this message again**.
    c. Click **OK**.
    - The presentation is automatically saved and the marked as final message appears above the presentation.

18. Close the presentation (Figure 6-155).

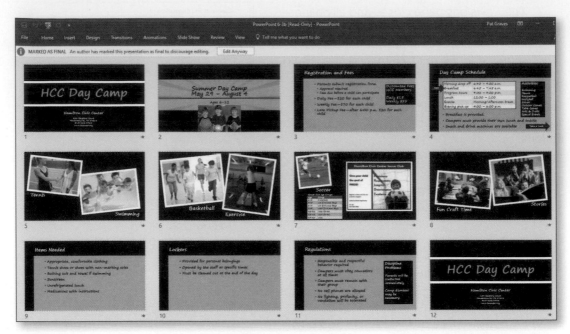

6-155 PowerPoint 6-3b completed

# Independent Project 6-4

At the Courtyard Medical Plaza, one of the physicians has been asked to speak to a community college organization about nutrition. For this project, you help the physician complete the presentation by adding content from other sources, creating custom shows, and exporting the presentation as a PDF file. [**Student Learning Outcomes 6.1, 6.3, 6.4, 6.6, 6.7**]

Files Needed: ***Nutrition-06.pptx***, ***Carbohydrates-06.docx***, and ***Calories-06.xlsx*** *(student data files are available in the* Library *of your SIMnet account)*
Completed Project File Names: ***[your initials] PowerPoint 6-4a.pptx*** and ***[your initials]***
***PowerPoint 6-4b.pdf***

## *Skills Covered in This Project*

- Create slides from a Word outline.
- Work with multiple PowerPoint windows.
- Use *Paste Special* to embed an object.
- Modify an embedded object.

- Use *Replace*.
- Create a custom slide show.
- Hyperlink to a custom slide show.
- Export a presentation as a PDF file.
- Add a password.

1. Open the presentation **Nutrition-06** and save it as [your initials] PowerPoint 6-4a.

2. Add slides from a Word outline.
   a. Display slide 13. Click the **New Slide** drop-down arrow and select **Slides from Outline** to open the *Insert Outline* dialog box.
      - Locate your student data files and select **Carbohydrates-06**.
   b. Click **Insert**.

3. Update slide layouts.
   a. Display slide 14, click the **Layout** button and select the **Section Header** layout.
   b. Click the **Reset** button to update the font.
   c. Select slides 15–18 and click the **Reset** button again.

4. Use *Paste Special* to embed an Excel chart and modify the embedded object.
   a. Open Excel and open the file **Calories-06** in your student data files.
   b. Select the **bar chart** and press **Ctrl+C**.
   c. Go to PowerPoint and select slide 6.
   d. Click the **Paste** drop-down arrow and select **Paste Special** to open the *Paste Special* dialog box.
      - Select **Paste**. In the *As* area, select **Microsoft Excel Chart Object**.
      - Click **OK** to close the *Paste Special* dialog box, and the object appears on your slide.

5. Modify the embedded object.
   a. Increase the chart size (approximate *Height* **5"**) (Figure 6-156).
   b. Double-click the **chart** to open the Excel *Ribbon*.
   c. Click text on the left of the chart to select *Y axis titles* and apply **Bold**.
   d. Repeat step 5c for the remaining text:
      - *X axis titles* below the chart
      - *Series numbers* on the green and gold bars,
      - *Legend* in the upper right.
   e. Click off the chart to return to PowerPoint.
   f. Center the chart on the slide.
   g. Close the worksheet in Excel without saving the file. Close Excel.

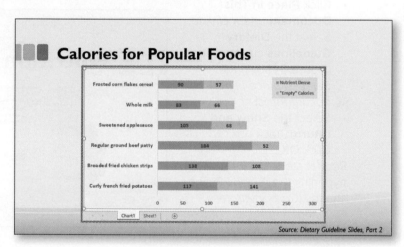

6-156 Editing an embedded Excel chart in PowerPoint

6. Use *Replace*.
   a. Display the first slide and click the **Replace** button to open the *Replace* dialog box.
      - Type U. S. (space once after U.) in the *Find what* box.
      - In the *Replace with* box, type United States.
      - Select **Match case** and click the **Replace All** button.
      - Click **OK** to close the dialog box indicating the number of changes.
   b. Click **Close** to close the *Replace* dialog box.

7. Create three custom slide shows.
   a. Click the **Slide Show** tab.
   b. Click the **Custom Slide Show** button and select **Custom Shows** to open the *Custom Shows* dialog box.
   c. Click the **New** button to open the *Define Custom Show* dialog box.
      - For the *Slide show name*, type Dietary Guidelines.

- On the left, click slides 2–13 and 25 to select them and click the **Add** button. The slides are listed on the right and renumbered (Figure 6-157).
- Click **OK** to close the *Define Custom Show* dialog box.

d. Repeat step 7c for a custom show named Carbohydrates, Fiber, Fat using slides 14–20.

e. Repeat step 7c for a custom show named Farm to Table using slides 21–25.

f. Click **Close** to close the *Custom Shows* dialog box.

8. Hyperlink to the three custom shows.

a. Select the "**Dietary Guidelines**" shape on slide 1.
- Be sure you select the shape and not the text within the shape.

b. Click the **Hyperlink** button [*Insert* tab, *Links* group] to open the *Insert Links* dialog box.
- Click **Place in This Document** under *Link to*.
- Select the **Dietary Guidelines** custom show (Figure 6-158) in the *Select a place in this document* list.
- Select the **Show and return** check box.
- Click **OK**.

c. Repeat steps 8a–b to hyperlink the remaining two shapes (*Carbohydrates, Fiber, Fat* and *Farm to Table*) to their respective custom shows.

d. Test the hyperlinks in *Slide Show* view to verify that each custom show opens, advances correctly, and returns to the linked slide. Press **Esc** to exit *Slide Show* view.

9. Select the **Cube** transition and click **Apply To All**.

10. Create a PDF file.

a. Click the **File** tab, choose **Export**, and select **Create PDF/XPS Document**.

b. Click **Create PDF/XPS**.

c. Change the file name to [your initials] PowerPoint 6-4b.

d. Select the **Open file after publishing** checkbox.

e. Select **Minimum size (publishing online)**.

f. Click the **Options** button to open the *Options* dialog box.
- For *Publish what*, select **Handouts** and check **Frame slides**.
- Deselect **Document Properties** (Figure 6-159).
- Click **OK** to close the dialog box.

6-157 Slides added to a custom show

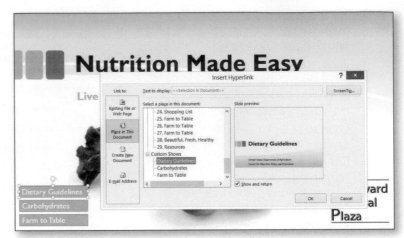

6-158 Hyperlink to a custom show

g. Click **Publish**.
   - The file opens in Adobe Reader.
   - Review the file then close Adobe Reader.

11. Encrypt a presentation with a password.
    a. Click the **File** tab, click the **Protect Presentation** button, and select **Encrypt with Password** to open the *Encrypt Document* dialog box.
    b. Type the password Project6-4 then click **OK** to open the *Confirm Password* dialog box.
    c. In the *Reenter password to confirm* text box, type Project6-4.
    d. Click **OK** to close the dialog box.

12. Save and close the *[your initials] PowerPoint 6-4a* presentation (Figure 6-160).

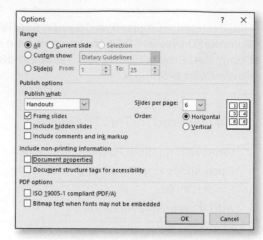

6-159 *Options* dialog box for saving a PDF file

6-160 PowerPoint 6-4a completed

# Independent Project 6-5

The Pool & Spa Oasis has prepared a presentation to feature its services and educate customers about how to maintain their pools and spas. The *Slide Master* includes a background video to emphasize the soothing nature of water. For this project, you add content from other sources and compare presentations to consider reviewer comments and changes.
[Student Learning Outcomes 6.1, 6.2, 6.3, 6.5]

Files Needed: ***SummerFun-06.pptx, SafeWater-06.pptx, WaterQuality-06.docx*** and
***SummerFunReview-06.pptx*** *(student data files are available in the* Library *of your SIMnet account)*
Completed Project File Names: *[your initials] **PowerPoint 6-5a.pptx*** and *[your initials]*
***PowerPoint 6-5b.pptx***

## *Skills Covered in This Project*

- Work with multiple PowerPoint windows.
- Copy slides from another presentation.
- Embed a file.
- Add and rename sections.

- Add a custom *AutoCorrect* entry.
- Insert comments.
- Compare presentations.
- Accept or reject changes.

### *Part A*

1. Open the presentation ***SummerFun-06*** and save it as [your initials] PowerPoint 6-5a.

2. Open a second presentation and arrange two PowerPoint windows side-by-side.
   a. Open the ***SafeWater-06*** presentation.
   b. Click the **Switch Windows** button and select **[your initials] PowerPoint 6-5a**.
   c. Click the **Maximize** button so PowerPoint fills the screen if your window is not already maximized.
   d. Click **Arrange All** and your *[your initials] PowerPoint 6-5a* (destination) presentation is on the left and the *SafeWater-06* (source) presentation is on the right.
   e. Change to *Slide Sorter* view and adjust the *Zoom* to approximately **90%** so you can see all slides in both presentations.

3. Copy slides from the source presentation and paste them in the destination presentation.
   a. In the source presentation on the right, select slides 1–5 (Figure 6-161) and press **Ctrl+C**.
   b. Select *[your initials] PowerPoint 6-5a* to activate it.
   c. Click after slide 8, and press **Ctrl+V**.
   d. Save the ***[your initials] PowerPoint 6-5a*** presentation with the new slides.

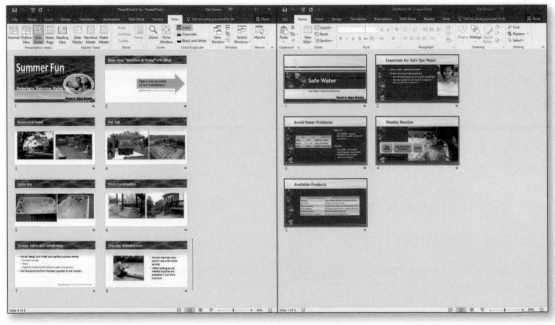

6-161 Two presentation windows displayed using *Arrange All*

    e. Close the **SafeWater-06** presentation.

    f. Maximize your PowerPoint window or restore it to the size you prefer.

4. Edit objects on the pasted slides to blend with the current presentation.

    a. Double-click slide 10 to open it in *Normal* view.

       • Move the picture of a girl down slightly and away from the slide edge.

    b. Display slide 11 and select the table.

       • Apply the **Themed Style 1 – Accent 1** table style.

       • Center the table in the white space at the left of the slide.

    c. Display slide 13 and select the table.

       • Apply the same **Themed Style 1 – Accent 1** table style.

       • Center the table horizontally on the slide.

    d. Display slide 12 and select the *SmartArt* graphic.

       • Click the **Change Colors** button and select the **Colored Fill – Accent 1** style.

       • Select the text box below the *SmartArt* graphic and change the *Shape Fill* to **No Fill** (Figure 6-162).

5. Add a custom *AutoCorrect* entry.

    a. Click the **File** tab to open the *Backstage* view and click the **Options** button.

    b. Click the **Proofing** button and select the **AutoCorrect Options** button to open the *AutoCorrect* dialog box.

       • Type Bromene in the *Replace* box.

       • Type Bromine (Figure 6-163) in the *With* box.

       • Click **Add**.

       • Click **OK** to close the *AutoCorrect* dialog box.

    c. Click **OK** to close the *PowerPoint Options* dialog box.

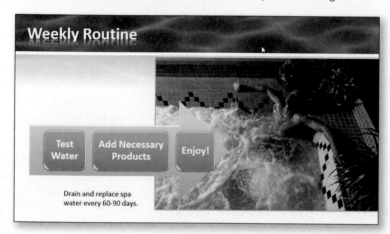

6-162 Slide objects adjusted for the current theme

6-163 *AutoCorrect* dialog box

6. Embed a PDF file.

    a. Insert a new slide after slide 13 with the *Title Slide* layout.

    b. Type Pool School! for the slide title and delete the subtitle placeholder (Figure 6-164).

    c. Click the **Object** button and select **Create from File**.

       • Locate your student data files and select **WaterQuality-06**.

       • Click **OK** to insert the file and close the dialog boxes.

    d. Increase the object size (approximate *Height* **7"**) and place it on the right.

7. Add and rename sections.

    a. Change to **Slide Sorter** view and adjust your *Zoom* percentage so you can see all slides.

    b. Add a section after slide 1.

    c. Rename the **Untitled Section** Installations (Figure 6-165).

6-164 Embedded PDF file

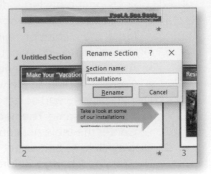

6-165 *Rename Section* dialog box

   d. Add another section after slide 8 and rename it
      Safe Water.
   e. Rename the *Default Section* (before slide 1) Introduction.

8. Insert comments.
   a. Double-click slide 2 to open it in *Normal* view.
   b. Add a new comment:
      • Type Should we show when this special promotion ends?
        (Figure 6-166).
      • Move the comment icon near the promotion text.
   c. Select slide 5 and add a new comment:
      • Type Replace the picture on the right to show the swim spa
        filled with water and the jets running.
      • Move the comment icon near the top of the
        picture.
   d. Close the *Comments* pane.

6-166 Comment inserted

9. Save the *[your initials] PowerPoint 6-5a* presentation.

## Part B

10. Compare presentations.
   a. With *[your initials] PowerPoint 6-5a* open, click the **Compare** button.
      • Locate your student data files, select ***SummerFunReview-06***, and click **Merge**.
   b. Save this merged version as [your initials] PowerPoint 6-5b.

11. Review and delete comments.
   a. Display slide 2, the first slide with a comment.
   b. Click one of the comment icons to open the *Comments* pane.
      • Read the slide 2 comments, and delete them.
   c. Click the **Next** button to go to the next comment on slide 5.
      • Read and delete the comments.
   d. Close the *Comments* pane.

12. Accept and reject changes.
   a. Begin your review on slide 2 and change the following:
      • Select the **Freeform 7** change in the *Revisions* pane and check the change icon on the slide to
        see the reviewer's change. Leave the items checked to accept them.

- Select the **TextBox 2** change in the *Revisions* pane and check the change icon on the slide to see the reviewer's change. Reject this change to keep the text box in its original location (Figure 6-167).

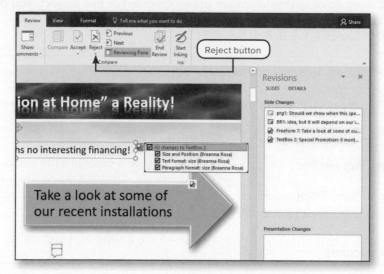

6-167 Click *Reject* to not accept a change

b. Go to the next reviewer change on slide 7.
- Check the reviewer change icon for the **Content Placeholder 1** to add another bulleted item to the list
- Move to slide 8 and check the change icon to accept changes.
c. End the review and click **Yes** to confirm. The *Revisions* pane closes.

13. Select the **Ripple** transition and the **From Top-Left** effect option. Apply to all slides.

14. Save and close the presentation (Figure 6-168).

6-168 PowerPoint 6-5b completed with inserted sections in *Slide Sorter* view

# Independent Project 6-6

At Solution Seekers, Inc., one of the consultants has been asked to give a seminar. The clients want to learn more about using color to create unique presentations. For this project, you paste slides from another presentation, replace fonts, add sections, and create custom shows.
[Student Learning Outcomes 6.1, 6.3, 6.4, 6.6, 6.7]

Files Needed: ***ColorChoices-06.pptx*** and ***ColorUse-06.pptx*** *(student data files are available in the* Library *of your SIMnet account)*
Completed Project File Names: *[your initials] PowerPoint 6-6a.pptx*, and *[your initials] PowerPoint 6-6b.jpg*

### *Skills Covered in This Project*

- Work with multiple PowerPoint windows.
- Copy slides from one presentation to another.
- Use *Replace*.
- Add and rename sections.

- Create a custom slide show.
- Hyperlink a custom slide show.
- Inspect a presentation.
- Check for compatibility.
- Save a slide as a picture.

1. Open the presentation ***ColorChoices-06*** and save it as [your initials] PowerPoint 6-6a.

2. Arrange two PowerPoint windows.
   a. Open the presentation ***ColorUse-06***.
   b. Select **[your initials] PowerPoint 6-6a** to activate it.
   c. Maximize your PowerPoint window so it fills the screen.
   d. Click **Arrange All** so both presentations display.
   e. Change to *Slide Sorter* view and adjust the *Zoom* to approximately **60%** in both presentations (Figure 6-169).

6-169 Two presentation windows displayed using *Arrange All*

3. Copy, paste, and format slides.
   a. Select slides 5, 6, and 8 in the source presentation on the right. Press **Ctrl+C**.
   b. Select your current presentation to make it active and click after slide 14. Press **Ctrl+V**.
   c. Select the pasted slides. Change the layout to **1_Title and Content white**.
   d. Save your *[your initials] PowerPoint 6-6a* presentation with the new slides and close the **ColorUse-06** presentation.
   e. Double-click slide 15 to open it in *Normal* view.
   f. Restore your PowerPoint window to the size you prefer.
   g. Delete the content placeholder behind the group of pictures.
   h. Select the group of pictures and move the pictures slightly up and to the right.

4. Replace a font.
   a. Display slide 1.
   b. Click the **Replace** drop-down arrow and select **Replace Fonts**.
   c. Select **Corbel** in the *Replace* box.
   d. Select **Trebuchet MS** in the *With* box (Figure 6-170).
   e. Click **Replace** and close the dialog box.
      • The font is changed in the presentation (Figure 6-171).

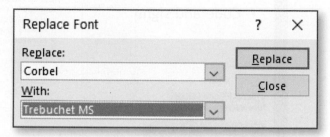

6-170  *Replace Font* dialog box

5. Create two custom slide shows.
   a. Open the *Custom Shows* dialog box.
   b. Click **New** to open the *Define Custom Show* dialog box.
      • Type **Color Meaning** for *Slide show name*.
      • Select slides 3–12 and add them so they are also listed on the right under *Slides in custom show* (Figure 6-172).
      • Click **OK**.
   c. Click the **New** button again.
      • Type **Presentation Colors** for *Slide show name*.
      • Select slides 13–24 and add them on the right.
      • Click **OK** and then close the *Define Custom Show* dialog box.
   d. Close the *Custom Shows* dialog box.

6-171  Title slide with font replaced

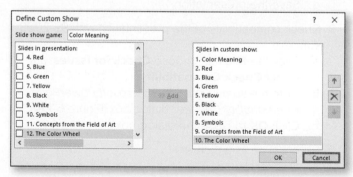

6-172  Slides added to a custom show

6. Hyperlink to the two custom shows.
  a. Select the "**Color Meaning**" shape on slide 2.
    • Click the **Hyperlink** button and link to the *Color Meaning* custom show (Figure 6-173).
    • Select **Show and return**.

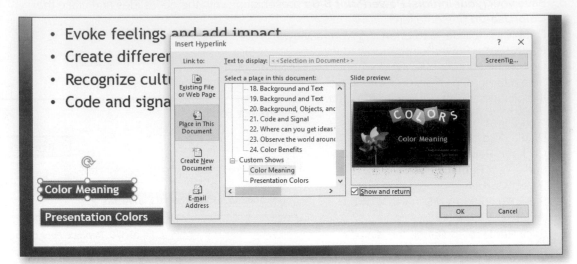

6-173 Prepare a hyperlink to a custom show

  b. Repeat step 6a for the "Presentation Colors" shape.
  c. Test the hyperlinks in *Slide Show* view to verify that each custom show opens and advances correctly.

7. Select the **Wipe** transition with the **From Left** *Effect Option* and click **Apply To All**.

8. Inspect the presentation.
  a. Click the **File** tab, choose **Check for Issues**, and select **Inspect Document**.
  b. Click **Yes** if you are prompted to save.
  c. Deselect the **Document Properties and Personal Information** check box.
  d. Click **Inspect**.
  e. In the *Document Inspector* dialog box, click **Remove All** after *Invisible On-Slide Content* if a notation appears.
  f. Click **Close** to close the dialog box.
  g. Save the presentation.

9. Check compatibility of the presentation with 97-2003 software.
  a. Click the **File** tab, choose **Check for Issues**, and select **Check Compatibility**.
  b. Note the summary on the *Microsoft PowerPoint Compatibility Checker* dialog box (Figure 6-174).
  c. Click **OK** to close the dialog box.

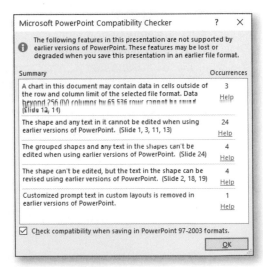

6-174 *Compatibility Checker* dialog box

10. Save a slide as a picture.
  a. Display slide 3.
  b. Choose **Export** on the **File** tab and select **Change File Type**.

c. Select the **JPEG File Interchange Format** file type (Figure 6-175) and click **Save As** to open the *Save As* dialog box.

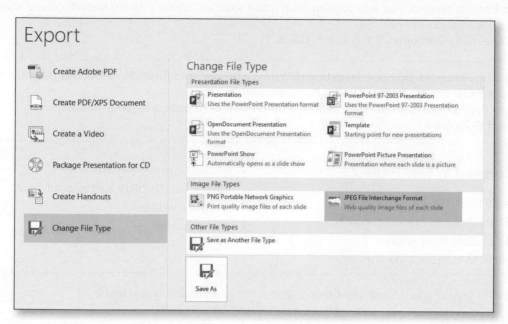

6-175  Export with the JPEG file format

d. Type the file name [your initials] PowerPoint 6-6b.
e. Click **Save**. On the dialog box that opens, click **Just This One** to save the current slide only.

11. Save and close the presentation (Figure 6-176).

6-176  PowerPoint 6-6a completed

# Improve It Project 6-7

A financial adviser at Dawson Financial Group is speaking to a student organization about saving and investing. For this project, you add content from other sources, create custom shows, create a video and mark the presentation as final.
[Student Learning Outcomes 6.1, 6.4, 6.5, 6.6, 6.7]

---

Files Needed: *Finances-06.pptx*, *InvestmentStrategy-06.pdf*, and *SmallSave-06.xlsx* (student data files are available in the Library of your SIMnet account)
Completed Project File Names: *[your initials] PowerPoint 6-7a.pptx* and *[your initials] PowerPoint 6-7b.mp4*

---

## Skills Covered in This Project

- Embed a file.
- Use *Paste Special* to link an object.
- Create custom slide shows.
- Hyperlink to custom slide shows.
- Inspect a presentation.
- Check accessibility and add *Alt Text*.
- Create a video.
- Mark as final.

---

1. Open the presentation *Finances-06* and save it as [your initials] PowerPoint 6-7a.

2. Embed a PDF file.
   a. Display slide 11. Insert the object *InvestmentStrategy-06*, which is a PDF file.
   b. Change the *Height* to **6"** and move the object to the right (Figure 6-177).

3. Use *Paste Special* to link to an object.
   a. Open Excel and open the file *SmallSave-06*.
   b. Copy the chart that shows the amount of accumulated money by day, week, month, and year.
   c. Switch to PowerPoint and select slide 4.
   d. Click the **Paste** button and select **Paste Special**.
   e. Select **Paste link**.
   f. Click **OK** and the chart appears on your slide.
   g. Switch to Excel and change the "Year" amount to 1,277.
      - Save the Excel file and the change is automatically reflected on the slide 4 chart.
      - If the chart does not update in PowerPoint, then right-click the chart and select the **Update Link** option from the context menu.
      - Increase the chart *Height* to **5"** and move it slightly to the right (Figure 6-178).
   h. Close the worksheet and close Excel.

6-177 PDF file embedded in PowerPoint

4. Break the link to an object.
   a. Select **Info** on the *Backstage* view.
   b. Click **Edit Links to Files** and select ***SmallSave-06***.
   c. Break the link and close the dialog box.

5. Create two custom slide shows.
   a. Click the **Slide Show** tab and the **Custom Slide Show** button; then select **Custom Shows**.
   b. Click **New**.
      • Name the custom show Save.
      • Add slides 2–4 and 7.
   c. Click **New** to create a second custom show.
      • Name it Invest.
      • Add slides 5, 6, and 8–11.
   d. Click **OK** and then close the *Custom Shows* dialog box.

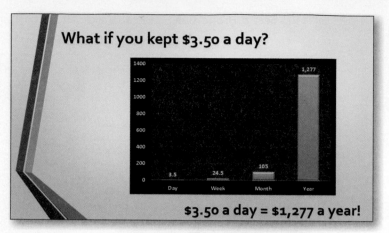

What if you kept $3.50 a day?

$3.50 a day = $1,277 a year!

**6-178** Linked Excel chart in PowerPoint

6. Create a hyperlink for each custom show.
   a. Use the shapes below the camera on slide 1.
   b. Select **Show and return**.
   c. Test the hyperlinks.

7. Insert comments.
   a. Display slide 4 and click the **New Comment** button [*Review* tab, *Comments* group] to open the *Comments* pane.
      • Type It would be good to add another chart showing how much $1,277 a year would generate in 10 years with current interest rates.
   b. Display slide 7 and click the **New** button at the top of the *Comments* pane.
      • Type Remind people that their preferences may differ from the images shown here.
      • Move the comment icon near the top of the *SmartArt* graphic.
   c. Close the *Comments* pane.

8. Apply the **Window** transition to all slides.

9. Inspect the presentation.
   a. Click **Check for Issues** on *Backstage* view and select **Inspect Document**.
   b. Click **Inspect**.
   c. Click **Remove All** after *Document Properties and Personal Information* but do not remove *Comments and Annotations*.
   d. Close the dialog box.

10. Check accessibility and add *Alt Text*.
    a. Click **Check for Issues** on *Backstage* view and select **Check Accessibility**.
    b. Select **Picture 2 (Slide 4)** in the *Accessibility Checker* pane under *Missing Alt Text* and the linked chart is selected.
    c. Right-click the chart and choose **Format Picture**.

d.  Click the **Size & Properties** button and click **Alt Text** (Figure 6-179).

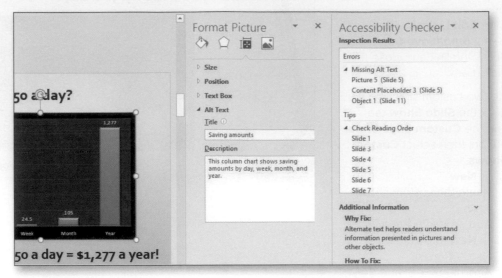

6-179  Add *Alt Text* to identify the linked chart

e.  Type the title and the description text as shown in the following table.
f.  Repeat for the remaining items listed in the *Accessibility Checker* pane.

| Item | Title Text | Description Text |
| --- | --- | --- |
| Picture 2 (Slide 4) | Saving amounts | This column chart shows saving amounts by day, week, month, and year. |
| Picture 5 (Slide 5) | Money | This picture shows a stack of money. |
| Content Placeholder 3 (Slide 5) | Invest | This diagram shows that consistent saving plus compound interest equals significant growth. |
| Object 1 (Slide 11) | Announcement | DFG promotion |

g.  Close the *Format Object* and the *Accessibility Checker* panes.
h.  Save the presentation.

11. Create a presentation video.
    a.  Choose **Export** on *Backstage* view and select **Create a Video**.
    b.  Choose the **Low Quality**, **Don't Use Recorded Timings and Narrations**, and 3:00 second for *Seconds to spend on each slide*.
    c.  Click **Create Video** and name the video [your initials] PowerPoint 6-7b.
    d.  Choose the **MPEG-4 Video** file type and save the video.

12. Mark the presentation as final.
    a.  Click **Protect Presentation** on *Backstage* view and select **Mark as Final**.
        •  A dialog box opens.
    b.  Click **OK**.
        •  Another dialog box opens with the final version message.
    c.  Click **OK**.
        •  The presentation is automatically saved.

13. Close the presentation (Figure 6-180).

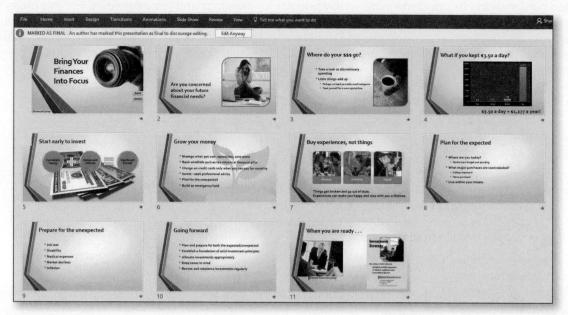

6-180 PowerPoint 6-7a completed

# Challenge Project 6-8

For this project, search online for information about how mobile apps can support team collaboration. Create a presentation about this topic. Include cautions about sharing private or sensitive data. List some of the products and their prices in a spreadsheet and link to it in PowerPoint. Describe features and capabilities.
[**Student Learning Outcomes 6.1, 6.2, 6.3, 6.6**]

File Needed: None
Completed Project File Name: *[your initials] **PowerPoint 6-8.pptx***

Create a new presentation and save it as [your initials] PowerPoint 6-8. Modify your presentation according to the following guidelines:

- Select an appropriate theme and colors.
- Identify the most common categories of mobile apps and describe them.
- Use Excel to list some of the products and their prices.
- In PowerPoint, link to the price list in Excel.
- Add sections to divide the presentation into logical groups.
- Add *AutoCorrect* entries to recognize three trade names for web apps or devices.
- Use other proofing options as needed.
- Inspect the presentation and mark it as final.

# Challenge Project 6-9

Video conferencing has become increasingly popular for meetings and job interviews. For this project, search online for information about how to prepare yourself to appear professional when the camera is on you. Discuss both verbal and nonverbal behaviors that are important during a video conference. Share your presentation with a friend or colleague and ask that person to provide feedback with the *Comments* feature of PowerPoint. Compare the presentations and use those comments and any changes to improve your presentation.
[**Student Learning Outcomes 6.1, 6.3, 6.4, 6.5, 6.6, 6.7**]

File Needed: None
Completed Project File Name: *[your initials] PowerPoint 6-9.pptx*

Create a new presentation and save it as [your initials] PowerPoint 6-9. Modify your presentation according to the following guidelines:

- Select an appropriate theme and colors.
- Create slides that include information about what you need to do before a video conference to prepare yourself.
- Create slides that include information about behaviors that are important during a video conference.
- Use proofing options as needed.
- Prepare two custom shows within your presentation.
- Create hyperlinks to begin each custom show.
- Insert comments for a reviewer and distribute the presentation for review.
- Compare your original presentation and the reviewed presentation by merging them.
- Consider comments and delete them; consider changes and accept or reject them.
- Check the presentation for accessibility and add *Alt Text* as needed.
- Save a slide as a picture.

# Challenge Project 6-10

Good manners never go out of style. For this project, create a presentation that provides tips on business etiquette. Use online sources such as emilypost.com, etiquettescholar.com, missmanners.com, netmanners.com, or other similar sites. Work with another student to divide this project into two parts. Each of you should prepare slides and when they are complete you can combine them into one presentation.
[**Student Learning Outcomes 6.1, 6.2, 6.3, 6.4, 6.5, 6.7**]

File Needed: None
Completed Project File Name: *[your initials] PowerPoint 6-10.pptx*

Create a new presentation and save it as [your initials] PowerPoint 6-10. Modify your presentation according to the following guidelines:

- Prepare two presentations and combine them by pasting slides from the source presentation into the destination presentation.

- Select an appropriate theme and colors.
- Create slides that include information about behaviors that are important regardless of technology use.
- Create slides that include information about behaviors that are important as a result of technology use.
- If possible, take your own photos to illustrate several good and bad behaviors.
- Use proofing options as needed.
- Rearrange slide order as needed.
- Prepare custom shows for the major topics of the presentation.
- Create hyperlinks to begin each custom show.
- Create a presentation video.

# CHAPTER 7

# Using OneDrive, Office Online, Office Mix, and Sway

**POWERPOINT**

## CHAPTER OVERVIEW

Both Office 2016 and 365 integrate "cloud" technology so you can store your files online in Microsoft's *OneDrive* and use *Office Online*. Cloud services enable you to work on your files from anywhere you can use a computer with Internet access.

PowerPoint Online enables you to either start presentations or edit existing presentations and show them online. However, not all features of the full versions of PowerPoint are available. A new application, *Office Mix*, expands options of PowerPoint and adds interesting interactive features for presenting online. *Sway* is a new application that also provides many new features for presenting online.

---

### STUDENT LEARNING OUTCOMES (SLOs)

After completing this chapter, you will be able to:

**SLO 7.1**  Modify Office account settings and use add-ins (p. P7-453).

**SLO 7.2**  Use *OneDrive* to create, upload, move, copy, delete, and download files and folders (p. P7-457).

**SLO 7.3**  Share *OneDrive* files and folders (p. P7-462).

**SLO 7.4**  Open, create, and edit a presentation in *PowerPoint Online* and add comments (p. P7-468).

**SLO 7.5**  Use *Office Mix* to create an interactive online presentation with multimedia and to create presentation videos (p. P7-478).

**SLO 7.6**  Use *Sway* to create an interactive online presentation with multimedia (p. P7-489).

---

### CASE STUDY

For the Pause & Practice projects in this chapter, you use Microsoft cloud services to save, edit, and share presentations for the Eye Care Clinic at Courtyard Medical Plaza and Life's Animal Shelter.

***Pause & Practice 7-1:*** Customize Office account settings, use an add-in, and use *OneDrive* to upload files, create folders, move files, and share a file.

***Pause & Practice 7-2:*** Use *OneDrive* and *PowerPoint Online* to create, edit, add comments, and share a presentation.

***Pause & Practice 7-3:*** Use *Office Mix* to create a screen recording video and a slide recording for an online presentation with interactive elements.

***Pause & Practice 7-4:*** Use *Sway* to create an online presentation with multimedia.

# Modifying Office Account Options and Using Add-ins

When you purchase and install Office 2016 or 365, you set up your account with a user name and password. If you upgrade from Office 2013 to Office 2016, many of your settings are automatically transferred. You can view and customize your Office account settings on the *Backstage* view, add connected services such as LinkedIn or Twitter, and install Office add-ins for extra features in all Office applications.

> **MORE INFO**
>
> If you don't have a Microsoft account, you can create a free account at https://signup.live.com.

## Microsoft Account Information

Office 2016 and 365 provide portability of your files and account settings so you can work from different locations. When you use Windows 10, you sign in to your Microsoft account with your user name and password. Microsoft Office uses this information to apply your Office settings to the computer you are using. Your information displays in the upper right corner of the PowerPoint window (Figure 7-1). *Account Settings* is a link that will open the *Backstage* view where you can change Office settings.

7-1 Microsoft account information

> **MORE INFO**
>
> If you are using an older version of Windows, you may be prompted to sign in to your Microsoft account when you open an Office 2016 application or file.

Your Microsoft account also signs you in to other free Microsoft online services, such as *OneDrive*, *Office Online*, and *Sway*. You will use each of these services in this chapter.

7-2 Sign in to a Microsoft account

**HOW TO: Sign in and Use Microsoft Account in PowerPoint**

1. Open PowerPoint.
2. Click the **Sign in** link in the upper right corner of the PowerPoint window if you are not signed in with your Microsoft account.
   - A *Sign in* dialog box opens.
   - Type your Microsoft account email address, click **Next**, and another *Sign in* dialog box opens (Figure 7-2).
   - Type your password and click **Sign in**.
   - Your name appears in the *Title* bar on the upper right corner of the PowerPoint window.

3. Click your name (see Figure 7-1).

4. Click the **Account settings** link to open the *Account* area on the *Backstage* view (Figure 7-3).

    - Alternatively, you can click the **File** tab and select **Account** on the left.
    - Your account information displays.

5. Click the **back arrow** to return to PowerPoint.

7-3 Office account information and settings

### Office Background and Theme

You can change the ***Office Background*** and ***Office Theme*** in the *Account* area on the *Backstage* view or in the *General* category in the *PowerPoint Options* dialog box. Choose from one of several backgrounds to display a graphic pattern in the upper right corner of the application window. Select a theme to show different colors on the *Ribbon*, the *Backstage* view, and dialog boxes. Your selections apply to all Office applications you use. The Office 2016 default *Office Theme* is *Colorful* (see Figure 7-3).

### Connected Services

Office 2016 allows you to connect to online services in the *Account* area on the *Backstage* view. Your current services are listed in the ***Connected Service*** area (see Figure 7-3). You are usually prompted to enter your user name and password when you click the **Add a service** drop-down list and select a service. Connected services can be removed, too.

The following services are available (Figure 7-4):

7-4 Add an online service to your Office account

- ***Images & Video:*** Facebook for Office, Flickr, and YouTube
- ***Storage:*** Office365 SharePoint and *OneDrive*
- ***Sharing:*** Facebook, LinkedIn, and Twitter.

## Office Add-ins

Office ***add-ins*** are programs that provide additional features to your Office software similar to the "apps" on your smart phone. For example, you can add a dictionary, an encyclopedia, a search tool, or many other apps such as visualization tools and free stock photos that are especially helpful for PowerPoint. These programs are provided by Microsoft and other suppliers, and new ones are added regularly. Many add-ins are free while others require purchase.

## ▶ HOW TO: Install an Office Add-in

1. Open PowerPoint.

2. Click the **Store** button [*Insert* tab, *Add-ins* group] to open the *Office Add-ins* dialog box (Figure 7-5).

   - Featured apps display with thumbnails and a brief description.
   - Select a category on the left to filter the list.
   - Use the search box to find an add-in for a specific topic.
   - Click the link at the bottom of the dialog box to see more add-ins for PowerPoint.
   - Click **My Add-ins** to display currently installed add-ins.

3. Select an add-in and a dialog box opens that contains information about the program.

4. Click the **Trust It** button to install the add-in.

   - The *Add-in* pane opens on the right (Figure 7-6) or the add-in opens as an object on your slide such as the *Multiple Response Poll* shown in Figure 7-7.
   - Depending on the add-in you select, you may be taken to a web site to complete installation.
   - You must be online for the add-in to start and load content.

5. Close the add-in by closing the *Add-in* pane or deleting the add-in object on the slide.

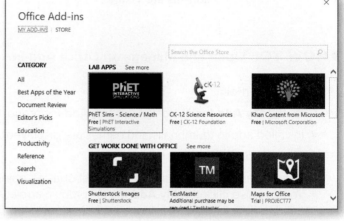

7-5 *Office Add-ins* dialog box

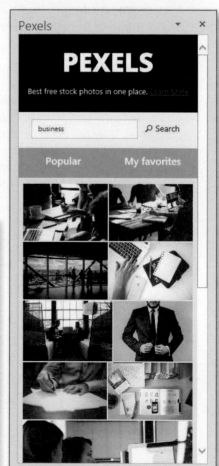

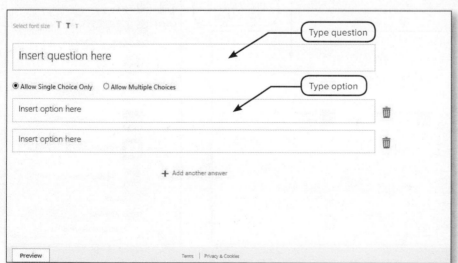

7-7 *Add-in* object

7-6 *Add-in* pane

## Open and Manage Office Add-ins

After installing add-ins, you can view the installed add-ins, open add-ins, and manage which add-ins are visible.

▶ **HOW TO:** Open and Manage an Office Add-in

1. Open PowerPoint.
2. Click the **My Add-ins** button [*Insert* tab, *Add-ins* group] to open the *Office Add-ins* dialog box (Figure 7-8).
   - Installed add-in thumbnails and names are displayed.
3. Select an add-in and click **OK** to open it.
   - The add-in opens in a pane on the right or as an object on the slide.
   - You can also click the **My Add-ins** drop-down arrow [*Insert* tab, *Add-Ins* group] (Figure 7-9) to display recently used add-ins and then click one of those names to open it.
4. Manage your add-ins on the *Insert* tab.
   - Click the **My Add-ins** drop-down arrow (see Figure 7-9) and right-click an add-in name in the list.
   - Select **Remove from list** or **Add Gallery to Quick Access Toolbar**.
5. Manage your add-ins at the *Office Store*.
   - Click the **My Add-ins** button [*Insert* tab, *Add-Ins* group] to open the *Office Add-Ins* dialog box.
   - Click the **Manage My Add-ins** link (see Figure 7-8).
   - Sign in to your Microsoft account if necessary.
   - An Internet browser window displays the add-ins downloaded from the Office *Store* and visible on your *Office Add-Ins* dialog box. They are listed here as *Visible apps* under *My Apps for Office and SharePoint* (Figure 7-10).
   - Click **Hide** in the *Action* column if you do not want the add-ins to appear in the *Office Add-ins* dialog box.
   - Click **Hidden** at the top of the window to see any add-ins previously hidden.
   - Click **Retrieve** on the *Hidden* list to move an add-in to the *Visible Apps* list.

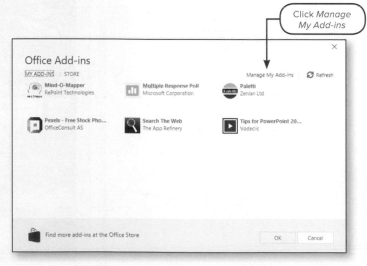

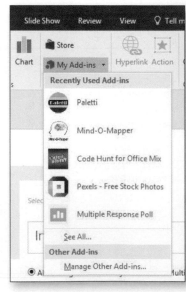

7-8 *Office Add-ins* dialog box, *My Add-ins*      7-9 Right-click to manage *My Add-ins*

My Apps for Office and SharePoint

Visible apps (5)                                                          SHOW: Visible | Hidden

| | Name | Status | First acquired | Expires on | Action | Comments |
|---|---|---|---|---|---|---|
| | Paletti<br>Word 2013 or later,<br>PowerPoint 2013 or later,<br>Word Online | Free | 5/24/2016 | | Hide | |
| | Multiple Response Poll<br>PowerPoint 2013 Service Pack<br>1 or later, PowerPoint Online,<br>PowerPoint for iPad | Free | 5/24/2016 | | Hide | |
| | Pexels - Free Stock Photos<br>PowerPoint 2013 or later,<br>PowerPoint Online, Word<br>2013 or later, Word Online | Free | 5/24/2016 | | Hide | |
| | eFax App for Word<br>Word 2013 or later | Free | 6/8/2013 | | Hide | |
| | Search The Web<br>Project 2013 or later, Excel<br>2013 or later, Excel Online,<br>Word 2013 or later,<br>PowerPoint 2013 or later | Free | 6/3/2013 | | Hide | |

7-10 *My Apps for Office and SharePoint*

---

**SLO 7.2**

# Using OneDrive

When you save files in PowerPoint, one of your available storage locations is *OneDrive*. You will see this location listed on the *Backstage* view when you select **Save As**. *OneDrive* is an online service that provides private and secure "cloud" storage. You can access files saved on *OneDrive* from any computer that is online. You are not limited to one computer or portable storage device.

Use *OneDrive* to store files, organize them in folders, and manage files by renaming, moving, removing, or sharing them. Through *OneDrive*, you can also use *Office Online* to create and edit your files. You can access *OneDrive* in more than one way as you will see in the upcoming sections.

If you don't have a Microsoft account, you can create a free account at https://signup. live.com.

 **MORE INFO**

While *OneDrive* requires a user name and password to sign in, no online accounts are 100 percent secure. Never store highly sensitive or confidential documents online.

## Use OneDrive in a File Explorer Window

With Windows 10, your *File Explorer* window will show *OneDrive* as a folder similar to your *Documents* or *Pictures* folders that you use when opening and saving files (Figure 7-11). You can create folders and rename, move, or delete files from your *OneDrive* folder. In *PowerPoint Options*, you can set *OneDrive* as the default save location.

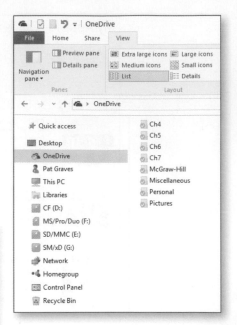

7-11 *OneDrive* folder displayed in a *File Explorer* window

> **MORE INFO**
>
> If you are using Windows 7 or 8, search online for the *OneDrive desktop app for Windows*. Download and install it on your computer. Then the *OneDrive* folder is available in the File Explorer window.

The difference between the *OneDrive* folder and other Windows folders is the physical location where files are stored. If you save a presentation in the *Documents* folder on *This PC*, the file is stored on the hard drive on your computer. You have access to this file only when you are using your computer. When you save a presentation in your *OneDrive* folder, the file is stored on both your computer and the *OneDrive* cloud storage. You have access to the file from your computer *and* from any other computer with Internet access.

> **MORE INFO**
>
> To access your *OneDrive* folder on your computer, you must be logged in using your Microsoft account.

> **MORE INFO**
>
> If you save to your *OneDrive* folder on your computer when you are offline, your changes sync to your online *OneDrive* when you reconnect later.

## Use OneDrive Online

In addition to accessing the *OneDrive* folder on your computer when you open or save files, you can access your *OneDrive* files from a web page using an Internet browser. You sign in to the *OneDrive* web page using your Microsoft account.

The appearance of the page may vary slightly depending on the browser you are using. Figures in this book show the Google Chrome browser. The online environment changes regularly, so figures might be slightly different from what is currently available.

## ▶HOW TO: Use OneDrive Online

1. Open an Internet browser Window and go to the *OneDrive* web site (https://onedrive.live.com) sign in page.
   - You can use any Internet browser to access *OneDrive* (Microsoft Edge, Google Chrome, or Mozilla Firefox).
2. Click the **Sign in** button.
3. Type your Microsoft account email address and click **Next** (Figure 7-12).
4. Type your password on the next screen.
   - If you are using your own computer, select the **Keep me signed in** check box to stay signed in to *OneDrive* when you leave the page and then return to it.

7-12 Sign in to *OneDrive* (https://onedrive.live.com)

5. Click the **Sign In** button to go to your *OneDrive* web page (Figure 7-13).
   - *OneDrive* category names (*Files*, *Recent*, *Photo*, *Shared*, or *Recycle bin*) are listed on the left under the *OneDrive* heading.
   - If you have Office installations on multiple computers associated with your Microsoft account, you will see a *PCs* category that displays your computer names.
6. Sort and view options are available on the *OneDrive* page in the upper right corner of the window (Figure 7-14).
   - Click the **Sort** drop-down list to select a sort option.
   - Click the **View** button to select **List** or **Tiles** view to change how files and folders display. In Figure 7-13, the *List* view is selected.

7-13 *OneDrive* category and folder names

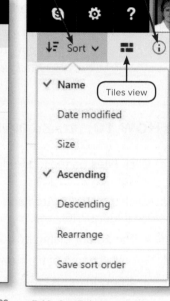

7-14 *OneDrive* sort and view options

7. Click the **Files** button on the left to display your folders and files.
8. Click the selection **circle** before a file or folder name (in *List* view) or on a tile (in *Tile* view) to select it.
   - Use buttons and drop-down menus at the top of the *OneDrive* window to perform actions on selected files and folders (Figure 7-15).
   - Click the **Information** button on the right to display details about a selected file or folder.

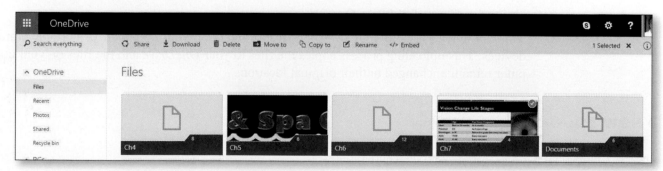

7-15 *OneDrive Menu* bar with files shown in *Tiles* view

9.  Click a file or folder to open it.
    - If you click an Office file, it opens in the appropriate Office Online application (see *SLO 7.4: Using PowerPoint Online*).
    - If you click a folder, the folder opens and displays the contents. Click **Files** on the left to return to the list of all *OneDrive* files.
10. Click your name or picture in the upper right corner and select **Sign out** to sign out of *OneDrive*.

> **MORE INFO**
>
> If you are using a public computer, do not select the **Keep me signed** *in* check box. You do not want your *OneDrive* files available to the next person who uses the computer.

## Create a Folder

In *OneDrive*, you can create folders to organize your files. Changes you make online will apply to the *OneDrive* folder on your computer, too. The new files and folders will appear on *Backstage* view, in *Open* and *Save* dialog boxes, and in the *File Explorer* window.

## ▶ HOW TO: Create OneDrive Folders

1.  Click **Files** on the left to display the contents of your *OneDrive* folder.
2.  Click the **New** button and select **Folder** from the drop-down list (Figure 7-16).
    - The *Folder* dialog box opens.
3.  Type the name of the new folder and click **Create**.
    - A new folder is created and its name is added to your list.
4.  Click a folder name to open it.
    - You can create a new folder inside an existing folder, or you can upload files to the folder (see the following *Upload a File or Folder to OneDrive* section).
    - Click **Files** on the left to return to the main *OneDrive* folder.

7-16 Add a new *OneDrive* folder

## Upload a File or Folder to OneDrive

You can upload files to your *OneDrive* from folders on your computer or portable storage devices. This uploading process copies the files to your *OneDrive* and the files on your computer remain unchanged in their original location.

## ▶ HOW TO: Upload a File or Folder

1.  Click **Files** on the left to display your files and folders.
    - If you are uploading a file to a specific folder, click the folder to open it.

2. Click the **Upload** button and select **Files** or **Folder** (Figure 7-17).

   - If you choose **Files**, the *Open* dialog box opens.
   - If you choose **Folder**, some browsers (such as Google Chrome) will open a different dialog box where you choose a folder (Figure 7-18).

3. Select the file or folder to upload to your *OneDrive* and click **Open**.

   - You can select more than one file. Press **Ctrl** when you click to select non-adjacent files, press **Shift** when you click to select a range of files, or press **Ctrl+A** to select all files in a folder.
   - An upload status message appears in the upper right corner.
   - The files or folders you upload appear in the *Files* area of *OneDrive*.

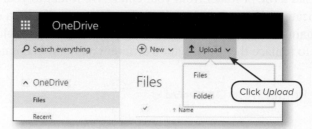

7-17 Upload a file or folder to *OneDrive*

7-18 *Browse For Folder* dialog box

---

> **ANOTHER WAY**
>
> A quick way to upload files to *OneDrive* is to drag and drop files. Open both your *File Explorer* window and your browser window and arrange them so you can see both windows. Select the files you need in *File Explorer* and simply drag them to the appropriate folder on *OneDrive*. This procedure copies the files but it does not move them.

### Move, Copy, or Delete Files and Folders

You are familiar with how to move, copy, and delete files and folders using the *File Explorer* window on your computer. The process is a little different in *OneDrive* because it is an online environment.

▶ **HOW TO:** Move, Copy, or Delete OneDrive Files

1. Click the selection circle for the file or folder name you want to move or copy.

   - In *List* view, the selection circle is to the left of the file or folder name.
   - In *Tiles* view, the selection circle is in the top right corner of the file or folder tile.
   - Select multiple items if they will move or be copied to the same location.

2. Click the **Move to** or **Copy to** button and a *Move item to* or *Copy item to* pane opens on the right (Figure 7-19).

3. Select the name of the destination folder where you want to move or copy the selected items.

   - Click **New Folder**, if necessary, to create a folder for moved or copied items.

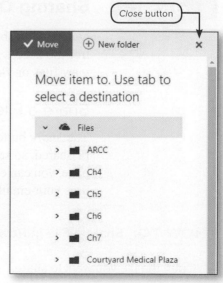

7-19 Move a *OneDrive* file

4. Click the **Move** or **Copy** button to close the pane and move or copy the selected items.
   - Press **Esc** or click the close button to cancel the process and close the pane.
5. Click the selection circle for a file or folder to delete.
   - Click the **Delete** button.
   - A status message appears on the upper right with an **Undo** button you can click to restore the file or folder. *Undo* is only available immediately after you delete.

### Download a File or Folder

You can download a file or folder from your *OneDrive* folder to your computer or a computer in a different location. When you download files from *OneDrive*, a copy is downloaded and the original remains on *OneDrive*. After editing the file, you can upload it to *OneDrive* using the same name to replace the file or with a different name to maintain both versions.

▶ **HOW TO:** Download a File or Folder from OneDrive

1. Click the selection circle for the file or folder name you want to download.
   - In *List* view, the selection circle is to the left of the file or folder name.
   - In *Tile* view, the selection circle is in the top right corner of the file or folder tile.
   - If you select more than one file or a folder to download, a compressed (zipped) folder downloads with the files or folders you selected.
2. Click the **Download** button. The download actions differ slightly based on the browser you are using and how it is configured.

   - The file or folder name may appear at the bottom of the *OneDrive* window (Figure 7-20), and the file or folder will be saved in your *Downloads* folder. You can transfer the file or folder from that location to the appropriate location.
   - The *Save As* dialog box may open. Select an appropriate location and file name then click **Save**.

   7-20 Downloaded file from *OneDrive*

**SLO 7.3**

## Sharing OneDrive Files and Folders

*OneDrive* enables you to collaborate with other people by sharing files or folders. You control the access they have to the items you share by assigning permission so users can only view files or view and edit files.

### Share a File in PowerPoint

The *Share* button in PowerPoint is in the upper right. However, a file must be saved online to be shared, so save your presentation to an appropriate folder on *OneDrive*. Then, in the *Share* pane, you can enter email addresses, set the permission level, and type a message. PowerPoint uses your email address to send the message.

▶ **HOW TO:** Share a File in PowerPoint

1. Open the file you want to share.
   - Save the file to *OneDrive* if it is not already saved.

2. Click the **Share** button in the upper right corner of the PowerPoint window to open the *Share* pane (Figure 7-21).

3. Type or select the email address under *Invite People* for the person with whom you are sharing the presentation.

   - If Outlook is your email program, you can add addresses from your *Outlook Contacts*. Click the **Address Book** button to the right of the *Invite People* text box, select the recipient name, and click **OK**.
   - If you include multiple addresses, separate each with a semicolon.

4. Click the **Permission** drop-down list and select **Can edit** or **Can view**.

   - The *Permission* drop-down list and the *Message* text box do not display until you type an email address in the *Invite people* text box.

5. Type a brief message to the recipient(s) in the *Message* text box.

6. Click the **Share** button to send the sharing invitation email.

   - The people you have chosen receive an email containing a link to the shared file on *OneDrive*.

7. Close the *Share* pane.

> **► ANOTHER WAY**
>
> You can also open the *Share* pane from the *Backstage* view. Click the **File** tab, click **Share**, select **Share with People**, and then click the **Share with People** button.

7-21 Share a presentation

## Create a Sharing Link

A *sharing link* is a hyperlink that you copy and email to others so they can access your file on *OneDrive*. You specify *Edit link* or *View-only link*. You can change the sharing permission or remove sharing on a file or folder. The *Details pane* on the right displays properties of the selected file or folder.

- Click **Get a link** to generate a link to send to recipients using your own email account.
- You can post the link on Facebook, Twitter, or LinkedIn.

### ▶ HOW TO: Create a Sharing Link

1. Open the file stored on *OneDrive* that you want to share.

2. Click the **Share** button in the upper right corner of the PowerPoint window to open the *Share* pane.

3. Click **Get a sharing link** at the bottom of the *Share* pane (see Figure 7-21).

4. Click the **Create an edit link** or **Create a view-only link** button (Figure 7-22).

   - A link is created and displayed.
   - The displayed name of this link depends on the sharing permission of the file.

5. Click the **Copy** button (Figure 7-23).

   - You can paste the copied sharing link in an email message, a document, a presentation, or an online location.

7-22 Get a sharing link in the *Share* pane

7-23 Copy a sharing link in the *Share* pane

6. Click the **Back** arrow to the left of **Get a sharing link**.
   - The main *Share* pane displays.
7. Close the *Share* pane.

## Change Sharing Permission

After sharing your *OneDrive* file with others, you can change the sharing permission or remove permission to edit the file. If you created a sharing link, you can disable the sharing link.

▶ **HOW TO:** Change Sharing Permission

1. Open the shared file.
2. Click the **Share** button in the upper right corner of the PowerPoint window to open the *Share* pane.
3. Right-click a name of one person with whom you have shared the file.
   - Select **Remove User** or **Change permission to: Can view (or Can edit)**.
4. Right-click the sharing link and select **Disable Link** (Figure 7-24).
   - You can also click **Copy Link** to copy and share the link with others.
5. Close the *Share* pane.

7-24 Disable or copy a sharing link

## Other Sharing Options in PowerPoint

PowerPoint has more ways to share files with options available by clicking the *Share* button on the *Backstage* view (Figure 7-25).

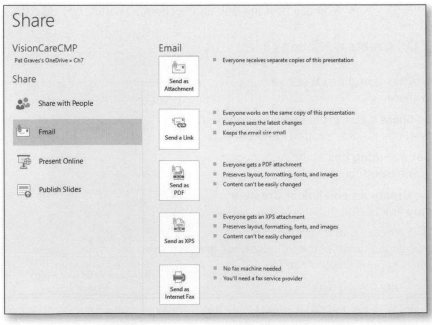

7-25 *Share Email* options in PowerPoint

- *Email:* When you use Microsoft Outlook, you can choose *Send as Attachment, Send a Link, Send as PDF, Send as XPS,* or *Send as Internet Fax.* The last option requires a fax service provider.
- *Present Online:* Access to the **Office Presentation Service** is provided with your Microsoft account. Your presentation is saved online with a link created that you can share with people. Invited people can view your presentation in a web browser and can download the presentation if you enable this option.
- *Publish Slides:* Slides are stored in a location such as Microsoft's SharePoint site (which is available for a monthly subscription fee). Several SharePoint products exist that provide cloud-based service for businesses and individuals to share and collaborate.

## Share a File or Folder in OneDrive

The process for sharing a file in *OneDrive* is similar to sharing a file or folder within PowerPoint. You can control the permission levels and send an email with a link to the shared file.

▶ **HOW TO:** Share a OneDrive File or Folder

1. Sign in to your *OneDrive* account.
2. Click the selection circle for the file or folder to share.
   - When you share a folder, users have access to all files in the folder.
3. Click the **Share** button to open the *Share* window with two options: *Get a link* and *Email* (Figure 7-26).
4. Click **Get a link** to generate a link that you can send to recipients.
   - Click **Copy** (Figure 7-27). You paste this sharing link in an email message, a document, a presentation, or an online location.
   - By default, **Allow editing** is selected so the recipient will be able to edit the file.
   - Click **Anyone with this link can edit this item** to deselect **Allow editing** if you want the recipient to be able only to view the file.
   - Click the **More** link to display more viewing options to share the file on Facebook, Twitter, or LinkedIn.
5. Click **Email** (Figure 7-28) to send a message with a sharing link.
   - Type the email address(s) in the first text box. Press **Tab** to add another address.
   - Type a brief message in the text box.
   - Click the **Share** button. The recipients will get an email with a link to the shared file or folder.

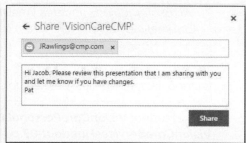

7-26 *Share* options in *OneDrive*

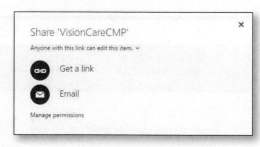

7-27 Copy a sharing link in *OneDrive*

7-28 Send a sharing email message in *OneDrive*

## Change Sharing Permission in OneDrive

In *OneDrive,* the **Information** pane displays properties of a selected file or folder and add people to share. You can change sharing permission or remove sharing on a file or folder.

## ▶ HOW TO: Change or Remove OneDrive Sharing

1. Select the shared file or folder in your *OneDrive* account.

2. Click the **Information** button in the upper right corner to open the *Information* pane (Figure 7-29).
   - A portion of the file is displays at the top of the pane with its file name.
   - Under *Sharing*, people who have permission to view or edit the selected item and their email addresses are listed.

3. Click **Add People** to open a *Share* dialog box to get a link or send a sharing email to others.
   - Click **Get a link** and the link is displayed at the bottom of the *Information* pane.

4. Change sharing permission or stop sharing for each recipient by clicking the **Permission** drop-down list (**Can Edit** is shown in Figure 7-29) and selecting **Change to view only**, **Allow edit**, or **Stop Sharing**.

5. Copy a sharing link in the *Information* pane by clicking the link and pressing **Ctrl+C**.

6. Remove a sharing link from the *Information* pane by clicking the **X** (*Disable link*) on the right to open the *Remove link* dialog box (Figure 7-30). Click **Remove link**.

Remove link                                   ✕

If you want to share this item again, you'll need to create a new link.

**Remove link**        Cancel

7. Close the *Information* pane.

7-30  Remove a sharing link

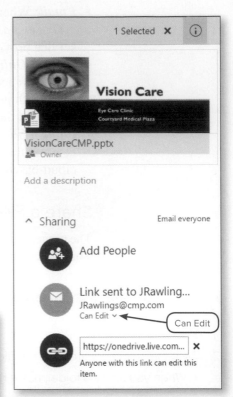

7-29  Change or remove sharing permissions in the *Information* pane

---

# PAUSE & PRACTICE: POWERPOINT 7-1

**Note to Instructor and Students**:

> *If you do not have a Microsoft account, go to* https://signup.live.com *to create one. See the Microsoft Account Information section in* SLO 7.1 Modifying Office Account Options and Using Add-ins.

> *Microsoft regularly updates OneDrive. Instructions and figures in this project (created with Google Chrome) may differ slightly from how this application displays in your Internet browser.*

For this project, you work with files from the Eye Care Clinic at Courtyard Medical Plaza. You change your Microsoft account settings and add an add-in. You also upload files to your *OneDrive* folder and create a folder online, move files, delete a folder, and share a file.

---

Files Needed: ***VisionCarePersonal-07.pptx***, ***VisionCareServices-07.pptx***, ***VisionCareServicesHandout-07.pdf***, and ***Vision-07.jpg*** *(student data files are available in the* Library of your SIMnet account)
Completed Project File Name: None *(files uploaded/arranged and one file shared on OneDrive)*

---

1. Open the presentation ***VisionCareServices-07***.

2. Customize your Office account settings.
   a. Click the **File** tab and select **Account** to display your account information on the *Backstage* view.
   b. Click the **Office Theme** drop-down list and select **Dark Gray**.

c. Click the **Office Background** drop-down list and choose **Geometry**.

d. Edit the list of *Connected Services*.
- If YouTube is not listed, click the **Add a service** drop-down list.
- Select **Images & Videos**, and click **YouTube** (Figure 7-31).
- YouTube is added to the *Connected Services* list.

e. Click the **Back** button to return to *Normal* view.

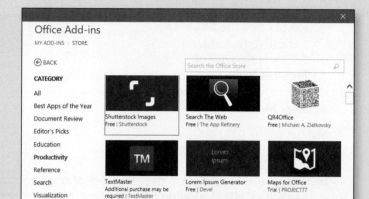

7-31 *Add a service* options

3. Add an Office add-in.
a. Click the **Store** button [*Insert* tab, *Add-ins* group] to open the *Office Add-ins* dialog box.
b. Click **Productivity** in the *Category* area (Figure 7-32).
c. Select an app of your choice and a dialog box opens with information about the add-in.
d. Click **Trust it** and the add-in is installed. The add-in opens in the *Add-in* pane or in a separate object.
e. Close the *Add-in* pane or object.

4. Close the presentation without saving and exit PowerPoint.

7-32 *Office Add-ins* dialog box with information about the add-ins

5. Sign in to *OneDrive* online.
a. Open an Internet browser window and type onedrive.live.com to go to Microsoft's sign in page.
b. Click **Sign in** on the *Title* bar on the right.
c. Type your Microsoft email address and password to sign in to *OneDrive*.

6. Create a new folder and upload files.
a. Verify that **Files** is selected on the left to display the contents of your *OneDrive* folder.
- Click the **List** view button (Figure 7-33), if necessary, so your screen displays file names rather than tiled images.

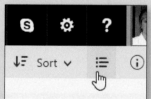

7-33 *List* view button

7-34 Create a *OneDrive* folder online

b. Click the **New** button and select **Folder** from the drop-down list (Figure 7-34).
c. Type Courtyard Medical Plaza and click **Create**.
d. Open the *Courtyard Medical Plaza* folder.
e. Click the **Upload** button and select **Files** to open an upload dialog box.
- Remember, the name of this dialog box varies depending on the Internet browser you are using.
f. Locate your student data files and select *Vision-07*, *VisionCarePersonal-07*, *VisionCareServices-07*, and *VisionCareServicesHandout-07* from your student files.
g. Click **Open** and the files will upload.

7. Create a subfolder and move a file.
a. Click the **New** button and select **Folder**.

b. Type CMP Marketing and click **Create**.
   - A subfolder is created within the *Courtyard Medical Plaza* folder (Figure 7-35).
c. Click the selection circle before ***VisionCareServices-07***.
d. Click the **Move to** button to open the *Move* pane (Figure 7-36).
e. Click the **Courtyard Medical Plaza** folder to display subfolders.
f. Select the **CMP Marketing** subfolder.
g. Click **Move**.

7-35 Create a *OneDrive* subfolder online

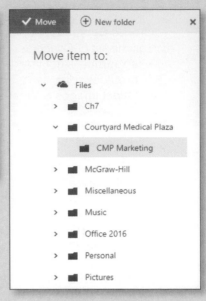

7-36 Move a file to a subfolder

8. Move a file by dragging.
   a. Click the selection circle before *VisionCareServicesHandout-07*.
   b. Drag the selection circle over the **CMP Marketing** folder name and release.
   c. Click the **CMP Marketing** folder to open it and confirm that both files are moved.

9. Share a file.
   a. Select the ***VisionCareServices-07*** file in the **CMP Marketing** subfolder.
   b. Click **Share** in the menu bar to open the share dialog box.
   c. Click **Email** and another dialog box opens.
   d. Type your instructor's email address and a brief message (Figure 7-37).
   e. Click **Share** to send the sharing email to your instructor.

10. Click your picture in the *OneDrive Title* bar and select **Sign Out**.

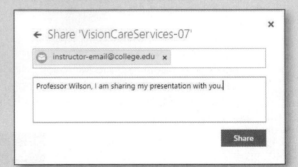

7-37 Send a sharing email

---

## Using PowerPoint Online

***Office Online*** is a scaled-down version of *Office 2016/365* that is available to you at no cost when you sign in to your Microsoft account at https://onedrive.live.com.

The available applications, including ***PowerPoint Online*** are shown in Figure 7-38. Purchasing the *2016/365* software is not required to use these applications. Each online application works in the same way, but not as many features

7-38 *Office Online* applications

are available. You can use *Office Online* to create, edit, print, share, and insert comments on files. When you need more features, you can open *Office Online* files in their respective *Office 2016/365* applications installed on a desktop or notebook computer.

Microsoft is continuously improving and upgrading these applications and the online experience of working with *Office Online*. The figures shown in this section, using Google Chrome, may look slightly different than what you see when you access *Office Online* at a later date or in a different browser.

In addition to editing presentations, in *PowerPoint Online* you can display your presentation in *Slide Show* view or *Reading* view. This capability is very important because you could display your presentation from any computer even when PowerPoint is not available. The following sections will focus on how to use *PowerPoint Online* and explain some of the differences in using the online version of PowerPoint.

## Edit a Presentation in PowerPoint Online

*Office Online* is very similar to the desktop version of *Office 2016/365* and has the familiar *Ribbon*, tabs, and groups. You can start a presentation using the *PowerPoint Online* application within *Office Online*, or you can open and edit the PowerPoint files you have stored on *OneDrive*.

When you select a file in the *OneDrive* browser window, *Office Online* opens your file in **read-only mode** in the appropriate program. For example, if you select a PowerPoint presentation, your presentation opens in *PowerPoint Online* and you could click **Start Slide Show** to display it in *Slide Show* view. To make changes to the presentation, you click **Edit Presentation** and choose the **edit mode** that you need. Select **Edit in Browser** to work in *PowerPoint Online* or **Edit in PowerPoint** to work with PowerPoint installed on your computer.

---

### ▶ HOW TO: Edit a PowerPoint Online File

1. Sign in to your *OneDrive* account.
2. Click the name of a PowerPoint file in the file list on *OneDrive* (Figure 7-39).
   - The presentation opens (read-only mode) in *PowerPoint Online* in a new tab in your browser (Figure 7-40).
   - Alternatively, you can click a file's selection circle, click the **Open** button, and select *Open in PowerPoint Online* or right-click the file name and select **Open in** *PowerPoint Online*.
   - The opened file displays in read-only mode to make it easy to use *Slide Show* or *Reading* view.
   - You cannot edit a file in read-only mode.

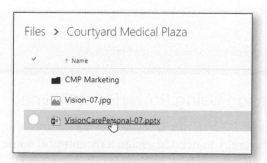

7-39 Open a presentation in *PowerPoint Online*

7-40 A presentation opened in *PowerPoint Online*, read-only mode

3. Click **Edit Presentation** and select **Edit in Browser** (Figure 7-41) to edit the file in *PowerPoint Online*.

- Alternatively, click **Edit in PowerPoint** to open the file in the full version of PowerPoint on your computer as long as Office 2016/365 is installed.
- Choose this option if you need certain features that are not available online.

7-41 Change from read-only mode to edit mode in *PowerPoint Online*

4. Edit and format in *PowerPoint Online* (Figure 7-42).

- The *File*, *Home*, *Insert*, *Design*, *Transitions*, *Animations*, and *View* tabs are on the *Ribbon* in *PowerPoint Online*. Other Office applications will display different tabs.

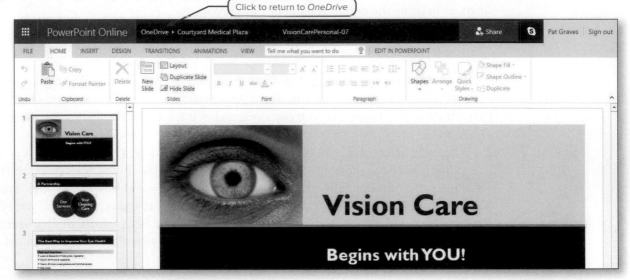

7-42 The *PowerPoint Online Ribbon*

- You can edit and change formatting, apply styles, and cut, copy, and paste selected text. Font sizing and gallery options are limited.
- When using *PowerPoint Online*, advanced formatting for text boxes, pictures, charts, and *SmartArt* might not display as they do when you open the presentation in *PowerPoint 2016/365*.
- *Slide Sorter* view is not available.
- Click **Edit in PowerPoint** on the *Ribbon* to open the presentation in *Office 2016/365* on your computer.

5. Click the **File** tab and choose **Save As** if you want to save to a different location.

- In *PowerPoint Online*, your file is automatically saved as you are working.

6. Close the browser tab to return to your *OneDrive* folders and files.

- Alternatively, click the **OneDrive** link in the *Title* bar to return to your *OneDrive* folders and files. The presentation is automatically saved and closed.

> **MORE INFO**
>
> The *PowerPoint Online Ribbon* displays in edit mode but not in read-only mode.

## Create and Save a Presentation Using PowerPoint Online

When you create a new presentation in *PowerPoint Online*, it is saved on your *OneDrive* when you close the presentation. Therefore, you need to assign a meaningful name and select an appropriate folder rather than accepting the default settings.

## ▶ HOW TO: Create and Save a Presentation Using PowerPoint Online

1. Sign in to your *OneDrive* account.

2. Select the folder where you want to create a new file.

3. Click the **New** button and select **PowerPoint presentation** from the drop-down list (Figure 7-43) to open a new presentation in edit mode.

4. Rename the presentation by clicking the default name in the *Title* bar and typing a new name (Figure 7-44).

   - In *PowerPoint Online*, your file is automatically saved when you close the presentation.
   - Click the **File** tab and choose **Save As** if you want to save to a different location.

5. Prepare your presentation slides and apply formatting as desired.

6. Close the browser tab to close the current file and return to your *OneDrive* folders and files.

7-43 Create a new presentation in *PowerPoint Online*

Replace the default file name text

7-44 Rename a presentation in *PowerPoint Online*

## Create and Edit Objects Using PowerPoint Online

Creating graphic objects in *PowerPoint Online* is a little different than when using *PowerPoint 2016/365*. Several of the differences are as follows:

- **Format Background:** Themes and variants are available, but formatting the background is limited to selecting a *Solid Fill* or *Picture from File*.
- **Layouts:** Choose a layout at the time you add a slide. You can change layouts later.
- **Shapes:** When you select the **Shape** tool, a shape is inserted on your slide and it can be resized by dragging the sizing handles. You cannot click and drag to draw the shape. The *Edit Points* feature is not available.
- **Text Box:** When you click the **Text Box** button [*Insert* tab, *Text* group], a text box is inserted on the slide. It can then be edited and resized. You cannot click and drag to draw the text box.
- **Tables:** Insert a table on a new slide with the *Title and Content* layout by clicking the **Table** icon and entering the number of rows and columns on the *Insert Table* dialog box. To add a table to an existing slide, click the **Table** button and drag to select columns and rows. However, no *Insert Table* dialog box is available.
- **SmartArt:** Insert a *SmartArt* graphic on a new slide with the *Title and Content* layout by clicking the *SmartArt* icon. A *SmartArt* graphic appears on the slide. Click the **SmartArt Tools Design** tab to choose a different layout from the gallery. The gallery does not include all the categories of layouts as in *PowerPoint 2016/365*. *Change Colors* includes variations of all your theme colors; *Styles* includes several options but they are not arranged in categories. To insert a *SmartArt* graphic on an existing slide, click the **SmartArt** button [*Insert* tab, *Illustrations* group] and select from the available layouts in the gallery.
- **Charts:** No chart features are available.
- **Pictures, Online Picture, and Online Video:** Add these objects on a new slide with the *Title and Content* layout or on an existing slide by clicking their respective buttons in the *Drawing Tools Format* tab.
- **Transitions and Animations:** Each feature is limited to about five options.

## Print a Presentation Using PowerPoint Online

When you print in *PowerPoint Online*, a PDF (Portable Document Format) file is created before you select your print options. Each slide appears on a page; no other options for printing are available online. You can print from either read-only or edit mode.

### ▶ HOW TO: Print an Office Online File

1. Sign in to your *OneDrive* account and locate the presentation you need to print in your *Files* list.

2. Click the file name to open the presentation in *PowerPoint Online*.
3. Click **Edit Presentation** and select **Edit in Browser**.
4. Click the **File** tab.
5. Select **Print** and click the **Print to PDF** button (Figure 7-45).

   7-45 *Print to PDF*

   • A message box may open asking you to click to view your PDF file.
   • The printable PDF file opens in a *Print* window with a preview of the document on the right (Figure 7-46).
   • Only full-size slides will print with each slide on a separate page.
   • Choose from the available print options.
   • If you need to print handouts or use other print options, open the file in *PowerPoint 2016/365*.

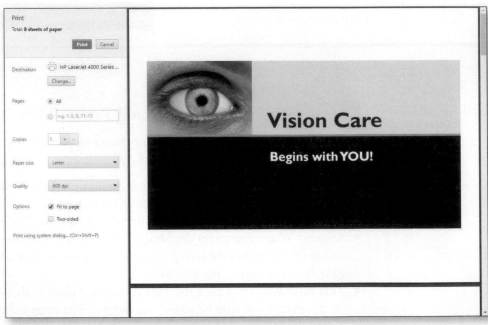

6. Click the **Print** button.

7-46 Preview the PDF file

## Share a Presentation in PowerPoint Online

The process for sharing a file in *PowerPoint Online* is similar to sharing a file in *OneDrive*.

### ▶ HOW TO: Share a Presentation in PowerPoint Online

1. Open a presentation in *PowerPoint Online*.
2. Select the file you plan to share. Click **Edit Presentation** and select **Edit in Browser** to open the file in *PowerPoint Online*.
3. Click the **Share** button in the *Title* bar to open the *Share window*.

   • The *Share* window opens.
   • Choose *Invite people* (send an email) or *Get a link*.
   • You can also click the **File** tab, select **Share**, and then click **Share with people** to open the *Share* window.

4. Send a sharing email (Figure 7-47).

- Select **Invite people** and type the recipient's email address. Press **Tab** to add the email address for another recipient.
- Type a brief message.
- Assign permission by clicking the **Recipients can edit** link and selecting **Recipients can only view** or **Recipients can edit**.
- You can also require recipients to sign in to their Microsoft account to view or edit the file by selecting **Recipients need to sign in with a Microsoft account** from the drop-down list.
- Click the **Share** button and recipients will receive an email containing a link to the shared file.
- Click **Close** to close the *Share* window and return to the *PowerPoint Online* presentation.

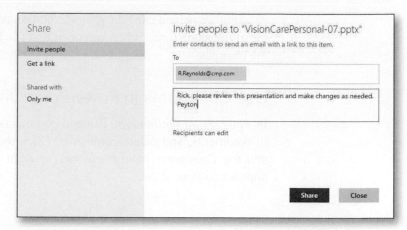

7-47 Share a *PowerPoint Online* file

5. Create a sharing link to send to others (Figure 7-48).

- Click the **Share** button to open the *Share* window.
- Click **Get a link** and choose **View Only**, **Edit**, or **Public** from the *Choose an option* drop-down list.
- Click the **Create link** button and a link displays.
- Copy the sharing link and paste it in an email or online location to share the file.

7-48 Create a sharing link in *PowerPoint Online*

6. Click **Close** to close the *Share* window and return to the *PowerPoint Online* presentation.

## Collaborate in PowerPoint Online

When you give others permission to edit your file, *PowerPoint Online* enables them to access and revise your file. If two or more people are working on the same file in *PowerPoint Online* at the same time, information about others editing the file displays in the upper right (Figure 7-49). In the *Thumbnail* pane, an icon displays beside the current slide of another person sharing the file (Figure 7-50). Revisions made by another person are reflected very quickly in your presentation.

7-49 Additional people are collaborating on a shared file

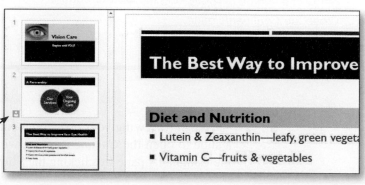

Indicates another person is editing

7-50 The icon shows the current slide of another person editing the presentation

Another person can edit your shared file using *PowerPoint Online* when you are not working at the same time. When you open that file later from your *OneDrive* account, you will see the changes.

## Use Comments in PowerPoint Online

In *PowerPoint Online*, you can add comments to a file, review comments from others, reply to comments, and delete comments. Click the **Comments** button [*Insert* tab] in edit mode, and the *Comments* pane opens on the right. When you add a comment, a comment icon appears on your slide.

---

▶ **HOW TO:** Add Comments in PowerPoint Online

1. Open a file in *PowerPoint Online*, select **Edit Presentation**, and select **Edit in Browser**.
2. Select the slide where you want to add a comment.
3. Click the
   **Comments**
   button [*Insert*
   tab, *Comments*
   group] to open the
   *Comments* pane.
   * In the *Comments*
     pane, your name
     automatically
     appears with
     space for your
     comment.

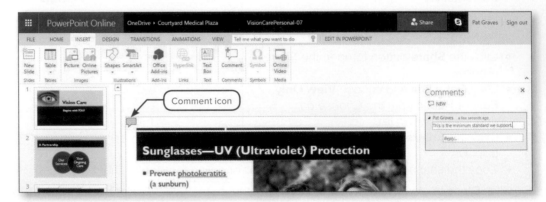

7-51 Adding comments in *PowerPoint Online*

4. Type your comment
   and press **Enter**.
   * A *Reply* box appears below your comment (Figure 7-51).
   * A comment icon displays on the slide in the upper left corner.
   * You can move the comment icon. Place it near an object to help
     a reviewer understand that your comment relates to that particular
     object.
5. Reply to a comment in the box that appears below each comment
   (Figure 7-52).
6. Click **New** to add a second comment.
7. Remove a comment by clicking the **Delete** button.
8. Close the *Comments* pane.

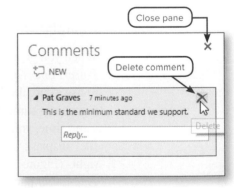

7-52 *Comments* pane

---

When reviewing your own comments or comments from others, click a comment icon on a slide to open the *Comments* pane, which appears on the right. Alternatively, you can open the *Comments* pane by clicking the **Show Comments** button [*View* tab, *Show* group].

***Note to Instructor and Students***:

*If you do not have a Microsoft account, go to* https://signup.live.com *to create one. See the Microsoft Account Information section in* SLO 7.1: Modifying Office Account Options and Using Add-ins.

*Microsoft regularly updates* OneDrive *and* Office Online. *Instructions and figures in this project (created with Google Chrome) may differ slightly from how these applications display in your Internet browser.*

For this project, you edit a file for the Eye Care Clinic at Courtyard Medical Plaza that you uploaded to your *OneDrive* in *PowerPoint 7-1*. You edit this presentation in *PowerPoint Online*, add comments, and share the presentation. Then you create a new presentation using *PowerPoint Online* and rename files.

File Needed: ***VisionCareServices-07.pptx*** *(on OneDrive)*
Completed Project File Names: ***[your initials] PP P7-2a.pptx*** and ***[your initials] PP P7-2b.pptx*** *(on OneDrive)*

1. Open an Internet browser page and sign in to your *OneDrive* account (https://onedrive.live.com).

2. Prepare folders and files if necessary.
   a. The *Courtyard Medical Plaza* folder and the *CMP Marketing* subfolder were prepared and four files uploaded in *Pause and Practice PowerPoint 7-1*.
   b. If you did not create these folders, return to that project and complete steps 6–8.

3. Edit a file in *PowerPoint Online*.
   a. Click the **Courtyard Medical Plaza** folder and then the **CMP Marketing** folder to open it.
   b. Click the ***VisionCareServices-07*** file to open it in read-only mode in *PowerPoint Online*.
   c. Click the **Edit Presentation** button at the top and select **Edit in Browser** from the drop-down list to open it in edit mode.
      • In *PowerPoint Online*, the file is saved automatically as you make changes.
   d. Display slide 1. Select the subtitle and change the font size to **40 pt**.
      • Increase the size of the placeholder for this larger text.
   e. Display slide 2. Insert a text box.
      • Click the **Text Box** button [*Insert* tab] and a text box appears in the center of the slide over the *SmartArt* graphic.
      • Select the text box and drag it to the upper left.
      • Type **Our Services**.
      • Change to left alignment.
      • Change the font size to **54 pt**. and apply **bold**.
      • Resize the text box so the words fit on one line.
      • Position this text box as shown in Figure 7-53 and move the *SmartArt* graphic down slightly.

4. Add a comment to the presentation.
   a. Display slide 3. Click the **Comment** button [*Insert* tab, *Comments* group] to open the *Comments* pane.
   b. Type **We need to develop a separate presentation about eye exams for children.** in the box after your name (Figure 7-54).
   c. Close the *Comments* pane.

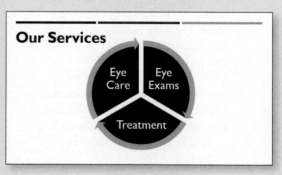

7-53 Text box added

7-54 Comment added

5. Share the presentation with your instructor.
   a. Click **Share** in the *Title* bar to open the *Share* window (Figure 7-55).
   b. Verify that **Invite people** is selected.
   c. Type your instructor's email address and a brief message.

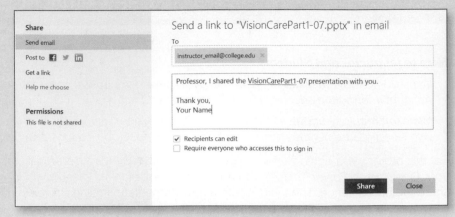

7-55 Share a presentation

   d. Click the permissions drop-down list and select the **Recipients can only view** option.
   e. Click **Share** to send the sharing email to your instructor.
   f. Click the **OneDrive** link in the *Title* bar to return to your *OneDrive* folders.
   g. Close the browser tab and return to your previous browser tab.

6. Create a new presentation in *PowerPoint Online* and apply a theme.
   a. Click the **Courtyard Medical Plaza** folder to open it.
   b. Click the **New** button and select **PowerPoint presentation**.
      • *PowerPoint Online* opens in edit mode with a blank presentation.
   c. Click the default file name in the title and type a new file name, **Children Exams**.
      • The file is automatically saved as you develop your presentation.
   d. Click the **Design** tab, click the **More Themes** button to open the *Themes* gallery, and click the **Savon** theme to apply it.
   e. Click the title placeholder on the slide and type **Eye Exams for Children** for the presentation title.
      • Press **Enter** after "Exams" so the text fits on two lines (Figure 7-56).

7-56 Title slide

7. Add a slide and create a *SmartArt* graphic.
   a. Click the **New Slide** button [*Home* tab, *Slides* group], select the **Title Only** layout, and click **Add Slide**.
   b. Type **Recommended Ages** for the slide title on slide 2.
   c. Click the **SmartArt** button [*Insert* tab, *Illustrations* group] to open the gallery.
   d. Click the **Basic Chevron Process** layout.
   e. Click the first shape and bullets appear (Figure 7-57).
      • Start with the top bullet and type **6 Months**.
      • Press the down arrow and type **Age 3**.
      • Press the down arrow and type **Age 5**.

7-57 Typing *SmartArt* text

f. Delete any remaining bullets if necessary.
- When you click anywhere on the slide, the text appears in the three shapes.
- Resize the *SmartArt* graphic as shown in Figure 7-58.

8. Add a slide with bulleted text.
   a. Click the **New Slide** button [*Home* tab, *Slides* group], select the **Title and Content** layout, and click **Add Slide**.
   b. Type the slide 3 title Eyesight Skills for Learning.
   c. Type the following items in the content placeholder.
      - Near and distance vision
      - Eye coordination and movement
      - Focusing skills
      - Peripheral awareness
      - Hand-eye coordination
   d. Increase the bulleted list font size on slide 3 to **28 pt**.

9. View the presentation.
   a. Click the *Reading* view button [*Status* bar] to return to view mode.
   b. Click the *Slide Show* button [*Status* bar] to view the presentation.
   c. Click the *OneDrive* link to return to your files.

10. Rename files.
    a. Open the **CMP Marketing** folder.
    b. Click the selection circle to select the ***VisionCareServices-07*** file.
    c. Click **Rename** in the menu bar.
       - You may need to click the **Other Things** icon if your window is not wide enough to display all options. Select **Rename** from the drop-down list (Figure 7-59).
       - Type [your initials] PP P7-2a and press **Enter** (Figure 7-60).
       - Deselect the **[your initials] PP P7-2a** check box.

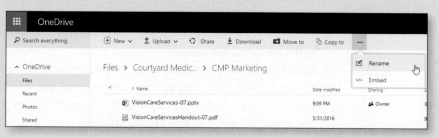

7-58 Completed *SmartArt* graphic

7-59 Rename a file

7-60 PP P7-2a completed

d. Open the **Courtyard Medical Plaza** folder.
  - Select the ***Children Exams*** presentation and rename it [your initials] PP P7-2b (Figure 7-61).

11. Select **[your name]** in the upper right corner and select **Sign out** from the *Account* drop-down list.

7-61 PP P7-2b completed

SLO 7.5

## Using Office Mix for Interactive Online Presentations and for Videos

Now that you have learned to use PowerPoint's advanced features, you can create dynamic and creative presentations to support a speaker and to create stand-alone presentations for users to view independently. You can add different forms of media to enliven a presentation or save an entire presentation as a video including music or narration. With *Office Online*, you have learned how to share your presentation by making it available online. An audience can be one or more people in any location.

Now *Office Mix*, an add-in for PowerPoint, provides more flexibility in how you record a presentation and makes it easy to create online presentations with engaging content and interactivity. You start with the familiar PowerPoint commands to develop content on slides and save your presentation as a PowerPoint file (.pptx). Then you include the following options as needed:

- Insert video, audio, screenshots, and screen clippings.
- Draw with real-time digital inking.
- Use screen recording to create a video of anything on your computer screen such as a software demonstration.
- Insert interactive elements such as quizzes, online videos, and web pages.
- Create a slide recording to capture the entire presentation including handwriting with digital ink if your computer or tablet has a touch screen. If your computer also has a camera and microphone, you can record yourself speaking.
- Upload your *Mix* to save it to the cloud and create an online interactive presentation or export it as a video.
- Share a link so others can view your *Mix* on any device (computer, tablet, or phone) with a web browser.
- Use analytics to study data regarding viewers' use patterns and quiz results.

Samples of visually stunning presentations are available on https://mix.office.com for inspiration and learning. For example, educators can prepare media-rich, interactive lessons that can work with many learning management systems. Business people can prepare reports and presentations that engage an audience in a much more compelling way than with more traditional methods.

After you download *Office Mix*, a new *Mix* tab appears on your PowerPoint ribbon. The *Mix* tab [*Insert* group] has three commands you have already learned to use from the *Insert* tab: *Screenshot*, *Insert Video*, and *Insert Audio*.

Develop your slides as you would for a presentation, or use a "picture book" approach where you write the text in paragraphs to be read by a single user as slides advance. Plan for places that need more time for the viewer to absorb information. Use animation to build slide content as it is discussed.

A video of yourself providing introductory comments would make the presentation more personal for viewers. If you insert a video file, introduce it on the previous slide because the video will play automatically when a slide advances. You can record a video of yourself giving the presentation, too, that would appear in a thumbnail size on each slide.

Once your recording is completed, you have a *Mix* to upload to a Microsoft secure cloud server where it is private until you add permission and sharing options.

The following sections show how to download *Office Mix* and explain the new features that *Office Mix* provides.

### ▶ HOW TO: Download Office Mix

1. Close PowerPoint if it is open.
2. Go to https://mix.office.com (Figure 7-62).
3. Click the **Get Office Mix** button.
4. Sign in with your Microsoft account info.
   - Your download should start automatically.
5. Click **OfficeMix.Setup.exe** that appears in the *Status* bar.
   - You may be asked to save *OfficeMix.Setup.exe* depending on the browser you are using.
   - Check **I agree to the license terms and conditions** and click **Install**.
   - If you are asked to authorize changes to your computer, click **Yes**.
   - After installation, PowerPoint automatically loads with the new *Mix* tab (Figure 7-63).
6. Click one or more of the tutorials listed in the *Welcome* pane to review that content.
   - Video tutorials will open in a browser window.

7-62 *Office Mix* **home page**

7-63 *Office Mix* **downloaded**

## Screen Recording

A *Screen Recording* creates a video of on-screen actions that can include audio narration. For example, you could record a series of slides, an illustration being drawn, or a software demonstration. *Screen Recording* works somewhat like a *Screen Clipping* because you start on the slide where you want the recording to appear. Then when you click the **Screen Recording** button [*Office Mix* tab, *Insert* group], the previous file (such as a document, web page, worksheet, or presentation) will be grayed out. You drag to select the recording area that shows as a rectangle with a red dashed border. The rectangle cannot be moved, but you can redraw it if necessary. Content behind the rectangle can be moved. It is possible, also, to record movements of your pointer and text entry to demonstrate a particular software feature. Use buttons on the *Recording* toolbar that opens at the top of your screen to redraw a selection area, begin the recording, and end the recording.

The recording is embedded as a video on the slide where it was made. Therefore, PowerPoint's video editing tools are available. You can add a video style, insert a poster frame, change its shape, or use other editing features such as trimming.

## ▶ HOW TO: Create a Screen Recording

1. Open PowerPoint and open the presentation where you need to play the recording.

2. Open the other application and file that you want to record.

3. Position it on your screen so the area to be recorded is visible.

4. Return to PowerPoint and select the slide where you want a screen recording to appear.

5. Click the **Screen Recording** button [*Office Mix* tab, *Insert* group] (Figure 7-64).

   • Your previous file is grayed out.

7-64 *Record and Insert* groups on the *Mix* tab

6. Drag to select the area to be recorded.

   • A *Recording* toolbar appears at the top of your screen (Figure 7-65).

7. Click the **Pin** icon so this toolbar remains visible.

   • Leave the *Recording* bar unpinned if it is in the way of your recording. To use it, point to the top of your screen, and it will appear.
   • If you have difficulty selecting the recording area, click the **Select Area** button on the *Recording* toolbar and try again.

7-65 *Recording* toolbar

8. Click the **Record** button and a countdown begins.

9. Complete your activity in the recording area.

   • This example shows a demonstration for cropping a rectangular image to create a round image in a two-step process (Figure 7-66).

10. Click the **Stop** button when your recording is complete.

    • The recording appears as a video in your presentation (Figure 7-67).
    • Use video editing or playback tools as needed.

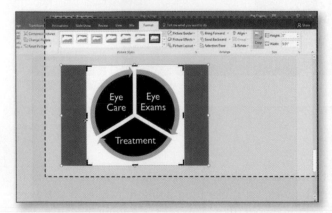

7-66 *Screen Recording* of a cropping demonstration

7-67 Completed video of a cropping demonstration

You can save your screen recording as a video for future use in other presentations or online. Right-click the video and select **Save Media As** from the context menu to open the *Save Media As* dialog box. Name the file and click **Save**.

## Add-ins for Quizzes, Polls, and Videos

In *SLO 7.1: Modifying Office Account Options and Using Add-ins*, you learned to select and download add-ins. The process works the same way from the *Mix* tab. Click the **Quizzes Video App** button to open the *Lab Office Add-ins* dialog box that shows applications in Microsoft's *Store*. Quiz add-ins include *Free Response Quiz*, *Multiple Choice Quiz*, *Multiple Response Poll*, and *True False Quiz*. Select and download the particular add-in that you want to use. Then in the future, the app is available in *My Add-ins* on the *Lab Office Add-ins* dialog box as long as you have an online connection.

Quiz questions enable you to involve your audience in your presentation because user input is required. However, be sure to use a separate slide for your question because you cannot have a screen recording and a question on the same slide.

---

### ▶ HOW TO: Install a Quiz Add-in and Type a Question

1. Select the **Mix** tab in PowerPoint.
2. Click the **Quizzes Video Apps** button [*Insert* group] to open the *Lab Office Add-ins* dialog box (Figure 7-68).
   - You must be online for the add-in to load and show content.
   - Quizzes and polls are listed first.
   - Select a quiz or poll and another dialog box opens with descriptive information.
   - Click **Trust It** to load the application.
   - The add-in opens as an object on your slide such as the *Multiple Choice Quiz* shown in Figure 7-69 with boxes for your question and responses.
3. Type your question and one or more responses depending on the type of question selected (Figure 7-70).
   - A floating formatting toolbar is available for all quizzes and polls.
   - Click the **Lightbulb** to add a hint.
   - Select from the options to control the number of correct answers, allow answers to be shuffled, allow retry, or limit the number of attempts to answer a question.

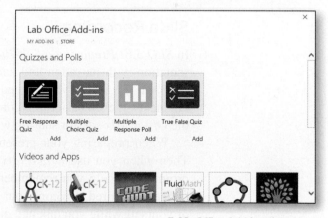

7-68  *Office Add-ins* dialog box

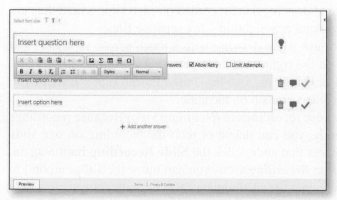

7-69  *Multiple Choice Quiz* object

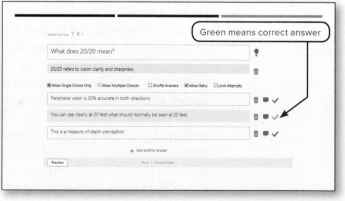

7-70  **Question items entered**

4. Select from other options:
   - Click **Delete** (the *Trashcan*) to remove an option.
   - Click the **Balloon** to provide feedback on a response.
   - Click the **Check Mark** to indicate correct and incorrect answers. Green means correct.
5. Click **Preview** to see the question on the slide (Figure 7-71).
6. Click off the object to leave editing mode.
7. Repeat this process to add more questions.
8. Save your presentation and then test each question in *Slide Show* view.

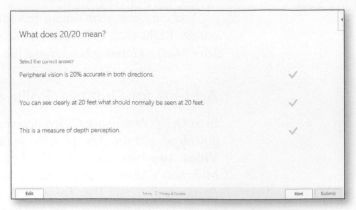

What does 20/20 mean?

Select the correct answer

Peripheral vision is 20% accurate in both directions. ✓

You can see clearly at 20 feet what should normally be seen at 20 feet. ✓

This is a measure of depth perception. ✓

Edit          Terms | Privacy & Cookies          Hint   Submit

**7-71** Preview completed question

More than one question may fit on one slide if you resize the question area. You can review and test all questions in *Slide Show* view.

When viewing a *Mix*, the user selects a question answer and clicks the **Submit** button. If the wrong answer is selected, the user receives a response to try again. A correct answer is required on each question before the user can advance to the next question. With a correct answer, the viewer receives confirmation and a **Continue** button appears. Press **Continue** to advance to the next question or slide.

Make this interaction clear for users by providing an instruction in your introductory comments to click links to advance through questions.

## Slide Recording

In *SLO 3.8: Preparing a Self-Running Presentation* you learned to create a stand-alone presentation with narration and automated timing. And in *SLO 6.7: Saving and Exporting in Different File Types* you learned to export your presentation as a video. The new *Office Mix* tab makes it even easier to record a presentation, and with interactivity. You can upload it on the *Office Mix* site for sharing with others or export it as a video for use offline.

When preparing your presentation to be recorded, type speaker notes with your slides. Then when you use *Office Mix* to record, those notes appear above your slide like a teleprompter to help you remember what you need to say while each slide displays. A microphone is required to record your voice. If your computer has a camera, you can create a video of yourself while you talk and display it in *Thumbnail* or *Full Screen* size during playback.

As you advance through slides giving your presentation, the different media you are using (voice, animation, transitions, video, and drawings) are recorded on each slide where they are used. They become part of your PowerPoint presentation—not separate files.

*Inking* tools and colors are easy to use when drawing with a touch screen or stylus, and a mouse works, too. These tools are on the right with three pens that draw lines in different thicknesses. The *Eraser* removes all drawings on a slide. Unlike PowerPoint's *Eraser*, you cannot remove individual lines while others remain on the slide.

Once slides are recorded, preview your recordings in *Recording* view. Because recordings are saved with each slide independently, you can delete or redo the recording on one slide without affecting other recordings. Select that slide, click the **Slide Recording** button again, and redo that slide only. After you close *Recording* view, you can move the slides around in PowerPoint using drag and drop or cut and paste. A thumbnail video can be moved anywhere on the slide. The audio (and video if used) remains with the slide where it was recorded.

# ▶ HOW TO: Create a Slide Recording

1. Select the slide where you will begin recording.

2. Click the **Slide Recording** button [*Mix* tab, *Record* group] and *Slide Recording* view opens (Figure 7-72).

   - Controls to record and navigate through slides appear above the slide.
   - Slide notes appear like a teleprompter.
   - Other controls are on the right.

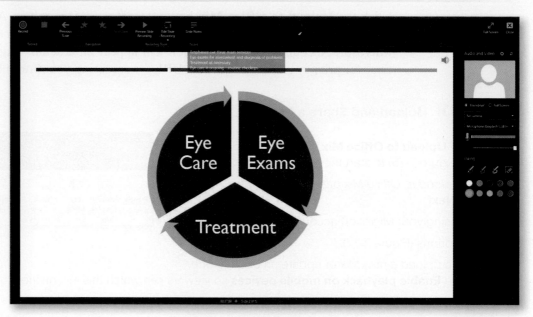

7-72 *Slide Recording* view

3. Click the **Record** button on the upper left.

   - Once recording begins, the dashed border changes to red and timing begins.

4. Advance through slides and record your voice (and video if possible) as you give your presentation.

   - Refer to speaker notes at the top of slides (see Figure 7-72).
   - Click the **Next Slide** button after you finish your comments on each slide.
   - Recordings are saved on each slide where they are made.
   - Click the **Pause** button to temporarily stop recording and then click **Record** when you are ready to begin again.

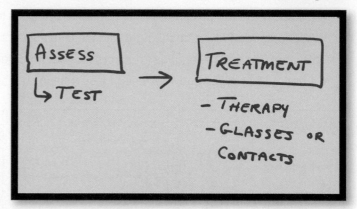

7-73 Drawing with a *Thick Pen*

5. Use *Inking* tools to draw on slides.

   - Select the color you want to use then select **Fine Pen, Medium Pen**, or **Thick Pen**.
   - Draw with a stylus, your finger, or a mouse (Figure 7-73).
   - Click the **Eraser** to remove all drawings on the slide.

6. Click the **Stop** button to end the recording.

7. Click **Preview Slide Recording** to view the presentation in *Slide Show* view with audio and video recordings.

8. Click **Edit Slide Recording** and choose *Trim Slide Recording, Delete Slide Recording,* or *Delete All Recordings*.

   - Remove any excess time from the beginning or end of the recording by trimming (Figure 7-74).

9. Click the **Recording** button to redo the recording on one slide.

10. Close *Recording* view when your presentation is complete.

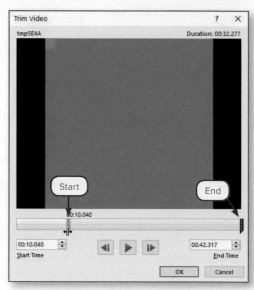

7-74 Trim audio

## Upload and Share a Mix

Click the **Upload to Office Mix** button to get your *Mix* online. A validation is performed to check for any conflicts, and then you must sign in to the *Office Mix* web site with your Microsoft Account. Your presentation will appear on a details page so you can control settings for privacy and sharing with a URL for accessing your presentation online.

### ▶ HOW TO: Upload and Share a Mix

1. Click the **Upload to Office Mix** button [*Mix* tab, *Mix* group] (Figure 7-75) to start the uploading process.

   - The *Upload to Office Mix* pane opens (Figure 7-76). Click **Next**.

2. Sign in using your Microsoft account information.

3. Select options (Figure 7-77):

   - Click to upload a new *Mix* or update an existing one.
   - Click to **Enable playback on mobile devices** so viewers can watch this mix offline. This option creates a video.

4. Click **Next**.

   - The uploading progress is tracked in the pane.

5. Click **Show me my mix** and the *Mix* details page opens in a browser window.

   - Your uploaded *Mix* is on the right with the URL address displayed.

6. Enter the *Title* and *Categories* (required) for your *Mix* (Figure 7-78).

   - Enter a *Description* and *Tags* used for searching.

7-75 *Mix* tab commands

7-76 *Upload to Office Mix* pane

7-77 Upload options

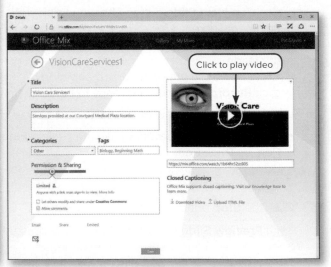

7-78 Uploaded *Mix* showing *Details* page

7. Choose the *Permission & Sharing* option.

   - By default, anyone with a link must sign in to view so your *Mix* is private.
   - Select the options for sharing or allowing comments if appropriate.

8. Click **Save**.

The option for *Closed Captioning* is helpful for situations where viewers might not be able to hear the presentation well. You must select **Enable playback on mobile devices** during the upload process, download your *Mix*, send it to a site that will create TTML (Timed Text Markup Language) files for video captions, and then you upload the TTML file. Refer to instructions in the *Office Mix Knowledge Base* for detailed procedures. When finished, preview your *Mix* to be sure close caption text is correctly synchronized to the video.

## Play a Mix

On the details page when you first upload a *Mix*, the *Mix* appears on the right. Click the **Play** button to view your *Mix*. When you access the *Office Mix* site later, click **My Mixes** to view all the *Mixes* you have uploaded and select the one you want to play.

▶ **HOW TO:** Play a Mix

1. Upload a *Mix* so you are on the *Office Mix* details page.
   - Your *Mix* appears on the right (Figure 7-79).
2. Click the **Play** button (in the middle of the slide or in the lower left) to view your *Mix* from the beginning.
3. Click the **Full Screen** button (lower right).
4. Play the *Mix* starting at different locations using one of the following methods:
   - Click a white marker on the timeline at the bottom of the player window. These markers indicate where a new slide starts.
   - Drag the playhead to start playback at any location.
   - Click the **Table of Contents** button below the *Mix* to display slide thumbnails (Figure 7-80).
   - Click a thumbnail to start playback on that slide.
   - Close the *Table of Contents* to return to your *Mix*.
5. Adjust volume as needed.
6. Click the **Full Screen** button to return to normal size.
7. Click **My Mixes** to view your uploaded files.
8. Select from the following linked information as needed. After you select an option and read the results, click the browser's **Back** button to select another option.

7-79 *Office Mix* playback

7-80 *Office Mix Table of Contents*

- **Details:** Title, description, category information, and sharing options.
- **Analytics:** Data about slides, visitors, and exercises. Click **More** to view data specific to each viewer.
- **Discussion:** Data will appear if you allowed discussion.
- **Presentation:** Click to download the presentation.

9. Click **Watched Mixes** to view any *Mix* that you previously viewed.

10. Click **Gallery** in the *Title* bar to view *Office Mixes* in many different categories.

11. Click your name and then **Sign Out** to return to the *Office Mix* main page. Close your browser window.

## Examine Analytics

*Office Mix* records data about how people are viewing your *Mix*. On the *My Mixes* page, click **Analytics** to view data about your uploaded *Mix*. You can analyze use patterns to gain insights and have a better understanding of how your material is meeting the goal for which it is intended. Then, based on your understanding, you can develop solutions to improve your results.

For example, data is recorded by slides to measure the number of views, duration, and average time spent on a slide. Visitor statistics are recorded with results on quizzes and polls. This information might be used to identify an area of the presentation that was engaging because users viewed it multiple times. Or, if a high drop-off rate was identified, you might need to condense information or remove detail to maintain participation.

In an educational or training course, you could check student progress, see who watched the presentation, and see how quiz questions were answered. Quiz results generate the number of correct answers plus the number of attempts to get a correct answer and the choices made that were not correct. Identifying a large number of wrong choices could guide content changes to clarify concepts so these misunderstandings do not occur. Data can be exported to Excel for further analysis and reporting.

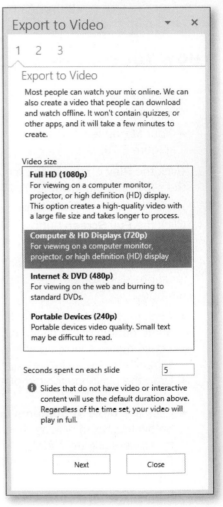

7-81 *Export to Video* pane

## Export a Mix

To create a video of your *Mix* for noninteractive viewing, click the **Export to Video** button [*Mix* tab, *Video* group] (see Figure 7-75). You can select full high definition or a lower quality to control file size (Figure 7-81). As when creating a video in PowerPoint, the number of seconds each slide is displayed can be specified if timings are not used in the presentation. Be sure to use timings when you need to vary the time each slide displays. The MP4 video format records all slides, transitions, and audio recordings. Interactive content is removed.

***Note to Instructor and Students***:

*If you do not have a Microsoft account, go to https://signup.live.com to create one. See the Microsoft Account Information section in SLO 7.1: Modifying Office Account Options and Using Add-ins.*

*Microsoft regularly updates Office Mix. Instructions and figures in this project (created with Google Chrome) may differ slightly from how this application displays in your Internet browser.*

For this project, you add the new *Mix* tab to PowerPoint. You record an interactive presentation for Life's Animal Shelter to create a *Mix* with a screen recording of pets available for adoption. You upload your *Mix* to Microsoft's *Office Mix* site and share it.

Files Needed: ***DogTraining-07.pptx*** and ***AdoptablePets-07.pptx*** *(student data files are available in the Library of your SIMnet account)*
Completed Project File Names: ***[your initials] PP P7-3.pptx*** *(before uploading)* and ***Dog Training*** *(shared at https:/mix.office.com)*

1. Close PowerPoint if it is open.

2. Install *Office Mix*.
   a. Go to https://mix.office.com and click the **Get Office Mix** button.
   b. Sign in with your Microsoft account.
   c. Click **OfficeMix.Setup.exe** that appears in the *Status* bar.
      • You may be asked to save OfficeMix.Setup.exe depending on the browser you are using.
   d. Check **I agree to the license terms and conditions** and click **Install**.
   e. Click **Yes** to authorize changes to your computer.
   f. Open PowerPoint and confirm that the new *Mix* tab is available.

3. Create a *Screen Recording*. Include audio if your computer has a microphone.
   a. Open ***AdoptablePets-07*** from your student data files.
   b. Open ***DogTraining-07*** from your student data files and save it as [your initials] PP P7-3.
   c. Select slide 6 and click the **Screen Recording** button [*Mix* tab, *Insert* group].
      • The *Adopt-ablePets-07* presentation will display and your screen will be grayed out.

4. Drag to select all of slide 1 in the *AdoptablePets-07* presentation to define the area to be recorded (Figure 7-82).

7-82 *Screen Recording* selection area

5. Click the **Record** button in the *Recording* toolbar at the top of your screen.
   a. Read these comments to record audio on the first slide.
      We have many pets available at Life's Animal Shelter now.
      Here are just a few. Come in and take look.
      Forever homes and foster homes are needed.
   b. Press **Page Down** or the down arrow to go to the next slide.
      • You can also click the **Next Slide** button.
   c. Record the dog's name and breed for each picture as you go through slides 2–5.

6. Point to the top of your screen so the *Slide Recording* toolbar is visible and click the **Stop** button to end your recording.
   a. You can also press **Windows + Shift + Q** to end your recording.
   b. The recording appears as a video in your presentation.

7. Apply the **Moderate Frame, Black** video style (*Moderate* category).
   a. Align the top of the video with the orange shape on the right.
   b. Click the **Align** button and select **Align Center**.

8. Close the **AdoptablePets-07** presentation without saving.

9. Add a quiz question.
   a. Select slide 8. Click the **Quizzes Videos Apps** button [*Mix* tab, *Insert* group] to open the *Lab Office Add-ins* dialog box.
   b. Select the **Multiple Choice Quiz** and then click **OK**.
      • If this quiz is not in the *My Add-ins* list, click the **Store** link.
      • Select the **Multiple Choice Quiz** and then click **Add**.
   c. Type a question and four responses as follows:
      How long should your dog be confined at the beginning of training?
      2 days
      1 week
      2 weeks
      3 weeks
   d. Select **Allow Single Choice Only** and **Allow Retry**.
   e. Select **2 weeks** as the correct answer (Figure 7-83).

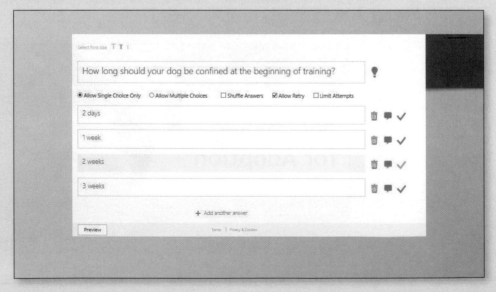

7-83 *Multiple Choice Quiz* object

10. Save your *[your initials] PP P7-3* presentation with these changes.

11. Create a *Mix*.
    a. Delete slide 6 because the video will not record when making a *Mix*.
    b. Select slide 1 and click the **Slide Recording** button.
       • *Recording* view opens with the first slide displayed (Figure 7-84).
    c. Click **Record**. Use notes and your own comments to record the audio for each slide.
       • No recording can be made on the slide with the quiz question.

12. Upload a *Mix*.
    a. Click the **Upload to Office Mix** button [*Mix* tab, *Mix* group].
    b. Click **Next** and sign in to your Microsoft Account if you are not already signed in.
    c. Click **Show me my mix** in the *Upload to Office Mix* pane when uploading is complete.

13. Edit *Mix* details.
    a. Leave the title as shown.
    b. Type the *Description* LAS Dog Training.
    c. Change *Categories* to **Other**.
    d. Type the *Tags* dog training and pet adoption.
    e. Click **Save**.

14. Sign out of the mix.office.com site.

15. Close your presentation and close PowerPoint.

7-84 *Slide Recording* pane as the presentation begins

## Using Sway for Interactive Online Presentations

*Sway* is an online presentation application available through your Microsoft account that you access in *OneDrive* or at https://sway.com. *Sway* can be used to create a presentation that supports a speaker, but its main focus is to create a stand-alone product that tells a complete story (whatever the topic might be) using a multimedia approach. You provide the content and *Sway's* design engine controls many aspects of design for web and mobile devices and adapts to the device size.

The presentation you create in *Sway* is also referred to as a *Sway*. Now that you have worked with PowerPoint's advanced features, you will quickly learn how to apply this knowledge to build creative *Sway* presentations. Get ideas by reviewing sample *Sways*. Tutorials are available from within *Sway*, too.

A variety of content imported from other files and sources can make your presentation interactive. Instead of a slide show, *Sway* uses a ***storyline***. Instead of slides, *Sway* uses ***cards***. Cards can be combined into a ***group***. You can set up your *Sway* to display almost like a slide show where you change cards horizontally to show your content. Or you can arrange all your content vertically so you scroll down like a long web page. Share a *Sway* in the same way you share a PowerPoint presentation by providing a link, share it on a social media site, or make it public. Once you have created a *Sway*, go to https://sway.com/my where you will see available *Sways* after you sign in to your Microsoft account.

## ▶HOW TO: View a Sample Sway

1. Go to https://sway.com and sign in using your Microsoft account.
   - If you are already signed in to your Microsoft Account on *OneDrive*, click the **List of Microsoft Services** button and select **Sway** to open the application (Figure 7-85).
   - The *My Sway* home page shows several thumbnails of sample *Sways*.
2. Click one of the *Sway* thumbnails to open a featured *Sway*.
   - The *Cards* pane is on the left, the *Storyline* pane is in the center, and the *Preview* pane is on the right (Figure 7-86).
   - The panes are dynamic because they resize based on what you are doing.
   - Buttons at the top of each pane are used to minimize or maximize the pane.
3. Scroll the *Storyline* pane to see the cards represented by a white rectangle.
   - Cards may be grouped to organize content with a gray rectangle behind each group of cards.
   - Some grouping appears automatically.
   - Cards contain text, pictures, and other media.
   - Click the arrow at the top left of a group of cards to expand or collapse the group.
   - Click buttons (*Close Storyline*, *Open Storyline*, *Maximize Storyline*, and *Restore Preview*) at the top of the *Storyline* pane to feature different panes.
4. Click the *Preview* pane to playback the *Sway*.
   - The *Storyline* pane collapses and moves to the left.

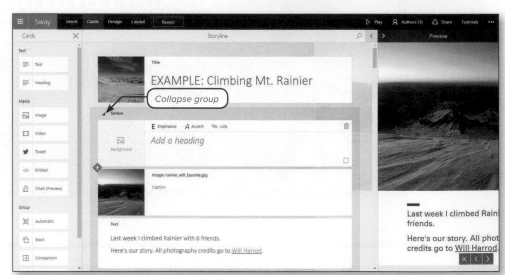

7-85 *List of Microsoft Services* **button and applications**

7-86 The *Sway* application with dynamic panes

5. Play the *Sway* to see the content, how it is arranged, and how you navigate.
   - Click **Play** on the *Menu* bar (Figure 7-87) to go into viewing mode.
   - Scroll right or down to view the *Sway*.
   - *Sway* layout determines if the content appears horizontally or vertically.
   - Navigation buttons are used for horizontal layouts.

7-87 Preview a sample *Sway* to see how content displays

6. Return to edit mode.
   - Point to the upper right and buttons appear.
   - Click **Edit** (pencil icon) (Figure 7-88) to return to edit mode.
   - If the *Storyline* pane is not displayed, click **Open Storyline** [*Menu* bar] to the left of the *Preview* pane.
   - If the *Cards* pane is not displayed, click **Cards** [*Menu bar*] to open the pane.
7. Click **More Options** [*Menu* bar] and click **My *Sways*** to return to the *My Sway* home page or to sign out.

7-88 Click *Edit* to return to edit mode

The *Sway Menu* bar (Figure 7-89) across the top of the window provides options described in the following list.

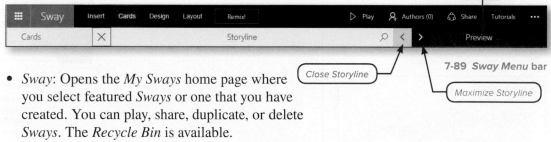

7-89 *Sway Menu* bar

- *Sway*: Opens the *My Sways* home page where you select featured *Sways* or one that you have created. You can play, share, duplicate, or delete *Sways*. The *Recycle Bin* is available.
- *Insert*: Opens a pane to browse *Sway* content or select from many different sources.
- *Cards*: Opens a pane that displays the *Cards* used to build content.
- *Design*: Opens a gallery of built-in colors, textures, and typography that controls font settings.
- *Layout*: Opens a gallery of navigation options to scroll vertically (default), scroll horizontally, or to optimize *Sway* for a presentation.
- *Remix!*: Applies a new built-in design. Once you have used *Remix!*, buttons appear so you can *Undo* or *Redo* an action.
- *Play*: Previews your content so you view it the way others will see your *Sway*.
- *Authors*: Provides a link so you can invite others to edit your *Sway* and lists current authors.
- *Share*: Provides options to share your *Sway* publicly, share with friends using social media sites, or embed your *Sway* on a web site.

- *Tutorials*: Opens a YouTube site in a browser window with video tutorials that demonstrate how to use *Sway* features.
- *More Options*: Opens a drop-down list of options to return to *My Sways*, create or duplicate a *Sway*, provide feedback, or sign out.

## Create a Sway from a PowerPoint Presentation

You can create a *Sway* by importing a presentation. It's file size must be less than 20MB. The presentation may appear in a vertical layout, but you can change that after you review the content if you prefer a horizontal layout.

> **HOW TO:** Create a Sway from a PowerPoint Presentation

1. Go to https://sway.com and sign in using your Microsoft account.
2. Click **Import** [*Menu* bar] (Figure 7-90) on the *My Sway* home page.
   - An *Open* dialog box displays where you select a file to import.
   - Navigate to your files and select the PowerPoint presentation that you want to use. Click **Open**.
   - *Sway* opens with the content of the presentation divided into cards.
   - Cards may be grouped in the *Storyline*.
3. View your *Sway*.
   - Click anywhere in the **Preview** pane to view your *Sway* (Figure 7-91).
   - Click the **Open Storyline** button to return to your *Sway* cards that were created from PowerPoint slides. Scroll down the page or click buttons in the lower right to navigate.
   - Click **Play** [*Menu* bar] to view your *Sway* as it will appear to others.
   - Click **Edit** (pencil icon) to return to the *Storyline*.

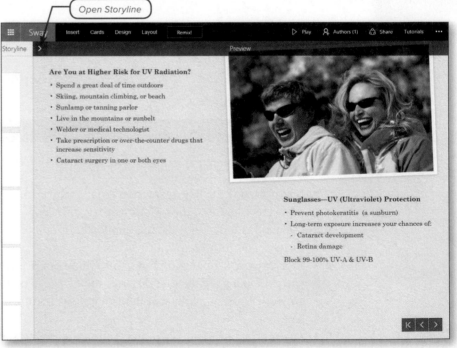

7-91 The *Sway* application with dynamic panes

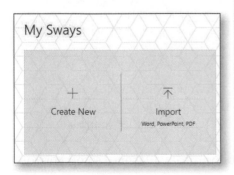

7-90 *Create New* or *Import*

Not all content converts well into the *Sway* format. Examine your content and modify it as necessary for this online application. As you are working, *Sway* automatically saves your content.

## Customize Sway Design Colors and Other Effects

The *Design* gallery provides built-in designs that control colors, background textures, and typography for font settings. The gallery displays thumbnails arranged in rows with arrows to click so more options can be displayed at one time. Think about your presentation content when you make choices that will compliment your presentation in style and tone. Clarity is always important.

The various designs also have different types of navigation, animation effects, and picture layouts applied. Click **Remix!** to quickly try different options by cycling through several random choices. Click **Undo** to revert to a previous choice. Then you can further customize settings.

With each picture that you use, *Sway* decides how to position it, what part of the picture is most important, and determines its focus points. Adjust these settings if the picture's positioning does not seem appropriate.

---

### ▶ HOW TO: Remix and Customize a Sway Design

1. Display your *Sway* in edit mode.

   - If necessary, go to https://sway.com and sign in using your Microsoft account.
   - Click your *Sway* to open it.

2. Remix your *Sway*.

   - Click **Remix** [*Menu* bar] (see Figure 7-89) and *Sway* applies a different design.
   - Click **Undo** [*Menu* bar] to restore the original design.
   - Click **Remix** again to try a different design.
   - Repeat to cycle through different combinations of design and navigation.

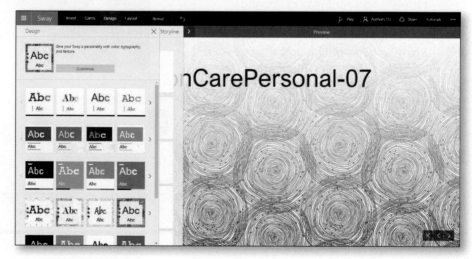

7-92 *Sway Design* gallery

   - Horizontal layouts have directional arrows at the lower right to change from card to card.

3. Use the *Design* gallery (Figure 7-92) to select a different design.

   - Click **Design** [*Menu* bar] to open a gallery of built-in designs.
   - Click the right arrow on each row of thumbnails to see different color and font combinations for that particular layout.
   - Select a design to apply it.

4. Customize the current design by clicking the **Customize** button at the top of the *Design* pane and selecting from the following options.

   - ***Color inspiration:*** Select one of the picture thumbnails to create a color palette from that image. Click the right arrow to see more.

- **Color palettes:** Choose from 12 or more color combinations.
- **Font choices:** Click the drop-down list and scroll down to select from many different font pairs.
- **Animation emphasis:** Drag a slider to change from *Subtle*, *Moderate*, or *Intense*.
- **Text size:** Drag a slider from *Small*, *Normal*, and *Large*.

5. Customize how your *Sway* displays.

- Click **Layout** [*Menu* bar] to open the *Layout* pane on the left.
- Select from one of three options: **Scrolls vertically**, **Scrolls horizontally**, or **Optimized for presentation**.

6. Adjust a picture's *Focus Points*.

- Click a picture that is not displaying effectively for your purpose and options appear (Figure 7-93).
- Click **Focus Points** to open the *Focus Points* pane.
- Select **The entire image is important** if you want all of the picture to show.
- Click (or tap) on an area of the picture to mark what is important on the picture and a circle appears (Figure 7-94).
- Click again to add another *Focus Point*. Multiple points can be used.
- *Sway* instantly repositions the picture based on your selections.
- Click a circle to remove it.

7-93 Picture options

7. View your *Sway* with your new design.

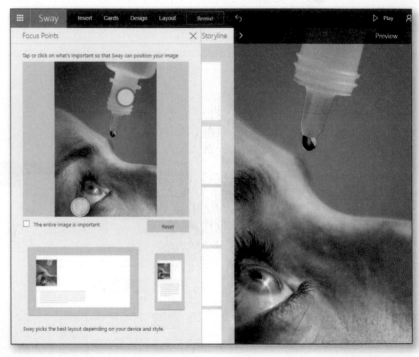

- Click **Preview** in the upper right to view your *Sway*.
- Click the **Open Storyline** button to return to your *Sway* cards and groups.
- Click **Play** [*Menu* bar] to view your *Sway* with navigation and animation.
- Click your browser's **Back** button to return to *Sway*. Your *Sway* automatically saves.
- Notice that the first picture in your *Sway* appears in the thumbnail with the presentation title and date.

8. Click **More Options** and select **Sign Out**.

9. Close your browser to close *Sway*.

7-94 Change *Focus Points*

> **MORE INFO**
>
> If you are developing your *Sway* using a public computer, be sure you sign out of your account when you are finished.

## Add Content with Cards

*Sway* content is controlled with *Cards* that you add to your *Storyline* and organized by sequencing and grouping. Every *Sway* starts with a *Title Card*, and you select from the following card types to build your content:

- **Text:** *Text* or *Heading*
- **Media:** *Image, Video, Tweet, Embed,* or *Chart (Preview)*
- **Group:** *Automatic, Stack, Comparison, Slideshow,* or *Grid*

Select a card and then click a card type in the *Cards* pane to add a new card to the storyline after your selected card. A green diamond (*Insert Content* icon) shows where content will be inserted (Figure 7-95). You can also drag a card to the storyline to control where it is positioned. You can rearrange cards by dragging, too.

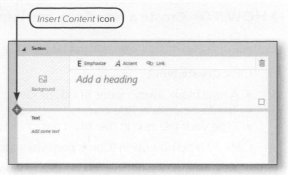

7-95 *Heading* card and *Insert Content* icon

Many options are available for cards such as interactive photo stacks, comparisons, slide shows, maps, tweets, videos, charts, and more.

When you click **Insert**, *Sway* provides a listing of suggested sources arranged in a gallery (Figure 7-96). Click one of these items and images as well as web articles appear (Figure 7-97). Drag one or more items into your storyline or click terms at the top of the pane to consider related content.

When using suggested sources, remember that you are responsible for appropriate use and permission or licenses that may be required. Click the **Upload** link to locate your files and upload your own content.

The next *How To* will show you several different ways to insert cards and add content.

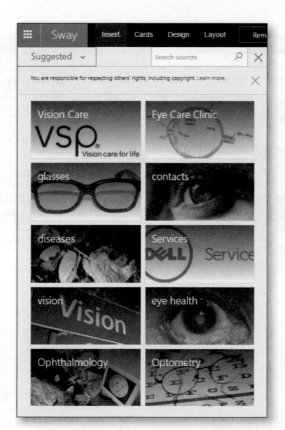

7-96 Suggested content

7-97 Many available content sources

## ▶HOW TO:  Create a New Sway and Insert Content on Cards

1. Go to https://sway.com and sign in to *Sway* using your Microsoft account.
2. Click **Create New**.
   - A new blank *Sway* opens in edit mode.
   - The first card is a *Title* card.
   - Type your title text in the *Title* card.
3. Click a *Heading* button [*Cards* pane] to insert a *Heading* card.
   - A heading identifies a group of cards similar to a slide title.
   - Options appear at the top of all cards.
4. Click a *Text* button [*Cards* pane] to insert a *Text* card.
   - Type paragraph or listed text in the card.
5. Select card options at the top of each card. Available options vary depending on the type of card (see Figures 7-95 and 7-98) and how they are applied vary based on the selected design.
   - ***Heading:*** Will convert the first text item to a heading card.
   - ***Emphasize:*** Applies bold, underline, color, or highlight to emphasize selected text.
   - ***Accent:*** Applies italics, soft glow, shadow, or saturation to add a subtle emphasis.
   - ***Bullets:*** Adds bullets to a list.
   - ***Numbers:*** Adds numbers to a list.
   - ***Link:*** Enables you to insert a Web link.
   - ***Subtle:*** Moderate or Intense options apply to all card content.
   - ***Delete:*** Removes the card.
   - ***Focus Points:*** Available on image cards to change how an image displays.
6. Press the up or down arrows to change the *Insert Content* position on the storyline.
7. Select a source and let *Sway* select the appropriate card.
   - Click **Insert** [*Menu* bar] and select a *Suggested* source (Figure 7-98).
   - *Sway* displays suggested content, but you can also search for content or select from *OneDrive* or social media sites.
   - Alternatively, click **Suggested** and then select **Upload** to locate your file in the *Open* dialog box and click Open.
   - The type of card inserted depends on the type of file you selected.
8. Click the space between cards and buttons appear so you can select the type of card for that position.
   - Click one of the buttons to insert a heading, text, or image card, upload content on a new card, or open the *Cards* pane (Figure 7-99).

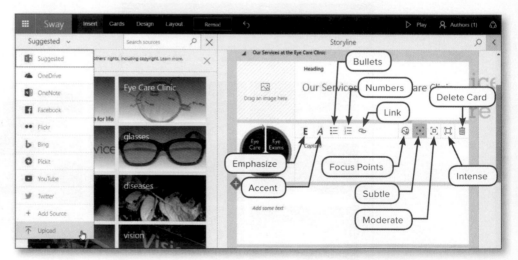

**7-98** Select *Upload* option

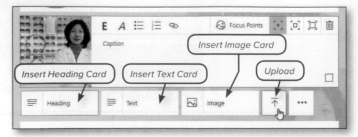

**7-99** *Upload* button for a new card

9. Insert a picture group.

   - Drag an **Automatic** group card to your storyline.
   - Click the **Group Type** button to open the *Group Type* pane and select the **Stack** group (Figure 7-100).
   - Click the card to add an image.
   - Click **Suggested**, select **Upload**, and select pictures from your files.
   - Click **Preview** and move to where your stack is displayed (Figure 7-101).
   - Click the stack several times to flip through the pictures.
   - Click **Open Storyline**.

10. Create a chart.

    - Drag a *Chart* card to your storyline.
    - A column chart appears with a *Subtle* effect (smallest size). Click the **Subtle** button to change to *Moderate* (larger) or *Intense* (full-screen).
    - Click to preview the chart (Figure 7-102).

11. Click the chart preview to edit. Three buttons appear in the upper right corner with various options (Figure 7-103):

    - ***Chart Type:*** Choose from column, bar, line, pie, and area charts with variations for each one.
    - ***Data:*** Enter data and toggle between *Row Header* and *Column Header*.
    - ***Settings:*** Add a chart and axis titles, show values, and show grid.

12. Edit content in preview mode.

    - Click text you need to revise, emphasize, or delete.

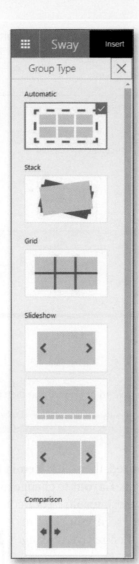

7-100 *Group Type* pane

7-101 Picture *Stack* group

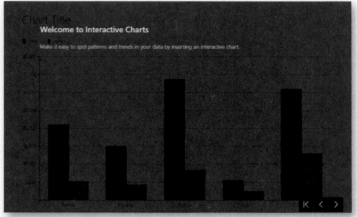

7-102 Chart as it first appears, *Moderate* size

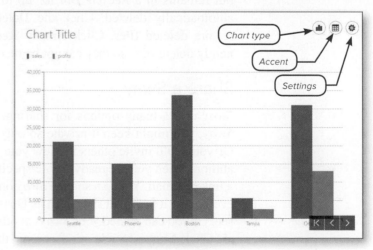

7-103 Edit chart

- The contents of one card is selected, the remaining screen is grayed out, and buttons appear (Figure 7-104).
- Click **Edit** and a card opens so you can change wording or correct errors (Figure 7-105). For pictures, you can adjust the *Focus Points*.

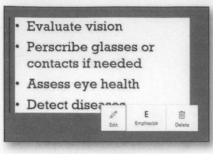

7-104 Text selected in *Preview* mode

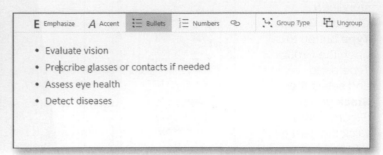

7-105 Edit text on card

- Alternatively, text can be edited on each card in the storyline.

---

Once your cards are prepared and organized, then click **Remix** to try different designs. Click **Design** to further customize the design. Click **Layout** to change navigation. Click **Preview** and **Play** frequently while you are working to check results. Your content is automatically saved.

*Sway* does not have a backup function, so if you want to maintain a second version of your *Sway*, then resave it using a different name.

On your *My Sways* page under the *Edited* link, your *Sways* are shown as thumbnails. Click the **More Options** button on a *Sway* thumbnail and select from **Play**, **Share**, **Duplicate** or **Delete**. When you click **Delete**, you will be asked for confirmation. The *Sway* is deleted from your *My Sways* group but remains in a *Recycle Bin* for up to 30 days and then is automatically deleted. Click the **Deleted** link to view or restore deleted files. Click **Empty Recycle Bin** to permanently delete files so they cannot be recovered.

7-106 *Share* options

## Share a Sway

*Sway* offers many options for sharing. While developing a *Sway*, you might keep it private so only you see the content. Or you could invite others to view your *Sway* to edit as a co-author. When you are ready, invite specific people by sending a link by email. You can share a *Sway* on social media sites or even make it public at sites such as Docs.com for everyone to see. Or you can embed your *Sways* at other web sites or blogs.

Click **Share** in edit mode or on the *My Sway* page to access your options (Figure 7-106).

***Note to Instructor and Students***:

> *If you do not have a Microsoft account, go to* https://signup.live.com *to create one. See the Microsoft Account Information section in* SLO 7.1: Modifying Office Account Options and Using Add-ins.

> *Microsoft regularly updates Sway. Instructions and figures in this project (created with Google Chrome) may differ slightly from how this application displays in your Internet browser.*

For this project, you will start with the same file you used in *Pause & Practice 7-3* about dog training to create an online presentation using *Sway*. You will import it to create cards and modify content by grouping cards, applying options, adding a video, and changing the design. Then you will share your *Sway*.

Files Needed: ***DogTraining-07.pptx***, ***PillowPup-07.mov***, and ***DogWalk-07*** *(student data files are available in the* Library *of your SIMnet account)*
Completed Project File Name: ***Dog Training*** *(shared on* https://sway.com*)*

1. Go to https://sway.com and sign in using your Microsoft account to open the *My Sway* page.

2. Import a presentation.
   a. Click **Import** [*Menu* bar] and the *Open* dialog box appears.
   b. Locate your student data files.
   c. Select ***DogTraining-07*** and click **Open**.

3. Scroll down to see the cards that were prepared. Notice that no cards are grouped.

4. Click **Preview** (upper right corner) and click the **Move Forward** button (lower right corner) to move horizontally through the content.

5. Click **Layout** [*Menu* bar] and select **Optimized for presentation** (Figure 7-107).

6. Click **Design** [*Menu* bar] to open the *Design* pane.
   a. Click the right arrow on the third row until you locate and select **Style 3, Variation 36**.

7. Customize the design colors and fonts.
   a. Click the **Customize** button.
   b. Click the right arrow under *Color inspiration* (Figure 7-108) and then select the picture of a woman

7-107 Selected layout is *Optimized for presentation*

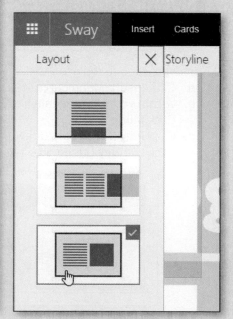

7-108 *Customize* settings after the presentation is imported

holding up a stick while training a dog (first picture in the second group), **Color Option: 4**. (*Note: Color Option numbering may vary.*)
- A check appears on the picture to indicate selection.
c. Click the solid blue palette, **Color Palette: 3**, under *Color palettes*. (*Note: Color Palette numbering may vary.*)
d. Click the down arrow under *Font Choices* and scroll down to select the **Quire Sans** and **Univers Condensed** font pair.
e. Click **Intense** for *Animation emphasis*.
f. Click **Large** for *Text size* (Figure 7-109).
g. Click **Cards** [*Menu* bar] and the *Design* gallery automatically closes when the *Cards* pane and *Storyline* appear.

8. Click **Play** [*Menu* bar] to view these changes.
a. Click the navigation right arrow to move through your content.
b. Point to the upper right of your *Sway* window so buttons appear.
c. Click **Edit** to return to your storyline.

9. Adjust a picture.
a. Select the *Image* card with a picture of a man walking a dog.
b. Click **Focus Points** to open the *Focus Points* pane.
c. Select **The entire image is important**.
d. Click **Cards** and the *Focus Points* pane automatically closes.

7-109 *Customize* settings after changes

10. Select the *Text* card with "Does This Look Familiar?" and click **Moderate** in the upper right corner of the *Text* card.

11. Select the *Image* card with a picture of a puppy destroying a pillow. Click **Delete Image Card** in the upper right corner of the *Image* card (Figure 7-110).

12. Insert a video to replace the deleted picture.
a. Click **Insert** [*Menu* bar], click **Suggested**, and then click **Upload**.
b. Locate your student data files, select *PillowPup-07*, and click **Open**.
c. Click **Moderate**.
d. Click **Play** [*Menu* bar] to review your *Sway*.
e. Click the **Play** button on the video to play it.

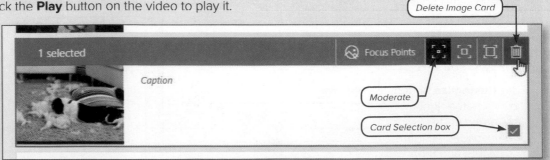

7-110 Selected card to delete

f. Point to the upper right of your *Sway* window so buttons appear.

g. Click **Edit** to return the *Storyline*.

13. Adjust a picture.

   a. Select the *Image* card with the picture of arrows.

   b. Click **Moderate**.

   c. Click **Focus Points** to open the *Focus Points* pane.

   d. Select **The entire image is important**.

   e. Click **Cards** [*Menu* bar] and the *Focus Points* pane automatically closes.

14. Select the *Text* card with "Training" and click **Delete**.

15. Group an *Image* and a *Text* card and then edit text.

   a. Click **Automatic** in the *Cards* pane.

   b. Click the **Card Selection** box (lower right corner) to select both the *Image* card of the woman training the dog and the *Text* card with bulleted text.

   c. Drag both selected cards into the *Group: Automatic* card.

   d. Type the word Training on the first bulleted line and press **Enter**.

   e. Select the word "Training" and click **Bullets** to remove the bullet and click **Emphasize** (Figure 7-111).

   f. Select the *Image* card and click **Focus Points**.

   g. Select **The entire image is important**.

   h. Click **Cards** [*Menu* bar].

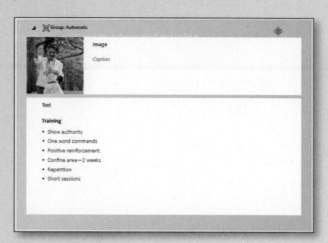

7-111 Two cards arranged in an *Automatic* group

16. Group a *Text* card and an *Image* card.

   a. Click **Automatic** in the *Cards* pane.

   b. Click the **Card Selection** box (lower right corner) to select both the *Text* card with "When you master the basics" and the *Image* card with the picture of two dogs.

   c. Drag both selected cards into the *Group: Automatic* card.

   d. Select the *Image* card and click **Focus Points**.

   e. Select **The entire image is important**.

   f. Click **Cards**.

17. Select the last *Image* card and click **Delete Image Card**.

18. Insert a picture on the *Title* card.

   a. Scroll up and select the *Title* card.

   b. Click **Insert** [*Menu* bar], click **Suggested**, and then click **Upload**.

   c. Locate your student data files, select ***DogWalk-07***, and click **Open**.

   d. Click **Play** [*Menu* bar] to see how this image is automatically animated to scroll down.

   e. Click **Edit** to return to edit mode.

19. Click **Play** [*Menu* bar] and review your entire *Sway* (Figure 7-112).

7-112 Completed storyline with two groups collapsed

20. Share your *Sway*.
    a. Click **Share** [*Menu* bar].
    b. Click **More options** [*Share* drop-down list] and remove the checks for all other options such as duplicating, changing, or showing a footer.
    c. Copy the URL address shown in the text box below *Share with friends*.
    d. Sign in to your email program and compose a message to your instructor.
    e. Paste the URL address in the message and send.
    f. Close your email program.
    g. Sign out of *Sway* and close your browser window.

# Chapter Summary

**7.1** Modify Office account settings and use add-ins (p. P7-453).

- The *Account* area on the *Backstage* view provides information and account customization options.
- Your Office account information and settings are available whenever you sign in to PowerPoint (or any Office application) using your Microsoft account.
- Change the **Office Background** in the *Account* area on the *Backstage* view.
- Add **Connected Services** to your account to access online services for **Images & Videos**, **Storage**, and **Sharing**.
- **Add-ins** are programs that provide additional features to your Office software. Office add-ins are available in the *Store*, and add-ins previously installed display in the *My Add-ins* area.

**7.2** Use *OneDrive* to create, upload, move, copy, delete, and download files and folders (p. P7-457).

- **OneDrive** is a cloud storage area provided by Microsoft.
- Sign in to *OneDrive* using your Microsoft account from any computer that has Internet access.
- If you use Windows 10, *OneDrive* is listed as a storage location when you save files. You access those files in a *File Explorer* window or on your *OneDrive* using an Internet browser.
- *OneDrive* enables you to upload files, create folders, and move, copy, delete, and download files.
- When you upload a file to *OneDrive*, the original file on your computer is unchanged and a copy is saved on *OneDrive*.
- When you download a saved file from *OneDrive*, the file is copied to your computer.

**7.3** Share *OneDrive* files and folders (p. P7-462).

- Files on *OneDrive* can be shared with others, and you control whether files can be viewed only or if others can edit files.
- Use the *Share* command to send an email message with a link to a shared file.
- Create a **sharing link** and copy it into an email message, a document, or in an online location so recipients can click the link to view or edit your file.

- For a shared file, sharing permission can be changed or removed.
- Files can be shared when using PowerPoint as long as the file is saved on *OneDrive*.

**7.4** Open, create, and edit a presentation in *PowerPoint Online* and add comments (p. P7-468).

- **Office Online** is available at no cost with your Microsoft account.
- Use of *Office Online* does not require that *Office 2016/365* is installed on your computer.
- *Office Online* applications are accessible through *OneDrive* or online at https://onedrive.live.com.
- **PowerPoint Online** is one of the *Office Online* applications, and it is used to create, edit, and share presentations.
- *PowerPoint Online* can display presentations in *Slide Show* view.
- Sharing a presentation enables others to view your file or make changes if you have given them permission. More than one person can edit the file at the same time in *PowerPoint Online*.
- You can add comments, reply to comments, or delete comments in presentations while using *PowerPoint Online*.

**7.5** Use *Office Mix* to create an interactive online presentation with multimedia and to create presentation videos (p. P7-478).

- *Office* Mix is a PowerPoint add-in.
- *Office Mix* extends the capabilities of PowerPoint.
- A *Screen Recording* creates a video of anything on your computer screen such as a software demonstration. The video can be saved for use in a different program.
- *Office Mix* can include interactive elements such as quizzes.
- A *Slide Recording* captures your entire presentation and can include handwriting, audio, and video.
- Upload a *Mix* to Microsoft's site https://mix.office.com for online viewing and to share with others.
- *Analytics* enable the study of viewer's use patterns and quiz results.
- Export a *Mix* to create a video of your presentation.

**7.6** Use *Sway* to create an interactive online presentation with multimedia (p. P7-489).

- **Sway** is an online presentation application available with your Microsoft account.
- *Sway* is accessible through *OneDrive* or at Microsoft's site https://sway.com.
- The presentation you create in *Sway* is also referred to as a *Sway*.
- *Sway* uses a **storyline** with content arranged in **cards** that can be combined in different **groups**.
- *Sway* can arrange content in vertical or horizontal layouts.
- *Remix!* is an option that provides a quick way to try out different designs with varying layouts, textures, and fonts.
- A PowerPoint presentation can be imported into *Sway* and then modified for online viewing in this different application.

- *Sway* arranges pictures differently based on a particular design and layout. How they display can be modified using *Focus Points*.
- *Sway* provides extensive suggested content and makes it easy to locate and upload related sources.
- Share a *Sway* by inviting others to view it or edit your content. You can also share your *Sway* on social media or sharing sites.

## Check for Understanding

The SIMbook for this text (within your SIMnet account) provides the following resources for concept review:

- Multiple choice questions
- Matching exercises
- Short answer questions

**Note to Instructor and Students**: *For projects in this chapter, you use your Microsoft Account, OneDrive, PowerPoint Online, Office Mix, and Sway. If you don't have a Microsoft account, create a free account at* https://signup.live.com. *See the Microsoft Account Information section in* SLO 7.1: Modifying Office Account Options and Using Add-ins.

*Microsoft regularly updates these applications. Instructions and figures in these projects (created with Google Chrome) may differ slightly from how these applications display in your Internet browser.*

## Guided Project 7-1

For this project, you revise a presentation about home staging for Placer Hills Real Estate. You create a *OneDrive* folder, upload files, edit a presentation using *PowerPoint Online* and share the presentation.
[**Student Learning Outcomes 7.2, 7.3, 7.4**]

File Needed: ***HomeStaging-07.pptx*** *(student data files are available in the* Library *of your SIMnet account)*
Completed Project File Name: *[**your initials**] **PowerPoint 7-1.pptx** (on OneDrive)*

### Skills Covered in This Project

- Sign in to *OneDrive*.
- Create a *OneDrive* folder.
- Upload a file to your *OneDrive* folder.
- Edit a presentation in *PowerPoint Online*.
- Share your presentation.

1. Open the presentation ***HomeStaging-07***. Save it as [your initials] PowerPoint 7-1 on your computer in the location where you store your solution files and then close the presentation.

2. Sign in to *OneDrive* using your Microsoft account.
   a. Open an Internet browser window and go to https://onedrive.live.com.
   b. Click the **Sign in** button.
   c. Type your Microsoft account email address and click **Next**.
   d. Type your Microsoft account password and click **Sign in** to go to your *OneDrive* page.

3. Create a new folder and upload files to your *OneDrive*.
   a. Click **Files** on the left, if necessary, to display your *OneDrive* folders and files.
   b. Click the **New** button and select **Folder** from the drop-down list (Figure 7-113).
   c. Type Placer Hills Real Estate as the name for the new folder and click **Create**.

4. Upload files to your *OneDrive* folder.
   a. Click **Files** view, if necessary, so your screen displays file names rather than thumbnail images.

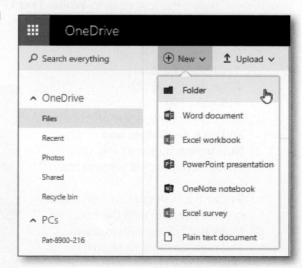

7-113 Create a new folder in *OneDrive*

b. Click the **Placer Hills Real Estate** folder (not the check box) to open it.

c. Click the **Upload** button, click **Files**, and select the *[your initials] PowerPoint 7-1* file from your solution files. Click **Open**.
   - The file is added to the *Placer Hills Real Estate* folder.

5. Open a file for editing in *PowerPoint Online*.

   a. Click the *[your initials] PowerPoint 7-1* file to open it in *PowerPoint Online* in read-only mode.

   b. Click the **Edit Presentation** button at the top and select **Edit in Browser** from the drop-down list.

7-114 Subtitle text duplicated with resizing and font size changes

6. Change text on the title slide.

   a. Display slide 1. Select the subtitle and change the font size to **36 pt**. [*Home* tab, *Font* group].
      - Move the subtitle placeholder up and to the left as shown in Figure 7-114.
      - Press **Ctrl+D** to duplicate.

   b. Edit the duplicated text box on slide 1.
      - Replace text with the company name, Placer Hills Real Estate.
      - Change the font size to **20 pt**.
      - Resize the text box. While you resize, the text appears condensed but it restores to its correct size when you release the sizing handle.
      - Position it in the lower right corner.

7. Add a slide.

   a. Display slide 7. Click the **New Slide** button [*Home* tab, *Slides* group] and select the *Title and Content* layout.

   b. Click **Add Slide**.

8. Edit the new slide.

   a. Display slide 8. Type the title For Assistance, Call.
      - Change the font color to **White, Text 1** [*Home* tab, *Font* group].
      - Select the bulleted text placeholder and type:
      Emma Cavelli, Listing Agent
      Placer Hills Real Estate
      7100 Madrone Road
      Roseville, CA 95722
      916-450-3300

   b. Select the bulleted text placeholder and click the **Bullets and Numbering** button [*Home* tab, *Paragraph* group] to remove the bullets.

   c. Resize the bulleted text placeholder on the right side to fit the text.

   d. Move both placeholders down and position them as shown in Figure 7-115.

7-115 New slide added

9. Apply a transition.
    a. Click the **Fade** transition [*Transitions* tab, *Transition to This Slide* group].
        - Notice that transition options are limited.
    b. Click **Effect Options** and select **Smoothly**.
    c. Click **Apply to All**.

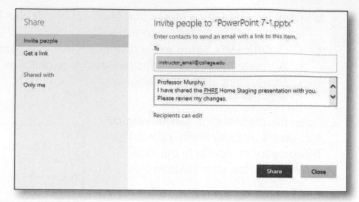

7-116 Share a presentation

10. View the presentation.
    a. Click the **Reading** view button to return to view mode.
    b. Click the **Slide Show** button to view the presentation in *Slide Show* view.

11. Share the presentation with your instructor.
    a. Click **Share with People** in the *Menu* bar to open the *Share* window (Figure 7-116).
    b. Select **Invite People** on the left.
    c. Type your instructor's email address in the *To* area.
    d. Type a brief message in the body area.
    e. Verify that **Recipients can edit** is displayed.
    f. Click **Share** to send the sharing email to your instructor.
    g. Click **Close** to close the *Share* window.

12. Click the **OneDrive** link at the top to return to your *OneDrive* folders. The file is automatically saved and closed.

13. Click your name in the upper right and select **Sign Out**.

## Guided Project 7-2

For this project, you work on a presentation for the Hamilton Civic Center about being more active. You download *Office Mix* and create a slide recording with an interactive question using an add-in. Include audio and video if a microphone and camera are available. Then upload your *Mix* and share it with your instructor. You also save the presentation as a video.
[Student Learning Outcomes 7.1, 7.5]

File Needed: ***GetMoving-07.pptx*** (*student data files are available in the* Library *of your SIMnet account*)
Completed File Names: *[your initials] **PowerPoint 7-2a.pptx**,* **Get Moving for a Healthy Lifestyle** on https://mix.office.com, *and **[your initials] PowerPoint 7-2b.mp4***

### Skills Covered in This Project

- Download *Office Mix*.
- Install an add-in.
- Create an interactive question.
- Create a slide recording.
- Upload to the *Office Mix* site.
- Share your *Mix* with your instructor.
- Export your *Mix* as a video.

1. Download *Office Mix* if it is not yet available on your computer.
    a. Open an Internet browser window and go to https://mix.office.com.

b. Click the **Get Office Mix** button and sign in with your Microsoft account.
   - The download starts automatically.
c. Click **OfficeMix.Setup.exe** that appears in the *Status* bar.
   - Agree to the license terms and authorize changes.
   - PowerPoint automatically loads with the *Mix* tab.

2. Open the presentation **GetMoving-07** and save it as **[your initials] PowerPoint 7-2a** on your computer in the location where you store your solution files.

3. Install a quiz add-in and type a question.
   a. Display slide 6. Select the **Mix** tab in PowerPoint.
   b. Click the **Quizzes Video Apps** button [*Insert* group] to open the *Lab Office Add-ins* dialog box (Figure 7-117).
   c. Select the **Free Response Quiz**.
   d. Click the **Add** button.
      - The question object appears on the slide.
   e. Type **What extra activities can you do tomorrow?** in the question box (Figure 7-118).
   f. Click the slide background to leave the question edit mode.

4. Prepare to record the presentation.
   a. Display slide 1. Click the **Notes Page** button [*View* tab, *Presentation* views].
   b. Read the notes for slide 1 and then click the **Next slide** button (or press **Page Down**).
   c. Repeat to review all slide notes.
   d. View all slides in *Slide Show* view so you see where animation occurs automatically and where you need to click.

5. Create a *Slide Recording*.
   a. Display slide 1. Click the **Slide Recording** button [*Mix* tab, *Record* group] and *Slide Recording* view opens displaying the title slide (Figure 7-119).

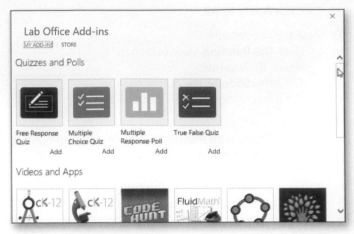

7-117 *Office Add-ins* dialog box

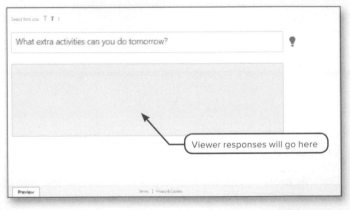

7-118 *Free Response Quiz* object

7-119 *Slide Recording* view

b. Use the *Slide Notes* to guide what you say as each slide displays.
c. Click the **Record** button to begin the recording.
   - The title slide transition and animation are recorded.
   - Record your comments and click the **Next Slide** button.
   - Click **Next Animation** to add the *SmartArt* shapes. Make your comments and click the **Next Slide** button.
   - Click the **Pause** button if necessary and then click **Record** when you are ready to begin again.
d. Advance through all slides making your comments from slide content and notes.
   - Be sure you have finished your comments related to each slide before advancing to the next slide.
e. Click the **Stop** button to end the recording.

6. Preview and make adjustments if necessary.
   a. Click **Preview Slide Recording** to view the presentation in *Slide Show* view.
   b. Make corrections if needed.
      - Click the **Recording** button to redo the recording on one slide.
      - Click **Edit Slide Recording** and choose **Trim Slide Recording** to remove unwanted audio from the beginning or end of the recording.
   c. Close *Slide Recording* view when your presentation is complete.

7. Save your presentation. Now you have a *Mix* with the interactive question and slide recording.

8. Upload a *Mix*.
   a. Click the **Upload to Office Mix** button [*Mix* tab, *Mix* group] to start the uploading process.
      - The *Upload to Office Mix* pane opens.
      - Click **Next** and sign in to your Microsoft account if necessary.
      - Select **I'm uploading a new mix**.
      - Click **Next** again and the uploading progress is tracked.
   b. Click **Show me my mix** and https://mix.office.com opens with the details page for your uploaded *Mix*.

9. Add *Mix* details.
   a. Type the *Title* Get Moving for a Healthy Lifestyle.
   b. Type the *Description* A presentation for the Hamilton Civic Center about being more active.
   c. Change *Categories* to **Other**, if necessary.
   d. Change *Tags* to health and fitness.
   e. Click **Save** (Figure 7-120).
   f. Copy the URL address below the video on the right.
   g. Click the **Email** link and compose a brief message to your instructor and paste the URL.

10. Play your *Mix* from the *Details* page.
    a. Click the **Play** button to view your *Mix* from the beginning.

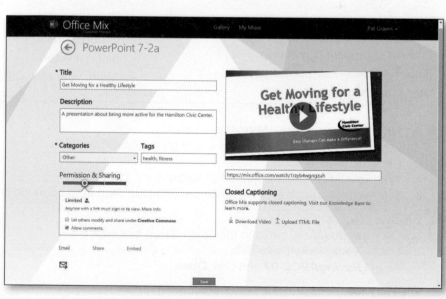

7-120 Uploaded *Mix* showing *Details* page

b. Click the **Full Screen** button.
  - When complete, click the **Full Screen** button again to return to normal size.
c. Click **My Mixes** to view your uploaded file.

11. Click your name in the upper right corner and select **Sign out**.

12. Export a video.
  a. Go to your *[your initials] PowerPoint 7-2a* presentation.
  b. Click the **Export to Video** button [*Mix* tab, *Video* group].
  c. Select **Internet & DVD (480p)** and click **Next**.
  d. Select the location where you save your files and change the file name to [your initials] PowerPoint 7-2b.
  e. Click **Save**.
    - As the video is created, you can watch the progress on the status bar.
    - When the video has been exported, click **Close**.
  f. Use *File Explorer* to locate the exported video file. Double-click the file name to preview your video.
  g. Close the open files.

# Guided Project 7-3

For this project, you redesign a promotional presentation for the American River Cycling Club. Using *Sway*, you insert a PowerPoint presentation and modify it for this online application. You will customize the design with a texture and different font, group cards, insert a video, and then share your *Sway*. [**Student Learning Outcome 7.6**]

Files Needed: ***RacingARCC-07.pptx*** and ***StartYoung-07.mov*** *(student data files are available in the Library of your SIMnet account)*
Completed Project File Name: ***American River Cycling Club*** *on* https://sway.com

## Skills Covered in This Project

- Sign in to https://sway.com.
- Import a PowerPoint presentation.
- Apply a design.
- Customize colors and fonts.
- Group cards.
- Insert a video.
- Share your *Mix* with your instructor.

1. Sign in to *Sway* using your Microsoft account.
  a. Open an Internet browser window and go to https://sway.com.
  b. Click the **Sign in** button.
  c. Type your Microsoft account email address and click **Next**.
  d. Type your Microsoft account password and click **Sign in** to open the *My Sways* page.

2. Import a presentation.
  a. Click **Import** [*Menu* bar] and the *Open* dialog box appears.
  b. Locate your student data files.
  c. Select ***RacingARCC-07*** and click **Open**.

3. Click **Layout** [*Menu* bar] and select **Optimized for presentation**.

4. Click **Design** [*Menu* bar] and select **Style 1, Variation 3** in the first row.

5. Click the **Customize** button and apply the following changes:
   *Color inspiration*: Picture of a rider on a hill above a lake (Figure 7-121)
   *Color palettes*: **Color Palette: 4**
   *Font choices*: **Arial Nova/Arial Nova**
   *Animation emphasis*: **Moderate**

6. Click **Preview** and the right navigation arrow to move horizontally through the content.

7. Add an image to the *Title* card.
   a. Click **Cards** [*Menu* bar].
   b. Scroll down the cards and select the picture of a rider on a hill. Drag that picture to the *Background* image placeholder on the *Title* card.
   c. Select the text and click **Emphasize**.
   d. Click **Focus Points** to open the *Focus Points* pane.
   e. Select **The entire image is important** (Figure 7-122).
   f. Click **Cards** again and the *Focus Points* pane automatically closes.

8. Select the *Text* card "**Promoting Fun and Fitness**" and click **Delete Text Card**.

7-121 Customize a *Sway* design

9. Adjust a picture.
   a. Select the first *Image* card with one rider (yellow shirt).
   b. Click **Intense**.
   c. Click **Focus Points**.
   d. Select **The entire image is important**.
   e. Click **Cards** [*Menu* bar].

10. Group cards and then edit text.
    a. Click **Automatic** in the *Cards* pane.
    b. Click the **Card Selection** box (on the card lower right) for both the *Image* card of the rider and the *Text* card with bulleted text "**Racing Opportunities**."
       • The *Menu* bar turns green and the card has a green border to show it is selected.
    c. Drag both selected cards into the *Group: Automatic* card.
       • When you drag one of the selected cards, they will both move.
    d. Copy the text from the *Text* card "**Competitive Cyclists**" and paste that text above "Racing Opportunities" as shown in Figure 7-123.

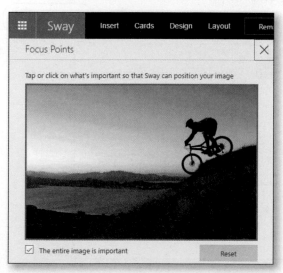

7-122 Change an option on *Focus Points*

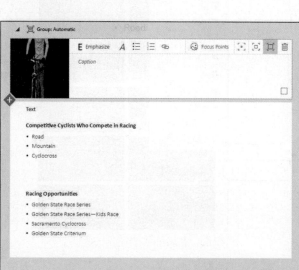

7-123 *Image* and *Text* cards in an *Automatic* group

e. Select the first line of text and click **Emphasize**.
f. Select the three words and click **Bullets**.
g. Press **Enter** twice before "Racing Opportunities" to add space.
h. Select the *Text* card "Competitive Cyclists" and click **Delete Text Card**.

11. Change how a picture displays.
    a. Select the picture with multiple riders.
    b. Click **Intense**.

12. Insert text.
    a. Select the *Text* card that says "Which Team is Right for You?" after the picture of multiple riders.
    b. Edit the text so it reads **Which Club Racing Team Is Right for You?**

13. Adjust text spacing.
    a. Select the *Text* card with "ARCC organizes . . ." after the racing club team.
    b. Delete soft returns in the two sentences so both sentences align at the left (Figure 7-124).

14. Group a *Text* and an *Image* card and then edit text.
    a. Press the down arrow as needed to move the *Insert Content* icon between the last two cards.
    b. Click **Automatic** [*Cards* pane].
    c. Select the last *Image* card of the rider and the *Text* card with "American River Cycling Club."
    d. Drag both selected cards into the *Group: Automatic* card.
    e. Drag the *Image* card below the *Text* card if necessary.
    f. Click **Moderate** on the *Image* card.
    g. Select the *Text* card and place your insertion point after "Club."
    h. Press **Enter** four times.
    i. Type **Promoting Fun and Fitness.**

15. Click above this group to move your *Insert Content* icon.

16. Click **Video** [*Cards* pane] to insert a *Video* card.
    a. Click **Insert** [*Menu* bar], click **Suggested**, and then click **Upload** (see Figure 7-124).

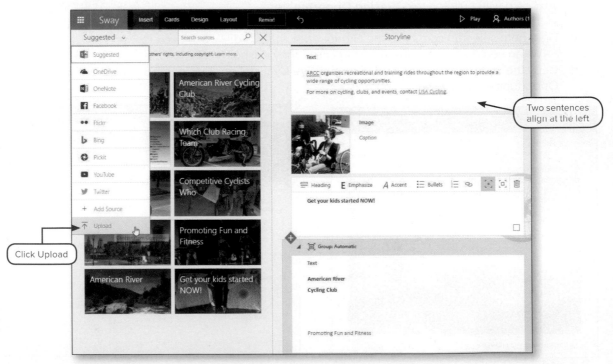

**7-124** Select *Upload* option

b.  Locate your student data files, select **StartYoung-07**, and click **Open**.
   c.  Click **Moderate** on the *Video* card.

17. Click **Play** [*Menu* bar] and click the navigation arrows to review your entire *Sway* (Figure 7-125).
   a.  Click the **Play** button on the video to view the video.

18. Click **Edit** to return to edit mode.

19. Share your *Sway*.
   a.  Click **Share** [*Menu* bar].
   b.  Click **More options** [*Menu* bar] and remove the checks for the items listed there.
   c.  Copy the URL address.
   d.  Open your email program and create a message to your instructor.
   e.  Paste the URL address in the message and send.

20. Click **Sway** [*Menu* bar] and you'll see your uploaded *Sway*.

21. Click **More Options** [*Menu* bar] and select **Sign out**.

**7-125** *Share* options

# Independent Project 7-4

For this project, you work on a presentation about stress for the Courtyard Medical Plaza. You upload a file to a *OneDrive* folder, rename a file, edit a presentation and add a comment using PowerPoint Online. You also invite your instructor to share your file.
[**Student Learning Outcomes 7.2, 7.3, 7.4**]

File Needed: **Stress-07.pptx** *(student data files are available in the* Library *of your SIMnet account)*
Completed Project File Name: **[your initials] PowerPoint 7-4.pptx** *(on OneDrive)*

*Skills Covered in This Project*

- Sign in to *OneDrive*.
- Create a folder.
- Upload a file to *OneDrive*.
- Rename a file.
- Edit a presentation in *PowerPoint Online*.
- Add a comment to a slide in *PowerPoint Online*.
- Share the presentation.

1.  Open an Internet browser and sign in to your *OneDrive* account (https://onedrive.live.com).
   a.  Click **Files** on the left to display the contents of your *OneDrive* folder.
   b.  Click **New** and select **Folder**.
   c.  Name the folder CMP Seminars.
   d.  Click the selection circle for the **CMP Seminars** folder and click **Move to**.
      •  Select **Courtyard Medical Plaza** folder in the *Move* pane and click **Move** at the top of the *Move* pane.
      •  If you do not have this folder, create it and then move the *CMP Seminars* folder.

2. Upload a file.
   a. Click the **Courtyard Medical Plaza** folder to open it and then click the **CMP Seminars** folder to open it.
   b. Click the **Upload** button and select **Files**.
   c. Locate your student data files and select *Stress-07*. Click **Open**.
      • You may need to refresh your browser window to display the file.
   d. Click the selection circle for *Stress-07* to select the file.
   e. Click the **Rename** button and name the file [your initials] PowerPoint 7-4.

3. Open the file *in PowerPoint Online*.
   a. Click the *[your initials] PowerPoint 7-4* file to open it in read-only mode in *PowerPoint Online*.
   b. Click the **Edit Presentation** button at the top and select **Edit in Browser** from the drop-down list.

4. Insert *SmartArt*, apply styles, and adjust object positions.
   a. Display slide 2 and delete the title placeholder.
   b. Click the **SmartArt** button in the content placeholder.
      • Shapes automatically appear.
   c. Click the **More** button [*SmartArt Tools Design* tab, *Layouts* group] to open the *SmartArt* gallery.
      • Select the **Diverging Arrows** layout (Figure 7-126).

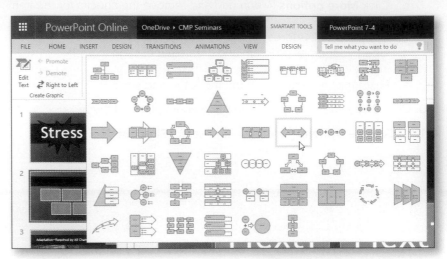

7-126 *SmartArt* layouts in *OneDrive*

   d. Select the left shape and bullets automatically appear.
      • Type **Eustress** and **Distress** after the first two bullets (Figure 7-127).
      • Click the slide background and the text appears on the two arrow shapes.
   e. Select the *SmartArt* graphic. Click the **More** button [*SmartArt Tools Design* tab, *SmartArt Styles* group] and select the **Intense Effect**.
   f. Select the picture of the woman. Click the **Bring Forward** button [*Picture Tools Format* tab, *Arrange* group] and select **Bring to Front**.
   g. Move the picture to the middle over the two arrows (Figure 7-128). Resize the *SmartArt* graphic if necessary.

7-127 Adding *SmartArt* text

5. Add titles on two slides.
   a. Display slide 4. Select the title placeholder and type The "Always On" World We Live In.
   b. Display slide 6. Select the title placeholder and type **My Prescription?**

7-128 Picture moved over *SmartArt*

6. Apply a transition.
   a. Click the **Transitions** tab and select the **Fade** transition.
   b. Click **Effect Options** and select **Smoothly**.
   c. Click **Apply to All**.

7. Add comments.
   a. Display slide 5 and click the **Comment** button [*Insert* tab, *Comments* group] to open the *Comments* pane.
   b. Type Should we include other items? We could change this to a two-column layout if necessary. (Figure 7-129).
   c. Close the *Comments* pane.

7-129 Add a comment

8. View the presentation in *Slide Show* view.
   a. Click the **Reading** view button to return to view mode.
   b. Click **Start Slide Show**.
   c. Review all slides.

9. Send an email message to your instructor.
   a. Click **Share with people**.
   b. Select **Invite people** on the left.
   c. Type your instructor's email address in the *To* area.
   d. Type a brief message in the body area.
   e. Confirm that **Recipients can edit** is displayed.
   f. Click **Share** to send the sharing email to your instructor.
   g. Click **Close** to close the *Share* window.

10. Click the **OneDrive** link at the top to return to your *OneDrive* folders. The file is automatically saved.

11. Click your picture in the upper right and select **Sign Out**.

## Independent Project 7-5

For this project, you download *Office Mix* if it is not available on your computer. You then use the *Screen Recording* feature of *Office Mix* to capture an animation sequence adapted from a previous *Pause & Practice* project. You will use video editing tools to modify the recording and then save it as a countdown video.
[**Student Learning Outcomes 7.1, 7.5**]

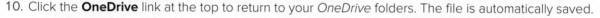

File Needed: ***Countdown-07.pptx*** *(student data files are available in the* Library *of your SIMnet account)*
Completed Project File Name: *[your initials]* **PowerPoint 7-5.mp4**

### Skills Covered in This Project

- Download *Office Mix*.
- Prepare to record.
- Create a screen recording.
- Save as a video.
- Share your video.

1. Download *Office Mix* if it is not yet available on your computer.
   a. Open an Internet browser window and go to https://mix.office.com.
   b. Click the **Get Office Mix** button and sign in with your Microsoft account information.
      - The download starts automatically.

c. Click **OfficeMix.Setup.exe** that appears in the *Status* bar.
d. Agree to the license terms and authorize changes.
   - PowerPoint automatically loads with the *Mix* tab.

2. Open the presentation **Countdown-07** from your student data files. This is a single slide with stacked animated objects (Figure 7-130).

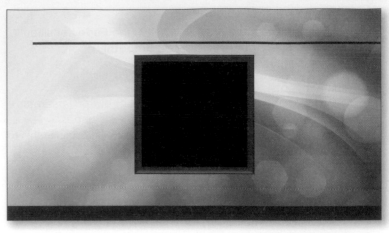

7-130 **Slide with animated countdown**

3. Click the **Slide Show** button then click the slide background to begin the animated countdown from numbers 10 to 1.
   a. Notice the size of the square that is positioned in the middle of the slide. You will need to capture this square in *Slide Show* view when you record.
   b. Press **Esc** to return to the slide.

4. Open a new blank presentation.
   a. Change the slide layout to **Blank** [*Home* tab, *Slides* group].
      - This slide will contain only the slide recording.
      - Recall that a *Screen Recording* is similar to a *Screen Clipping* in that the capture is taken from the file previously viewed.

5. Create a *Screen Recording* on the blank slide.
   a. Click the **Screen Recording** button [*Mix* tab, *Insert* group].
      - The screen appears grayed out.
      - You can move objects around on the screen, activate buttons, or redraw the selection area.
      - Recording does not start until you click the **Record** button.
   b. Click the **Slide Show** button on the *Status* bar so the countdown black square with the gray frame is shown at full screen size.
   c. Click the **Select Area** button on the *Recording* toolbar and redraw the selection area around the gray frame (Figure 7-131).
      - Be careful that you select the frame only and not the yellow background.
      - If excess space is captured, you can crop the video later.

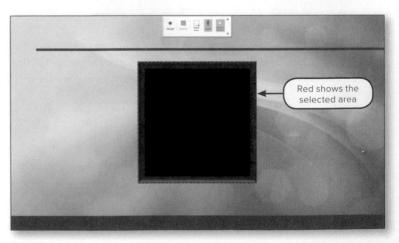

Red shows the selected area

7-131 *Screen Recording* selected area

d. Click the **Record** button (Figure 7-132) to begin recording. You will see 3, 2, and 1. Then click the slide background to start the animation of the number countdown.
   - Do not move your pointer into the area being captured.
   - Be ready to point to the top of your screen when the animation is complete.
   - You can trim the video later if you use it in another PowerPoint presentation.

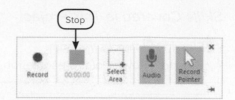

7-132 *Recording* toolbar

e. Point to the top of your screen and click the **Stop** button after the last number appears to end the recording.
   - The new video appears on the blank slide.

6. Click the slide show background to activate that presentation and press **Esc** to end the slide show.

7. Select the presentation with your blank slide and video.

8. Click the **Play** button to test the video (Figure 7-133).
   a. Be sure that all of the gray frame on the countdown square is visible.
   b. Record again if necessary.

9. Change the video *Height* to **5"** [*Video Tools Format* tab, *Size* group] and the *Width* automatically adjusts.

10. Right-click the video and select **Save Media As** from the context menu to open the *Save Media As* dialog box. Name the file [your initials] PowerPoint 7-5 and click **Save**.

11. Close the **Countdown-07** and the blank presentations.

7-133 Testing the countdown video

## Independent Project 7-6

For this project, prepare an online presentation for employees at Paradise Lakes Resort about up-selling services. You import a PowerPoint presentation into *Sway*, choose a layout and design, customize a design, modify existing cards, and add text.
[**Student Learning Outcome 7.6**]

File Needed: ***Up-SellServices-07.pptx*** (student data files are available in the Library of your SIMnet account)
Completed Project File Name: ***Up-Sell Services*** (shared at https://sway.com)

## Skills Covered in This Project

- Sign in to https://sway.com.
- Upload a PowerPoint presentation.
- Apply a design and layout.
- Customize the design.
- Delete and group cards.
- Add text.

1. Sign in to *Sway* using your Microsoft account at https://sway.com.

2. Click **Import** and select ***Up-SellServices-07*** from your student data files. Click **Open**.

3. Click **Layout** and select **Scrolls Vertically** if it is not already selected.

4. Click **Design** and select **Style 2**, **Variation 13**.

5. Click **Customize** and change the following:
   - *Color inspiration*: **Color Option:2**, (Picture of *SmartArt*)
   - *Color palettes*: **Color Palette: 2**
   - *Font choices*: **Ford's Folly/Tahoma**
   - *Animation emphasis*: **Intense**
   - *Text size*: **Large**

6. Click **Cards** and select the *Title* card. Select the text and click **Emphasize**.

7. Select the *Text* card "Focus on Up-Service, Not Up-Selling."
   a. Select the text and choose **Emphasize** and **Moderate**.

8. Insert a new *Text* card and type Paradise Lakes Resort.

9. Group the two *Text* cards with an *Automatic* group (Figure 7-134).

10. Click **Play** to test these changes (Figure 7-135).

7-134 Grouped cards

7-135 Top of *Sway* page using *Scrolls Vertically* layout

11. Select the *Text* card with "Customer Service . . ." and click **Moderate** (see Figures 7-134 and 7-136).

12. **Select** the *Text* card with "Focus on . . ." and click **Moderate**.

13. Select the *Image* card with *SmartArt*.
    a. Click **Focus Points** and confirm that **The entire image is important** is selected.
    b. Click **Moderate** (Figure 7-137).

14. Delete the *Text* card with "Our Goal?"

15. Edit the last text card so it reads **Our Goal . . . A Great Customer Experience** and then select the text and click **Emphasize** and **Moderate**.

16. Click **Play** to test these changes (Figure 7-138).

17. Share your *Sway* with your instructor.

18. Click the **More Options** button and select **Sign out**.

7-136 List with *Emphasis* and *Moderate* applied

7-137 *SmartArt* with *Moderate* applied

7-138 Edited text

## Improve It Project 7-7

For this project, prepare an online presentation about garden planning for Classic Gardens and Landscapes. You import a PowerPoint presentation into *Sway*, modify existing cards, create a picture stack, and add suggested online content.
[**Student Learning Outcome 7.6**]

*Instructors: Student solutions will vary slightly depending on the online source material that they include.*

File Needed: **Gardens-07.pptx** *(student data files are available in the Library of your SIMnet account)*
Completed Project File Name: **Garden Planning** *(shared at* https://sway.com*)*

## Skills Covered in This Project

- Sign in to https://sway.com.
- Upload a PowerPoint presentation.
- Apply a design and layout.
- Customize the design.
- Delete and group cards.
- Create a stacked image group.
- Insert media from recommended sources.

1. Sign in to *Sway* using your Microsoft account at https://sway.com.

2. Click **Import** and select **Gardens-07** from your student data files. Click **Open**.

3. Click **Layout** and select **Optimized for presentation**.

4. Click **Design** and select **Style 6**, **Variation 1**.

5. Click **Customize** and change the following:
   *Color inspiration*: No change
   *Color palettes*: **Color Palette: 1**
   *Font choices*: **Cavolini/Arial Nova**
   *Animation emphasis*: **Intense**
   *Text size*: **Large**

6. Click **Cards** and select the *Title* card.
   a. Edit the text so it reads Garden Planning.
   b. Highlight the text and click **Emphasize**.
   c. Insert the **SpringTulips-07** image from your student data files as the background image for the *Title* card.
      - Notice the *Heading* card "Planning for All Seasons."
      - For this particular design, all remaining cards are grouped under this heading as you can see in the *Storyline* by the gray rectangle behind them.
      - When you click **Preview** or **Play**, the heading appears at the top of your window.
   d. Preview your *Sway* (Figure 7-139).
      - Notice the arrangement of slide content with this design.
      - The image card for the company logo requires no change.

7. Delete the *Text* card with "Gardens."

8. Change the *Text* card with "Our Services."
   a. Click **Moderate**.
   b. Delete the text "Classic Gardens and Landscapes" (Figure 7-140).

7-139 *Title* card preview

7-140 Bulleted text

9. Delete the *Text* card with "Beautiful Entryways."

10. Create an image group after the "Our Services" card.
    a. Click **Stack**.
    b. Drag the next three image cards into the *Stack* group.

11. Delete the *Text* card with "Informal Gardens."

12. Add cards to the *Stack* group.
    a. Select the next three *Image* cards and drag them into the *Stack* group.
    b. Preview your *Sway*. When the pictures appear, click to go through all images in the stack (Figure 7-141).

7-141 *Stacked Image* group

13. Create another group.
    a. Click **Automatic**.
    b. Drag the *Text* card with "It Begins . . ." into the group. Click **Moderate**.
    c. Drag the *Image* card with a picture of a landscape drawing into the group.
       • The *Text* card is above the *Image* card.

14. Create another group.
    a. Click **Automatic**.
    b. Drag the *Text* card with "Then a Photo . . ." into the group. Click **Moderate**.
    c. Drag the *Image* card with a picture of planted garden into the group.
       • The *Text* card is above the *Image* card (Figure 7-142).

7-142 *Automatic* group

15. Select the *Text* card with "We Provide" and click **Moderate**.

16. Select the *Text* card with "Available Products" and click **Moderate**.
    a. Highlight the text "Classic Gardens and Landscapes" and press **Ctrl+C**.
    b. Delete this text and any extra space below the last bulleted item.
    c. Paste this text before the phone number on the last card. Click **Moderate**.
    d. Press **Enter** so the company name and phone number are on two separate lines.

17. Play your *Sway*.

18. Add content from *Sway*'s *Suggested* sources and create a group.
    a. Click **Insert** to open the *Suggested* pane.
    b. Search for "shade trees."

c. Select three images with a pixel width (the first number shown) about 500. Click **Add** to insert them on three *Image* cards.

d. Select one video (an icon displays on the thumbnail). Click **Add** to insert it and a *Video* card is created.

e. Click **Grid** and drag the *Image* and *Video* cards into that group.

19. Play your *Sway* to see how this group appears. View the video.

20. Share your *Sway* with your instructor.

21. Click the **More Options** button and select **Sign out**.

## Challenge Project 7-8

Create a presentation using *PowerPoint Online* for a student group, organization, or work team. Share the presentation with members, determine the goal for your project, and plan how each person will contribute. Collaborate by storing all related files in a *OneDrive* folder, co-authoring and editing the presentation, and providing feedback through comments.
[Student Learning Outcomes 7.2, 7.3. 7.4]

File Needed: None
Completed Project Folder and File Names: **New *OneDrive* folder and files**

Create a *OneDrive* folder to store your presentation and related files. Modify your *OneDrive* folder according to the following guidelines:

• Create a *OneDrive* folder for your presentation project.
• Upload files.
• Move or copy files as needed.
• Use *PowerPoint Online* to create or revise your presentation.
• Insert comments.
• Share files with group members.
• Share your final presentation with your instructor.

## Challenge Project 7-9

Design an example to show how to use PowerPoint's new *Morph* feature to create animation effects. Include several different effects and plan your instructional sequence to explain how to create the effects. Use the *Office Mix Screen Recording* feature to record screen movements and to record your comments. Save your recording as a video.
[Student Learning Outcomes 7.1, 7.5]

File Needed: None
Completed Project File Name: *[your initials] PowerPoint 7-9.mp4*

Create a *Screen Recording* for this project according to the following guidelines:

- Install the *Office Mix* add-in if it is not available on the computer you are using.
- Design a slide, your final slide, with text and graphic objects in an interesting layout.
- Duplicate this slide and modify slide objects by changing size, fonts, color, etc.
- Move the modified slide before the final slide and apply the *Morph* transition to the final slide.
- Test all movements and changes and adjust as needed.
- Plan how you will capture the screen action in a demonstration and how you will describe the effects. Prepare notes to use as a reference during your recording.
- Create a *Screen Recording* and save it as a video.
- Share the file with your instructor.

## Challenge Project 7-10

Create an eCard for a friend or family member using *Sway*. Insert pictures, text, and video (if available) to tell a story in an interesting way to celebrate a birthday, an anniversary, or just a special day. Share your *Sway*.
[**Student Learning Outcome 7.6**]

File Needed: None
Completed Project File Name: *(shared on* https://sway.com*)*

Create a *Sway* for this project according to the following guidelines:

- Collect media resources and consider how they should be sequenced and combined.
- Develop all content in *Sway* or create part of your material in PowerPoint and then import it.
- Select a design and navigation that is appropriate for your *Sway* topic.
- Customize colors, fonts, and emphasis effects.
- Build your content and use different types of groups to combine related material.
- Arrange pictures in interesting group layouts (stack, grid, etc.).
- Apply individual effects on cards as needed.
- Share the URL for your *Sway* with your instructor.

# appendices

# Office 2016 Shortcuts

## Using Function Keys on a Laptop

When using a laptop computer, function keys perform specific Windows actions on your laptop, such as increase or decrease speaker volume, open Windows *Settings*, or adjust the screen brightness. So when using a numbered function key in an Office application, such as **F12** as a shortcut to open the *Save As* dialog box, you may need to press the *function key* (**Fn** or **fn**) on your keyboard in conjunction with a numbered function key to activate the Office command (Figure Appendix A-1). The *function key* is typically located near the bottom left of your laptop keyboard next to the *Ctrl* key.

**Appendix A-1
Function key**

## Common Office 2016 Keyboard Shortcuts

| Action | Keyboard Shortcut |
|---|---|
| Save | **Ctrl+S** |
| Copy | **Ctrl+C** |
| Cut | **Ctrl+X** |
| Paste | **Ctrl+V** |
| Select All | **Ctrl+A** |
| Bold | **Ctrl+B** |
| Italic | **Ctrl+I** |
| Underline | **Ctrl+U** |
| Close *Start* page or *Backstage* view | **Esc** |
| Open *Help* dialog box | **F1** |
| Activate *Tell Me* feature | **Alt+Q** |
| Switch windows | **Alt+Tab** |

## PowerPoint 2016 Keyboard Shortcuts

| Action | Keyboard Shortcut |
|---|---|
| *File Management* | |
| Open a new blank presentation | **Ctrl+N** |
| Open an existing presentation from the *Backstage* view | **Ctrl+O** |
| Open an existing presentation from the *Open* dialog box | **Ctrl+F12** |
| Open *Save As* dialog box | **F12** |
| Save | **Ctrl+S** |
| *Editing* | |

*(continued)*

| Action | Keyboard Shortcut |
| --- | --- |
| Cut | **Ctrl+X** |
| Copy | **Ctrl+C** |
| Paste | **Ctrl+V** |
| Duplicate slides | **Ctrl+D** |
| Undo | **Ctrl+Z** |
| Redo | **Ctrl+Y** |
| Soft return, causes text to word wrap to the next line | **Shift+Enter** |
| *Slide Movement in Normal View* | |
| Move to first slide | **Home** |
| Move to last slide | **End** |
| Move to next slide | **Page Down** or **down arrow** |
| Move to previous slide | **Page Up** or **up arrow** |
| Move from the slide title to the body placeholder | **Ctrl+Enter** |
| *Slide Movement in Slide Show View* | |
| Start a presentation slide show from the beginning | **F5** |
| Open *Presenter View* and start a slide show | **Alt+F5** |
| Advance to the next slide | **N, spacebar, right arrow, down arrow, Enter,** or **Page Down** |
| Go to the previous slide | **P, Backspace, left arrow, up arrow,** or **Page Up** |
| Go to a particular slide | Slide number, **Enter** |
| Go to a particular slide by opening *All Slides* dialog box and selecting a slide title | **Ctrl+S** |
| Go to a hidden slide | Slide number, **Enter** or **H** if the next slide is hidden |
| Blanks the screen to black | **B** or **period** |
| Blanks the screen to white | **W** or **comma** |
| Zoom in | **Plus sign** |
| Zoom out | **Minus sign** |
| Stop or restart an automatic show | **S** |
| *Ink Markup in Slide Show View* | |
| Change pointer to pen | **Ctrl+P** |
| Change pointer to arrow | **Ctrl+A** |
| Change pointer to eraser | **Ctrl+E** |
| Show or hide ink markup | **Ctrl+M** |
| Erase markings on the screen | **E** |

# glossary

**.potx** PowerPoint file format for templates.

**.pptx** PowerPoint file format for presentations.

**3-D Rotation** Style effect that includes parallel, perspective, and oblique options to create an illusion of depth; available for shapes, *SmartArt,* and charts.

## A

**Action Buttons** Shapes that automatically have an action such as *Previous, Next, Beginning,* or *Home* when clicked during a slide show; customize options to control what happens with a *Mouse Click* or *Mouse Over* action.

**Add a Digital Signature** Feature that helps to ensure integrity by creating a read-only presentation that is marked as final.

**Add Shape** *SmartArt* command that inserts a shape in relation to the selected shape.

**add-ins** Programs that provide additional features to Office software.

**adjustment handle** Yellow circle used to change shape curves or points.

**Align** Feature used to arrange objects evenly on the slide or in relationship to each other; horizontal alignment includes left, center, right and vertical alignment includes top, middle, and bottom.

**Alt Text** Alternative text that identifies a picture or graphic object; used with screen readers to accommodate individuals with visual impairments.

**animation** Movement of objects on a slide.

**Animation Painter** Tool that copies animation settings and applies them to another object in the same way the *Format Painter* copies format settings.

**Animation Pane** Pane that displays animation settings for multiple objects and multiple effects.

**animation tag** Small numbered box that appears on the slide next to an animated object when the *Animations* tab is active.

**Area chart** Chart type that shows data changes over time, emphasizes the total value of a trend.

**Arrange All** *View* option that displays tiled windows so you can see all open presentations at the same time.

**Arrows** Line style that provides arrowheads or other shapes for both ends of a line.

**Artistic Effects** Picture effects that resemble creative painting techniques such as *Pencil Sketch, Line Drawing, Watercolor Sponge, Glass, Plastic Wrap,* and many others.

**aspect ratio** The ratio of width to height; affects slide, picture, and other object sizing.

**audio** A digital file inserted in a presentation that plays music or audio recordings such as sounds or a voice recording; can be recorded within a presentation.

**AutoCorrect** Feature that automatically corrects commonly misspelled words.

**AutoFormat** Feature that replaces various punctuation marks as you type.

**Axis Title** Chart element that names the horizontal and vertical axes.

## B

**Background Style** Option that changes slide background and text colors to light or dark variations.

**Banded Columns** Table style option featuring columns that have alternating colors.

**Banded Rows** Table style option featuring rows that have alternating colors.

**Bar chart** Similar to column charts except bars are horizontal.

**Bevel** Style effect option that applies light and dark areas to create a dimensional appearance so objects and text look raised or inset.

**Bookmark** Feature that designates a specific location in an audio or video file; can be used to start an animation effect.

**border** Line around text, paragraph, page, cell, table, or graphic object.

**Brightness** Picture correction option that darkens or lightens a picture by adding white or black.

**build** Animation technique that makes items gradually appear on a slide to focus attention; also called *progressive disclosure.*

## C

**Cards** Used in *Sway* to contain text, pictures, and other media.

**Cascade** *View* option that displays each presentation in a separate, layered window with its own *Ribbon.*

**case** Typographic term for capitalization; small letters are lowercase and capital letters are uppercase.

**category** Group of data values from each row in a spreadsheet.

**cell** Intersection of a column and a row.

**Cell Margin** The space between the border lines of a cell and the text in the cell.

**Change Colors** Command that displays different theme color combinations for *SmartArt* layouts and charts.

**Change Picture** Command that replaces one picture with another while retaining the same size and effects.

**chart** A visual representation of numeric data.

**Chart Area** The background area where the entire chart is displayed in a frame.

**Chart Element** Separate, selectable, editable object in a chart.

**Chart Floor** Area at the bottom of a 3-D chart.

**Chart Style** Combination of colors and effects for a chart and its elements.

**Check Accessibility** Feature that identifies potential issues that users with disabilities may have with your presentation when using a screen reader or other adaptive resources.

**Check Compatibility** Feature that examines a presentation for compatibility issues between the current version of PowerPoint and versions before 2007.

**Clipboard** Location where multiple copied items from an Office file or other source such as a web page are stored.

**Color Saturation** Option that controls the intensity of the colors in a picture; colors that are vibrant are highly saturated and colors that are muted have a low saturation level.

**Color Tone** Option that controls temperature values to make a picture's colors more cool or warm.

**Colorful** Option that provides varied colors for *Chart Styles* and *SmartArt Styles*.

**column** Vertical grouping of cells in a table or spreadsheet; vertical area of text in a document or slide.

**Column chart** Shows a comparison of values or data changes over time displayed in columns that may be grouped or stacked.

**Combo chart** Combines two charts such as a column chart with a line chart.

**Comments** Collaboration feature that allows users to add notes on presentation slides without altering the design of slides.

**Compare** Collaboration feature that allows users to merge an original presentation with a revised presentation to consider reviewer feedback.

**Compress Media** Feature used to improve playback performance and to reduce presentation file size; different quality levels are available.

**Compress Pictures** Command that reduces presentation file size by reducing picture resolution.

**Connected Service** Services users can add to Office programs for images and video, storage, and sharing.

**Connector Lines** Tools that attach two or more shapes for custom diagrams; lines are available in different shapes.

**constrain** Keep lines straight, circles round, and rectangles square; press **Shift** or **Ctrl** when resizing.

**Contrast** Picture correction option that adjusts the difference between the picture's lightest and darkest colors.

**Copy** Duplicate text, objects, or slides.

**Corrections** Feature that improves picture appearance by adjusting *Sharpen, Soften, Contrast,* and *Brightness* options.

**crop** Trim unwanted areas of a selected picture.

**cropping handles** Black handles that appear on the corners and sides of pictures that you can drag to remove part of the picture.

**crosshair** Plus sign pointer used to draw a shape.

**Curve** Line tool used to draw smooth curves; a line is formed each time you click and the line curves as you change direction.

**Custom Path** A type of *Motion Path* animation; you draw the path that an animated object follows.

**Custom Slide Show** Feature that creates a presentation within a presentation by creating a list of slides that can be arranged in any order.

**Cut** Remove text, objects, or slides.

**Cycle** *SmartArt* layout type used to illustrate a continuing sequence or concepts related to a central idea.

# D

**Dashes** Line styles that combine dots and dashes to make different patterns.

**Data Label** Used to identify data series or its individual points; may include values.

**Data Marker** The graphical representation of values shown as columns, bars, slices, or data points.

**data series** A group of related values graphed by columns, bars, slices, or other objects in a chart.

**Data Table** Columnar display of values for each data series in a chart located below the chart.

**Delay** Animation timing command used to make an animation begin at a specified time.

**Delete** Remove text, objects, or slides.

**direction handles** Line tool used to change the curve of a line between two points.

**Distribute** Feature that creates even spacing between multiple slide objects.

**Duplicate** Create a copy of an object or a slide.

**Duration** Length of time; controls the speed of transitions and animations in a slide show.

# E

**edit mode** *PowerPoint Online* view where users can edit a file, add comments, and save a file.

**Edit Points** Editing feature used to change the curve or direction of a line or shape.

**Effect Options** Command that controls the direction of slide transitions and animation movement.

**Effects** Formatting feature such as *Shadow, Glow,* or Soft Edges added to *WordArt,* shapes, or pictures.

**embed** Insert an object from another application; the source program is used from within PowerPoint for editing, but the object in PowerPoint can be changed independently and the source file is not affected.

**embed code** Instructions that enable linking to and displaying a video within PowerPoint; requires an Internet connection.

**Embedded TrueType fonts** Option that saves presentation fonts for display on a different computer.

**Emphasis** Animation effect that calls attention to an object that remains on the slide.

**Encrypt with Password** Feature that protects a presentation from being opened and edited; a password is required to open a presentation.

**Entrance** Animation effect that occurs when an object appears on the slide.

**Exit** Animation effect that occurs when an object leaves the slide.

**explode** Separate pie chart slices.

**Export** Save a presentation in different formats to use in another program or application.

**Eyedropper** Feature in PowerPoint used to match colors.

# F

**Fade In** Effect that causes an audio to gradually reach full volume or a video to gradually come into focus.

**Fade Out** Effect that causes an audio to gradually decrease volume or a video to gradually blur out.

**Find** Feature that searches for specific text and/or formatting.

**Flip** Drawing option used to make an object point in different directions or create a mirror image.

**footer** Displays content at the bottom of a document page, slide, or object.

**Format Painter** Tool that duplicates formatting choices such as font, font size, line spacing, indents, bullets, numbering, styles, etc. from one selection to another selection.

**Freeform** Line tool used to draw both straight and curved lines; when the end of the line you draw touches the beginning of the line, a shape is created with a solid fill color.

# G

**Glow** Style effect option that provides a colored area around an object that fades into the background color.

**Gradient** Option that blends two or more colors or light and dark variations of the current fill color in different directions.

**Grayscale** A range of shades of black in a display or printout.

**Gridlines** Evenly spaced vertical and horizontal lines on a slide in *Normal* view that aid in object alignment; also the horizontal or vertical lines that appear in a chart area.

**Group** Connect multiple objects as one object. Also, area on a tab that contains related commands and options.

**Guides** One vertical and one horizontal line in the middle of the slide that you can move to check for consistent alignment; guides display in *Normal* view but not in *Slide Show* view.

# H

**Handout** Option that displays or prints 1–9 slides on a page.

**Handout Master** Feature that stores information about handout backgrounds, layouts, and fonts.

**header** Displays content at the top of a document, slide handout, or object.

**Header Row** First row of a table.

**Hierarchy** *SmartArt* layout type used to illustrate a decision tree or top-to-bottom relationship such as an organization chart.

**Highlighter** Tool used to write or draw on a slide in *Slide Show* view.

**horizontal alignment** Content positioning option that aligns material in relation to the left, center, right, or middle (justified) of the page or slide; can also refer to the position of objects in relation to each other.

**hyperlink** Connection between two locations applied to text or objects; when you click a hyperlink, you move to a different slide, presentation, application, or web site.

# I

**Information pane** Displays properties of a selected file or folder on *OneDrive*.

**ink annotations** Markings that call attention to information you mark by writing or drawing on slides.

**Ink Color** Option that controls the pen color when writing or drawing on slides during a presentation.

**Inspect Presentation** Feature that examines a presentation for hidden content, properties, or personal information that you may not want to share.

# K

**kiosk presentation** Self-running slide presentation that automatically loops.

# L

**laser pointer** *Slide Show* feature that displays a small dot on the screen during a presentation; also available on remote control devices.

**layout** Controls the position of placeholders on a slide.

**Legend** Descriptive text or key that describes a data series and identifies it by color.

**Line chart** Chart type that shows data changes over time.

**link** Insert an object from another application that remains connected to the source document; the object opens in a separate window for editing in the source program and changes also appear in the PowerPoint object.

**List** *SmartArt* layout type used to illustrate non-sequential or grouped information in a graphical list.

**Lock Drawing Mode** Feature used to draw more than one of the same shape.

**loop** Cycle continuously in a slide show from beginning to end and automatically repeat.

**luminosity** Affects the lightness and brightness of a color.

# M

**Mark as Final** Feature that makes a presentation a read-only file; protects a presentation from being accidentally altered.

**Matrix** *SmartArt* layout type used to illustrate the relationship of four parts to the whole.

**media controls** Area visible below an audio or video object that controls play, pause, move back, move forward, mute, and unmute; also displays elapsed time.

**Merge Cells** Command that combines two or more cells in a row or column.

**Merge Shapes** Feature that combines two or more stacked shapes to create a single, new shape.

**metadata** Document properties stored with the file.

**Monochromatic** Color combinations containing only shades of one color; color option for *Chart Styles*.

**Morph** A transition that creates an animation effect by blending the objects on one slide to the same objects with different colors, sizes, or positions on a second slide.

**Motion Path** Type of animation that provides predefined paths for the direction of movement of an animated object.

**multimedia** Broad range of digital media that includes text, pictures, audio, and video combined with dynamic motion and interactivity; also called *rich media*.

# N

**Normal view** Default view option where you enter the content of slides and move between slides as you develop them.

**Notes Master** Feature that stores information about notes page backgrounds, layouts, and fonts.

**Notes Page view** Option that displays each slide on a page with space below the slide where you can type speaker notes.

# O

**Object linking and embedding (OLE)** Technology developed by Microsoft for sharing objects between different Microsoft Office applications.

**Office Mix** An add-in for PowerPoint that provides flexibility in recording a presentation, supports interactive content, and enables a presentation to be shared online.

**Office Online** The online version of Microsoft Office that is available through a web browser.

**OneDrive** Online (cloud) storage area that is a part of your Microsoft account where you can store and access documents from any computer that is online.

**Optimize Compatibility** Feature used with media files to improve performance for a presentation that is displayed on different computers.

**Outline view** Option that expands the pane at the left of the slide area to show slide titles and bulleted text.

# P

**Package Presentation for CD** Feature that saves a presentation and related files to a CD or a folder.

**Paste** Place text or objects that have been stored on the *Clipboard* in a new location.

**Paste Options** Options that control whether an object being inserted uses destination or source formatting.

**Paste Special** Feature used to insert objects as either embedded or linked objects.

**Pattern fill** Shape fill option that applies a mixture of two colors in various dotted or crosshatch designs.

**Pen** Tool used to write or draw on a slide in *Slide Show* view; also used in *Normal* view to draw tables and edit border lines.

**Photo Album** Feature that creates a presentation from a group of pictures with one, two, or four pictures on a slide.

**Picture Effects** Command used to apply effect options, such as *Shadow* or *Glow*, to pictures.

**Picture fill** Shape fill option that inserts a picture from a file or search.

**Picture Layout** *SmartArt* layout type used to show pictures as integral parts of many different diagrams.

**Pie chart** Shows the values in a data series in proportional slices that make up a whole pie.

**pixel** Abbreviated term for picture element, a single unit of information about color.

**placeholders** The area of a slide where you can add text, tables, charts, and pictures.

**point** Small black square on a line that controls where a line curves or changes direction; also called a vertex.

**Poster Frame** Picture displayed as a preview image at the beginning of a video.

**PowerPoint Designer** Feature that provides a variety of suggested layouts for slides with picture content.

**PowerPoint Online** A presentation application in *Office Online*.

**Presenter View** Feature that displays slides, speaker notes, a timer, and features helpful for a speaker; can be displayed on one monitor or with a second monitor or projector to also display the presentation at full-screen size.

**Print Settings** Options to control what and how printing occurs.

**Process** *SmartArt* layout type used to illustrate sequential steps in a process or workflow.

**Proofing Language** Tool that allows you to choose a dictionary for a language so you can apply appropriate spell checking and grammar rules.

**Properties** Information recorded in a file such as title, author name, subject, creation date, etc.

**Pyramid** *SmartArt* layout type used to illustrate proportional or interconnected relationships.

# R

**Reading view** Option that displays a slide show at full-screen or alternate window size determined by the viewer.

**read-only mode** *PowerPoint Online* view where users can view but not edit a file.

**Recolor** Option that changes picture colors to different monotone color variations.

**Record Audio** Feature used to create an audio file.

**Reflection** Style effect option that shows a mirror image below an object.

**Regroup** Connect ungrouped objects that were previously grouped.

**Rehearse Timings** Feature that helps to judge the pace of the presentation.

**Relationship** *SmartArt* layout type used to illustrate concepts that are connected such as contrasting, opposing, or converging.

**remote control** Device that enables a speaker to control a slide show when he or she steps away from the computer during a presentation.

**Remove Background** Feature used to remove picture areas without affecting the original picture; the area removed appears transparent.

**Reorder Animation** Animation timing command used to adjust animation sequence.

**Replace** Feature that enables you to change words that match your specifications.

**resize pointer** Pointer used to change the size of a graphic object or a table column or row.

**RGB model** Typically used for computer displays; colors are formed by blending values for *Red, Green,* and *Blue*.

**rich media** Broad range of digital media that includes text, pictures, audio, and video combined with dynamic motion and interactivity; also called *multimedia*.

**Rotate** Drawing option used to make objects angle.

**rotation handle** A circular arrow used to turn an object in different directions.

**row** Horizontal grouping of cells.

**Ruler** Vertical or horizontal guide that displays measurements above the slide and on the left with markers that indicate the current margin and indents.

# S

**sans serif** Category of fonts that do not include structural details at the ends of letter strokes.

**saturated** Colors are intense and vibrant.

**Screen Clipping** Feature that copies a portion of an application window and displays it on a slide.

**Screen Recording** Feature that creates a video of on-screen actions that can include narration such as a software demonstration.

**Screenshot** Feature that copies an entire application window and displays it on a slide.

**ScreenTip** Text that displays when the user points to a hyperlink.

**Scribble** Line tool used to draw a continuous line; similar to writing.

**Sections** Organization feature used to divide a presentation using major topics; during a slide show, sections are not visible.

**serif** Category of fonts that includes structural details at the ends of letter strokes.

**Set Transparent Color** Feature that removes one color from a picture; used to remove solid backgrounds.

**shading** Fill color applied to text, paragraph, page, cell, table, or graphic object.

**Shadow** Style effect option that provides dimension by inserting a shadow behind or below an object.

**Shape** Graphic object that can be drawn, such as a line, arrow, circle, or rectangle.

**Shape Effects** Command used to apply effect options, such as *Shadow* or *Glow*, to objects.

**Sharing** Making a presentation available to others through various methods online.

**Sharing Link** A hyperlink that you can copy and email to others so they can access your file on *OneDrive* or other online applications.

**Sharpen** Picture correction option that makes picture details more evident.

**sizing handles** White circles on the corners and sides of an object that are used to resize the object.

**Slide Master** Feature that stores information about slide backgrounds, layouts, and fonts for each theme.

**Slide Recording** Feature that captures an entire presentation; may include handwriting with digital ink, narration, or a speaker video.

**Slide Show view** Option that displays slides in sequence at full-screen size for audience viewing.

**Slide Sorter view** Option that displays slides as thumbnails.

**Smart Guides** Temporary lines that appear when your objects are aligned or spaced evenly.

**Smart Lookup** Feature that displays the definition and additional information from the Internet of a selected word or selected words.

**SmartArt graphics** Diagram layouts used to illustrate concepts such as processes, cycles, or relationships.

**SmartArt Styles** Gallery that displays different effects for emphasizing shapes within *SmartArt* layouts.

**Soft Edges** Style effect option that creates a feathered edge, which gradually blends into the background color.

**Soften** Picture correction option that creates a color blending effect.

**Speaker notes** Reminders to help the speaker present; entered into the *Notes* pane and visible in *Notes Pane* view.

**Spelling** Feature that identifies misspelled words and gives the user word choice options to correct spelling.

**Split Cells** Command that divides a single cell into two or more cells.

**spreadsheet** In PowerPoint, data displayed in columns and rows to create a chart.

**stacking** Layering multiple shapes or objects.

**Standard 4:3** Slide display option size that uses a 4:3 aspect ratio.

**Standard Colors** Ten colors that are not affected by *Theme Color* changes.

**Start** Animation timing command that controls when animation begins.

**Storyline** Used in *Sway* to organize all content and control how it is displayed.

**Style galleries** Collection of preset effects for text, shapes, pictures, or other objects.

**Sway** An online presentation application available through your Microsoft account.

**Switch** *View* option that allows movement between open presentations; only one presentation displays at a time.

# T

**tab stops** Markers on the ruler that indicates text indenting; spaced by default at every one-half inch.

**table** Shows data in an organized, easy-to-read format with information arranged in columns and rows; in Access, database object that stores a collection of related records.

**Table Style Options** Built-in formats for tables, which include a variety of borders, shading, alignment, and other options.

**Table Styles** Gallery of built-in table formats which include a variety of borders, shading, alignment, and other options.

**Template** Predesigned and ready-to-use document, workbook, database, or slide presentation that includes formulas, formatting, viewing options, and sample content; a PowerPoint template has a .potx file extension.

**text box** Area where you can type text.

**Text Direction** Option to arrange text horizontally, rotated, or stacked within a cell or text box.

**Text Effects** Command used to apply effect options, such as *Shadow* or *Glow*, to text.

**Text Pane** Area where you enter text for *SmartArt* shapes.

**Texture fill** Shape fill option that applies an image such as woven fabric or wood.

**Theme** Collection of fonts, colors, and effects that you can apply to an entire document, workbook, or presentation; provides consistent background graphics.

**Theme Colors** Set of background and accent colors.

**Theme Fonts** Pair of fonts used for a presentation's headings and body text.

**Thesaurus** Resource tool that lists synonyms for a selected word.

**thumbnails** Small picture of an image or layout.

**Tick Marks** Lines of measurement on an axis that helps to interpret values.

**Tile** Fill option that causes a picture to be repeated to fill a slide area or shape.

**Title and Content** Slide layout provided by the *Slide Master* for most slides in a presentation.

**Title Slide** Slide layout provided by the *Slide Master* for the first slide of a presentation.

**Total Row** Table style option showing color and text emphasis.

**Transform** Text effect used to change the shape of words.

**Transition** Visual effect that occurs when one slide changes into another slide.

**Translate** Feature that converts words or short phrases to a different language.

**Transparency** Color setting that is adjusted by percentage to allow the background to show through objects.

**Trigger** Setting applied to a slide object so that when the object is clicked, the animation starts.

**Trim** Tool that removes playback time from the beginning or end of audio and video files.

# U

**Ungroup** Separate grouped objects so you can modify them independently.

**user name** Name used when Microsoft Office is installed on a computer; by default, this is the author name for each presentation.

# V

**Variants** Theme designs showing different color combinations.

**vector** Graphic file format used to create drawings based on angles and points.

**vertex** Small black square on a line that controls where a line curves or changes direction; also called a point.

**vertical alignment** Content positioning option that aligns material in relation to the top, middle, or bottom of the slide; can also refer to the position of objects in relation to each other.

# W

**Walls** Areas of a 3-D chart that create an illusion of depth.

**Weight** Thickness of an outline measured in points.

**Widescreen (16:9)** Default slide display option size that uses a 16:9 aspect ratio; 16:10 is also available.

**WordArt** Displays text as a graphic object with preset text effects that can be modified.

# Z

**Zoom** Change file display size.

# index

## Symbols

#####, P2-112
3-D Column Chart, P2-115
3-D pie chart, P2-117
3-D Rotation, P2-74
4:3 aspect ratio, P3-167
6 Slides Horizontal, P1-44
7 point star, P4-242
16:9 aspect ratio, P3-167
16:10 aspect ratio, P3-167

## A

Accent colors, P2-75, P3-147
Accept or reject changes, P6-399 to P6-400
Accessibility Checker pane, P6-405, P6-406
Accessibility issues, P6-405 to P6-407
Account settings, P7-454
Action buttons, P2-71, P5-312 to P5-313, P6-391
Action Settings dialog box, P5-313
Add a Digital Signature, P6-410
Add a service drop-down list, P7-454
Add Animation button, P3-156, P5-293, P5-297, P5-298, P5-299, P5-300, P5-301, P5-302, P5-324
Add Assistant, P2-105
Add Bookmark button, P5-320
Add Gradient Stop, P2-76
Add gradient stop button, P3-152
Add-in, P7-454 to P7-456
Add-in object, P7-455
Add-in pane, P7-455
Add Section, P6-377
Add Shape button, P2-105
Add Shape options, P2-106
Add shapes, P2-105 to P2-106
Adding content from other sources, P6-366 to P6-376
    copying slides from another presentation, P6-369 to P6-370
    create handouts in Word, P6-417
    creating slides from Word outline, P6-366 to P6-367
    linking and embedding Office objects, P6-370 to P6-374
    Paste Options and Paste Special, P6-374 to P6-376
    summary/review, P6-420
Address Book button, P7-463
Adjust pane size, P1-9
Adjustment handle, P2-71, P2-72, P4-212
Adobe Flash file (.swf), P5-317
Advance Slide options, P1-40
After Animation drop-down list, P5-295
.aiff, P5-316
AIFF file (.aiff), P5-316
Align
    cells (table), P2-98
    options, P1-18
    picture, P1-39
Align Bottom, P1-18
Align button, P1-18, P4-216
Align Center, P1-18
Align Left, P1-18
Align Middle, P1-18
Align Right, P1-18
Align Text button, P4-210

Align Top, P1-18
All at Once, P5-294, P5-295
Allow edit, P7-466
Alt Text, P6-406
Analytics, P7-486
Animate text drop-down list, P5-295
Animation, P3-155 to P3-157, P3-185, P5-293 to P5-306
    Animation Painter, P5-297
    charts, P5-298 to P5-299
    chevron pointing up/down, P5-297
    Custom Path, P5-302, P5-333
    Delay time, P5-296
    dim text, P5-293 to P5-294
    duration, P5-296
    Emphasis effects, P5-294
    Entrance effects, P5-294
    Exit effects, P5-294
    keyboard shortcuts, P5-295
    lists, P5-293 to P5-295
    logical, intuitive, and not disorienting, P5-328
    Morph transition, P5-302 to P5-306
    Motion Path, P5-300 to P5-302
    pointers/tips, P5-293, P5-328
    reorder animation sequence, P5-296 to P5-297
    Slide Sorter view, P5-295
    SmartArt graphic, P5-299 to P5-300
    sound, P5-324 to P5-325
    Timing tab, P5-296
    trigger, P5-296, P5-320, P5-321
    trigger animation with video bookmark, P5-320 to P5-321
    uses, P5-293
Animation gallery, P5-293, P5-294
Animation numbers, P3-156, P3-157
Animation Painter, P5-297
Animation Painter button, P5-297
Animation pane, P5-293
Animation Pane button, P5-296, P5-298, P5-320
Animation tag, P5-293, P5-297
Animation timing and duration, P3-157
Animation trigger, P5-296, P5-320, P5-321
Animations gallery, P3-155
Animations tab, P3-156, P5-297
Annotation pens, P3-176 to P3-177
Apply to Selected Slides, P1-31
Area chart, P2-109
Arrange All, P6-368, P6-369
Arrows, P2-74
Artistic Effects, P4-241
As One Object, P5-294, P5-295
.asf, P5-317
.au, P5-316
AU file (.au), P5-316
Audio and video content, P5-316 to P5-329
    add sound to animation, P5-324 to P5-325
    audio file formats, P5-316
    best results -- .m4a audio files/.mp4 video files, P5-316
    bookmark, P5-319 to P5-321
    codec, P5-316
    compress media, P5-326 to P5-327
    create a video, P1-14
    delivery techniques, P5-328 to P5-329
    editing options, P5-319
    embed code, P5-318
    formatting, P5-325 to P5-326
    hide during show, P5-323

insert audio or video file, P5-317, P5-318
    keyboard shortcuts, P5-323
    Loop until Stopped checkbox, P5-322
    media compatibility, P5-326
    media controls, P5-319
    mute/unmute, P5-320
    online video, P3-158 to P3-160, P3-185
    play and hide options, P5-323
    Play Audio dialog box, P5-323
    playback options, P5-322 to P5-323
    pointers/tips, P5-327 to P5-329
    poster frame, P5-325, P5-334
    presentation video, P6-416 to P6-417
    record audio, P5-324
    Rewind after Playing checkbox, P5-322
    rewind options, P5-322
    start, P5-322
    summary/review, P5-333 to P5-334
    trigger animation with video bookmark, P5-320 to P5-321
    trim and fade, P5-322
    trim audio and video, P5-321
    video file formats, P5-317
    video quality, P5-328
    Video Styles group, P5-326
    volume, P5-322
    YouTube video, P5-318
Audio and video keyboard shortcuts, P5-323
Audio bookmark, P5-320
Audio button, P1-23, P5-324
Audio file formats, P5-316
Audio Tools Format tab, P5-319, P5-325
Audio Tools Playback tab, P5-319, P5-322
AutoCorrect, P1-22, P6-383, P6-384 to P6-385
AutoCorrect dialog box, P6-384
AutoCorrect Options button, P6-384
AutoFormat, P6-383 to P6-384
AutoFormat As You Type tab, P6-385
Automatically extend display when presenting on laptop or tablet, P3-168
.avi, P5-317
Axis Titles, P2-111

## B

Background color, P3-150 to P3-155
Background gradient fill, P3-152
Background graphics, P4-228 to P4-229
Background picture fill, P3-152 to P3-153
Background Removal tab, P4-243, P4-244
Background shapes, P4-229
Background Styles, P1-31, P3-152
Background Styles button, P3-151
Backstage view, P1-3, P1-6
Backup copies of presentation, P3-167
Balloon, P7-482
Banded Columns, P2-96
Banded Rows, P2-96
Bar chart, P2-108
Begin and End Arrow size, P2-75
Begin and End Arrow type, P2-75
Best scale for Slide show, P3-159
Bevel, P2-74
Bevel Rectangle picture style, P4-240
Bilingual Dictionary, P6-389
Bilingualism, P6-387 to P6-389
Bing search engine, P2-87
Black or unblack slide show, P3-170, P3-171
Blank layout, P1-14, P1-15